Downtime

Downtime

The Twentieth Century
in Slow Motion

Mark Goble

Columbia University Press

New York

Columbia University Press
Publishers Since 1893
New York   Chichester, West Sussex
cup.columbia.edu

Copyright © 2025 Columbia University Press
All rights reserved

Library of Congress Cataloging-in-Publication Data
Names: Goble, Mark, author.
Title: Downtime : the twentieth century in slow motion / Mark Goble.
Description: New York : Columbia University Press, 2025. |
Includes bibliographical references and index.
Identifiers: LCCN 2024048139 (print) | LCCN 2024048140 (ebook) |
ISBN 9780231219150 (hardback) | ISBN 9780231219167 (trade paperback) |
ISBN 9780231562546 (ebook)
Subjects: LCSH: Cinematography—Special effects. | Space and time—Philosophy. |
Space and time in motion pictures. | Space and time in literature.
Classification: LCC TR858 .G65 2025 (print) | LCC TR858 (ebook) |
DDC 778.5/345—dc23/eng/20241029
LC record available at https://lccn.loc.gov/2024048139
LC ebook record available at https://lccn.loc.gov/2024048140

Printed in the United States of America

Cover design: Julia Kushnirsky
Cover image: Jeff Wall, *Milk*, 1984. Courtesy of the artist.

GPSR Authorized Representative: Easy Access System Europe, Mustamäe tee 50,
10621 Tallinn, Estonia, gpsr.requests@easproject.com

Contents

List of Illustrations ix

Introduction: Slow Motion, Very Quickly 1

PART I
A Theory in Slow Motion

1. At the Movies to the End of Time 19
2. Almost Freeze Frame 31
3. From Zero to Slow 40
4. Experiments in Time 58
5. Slow-Motion Modernism 65
6. Escape Velocities 73
7. Technological Aesthetics 80
8. New Media, Slow Media 92
9. What We See in Slow Motion 98

PART II
Modernity at Any Speed

10. Some Literary Histories of Slow Motion   117
11. Modernity's Slow Start   125
12. Faulkner at the Speed Limit   130
13. Snopes at Rest   136
14. *Remainder*'s Instant Replays   142
15. *Austerlitz*'s Traumatic Pauses   148
16. Being in Racial Time: *Daughters of the Dust*   155
17. We Have Always Been in Slow Motion: *The Discovery of Slowness*   165
18. DeLillo, Slowing Down   177
19. From 9/11 to JFK in Slow Motion   183
20. *Underworld*: How Slow Is Now?   190
21. A "Sixties Incandescence": Periodizing Slow Motion   198

PART III
Forever '68

22. *Bonnie and Clyde* and Slow and Fast   209
23. Posthistoric Prehistoric Modernism: *2001: A Space Odyssey*   238

24. How the West Slows Down:
Sergio Leone and the Long Struggle   266

25. *The Wild Bunch*, or the Pains of Being Sam Peckinpah   291

26. Antonioni's Art of Excess: *Zabriskie Point*   314

....

Acknowledgments 343

Notes 347

Bibliography 373

Index 385

Illustrations

Figure 1.1. Robert Smithson, *Spiral Jetty* (1970)   27

Figure 1.2. Robert Smithson, still from *Spiral Jetty* (1970)   29

Figure 2.1. Hiroshi Sugimoto, *Tri-City Drive-In, San Bernardino*, 1993   32

Figure 2.2. Hiroshi Sugimoto, *Proctor's Theater, Troy*, 2015   34

Figure 2.3. Still from *Goodbye Dragon Inn* (2003)   37

Figure 3.1. Still from "Annabelle Serpentine Dance," 1894–5   41

Figure 3.2. Still from *Entr'acte* (1924)   43

Figure 3.3. Still from *The Blood of a Poet* (1930)   48

Figure 3.4. Still from *Man with a Movie Camera* (1929)   50

Figure 3.5. Still from *What Price Hollywood?* (1932)   52

Figure 3.6. Still from *L'Atalante* (1934)   54

Figure 3.7. Still from *Zéro for Conduite* (1933)   55

Figure 3.8. "The trick was blown" by the time Stanley Cavell saw this moment in slow motion from *The World of Henry Orient* (1964)   56

Figure 4.1. Only Astaire is in slow motion in this sequence from *Easter Parade* (1948)   60

Figure 4.2. These beads fall in slow motion decades before the iconic bullets in *The Matrix* in a still from *By the Bluest of Seas* (1936)   64

Figure 6.1. Still from *Point Blank* (1967)   77

Figure 8.1. Still from *The Flash* (2017)   93

Figure 8.2. Still from *The Quintet of the Astonished* (2003)   94

Figure 9.1. Still from *The Seven Samurai* (1954)   99

Figure 9.2. Still from *The Seven Samurai* (1954)   100

Figure 9.3. The aesthetics of slow motion   103

Figure 10.1. Google Ngram "slow motion"   119

Figure 10.2. HathiTrust Bookworm "slow motion"   119

Figure 10.3. "slow motion" in media studies database   120

Figure 15.1. A time-stamped image of the Holocaust from Sebald's *Austerlitz*   151

Figure 16.1. Slow motion and step printing in two stills from *Daughters of the Dust* (1991)   159

Figure 16.2. Still from *Daughters of the Dust* (1991)   161

Figure 16.3. Still from *Daughters of the Dust* (1991)   161

Figure 16.4. Still from *Daughters of the Dust* (1991)   162

Figure 16.5. Still from *Daughters of the Dust* (1991)   164

Figure 22.1. Stills from *Bonnie and Clyde* (1967)   220

Figure 22.2. Queer slapstick in a still from *Bonnie and Clyde* (1967)   223

Figure 22.3. Zapruder film homage in a still from *Bonnie and Clyde* (1967)   228

Figure 22.4. Still from *Bonnie and Clyde* (1967)   230

Figure 22.5. Still from *Bonnie and Clyde* (1967)   231

Figure 22.6. The agony of Clyde's postmortem ecstasy in two stills from *Bonnie and Clyde* (1967)   232

Figure 22.7. Stills from *Bonnie and Clyde* (1967)   232

Figure 22.8. Still from *Bonnie and Clyde* (1967)   237

Figure 23.1. Stills from *2001: A Space Odyssey* (1968)   244

ILLUSTRATIONS   xi

Figure 23.2. The fastest 4 million years in narrative cinema in a still from *2001: A Space Odyssey* (1968) 249

Figure 23.3. Bingham Canyon Mine in Cinerama in a still from *How the West Was Won* (1962) 251

Figure 23.4. Monument Valley and Monument Valley on drugs in stills from *How the West Was Won* (1962) and *2001* (1968) 253

Figure 23.5. Still from *2001: A Space Odyssey* (1968) 260

Figure 24.1. Franco Nero, not yet moving in slow motion, in *Keoma* (1976) 277

Figure 24.2. Still from *The Good, the Bad, and the Ugly* (1966) 277

Figure 24.3. Still from *The Good, the Bad, and the Ugly* (1966) 280

Figure 24.4. Google Earth photos of Sad Hill Cemetery's location in Spain, circa 2006 280

Figure 24.5. It's always 1968 in Leone's *Once Upon a Time in America* (1984) 286

Figure 24.6. Henry Fonda as modernist sculpture in *Once Upon a Time in the West* (1968) 288

Figure 24.7. Still from *Once Upon a Time in the West* (1968) 289

Figure 24.8. A Leone non-site, Monument Valley 290

Figure 25.1. Stills from *Junior Bonner* (1972) 297

Figure 25.2. Pike can still get it up in a still from *The Wild Bunch* (1969) 303

Figure 25.3. Burt Lancaster does not stick the landing in this still from *The Swimmer* (1968) 304

Figure 26.1. Still from *Zabriskie Point* (1970) 316

Figure 26.2. Still from *Zabriskie Point* (1970) 317

Figure 26.3. Still from *Zabriskie Point* (1970) 318

Figure 26.4. Still from *Zabriskie Point* (1970) 319

Figure 26.5. Stills from *Zabriskie Point* (1970) 320

Figure 26.6. Real estate porn in *Bad Boys II* (2003) 325

Figure 26.7. The thrill of victory in *Zabriskie Point* and *Star Wars* (1976) 325

ILLUSTRATIONS

Figure 26.8. Stills from *Zabriskie Point* (1970) 329

Figure 26.9. Still from *Zabriskie Point* (1970) 329

Figure 26.10. Antonioni showing actors what he wants on the *Zabriskie Point* set in 1969 330

Figure 26.11. Harold "Doc" Edgerton, atomic explosion (1952) 335

Figure 26.12. The Slo Mo Guys accidentally remake *Zabriskie Point* in a still from "Exploding Fruit in 4K" (2018) 336

Figure 26.13. An "exploded view" 338

Figure 26.14. Stills from *Crossroads* (1975) 341

Downtime

Introduction

Slow Motion, Very Quickly

The first time we see slow motion in the 2012 film *Dredd* it's a cheap trick, but it doesn't look it. We've just barely gotten our introduction to the brutal world of Mega City One and the fascist cops—who are also the judges, juries, and executioners who keep its "peace"—when Judge Dredd, played by Karl Urban, answers a call to apprehend three suspects speeding down some crowded streets "under the influence of narcotics." When we cut from Dredd and his sleekly futuristic motorcycle to the interior of the van he's chasing, the close-up on the criminal in the passenger seat shows him with an inhaler pressed against his lips, radiant and sparkling like nothing else in the dark Johannesburg streets that served as the film's exterior locations. The actor's brown skin glows with blown-out highlights, tiny lens flares pop from the translucent cartridge held up to his mouth, and silver smoke drifts beautifully across his face and back into the van, where we see another figure similarly entranced by whatever drug has so decelerated their sense of time—while rendering their ugly world so vivid—that they can barely hear the distorted, low-pitch screaming of the driver.

This opening chase does not last long, and all the criminals are dead after a couple minutes of action that has no more slow motion because, as we'll eventually discover, *Dredd* only features slow motion when someone in the film is on the drug whose sale and manufacture is the central business of Lena Headey's fearsome gangster Ma-Ma, whom Dredd of course will kill. But not before she has a final hit of her own product, street name "slo-mo," which means that when Dredd throws her out of a two-hundredth-story window, she experiences her fatal fall at "1 percent its normal speed" and we experience it as a spectacle of heightened color, ridiculous detail, and horrid grace. Her dying fall is actually too fast according to the temporality of "slo-mo" in the film. I'm too polite to say my guess for Lena Headey's weight, but an online "Splat Calculator" would put Ma-Ma's time of death at around fourteen seconds after Dredd passes his sentence.

Dredd clocks in at a lean ninety-five minutes, and spending another twenty-four minutes on how Ma-Ma's fall would feel on "slo-mo" would be a waste of time. Though it could take even longer: The Phantom Flex digital cameras that cinematographer Anthony Mantle used to shoot the "slo-mo" sequences of slow motion in *Dredd*—which required him to devise the first handheld 3-D rig and several other innovations—were capable of filming at 3,000fps (frames per second) and thus stretch her fall nearly to half an hour. *Dredd* saves a lot of time along the way by rigorously avoiding any use of slow motion for all the fight scenes, gun battles, and explosions where we would, in a twenty-first-century action film, expect to find it. There is plenty of "slo-mo" in *Dredd*, but only when our brains as viewers are on drugs. The film does not add much to the recycled dystopianism of the original *2000 AD* comic, but it has some style and knows that we have all seen enough slow motion to have the highest tolerance for its effects. It takes a lot, in other words, to engineer a film in 2012 that, like a weird ultraviolent version of Joseph Conrad's hope for modern art, is to make us really see slow motion like it was something new. As if, as an effect, it still was special.

■ ■ ■

The last reference to slow motion in Cynthia Ozick's *The Messiah of Stockholm* (1987) is a cheap shot, but I take her point. Lars Andemening, the Swedish book reviewer and frustrated intellectual at the center of the novel, has worse problems than his annoying colleague Gunnar—like believing he is the son of Bruno Schulz, the tragic Polish writer who was murdered by Nazis in 1942—but it's much easier for Lars to see why Gunnar bothers him than to face the facts of his delusion. As the most popular reviewer at the paper where they work, Gunnar "peppered his columns with *slow motion, back alley, big deal, wisecrack,* even *so what*," a litany of Americanisms or "vulgarities" that Lars cannot abide.[1] Such concessions to the reading public—that much prefers Gunnar's breezy, "cosmopolitan" discussions of the latest bestsellers to Lars's obscure intellectualism—don't seem like they should matter much in the late eighties, when neither film nor U.S. popular culture were exactly avant-garde arrivals to Europe. Perhaps it is Gunnar's easy use of English that is more disturbing than his mention of the slow motion that would have been, even for an absurdly preoccupied figure like

Lars, a familiar feature of twentieth-century cinema—already prominent in the work of the modernist filmmakers Lars might recognize as worthy counterparts to the surrealist vision of Schulz's own fiction.

Lars obviously wouldn't be caught dead at any of the top-ten worldwide box office hits for 1987, seven of which (*Fatal Attraction*, *Beverly Hills Cop II*, *Dirty Dancing*, *The Living Daylights*, *Lethal Weapon*, *Predator*, and *The Untouchables*) feature at least one scene in slow motion. Nothing unusual here. If anything, slow motion has only become more popular and conventional in films across the range of genres that dominate global cinema. Lars is old enough to remember when a romantic musical or sophisticated thriller might not employ slow motion; he is "already well into graying" and, though he was probably too lost in his fantasies to pay very close attention, would have been the perfect age to witness the explosion of slow motion in visual culture at the end of the 1960s that I'll consider here.[2] He is, in fact, a perfect case for reckoning with the prominence of slow motion as a media and technological aesthetic that patterns twentieth-century and contemporary life in countless forms. Including, or so it would seem, the unconscious of the otherwise devoutly unpopular Lars Andemening, who is the very opposite of the intended audience for a movie like *Predator* or *Lethal Weapon*—and would probably find *Dredd* too abominable to suffer—yet imagines himself reading the serious books he loves "meticulously, as if, swimming, he were being filmed in slow motion."[3] Actually, for Lars, this is the telling symbol of his resistance to the modernity that Gunnar vibrantly and trashily embodies. It makes for a compelling picture of slow reading as an analogue to the other forms of slowness (slow food, slow cinema, slow travel) that I should probably appreciate since somebody like me is precisely whom Lars and Ozick are writing for. I do, but not without some hesitation. I also like slow motion at its most outrageous, and this book is in part about how hard it is sometimes to tell the difference between the high-speed world of shameless thrills that slow motion tries to capture and the art that slow motion tries to make from time and its technologies.

■ ■ ■

There is more slow motion than I know what to do with in Jean-Luc Godard's *Historie(s) du cinéma* because it was a cheap option, which is fine because it's still Godard. As we will see, slow motion is not particularly prominent in the French New Wave, despite the influence that Godard, Truffaut, and others had on the New American Cinema of the late sixties, which I'll be arguing marks the moment when slow motion goes from being a relatively minor element of modernist cinema and various documentary genres to the single most popular special effect in global film and media culture. Godard first employs slow motion in some of his television work from the early 1970s and then at length and with tremendous self-consciousness in *Suave qui peut* (1980), his return to a more familiar mode of narrative cinema after his years of radicalism, video, and antic experimentation with the Dziga Vertov Group. In parts of the English-speaking world, *Suave qui peut* was released with *Slow Motion* as its title, though the way that Godard exploits the effect has everything to do with how he spent the seventies. The slow motion in his *Slow Motion* is achieved with video processing and step printing; instead of filming at higher frame rates, like we see in *Dredd* and Lars in *The Messiah of Stockholm* would not have seen in *The Untouchables*, Godard transferred his 35mm footage to video and manipulated playback speeds in postproduction or achieved a singularly blurred, haltering version of slow motion by making multiple images of individual frames and then inserting them into the finished film.

His indulgence of these techniques is more extreme in *Historie(s) du cinéma*, his magisterial and impenetrable reflections on the twentieth century and its most iconic medium. I won't try to summarize the argument of Godard's *Historie(s)*, but anybody who has watched any of its episodes will recall how he aggressively slows film down to a delirious mix of speeds and stills through the use of video effects. Slow motion has become a historical aesthetic in *Historie(s) du cinéma* not just because it represents a figure of modernity as Lars might like to "read" it but also because we see it being outmoded in real time, replaced by video in a wilder and more diverse media ecology. I remember playing around with slow motion for less high-minded reasons on a VCR my parents had sometime in the 1980s. Unlike Godard, they definitely weren't early adopters, but still: The trajectory of slow motion from special effect to default mode is largely set in place by the emergence of video technologies, from instant replay in TV sports beginning in the early sixties to the endless accumulations of "fails" and supercuts on YouTube or to the unknowably vast and already vanishing archive of digital video shot on iPhones that aren't quite as fast (yet) as the Phantom Flex cameras used for *Dredd* but are getting close to the Phantom 2K rigs that Anthony Mantle used for Lars Von Triers's *Antichrist* in 2009. On the one hand, *Antichrist* looks much better at 1000fps than what I can do at 240fps with my phone; on the other hand, thankfully none of the slow motion I've shot of kids and pets looks anything like *Antichrist*. In the end, though, slow motion remains inescapable.

■ ■ ■

INTRODUCTION   5

The slow motion that helps save the world in Kim Stanley Robinson's 2020 novel *The Ministry for the Future* might be a cheap solution, but I hope it works. "Project Slowdown" is a massive enterprise of glacier restoration that Robinson imagines as one of many answers to the climate crisis in his surprisingly popular epic of technological development, resource economics, bureaucratic cooperation, and violent ecoterrorism. I was surprised, anyway, when former president Obama named it as one of his favorite books of the year, given how clearly Robinson argues that the three things I just listed that Obama no doubt likes a lot will finally fail to make a difference without the threat of the other thing it's hard to see him championing. One of these things is not like the others. Long before Robinson reveals that geoengineering at scale has saved our planet's glaciers, a series of targeted assassinations and acts of sabotage have helped persuade the nations of the world that human beings and commodities, for the good of everyone, must start traveling in slow motion. Literally: "Because they were slow," a future of solar-powered cargo ships demands new logistics for global trade, and traveling by sail and hydrofoil once again requires budgeting eight days for an Atlantic crossing. "It was adapt or die," writes Robinson, and since "they weren't going to be able to stop the saboteurs," the only choice was to slow down.[4] For the first time in centuries, the capitalist "annihilation of space by time" that Marx originally observed in the *Grundrisse* starts to reverse, and the "time-space compression" that marks modernity comes to a deliberate halt.[5] Not that Robinson is entirely utopian in his calculations about what such a change would mean since, as one of his heroic bureaucrats discovers on her inaugural voyage in a newer, slower world, the ocean was "beautiful" *and* "she was getting her work done. So—where had this obsession with speed come, why had everyone caved to it so completely?" She may have been forced into slow motion to save her life—and the only world she knows—but like the rest of us she is still always on the clock.[6]

■ ■ ■

This book is about all this slow motion, which follows from the slow motion we've been seeing on our screens for more than a century now and which explodes in popularity and scope after the late sixties. I am interested in the history and cultural shape of a form that begins as a technological capacity—an instance of what Susan Sontag once described as the "discussable technology of camera movements, cutting, and composition" that makes for film's "vocabulary of forms"—which then becomes a special effect and now flourishes as a pervasive imagery of time as we experience it in the modern world: variously uneven, punctuated and accelerated, dragging and expanding, beautiful, traumatic, endless, and commodified. When Sontag published "Against Interpretation" in 1964, there would not have been nearly so much slow motion for her to see, which is why I will be insisting on showing, against her own example, not just "*how it is what it* is" but very much "*what it means*."[7] From early cinema to modernism to Hollywood and beyond, I will track how slow motion emerges as a media aesthetic and how we might understand its resonance as a metaphor and figure across a wildly incomplete but I hope coherent-enough sample of twentieth-century culture. After all, if we know anything about slow motion today, it's that there is too much of it. The arguments I will be pursuing in the three parts of this book are not intended as the only explanation for why this may be so, but they tell a story about slow motion that speaks to its significance as more than just a special effect that does not seem so special anymore. I start with film history because that is where slow motion comes from, but then I turn to a series of literary figures that lets us see it working as a symbolic form to help us understand aspects of modernity. This literary history also suggests why the specific films of the late sixties that I read at length in the last section of this book—*Bonnie and Clyde* (1967), *2001: A Space Odyssey* (1968), *Once Upon a Time in the West* (1968), *The Wild Bunch* (1969), and *Zabriskie Point* (1970)—can be seen to mark the moment when slow motion both achieves a concentrated force as a visual language of historical crisis and also arrives at the almost stupidly extensive visibility that it has for us today.

I want to tell a story about slow motion and the twentieth century that is arguably exhaustive, but I also realize that it is only partial. The film and literature that I know best reflects my training as an Americanist, and the gravity of Hollywood cinema as slow motion's most abundant ecosystem, so to speak, means that this project has been influenced by the biases and preferences of this institution and how it has historically distributed attention along lines of gender, class, and race. I know, in other words, that I have not nearly seen enough slow motion even though I have probably seen as much as almost anyone. Yet there is always more and probably too much slow motion, so the examples I've assembled here will be pushed to their very limits.

The first reference to slow motion in a work of U.S. fiction that gives some sense of these limits occurs about halfway through William Faulkner's 1932 *Light in August*. He was on his way to Hollywood as it was being published, but it is very hard to know if he has any specific film in mind when he pictures Joe Christmas, racially ambivalent and perpetually tormented, in an image that, like so much of Faulkner, only gets stranger with time: "It—the horse and the rider—had a strange, dreamy effect, like a moving picture in slow motion as it galloped steady and flagging up the street and toward the old corner where he used to wait, less urgent perhaps but not less eager, and more young."⁸

I won't try to rush through a whole argument about Faulkner in these few sentences. Is this an allusion? I don't know. There had only been a handful of feature films to use slow motion as of 1932, and I wouldn't want to bet that Faulkner had seen any of them. But sports newsreels featuring slow motion were already common in the silent era; the rendering of a horse and rider and their "attitude of terrific speed" into a visual form of "spent and terrific slowness" is one place where film begins with Muybridge and his motion photography of Leland Stanford Jr.'s horse Occident in 1878. Jordan Peele's *Nope* (2022) comes at this history of media, identity, and time from a much different perspective than does *Light in August* but similarly decides that there is no way to understand the twentieth century and after without remembering the technologies that make it possible to look at its violence and beauty and to make them occasionally feel like each other. Peele's spectacular monster movie starts with uncanny Muybridge images of a black jockey at almost but not quite normal speed. Faulkner may have gotten there first, but here we are, almost one hundred years later, and we barely seem to have moved at all. Does this mean we're going fast or slow or both at the same time?

■ ■ ■

Slow motion is an art and artifact of speed we do not see. Every instance of slow motion is an image of speed transformed by technology into something else entirely, making it at once a symbol for the experience of modern, mediated times outside the narrow bandwidths of human perception but also one of the most popular aesthetic forms depending entirely on the ways machines can see the world without us. Until this recent era of digital filmmaking introduced a new array of technologies for accelerating or decelerating moving images—first by way of "speed ramping" or "time remapping" with professional editing software products like Adobe Premiere Pro and, eventually, on smartphones starting with the Samsung i8000 Omnia II (2009) and iPhone 5S (2013)—slow motion was made by shooting at faster frame rates than the 16 to 24fps that was established in the era of early cinema as the standard for reproducing the illusion of motion. The introduction of sound cinema in the 1920s inspired the need for a universal fixed frame rate, and engineers at Western Electric, working with filmmakers at Warner Bros., soon set it at 24fps. Theaters could adopt this standard with minimal disruption to the widespread practice of showing films that had been shot at 16–20fps at 24–28fps instead. Though only reducing runtimes by a few minutes, these slight accelerations marginally increased audience turnover and theater profits. Of course, since all these frame rates had to be "cranked" by hand before motorized cameras and projectors were also invented, there is no way to know for sure how much "undercranked" or accelerated motion spectators really saw, nor how much "overcranked" slow motion was accidentally experienced when film shot at 24fps was projected at 16 or 20fps. The history of film might well begin in slow motion and only later pick up speed, or maybe it started too fast and has been slowing down ever since.

Soon enough, however, it is understood that faster and still faster frame rates make for slow and then slower motion, with camera speeds of 48, 72, or 96fps producing motion at one-half, one-third, or one-quarter normal. For the rest of the twentieth century and up to the present, imaging technologies—first analog, then digital—get only faster, and so slow motion gets even slower. Consumer-grade mirrorless cameras and GoPro rigs easily shoot at frame rates that were unseen outside of laboratories and soundstages before the 1950s, and YouTube auteurs such as Gavin David Free and Daniel Charles Gruchy, or "Gav" and "Dan" as they are known on their channel called "The Slow Mo Guys," can make masterpieces like "Opening a Condom in a Wind Tunnel" (2019) or "Diving Into 1000 Mousetraps in 4K Slow Motion" (2017) with the flair of a demented, backyard Stanley Kubrick on gear that might cost as much as a nice car but just the barest fraction of the budget for a Marvel movie.[9]

This book does not exactly tell the story of the technologies that make slow motion slower, faster, and cheaper over the course of the twentieth century and after, but this is one reason why *2001: A Space Odyssey* required so much elaborate and expensive design to imagine the origins of humanity in slow motion while a film like *Dredd* seems utterly generic for going even slower. From the invention of cinema to the late sixties, slow motion is a relatively minor aspect of film style and language across a range of modernist experimental shorts and features, appearing in sports newsreels and documentaries and ultimately in just a few dozen feature films as the narrative conventions of the studio system were codified around the world. Last time I checked, a search for "slow motion" on YouTube promised more than 200,000,000 videos. I am interested in the archaeology of media that such staggering numbers force us to consider. Yet relatively little of this larger media history—of high-speed cameras and visual effects, of optics and scientific imaging, of software engineering and computer graphics—figures in the films and texts that let us understand what slow motion says about the time we keep and spend with our technologies in the modern world.

I am not suggesting that the speed that makes slow motion possible—that *makes* slow motion—is always part of what slow motion is about or is the secret of its appeal to all the filmmakers, writers, and artists whose works I will examine here. The mechanics of slow motion as technique were widely known from the first moments of film's history as a medium, and many of the books that I read to trace slow motion's shape and meaning in the twentieth century are, not surprisingly, by authors such as William Faulkner, W. G. Sebald, Tom McCarthy, and Don DeLillo, whose fictions are patterned on a poetics of the moving image. Slow motion represents perhaps the most singularly popular and visible result of what Shane Denson describes as "the discorrelation of images": a breakdown in older ways of seeing and perceiving in the wake of new technologies that depend on "[temporalities] no longer tuned to that of their human receivers." For Denson, it is primarily through "post-cinematic cameras and screens" and the "computational agencies" on which they depend that we experience the increasingly "'time-critical'" processes (in language we both borrow from Wolfgang Ernst) and the "material and sensory relations at the microtemporal level" that are often said, by Denson and others, to determine the forms and genres of our contemporary visual culture. "Older relations," Denson writes, "such as that between a human subject and a photographically fixed object ... are dissolving, and new relations are being forged in the microtemporal intervals of algorithmic processing."[10]

Or maybe not. We need more languages to help us understand the otherwise incomprehensible speeds at which digital technologies can operate. But thinking about or even *in* slow motion—which is maybe the only the way, as human beings, we still can think in the futures we are making now—is also to remember that modernity has been effectively too fast for us forever. It is dazzling and occasionally despairing to reckon with a world of real-time operations happening by the millions and billions every second, but perhaps it is just as important to look back on a medium that had already left us far behind at 24 fps. Slow motion is already going faster than we can ever know as "human receivers" and has been speeding past us since the invention of film. This book explores slow motion as both a cinematic relic and a foundational, ongoing, and utterly pervasive form of "time-axis manipulation," which is how Friedrich Kittler would describe it even while dismissing what we see of it as "eyewash."[11] Slow motion is deeply primordial in its appeal, not just as a technology that emerges alongside cinema and tests its limits from the beginning but also as a figure for so many of the ways that modern life inflicts its temporalities and speeds on us, whether or not we know how fast or slow they really are. In slow motion they are always both at the same time.

Writing in the 2003 catalogue for *The Passions*, Bill Viola's major installation of HD videos, the opera director Peter Sellars makes a claim that I find embarrassingly clear about some ideas that this book will deny at almost every turn despite the fact they are, more embarrassingly still, crucial for its origins. "Slow motion is inherent in history," Sellars writes with no sense for what he means by "history," before continuing to advance the equally bombastic proposition that "slow motion is the very process of philosophy, the careful consideration of minute detail." "Even more essentially," he adds, "slow motion opens out onto the path of enlightenment itself."[12] It frankly would be weird for me to altogether disagree since I must obviously believe slow motion can help illuminate *a* history and provide *some* enlightenment about the conditions of technological modernity and its experiences of time and temporality and the many, many speeds, not one of which I'd offer as the sole truth of multiple philosophies and politics, a truth that we need to grasp it as it rushes by and grinds away. It is also the case that while I actually haven't been working on this book since I first saw Viola's exhibit at the Getty in 2003, it has been, like most scholarly work, a long time coming for many reasons—many of which bear on questions of how we value the labor that goes into all the care we take as critics for whom the "consideration of minute detail" is finally a way of life.

In his "Textual Analysis of a Tale by Edgar Poe," which Roland Barthes wrote just a couple years after publishing *S/Z*, he promises a mode of criticism that "shall leave to our analysis even the pacing of the *reading*: simply, this reading will be, as it were, filmed in *slow motion*."[13] Barthes does not press the visual connection to film or present his methodology in any terms more allegorical than the slightly hesitating gesture that he uses to introduce the analogy in the first place. Nor does he make any larger argument that reading in slow motion ("*au ralenti*") is ethically superior or redemptive, which is an almost mandatory feature of the many defenses of "slow reading" that have appeared while I've been working slowly on this book and that, like the various "slow" movements that will also eventually find their way into the pages that follow, express a series of anxieties about and resistance to a Western culture of modernity defined by its perpetual acceleration and pursuit of speed in every possible endeavor, from a just-in-time economy of relentless productivity to the "Global War on Terror," or "GWOT" if you're in a hurry, whose artificially accelerated pace and reckless, frantic scope looms over Sellars's adoration of Viola's magic on the bleeding edge of video technology at the turn of the twenty-first century.[14] Unlike the Old Master iconographies that Viola put into radically decelerated motion for his *Passions*, the film and visual culture that has inspired this book is more familiar to us in the happily degraded glories of the fight scenes and action sequences that we know from global blockbuster cinema, though as we'll discover, these have their roots in modernist experiments with time and seeing, as well as various non-narrative filmmaking modes (sports highlights, scientific and industrial film, forensic analysis) that are not exactly where we are used to looking for the major influences on slow-motion connoisseurs like Michael Bay or Zach Snyder. This is just one reason why I find Sellars's sentiments about slow motion hard to take and why I'm also not sure if this book is seeking "to clear attentional ground," like another of its major influences, Lutz Koepnick, "for a radical rupture in the temporal fabric" of the present.[15] I'll settle for Barthes's no more modest but not so reverently phrased aspiration that by proceeding in slow motion we might better know the "structuration" of our time, a project that demands not just serious contemplation but also a willingness to get lost occasionally in the various "codes," or the "supra-textual organization of notations," that he names simply as the "associative fields" that are "constitutive of the writing of the world."[16] The readings here are deliberate, perhaps relentlessly so. I assure you they're going as fast as I think they possibly can. There is no slow motion without speed, though it won't always look like it in the book you are about to read.

■ ■ ■

Slow motion is a measure of speed, an index to a velocity that appears to us like something else entirely. But slow motion can do more, and my interest in its history and aesthetics extends beyond the world of film where it originates and beyond the ways that it might symbolize the very character of criticism as a kind of labor of attention or duration or even care. My own investment in slow motion—my love, I think it fair to say, for how it works and means—is nowhere near as personal or consequential as that which Denise Riley writes about in her poetic reflections on loss in *Time Lived, Without Its Flow*. In the wake of her son's death, Riley describes the "sensation of having been lifted clean out of habitual time," the feeling of "so very little movement" that her perceptions of time's "capacity to be baggy" risk her own undoing since "the self itself, declares Hegel, belongs to time. . . . Time *is* the being of the self." I didn't write this book fast enough for my parents to get to see it. But I took long enough that now my daughter won't have to wait to read it. I lost some time during the pandemic, but who's to say this book would have been better if I had finished it a little faster? Books don't just take time; they make something real out of what Riley calls an "elaborate, dynamic, silent temporal abundance" that comes from "the living with the living, and the living with the dead."[17]

But time, whether slow or fast or both at once, also is the being of the world—and especially of the modern world that we have been trying to know for centuries. There isn't much poetry, nor should there be, in Koepnick's vision of modernity as a network of "invisible transnational dynamics" that render the present "as a multiplicity of incompatible temporalities, memories, and narratives," each of which unfolds across "space as a nestled array of sensory and highly mediated data, a fold of various elsewheres amid the here and now."[18] This is knotty language, shot through with allusions to theories and intellectual frameworks that scholars like Koepnick and I—and probably many of this book's readers—spend years trying to read and comprehend to place our work within a set of conversations that have been going on decades, if not longer, and that we hope will still be possible for futures we won't live to see. "Modernization," writes Kristen Ross, is "not an event but a process, made up of slow- and fast-moving economic and social cycles."[19] This painfully open secret about contemporary capitalism is perhaps becoming harder to keep as both its ideology of perpetually accelerating growth and its assumptions of de facto permanence are being newly challenged from a range of economic, political, and ecological perspectives that have informed this book at every turn.[20] They will rarely be a focus in the pages that follow, but they map this book's historical horizon and the ground on which its claims about slow motion's technical and figurative significance are reckoned.

Slow motion captures and transmutes into aesthetic form the two most dominant temporalities of modern life. Slow motion is, to borrow from Edna Duffy, "a new pleasure" that *depends* on the "increased regime of speed" that we have come to make synonymous with modernity and the experience of time-space compression, first explored by Marx and now articulated so fully in the work of critics such as David Harvey.[21] It is also a media aesthetic that is literally the image of progress as it slows down, perhaps along the way to stopping altogether—a stasis that slow motion cannot show us but that it often teases. Violence and death are two of its most ready subjects for good reason, as we will see. But I am just as interested in how slow motion registers—at a far more abstract level that I will try to make almost as visceral—a feeling that, to borrow from Harmut Rosa, "the current epoch is characterized by the way all motion seems to come to an end," all of its "utopian energies" already "exhausted because all the intellectual and spiritual possibilities appear to have been tried."[22]

I won't speculate about how many of the 187,000,000 Google hits for "living in slow motion" speak to the "frenetic standstill" that Rosa takes from Paul Virilio to put some writerly flesh on the sociological bones of what Rosa later terms the *"processes of rigidifcation"* that are dead ringers for the advances and accelerations that capitalism must sustain. Again, Ross is helpful here for being more concrete about the stakes and more specific about why the 1960s represent a signal period of crisis for the fantasy that "capitalist modernization presents itself as timeless," the illusion of a "changeless world" in all the ways that really matter, "functioning smoothly under the sign of technique" in a society "devoid of class conflict." Within the workings of slow motion, maybe we can track some of the "seemingly unrelated temporal spans" that the ecologist Andreas Malm argues are the defining and depressing features of living in a "now that is non-contemporaneous with itself" since every instant is actually a "*conjuncture* [that] combines relics and arrows, loops and postponements that stretch from the deepest past to the most distant future."[23] If capitalist modernity is an "era of diachronicity," as Malm says, then it makes perfect sense to watch it happening in but also *as* slow motion, its many speeds and temporalities combined and somehow mystified in what is almost certainly the most obvious way that any of us have ever seen.

■ ■ ■

This book follows slow motion along three connected and ultimately convergent arcs. In each section, I trace a history of slow motion across different forms of media and at different scales of cultural time. Part 1 is an account of where we see slow motion in cinema before the sixties and looks at how it appears in some of the founding works of film history and theory. Here I will explore the aesthetics of slow motion as a special effect in ways that might occasionally feel familiar but also a little arcane. There will be a necessarily speculative framework that structures aspects of my argument since it is impossible to reconstruct a complete archive of slow motion: It was visible not just in feature films but also in newsreels, documentary shorts, scientific and industrial filmmaking, and various nonfiction or experimental genres. It is possible, on the other hand, to catalogue most of the slow motion that appeared in fiction films produced by studios in the United States and Europe, and these examples will let me propose a series of explanations for why slow motion matters, why it eventually takes the forms we know today, and, more importantly, why very little of what we see in slow motion before the moment of "1968" predicts its staggering proliferation and popularity in the final decades of the twentieth century and on into a twenty-first century that has only witnessed its continuing acceleration.

Turning next to a broader literary field, part 2 examines how slow motion became a central metaphor for writers who are themselves preoccupied with the ways in which history is mediated and transformed by new and old technologies like film. Fantasies of speed and technophilic delusions do not define the whole of modernism in the twentieth century nor even the narrower channels of Anglo-American and European high culture that have been disproportionately significant to so many critical discussions of the period. But these discourses are crucial to the matrix of aesthetic and institutional forces from which slow motion emerges in the forms that we know best. Alongside works by writers such as William Faulkner, Don DeLillo, W. G. Sebald, Tom McCarthy, and Sten Nadolny—an admittedly eccentric assembly of writers who do share more in common than just a fascination with slow motion—a single cinematic case study, Julie Dash's 1991 film *Daughters of the Dust*, will here help us understand how slow motion operates as a reflection on and, more weirdly, *of* the speed that it obscures and mystifies and holds up to aesthetic scrutiny. We will come to see how slow motion is part of the dream-work for a culture of technology that has accelerated past our perceptual capacities and increasingly represents a system of productive forces that have no interest in human time or temporalities that cannot be materialized as profits, commodities, or outputs for an economy that could well be the end of us in the long run that is getting shorter by the day. Not every reference to slow motion invokes its cinematic archaeology, much less the "slow violence" that Rob Nixon has helped establish as a symbol of modern life's assault on us.[24] Nor does just any mention of slow motion invoke the "slow time" that Jonathan Sachs describes as an invention of the Romantic period and its early reckoning with the sheer pace of change during the Industrial Revolution and with the vast, inhuman temporalities opened up by the discoveries of Charles Lyell and Charles Darwin. But we will consider several works that precisely turn on all the ways that modernity is a form of what Sachs, borrowing from Claude Lévi-Strauss, terms a "hot chronology," where we feel terminally immersed in a culture of "intense acceleration" that also "slows down most of those who experience it."[25] We don't necessarily need slow motion to show us what modernity really looks like or to describe the mix of speeds that makes it, if not traumatic, still too much for most of us to bear for the duration. But the works that I examine in part 2 look for moments in slow motion that try to tell us how to stop it all while we still can.

These critiques of speed and temporality will lead us to the landscape of the late sixties and the mythologies that surround its intersecting social movements—some ascendant, some fleeting, some retrospective, but all insisting that the time of Western modernity should finally be up. There are some anticipations of this argument in my opening account of Robert Smithson, who makes a slow-motion masterpiece at *Spiral Jetty* to test the limits of how modernism can embody time and then makes a film, also entitled *Spiral Jetty*, that uses slow motion to imagine a particularly ironic end to human progress. Smithson imagines something like the apocalypse of entropy that Jean Louis Schefer pictures in *The Ordinary Man of Cinema*: "as if all action had already been relieved by a pervasive wearing down of all sense of expectation, leaving nothing in the midst of these many movements but a heaping pile of dust."[26] But there is nothing especially obscure or abstract about the slow motion that I examine in part 3. I look at how a sense of the events of "1968" are put on high display in the slow motion that patterns five films from the period, each abundantly iconic on its own but that have never been explored together for the ways they make slow motion into the most widespread and persistent way of visualizing time as shaped and structured by technology. As we'll see, *Bonnie and Clyde* does not "invent" slow motion in 1967, yet, by the end, and with ample help from *2001*, *Once Upon a Time in the West*, *The Wild Bunch*, and *Zabriskie Point*, we'll also see that it does. Or put differently, there is more slow motion than we might think in modern culture before the late sixties, but it is this period's lasting iconography—of bodies taking bullets, of Kubrick's majestic floating bones and spaceships, of distended acts of violence and endless explosions—that sets the terms for how slow motion has looked ever since. Slow motion is as old as film, and maybe even older as an aesthetic of modernity. But we have to wait until the sixties for it to become, in a span of only months, a suddenly symbolic form of history in crisis and then, almost immediately and forever after, a little bit generic as a media aesthetic. But generic need not mean exhausted.

"Textual analysis," writes Laura Mulvey in *Death 24x a Second*, "has always generated a tension between a coherent narrative 'whole' and its forward drive and the desire to slow down the movement of film so that time itself becomes palpable."[27] Mulvey's book was one of the most important early and defining influences on my own, and the dialectic she describes has shaped this project from the start. I was interested in where slow motion began in hopes of figuring out the story of why it ends up everywhere. And then the more I realized that it really doesn't have a point of origin and that even the first critics to observe slow motion wrote as if it had always been around, the more I understood that I had to find another shape in which to trace its presence in and through and past a twentieth century that sometimes feels like yesterday or like ancient history or like it will never end.

Slow motion is a phenomenon of speed that emerges almost at the very instant film and modern visual culture are invented; slow motion is an aesthetic that settles to the margins of modernism and modernity until it almost literally explodes into a media effect so dominant and inescapable that it is hard to believe it ever wasn't. Mulvey has almost nothing to say about slow motion, despite the fact that the critical tradition that she exemplifies—and that this book, however imperfectly, tries to extend—is devoted to discovering the "hidden past that might or might not find its way to the surface" when we imagine "different relations to time." She spots the single fleeting moment of slow motion in *Peeping Tom* (1960) and elegantly explains on her commentary track for the Criterion DVD how the director, Michael Powell, achieved it. But she isn't really interested in such tricks or half measures. The "unglamorous mechanics" of slow motion, if I might borrow another phrase from Mulvey, leave us deliriously suspended within the "opposition between stillness and motion that reverberates across the aesthetics of cinema."[28] As we have learned from critics such as Stuart Burrows, Louise Hornsby, and Alix Beeston, there were other aesthetic projects besides film that provocatively stress experiments in composure, stillness, or static fragmentation—often drawing on photography—and that reflect on the power and allure of movement, speed, and progress as defining the default velocity of modern life.[29] Slow motion, though, is not and never stillness. It is among the "extraordinary motion forms" that, as Jordan Schonig richly explores, can help us better imagine the "pleasure of beholding movement of all kinds" and the different phenomenologies of watching bodies come and sometimes slowly go or better describe how duration shapes the rhythms of both everyday perception and the temporal arts that we encounter along the way.[30]

But I also want to take Mulvey at her word when she insists that if something we expect to move slows down enough, we face the image not just of stillness or delay or rest but finally the prospect of its death as well. "Death as a trope," she writes, embodies the "stillness" of narrative cinema, which can "suggest a return of the repressed stillness on which cinema's illusion of movement depends."[31] Not everything dies slowly, of course, and there are some things that can't die fast enough. Slow motion is forever in between velocities and temporalities, which is fitting because if it is another of the metaphors for death that film has given us, it is just as certainly a metonymy for a modern world of speed that never seems to stop, a spectacular part of a whole culture of acceleration that at times, strangely enough, we cannot see any other way.

PART I
A Theory in Slow Motion

I
At the Movies to the End of Time

It is a shame that Robert Smithson didn't have more time for the movies, not that much of what he was seeing in the early 1970s made him happy. But he watched anyway, even though he doesn't know which might be worse: to admit that Hollywood has declined into a ruin of exhausted visual forms and anachronistic genres or to know that this will be true until the end of time. Writing one year after he completed his most celebrated project—the Utah earthwork *Spiral Jetty* (1970), which has, since reappearing after almost three decades under water, become the single most recognizable icon of contemporary land art from the period—Smithson's 1971 *Artforum* essay, "A Cinematic Atopia," is set far from the depopulated spaces of the U.S. West, where his too-short career witnessed its most significant accomplishments. At the movies, Smithson pictures himself at a site that is no place at all. "One forgets where one is sitting," and then, he observes, "the outside world fades as the eyes probe the screen," noting that "one thing all films have in common is the power to take perception elsewhere."[1] Smithson has a fairly rarefied complaint to make about "a notion of the abstraction of films," but this is less an argument he develops and more of an excuse to voice a series of conventional, even pedestrian disappointments. His vision of "a pure film of lights and darks" fades "into a dim landscape of countless westerns. Some sagebrush here, a little cactus there, and hoofbeats going nowhere." He isn't thinking about any movie in particular, and he can't, or so he says, remember "a single film I liked, or even one I didn't like," out of the years that he's spent "swallowed up in a morass of Hollywood garbage" (138). "The thought of a film with a 'story' makes me listless," Smithson grumbles, sounding like nothing so much as a bleak, inverted echo of Frank O'Hara's poem "To the Film Industry in Crisis." Except where O'Hara loves what he sees dying, Smithson blames the victim for the crisis. "How many stories have I seen on the screen?" Smithson asks, and what about "all those 'characters' carrying out dumb tasks. Actors doing exciting things"? Smithson has seen movies come and go and vanish "somewhere at the bottom of my memories," more wreckage in a "tangled mass" of twentieth-century media amid the "sunken remains of all the films I have ever seen . . . stagnant pools of images that cancel each other out." Born in 1938, Smithson would have been a child when movie attendance in the United States was at its highest, and he was almost certainly among the 90 million people—from a population of just over 140 million—who visited a theater in 1946, the year most often cited as Hollywood's peak moment of cultural and commercial dominance. It was all downhill from there, and as a connoisseur of "entropy" or "energy-drain," we should not be surprised that Smithson takes sardonic pleasure in signs that cinema is spilling out "into a state of stupefaction."[2] Yet there is sadness as he takes biting inspiration from the ends of things. "It's enough," he writes, "to put one into a permanent coma."[3]

And yet, Smithson was an avid and intrepid moviegoer. A "devoted cinephile," writes Michael Ned Holte, he "haunted the Anthology Film Archive with its 'essential repertory' of avant garde cinema, as well as the 'crummy baroque' cinemas on 42nd Street, screening B-movie gems."[4] Thus we are ready when Smithson stirs from his figurative coma to namedrop Akira Kurosawa's *Ikiru* as a potential favorite, only to immediately suffer an entropic relapse when he concludes that "Japanese films are too exhausting" and that Satyajit Ray is good "for a heavy dose of tedium, if you're into tedium" (139). "Actually," Smithson confesses, he prefers the "lurid sensationalism" of Alfred Hitchcock, which perhaps helps explain the remarkable homage to *North by Northwest* (1959) that several critics have identified toward the end the film *Spiral Jetty* (1970), produced alongside the earthwork, with Smithson running nowhere along the recently constructed earthwork while a loud and seriously determined helicopter follows him for nearly three full minutes. Smithson's billowing white shirt appears almost as out of place on the arid shores of the Great Salt Lake as Cary Grant's sharp gray suit on the plains of South Dakota, and such deeply inside jokes are not infrequent in Smithson's work and especially in his writings.

"A Cinematic Atopia" includes thirty-six stills from *Spiral Jetty*, but Smithson does not say anything about his own filmmaking. That said, he more than establishes his credentials as a fellow traveler of the cinematic avant-garde with a fairly cutting mention of Gene Youngblood's (then) new book *Expanded Cinema* (1970)—which, for Smithson, imagines cinema "expanding into a deafening pale abstraction controlled by computers"—alongside a thermodynamic entendre about the "deteriorated images of Hollis Frampton's *Maxwell's Demon*" and assorted references to George Landow's "depraved animation," Kenneth Anger, and Michelangelo Antonioni (139–40). Yet Smithson barely registers the abundance of legendary figures and future icons of cinematic modernism at a moment that is celebrated for its mix of earlier-twentieth-century avant-gardes, the New Wave and other postwar European movements, global national cinemas, and the stranger fringes of Hollywood and the New American Cinema. Smithson's pose stays remarkably impassive. "We are faced with inventories of limbo," he complains (139). And so he probably is not heartened by the excellent company he keeps in this issue of *Artforum* dedicated to "the present flowering of cinema in this country," as Annette Michelson writes in her "Forward," where she argues for "the urgency of recognition for an achievement whose importance will eventually be seen as comparable to that of American painting in the 1950s and onwards."[5] "Eyes were still very much on American art," writes John Roberts of the 1960s, since even after the era of abstract expressionism, the United States was still "the post-war court of arbitration on modernity."[6] Or, this was still the time of "hegemonic modernism," in Miriam Hansen's devastatingly efficient formulation.[7] This is the assumption looming in the background over Michelson's strong claim, which captures something of the swagger—parochial and unearned in retrospect but nonetheless persuasive—that remained of midcentury modernism as the 1970s began. It also gives a sense of what was at stake for Smithson to stay so listless in response to such an exuberant statement of artistic progress and national accomplishment. "The ultimate film goer would be a captive of sloth," his perceptions "among the flickering shadows ... would take on a kind of sluggishness" (141). A "hermit dwelling among the elsewhere," Smithson's ideal viewer seems unlikely to feel much "urgency" over anything, much less for the achievements of modern cinema in America (142). "He would not be able to distinguish between good or bad films" as "all would be swallowed up into an endless blur" (142). Smithson understands that the movies have become another place where the trajectories and technologies of modernism are unthinkingly celebrated and confirmed. Smithson wants to bring all this to the slowest and most excruciating of stops, "all films ... brought into equilibrium—a vast mud field of images, forever motionless." It doesn't matter if you're watching Godard or Kurosawa, Hitchcock or Hollis Frampton: At the movies of "A Cinematic Atopia," everybody knows this is nowhere.

Many of the ideas and turns of phrase that I find most striking in "A Cinematic Atopia" appear for the first time in Smithson's most famous piece of writing, "Entropy and the New Monuments" (1966), which not only championed the work of Donald Judd, Dan Flavin, Robert Morris, and other minimalists with gnostic gusto but also gestured toward the discourses and aesthetics that would inform his "nonsites" and later earthworks that pushed against the limits of "classical time and space."[8] Here we find Smithson looking on with admiration at sculptures that intimate just how "the whole universe will burn out and be transformed into an all-encompassing sameness" (11). And here too we find Smithson at the movies, grouping his favored artists by their preferences for the "'blood and guts' of horror movies" or the "cold steel" of science fiction, many of which we can assume they saw in the same "crummy baroque and rococo" theaters around Forty-Second Street (16–17). Smithson catalogs a canon of genre films from *Creation of the Humanoids* ("Andy Warhol's favorite movie") and Mario Bava's *The Planet of Vampires* ("movie about entropy") to *Creature from the Black Lagoon* and *Abbott and Costello Meet Frankenstein* (17). While these are not the sorts of films that Michelson thinks her *Artforum* readers should know better, she probably would have appreciated the philosophical prestige that Smithson grants them. "Time is compressed or stopped inside the movie house," he writes, "and this in turn provides the viewer with an entropic condition" (17). Having not set foot in a theater for a couple years while I was writing portions of this book during the COVID pandemic, I might point out that life gives us plenty of entropic conditions anyway. Nor should we understand Smithson's sense of temporal compression or even stoppage as romantic or escapist, despite the fact that going to the movies was the opposite of an event for much of the past century—the epitome of distraction, aimless entertainment, or just killing time.

It is exactly the strange mix of speeds and temporalities that Smithson links to the experience of watching movies that makes him a compelling figure for helping us understand how, over these very years in the late 1960s, cinematic slow motion emerges as a signature motif of visual culture in the United States and beyond. More importantly, Smithson lets us see how slow motion crystallizes—to borrow one of his own metaphors for how "time is deranged" by the materialities of art—the broader contours of a whole culture of modernity and technology, from literature to new media, that is represented and embodied with each instance, figurative or viewed, of what must by any measure be considered the very least special effect.[9] Smithson's "nonsites" don't at all negate the sites to which their matter, maps, and diagrams refer. They are extensions and experiments with differential perceptions of space, and we hear anticipations of their logic when Smithson says that "to spend time in a movie house is to make a 'hole' in one's life" (17). This book is about the hole slow motion makes in a culture of speed.

∎ ∎ ∎

In the almost forty years since Stephen Kern's defining work in *The Culture of Time and Space*, critics and scholars have considered with increasing refinement and sophistication how "the cinema portrayed a variety of temporal phenomena that played with the uniformity and the irreversibility of time."[10] The rich collection of essays put together by Leo Charney and Vanessa R. Schwartz's *Cinema and the Invention of Modern Life* extended both the range of where we could look to find film's cultural influence and the institutions, practices, and technologies that informed its development.[11] Sara Danius and Susan McCabe each illuminate how film patterned the conceptual and aesthetic horizons of writers from the late nineteenth and early twentieth centuries as they attempted at once to depict, in McCabe's terms, "bodily experience and sensation along with an overpowering sense of the unavailability of such experience except as mediated through mechanical reproduction."[12] Their work in modernist literary studies—which was influential for my own and other "new" modernist accounts of literature and media in the first part of the century—reflects a larger turn toward more searching engagements with the experience of cinema as a defining cultural feature of the first half of the twentieth century. These modernist critics were following from the indispensable writings of Miriam Hansen, who proposed that cinema needs to be understood less for what it showed than for what it "brought into optical consciousness [by opening] up hitherto unperceived modes of sensory perception and experience [and] a different organization of the daily world."[13] Hansen insisted that it was hard even to conceive of modern culture without first acknowledging the centrality of film, which was not just the dominant mass medium of a particular artistic period but more profoundly constituted "the single most expansive discursive horizon in which the effects of modernity were reflected, rejected or denied, transmuted or negotiated."[14] Hansen's point is absolute and universal but also provocatively vague and subject to all manner of qualifications and demands for specificity—which is, of course, what categorical statements are designed to invite but also to transcend. This is why the equally influential work of Mary Ann Doane seems significant for the sharper edges it puts on a similarly sweeping argument about the modernity that cinema reveals. "Modernity was perceived as a temporal demand," Doane writes, but there were designs on this demand that asked more of subjects than that they just accommodate new perceptual skills and capabilities.[15] Cinema is one of several new "technologies of representation" at the turn of the twentieth century that participate in the "rationalization of time characterizing industrialization and the expansion of capitalism."

It is not that slow motion simply symbolizes another order of "modernity" or the "emergence," borrowing now from Doane, of another "cinematic time" that we have somehow overlooked. Slow motion, as we will see, is part of twentieth-century culture from its earliest beginnings and embodies many of the same fundamental inspirations as the oldest fantasies of fully capturing movement in words or images. Slow motion is already precinematic and permanently belated in all the ways that cinema too is not so much a singular invention as a gradually codified assembly of technological innovations, social practices, and the "converging of various obsessions with . . . integral realism," as André Bazin once wrote, that we may or may not still believe add up to a "myth of total cinema."[16]

We are on the other side of slow motion's definitive and spectacular proliferation after the late 1960s, and it has become so impossible to miss that it can be hard to see and value as not just an effect of media—a byproduct of ever faster cameras on studio lots and soundstages, in stadiums, labs, homes, and finally phones—but also as an exemplary instance of the "time-critical media processes" that Wolfgang Ernst describes as transforming time itself "from a metaphysical signified to technical availability" that "communicates its processuality to humans." This is some especially spiky language, and it wants to stress the constant and abiding presence of technologies that decelerate and analyze the flow of time—from the "trivial machine of the clock" to "photography, cinematography, and computer games," as well as all manner of scientific instruments and devices for exploring the "micro-temporal . . . in electrophysics itself"—that have always shaped and shadowed our reflections and representations of temporality, our "Dasein-critical" perceptions, intuitions, and iconographies that show how "reified time . . . subliminally intervenes in human experience as such." "Time is the subject and object of technologies," Ernst plainly states, and we are the "human time sensor[s]" that have created whole philosophies to gain a purchase not only on the "infra-temporal domain of the smallest moments" but also on the "gradual ongoing transformations that are not noticed by people at all due to their slowness." The present is the only "window of perception" that unfolds at speeds that we can match and process; this is, for Ernst, the very essence of its limited utility in a world where the intensification of "chrono-technical production" is measurable at every turn though almost utterly invisible to us. "The power of media," he writes, "is that their temporal process becomes imperceptible."[17]

Yet even as I am drawn to the stark and explicitly inhuman methods of analysis that distinguish Ernst's media archaeology, it does not come naturally to me. There will, I promise, be some discussions of frame rates, shutter speeds, and CGI along the way, but up against the daunting technicality of Ernst and other figures in European media studies—or else in light of writers such as John Durham Peters, Lisa Gitelman, Tung-Hui Hu, and Jonathan Sterne, who don't write media history to grind a philosophical axe or two—my approach to slow motion is positively retrograde. Slow motion, across its many incarnations from early cinema and high-speed photography to Hollywood blockbusters and digital imaging, might lack the technical specificity to warrant being called a "format," in Sterne's sense, but it does let us reflect on the "concept of mediality ... and invites us to ask after the changing formations of media, the contexts of their reception, the conjunctures that shaped their sensual characteristics, and the institutional politics in which they were enmeshed."[18] Somewhat awkwardly conceptualized as everything from a standard visual technique to the very signature of modernist aesthetics—a practice of the avant-garde then incorporated and debased by the sheer scale and economics of Hollywood—slow motion is occasionally mentioned in foundational discussions of film style as if all its meanings have already been confirmed. This is one reason why I think slow motion has been dismissed so quickly as a device or gimmick after the relatively short period—call it a "long" 1968—that establishes the basic shape it takes in film and visual culture more or less up to the present. But when we watch the films that make slow motion seem so obvious in retrospect, we see that they are themselves preoccupied with questions of speed and change, with narratives about the violence of historical progress and the costs and consequences of trying to endure the endless epoch of capitalist modernity, even as it might be dying.

The perception of time as forever varying in both its speeds and its velocities is not invented in the twentieth century, nor is it solely the product of cinema or the network of technologies and practices that this term has come to embody for critics who now argue for its persistence, its decline, or both. Film offers, in the United States and beyond, an eminently available set of metaphors or figures for a technology whose essence is "by no means anything technological," to invoke some familiar Heidegger—for thinking through experiences of mediated time. Heidegger says that technology must be confronted not simply as a set of "means" or instrumentalities but rather as a "way of revealing," as an "enframing" of the world that is the very ground on which experience takes place.[19]

Heidegger published his essay "The Question Concerning Technology" in 1954, but it was not translated into English until 1977; Smithson never read it, though in a very literal way it does "enframe" the epoch of his brief career.[20] Smithson mined all sorts of books for his ideas on time and art, from pulpy science fiction and the somewhat more gentrified work of J. G. Ballard to anthropology and physics textbooks and more. It seems unlikely that Smithson would have known

Blaise Cendrars's fascinating sketch "High Speed and Slow Motion" ("Cinéma accéléré and cinéma ralenti") published in his 1963 *Ouvres complètes*, which imagines an epoch after human life on earth as a time-lapse series of intensely static scenes of nature that shift into "slow motion" as "the shapes of all the annihilated beings" magically reappear just before "blackened, bloody earth liquefies" with the final heat death of the sun.[21] But Smithson was clearly drawn to writers who were preoccupied with time beyond the limits of perception and were willing to speculate about how much passed beneath the threshold of the narrow range of speeds and short durations we could process. As Gary Shapiro and Pam Lee both point out, the influence on Smithson of George Kubler's 1962 book *The Shape of Time: Remarks on the History of Things* is particularly revealing—though again, not in quite the arcane sense that comes with Heidegger. Kubler likely informs Smithson's reflections on the speed of things in 1966, where his own logic seems to echo Kubler's, for whom "there are only two significant velocities": "One is the glacier-like pace of cumulative drift in small and isolated societies.... The other, swift mode resembles a forest fire in its leaping across great distances." The symbolism here is conventional, even romantic in the way it renders natural occurrences as timepieces for measuring phenomena that human beings might have difficulty comprehending. At other places, though, Kubler speaks in a different language of historical analogy and exploits the temporalities of film and media in hopes of capturing the qualities of transformation that our perceptive apparatuses have trouble processing even when their scales are not anything so sublime. "Certain types of motion appear when we look at time as an accumulation of nearly identical moments drifting by in minute changes toward large differences amassed over long periods." "Motion," Kubler continues, "is perhaps a misnomer for the changes" that happen in this way, despite that fact that they "describe through time an appearance of motion like that of the frames of a film, recording the successive instants of an action, which produce the illusion of movement as they flicker past the beam of light."[22]

Cinema operates here less as a technology than as the center of a fiction about modernity and its comingling of speeds, a fiction that provides what Donald Davidson would call a "conceptual scheme" that still governs our thinking about modernity and modernisms no matter how much we pluralize the latter.[23] Speed and acceleration, for reasons that are both obvious yet still worth questioning, are defining features of modern life, which is then defined not so much dialectically but just reflexively as the historical period when everything starts to go faster. But these feedback loops work to prevent us from understanding all the ways that, as Lutz Koepnick writes, slowness is also an aesthetic "of the contemporary" and not a residual, prelapsarian, or redemptive temporality with purer motives or truer claims on the experience of durée.[24] Slow motion is a signature effect of modern technologies of representation, one that might look on the surface like it is out of sync but that is utterly dependent on the speed we don't see behind it.

■ ■ ■

Slow motion is present everywhere at the site of Smithson's *Spiral Jetty* (figure 1.1). A gradual rise in the Great Salt Lake's water levels submerged the entire construction from 1973 to a brief period in the early 1990s before it disappeared again between 1993 and 1996. In the years since, it has been possible to see the slow formation of salt crystals change *Spiral Jetty*'s color and brightness, and at a level of detail no one can perceive, even its outline and dimensions are slowly growing as the salt deposits solidify. In this respect, the project weirdly accelerates the processes of geological time that are otherwise, as Kubler and Smithson would remind us, "glacier-like" and invisible to us. In both James Benning's film about *Spiral Jetty* (*Casting a Glance* [2007]) and Tacita Dean's more elaborate reimagining of Smithson by way of J. G. Ballard (*JG* [2013]), there is imagery

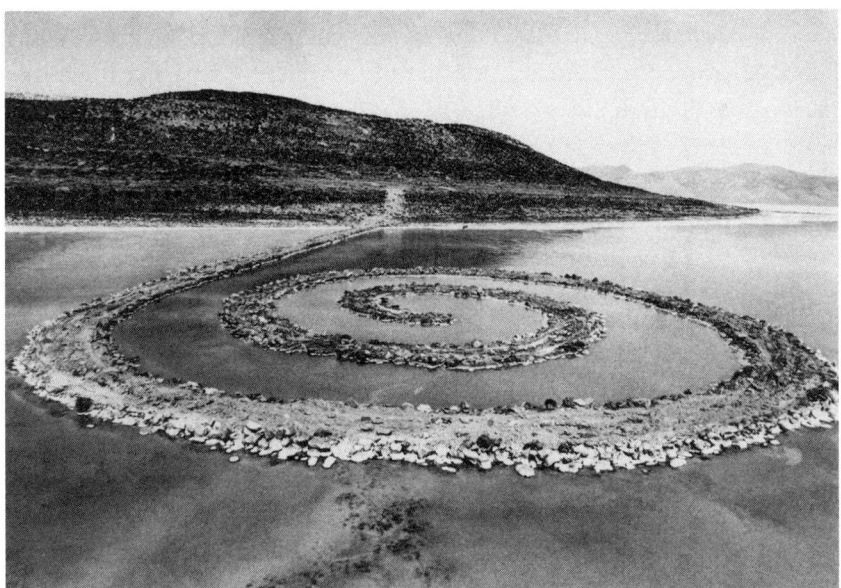

FIGURE 1.1 Robert Smithson, *Spiral Jetty* (1970).

Source: © 2025 Holt/Smithson Foundation and Dia Art Foundation / Licensed by Artists Rights Society (ARS), NY.

that depicts the salt-swept tableaux and stalactites of the western landscape as if it were an Arctic scene of drifting snow and polar ice. Benning and Dean are drawn to Smithson's monument at least in part as a reflection of what Walter Benjamin called the "petrified unrest" of modern life itself, which can make ruins out of even the most recent past.[25] These films signal, along with popular books, abundant travel writing, and official tourist marketing from the state of Utah, the belated confirmation of *Spiral Jetty*'s stature as a canonical example of land art.[26] It only took forty or fifty years, which is fast or slow, depending on your baseline for the speed of high culture as an institution.

There is also some slow motion in *Spiral Jetty*, the 1970 film that Smithson and Nancy Holt made with Robert Logan, Barbara Harris, and Robert Fiore. With its opening shots of solar flares and eerily red-filtered sequences made in the old dinosaur room at New York's American Museum of Natural History, there is no mistaking the film's devotion to registering the uncanniness of inhuman time. Its last shot—of the editing room where *Spiral Jetty* (the film) has been assembled beneath a giant, black-and-white photograph of *Spiral Jetty* (the artwork)—shows how time can be materialized by media technologies and natural processes alike. But I am just as interested in the slow motion that is literally present in the film—and that goes unremarked in every account of *Spiral Jetty* I have read.

We see in *Spiral Jetty* several sequences of the actual construction of *Spiral Jetty* on the ground in Utah, with the growling mechanical roar and lumbering power of backhoes and dump trucks meant to signify, without much subtlety, that versions of the dinosaurs still roam on these foreboding landscapes, terrible beasts of diesel engines and hydraulic augers and tiltrotators. When the dump trucks drop their loads of rocks and dirt into the water (figure 1.2), the slow motion is noticeable, though again not especially dramatic. I am not surprised that no viewer or critic has seemed to notice it for over fifty years—the same fifty years that witness the staggering proliferation of slow motion from its relative rarity before 1968 to its almost preposterous ubiquity today. There is no way to know who filmed these shots in *Spiral Jetty* because Smithson, Holt, and Fiore shared the job of cinematographer. But Fiore was the most professional and had already shot footage for Richard Serra and Brian DePalma as well as doing secondary camerawork on Albert and David Maysles's *Gimme Shelter*. He would go on to film the iconic bodybuilding documentary *Pumping Iron* (1977), where Arnold Schwarzenegger is the monster slinging heavy metal like it weighed nothing. So he might deserve the credit for these shots, which would have been trickier to film, given the faster shutter speeds of slow-motion photography back then and the extra care required when shooting in natural light. Then again, these sequences are nothing special: You must watch closely to see the water

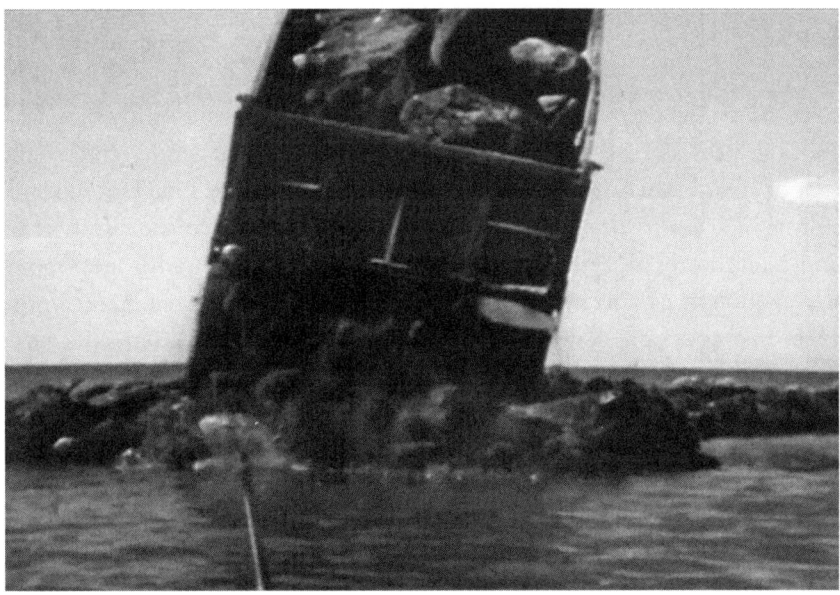

FIGURE 1.2 Robert Smithson, still from *Spiral Jetty* (1970).

Source: © 2025 Holt/Smithson Foundation / Licensed by Artists Rights Society (ARS), NY.

hanging in the air just slightly longer than it should as the rocks explode its surface, and then you start to see that the rocks themselves are falling with just marginally more grace and detail than they should have to the naked eye. Smithson's Bolex H16 could film at 8, 16, 24, 32, or 64fps, or frames per second, and I'd guess this was shot at 32fps (with 16fps as the film's normal speed) because it looks entirely "natural" when played twice as fast on my laptop. I could be wrong, but what's a few split seconds against the endless wastes of time itself?

In the pages that follow, I take my inspiration from Siegfried Zielinski's idea that we should examine a "deep time of the media" that wanders back and forth through centuries of material forms and cultural practices even if, at the end of the figurative day, we will largely stay in the merest shallows of the incomprehensible durations that Zielinski invokes, like many others, in the wake of John McPhee's popularization of this concept in his book *Basin and Range* (1980).[27] I will get to deeper times eventually, but only as they emerge at sudden and surprising intervals within the far shorter history of a specific media form that lets us think about the speed of modern life and its technologies in different and sometimes contradictory ways. Slow motion, after all, would seem the worst way to picture change over vast epochs of time because the very essence of its technological identity is the ability to render smaller all-but-instantaneous events as distended spectacles of detail and information. For a genuinely "deep time" media history, a century or two is not enough to avoid turning a gradual and largely invisible network of small advances and aesthetic gestures into a pageant of "firsts" and breakthrough innovations of exactly the kind that modern culture tends to fetishize. Somewhere amid the blur of cinematic history that Smithson absorbs in such encompassing abstraction there is another story about slow motion that I start here because these isolated moments from the art world of the 1960s not only show us how a minor modernist device becomes the most pervasive special effect in global visual culture but also help us think through all the speeds at which modernity unfolds.

In a short piece from 1968 entitled "The Monument: Outline for a Film," Smithson imagines a final sequence involving "a series of *tableaux vivants*" made with "rapid zoom shots onto faces, hands" to give the effect of "statues breaking and crumbling." Mixing art-historical citation and montage theory, it is worth wondering how seriously Smithson would have taken film if he hadn't died so young. This unfinished and unfinishable "monument" wasn't supposed to end in entropy but rather with "Dancing—slow motion, 'Vanilla Fudge' play rock and roll."[28] This is one way slow motion could look by the late 1960s—the easy shorthand for a period aesthetic that would go perfectly with the heavy psychedelic sounds of Vanilla Fudge and their sludgy covers of the Beatles and the Supremes. But why did it take so long to get there?

2

Almost Freeze Frame

I want to trace two histories of slow motion. The first begins much later and takes us right up to the present. The second begins with the origins of film and takes us up to the 1960s. The first is arguably shorter—almost brief enough to capture with a single image.

Since the mid-1970s, the Japanese photographer Hiroshi Sugimoto has been taking pictures of places to watch movies as part of an ongoing series he calls *Theaters*. No matter what proscenium we see or whether we are outdoors and amid the ruins, the central feature of every image remains the same: a dense white field of light, luminous, like a portal to another dimension, but also singularly flat, in contrast to the classical perspectives of the architectural interiors of old movie palaces like Radio City Music Hall or the Cinerama Dome or to the surrounding landscapes that recede behind the glowing screens of drive-ins, like the one we see in 1993's *Tri-City Drive-In, San Bernardino* (figure 2.1). The Tri-City Drive-In closed in 1993, right around the time Sugimoto would have visited.

Every picture in the *Theaters* series involves a push and pull between the site where a particular film is showing and the generic, abstract scene of cinema that illuminates the image. Only in an early 1976 "experiment" that Sugimoto took at St. Marks Cinema in Manhattan's East Village do we see any people in his pictures of the movies; after this proof-of-concept photograph, all the others were taken in empty theaters. These are not exactly pictures of "theaters" as places where we watch movies sitting next to other people; Sugimoto's original ambition, which he says came to him in a "near-hallucinatory vision," was to *"shoot a whole movie in a single frame,"* or, as he would later write, "my dream was to capture 170,000 photographs on a single frame of film."[1] "To watch a two-hour movie," according to Sugimoto, "is

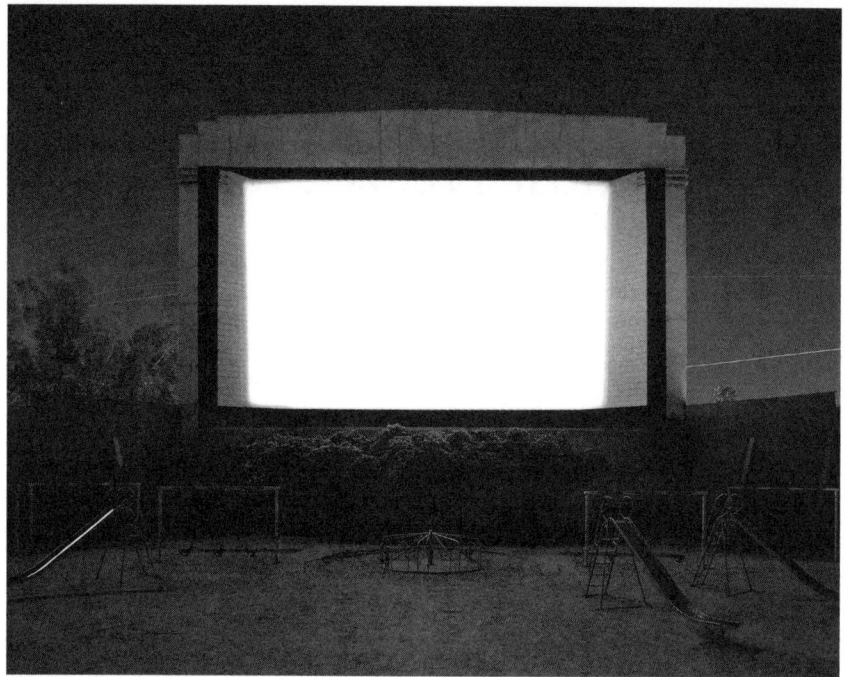

FIGURE 2.1 Hiroshi Sugimoto, "Tri-City Drive-In, San Bernardino," 1993.

Source: © Hiroshi Sugimoto, courtesy Fraenkel Gallery, San Francisco.

simply to look at 172,800 photographic afterimages." His math is as impeccable as his commitment to a certain logic of medium-specificity that grounds film in what Bazin famously called "the ontology of the photographic image."[2] All of his *Theaters* are empty by design because, with the aperture on his large-format camera set to its maximum, any people sitting in the seats would look like blurs or smudges, even ghosts, since their every shift and little movement—not to mention trips for popcorn or the bathroom—would be apparent with Sugimoto's shutter kept wide open for the duration of the running time of the movie he is screening. In a recent book revisiting these now iconic photographs, he lets us know more about the films he watched while rendering them invisible. The book is called *Snow White*, which is the movie pictured—but not for us to see—in one of the photographs inside. There is a great deal of humor in Sugimoto's writings throughout *Snow White*, suggesting that a project that began in hopes of realizing "something awe-inspiring and divine," perhaps even "the 'excess of death'" itself, has become, at least in part, a project of deadpan media historicism too. To witness these films in the slowest motion might give us something beautiful and blank, the movies as virtual "still lifes" in an era of digital cinema and whatever ontologies come with it.

Sugimoto's photographs are arresting at first glance and studiously remote as feats of long-exposure technique and documents of media archaeology. The nostalgia in which they traffic—for any viewers with memories of going to the movies—is obvious, no matter the rigor of Sugimoto's austere erasures of film history. That the screen in *Tri-City Drive-In, San Bernardino* illuminates an empty playground suggests that this theater has already been repurposed once and stands utterly devoid of any human presence. The midcentury architectural details and Cold War aura of drive-ins in America—which became popular in the years after World War II, with over four thousand in operation in the early 1950s—lends this scene a distinctly apocalyptic glow, as if the invading body snatchers have just left or the horizon is glowing from nuclear fallout. At one level, the genius of Sugimoto's vision is that I can easily imagine this might be where John Travolta's "Danny" sang the fifties simulacrum "Sandy" to Olivia Newton-John in *Grease* (1978), but I can also find everything I need to see this as a version of an atomic test site, "predicated," as Jennifer Fay writes, "on the technological and biological disposability and replaceability of the subject."[3]

Alongside these iconographies and atmospherics, Sugimoto's *Theaters* summon a whole host of art-historical precedents and citations. Though the visual textures of a painting like Kazimir Malevich's *White on White* (1918) or Agnes Martin's *White Stone* (1964)—much less the wrought surface of Robert Ryman's *Bridge* (1980)—are flat-out busy when compared to Sugimoto's screens, they can all be grouped together in a tradition of artistic gestures, from modernism to minimalism, that aestheticize the negative capability of the picture plane. In his own medium, Sugimoto can be situated in a history of long-exposure photography that reaches back to Nadar and other early figures who had to manage shutter "speeds" that ranged from several seconds to nearly twenty minutes. The fine white lines that crisscross *Tri-City Drive-In* are not power lines or cables but rather the tracks of stars proceeding across the night sky during the eighty-two minutes of exposure Sugimoto engineered; this is one of several pictures in *Theaters* that could be discussed as fine-art forms of scientific imaging or time-lapse photography as practiced by countless astronomers and amateur observers since the publication of Edward Skinner King's *A Manual of Celestial Photography* (1931). For Mary Ann Doane, Sugimoto's project is best understood in terms drawn from the philosophy of Henri Bergson, which she uses brilliantly to explore how these pictures participate in "synchronic spatial network of other media" and so end up rendering time as space despite themselves.[4] Michael Fried puts Sugimoto with Jeff Wall and Cindy Sherman, arguing that their photographs function at a certain distance from the "theatricality" of filmic experience, explicitly revisiting the terms of his debates with Judd and Smithson from the 1960s.[5] Sugimoto's *Theaters*, in short, leave a lot of space for critics to project their arguments.

One could hardly ask for a less charming description of *Tri-City Drive-In* than Wolfgang Ernst's account of "intermediality," which fixates on the ways that "temporally serial data" in digital formats "are thus ... retranslated into spatial orders again—reminding us of the premodern cultural engineering of memory (*ars memoriae*)."[6] But this language can focus our attention on the broader shape of Sugimoto's project, which may have started as a way of representing cinematic motion in the stillness of a single photographic image but has turned into—by the very nature of its four-decade duration and increasingly global scope—a slower and more recognizable commemoration of a modernity that might be vanishing before our eyes. The latest of the *Theaters* that Sugimoto has included in the series are flamboyantly abandoned and in exquisite states of disrepair; in photographs like *Proctor's Theater, Troy* (2015) (figure 2.2),

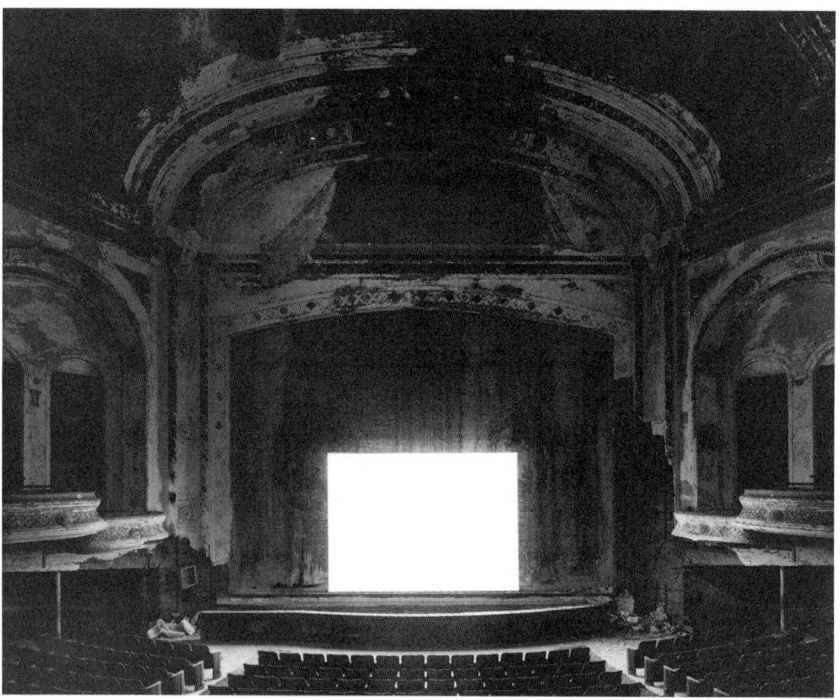

FIGURE 2.2 Hiroshi Sugimoto, "Proctor's Theater, Troy," 2015.

Source: © Hiroshi Sugimoto, courtesy Fraenkel Gallery, San Francisco.

the glowing white screen at the center of the image, fittingly proportioned in the old-fashioned 4:3 "Academy ratio," gleams before a torn and tattered curtain on a half-destroyed proscenium. Every surface that we see—save for the screen—has lost its finish, and more dramatic damage is piled up as trash and rubble at both corners of the stage. There is too much of this space's bare life on full display: The grubby textures of the beams are revealed behind the plaster; the lath from inside the walls has been "exposed" from years and decades of neglect that precede the time it took to make this painfully slow picture, which is also just a passing glance only fleetingly evoking the temporality of this solid structure turning into dust.

Susan Stewart writes: "Artists of ruins... give us a sense not only that the material resists meaning, but also materiality at times cannot bear up under a surplus of meaning" because, she adds, "these aspects of the ruin are tied to the inherent violence of all representation, which reifies or fixes the object, making living things dead and bringing dead things to life."[7] There has always been something melancholic about these *Theaters* and their structuring absence of the moving image stopped in and out of time. But *Proctor's Theater, Troy* is also sort of sad. This looks a lot like "ruin porn," as this genre of iconography came to be called in the early 2010s, when its emergence in such proximity to the financial crisis and Great Recession of 2007–2009 made for arguments about the exploitative ethics of visual motifs dependent, for the most part, on the destructiveness of capitalism and the radically uneven consequences of deindustrialization.[8] The itinerary we can reconstruct for Sugimoto from these later photographs is a Rust Belt geography—Troy, New York; Kenosha, Wisconsin; Detroit, Michigan—that seems overdetermined to make cinema's slow ruination into a figure for the decline and fall of the American century. Sugimoto seems to mystify these extinction sites, as if the people who once went to the movies have simply followed the light to somewhere beyond this suffering and decay.

We get closer to the slow motion that we actually do see at the movies—wherever we might see them now—at another theater altogether as empty as any of Sugimoto's despite the fact that it remains in operation on the night we are taken to it in Tsai Ming-Liang's 2003 film, *Goodbye, Dragon Inn*. Set during and right after the final screening of King Hu's *wuxia* epic *Dragon Inn* (1967) at the Fu-Ho Grand Theater in Taipei, Taiwan—with the theater set to close for good—this film consolidated Tsai's status as a leading figure in global art cinema and a festival celebrity, which he had achieved already with the success of features such as *Rebels of the Neon God* (1992), *Vive L'Amour* (1994), and *The Hole* (1998). The plot of *Goodbye, Dragon Inn* is sparse and schematic: A female employee who sells tickets and cleans up at the theater spends much of the night trying to find the projectionist, played by the Tsai regular Lee Kang-sheng, while a Japanese tourist wanders the same aisles, halls, and bathrooms amid the phantom presences of an audience we don't know for sure is real, including two actors (Chun Shih and Tien Mao) making cameos from Hu's original. The Fu-Ho Grand Theater is not dilapidated yet in *Goodbye, Dragon Inn*, but it is surely on its way; the film is full of long shots where we are given ample time to notice all the peeling paint, cracked tiles, dodgy staircases, and accumulating rubbish that renders the interiors (shot on location) biomorphic and affectingly organic, an effect that appears calculated, in part, to make the theater feel like an extension of the "Ticket Woman" herself, whom Shiang-chyi Chen plays as a disabled woman who walks with an acute, heavy, hesitating limp. Her character's disability is handled without much drama or detail, but in a film where almost no one speaks, it effectively defines her character. The slowness of her walk is the very opposite of the gliding dolly tricks, wire work, and kung fu choreography we see in passing moments of *Dragon Inn* as projected on the Fu-Ho Grand Theater's screen.

Her slow walk quite literally sets the pace for what has, I think, become the film's most famous sequence, which also marks one of the exemplary set pieces of the "slow cinema" that Tsai has come to represent. At just over an hour into the film, the lights come up on the empty seats, which are framed for us at a perspective that puts us near the screen but angled to give a greater sense of depth and scale (figure 2.3). The woman enters from the right side of the frame and works her way across the space and up and down the rows for almost three full minutes, stooping laboriously a couple times over her broom and dustpan. It takes her three minutes to cross the screen, and then Tsai lets us linger for more than another two minutes on the emptier emptiness she leaves behind. Like Beckett's "Unnamable," she must go on, she can't go on, she will go on. Until we cut to the next scene, we are watching the equivalent of a photograph of cinema, the motion of the apparatus going on invisibly but making nothing move on screen. Here is a kind of slowed motion that lacks the suddenness and inherent drama of the freeze-frame, a "reduction in time," as Smithson might say, that still takes place *in* time as it "annihilates the value of the notion in 'action' in art."

For the past decade, Tsai has been regularly mentioned in almost any discussion of "slow cinema," a subgenre of global art film that began to coalesce into a recognizable style in the 2000s and became something of a flashpoint for many critics after Nick James, then writing in 2010 as the editor of *Sight and Sound*, signaled his growing impatience with a mode of "passive-aggressive" movie that increasingly "demand[s] great swathes of our attention to achieve quite fleeting

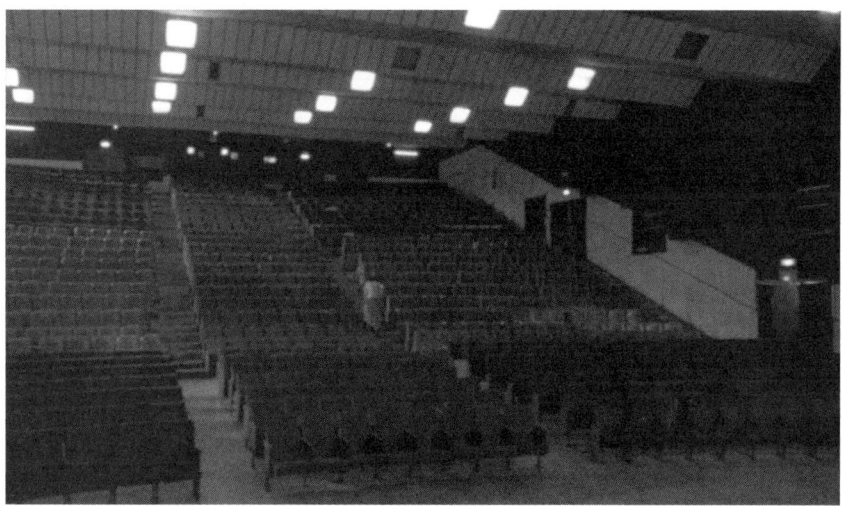

FIGURE 2.3 Still from *Goodbye, Dragon Inn* (2003).

and slender aesthetic and political effects."[9] Against the "declining shot lengths of assaultive post-continuity editing," writes Erika Balsom, slow cinema emerged as something of a "reaction formation to that same condition, a dialectical response to withering attention spans and tiny, portable screens."[10] Both film bloggers and mainstream critics responded to James's complaints, with some aggressively outraged that one of the last remaining magazines still covering film festivals and "serious" cinema from around the world "would publish such anti-intellectual banter" and others, such as the film theorist Steven Shaviro, offering qualified agreement about the "oppressive sense .. in which the long-take, long-shot, slow-camera movement, sparse-dialogue style has become entirely routinized."[11] When Manohla Dargis and A. O. Scott eventually caught up to the debate the following year, their diverging responses to Terence Malick's *Tree of Life* allowed them to discuss Reichardt, Tarr, Weerasethakul, and more under the headline "In Defense of the Slow and the Boring."[12] Scholars, theorists, and academic critics have continued these debates ever since. Writing about Kelly Reichardt, Katherine Fusco and Nicole Seymour largely reject conceiving of slow cinema as "a kind of pastoral for the present moment, a respite from our technologically saturated, nature-alienated, Hollywood-blockbuster-centered era," and several of Tsai's best critics would agree with them.[13] Still, others are more than willing to admit that admiring "slow cinema" is, as Ira Jaffe puts it, a way of "countering the cinema of action," and so analogies to the global

Slow Food movement—and all the slownesses it has inspired, from Slow Travel and Slow Cities to Slow Gardening and Slow Sex—are solicited and welcomed.[14] Arden Reed invokes many of these somewhat flimsy projects of temporal resistance in his wonderfully searching account of "slow art" from the late eighteenth century to the present, where he proposes instead that we attend more to "the fact that modernity conjugates with speed serves to open spaces for slowness."[15]

But this is not what I find most compelling about the other forms of slow motion that we do see in *Goodbye, Dragon Inn*. Tsai's film observes its cinematic end times not only as they pervade a site and institution—"the whole aggregate," we might say, borrowing from D. A. Miller, "of film societies, archives [and] art houses where the religion of cinema was practiced" for much of the twentieth century and after—but also as they are incarnated or personified in the almost always barely moving bodies that we see on screen.[16] To anticipate an argument I will be making later about *Bonnie and Clyde*, I do not think it is at all an accident that the single film most responsible for popularizing slow motion as a special effect in global narrative visual culture is a work of unabashed and wistful cinephilia set amid a landscape marked everywhere by film in ruins. *Bonnie and Clyde* can be seen as an example of what Michel Chion calls "*ritualized film* [sic]," a mode he associates with the rise of "auteur cinema" by directors such as Hitchcock, Kurosawa, and Antonioni but that he ultimately and far more powerfully attributes to a sort of trauma in the medium of film itself whose aftermaths are radically deferred. I have more to say about Chion as well, but for now I want only to point out that he links "ritualized film" to the "hardening of time" that came with the transition to sound between 1926 and 1933. "Whereas the rates of shooting and projection had been relatively free to fluctuate in silent film," he argues, the "new mechanical standardization" that sound required meant that—and the echoes here of Doane are telling though entirely inadvertent—cinema became "an art that recorded time and no longer just movement." For Chion, "the ritualized film does not take clear shape until the 1960s," and he doesn't really speculate about the decades of delay that make his story so affecting. The films that get made in the protracted fallout are "essentially ceremonials" that include "set pieces of temporal bravura." Chion is thinking of sequences from *Playtime* (1967) and *Le cercle rouge* (1970) or from *2001: A Space Odyssey* (1968) and *Once Upon a Time in the West* (1968), two films that will concern us at great length in later chapters.[17]

Despite the high-art pedigree of Sugimoto's photographs, neither *Tri-City Drive-In* nor *Proctor's Theater, Troy* memorialize the type of film that might share gallery space beside them. In *Snow White*, as I said, Sugimoto discloses the movies that he screened for each of the pictures in *Theaters*, which both confirms specific timings for his very long exposures—as if 1 hour, 21 minutes glows any less than 1 hour, 34 minutes?—and the perversity of his selections, some of which show more teeth than we might expect from such reverent imagery so sincerely packaged. In Troy, New York, he tells us that the screen is illuminated by Stanley Kubrick's *Dr. Strangelove or: How I Learned to Stop Worrying and Love the Bomb* (1964). This is a classic to be sure, but not quite a museum piece either. Sugimoto's brief essay gives a deadpan summary of its plot and leaves us with his version of its final shots: "Hydrogen bombs detonate in a series of beautiful explosions."[18] Several of these explosions are in slow motion, though like much of the special effect's appearances before the later 1960s, they come and go spectacularly, without leaving much of a trace. This does mean, however, that the ruins of *Proctor's Theater, Troy* are even more postapocalyptic than the obvious iconography implies. Sugimoto likes this inside joke enough to rehearse it for other pictures featuring ruined theaters all but irradiated, we might say, by films paying homage to the horrors of atomic war—the original *Godzilla* (1954; in *Kenosha Theater, Kenosha*) and Stanley Kramer's somber allegory *On the Beach* (1959; in *Paramount Theater, Newark*)—or brightened by the equally destructive light of the killer asteroid from Mimi Leder's *Deep Impact* (1998; in *Metropolitan Opera House, Philadelphia*). The empty theater of *Tri-City Drive-In* speaks to the weirdest version of end times that we see in any of Sugimoto's photographs, though it does show a film that Smithson might have relished for its B-movie "blood and guts." This photograph shows us Sam Raimi's *Army of Darkness* (1993), a sequel to his two earlier *Evil Dead* films following the adventures of Ash Williams (played always and, I hope, forever by Bruce Campbell) and the zombies and other monsters that one particularly grisly form of dead media keeps bringing back to life. A book entitled the *Necronomicon* is behind all the destruction that we see in Raimi's film; it is a bonkers catalog of delirious crash-zooms and dolly shots that is also a museum of antique special effects from slow motion to claymation to goofy matte sequences and giant props. Amid Raimi's slapstick splatter and intentionally half-baked gore, the occasional slow motion in *Army of Darkness* seems stately and reserved. But we know that Sugimoto saw it. He wanted to make sure that it was consecrated as part of cinematic history that, like all the films showing in these dead *Theaters*, went by too fast to register much of anything at all.

3
From Zero to Slow

The other version of slow motion's history is the story of a visual effects technology, and though its origins will have to remain uncertain, we know where it ends up: *everywhere*. It is in more narrative films since 1968 than anyone could watch or count; in the vast and largely unchartable reaches of visual culture, from video art to scientific imaging to sports highlights to glossy Netflix food documentaries to YouTube, TikTok, and more; in who knows how many megabytes of video shot on our phones and stored away on hard drives, an anonymous archive of media that shows levels of technological proficiency that, for most of the twentieth century, only the most accomplished filmmakers could have achieved. No history of slow motion can hope to detail its absolute ubiquity as the single most pervasive special effect in global visual and media culture since the 1960s. What we might call the prehistory of slow motion and its omnipresence, on the other hand, is short enough to take at something like full speed—we hardly need to rush.

There are no sustained accounts of slow motion in any of the major works of film theory, criticism, or history that helped define film studies as an academic discipline in the first half of the twentieth century, nor are there any in any of the standard texts on narrative film, experimental film, or film style that continue to shape the field. This is not to suggest that slow motion goes unnoticed over all these decades. What I find striking is that even the earliest references to slow motion—in texts addressing film when its development as an artistic medium and emblematic institution of mass culture was still shifting and inchoate—sound like they assume that it has always been a part of cinematic representation and its techniques. Which is certainly the case: Consider the Edison short *Serpentine Dance* (or *Annabelle Serpentine Dance*) from 1894 or 1895, which featured a performer doing her burlesque version of the choreography that had made Loie Fuller a transatlantic sensation at the time. "Annabelle" does a more pedestrian series of kicks and jumps—in a costume that literalizes Fuller's billowy abstractions into butterfly motifs—against the familiar black void that William Dickson filmed against at the Edison Studios (figure 3.1). Sections of this film and other kinetoscope shorts distributed with the same title were among the first to feature hand-tinted color, making them particularly significant, considering they were also among the earliest motion pictures to be produced in the United States. The use of slow motion here would have been as visible to the viewer, though perhaps not quite as spectacular in its accentuation of the erotic movements on display. Audiences for the traveling Veriscope presentation of *The Corbett-Fitzsimmons Fight* (1897) would have had to wait until the film was almost over before seeing a slow-motion "replay" of Fitzsimmons's fourteenth-round body blow that won the fight by technical knockout, a sequence barely visible in surviving extracts of what was, at a running time of ninety to one hundred minutes, the first feature-length film. Perhaps it doesn't quite make sense to identify these early examples as slow motion in the way we'll

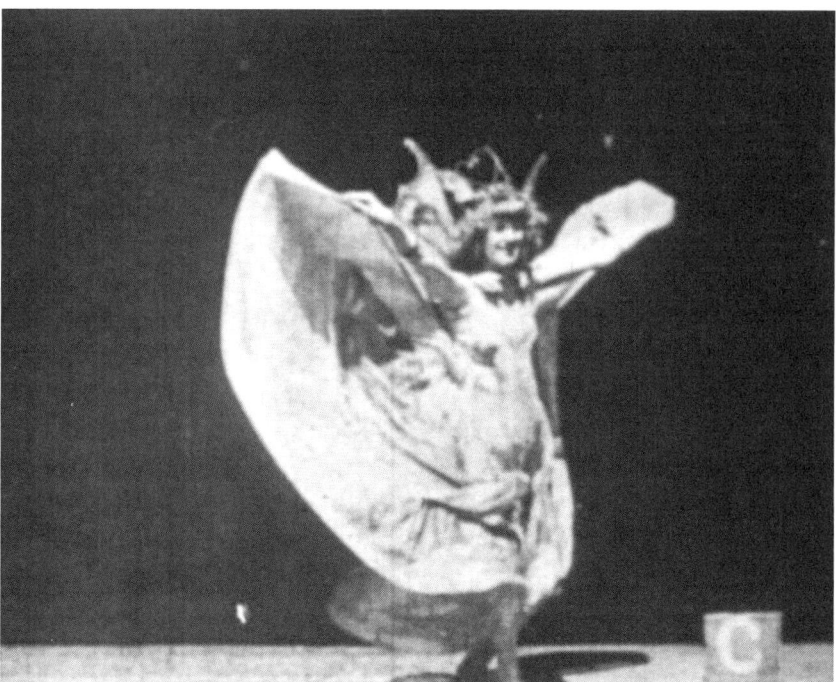

FIGURE 3.1 Still from "Annabelle Serpentine Dance," 1894–1895.

come to know it. Before motorized cameras and electrical projectors (both coming into operation in the early 1910s), it is theoretically possible that half of early cinema was, technically speaking, in slow motion—and the other half, accelerated—caused by the errors and inefficiencies of hand-cranked cameras and projectors that could not be calibrated for frame rates that varied from 16 to 24 per second well into the silent era. That said, the obvious slowness of Edison's *Serpentine Dance* appears deliberate when we think of how many other shorts from this same period—filmed at the same site by the same filmmakers—do not look like this at all. We can't know how this slow motion was seen in 1894, but it would seem that it left little trace—as if, perversely enough, it went by too fast for anyone to notice. It is certainly the case that film archivists and scholars such as Charles Musser, Noël Burch, and Laurent Mannoni—to say nothing of truly foundational figures like Terry Ramsaye and Georges Sadoul—probably came across these earliest examples of slow motion and more. Yet their collectively groundbreaking projects of film history span thousands of pages and mention slow motion only twice.[1]

I do not want to make too much of these omissions. The swirling curves and undulations of Edison's *Serpentine Dance* appear to have been filmed by "overcranking" the camera at significantly higher speeds than the 16fps frame rate for conventional viewing; since Edison and Dickson had designed a camera that could film at 30 or even 46fps, it would certainly have been possible for them to shoot a strip of images that, when shown at "normal" speed, would produce effects of temporal distention and decelerated action—or, said quickly, slow motion. But, as Barry Salt observes, before 1906 "intentional departures from a standard camera speed for expressive purposes were extremely rare."[2] He notes that a 1901 Cecil Hepworth short, *The Indian Chief and the Seidlitz Powder*, employs slow motion for its main gag: a racist bit involving the wrong mix of digestion aids resulting in a grotesquely bloated stomach that lifts an actor dressed in garish feathers off the ground before a small explosion brings him back to earth. The actor's comic leaps are filmed in slow motion so that the prop balloon stuffed in his shirt can seem to be defying gravity.[3] The visual effect is less dramatic than what we see in *Serpentine Dance*, but just as the Edison short uses slow motion to emphasize the "lyricism" of physical actions that would be less charming otherwise (and we'll return to slow motion's "poetic" connotations later), the Hepworth comedy discovers in this illusion of altered gravity another of slow motion's most fundamental on-screen iconographies. Yet slow motion remained vanishingly rare throughout the period, evidence that the plain fact of its technological possibility was not sufficient for most filmmakers to find a use for it. Even in the work of George Méliès, where there is little realism to prohibit trick shots and visual effects in wild abundance, I have not seen any sequences in slow motion—an absence that is particularly surprising given that some of his most celebrated films are set in environments (outer space in *A Trip to the Moon* [1902], underwater in *Under the Seas* [1907]) that allow for slow motion all but naturally to appear.

This helps explain why slow motion does not figure in histories of cinema trying to understand how dominant modes and languages of expression came to be codified in the first decades of the twentieth century. We can readily see films from the late 1890s and early 1900s working out the rules for—and, just as significantly, the resistances to and variations on—close-ups, shot-reverse-shot editing, narrative continuity, composition in depth, studio lighting, spectatorial perspective, location footage, and more, along with inventing or adapting countless genre conventions for both fictional and documentary cinema. But slow motion largely recedes from view until the 1920s. Its use in Rene Clair's *Entr'acte* (1924) is justifiably iconic: It opens with Erik Satie and Francis Picabia slowly bounding into the frame, and the goofy loping of the funeral procession in slow motion is a performance of lyrical, surreal resistance to the very "gravity" of the occasion (figure 3.2). The much briefer bit of slow motion in Abel Gance's *Au*

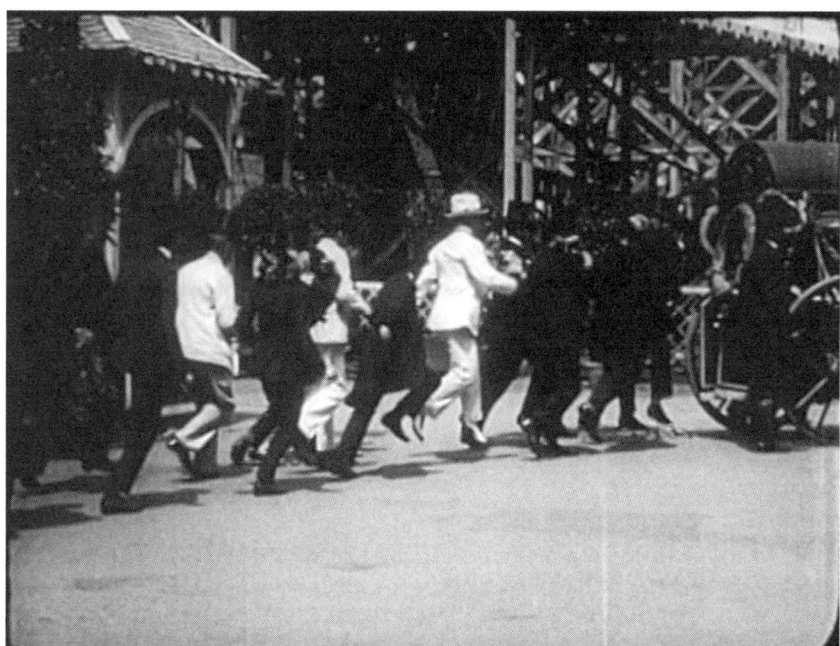

FIGURE 3.2 Still from *Entr'acte* (1924).

secours! (1924) is just one of many gags and gimmicks found in the haunted house where Max Linder tries to stay the night; many of the effects emulate Méliès, but when we see a character heavily bouncing in the air above a hidden trampoline, this would have been a new trick, though soon overwhelmed by the epic montages, tracking shots, and split screens of Gance's next film, *Napoléon* (1927). These sequences bring slow motion into the discourses of cinematic modernism as well.

Arnheim cites *Entr'acte* in the short section on slow motion from his 1933 book *Film*. He recalls the "ghastly deliberation" of the mourners as an "irresistibly comic effect . . . because one does not feel that one is seeing a retardation of normal running but a stylized take-off."[4] Writing in 1960, Kracauer also remembers slow motion first from Clair's *Entr'acte*, which he says "deliberately tried out everything that can be done within the medium in terms of fantasy and technique."[5] We cannot know if Benjamin has Clair or Gance in mind when he famously writes about slow motion in his "The Work of Art" essay, but we do know he had read Arnheim because he quotes him to powerful effect in a passage that has proved decisive for a whole network of modernist genealogies in art history and media theory:

> With the close-up, space expands; with slow motion, movement is extended. And just as enlargement not merely clarifies what we see indistinctly "in any case," but brings to light entirely new structures of matter, slow motion not only reveals familiar aspects of movements, but discloses quite unknown aspects within them—aspects which do not appear as the retarding of natural movements but have a curious, gliding character of their own. Clearly it is another nature which speaks to the camera as compared to the eye. "Other" above all in the sense that a space informed by human consciousness gives way to a space informed by the unconscious. . . . This is where the camera comes into play, with all its resources for swooping and rising, disrupting and isolating, stretching or compressing a sequence, enlarging or reducing an object. It is through the camera that we first discover the optical unconscious, just as we discover the instinctual unconscious through psychoanalysis.[6]

It is not too much to propose that this is where slow motion begins in modern culture, with a fairly circumscribed cinematic practice and minor format itself "enlarging" into a set of metaphors that try to capture how we see and feel differently through, and with, technologies and their pervasive patterning of human space and time. Benjamin does more with slow motion in a paragraph than I'll probably do in this entire book. But hopefully I'll make the long way worth it too.

Arnheim suggests that "slow motion has hardly been applied at all yet to artistic purposes" and notes instead that it has "been used almost exclusively in education films in order to show the individual phases of rapid movements," thus documenting and opening to visual scrutiny such actions as "the technique of a boxer or of a violinist, the explosion of a bomb."[7] While it is impossible to know exactly what short subjects Arnheim may have seen, there are numerous surviving silent-era newsreels that feature athletic performances in slow motion, such as British Pathé's 1924 *Running with Harold Abrams* or the Novagraph Film Corporation's *Golfer Bobby Jones Demonstrates His Golfing Technique* (1926). There were also newsreels of live sporting events that filmed portions of the action at Wimbledon or the Kentucky Derby in slow motion, but it is in the short films of individual athletes like Abrams or Jones instead that we see the full scope of the analytical aesthetic—the forensic imagining of human motion—that Arnheim notes in 1933. Novagraph does not appear to have left much of a mark in histories of silent cinema, but as early as 1923, the *New York Times* was reporting on a Novagraph movie camera that could reach shutter speeds of close to 1/1000th of a second for a film showing a hammer striking a ten-inch vacuum globe.[8] This lost work from the bleeding edge of 1920s media makes me think of a painting like Jean Siméon Chardin's *Soap Bubbles* (1733–1734) and of course invokes much longer histories of artistic and scientific efforts to capture events too fleeting and transient for human perception. I mentioned Muybridge and Marey in passing earlier, but their influential experiments in high-speed photography in the late nineteenth century set many of the terms for later sports or scientific filmmakers intent on registering human, animal, or material locomotion in rigorous, if not fetishized, detail. "Note the foot action," reads an intertitle in Novagraph's slow-motion look at every angle, flex, and posture of Bobby Jones's swing; the forward pitch and thrusting arms of Abram's vintage sprinting makes for some Olympic-level cubism on the track. A fox scrambling in slow motion up some rocks in the silent documentary *Wildlife on the Deserts of America's Great Southwest* (n.d.) is decidedly more graceful, and the women in another British Pathé short, *Cross Country Girl: A Slow Motion Study* (1922), might give Abrams a run for his money, if only at the level of form.

What slow motion reveals in all these bodies—almost as if the technology is incarnating them before our eyes—is a version of the "athletic beauty" praised by Hans Ulrich Gumbrecht, an aesthetic of sheer skill, prowess, competence, and physicality that renders athletes "into objects of admiration and desire."[9] It sometimes can be difficult to determine how slow motion operates as an aesthetic since it is characterized so frequently as circling between "aestheticizing" because it's "lyrical" or "lyricizing" because it illustrates some generalized "aesthetic" quality of motion. It is not just that sometimes in slow motion people look like they are nothing but their bodies, animated by all the forces working on or through them out of any individual's control. In slow motion, after all, Arnheim doesn't seem to see much difference between a boxer or a violinist or a bomb. At its upper limits—with faster cameras taking more and more pictures per second of elaborately "slower" motions—we soon are operating outside human time not only as a phenomenon of minds that only hold onto a "present" of about three seconds but also as imperceptible to the neurological and physiological durations that, as Jimena Canales has shown, were discovered and debated as nineteenth-century researchers became fixated on measuring "the precise *pace* of the brain."[10] As she demonstrates to great effect, a "tenth of a second" came to matter very intensely to psychologists, doctors, and other scientists working in the decades before and during Muybridge and Marey's experiments in high-speed imaging. The cinematic relics of the forgotten Novagraph Film Corporation had already, by 1923, accelerated past these fleeting increments of time—fast for sure, but still embodied in slow flesh and nerves—in the pursuit of "the systematic creation of multimedia systems," to borrow from Friedrich Kittler, that would "technically [replace]" the "individual sensory channels" and the terminally lagging measurements they produced.[11] These first instances of slow motion, in other words, do not just indicate some of the shapes its iconography will take in fiction and nonfiction film in the twentieth century; we catch glimpses, even here, of what Ernst calls "a media-technical event in cinematography" with the "time-critical intensification" of newly visible "spatial and temporal relations that are not accessible to human perception."[12] "This non-discursive tumult," Ernst adds with a posthuman flourish, represents "articulations of the real, which can only be registered by technical measuring media."

But there was already some patently unreal slow motion by 1933 that Arnheim overlooks. With all due respect to Kracauer, it would seem that Clair didn't "try out everything" that could be done in slow motion: In *The Thief of Bagdad* (1924) we see Douglas Fairbanks fighting a giant spider underwater in one of many of the film's extravagantly designed and wrought action sequences—many of which Fairbanks helped devise with the film's director Raoul Walsh and art director William Cameron Menzies. Though this film is often counted among the greatest spectacles of silent-era Hollywood, this instance of slow motion—the earliest I have been able to discover in a fiction film produced in the United States—almost never figures in accounts of its lavish sets and technical ambitions. Perhaps this is because the fight scene takes place after we have already witnessed outlandish stunts and special effects before Fairbanks's

"Ahmed" descends into the deep to pursue his quest, or perhaps it is because Walsh's use of slow motion is formulaic from the start, a visual motif borrowed from the iconography of sports and applied to Fairbanks's own signature athleticism. Paul Rotha, writing in *The Film Till Now* (1930), seems to have been one of the only critics of the era who recognized the singular appeal of slow motion in a film whose ambitions were hardly modernist. "The properties of the camera," he notes, "add grace to [Fairbanks's] sweeping curves of action."[13] In any case, *The Thief of Bagdad* is practically an allegory for how a Hollywood "cinema of effects," as Tom Gunning famously observed, trades on the "tamed attractions" that replace the more aggressive and self-conscious aesthetics of display that patterned both early cinema before 1907 and the avant-garde after 1922.[14]

The avant-garde, for better or worse, is maybe harder to vanquish than a monstrous spider: The curtains billow in slow motion in Jean Epstein's *The Fall of the House of Usher* (1928), another example of slow motion's use that Kracauer recalls and then dismisses for the "stagnant artificiality" of using such effects as mere "tokens of the supernatural."[15] Usher's psychological fragility manifests in things that move more slowly than we expect; they are the "objective correlatives" of his eventual derangement but also of Epstein's own commitment to the magic of *photogénie*, his elusive term for any number of revealed intensities of both aesthetic perception and affective intuition. "The slowing down of time," Epstein declares in *The Intelligence of the Machine* (1946), "increases death and matter": "Human beings become statues, the living merges with the inert, the universe devolves into a desert of pure matter without any trace of spirit."[16] Epstein's understanding of slow motion practically devolves into a retelling of Poe's original gothic tale of ambiguous immobility, but elsewhere it is clear that Epstein is profoundly fascinated by what he terms "the extreme malleability" of cinematic time. Béla Balázs says in his 1930 *The Spirit of Film* that slow motion, as an "optical camera technique" in Epstein's surrealism, means that "we see not narrative events, but the reaction of the psyche."[17] But recent critics caution against treating *photogénie* as a purely mental category or mystical placeholder for a shifting set of spiritual and aesthetic values. For Epstein, according to Trond Lundemo, cinema is a "machine able to defy the irreversibility of time and the second law of thermodynamics, as well as a means of access to the hidden movement and temporality of all objects."[18] An underwater sword fight with a spider might seem more dramatic than some drifting leaves and flowing curtains, but Epstein finally had bigger fish to fry in his use of slow motion.

Kracauer would not have seen the slow motion that James Sibley Watson and Melville Webber used in their own version of *The Fall of the House of Usher* (1928), which is a more energetic and expressionist adaptation, with a slow-motion shot of a hammer coming down to seal Madeline Usher in her coffin. But with Luis Buñuel's *Un chien andalou* (1929) and Jean Cocteau's *The Blood of a Poet* (1930), there is no mistaking that slow motion had become a signature technique of modernist and avant-garde cinema. In both films, slow motion comes at moments of violence and trauma; in Buñuel, Pierre Batcheff walks toward us in slow motion shortly after the "Seize an savant" title card appears and right before he is shot by his dark-suited doppelganger; in Cocteau, Enrique Riveros's "Poet" witnesses the victim of a firing squad crumple to the floor in slow motion, a simple sight gag that also might be quoting famous execution imagery from paintings by Goya or Manet (figure 3.3). There is nothing especially surprising about slow motion as it appears in either Buñuel or Cocteau, and their variations on surrealism will color how slow motion looks for generations of experimental filmmakers in the United States and elsewhere. The slow motion that opens Alexander Dovzhenko's *Zwenigora* (1928), on the other hand, can't avoid appearing as a shock when, right after the last introductory intertitle, we see a group of costumed riders fly and float across the screen from right to left, out of a wall of forest that completely fills the frame—there is no visual or narrative orientation for the weird suddenness of Dovzhenko's slow

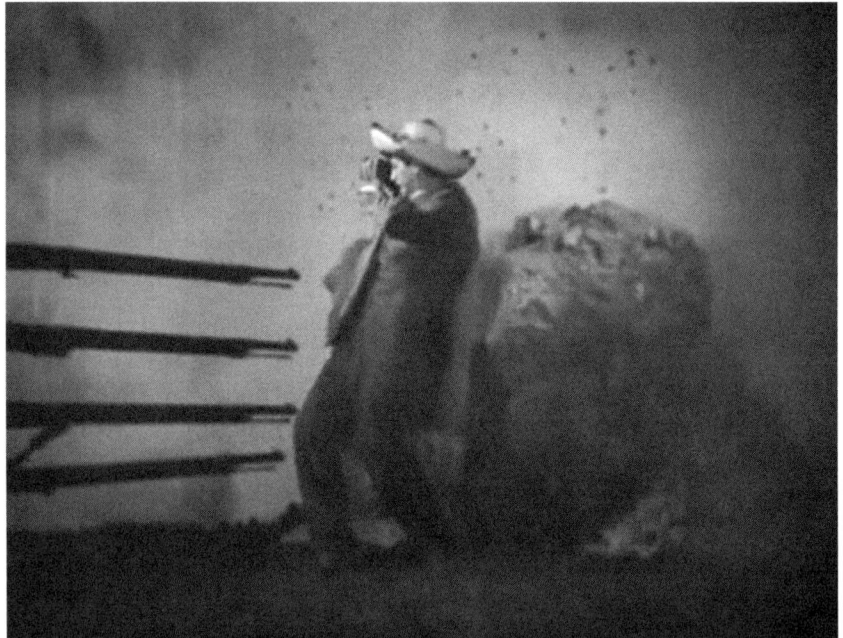

FIGURE 3.3 Still from *The Blood of a Poet* (1930).

motion as it dreamily erupts onto the screen long before we have a chance to acclimate to the film's abiding eccentricity and its departures from naturalist conventions. Rotha found the opening of *Zwenigora* "enchanting" as a sign of Dovzhenko's aesthetic "mysticism," which he suggests was part of why the film was "poorly received in Moscow and Leningrad" at a moment when the experimental exuberance of the revolution was fading into the protocols of socialist realism.[19]

In its own way, the brief slow motion punctuating a dance scene in Erich von Stroheim's *The Merry Widow* (1925) is equally unexpected since, like *Zwenigora*, the film is strongly narrative and, for the most part, generic in its mode of address and cinematic style. When John Gilbert's "Count Danilo" takes to the dance floor in slow motion with Mae Murry's "Sally O'Hara," it is easy at first to miss that they are waltzing across the screen in a display of grace that has been decelerated to a pace below the tempo of the romantic music we see the orchestra performing—which is, in the version of the film I've seen, the famous waltz that gives the film its name. These deviations from the early norms that had almost immediately come to pattern where and how slow motion could be employed look even more striking when we see slow motion exactly where we might expect to find it in a film whose every gesture and stylistic gambit aimed against the conventions of film language: In Dziga Vertov's *Man with a Movie Camera* (1929), we are treated to a constructivist barrage of stop motion, dissolves, shots in mirrors, and double exposures before we get slow motion in a montage of athletic exploits—two minutes of discus throws, high jumps, hurdling men, and hurdling women—contrasted, finally, to a suspiciously bourgeois race track and a trotting horse that slows and then grinds to an awkward halt (figure 3.4). It is as if Vertov wants to remind us that Muybridge invited motion photography, and thus helped film along its way too, because a robber baron like Leland Stanford Jr. had a bet to settle, which is why Occident was set galloping in front of cameras in the first place. Slow motion is heroic until it isn't, and then it turns into another dead form of Western art.

From advertisements in trade publications and listings in distributors' catalogs it is clear that the vast majority of slow motion occurred in short newsreel features on sports or other feats of physical performance (dance, parachuting, swimming) or in educational films that promised to let viewers see aspects of the natural world that would otherwise remain invisible at full speed. As with so much ephemeral or "useful cinema," neglecting these domains of visual culture not only invites us to reify the specific practices and institutions of theatrical exhibition as the experience of cinema as such but also blinds us to the many technical innovations and developments in special effects by filmmakers either

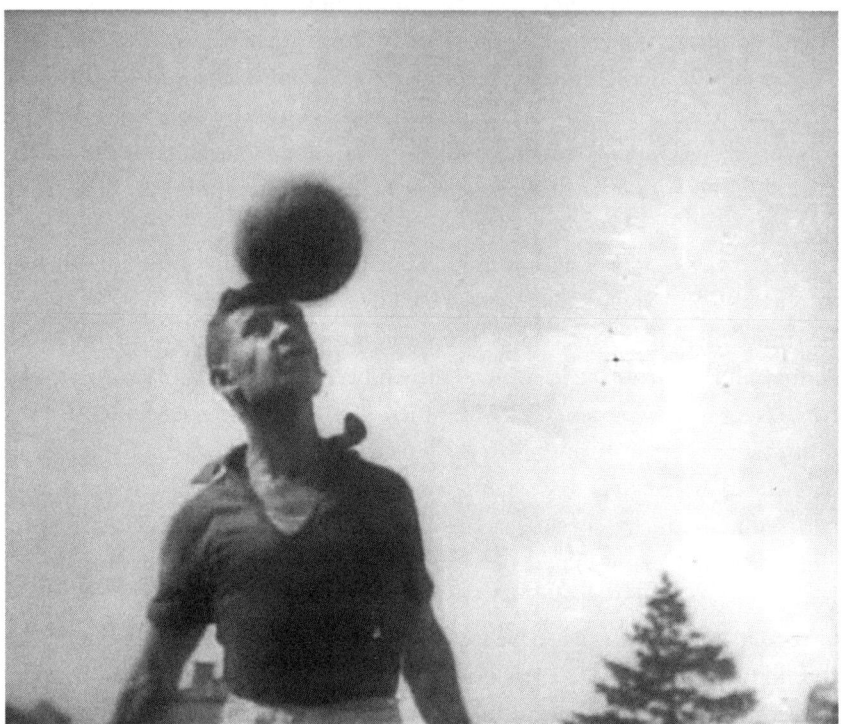

FIGURE 3.4 Still from *Man with a Movie Camera* (1929).

at the margins of the studio system and its uneven investments in industrial research and development or working outside Hollywood entirely in laboratories, factories, design firms, universities, or homes.[20] With all the time and every archive at my disposal it would still be hard to offer a complete account of slow motion as the twentieth century proceeds, but it is worth pointing out that much of it would have been seen in films with titles like *Lifting the Veil of Motion* (1924), *Secrets of Nature* (1930), *Car Stunting in Slow Motion* (1926), *South African Cricket Practice* (1929), or *The Polo That Is Water* (1933).

In his 1926 essay "The Horrors of Film," Edogawa Rampo asks his readers, "have you ever experienced the fear that comes from a movie filmed at high speeds?" His answer carries us to a gothic realm where "the air is heavy like mercury," a "fearsome and impenetrable climate" where "humans and animals alike force their way through the heavy atmosphere, staggering forward." From his description, it sounds like he is watching a short subject featuring a woman swimming underwater. But there is no grace or gliding in the imagery that Rampo sees on screen, and the breezy nightmares conjured up by Epstein feel merely "photogenic" when set against the "dance of drowning" Rampo experiences with this "disturbing new sensation for the modern world."[21]

Colette apparently enjoyed slow motion much more than Rampo, at least according to a 1920 review where she recounts how "'Ahs' or respectful ecstasy" greet a "'slow motion' shot [that] rose from the ground, immobilized itself in the air, then held on a sea gull suspended on a breeze." She stresses the physicality of slow motion's detailing of anatomy and action, observing the "undulation and the flexing of the wings, the mechanism of guiding and direction in the tail, the whole secret of flight, the whole simple mystery of aviation, revealed in an instant."[22] Dorothy Richardson, writing an installment of her "Continuous Performance" column for the landmark British film journal *Close-Up* in 1928, gets as completely swept away as Colette by the program of slow-motion documentary shorts that she recounts. "For it was a picture of runners at close quarters" near the end of a mile race, she narrates, and then "a caption spoke: 'Now see what our slow-motion camera can do.'" What had appeared as "desperate competition, agonised heads thrown back, open mouths agasp at the last effort for supremacy" is now diminished from a spectacle of pain to a comedy of "leaden limbs" and "air-clutching fingers" that prompt an "avalanche of laughter."[23] Neither the audience nor Richardson knows how to react to the "freakish incident of the new entertainment." But then, another "slow," as she labels them, begins, and this one shows a high jumper whose flight over the bar leaves "all lesser emotions . . . submerged in that of stupefaction at the sheer marvel of the levitations." Her brief essay is not the earliest account of slow motion that we have—Richard Abel includes mentions by Coctcau, Blaise Cendrars, and Marcel Gromaire that go back to 1919—but Richardson perhaps exemplifies most clearly how slow motion had no settled aesthetic in this period.[24] It could be traumatic or slapstick, a one-off gag or an inadvertent second coming of the suffering frozen on the face of the *Laocoön*. We will do well to remember this evidence of slow motion's wilder forms and more eccentric variants as its effects become less special.

By the early 1930s, then, we can see slow motion starting to become the visual effect that we recognize so immediately today—almost instantaneously, in fact, given how its most formulaic uses have been codified already into familiar motifs and tropes. In films as otherwise different from one another as George Cukor's *What Price Hollywood?* (1932) and Vselevod Pudovkin's *The Deserter* (1933), slow motion is used to dilate and extend the dying falls of men: In a beautifully composed shot from later in *The Deserter*, we see a worker throw himself into the dark waters in an act of suicidal despair, and in *What Price Hollywood?* (figure 3.5), the aging, alcoholic director Maximillian Carey shoots himself and

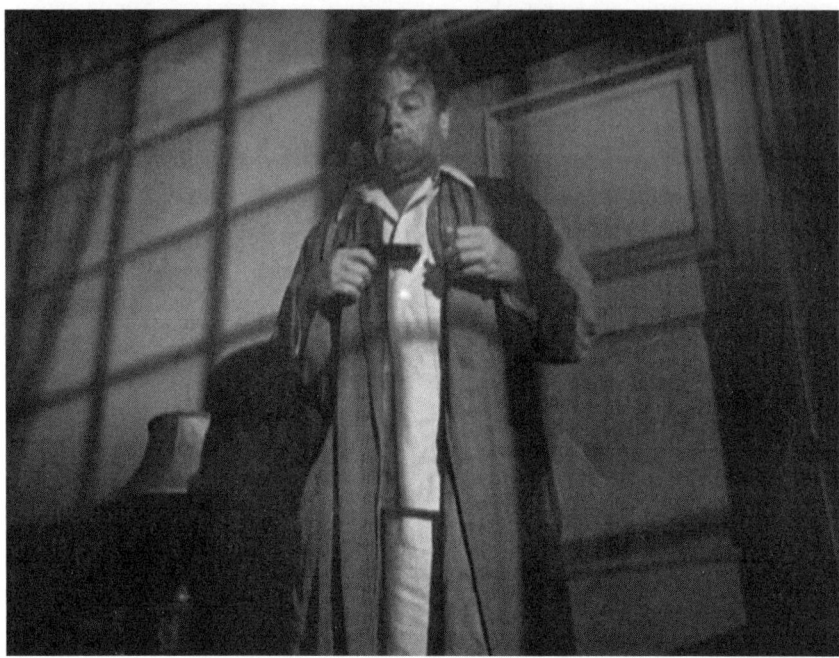

FIGURE 3.5 Still from *What Price Hollywood?* (1932).

then takes five full seconds to drop out of the frame and onto the floor (122 frames at 24fps). The whole sequence depends on an arresting barrage of montage effects and rakish angles that were in part designed by the avant-gardist Slavko Vokapić, who had directed *The Life and Death of 9413: A Hollywood Extra* (1928) and would become the chair of the film department at USC—a trajectory that makes this appearance of slow motion into a perfect symbol of how modernist film style gets institutionalized over time. *What Price Hollywood?* premiered in June 1932 and might very well be the first classical Hollywood feature to use slow motion in the sound era.

But it was a singular example only for a few weeks: In July, the Jack Oakie and W. C. Fields vehicle *Million Dollar Legs* featured a shot of Susan Fleming's character diving from a bridge in elegant slow motion, a show of female athletic prowess and pre-Code sensuality that is, among other things, a resplendent display of willful action that counters the imagery of Cukor and Pudovkin, where the effect is something that happens *to* bodies that would be better off without enduring it. Set during the Los Angeles Olympics, *Million Dollar Legs* also uses fast motion to depict a blazing runner from the fictional country of Klopstokia, but unfortunately uses no trick photography for any of the scenes where we are treated to the improbable spectacle of W. C. Fields, playing Klopstokia's president, performing various feats of muscular authority as the nation's literal and figurative "strongman" at the Olympics. Given that Fields rules a country whose name is a spoonerism for "stop clock," it is perhaps surprising that this slapstick comedy is not even more temporally adventurous.

This is not an issue for the very next Hollywood film to employ slow motion. August 1932 sees the debut of Rouben Mamoulian's *Love Me Tonight*, a musical comedy starring Maurice Chevalier as a Parisian tailor who charms his way into the aristocratic circles and affections of "Princess Jeanette" (Jeanette MacDonald). Though "Maurice" lacks the habits and wardrobe required for a fancy hunt, he compensates with the ability to disperse a riding party in slow motion, suggesting a fantastic ability to bend space and time. Writing in *The World Viewed* (1971), Stanley Cavell includes this scene as the earliest example of one of several "assertions in technique" or "automatisms," including slow motion, that reveal how certain aesthetic "devices"—along with freeze frames and split screens—draw our attention as viewers to the "condition of the physical bases of a medium and the achievement of art by means of them."[25] Cavell, as we'll see later, does not much like these gimmicks as a rule, slow motion least of all. If he ever saw *The Crime of Helen Stanley* (1934), the third installment of the otherwise forgettable Inspector Trent series starring Ralph Bellamy, he probably would not have thought much of the way Bellamy's detective tries to use slow motion to reveal who murdered the imperious actress Stanley on set during the filming of a production number. A helpful cinematographer approaches Bellamy and assures him that they can replay the footage "slowed down" so that the crime might be revealed like "action in the news weekly." While this is a good reminder of where and how slow motion circulated throughout the period before Cavell and many others tired of it, it is both wildly and technologically impossible: Unless the fictional cameras were shooting at high speed in the first place, there would be no way, in 1934 at least, to produce the slow motion that we later see in what the characters in the movie weren't yet calling "post." Not any longer though, thanks to digital speed ramping and now, in the blink of ninety years, consumer-grade AI that can simulate slow motion out of real-time video on the latest Samsung Galaxy.[26]

Cavell appreciates that the slow motion in *Love Me Tonight* manages to be "surprising," but he might not have appreciated some of the other visible slow motion in the period, such as the underwater sequences in Jean Vigo's documentary short *Taris* (1931) and final feature, *L'Atalante* (1934; figure 3.6). Vigo's technique is doubly assertive here, with Michel Simon's swimming in slow motion underwater while the superimposed image of his beloved drifts and turns in

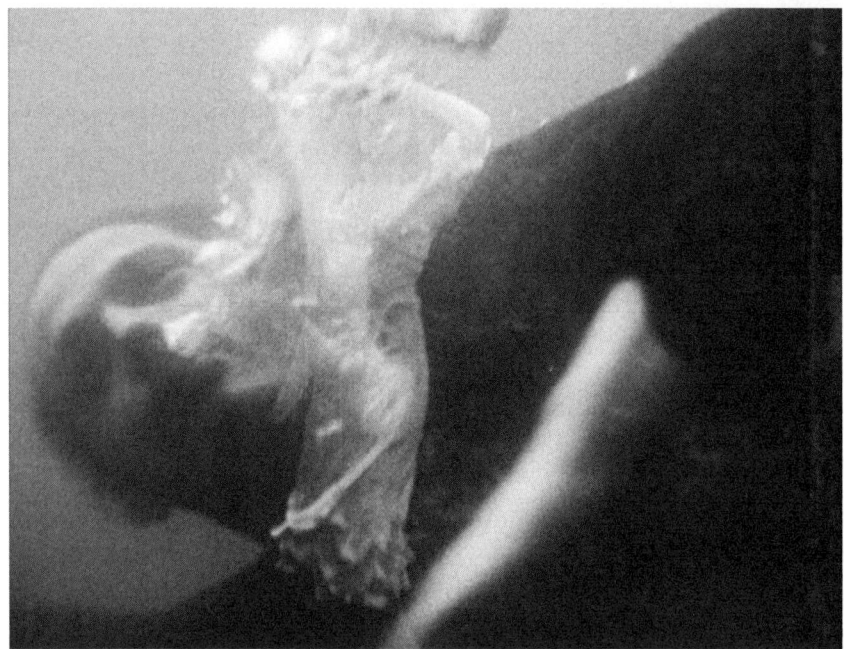

FIGURE 3.6 Still from *L'Atalante* (1934).

slow motion, too. "Ordinary swimming is *already* in slow motion," Cavell complains about the flagrance of this motif in certain films of the 1960s, "and to slow it further and indiscriminately only thickens it. It's about the only thing you can do to good swimming to make it ugly."[27] He would probably have kinder things to say about the exuberant, acrobatic pillow fight in Vigo's *Zéro de conduite* (1933)—feathers and half-naked boys flying in high defiance of both authority and gravity alike (figure 3.7).

All this slow motion, as well as a brief moment in Vigo's first film, *À propos de Nice*, was filmed by the cinematographer Boris Kaufman, the younger brother of Dziga Vertov, and also Mikhail Kaufman, who was educated in Paris and worked first in France before escaping to Canada during World War II. Before Elia Kazan hired him for *On the Waterfront* (1954)—which sticks to a vehement realism that does not accommodate slow motion—Kaufman spent a decade shooting shorts and documentaries, and even these meager credits made him the only Kaufman brother to keep working in the movies after the war. But after winning an Oscar for *On the Waterfront*, he became a prominent cinematographer in Hollywood, working again on some of Kazan's major films (*Baby Doll* [1956]; *Splendor in the Grass* [1961]), as well as those of Sidney Lumet. It was in

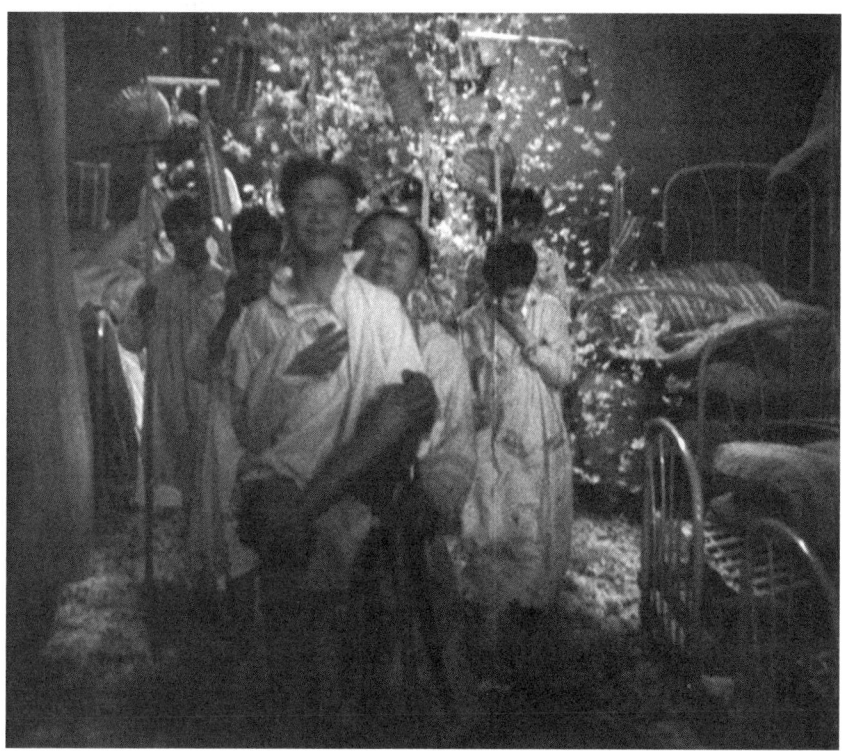

FIGURE 3.7 Still from *Zéro de conduite / Zero for Conduct* (1933).

Lumet's *The Pawnbroker* (1964) that Kaufman once again included a slow-motion sequence as part of Sol Nazerman's opening flashback onto the world and family that he lost during the Holocaust. It was perhaps only the sixth or seventh use of slow motion in a Hollywood feature, and its rendering of past trauma in (and *as*) slow motion becomes a crucial aspect of slow motion's pervasive symbolism and significance in later films, like Leone's spaghetti westerns or Peckinpah's blood-drenched epics, that are not exactly working in the somber historical tonalities of Lumet.

Cavell never seems to pick up on the slow motion in *The Pawnbroker*, though he hates its flashbacks to the Holocaust and the film's grotesque use of nudity and Blackness: Sol's memories of his wife's rape and death are prompted by the abject offer of sex by a nameless character played by Thelma Ortiz, and Cavell is right to call it "hopeless" in appealing to "a favorite speechless horror as a cover for the inability to respond." What Cavell finds ultimately immoral about this particular Hollywood innovation—*The Pawnbroker* was among the first films of the 1960s willing to break the Motion Picture Production Code and its absolute ban on nudity—is also part of what he doesn't like about slow motion, which indulges in the "vulgarity" of any technique "asserted" without regard for what it signifies, or, as he dismisses it, "for a fast touch of lyricism, throw in a slow-motion shot of a body in free fall." This is the "general message" of slow motion as it started to proliferate in the 1960s, he writes, "in everything from the high-jumping children in *The World of Henry Orient* ... to the floating women in television commercials honoring feminine hygiene." Cavell's antipathy to slow motion shows his disdain for the overtly "commercial" application of a technique—in films or on TV—that tries to manufacture an aesthetic experience by the mechanics of form alone.[28]

Again, Cavell places slow motion among a rogue's gallery of "assertions" for a reason, and the question that they too frequently fail to answer is: "What do they signify?"[29] For Boris Kaufman, the cinematographer for George Roy Hill's *The World of Henry Orient* (1964), which Cavell notably dislikes, slow motion probably signified enough already as an allusion to the camera work in *Zéro de conduite*; as two girls run and jump, one dressed in a fur, the other in bright red, they are taking the rebellious energies of an liberated French boys' school to the Manhattan streets (figure 3.8). Cavell's reading of the film might be ungenerous. That he pairs it with a reference to "feminine hygiene," as if this is the worst ad he can imagine for his readers, is not especially flattering, though given his profound attachment to screwball comedy, melodrama, and other "women's" genres, I don't want to make too much of the association either. What matters more is that, in 1971, Cavell is offering one of the very first accounts of slow motion that even attempts to articulate its meanings and artistic purposes. He is not usually seen as a founding figure in film studies along with Arnheim, Balázs,

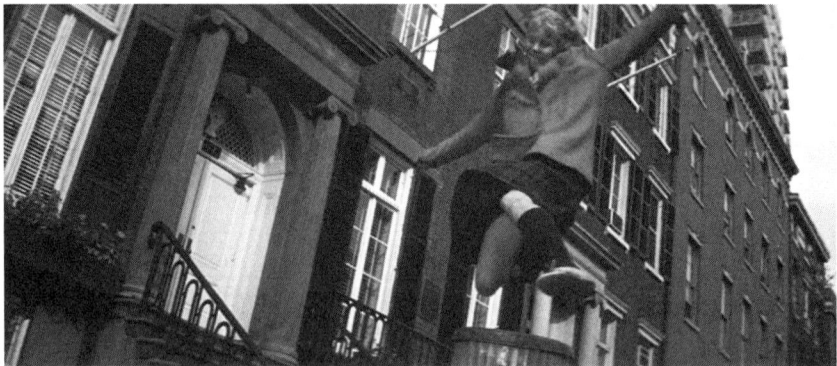

FIGURE 3.8 "The trick was blown" by the time Stanley Cavell saw this moment in slow motion from *The World of Henry Orient* (1964).

or Kracauer, but their own short reflections, along with a few densely encrypted sentences by Benjamin and a single column from Dorothy Richardson, would seem to represent the entire bibliography on slow motion as an aesthetic artifact of twentieth-century culture.

The only other examples of slow motion from before the 1960s that Cavell mentions are Leni Riefensthal and Akira Kurosawa, each of whom, as I'll detail soon, are crucial figures in its archaeology. Still, with just three documented instances at his disposal from before the release of *Bonnie and Clyde*—and with whatever ads and sports highlights he certainly would have seen—Cavell is more than ready to announce slow motion's fast decline just four years later. It happens in an instant, he says, because "the trick was blown."[30]

4
Experiments in Time

There is just one thing I have on Stanley Cavell as he was writing in 1971: I've definitely seen more slow motion. At the risk of speaking for everybody who has gone to the movies or watched TV since the 1970s or streamed video or YouTube since the 2000s, let me venture that *we all have*. Cavell may have already felt exhausted by the way slow motion had "blown" up as the 1960s ended, and the irony of his symbolism is sharp since, as we'll later see, explosions are one of the attractions in slow motion that we see the most. The earliest example in a feature-length film that I have found is from Vertov's *Three Songs About Lenin* (1934), which does not seem like a film that Cavell could possibly have seen. He cites the far more popular and influential *Olympia* (1938), directed by Leni Riefenstahl, a film that indulges in slow motion practically from its first frames and never goes very long without returning to it over almost four hours of running time. "Riefensthal's use of slow motion," Koepnick observes, "is essential to her peculiar construction of athletic beauty and embodiment" in *Olympia*, and she makes ample use of Kurt Neubert's skills as a cinematographer and the new DeBerie cameras he employed (massive machines, but able to film at 96fps) to "fuse the ethical, the epistemic, and the aesthetic into one single dynamic" that can save the body "from its own emphemerality."[1] The monumentality of Riefensthal's slow motion more than just survives in subsequent Olympic films and in the visual culture of sports in general; it patterns a great deal of the iconography of action and superhero films, right down to the absurdist CGI classicism of Zach Snyder. His four-hour version of *The Justice League* (2021)—a film in slow motion for over 10 percent of its length—is an epic of time-axis manipulation, speed ramping not just quivering muscles, body blows, and screams of agony but also spilled drops of coffee, hot dogs, and sesame seeds that become collateral damage of the violence he so lavishly mythologizes. If Cavell's resistance to slow motion speaks to even the slightest anticipation of its contemporary excesses, it's hard to blame him for sounding grumpy.

At the same time, there are good reasons for lingering a bit more in the decades of slow motion's antiquity, so to speak—especially since not every time we see it in the 1930s and the decades after does it look as disturbingly contemporary as it does in Riefensthal. For one, most of these early uses of slow motion are far more underdetermined than that of *Olympia* or even *The Thief of Bagdad*. In *Saratoga* (1937), starring Clark Gable and Jean Harlow, in her final role, the happy ending depends on determining the winner of a horserace with a photo finish that is so close that only what Lionel Barrymore's character calls the "more accurate" technology of slow-motion film can do the job. Of course, while everyone is watching the replayed conclusion of race for the victorious horse to be confirmed—we're rooting against "Moonray" so that Gable will lose his bet and marry Harlow—Barrymore complains that he "can't stand this much longer" and asks why "can't they run a little faster?" Given the generic logic of romantic comedy, slow motion here is only delaying the inevitable.

It can also, perversely enough, speed things along: The slow-motion dance number in *Carefree* (1938) is set to "I Used to Be Colorblind" and unfolds in a dream that proves to Ginger Roger's "Amanda" that she really does love her psychoanalyst, "Tony," played by Fred Astaire. This scene is better remembered for featuring the longest onscreen kiss the couple ever shared, but at least a portion of the erotic energy being displaced as onscreen dream-work is the slow-motion spectacle of transference set to music. And while by some measures this is the most sexually explicit performance they would share, Astaire at least would enjoy the pleasures of slow motion again on his own in *Easter Parade* (1948), where in the singular production number for "Steppin' Out with My Baby," Astaire dances at miraculously diminished speed in an elaborate matte shot before a chorus moving at the music's normal speed (figure 4.1).

These diversions into temporal fantasy and visual excess do not seem to have played much of a role in slow motion's subsequent—and sudden—formalization as a special effect in commercial narrative cinema later in the 1960s. Though there are more examples of slow motion in Hollywood productions of the classical era than we might expect, no single scene looms as legendary or iconic, and there is no discernible pattern or increasing frequency to their appearances over time. During the ten years between *Carefree* and *Easter Parade*, I haven't been able to find a single use of slow motion in a fiction film produced by any studio in the United States. In the listings of distribution

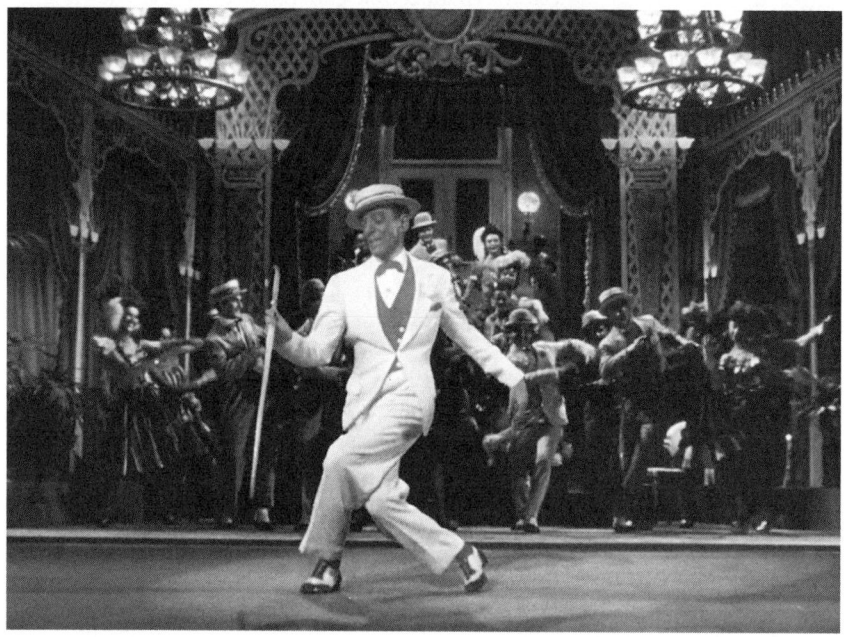

FIGURE 4.1 Only Astaire is in slow motion in this sequence from *Easter Parade* (1948).

catalogs and in ads from trade publications of the period, slow motion continues to be a selling point—a tamed attraction, to recall Gunning—for educational films and newsreel coverage of boxing, baseball, and other popular sports, but not in such overwhelming numbers as to suggest that it would have been seen regularly or consistently by most film audiences. The few exceptions that make me think this is the rule are somewhat eccentric or aggressively avant-garde. Sibley and Weber's *Lot in Sodom* (1933) is a gaudy showcase of visible techniques, structuring its exploration of the Bible's story of sin and retribution by way of animations, superimpositions, expressionistic passages of light and fog, and, yes, slow motion—the sin, in short, looks pretty good. Marianne Moore called it "the best art film" she had ever seen and praised it for the "genuine splendor" of the unspoken (but unmistakable) homoerotic allure of the slow-motion montage flaunting the bodies of "the men who vexed Lot by day." Given that she published this review in *Close-Up*, the high praise she heaps upon the film reads almost like she's trying to boost its Rotten Tomatoes score for modernists drawn to the "atmosphere" of Henry James's prefaces, "the later bloodcurdling poems of James Joyce," and "E. E. Cummings' elephant-arabesques."[2] Moore's gushing was not enough to canonize the film, however, at least outside discussions of American queer or independent cinemas. These discussions are also where we find accounts of such films as Sidney Peterson's *Mr. Frenhofer* (1949) and *The Lead Shoes* (1949), outlandish and challenging experiments in non-narrative film that render slow motion doubly strange by giving us scenes of tangos danced at not just dramatically distended tempos (in *Mr. Frenhofer*) but also shot in anamorphic lenses that bend and warp the geometries in the frame. Kenneth Anger's early film *Eaux d'Artifice* (1953), which follows a woman in eighteenth-century costume on her nighttime walk through the fountains and gardens of an Italian villa, is so voluptuous in its fetishization of splashing arcs of water and her measured step that it is hard to spot the subtle slow motion that Anger occasionally employs.

There is no missing the extensive slow motion in the work of Maya Deren, the midcentury's most prominent and visible independent filmmaker. She deploys it in the first minute of her first film, *Meshes of the Afternoon* (1943), to fixate on a telling moment of action (a dropped key) that starts its noirish plot, and then returns to it for a later close-up on a character's decelerated feet as she climbs a flight of stairs. Bodies fall in slow motion in *At Land* (1944); they ultimately dance in slow motion near the end of *A Study in Choreography for Camera* (1945); *Ritual in Transfigured Time* (1946) makes slow-motion "rituals" out of everything from a game of cat's cradle to a ballet's *jetés*. Deren's *Meditation on Violence* (1948) is not, as we'll soon see, the very first film to display martial-arts choreography in slow motion, but it is remarkably precocious in the way it dances between its exacting style and reflexive Orientalism. Slow motion is also a racialized aesthetic in some of the footage that was posthumously assembled into *Divine Horseman* (1981), the Haitian Vodou documentary inspired in part by her work on Gregory Bateson's ethnographic filmmaking in Bali and that for now will have to stand in for other uses of slow motion in visual anthropology, psychology, and research in the social sciences that, again, raise questions about whole genres that routinely are neglected in histories of style. In "An Anagram of Ideas on Art, Form and Film," Deren describes slow motion primarily as a scientific mode of vision. "Slow-motion is the microscope of time," she writes, and though she celebrates some "lyric sequences" of "birds photographed by an ornithologist interested in their varied aerodynamics," even the "emotional and psychological complexes" that slow motion reveals when turned on human beings is the product of "the agony of its analysis."[3]

Though not considered a scientific filmmaker, Deren reminds us that the history of slow motion also unfolds in educational or industrial films, or other types of "useful cinema," as Acland and Wasson term it. Jean Painlevé was both a darling of the French surrealists in the 1920s and a prolific scientific filmmaker and made some of the earliest underwater documentaries using camera technologies he himself devised. His 1933 *The Sea Horse* employs slow motion to see better the contractions of the tiny fish's beating heart, an ingenious accomplishment at the time that also shows how closely the imperatives of empirical observation could manifest as desires of the optical unconscious, and vice versa. In his 1937 short *The Fourth Dimension*, he explores the mathematics of space-time perception across a series of beautifully rendered diagrams and tableaux and also uses footage of a slowly falling orange to illustrate how three-dimensional objects would appear to flat beings whose reality is a single plane. George Sidney directed several classic musicals in Hollywood (*Annie Get Your Gun* [1950], *Kiss Me Kate* [1953], *Bye Bye Birdie* [1963]) and hardly swam in the same waters of global modernism as Painlevé, but his 1940 documentary short on Harold "Doc" Edgerton, whose pioneering work in high-speed photography we will come back to later, is a surrealist fantasia of cracking eggs, vortices of smoke, and, in a particularly astounding sequence, a golf ball sent exploding through a telephone book to demonstrate the power both of Charles Lacey's swing and of Edgerton's strobe lights and cameras. In such films we see the material world not just defamiliarized by the forensic temporalities of media technology but literally and figuratively "blown up" to scales no human can perceive so that we might better visualize the acute slowness of our own perceptive apparatus, our lagging, perpetually belated processing of information and experience while plodding through a reality that moves at speeds we cannot fathom. Or put differently, the aestheticization of machine time—of the ways in which only a technology can "see" our world—quickly emerges as one of slow motion's most important motivations, extending both directly and obliquely the legacies of Muybridge, Marey, and more.

There are moments in fiction films of the 1930s and 1940s where we see this impulse to the sheer technique of slow-motion cinematography contending with the strain of narrative expectation. Why, exactly, are the first creepy birds that Alfred Hitchcock ever shows us also in slow motion? When two girls discover a body on the beach near the beginning of *Young and Innocent* (1937), they recoil and turn away just as Hitchcock cuts to a tight close-up on some gulls flying at what appears to be half-speed. Maybe this is some "lyric" footage that he recycled from the anonymous ornithologist that Deren half-recalls about a decade later? The girls immediately gaze back upon the murder victim after a couple seconds of uncannily distended nature footage, which I guess is supposed to register the horror of what they see. But if these birds are the "screen image" of the girls' displaced trauma—the symbol of their shock or of their immediate identification with a corpse that looks like them—it is weird that their unconscious minds manage to deflect onto the same random imagery and even weirder that this is a perfectly clear vision at a focal distance that far exceeds that of the human eye. And for reasons that are equally mysterious, the villainous Sir Humphrey Pengallan, played by Charles Laughton in the otherwise forgettable *Jamaica Inn* (1939), jumps to his death in slow motion after belligerently shouting to the assembled crowd below that they will get the "spectacle" they wished for—though most viewers of Hitchcock's tonally strange costume drama about Cornish pirates in the early nineteenth century are, on the contrary, hoping it will end as soon as possible. We might more generously read these odd scenes as technical experiments that will eventually result in some of Hitchcock's most compelling sequences (*The Birds* in slow-motion miniature, the various falling bodies of *Vertigo*). Hitchcock will return to a form of slow motion in *Rear Window* (1954), when he uses step printing to double each frame of Grace Kelly's disconcertingly distended kiss with James Stewart early in the film, giving the sequence a slightly halting sense of blurred intensity that makes these earlier moments of slow motion feel much more provisional and uncertain in their aims. Much the same could be said of Akira Kurosawa's first use of slow motion in his debut feature, *Sanshiro Sugata* (1943), which does not directly feature a moment of actual martial-arts action involving the heroic judo master against the jujutsu fighters aligned against him. Instead, we suddenly see a body float across the frame—propelled by one of Sanshiro's brilliant throws—and then into a wall, where the man crumples, dead not so much from Sanshiro's judo, within the logic of the film, as from his own prideful insistence on a match to the death in the first place. Kurosawa will return to slow motion later for a dream sequence in *Drunken Angel* (1948) and, with far more consequence for Hollywood filmmakers in the late 1960s, for a death scene in *The Seven Samurai* (1957), which became a global sensation that both Arthur Penn and Sam Peckinpah would cite as precedent for their later iconographies of violence and decelerated carnage. Had either just seen *Sanshiro Sugata*, a lot less blood might have been so magnificently spilled.

 The absolute abundance of slow motion means that almost every early variation on its use has since flourished into a familiar set of film motifs or been reified as what Bob Rehak, writing about the development of "bullet time" in the 1990s, would call a "microgenre."[4] Thus when Mariya, played by Yelena Zumina in Boris Barnet's 1936 Soviet romance *By the Bluest of Seas*, breaks a necklace given to her by a sailor whose desires show a bit too much possessive individualism for the ethos of the collective farm she helps direct, it comes as a complete surprise—given the presiding naturalism of Barnet's style—when the jewels drop down her chest and bounce onto the floor in sparkling slow motion (figure 4.2). Yet for a contemporary viewer who has seen bullet casings by the thousand fall just as slowly—not to mention dozens of glasses and bowls slip from the hands of someone who has just heard the bad news or caught someone in the

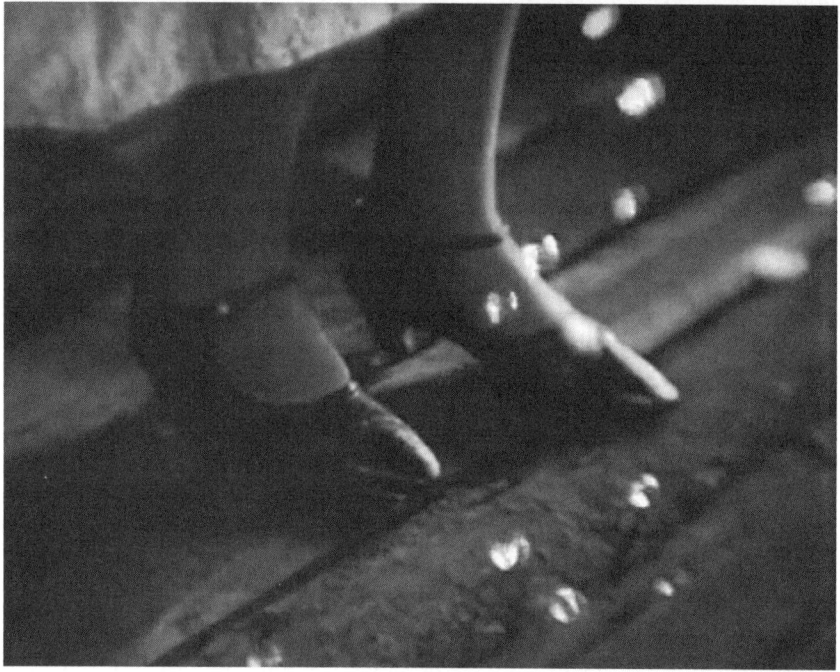

FIGURE 4.2 These beads fall in slow motion decades before the iconic bullets in *The Matrix* in a still from *By the Bluest of Seas* (1936).

act—or perhaps the broken string of pearls that land with maximum portent on the Gotham City pavement when in a Batman movie the young Bruce Wayne witnesses his mother's murder, this time, for the umpteenth time, the charm of seeing Mariya's crystals fall for the first version of this particular effect is tricky to hold onto. This brief instant of Mariya's devastation is impossibly prolonged in the material world, which almost seems determined to feel the suffering—and transmute it into something bearable, like art—that she herself will take in stride. Even as the sparking, falling jewels hang there in space, I can feel myself itching to Google just what the website TV Tropes confirms that we are catching at ground zero. It's the "slow-motion drop," in case you're wondering, which is a subtrope of the "dramatic drop."[5] From *The Bluest of Seas*, we can follow this particular motif to get to *Austin Powers: The Spy Who Shagged Me* (1999), *Run Lola Run* (1998), *The Usual Suspects* (1995), or *Ratatouille* (2007). Or, again in slow motion, we can arrive at the tumbling rocks of Smithson's *Spiral Jetty* as he plays with time and film on the shores of the Great Salt Lake. By this point in the 1960s, slow motion was not yet everywhere, but it was on its way.

5
Slow-Motion Modernism

Slow motion is a part of film's technical domain and stylistic language before, after, and apart from modernism—whether considered more narrowly in cinematic terms or more broadly, as I am doing here, as a network of aesthetic and cultural positions, emerging with special energy in the first decades of the twentieth century. Many of the positions taken by figures we might consider modernist—an unwieldy formulation, but one that honestly reflects the awkwardness and limits of the term—trade on formalisms (another term more awkward but more honest in the plural) that, as I have argued elsewhere, used ideas of medium specificity to work through the experience of new media technologies and the deeper economic and social transformations that they registered.[1] For one, there are biographical investments in modernism that matter a great deal for several filmmakers who come to be identified with the use of slow motion. This is obviously the case for figures such as Clair, Cocteau, Deren, Epstein, Buñuel, Vigo, Vorkapić, and Vertov, and though Clair's subsequent career departs from the avant-gardism of *Entr'acte* and Epstein does not make many films after World War II, Cocteau will return to slow motion to signature surreal effect in *La belle et la bête* (1946) and *Orphée* (1950), and Buñuel includes a transfixing slow-motion dream sequence in 1950's *Los olvidados*, a film that helped establish him as a global figure of Spanish-speaking cinema. The mix of tawdry realism and visual expressionism in Kurosawa's *Drunken Angel* speaks not only to the emergence of his status as an auteur in the 1950s but also to his engagements with Japanese and global modernisms when he was earlier contemplating a career as a painter. Modernism was effectively the family business for the Vertov/Kaufman brothers, and the fact that slow motion travels with Boris Kaufman from Jean Vigo's four films to the last years of the classic studio system in America makes him a transatlantic network of avant-garde technique unto himself. Nowhere, though, does slow motion look more modernist than in François Campaux's *Henri Matisse* (1946), which follows the aging painter around his studio in Vence but is punctuated by a startlingly decelerated scene that shows him sketching, each stroke and gesture literally producing still more modernism, however late, before our very eyes.[2]

Slow motion also provides a telling—but, all things considered, still infrequently appearing—sign of the emergence of what András Bálint Kovács calls "modernist art cinema" after World War II.[3] This terminology has its limits, and Kovács's perspective on the period is squarely European, but his work provides a helpful set of arguments for better understanding how filmmakers in France, Italy, and across Eastern Europe brought new stylistic innovations to commercial narrative cinema in the period while also codifying distinctive film histories and modes of writing, screening practices, marketing techniques, and affiliations with museums, universities, and festivals. From the cinematic canons promoted by the critics of *Cahiers du Cinema* that soon came to inform the New Wave in France to the neorealistic protocols of Visconti, Rossellini, and de Sica that shaped, though sometimes through rejection, the achievements of Fellini and Antonioni, there are many ways that these developments of the postwar decades remain critical parts of film's legacy infrastructure, so to speak: as an "art" medium that is definitely no longer new even when different national cinemas come to international attention (Hong Kong in the 1990s, South Korea in the 2000s, Greece in the 2010s) or when, as with figures such as Tsai, contemporary directors find ways to make cinema feel even slower when set against the high-speed rhythms of "intensified continuity" in Hollywood and beyond.[4] And to say that the directors of the New Wave or the Italian neorealists resisted many of the temporal conventions that dominated commercial fiction cinema in Europe and the United States is an understatement bordering on banality: European art films of the 1950s through the 1960s were fetishized—and nowhere more aggressively than in the New American Cinema of Hollywood around 1968—for their long takes, aimless dialogue, jump cuts, freeze frames, narrative discontinuities, distended or recursive timelines, and attenuated logics of cause and effect—for their abiding willingness, in other words, to highlight all the techniques that make time "cinematic" in its most dominant and suspicious forms.[5]

Kovács places these genres of art film after World War II within a genealogy that drew self-consciously on modernist precursors in literature, drama, and the visual arts. But he also structures his account as a response to the provocation of

Deleuze's singular insistence that there is a midcentury threshold or fault line (no figure really does him justice) between classical and modern cinema. "The difference," Kovács writes, "is to be found in their respective treatment of movement and time. Classical cinema articulates time through movement."[6] But after World War II—not that Deleuze would conceive these changes as mere reactions to historical events—we witness, as Deleuze writes in *Cinema II*, "the collapse of traditional sensory-motor situations . . . in the form these had in the old realism or the action image."[7] Now we have instead a "modern cinema," in Kovács's summary of Deleuze, that "does not represent a physical world" so much as those "'crystals of time'"—a resonant turn of phrase that Kovács borrows from *Cinema II*—"linked to one another by endless variation and multiplication." In the cinema of the "time-image" that Deleuze observes coming into being at midcentury, "time is no longer the measure of movement." Instead we see films enamored with a "pure optical and sound image" increasingly cut off from sequences of plot and action, films where "movement is the perspective of time: it constitutes a whole cinema of time."[8]

Yet there is hardly any more slow motion to be seen in this "cinema of time" after World War II than in the cinema of movement that preceded it. Nor does Deleuze have much interest in slow motion as such, though he does briefly admire Epstein's *The Fall of the House of Usher* for constituting "the maximum of movement in a form which is infinitely drawn out," and he later rhapsodizes about the "hydraulic" grace of Vigo's underwater scenes in *L'Atlante* and *Taris*. In Epstein or Vigo, "slow motion frees movement from its moving body," but this is as far as they can go.[9] These films remain, for Deleuze, within the domain of the "movement-image" and its more classical aesthetic. Slow motion is generally absent in the differently modernist cinema that Deleuze associates with the "time-image." Francois Truffaut inserts a small passage of slow motion in his 1957 short *Les mistons*, which he described as his first "real" film. But where his use of freeze frames and other showy gestures embodies one version of the New Wave ideal, this is the only slow motion that I have managed to see in any of his films. I am decidedly not a Jean-Luc Godard completist—a daunting task for even the most ardent cinephile—but there is no slow motion in his masterpieces of the 1960s from *Breathless* to *Week-end*, despite the formidable array of techniques and devices he puts on full display. Godard's first use of the effect—apart from some work for French TV in the mid-1970s—is *Suave qui peut* (1980), which was released as *Slow Motion* in the United Kingdom, making its step printing and other time-axis manipulations wonderfully self-reflexive.

In the rarefied circles of cinematic modernism after World War II, there is, then, surprisingly less slow motion than we might expect given how centrally the filmmakers we best remember from this period were interested in the experience and representation of time. For example, for a split second in Roberto Rossellini's *Paisan* (1946), it certainly looks as if the American soldier, Joe, tumbles out of the frame in slow motion when he is shot by snipers near the end of the film's first episode, but the effect is almost fleeting enough to be invisible.

There is no missing the slow motion, though, in *The Cranes Are Flying* (1957), which won the Palme d'Or at Cannes in 1958: Its director Mikhail Kalatozov and cinematographer Sergey Urusevsk conceived a very showy dream sequence for the moment when Boris is shot and, as he loses consciousness and dies, he sees a spinning vision of the forest where he has fallen become a sensational slow-motion fantasy of a marriage that now will never happen. The scene manages somehow to be even more melodramatic than the slow motion that Pier Paolo Pasolini turns to at two moments in *Mamma Roma* (1962), both of which—Anna Magnani's "Mamma" spinning with a child as she dances at a tawdry wedding and, later, her son, Ettore, walking out of view—foreshadow Ettore's excruciating death in prison despite all the torment and humiliations that Mamma Roma suffers on his behalf. Pasolini's cinematographer here, Tonnino Delli Colli, will come back in slow motion with a vengeance when he later works with Sergio Leone.

Critics from whom I've learned a lot have written that there is slow motion in Truffaut's *Jules and Jim* (1962) and Godard's *Pierrot le fou* (1965), as well as in Alain Resnais's *Last Year at Marienbad* (1961), another New Wave landmark of temporal complexity and philosophical torpor. Resnais does seem to have told his actors to perform some scenes with remarkable and disorienting slowness but did not film them moving very, very slowly in slow motion. And unless I missed it, neither Truffaut nor Godard use slow motion in the films they made in the decade of the New Wave's fullest flowering and cultural sway around the world. Neither the 1951 Bob Hope vehicle *The Lemon-Drop Kid* nor Henri Clouzot's 1953 thriller *The Wages of Fear* would have been New Wave favorites, and there is nothing especially modernist or avant-garde about their slow-motion sequences save for the fact that they are in the pretty exclusive company of Cocteau and Buñuel among the small handful of feature films to use slow motion at all in the 1950s. Few would place Yasuzo Masumura among these midcentury masters, despite his reputation in postwar Japan and the amazing use to which he puts slow motion in 1962's *Black Test Car*, a noir thriller about corporate espionage and industrial design that it is as far removed from Bob Hope's silliness as it is from New Wave visual poetry. But when the team from Tiger Motors stakes out a men's room window so that they can film the board meeting of their rivals at Yamoto—and then try to replay the footage in slow motion for a lip reader to figure out the price at which Yamoto will be rolling out the car whose specs they've stolen—we see one of the most self-conscious uses of the technique anywhere in film history before 1968, after which it will be much harder for any director to show us something in slow motion that we haven't seen before. The lip reading doesn't work, but the team at Tiger can't blame slow motion for the failure. The Yamoto chairman will only put the price down on a sheet of paper that is passed around the meeting. Slow motion might produce what Kracauer suggestively calls "temporal close-ups" on screen, but for all the technical prowess *Black Test Car* puts on show, what our heroes really needed was a bigger zoom.[10]

I won't name the critics who led me astray because I don't think their mistaken memories or omissions are any more revealing than those I've no doubt made myself while trying to do my best to catalog slow motion's history. The impossible abundance of slow motion in global visual culture from the end of the twentieth century and the first decades of the twenty-first beggars any claims to empirical authority about how many films have used it since the 1960s, and the numbers get only worse and even harder to comprehend when I think about the thousands of slow-motion replays I've seen on TV, the 42,200,000 results for "slow motion" on YouTube I just Googled, or even the dozens of examples of slow-motion video art I've seen over the years—more than a lot of people, but I bet far fewer than many who haunt galleries more than I do. I suspect that all this slow motion makes it difficult to realize that there was, not too long ago in the short-to-medium *durée* of aesthetic forms and media history—distinctly less of it in every way. Less slow motion in fewer films that were harder to see, fewer replays on fewer channels of not nearly so many sports, and not a single YouTube video from "The Slow Mo Guys," whose dedicated channel currently has just over 14 million subscribers who can watch just under three hundred examples of "offensively crisp slow motion footage," spanning over a decade, of the "guys" Gav or Dan themselves—sometimes I can't tell them apart— jumping onto a "Giant 6ft Water Balloon" or "Diving into 1000 Mousetraps" or suffering "Paintballs against BARE SKIN."

Aside from, again, making it sound fairly ridiculous even to suggest that any treatment of slow motion's place in modern and contemporary visual culture could possibly be complete, the scale and extent of all the films, genres, subgenres, and more ephemeral forms that have come to feature it make it hard, I think, to remember that it hasn't always been this way—despite the fact, as I have shown, that slow motion has also always been there. To excavate slow motion's history is, at one level, a project of finding "firsts" and moments when individual artists and filmmakers were able to "make it new," to invoke the modernist imperatives of Ezra Pound. The limits of this kind of modernism are many, from encouraging a disregard for genres and formal practices that do not aspire to the status of "art" in its most restrictive definitions to overselling avant-gardism and its aesthetic politics, as if slower and less perceptible histories of development, innovation, change, and, eventually, assimilation are always and forever to be taken as narratives of some originary form that then declines and falls into routine or, perhaps worse still, acceptance and popularity. There aren't many critics who still hold to these positions in anything like their purest and most embarrassing expressions, but the reflex can be hard to shake, especially when I'm tracking a particular media aesthetic that goes, in something of a straight line, from Buñuel to Michael Bay, from Rene Clair's surrealism to motion ramping in *The Raid 2*. Rather than search relentlessly for "befores" and "afters," most have learned the lessons of Raymond Williams and come to think about the subtler shifts among the categories of the "emergent," "dominant," and "residual" when thinking through—and against—the ways that the culture of modernity is shadowed by a rhetoric of perpetual progress that parallels that of capitalism.[11] Because often the discourse of modernity just *is* the rhetoric of capitalism, as Fredric Jameson reminds us: "Technological development lends itself irresistibly to subsumption under the empty narrative form of the break...even in our own historiographically far more self-conscious era, when everyone decries a 'technological determinism' that they secretly harbor in their heart of hearts." Setting aside his dubious projections about "our" secret historiographic fantasies—I'd like to think I have weirder dreams in my heart of hearts than technological determinism!—Jameson was right to notice, writing in 2002, that the sorts of skepticism we have had for decades about the events, "great men," and ideologies of history has been less rigorously applied to equally complex notions like technology or "new" media. "Modernity always had something to do technology," Jameson writes more bluntly elsewhere, "and thus eventually with progress."[12] Slow motion is a perfect and paradoxical sign of what this progress looks like in the twentieth century: It produces the aesthetic opposite of the high-speed photography that makes it possible, and the more we see of it, the less remarkable it seems, despite the fact that its wholesale proliferation tells us more about the meaning of our technological world than any handful of examples testifying to its residual aesthetic power.

So there is obviously a lot of slow motion from before the 1960s that I have never seen, not just in educational films, sports highlights, or industrial movies that have been lost or are sitting in archives that I'll never visit but almost certainly too in narrative films from around the world that I would never think to look for unless some previous critic, film historian, YouTube commenter, or fan had mentioned it already. The history of slow motion I have assembled here is meant to be provisional, and there is no single point of origin that lets us track its trajectory from a single moment in film and media history through literature, art, and twentieth-century culture in its endless variety of popular and elite forms. I'm writing from the vantage of a contemporary moment that is altogether "after" slow motion becomes pervasive. And while this might be exactly the sort of empty "break" that Jameson cautions us against, it does at least provide a retrospective rationale for why, beginning in the 1970s, it is almost impossible—and even pointless—to keep track of slow motion's individual appearances. It took me years to track down the sixty or so appearances of slow motion that I've listed to this point. My data is incomplete and unsystematically assembled; it has been an exercise in cinephilia, not empiricism. But as a point of reference, consider these sixty films in the following context: as I am writing, there are thirty-three titles in the Marvel Cinematic Universe, about a dozen in the DC Extended Universe; Zach Snyder has directed eight films that aren't part of DC's official continuity, such as it is, while Michael Bay has directed fifteen, and Guy Ritchie has directed fifteen films as I am writing, but let's say fourteen, since I doubt there is slow motion in 2002's *Swept Away* (and I'm unwilling to find out for sure). These are eighty-one examples of slow motion in the most obvious places I could think to look, and if I throw in the nine or so films directed by Lana and Lilly Wachowski, we're at ninety. Multiply the numbers globally across the national cinemas that make action films of any kind, or maybe assume that any film, aside from the rare costume epic or big-budget prestige drama, with production costs over $100 million (adjusted for inflation) or in the fortieth percentile and up (for a given year), and it will soon start to seem obvious that there have been thousands of films featuring at least some sort of slow motion since the 1970s, with a sharp acceleration in the 1980s with the rise of blockbuster cinema in post- or neoclassical Hollywood and also in the 2000s with the increasing use of CGI and digital speed ramping. I admit that this is speculative and that it would take a lot of work—and who knows how much time—to get a better grasp on slow motion's ludicrous omnipresence today.[13] Even if I'm a little off—what if there are closer to one hundred fiction films that use slow motion before 1968? or two hundred?—the fraction remains vanishingly small when set against its subsequent ubiquity. IMDb lists 13,970 releases in the 1940s; I've only found five that use slow motion. IMDb lists 2,236 releases for just 1956 alone, but only one in the United States that I have seen or read about—Akira Kurosawa's 1954 *The Seven*

Samurai—has any slow motion that anybody seems to have seen and noticed. As we'll see, this single example might be more directly consequential for *Bonnie and Clyde* than all the films and imagery I have dutifully assembled. And part of the reason why I am taking my time to get there is that slow motion goes so much faster after it ends this famous film with such exquisite and aggressive brutality.

6
Escape Velocities

There are limits to looking at mainly feature films in Europe and the United States to gauge slow motion's diffusion and codification in twentieth-century visual culture—limits that remain, at some level, methodologically insurmountable even when significant works of avant-garde or independent cinema are included, and with full acknowledgment that vast domains of sports coverage, industrial and scientific shorts, educational films, documentaries, newsreels, and pornography are even harder to account for. What I have done instead is trace references to slow motion in film history and criticism I have read on the assumption that this gives something like a core sample of the slow motion that finally emerges in such totality at the end of the century that it feels almost immediately residual and played out. When Cavell starts his discussion of slow motion with the imperative "Take slow motion," it's hard not to hear the implicit "please" that would finish off the one-liner. From the stupid technical brilliance of the Slow Mo Guys to endless listicles countingdown "6 of the Best Slow-Motion Action Scenes Ever" or "64 Stunning Slo-Mo Sequences in Movies—and What Makes Them Great"—it is all too easy to discover video essays that adoringly compile tropes like the "slow motion walk" or chart it through the work of fanboy directors like Bay and Snyder or, on artsier occasions, Wes Anderson, Quentin Tarantino, Martin Scorsese, Wong Kar-wai, or John Woo. We're always just a click from Googling ourselves to "Planet Slow Mo," a series started by the Slow Mo Guys in 2019 that officially had only twenty-four episodes but effectively describes the world of media in which we've lived for decades and will almost certainly outlast us. Slow motion has achieved the worst thing that can happen to an avant-garde or modernist technique: total victory everywhere.

Until around 1967 or so, there is little sign of how thorough this victory will be. What is remarkable instead is the slowness of slow motion's growth over the decades, given that it was technologically possible from the first moments of film's development. Motorized cameras with faster frame rates and greater film capacity become available in the 1920s, and better, cheaper film stocks matter, too, since slow motion goes through film faster and faster to produce slower and slower imagery for the screen. Digital filmmaking represents a whole different economy, but slow motion is already operationally "generic" by the 1980s and 1990s, long before the widespread transition away from celluloid. Technological innovations might help explain the fact that I've only seen (or read about) three examples of slow motion from before 1920 while managing to discover sixteen from the 1920s, fifteen from the 1930s, and fourteen from the 1940s—with who knows how many individual short-subjects, newsreels, and more besides. But the same degree of digging finds only nine titles from the 1950s, each of which I've listed, with one exceedingly notable exception given my interest here: Arthur Penn's debut feature, *The Left-Handed Gun* (1958). The numbers go up in the 1960s, especially, say, if each Andy Warhol "Screen Test" projected at 8 or 12fps is counted individually—there are hundreds—or if films like *Empire* (1964) count because they were shown at what was, for the silent era, a standard frame rate of 16fps, which would have looked like slow motion in the 1960s. Though of course the point of all these Warhol films is how little movement there can be in what we would still call movies. Dozens of films made by George Maciunas and others associated with the Fluxus movement employ slow motion, and while few of them are as iconic as works like "Disappearing Music for Face (Fluxfilm no. 4)" or "Eyeblink (Fluxfilm no. 9)"—twelve minutes of Yoko Ono slowly smiling or four minutes and thirty-one seconds of Yoko Ono slowly blinking—many of them are fascinated with prolonged and absurd temporalities applied to common, silly, or occasionally bawdy bodily performances.

These projects aside, slow motion doesn't seem especially prolific elsewhere in films from earlier in the 1960s: There are famous avant-garde examples such as Jack Smith's *Flaming Creatures* (1963) and Stan Brakhage's *Dog Star Man* (1961–1964). There is the gigantic spectacle of Kon Ichikawa's *Tokyo Olympiad* (1965), which at once evokes Riefenstahl's *Olympia* but also revises its antimodern pretense and cultishness. Brakhage also is occasionally credited with filming the original Downy fabric softener commercial and its iconic product drop onto a pile of plush and laundered towels, but whether or not this ad really has a secret provenance it still reminds us that television advertising began to incorporate slow motion in the early 1960s. By the same token, the slow-motion footage of

Tokyo Olympiad, though on another level of aesthetic mastery and style—its use of slow motion shifts between color and black and white, with sequences of high abstraction and granular realism building to its final appearance in the section on Abebe Bikila's win in the marathon—was preceded by television's gradual adoption of slow-motion instant replay for sports highlights in the early 1960s, with the widespread turn to videotape in Japan, Western Europe, Canada, and the United States.[1] One version of slow motion's origin story in TV sports begins with legendary ABC producer Roone Arledge taking inspiration from a "samurai epic"—the timing is right for this to be *The Seven Samurai*—that he sees while traveling in Japan sometime after 1956 to secure the rights for the Nippon Baseball All-Star game, with the technology then debuting for a college football game in 1961. Despite the breakthrough and the "dream-like grace" achieved by recording at half-speed for videotaped replay on a monitor, ABC apparently did not invest further money in the process Arledge claims to have invented. (His own memoir is fuzzy on the dates, and no footage of the game survives.) CBS producer Tony Verna devised a more elegant and effective process for slow-motion instant replay by using timed sound cues to index the game action on the secondary audio track of Ampex VTR-1000 tapes; technicians in the booth could then listen for these tones to rewind game tapes to various on-field occurrences. Verna's system had its first successful test during the Army-Navy game on December 7, 1963, which had been postponed after the assassination of John F. Kennedy, who had been planning to attend the game. "With all the patriotism involved," Verna recalls, at an Army-Navy game just two weeks after such a public loss, "screwing up" the heavily promoted launch of instant replay might have added "to the emotional cloud hanging over the nation."[2] Verna might sound a little melodramatic here in suggesting that Americans would be retraumatized by some minor technical difficulties amid the general anguish, but it turns out that Kennedy's assassination does, in fact, come to figure as a version of slow-motion's primal scene by the time we get to *Bonnie and Clyde*.

The increasingly widespread use of slow motion for TV sports coverage in the 1960s came just as newsreels and other shorts had all but disappeared as routine aspects of the cinematic experience. We might say, then, that this particular subgenre of slow motion was effectively domesticated by the end of the 1960s, while others, such as scientific or industrial films and other documentary shorts, became thoroughly segregated for nontheatrical exhibition in classrooms or museums or at conferences, conventions, or academic symposia. On the one hand, these shifts across media and institutions speak to the wholesale transformation of visual culture in the 1960s as television and video come to achieve forms of dominance that they will enjoy for decades. But on the other hand, what we observe for slow motion and its aesthetics are for the most part tradeoffs and transpositions, with a mostly steady state persisting from the 1920s to the 1960s. Nor do we find much evidence that Hollywood or other national cinemas, before the last years of the decade, were more invested in slow motion than in prior decades. Besides Boris Kaufman's slow-motion sequences in *The Pawnbroker* and *The World of Henry Orient*—both almost classical in their indebtedness to Vigo's modernism of the 1930s—we see scenes of decelerated violence in the grindingly realistic "angry young man" drama *This Sporting Life* (1963), starring Richard Harris as a coal miner whose exploits on the rugby pitch are shown as equally tortuous struggles to little gain. The battle scenes of Orson Welles's *Chimes at Midnight* (1965) unfold with immensely greater stakes but also look like slogs in the mud where Harris's futile masculinity would fit right in. Slow motion is a lot more fun in Richard Lester's *A Hard Day's Night* (1964), where it lets us see John, Paul, George, and Ringo floating through the air in lazy arcs set to "Can't Buy Me Love." Lester had worked with Tony Verna at a Philadelphia TV station in the 1950s, a startling coincidence given that they would cross paths in slow motion just a decade later.

The odds of two slow-motion pioneers meeting should be seen as longer still given that slow motion remained so rare: I've found just fourteen films before 1967, which is almost the same as the 1950s' nine, and not even statistically significant amid the nearly twenty thousand films released around the world over this period. Slow motion does distinguish some crucial and even iconic films in the years leading up to the release of *Bonnie and Clyde*. Martin Scorsese introduces his fetish for both slow motion and for Harvey Keitel in *Who's That Knocking at My Door?* (1967); Keitel, at least, does not appear in almost every film that he goes on to make. John Boorman's *Point Blank* (1967) was released in the United States just four weeks after *Bonnie and Clyde* debuted at the Montreal Film Festival and includes a devastating dream sequence—in slow motion, Lee Marvin tosses and turns while picturing his violent reunion with an old girlfriend he fears betrayed him—that is as stylish as any scene in this terminally stylish film (figure 6.1). But few viewers or critics seem to have noticed the scene in 1967, unlike the bullet-ridden finale of *Bonnie and Clyde*, which was to became iconic with such speed that it's easy to forget that it looked no more likely to become a hit on its modest budget of $2.5 million than Boorman's warped and existential revenge noir, a generic mix as off-putting to some, at least initially, as Penn's amalgamation of thirties gangsters, Dust Bowl nostalgia, and countercultural affect.

ESCAPE VELOCITIES   77

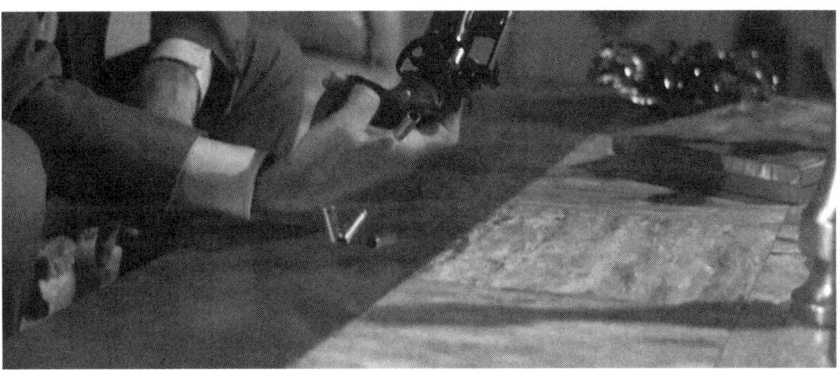

FIGURE 6.1   Still from *Point Blank* (1967).

All this to say, slow motion could have made it big in Hollywood much faster than it did. From the 1890s to the mid-1960s, it was continuously available as a technological possibility of the medium, a generic feature across a range of nonfiction modes, and a stylistic device with distinctive patterns for how it could be put to work aesthetically—as a tamed attraction in narrative cinema, as assimilated modernism—in movies from around the world. But it is not until the late 1960s that slow motion as we know it now entirely and at last arrives. The films that codify and popularize slow motion suddenly come at us quickly: *Bonnie and Clyde* in August 1967, Stanley Kubrick's *2001: A Space Odyssey* in April 1968, Sergio Leone's *Once Upon a Time in the West* in December 1968, Sam Peckinpah's *The Wild Bunch* in June 1969, and Michelangelo Antonioni's *Zabriskie Point* in February 1970. And there are more to see along the way that, though not quite so explicit in their iconographies of change and crisis, help make slow motion into the ubiquitous aesthetic that it remains, giving us a sense of the twentieth century as not just "long" but in some ways ongoing and enduring or, what is worse, unfinished and perhaps without an end in sight.

Thus it is worth remembering that the bewildering final shootout between Warren Oates and another Warren Oates in Monte Hellman's existential "acid Western" *The Shooting* (1966) is step printed to make even it more uncanny. Though Hellman's film was not widely distributed in the United States until 1971, there were many others that fared better at the moment even if they haven't aged as well. *Point Blank* is also released in August 1967; *How Sweet It Is!* in August 1968; *Goodbye, Columbus* in April 1969; *Easy Rider* in July 1969; *A Touch of Zen* in November 1971; and of course Peckinpah's own *Ballad of Cable Hogue* in March 1970, *Straw Dogs* in November 1971, *Junior Bonner* in June 1972, and *The Getaway* in December 1972; Kubrick's *A Clockwork Orange* in December 1971; and *Mean Streets* in October 1973. I've just listed seventeen notable and, in some cases, ridiculously iconic films from just over five years that feature, if not indulge, slow motion among their signature and most elaborate effects. There are obviously more examples—dozens? a hundred?—that I have not tracked down and never will since they represent the vaster expanses of slow motion that open up in the 1970s and beyond, an accumulation that stops being interesting as an undiscovered genealogy once it becomes too obvious to miss. This is not to say that there are not specific examples of slow motion since this extended "1968" that matter or conceive of something new against the background of the idiom's explosion and proliferation. To say slow motion is *now* exhausted would be a version of the same mistake of modernist avant-gardism that would insist it was already over by 1924 with *Entr'acte* or by 1934 with Vigo and then finally emptied out by Warhol in the 1960s.

Instead, the job at hand is to identify those examples of the form that most vividly reflect the experience of time as rendered by technology and that can help illuminate—at the level of both painfully incremental detail but also sometimes sweeping allegory—all the speeds at which the experience of modernity has been felt over the past century and longer. "Then times changed," writes Henri Lefebvre in 1962, just before slow motion started speeding up. "Technology began penetrating everyday life; there were new problems. And now, what can you see?"[3] From mechanical invention and special effect to media aesthetic and cultural iconography, slow motion emerges as a central figure for the modern "times" Lefebvre evokes. We can track its uses—on screen and off, as visualized in moving images or symbolized in literature—as a way of understanding how times change with technology and how this process functions in reverse as whole industries and networks of machines and media get older and rundown as the "twentieth century" we remember rightly as speed's epoch begins to look and feel in retrospect like the slowest decades any of us will ever know for ourselves. As a technology of the highest speeds appearing as their opposite, slow motion lets us ask whether the modern world we see is really always going quite so fast as we are conditioned to believe. It is hardly the only aesthetic form that lets us grasp modernity as, in Jameson's powerful abstractions, the juxtaposition of "radically different kinds of realities and temporalities," some of which pass by in what feels like the blink of an eye that then takes years or centuries to comprehend.[4] The history I am most interested in—which might not always parallel or run in the same direction as the "History" that Jameson capitalizes—will feature its own versions of the "dissonance" or "incommensurability" of overlapping and uneven times that are utterly familiar aspects of modern culture, which has proven itself more durable—which is to say, slower to fade away—than many, including Jameson, once thought. I choose to see this not as a sign of slow motion's timelessness so much as an expression of the fact that we are still living in and through the crisis that it helps us register. Or as Sarah Brouillette, Joshua Clover, and Annie McClanahan point out in respect to the grinding, declining "present" that has been happening to us collectively since more or less the late 1960s, "it's hard to build a robust philosophy of history around an economic theory for which time itself starts to slow down." "Capitalism in stagnation," they argue, demands that we think "in terms of stall, immobility, stasis."[5] Maybe the reason slow motion becomes so popular so fast is that it is the very image of modernity at terminal velocity, running out of steam but still with too much time that it can never, ever kill.

7

Technological Aesthetics

What do we see in slow motion that we don't see otherwise? Given its tremendous visibility and widespread use since the early 1970s, I was surprised to find that relatively few critics have talked about slow motion at any length or spent much time thinking through the form's history or poetics. Of course, the early accounts of Arnheim, Benjamin, Kracauer, and others remain endlessly provocative and rich. And there is, as I have said, a way in which Cavell is right to see even the infrequent instances of slow motion he could remember—though they were getting less so by the day in 1971—as already showing strain from overuse. For Cavell, even feminine hygiene can seem worth "honoring" in slow motion—which is the problem. But I suspect that he would have been no more persuaded by countless slow-motion gunshots, punches, car wrecks, tackles, strikeouts, falls, or crashes trying to impart a similarly inflated aura to masculinity. It's the repetitiousness and commercial showiness of slow motion that can make it mean less than it shows.

Cavell is practically alone among film theorists in mentioning slow motion, if only in part to condescend to it. It does not figure in Bazin, despite his abiding interest in film's relationship to the photographic image and its stillness, nor does it seem to have mattered much to Christian Metz, whose devotion to questions of identification and the psychology of spectatorship focuses on very different dimensions of film's language. Perhaps because slow motion remained, for most of the twentieth century, only a minor presence in the "classical" narrative cinemas of Hollywood and other centers of the industry, revisionist critics such as Peter Wollen, Stephen Heath, and Laura Mulvey tend to overlook it too since it was anything but essential to the semiotic systems whose ideologies they sought to expose and take apart. Even when explicitly concerned with "representations of time that can be discovered in the relation between movement and stillness," Mulvey's interest in narratives that "halt" or are rendered subject to "delay" pushes her toward the arrested temporality of the photograph or to an installation like Douglas Gordon's famous *24 Hour Psycho*—a dual-video projection of Hitchcock's masterpiece with its frame rate reduced to 2fps—that "opened up a Hollywood genre movie to the aesthetics of slow motion and thus to the traditions of the avant-garde film."[1] Like Doane, Garrett Stewart, Karen Beckman, Louise Hornby, and others trying to work through film's connection to the still image, Mulvey barely has more patience for slow motion than an aesthete like Cavell. Slow motion makes an artifice of cinematic time and flagrantly confuses many of the terms that critics focused on film's basis in photography try their hardest to keep clear: Does slow motion show us movement as it decelerates and freezes on its way to stillness, even if it will never get there? Or is slow motion insisting, however imperceptibly, on the ontological priority of movement in the world, forever failed for millennia by static visual media that give us only its illusion on stone walls, stretched canvases, or sheets of glossy paper? Motion, as Arnheim points out, "is the strongest visual appeal to attention."[2] And the Western preoccupation with what E. H. Gombrich calls the "*puntum temporis*" or "point in time" might be better seen, or so he argues in 1964's "Moment and Movement in Art," as a profoundly compensatory reaction to an "absurdity" of human psychology: "for we are not cameras but rather slow registering instruments that cannot take in much at a time.... Compared with the speed of a computer we are indeed slow in the uptake."[3] Or, as Jay Lampert concludes in a more specialized vocabulary, "delay is not an epistemic aporia, it is the real structure of temporality."[4] Slowness, to be brief, is the human condition.

This is not to say that every baroque explosion in *Transformers: Revenge of the Fallen* (2009) or the gloriously silly "power walk" of the astronauts and oil-rig workers in *Armageddon* (1998) must be a philosophical occasion. But slow motion is hard for some theories of film to explain and causes trouble for any metaphysics of the medium grounded on the "ontology of the photographic image," to evoke Bazin again. Cavell himself is working in this tradition throughout *The World Viewed*, and though he gets a bit "restless" with the language of "realism" that Bazin employs, he agrees that "the basis of the medium of movies is photographic, and that photography is *of* reality or nature."[5] With the shift from analogue technologies to digital media only intensifying these debates, Doane argues with compelling force and a degree of melancholy that the obsolescence of the "photochemical epistemology" means that we must revise the ways we have come to take for granted that cinema, even when departing radically from every type of realism we might imagine, still functions as what she calls a "deictic index," a visualizing of some "'this'... it points to and verifies."[6] Her thinking also begins with Bazin but reaches back to the semiotic terminology of Charles Sanders Peirce, who divided signs into "icons," which share a resemblance to the thing they represent; "symbols," which work operate by conventional associations; and the "index," which implies a "material connection between sign and object as well as an insistent temporality—the reproducibility of a past moment." Doane explores how photographs and, by extension, films can sometimes work iconically or symbolically but are always and inescapably indexical to the degree that any image produced by light striking a chemical emulsion on a material strip or plate—photography, in short—must have "an existential bond with its object."[7] There are hairs that we could try to split about the difference that it makes—or doesn't—if this existentially significant light ends up landing instead on the pixels and sensors of a digital camera. Lev Manovich and Sean Cubitt are both persuasive that we've been too invested for too long in a nostalgia for the materiality of analogue media and that we've accordingly hypostasized another exaggerated "break"—anxious and overdetermined—around a set of digital technologies that actually do things that older media have done for centuries.[8]

Slow motion has a strange ontology, if it has one at all. Like the photographic experiments of Muybridge and Marey, it captures motion incrementally, with a precision and exactitude that surpasses the perceptual apparatus of the human eye. By filming at frame rates higher than the images produced will be projected—often just two or four times faster in the Hollywood examples I've been discussing, but filming faster by factors of 10, 100, 10,000, and beyond was already possible for engineers in the 1940s—the camera gives us more motion than we need to represent the "real time" that would register if the images were shown at normal speed. In this, slow motion is particularly "manufactured," to return to Cavell on photography, and even more beholden to the "fact of mechanism" on which both still and moving pictures inescapably depend.[9] Whenever we suddenly see slow motion in a movie (or video or digital work) that had been going along at normal speed, no matter how we reconcile it to the narrative that contains it or to the style that otherwise defines the whole, what we are seeing is a show of *excess* at its most literal: Slow motion is an inverse but utterly precise and even "existential" index to how fast a camera films.

And the slower that slow motion goes, the more perverse and backward its ontology becomes. What we see in slow motion, simply put, is speed—but not for us. The "lyricism" that it intimates—which is rehearsed by every casual but largely empty description of how "graceful," "poetic," or "dreamlike" slow motion looks on screen—is the end product of a technology at work, and at velocities to which we are "nevertheless not present," borrowing from Cavell, or, as Kittler would say in his discourse of maximum inhumanity, "the different arrangement of a stream of temporal data" or, simpler still, "time axis manipulation."[10] In the genres of useful cinema and their video and digital versions today, these contradictions can be embraced as shows of wonder at the sheer impossibility of the higher and higher speeds technology can achieve—shutter times measured in the trillionths of a second, computers that crunch the ones and zeros of the images that they produce at even less conceivable rates measured in petaflops and operations by the quadrillion. But even for the glacial frame rates of slow motion in its most ancient, antique versions—a procession of Parisian artists in *Entr'acte*, a leaping comrade clearing the bar in Vertov—the camera has to go so fast that it might as well be magic from one of the "fantasies" that Kracauer just barely tolerates or a dream of the "optical unconscious" that Benjamin must speculate into existence as a figure for how we might still be able to see, slow as we are, a world whose pace and tempo isn't so much accelerated but estranged from human temporality at both its upper and lower limits.

The amazing resonance of Benjamin's notion of an "optical unconscious" in no small measure rests with the Freudian contexts that it invokes, contexts that inform generations of film theory and arguments about media technologies as versions of an "apparatus" that asserts not just a set of formal rules and visual perspectives when we watch but hails us into a larger network of ideologies and identifications that, like psychoanalysis, assumes that masculinity (white and bourgeois) is a default position of the very hardware that makes cinema happen. Slow motion, almost from its earliest incarnations in Edison, often looks like the indulgence of a technological power that wants to see and show what men want, almost as if offering voyeuristic access into the smallest intervals of time so that bodies can be more provocatively and even invasively displayed. If the "lyricism" of slow motion points toward its more soft-core aesthetics—the way it "eroticizes" or "poeticizes" actions that we might hardly notice, much less sexualize—its "visceral" spectacles of bodies undergoing the most extreme experiences of pain or pleasure are almost always conceivable as versions of pornography. The hundreds of ejaculating "squibs" of movie blood and hamburger that Peckinpah brought to Hollywood with *The Wild Bunch* are a kind of "money shot," after all, just not the sort that the Mitchell Brothers filmed in slow motion for *Behind the Green Door* (1972), where slow motion was definitely not the main attraction that got people to the theater but does reveal another aspect of its timeliness.[11] "If erotic stimulation," Leo Bersani and Ulysse Dutoit propose, "depends on the perceived or fantasized commotion of others, it becomes reasonable to put others into a state of maximal commotion." They're picturing Sade here, not slow motion, and the violence they explore in late Assyrian sculpture precedes Penn, Peckinpah, and Leone by more than a millennium. But they describe these ancient stone reliefs as uncanny anticipations of apparatus theory in all its psychoanalytic drama. They see figures in viscerally arrested actions who "mobilize our attention by distracting us from [their] own tragic immobility," showing in the absolutely slowest motion how quickly we can get from "nondesiring stillness of death" to "the sexual climax of masochistic fantasy"—and back again.[12]

But as sexy as all this sounds, it also can mystify slow motion as a technological aesthetic. As I've said, slow motion is always speed in different form. Though its meanings are not determined by its mechanics, they are always worth remembering. Slow motion describes a whole set of visual conventions for exhibiting the imagery produced by fast, then faster, and then ever faster cameras. N. Katherine Hayles says that the most significant new technologies of the twenty-first century aren't really media as we've inherited the term but rather processes of "nonconscious cognition" across a vast array of social systems, computer networks, and ecologies. There is no reason to think that she has Benjamin specifically in mind, but the echoes—and shift in emphases—are clear enough. Where modernist visual forms like slow motion provided a kind of afterimage of experiences at speed for aesthetic contemplation and second-order processing, the "technical cognitions" she discusses are not designed for us at all but aim "to keep consciousness, with its slow uptake and limited processing ability, from being overwhelmed." Slow motion as such, at least in the films and culture I am tracking here, does not go fast enough for the "temporal events" that matter most to Hayles, occurring as they do in high-speed trading networks or AI prototypes "at different points within a window of about 100 milliseconds." Yet slow motion is, apart from any of its artistic applications, an application of machine perception and, if not intelligence, than at least visualization. From historians of science such as Canales to media theorists such as Ernst, the development of "ultra-time-critical processes," as Ernst calls them, proves that "the effectiveness of technical media thus begins where the time resolution" of human being ends and then gives way to all manner of devices that overcome "the slowness of the human retina" to measure "the smallest physiological time intervals."[13]

Another way of putting this would be to notice just how readily slow motion can elicit or represent explicitly a sense of lived temporality in all its flexibility and subjectivity while also and absolutely functioning as an index to what Ernst describes, with considerable irony at Heidegger's expense, the "being-in-time of technical media."[14] Slow motion often looks like the very image of the experience of time that so many phenomenologists describe and fetishize, but accessed through the real time of the technologies and the inhuman speeds they index. Both Canales and Marta Braun track the emergence of Marey's motion photography from nineteenth-century psychophysics and research into the timing mechanisms of the body and its various visible and invisible reactions.[15] Novels of the same period, as Sue Zemka shows, also "have a fascinating relationship to the disappearing, unrepresentable duration," which for writers as differently inclined as Søren Kierkegaard and Dante Rossetti becomes a way to explore the shortest and most fleeting experiences as nothing less than "subjective moments of the human."[16] Across these cultural domains, then, we find a model of human physiology's "slow uptake" of sense perception, to borrow again from Hayles, which helps establish the scientific groundwork for the development of film.

But even figures operating at a significant remove from the world of early cinema have moments that seem almost perversely determined to summon the aesthetics and phenomenology of slow motion out of thin air—or other media. Music, for example, structures Edmund Husserl's account of "retentional modification" in *The Phenomenology of Internal Time-Consciousness*. Since a melody cannot, by definition, exist in the single note or chord we hear at any particular instant of the present, Husserl explains that even as the "tonal now ... passes over into modification," we can still direct "a ray of meaning" from "retention to retention," dragging these pieces of the past along with our immediate perceptions to make sense of what is always quickly passing by.[17] Husserl then mixes metaphors again to describe how perceiving a sequence of actions or events in space requires us to take this "now-apprehension" as just "the nucleus of a comet's tail of retentions referring to the earlier now-points of the motion" we are watching. The aura of the very recent past is like a halo that makes the present go by slower than consciousness allows, thickening temporality into a denser, richer medium—thick enough for Douglas Fairbanks to fight a spider in or to sustain the bouncing promenade of mourners of *Entr'acte* or lift the rebellious energies of youth in Vigo's *Zéro du conduite*. Slow motion becomes a sort of shorthand—maybe too easy for Cavell and others—for all the imaginative and qualitative dimensions of "pure" time that Bergson calls "duration" or *durée*, though he was often at pains to avoid any suggestion that his philosophies could be materialized in cinematic form.[18] Bergson insists that duration cannot be pictured in any medium, at any speed—though it sure seems like it would often have to be in slow motion if it were. Or, as William James observes in his *Principles of Psychology* (1890), "*the sense of haste goes with one measure of rapidity, that of delay with another*; and these two feelings harmonize with different mental moods."[19] Slow motion isn't just a measure of this harmony so much as it translates the mechanics of speed into a moody show of something else entirely.

The earliest accounts we have of slow motion from the 1920s and 1930s might vary in the analogies they use—does it look like motion remembered from a dream or described in lyric poetry? like hovering in air or floating in water?—but everyone from Arnheim and Benjamin to Rotha, Richardson, and Moore appear to have known exactly what they were watching without much philosophical self-reflection. The tremendous obviousness of slow motion, to put this point another way, serves to remind us that—notwithstanding claims to film's "realism" in Bazin and others—questions of mimesis or verisimilitude are always about media conventions, viewing practices, or vastly longer histories of representation. And we don't need to litigate any of them again to appreciate that David Bordwell is largely right, I think, when he says that "certain technical choices, such as slow motion . . . require experience of movies in order to be intelligible to viewers," but only to the degree that "ordinary thinking" handles all sorts of "genre-based or stylistic conventions" almost every time we encounter a cultural artifact; "no special instructions," he adds, "parallel to that of learning a code like language or even semaphore, is necessary to pick up the conventions of horror films or slow-motion violence."[20] It's tempting to quibble with Bordwell's easy assurances of transparency and wonder how they would apply to the "conventions" of the four-hour art film or a surrealist short. But this is only a problem if we believe that modernism is somehow *not* a genre whose conventions can be learned like any other. What Bordwell captures is the way that slow motion operates less as a modernist break with a set of practices preceding it and more as a minor but profoundly comprehensible aesthetic form that emerges simultaneously with cinema. Viewers did not have to learn to read slow motion any more—or less—than they had to learn what the "experience of movies" actually entailed. Though hardly present in the numberless profusion that we would attribute to such elemental forms as close-ups, cuts, or mise-en-scene, slow motion must still have been there all along. While slow motion has both a history and an archaeology, it looks almost the same if seen, as Bordwell's thought experiment suggests, as just another primitive materialization of cinema as such, as literally essential to the medium and invisible as an "automatism" as the flatness of the screen or the aspect ratio of the frame. Slow motion, to borrow from Quentin Meillassoux and so indulge in some philosophy after all, was never a technique that had to be invented, and no filmmaker, modernist or otherwise, ever had to make it new: Slow motion is and always was a kind of fossil in the cinematic record with an aura of "ancestrality" that precedes its individual instantiations or what Meillassoux would term its "givenness" for how it "retrojects a *seemingly* ancestral past."[21] Slow motion might be modern and "time-critical" in the way it measures and records sometimes infinitesimal moments at speeds that human beings can neither match nor really process, but as a technological representation of temporality, it invokes a deeper and more primordial aesthetic that feels as old and strangely enduring as the rocks and crystals Smithson made his medium for *Spiral Jetty*.

In her extraordinary account of slow motion, Vivian Sobchack attributes its aesthetic power to its ability to produce for viewers an experience of "revelation" and what she calls "an *extended sense of time*" that does not just permit us to gaze upon small details of action, trajectory, or force that emphasize the material physicality of bodies but more abstractly and essentially communicates "the *movement of movement* itself." Sobchack relies on a phenomenological vocabulary that does not immediately echo with Bordwell's stress on rational cognition, but her wonderfully sophisticated reading of slow motion—and easily, for me at least, the most influential—allows us to start thinking about why slow motion's visibility, in every way, intensifies and escalates in the 1960s. Like Bordwell, she assumes that slow motion represents more than a discrete effect or figure within the languages of cinema, that it is instead immanent to the medium of film as a "*residual premise* or *ground*," even for those periods—which is still most of narrative film's history, after all—when we don't see quite so much of it. This is why, Sobchack suggests, slow motion might be "tamed" in all the ways that Gunning teaches us—with early cinema's exuberant ecology of "attractions" progressively assimilated to a monoculture of "effects"—but can nonetheless endure and occasionally flash up as a genuinely uncanny and transfixing vision of those "alterior" or "differential" times and spaces that "we live but do not explicitly feel." She admits that slow motion "glorifies" a set of tropes that are endemic to the less appealing aspects of modernity's visual regime and its ideologies of surveillance, voyeurism, and control but that it simultaneously renders them as failing, finite, or obsolete in the face of timescales and temporalities that we can access through technology but that will always remain somehow unknowable to us—strange, uncanny, and "potentially sublime and dangerous" in Sobchack's terms—no matter what frame rates or resolutions might achieve. Slow motion serves as a "*memento mori* of modernity," returning us inevitably to the limits of the very technologies that let us see more of the world, at every speed, than any of us could see alone.[22] As slow motion goes still slower—which means, of course, as the technologies that make it possible go faster—perpetual acceleration looks more dreamy or lethargic, and we see relentless progress in actions that seem endlessly deferred and incomplete. Slow motion is neither slow nor fast but conditioned, as Ryan Bishop and John Phillips note, on the "relative powers of the single category 'speed,'" which modern life produces in abundance and dizzying variability.[23]

Let me take Sobchack at her word a bit more literally than she might like: Slow motion is what modernity looks like as it is dying, which it always is but never will, at least in time for any of us to witness. This is why, even when there is nothing especially tragic or serious about a sequence in slow motion—the comic version of the dramatic drop that leaves us crying over proverbially spilled milk, the distorted or silent scream of slapstick excess that gives us bathos in all its inappropriate grandeur—it is always haunted, however minimally, by the intimation of some serious violence. The more spectacular or baroque the latest variation on the form, the more it feels like a deliberate replay, not "instant" so much as self-regarding or monumental. Perhaps this also points to one reason that slow motion works so well as a YouTube genre and has spawned so many parodies, memes, and supercuts online: The same footage can look somber or hilarious depending on the context. Writing in 2006—when YouTube was still largely in its infancy and the first iPhone was a year away—it was maybe a little easier for Sobchack to advance the proposition that slow motion can invoke feelings of "wonder" or "astonishment" and bring forth "*physis*," in Heidegger's definition, as an ideal of "the inherent and self-generating energy of nature." Her seriousness is neither misplaced nor undesirable, however, despite the fact that watching the Slow Mo Guys try to eat a spoonful of cinnamon at 500fps or wasting what feels like centuries on compilations of "unflinching walks" or other slow-motion tropes does not exactly make me think that I'm gaining some perspective on what Heidegger—cited approvingly by Sobchack—calls the "frenziedness of technology," which he worried might "entrench itself everywhere" to such an extent that we'd be unable to see anything without it.[24] Slow motion can reveal the "*doubled poiesis*," as Sobchack suggests, of bodies and machines in modern culture—of *techne* and *physis* as "ambiguously convergent"— and yet, it can still in practice be a tremendous waste of time. I might more tentatively venture, with no nod to Heidegger at all, that slow motion shows us some of the ways that we spend time with technology and how technology makes the time we have to spend with it.

There is no reconciling this dialectic between slow motion's complete investment in the physics of embodied motion—in people, animals, or objects—and its equally profound dependence on a whole history of technologies, from early-nineteenth-century optical toys like the Thaumatrope to the latest Phantom TMX 7510 that shoots at 1.75 million fps, which at varying degrees betray, acknowledge, or breathlessly announce the limits of our abilities to perceive at speeds and times outside the narrowest of bandwidths. Thus for Malcolm Turvey, it seems almost obvious in retrospect that slow motion would emerge in both films and film criticism of the 1920s made by figures who were interested in "cinema's revelatory capacity" and ways of rendering into our field of vision "features of reality that are invisible in the sense that it is impossible for the human eye to see them without assistance."[25] At the bleeding edge of high-speed photography, machines such as the Phantom TMX match impossibly fast shutters to equally astonishing digital sensors—since, as the company's ad copy reminds us with a Spider-Man reference, "with increased speed comes the need for increased light"—to generate endless variations on the iconography of Edgerton's shattering dishes, ballistic spectacles, and displays of fluid dynamics. Even the most baroque action sequences or fight scenes don't require such extreme technologies, and Zach Snyder has yet to bloat and distend a single punch beyond a few seconds of screen time, no matter how long it feels like we're asked to watch all the body blows and other strenuous exertions that his films indulge. There is considerable resistance to identifying directors like Snyder, Bay, Ritchie, Gareth Evans (*The Raid*, *The Raid 2*), or Wilson Yip (*SPL*, the Ip Man series) as auteurs for their signature attachment to slow motion in all its tastelessness. Within the "revelationist tradition" that Turvey reconstructs, however, there is a certain logic to taking at least a short break from aesthetic judgment and stylistic preference to appreciate how utterly committed these directors are—along with older Hong Kong figures like John Woo or Tsui Hark or cult favorites like Paul W. S. Anderson (the Resident Evil franchise) or Lexi Alexander (*Punisher: War Zone*)—to a rarefied, if not always quite so critical, devotion to some of the techniques that modernists in the 1920s and 1930s, and Vertov most of all, saw not as special effects but rather as the very essence of cinema as such. "Slow-motion filming," Vertov writes, "was understood as the opportunity to make the invisible visible, the unclear clear, the hidden manifest, the disguised overt, the acted nonacted, untruth—kinopravda (i.e., *truth* obtained by cinematic means, in this cause, by means of the slow-motion eye)."[26] From the technological limits of scientific imaging to fight choreography, slow motion is a radical and compelling aid to human vision—an "extension of man," in McLuhan's dated but always helpful phrase—that, even when it fails to give us art, can't help but give us more to see. Like other mediums and machines that, in Turvey's words, "reveal truths about reality that are invisible to human perception," slow motion "*augments* our already existing capacity to find out about the environment around us."[27]

In the expanded field of temporal effects that cinema made possible and came to represent for much of the twentieth century, it would be hard to say that slow motion is the most significant or revolutionary. To borrow and adapt a particularly resonant phrase from Nöel Burch, slow motion is an "epistemological creation... of absolutely deliberate modernism."[28] Yet what it teaches us to know and see is both a dreamy world of movement—whether weightless and lyrical or visceral and graphic—as well as an abiding sense that even the times we feel most intensely in the being of our human bodies do not belong to us alone, or even to the realms of flesh and blood and matter that we see fetishized and amplified on screen. Slow motion thus ratifies "the analogical replication of movement" that Burch, for one, argues added "a decisive element to the production of photographic meaning" that enabled the development of cinema, which had to transcend the "semantic equivalent of movement" as it had existed in magic lantern shows and similar attractions and so achieve the "seamless concatenation of film frames which could make this semiosis as continuous and 'natural' as iconic signification itself." Of course, this all happened with slow motion, for the most part, operating on the margins of the dominant modes and conventions that mark this evolution, a relatively minor special effect that would eventually—though not very quickly, all things considered—translate some of a new technology's capacity for encoding and expanding time beyond our comprehension into an artistic language for depicting the most "human" dramas of rapture, glory, pain, or concentration. Just because it's probably more difficult now to take slow motion seriously than at any point in the history of the form, we should still be able to recognize what it represents and brings to life: "It experiments, distending time, dissecting movement," Vertov writes of slow motion as the material expression of the "kino-eye" in 1923, decades before his brother's camerawork would fail to impress Cavell.[29] He then immediately swerves onto an entirely different scale of time by also embracing how film, "absorbing time within itself, swallowing years, thus [schematizes] processes of long duration inaccessible to the normal eye." The reference here is likely to time-lapse photography, which, as we saw with Smithson and Sugimoto, depends on the literally slow motion of the camera to render transformations and events for human comprehension in an illusion of acceleration. But because Vertov is such an exuberant writer, we can't know for sure, or if he just means to invoke the normal—and also utterly inhuman—cuts and editing conventions that had, by the early 1920s, already been consolidated into the narrative modes that he saw as the opposite of his politicized and avant-garde technique. In any case, I want to suggest that even in slow motion we can start examining some of the histories—of cinema and otherwise—that Vertov is imagining, "thus schematizing," as he proposes, "processes of long duration inaccessible to the normal eye."

Or as Ernst puts much the same point after a century of what we've been encouraged to believe is nonstop, high-speed progress that has left both Vertov and modernism behind: "Media themselves also have their own duration and time, which go beyond what we could perceive as temporal with our bare eyes."[30] What we see in slow motion, finally, is a singular moment of technology and its effects, an instant that can feel like seconds, minutes, years, or eons. Not all these times are reflected in every version of slow motion that precedes the period in the 1960s that most radically expands its scope and popularity, but there are, as I've been arguing throughout, occasions when we can witness their convergence and phantasmatic resonance in sequences that often seem the very opposite of remarkable in films that are rarely remembered for them anyway. The history of slow motion has taken a long time to write because, I want to argue, in every way we are still living it.

8
New Media, Slow Media

That slow motion derives, at least in part, from the photographic experiments of Marey and Muybridge is undeniable. Muybridge's studies of human locomotion anticipate the fetish for athletic physicality that we see displayed by filmmakers such as Vertov and Riefenstahl, not to mention in the work of anonymous newsreel directors even earlier in the 1920s. And while Marey was notably uninterested in visual reproductions of motion that lacked an analytic component, his imagery of arrested speed directly influenced Futurist painters such as Umberto Boccioni and is latent in the streaming lines of force that comic book artists have used for decades to picture what it looks like to go faster than a speeding bullet—or far faster, as we see in his race between Barry Allen's "Flash" and Wally West's "Kid Flash" from the CW's series *The Flash* (figure 8.1). Edgerton's advances in stroboscopic imaging in the 1930s and after—he photographed a nuclear explosion with his Rapatronic camera in 1952—remain some of the twentieth century's most celebrated images of utterly slowed motion, but they represent the slightest fraction of the still pictures and films made by engineers and scientists pushing at the very limits of high-speed photography in classrooms, labs, and scientific conferences far removed from any of the places and sites that an image of the "movies" might conjure up. Burch observes a formative "detour via scientific and technical practices" that made it possible for photography, in the years immediately preceding the appearance of early cinema, to stop serving "as a substitute for academic painting" in ways that were crucial for the course of each medium in the periods that followed. But rather than seeing this as a single episode of divergence that is then corrected, it would be better to acknowledge that there are

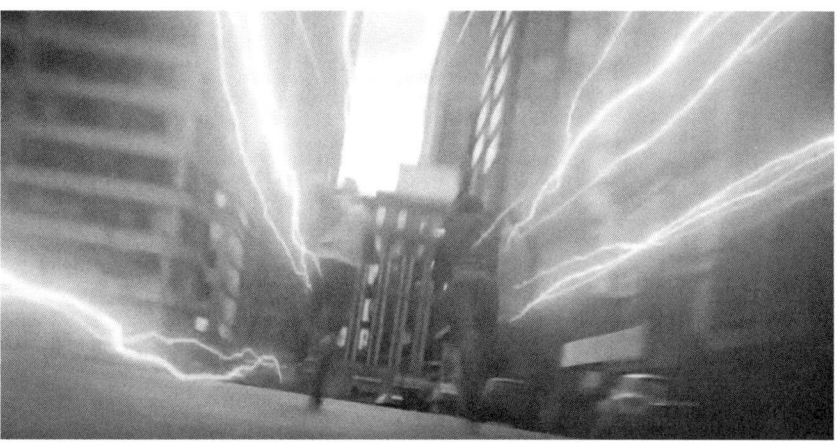

FIGURE 8.1 Still from *The Flash* (2017).

many branching paths and networks of shared preoccupations along which slow motion advances.

Nor is it much easier to process the lesser—but still profound—abundance of slow motion visible in the "high" media genres of video or installation art that differently shadow the traditions of narrative cinema that I've been investigating. Several of Warhol's most famous film projects, as I mentioned briefly earlier, are tests of duration and experiments in attentiveness and its alternatives, such as *Empire* or the *Screen Tests*. Almost the entirety of Bill Viola's long career, with the exception of earlier pieces like *Reverse Television* (1983), is a monument to the monumentality of slow motion across film and analog video to his extravaganzas in (and of) high-definition like *The Quintet Series* (2000) or *The Passions* (2003). I distinctly remember being overwhelmed by Viola's hardware, if not every work it helped create, when I first saw *The Passions* and his other blockbusters at the Getty in 2003, but there is no denying that his elaborate investment in digital video as a medium for spectacular slow motion helped mark the early 2000s as a period where many artists came to exploit the possibilities of HD cameras and displays—and cheaper, bigger hard drives—to pursue feats of deceleration that would have been all but technically impossible using celluloid film or videotape (figure 8.2). Viola shot *The Passions* at 300fps, and several of the most overwhelming pieces were projected on LCDs that would look pretty puny now at any Best Buy; today, my aging iPhone can almost match the speeds and resolution at which Viola filmed.

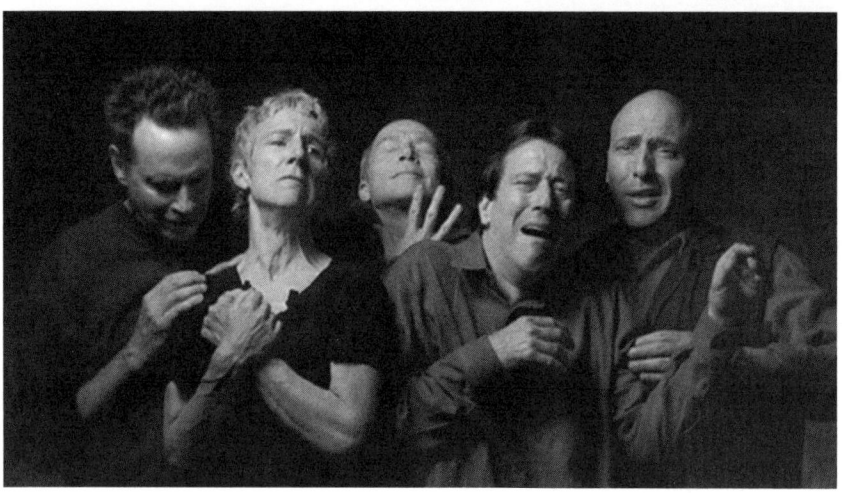

FIGURE 8.2 Still from *The Quintet of the Astonished* (2003).

For the 2007 performance piece and video installation *Fashionably Late for the Relationship*, R. Luke DuBois spent three days filming Lían Amaris Sifuentes as she spent three days going very slowly through the motions of getting ready for a date at an outdoor location they had staged in New York. DuBois then assembled and condensed seventy-two hours of footage into a digital film running just over an hour of blurred and dizzying time-lapse imagery set against the rushing speeds of urban life that constitute the scenic backdrop for Sifuentes's display of private temporality and female interiority. Like many of Viola's projects from this same period, DuBois and Sifuentes's undertaking is studious in its replication of "visual tropes of the old masters," and it's easy to identify the still-life trappings and portraiture conventions from which the performance and the film depart. What is maybe harder to process, looking back from over a decade of technological innovation and acceleration, is that DuBois had to rent a hotel room near the site to house the giant hard drives needed for his digital footage since, at the high resolution he was after, it took 10TB of space to store the seventy-two hours of material he shot. In 2024, a 10TB hard drive sells for around $250 and isn't much bigger than the Penguin classics edition of a long Victorian novel. And I suspect that similar illustrations of Moore's Law—or at least the way its predictions of geometrically increasing microchip capacity have played out in consumer electronics—could be discovered in the notes and working files of other artists for whom digital video in the first years of the twenty-first century was a primary medium for slow and then even slower motion. What Arden Reed calls the "slow art" of Sam Taylor-Johnson or Willie Doherty, whose 2007 Venice Biennale installation *Ghost Story* provides Lutz Koepnick with a case study in contemporary slowness, were almost certainly made with cameras and computers running at speeds that register as lumbering and outmoded to us now, former wonders of the cutting edge that were probably trashed or recycled years before Reed and Koepnick started writing about the "new media" art they helped make. Nothing ages faster than high technology. In this respect, the painterly and rampantly citational aesthetic that governs so many of these projects might almost be seen as the expression of an anxious technological unconscious: Only by aspiring to the institutional styles of art media like painting that we've learned to value and preserve for centuries can these icons of digital slow motion hope to outlast the plastics, circuit boards, and drives that structure their material existence, not to mention the software systems that sustain them in the only manner human beings can process.

Whether one admires such projects as canny works of what Richard Grusin and Jay Bolter would call painting's "remediation" in HD video or responds more skeptically to figures like Viola—Michael Fried, for example, describes *The Passions* as "a *ne plus ultra* of technologized theatricality," which is pretty much the ne plus ultra of Fried putdowns—I would simply observe that all this digital slow motion exists in a relationship of stark and absolute belatedness to the history of slow motion as a cinematic effect. This is more than just a plain fact of chronology and the decades that it took for video actually to become a dominant artists' medium in the 1970s and 1980s; nor is it enough, I think, to understand the use of extreme slow motion by these and other figures of the early 2000s as a simple consequence of cheaper and more available digital technologies making it possible for artists to shoot at frame rates that only the most expensive and advanced film cameras would have previously allowed and then to store and process footage whose bulk, expense, and fragility on celluloid would have been unworkable. Reed and Koepnick are both excellent on the durational modes of attention and experiences of distended temporality that so many contemporary video artists pursue, and art historians like Alex V. Uroskie have compelling accounts of the various trajectories that film took, as he puts it, from the "black box" to the "white cube" as many figures in the 1960s and after "intentionally sought to alienate the moving image from its customary home within the cinematic theater."[1] Thus Fried writes admiringly of Douglas Gordon—whose *24 Hour Psycho*, which decelerates and dilates Hitchcock's thriller as a series of projected stills, remains perhaps the most significant achievement in this genre—and fixes on all the ways he "takes a representative Hollywood movie and 'opaques' it by systematically denying the viewer access to the sort of near-total involvement in which the class movie experience has always been recognized to consist."² The "theatricality" that Gordon antagonizes, in other words, is not just the conceptual hobbyhorse that Fried was arguing over with Judd and Smithson in an era of late modernism. The prosaic institution of the movie theater—spiritualized by Sugimoto, excavated in *Goodbye, Dragon Inn*—is also rendered obsolete in these examples of slow motion, which might just as well be said to be reflections of film's aging and attenuation as a medium running out of steam over the course of the twentieth century. Fried would no doubt resist this effort to translate his aesthetic preferences into a sketched-out social history. But we don't need Fried's particular vocabulary—though it will keep coming back—to grasp just how the grandeur of slow motion for a figure such as Gordon is both a monument to a cinema in ruins and a calculated demolition of its temporality and deepest formal logic. "Slow motion," writes Philip Monk, "so radically distends the narrative construction of the film [Hitchcock's original] that another reality imposes itself.... The slow motion of *24 Hour Psycho* places us in a different temporal universe where there are no privileged moments."³ Gordon's version of Hitchcock is just as "cinematic" at one level in that its use of video has little to do with any challenge to the ontology of the photographic image, but on another level it is a flagrant violation of the film's medium specificity as a "narrative construction" that must automatically—if it is to *be* a narrative—show us that some moments are more important than others. Some must be permitted to pass by quickly so that others can be delayed or made to linger. Narrative is a medium of differential speeds, and, as Burch insistently argues in respect to early film, the "perennial question of cinema's specificity"—the ne plus ultra of modernist questions!—must be answered "within the broad spectrum of classical narrative in general." But as Fried implies, at slow motion's terminal nonvelocity there is no way to tell a story, or, returning to Burch, no way to maintain "the singular strength of [cinema's] diegetic production." Or as Monk explains more clearly: "In Gordon's version, the shower scene—the epitome of montage in *Psycho*—is no more significant than any other. In fact, 'scene' makes no sense when plot construction dissipates and montage is elided through protraction. Montage is the first victim of slow motion; the naturalistic duration film fictionality promotes is the second."⁴ Does this make "montage" Gordon's Marion Crane and "duration" his Milton Arbogast? I don't know how seriously we're supposed to take the allegory that Monk is playing with, but even as the most inside of jokes it helps make visible that slow motion means something different outside the forms of narrative cinema.

As we've just seen, slow motion can take us through film history and what comes after at such high speed that, perversely enough, it is easy to look past just how richly articulated and complex it was before figures like Viola and Gordon turned it into art. But for filmmakers at the end of the 1960s—and writers reflecting on the cinematic forms that they embraced—slow motion was already at the center of an ad hoc taxonomy of aesthetic gestures, ideologies, and affiliations. What I find striking about slow motion's cumulative appearances in narrative cinema before the 1960s is that we can see how much of its iconography had been established but that this, in and of itself, was clearly insufficient to provoke the rapid escalation in both its use and popularity in the aftermath of *Bonnie and Clyde*—when, to use a figure of speech that comes very close to being literally applicable, its popularity at last explodes. From the invention of cinema to the 1960s, slow motion makes barely any progress toward the global and pervasive visibility it now enjoys within a huge expanse of media and cultural forms—from gloriously stupid but occasionally brilliant wastes of time across the internet to scrupulously serious and rarefied works of art that are, in the cases of Viola and Gordon in particular, rapidly becoming canon for the "postmedium" contemporary. The styles of mainstream cinema and television where slow motion is now all but mandatory—from *The Matrix* sequels to the MCU, Michael Bay to *Baywatch*—fall somewhere in the middle, though my aim is not to erect a hierarchy that would rank, say, the truly breathtaking shootout in Johnnie To's *Three* (2016) against a YouTube supercut of "fails" or the somber richness (in every sense) of a Viola installation. I want to insist instead that all of this slow motion should be seen as part of a single network of technologies and forms and that its evolution was neither gradual over its twentieth-century course nor inevitable in its translation of a minor modernist motif into an essential aspect of media culture's lingua franca. That slow motion only really starts to gain this purchase on, well, everything, at a moment of crisis and political upheaval—in the United States and Hollywood but also, of course, everywhere around 1968—will later let us think about a series of iconic films in ways that will, I hope, challenge their mythologies even if I'm unwilling to abandon them entirely.

9
What We See in Slow Motion

There is no need for another reading of *The Seven Samurai* (1954), and certainly not from me. But I want to focus on its slow motion for two reasons: first, because we know that Arthur Penn saw it and cites it as the inspiration for his first use of slow motion in his almost entirely forgotten debut feature, *The Left-Handed Gun*, which in turn anticipates the spectacular slow motion that absolutely no one missed when it appeared in *Bonnie and Clyde*; and second, because the remarkable economy of the slow motion Kurosawa uses in *The Seven Samurai* makes for a particularly illuminating and concrete case study in the aesthetic dimensions of the effect as it plays out in narrative films more broadly. The scene is short and wouldn't take too long to discuss save for the fact that it manages to encode centuries of artistic discourse about the representation of time into less than two minutes of action.

This familiar scene takes place early in the film's story, when we are just beginning to get a feel for the pace of Kurosawa's epic and the rhythms of its plot and texture before the escalating action, brutalities, and deaths that finally bring it to a close. (Penn would have seen a version cut by fifty minutes for American audiences.) Shimada Kambei, played by Kurosawa regular Takashi Shimura, is an older samurai traveling in late medieval Japan who has been reduced to small jobs for subsistence wages as a mercenary. He enters a village where a thief has taken a hostage and barricaded himself in a hut that he refuses to leave on threat of killing the young boy that he has seized. Kamei agrees to save the boy for the price of two rice balls but then starts deliberately to shave his head, mystifying the villagers (and the viewer) until it becomes clear that he intends to disguise himself as a priest to approach the thief with just a small knife hidden in some ragged robes he borrows from a bystander. Toshiro Mifune's Kikuchiyo watches closely, along

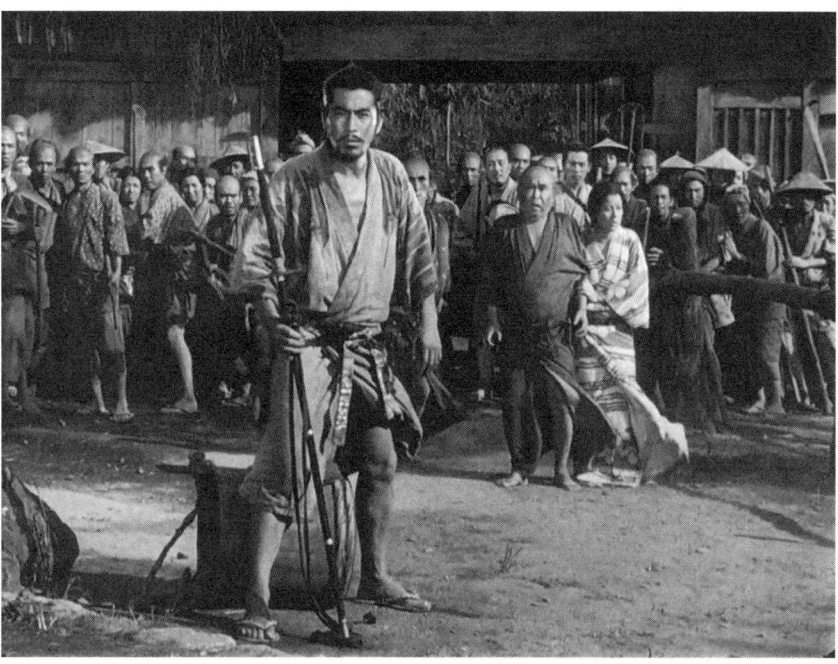

FIGURE 9.1 Still from *The Seven Samurai* (1954).

with a crowd of villagers, giving us two surrogates for whom the action is unfolding at a strictly measured pace across a series of long and medium shots, with a pair of close-ups suggesting that much of this performance, on Kambei's part, is being choreographed for Kikuchiyo's benefit (figure 9.1). The first and only moment of action occurs when Kambei rushes into the hut to free the child, not that there is anything to see: Whatever violence takes place inside during the few seconds after Kambei enters remains pointedly unseen, and aside from a single grunt, the thin cries of the kidnapped boy are all we hear. And then, with a woody clunk, the thief bursts out of the hut in slow motion, staggering a few steps into the courtyard, where he pitches awkwardly onto his toes, freezes for a brief instant, and then topples over dead—killed by his own sword, which we see covered in blood when Kambei tosses it onto the ground nearby (figure 9.2). The boy's mother runs to soothe her child, and Kikuchiyo walks toward the fallen body of the thief in a show of professional curiosity and grudging admiration for the samurai who has so elegantly dispatched an adversary that had him, so to speak, outgunned. That it is all staged masterfully and shot and edited with great style and precision is a catastrophic understatement. The whole sequence is a formalist field day. Nobody needs me to tell them that *The Seven Samurai* is pretty good!

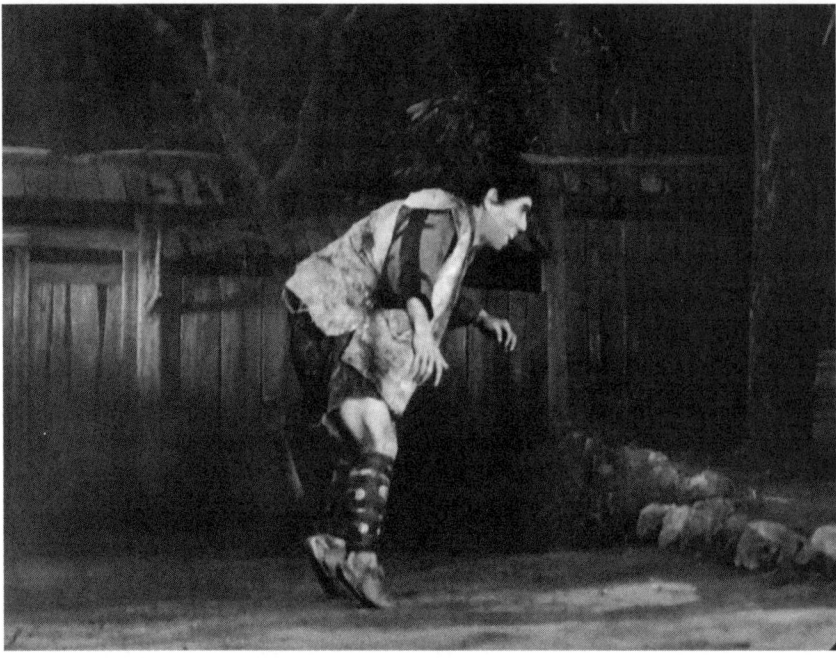

FIGURE 9.2 Still from *The Seven Samurai* (1954).

Still, this scene is odder than my summary lets on, and it is how Kurosawa employs slow motion that punctuates—as both emphasis and interruption—the terrific clarity and economy of style that he puts on display everywhere else. The fact that we don't see the killing blow is not especially surprising. Kambei's skill and speed are that much more powerfully affirmed for remaining mystified; like the single stroke Kyuzo, played by Seiji Miyaguchi, uses to dispatch the braggart who fatally challenges him to a real duel, the action is over almost before we have time to process it, which again makes the slow-motion fall of Kyuzo's antagonist—the only other instance in the film—an opportunity for us to appreciate a show of violence that we have and haven't seen. But this second example is far less involved than the elaborate extension of the thief's dying seconds earlier in the film. Both deaths loosely follow on the pattern of Kurosawa's first slow-motion sequence in *Sanshiro Sugata*, which also made a spectacle not of the hero's killing blow but of its consequences for his attacker's body, which becomes an icon of unseen action that is so forceful it requires the film itself to adopt a visual technique that has no precedent in its stylistic logic to that point. But the thief's death in *The Seven Samurai* is not simply filmed in slow motion so that it can look more dramatic or visceral and thus amplify—and give viewers more time to appreciate—the violent expertise to which it pays grisly tribute. This single dying fall, from the thief's sudden stumble out of the hut to his collapse onto the dusty ground, is composed of shots from three angles and distances that are then cut into a sequence of reaction shots that show the villagers and Mifune witnessing the same last few seconds in normal time, with the wind blowing through hair and rippling robes at 24fps and the spectators' gestures of surprise and panic and inchoate relief washing over them at regular speed. This mix of speeds prefigures some of the ways slow motion will appear in action cinema from the 1960s and beyond—in *Bonnie and Clyde* and *The Wild Bunch*, as we shall see, and today especially in sequences marked by the frantic pace of editing and shorter shot length in the mode of Bordwell's "intensified continuity." Contemporary digital techniques and speed ramping make it easy to depict a single action—or in a Zach Snyder film, every single action—across a wide range of time-axis manipulations without a cut or break as bodies, spears, or bullets decelerate and accelerate to whatever speeds the software used in post-production will allow.

Slow motion describes the temporality of the thief's dying seconds: Though we don't know it yet, we are already watching the door from which he'll rush out as a series of decelerated images since, without any cut to the thief's emergence from the hut, the waving blades of glass and swirling dust must also have been filmed at two or three times faster than normal speed. We can never know exactly how Kambei frees the boy and mortally wounds his kidnapper, but the shift into slow motion—which is practically just as invisible, I admit—lets us mark the action in time almost to the very 1/24th of a second captured in the first frame shot at higher speed. But this sort of temporalizing pedantry isn't really Kurosawa's point. As the scene continues in its montage back and forth from the thief's slow-motion death to the normal-speed reactions of the villagers, the tension escalates—or better, oscillates—between the increasingly singular and viscerally embodied experience of time as lived, though not for very long, by one isolated individual and a shared but strangely abstract experience of time as public, fixed, and perhaps even intractable in the face of human suffering or emotion. After all, if slow motion were simply an allegorical expression of subjective intensity and its affects, there is plenty here to go around. From William James to contemporary neuroscience, scientists and researchers have documented the ways that trauma, stress, or fear can radically distort and dilate the perception of duration, with accident victims remembering split seconds that felt like minutes, or, in James's pleasingly equivocal words, how *"a time filled with varied and interesting experiences seems short in passing, but long as we look back."*[1] But this scene would make for a weird fable of extreme cognition.

Certainly the thief's dying counts as "varied" experience in James's sense, and though he won't be around to do much looking back, slow motion in effect anticipates a version of the retrospective he could have had. But the thief is not the only interested onlooker. Mifune's younger samurai (who is only passing as a member of the warrior class) has an investment of his own in seeing how a master like Kambei performs when lives are genuinely at stake, and if this isn't enough, in the end, to expand and magnify his temporality as a spectator, it would be hard to say the same of the boy's mother, who stands off to Mifune's side in the background but prominently apart from the other villagers. This is a terrifyingly "interesting" experience for her. And even if we try to assume that the thief's death is somehow witnessed in slow motion by the crowd—that it is the intensity of their anxiety and attention that we are seeing in the decelerated spectacle—it becomes increasingly difficult to maintain this logic of identification as the structure of the scene comes into focus and as the juxtaposition of the two speeds settles into a rhythm that also comes to define two spaces, one in real time, where groups of everyday people watch powerful events unfold, and one in slow motion, where an individual who is an Other to the audience is left suspended in the agony that he deserves. There is nothing natural about the forward pitch of the thief's body as it is arrested for our view. That his posture almost looks like a stress position only confirms that his stark isolation and physical torments, however brief, are the punishments his crimes have earned. To use a term that's thrown about in descriptions of slow motion quite a bit—and that both Koepnick and Fried can help us understand more fully—everything about his death lacks *grace*, a term that each critic traces back to Friedrich Schiller, for whom it defined "a feature of bodies in motion" and "a playful harmony" of inner aspect and physical performance.[2] In Schiller's aesthetics, grace emerges around the indeterminate but compelling fascination of watching "what happens unintentionally when intentional movements are carried out, and also correspond to a moral cause."[3] Its utter absence here—filming the villagers at normal speed even precludes any accidental aestheticization of their response as witnesses or viewers—ratifies the immorality of the only figure who's left "hanging" for his transgressions, deprived of any dignity that a less ungainly execution might let him preserve.

This moment in *The Seven Samurai* also is exemplary for understanding slow motion as an aesthetic form, revealing with uncanny clarity so many of the ideas about time and technology that make the effect "special" across the broader expanses of the twentieth century in which it flourishes, from its emergence in early film and modernism to its achievement of such genuine saturation that it might not seem worth taking seriously at this late date. It's probably savvier to

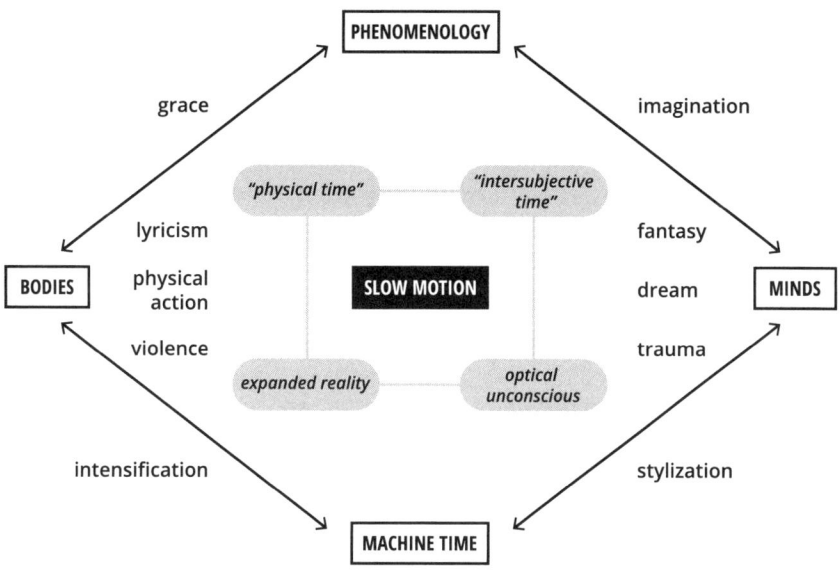

FIGURE 9.3 The aesthetics of slow motion. Designed by Patrick Kavanagh.

return to a figure of Kurosawa's stature as opposed to, say, YouTube masters like Gav and Dan to offer slow motion as a media aesthetic illustrating several of our most crucial discourses about temporality and the history of our attempts to capture it in art. Consider how the thief's death might look at the center of a constellation of terms and tropes that pattern discussions of slow motion in both film theory and criticism, as well as everyday conversations about the movies in which it features (figure 9.3). Unlike slow motion, Greimas squares have definitely fallen out of fashion. But I made one anyway to try to show a century of slow motion in a single frame.

We can immediately recognize the scene as a graphic and even conventional display—though it was, technically speaking, a startling innovation—of the differences between "physical time" in a world of clocks, communities, and shared reality and "intersubjective time" as deeply individual and dependent on the unique perceptions and ordeals that constitute our identity, few of which, thankfully, are as dramatic as getting stabbed by a wandering samurai. I'm taking these terms from Johannes Fabian's groundbreaking study *Time and the Other*, where they are used to highlight one of the most important vectors Western anthropologists developed to organize—as well as stigmatize and render "primitive"—the many global cultures whose deviations and departures from Anglo-European modernity helped constitute them as objects of inquiry for a whole series of white figures who were invested, as both agents of and romantic critics against, narratives of progress that could explain away or fetishize the presence of coeval histories in the present.[4] That Fabian reminds us that our languages of temporal experience are also, by necessity, racial and political gives us another reason to note that *The Seven Samurai* is very much a period piece, an elaborate exercise in anachronism (or allegory, or both) for Kurosawa that played very differently in the United States and Europe.

Another version of this opposition could be traced out of Plato's *Timaeus* and its categorical distinctions between a "physical" world of change and sense perception and an "eternal" world of forms that can be grasped solely by human reason turned inward on itself; or, in the Augustinian tradition, we find a parallel that's rough enough for my decidedly nonphilosophical purposes, in the famous inquiry into time's nature that takes place in chapter 11 of *The Confessions*, from which later Christian discourses all the way to T. S. Eliot's "Four Quartets" will explore how the "time of the world" must be differentiated from the "time of the soul" that ultimately transcends it. And we can find loose analogues, I think, for these temporal categories in Arnheim's and Benjamin's brief reflections on slow motion. Arnheim's stress on slow motion as a "technique" for examining "the individual phases of rapid movements" recalls the rhetoric of hyperempiricism and analysis that characterizes the motion photography of Marey and Muybridge and anticipates not only the iconography that we see in later scientific and industrial films but also in the detailed visual study of manual labor in Taylorism or ergonomics or of athletic performance using film, video, or computers to maximize efficiency by better understanding the mechanics of moving. Against this sense of an "expanded reality," we can juxtapose Benjamin's celebrated notion of the "optical unconscious," which functions at the same level of microscopic gestures visible only when we slow down fleeting intervals of time but also points away from the technocratic applications Arnheim cites in its borrowing from Freud and associations with surrealism, to cite just one modernist aesthetic of temporal distortion that we know Benjamin admired. But I don't think we can say that Benjamin believes film represents the dream states or reveries it evokes with the same exactitude that it lets us picture Harold Abram's gait or Bobby Jones's swing; we're dealing instead with images and objective correlatives, with second-order symbols that exist for viewers as a translated version of experiences that are unknowable in their original and inward-looking languages of self and mind. Arnheim and Benjamin offer modernized and more secular variations on a dialectic that tends to figure time as either sacred or profane; they reframe the tensions that flare up whenever the *chronos* of calendars and clocks is set against the *kairos* of charged moments that come to mean far more than any rational accounting can make sense of. Though of course these issues aren't really very secular for Benjamin either, no matter how inexorably his language—like that of Arnheim—encourages us to think about technology as the determining condition of modernity. Slow motion might also register as an illumination of the "messianic time" that Benjamin opposes to the "empty, homogenous time" that, in their own way, the movies try also to redeem. If only we could see Maurice Chevalier orchestrating horses in slow motion or Ginger Rogers as she spins and floats around Fred Astaire as angels of history, too.

Fantasy sequences in slow motion often turn on displays of physical action at its most lyrical, an often fuzzy term, suggesting qualities of ease, lightness, extension, and smoothness, that does come into particular focus when, as in *Carefree* or *Easter Parade*, we see Rogers or Astaire as they are dancing. Such scenes might also remind us that another reason why slow motion might be described so frequently as lyrical is that music and other extradiegetic sounds accompany the vast majority of sequences in slow motion since, as *Singin' in the Rain* (1951) definitively established, it's hard to maintain any measure of seriousness—much less passion—when the human voice is technologically decelerated. While pitch-shifting algorithms and other everyday practices in digital audio production can save most actors from the fate of Lina Lamont and Don Lockwood at the disastrous premiere of *The Dueling Cavalier*, which is turned into a comedy by all manner of mechanical breakdowns and malfunctions as their synced dialogue warps into incoherence when the film shifts suddenly into slow motion. We'll hear some uncanny echoes of this scene when Hal is shut down in Kubrick's *2001*, but it remains the case that most diegetic sound is isolated from the action in slow motion, save for the occasional crunch that is timed to land with the speed-ramped kick or punch that it accompanies or the explosions, crashes, or gunshots that don't need to be synchronized as precisely.

The map of slow motion I'm trying to outline here is not, however, intended as anything like a complete taxonomy of the emotions, affects, or situations—comic or tragic, violent or joyous, extreme or mundane—that have been rendered in a somehow heightened fashion by being deprived of their original velocity. If slow motion, to revisit Sobchack, registers the "*movement of movement*" itself, this wonderfully tautological phrase also helps us see how it might also simply give us *more* of anything that's there already, the cinematic equivalent of underlining or italicization. This is why I am ambivalent about trying to define slow motion's "lyricism" or its dreamlike qualities with much precision; or, to invoke another set of terms that often figures in discussions of film violence, the fact that slow motion is said to "aestheticize" some of the most extreme acts of brutality we can imagine is also, I think, an admission of its redundancy and the empty character of its emphasis. Various forms of physical action, whether lyrical or violent, show bodies looking maximally like bodies in slow motion—embodied with a vengeance, we might say. Yet slow motion can also, in the form of dream sequences or fantasy visions, appear as a cinematic language of pure interiority and mental experience, whether as moments of heightened consciousness or hypervivid flashbacks or as eruptions of unconscious traumas or desires that more prosaic temporalities can't adequately contain or express. Of course, bodies and minds are always connected, and particularly in slow motion: The phenomenology of Husserl, Bergson, or Heidegger gives us several overlapping lexicons to describe how all the lived experiences of time are bled of authenticity if subjected to the clocks, calendars, and other abstract systems that translate human temporality into quantities of seconds, years, or dollars. But as I've been arguing all along, slow motion is never *not* machine time too and so just as certainly speaks to all the ways that the modern experience of time is mediated and deeply technological, even when it looks like it's emerging from the physiology, materiality, and rhythms of our bodies or from the most internal workings of our minds and imaginations.

In practice, no single appearance of slow motion exemplifies just a single dimension of the categories and aesthetics that compose the field of possible meanings I've assembled around it here. In the Soviet film *The Cranes are Flying*, which triumphed at Cannes just a few years after *The Seven Samurai* was released, the furious show of cinematic technique that marks the moment Boris is fatally shot is narratively encoded as a dying vision, a montage of his desperate, mind's-eye dream of a future that is violently foreclosed. Like the similarly extravagant montage that accompanies Max's suicide in *What Price Hollywood?*, the indulgence in slow motion is also patently symbolic of the torments of the body at the threshold of the subject's nonexistence. Such framing and readymade interpretability is one of the ways that the attractions of modernist stylization at its most ornate—Dutch angles, expressionist chiaroscuro, spinning cameras, delirious montage, superimpositions, and, course, slow motion—are absorbed within and reconciled to the protocols of narrative cinema, which have always been more accommodating and flexible, even opportunistic, than the image of the institution that some genres of criticism occasionally dismiss in favor of the experimental or the avant-garde. It feels a little condescending, though, to dismiss entirely the notion that scenes like these, "tamed" as they may be, aren't also trying to use the conventions of a popular form to translate impossibly hard ideas—the "being-towards-death" of Heidegger, "*durée*" as a "qualitative multiplicity" in Bergson—into a ready visual vernacular. I'm not necessarily arguing that slow motion should be framed by these philosophies or by any others, but it's easy to imagine how they could circulate their way into the visual practices and intellectual associations of the filmmakers involved, which is just to say Cavell was probably right to spot the jumping children in *The World of Henry Orient* as already a cliché, but that doesn't mean George Roy Hill and Boris Kaufman weren't revisiting the spirited phenomenology of youthful rebellion that Kaufman had captured in Vigo's *Zéro de conduite* or the brash and silly surrealism of *Entr'acte*. And these foundational expressions of slow motion—made outside a studio system or on the margins of a national cinema—can't be admired for their daring modernism without acknowledging the plain technicity of film's power to play with speed and motion, making "art" from all the ways that, in Ernst's resonant formulation, "media as measuring instruments have exposed the various time regimes of life since the nineteenth century." As he goes on to remind us, "media themselves have their own duration and time, which go much beyond what we could perceive as temporal with our bare eyes."[5] For Ernst, this finally means that technologies like cinema, from the oldest surviving images on celluloid to the wonders of the Phantom TMX, can see more times than we can—both faster than our eyes and brains can process and slower than our restless, wandering focus will endure. But there is another way, I think, that slow motion operates as the "time" of a specific media: We can witness how its style evolves and replicates across a century or so of cinematic history, a "duration" that is long enough to matter for more than just the artificial confines of a decade or a period but still brief enough to grasp as a singular moment in a deeper history of technologies of representation reaching past even the broadest understandings of modernity. The archaeology of slow motion as a media aesthetic would take practically forever to construct in full, but just a few seconds of seeing it in action after all its many years of excessive visibility can tell us a lot of what we need to know about it as an artifact of modern life and temporality.

Nico Baumbach returns to Deleuze's concept of an "inclusive disjunctive synthesis" to describe a situation in which it becomes possible to take a set of ideas, categories, or propositions and "think them together in their mutual coexistence, while at the same time preserving their autonomy."[6] Thus the differences between bodies and minds as aspects of the self or between media theories and phenomenologies as explanatory frameworks are not reconciled or merged by slow motion as an aesthetic but rather remain visible and distinct as what they are (and aren't) as conceptual tools that can give us ways of making sense of why slow motion matters and how it works to express some of the historical conditions that the twentieth century required individuals—including many of us who are still around—to live through and, in a word, endure. For much of the past 120 years, slow motion remained a minor modernist peculiarity and technological contrivance that was largely circumscribed in its appearances and limited in its appeal to filmmakers and audiences alike. It is neither a secret sharer in all modernity's discourses and symbolisms nor a synthesis of the dialectical drives and forces it reflects upon and turns into a visual style that we see so much of now. Slow motion is a supremely *mediated* form—deeply and irrevocably in between photography and cinema, a self-conscious show of art's capacities that is often pretty tasteless, rendering bodies and minds for fetishized display, and suggesting always that the essence of our experiences of time are nothing, and also utterly, technological.

I dare say that adding another term to this constellation might not be the best way to reconcile the aesthetic categories, philosophical traditions, and media effects that describe the slow motion we can see in such abundance across the long expanse of the twentieth century—within which, for better or for worse, I would place our present too. Let me try, nonetheless, to risk both a mixed metaphor and another set of open questions by bringing several of the threads I've been pursuing together as explicitly as I can. What I want to say slow motion does, at the bottom of all the styles it animates and the temporalities it invokes, is to *valorize* motion itself. I realize this comes close to echoing Sobchack and her phenomenological understanding of slow motion as revealing that which really "moves" in movement, a circular argument that, as I have said, actually has a lot to teach us about film and the experiential concepts that come into view around it. And there are, too, aspects of slow motion that are sharply realized by thinking within some of the frameworks her work suggests. We don't need to share her investment in Heidegger, for example, or in Bergson, Husserl, or Maurice Merleau-Ponty—or even in a writer like William James, who isn't a strict phenomenologist at all—to appreciate that a number of figures emerge in the early twentieth century, in rough parallel with the development of cinema as a technology, for whom experiences of change over time, of flux and process, of things and beings understood as constantly in motion, constitute a central set of problems for modern philosophy. "Valorizing" motion might not be the most important project any of these figures undertakes, though it does come close for Bergson as his early studies of *durée* lay the foundation for the turn to full-blown vitalism later in his career. "Slow motion," writes Herbert Zettl in 1973's *Sight, Sound, Motion: Applied Media Aesthetics*, "is more a function of event *density*."[7] This is an idea that reveals another measure of slow motion's value.

In suggesting that slow motion is a cinematic and cultural form of valorizing motion, we can also witness some of the dramas of valorization that define modernity not just as an epoch of speed or acceleration in the abstract or even as dynamics of technology but rather—and with utter specificity—as vectors of capital. And while using "valorization" in this manner speaks to a host of internal debates with Marxist theory and Marxian economics that I can barely touch on here, from a broader historical perspective the idea that film emerges from and reflects upon the conditions of modern and contemporary capitalism is another version of common sense. In Doane and Hansen, as we've seen, the expanded field of temporalities to which film gives both technological form (as media) and social texture (as mass entertainment) must always be considered in parallel with the distinct—but also consciously and unconsciously connected—innovations in timekeeping, time management, and other modes of regulation that defined the workplaces of the industrializing urban spaces that produced, among other new commodities, the audiences for early cinema. We need not go so far as Burch, for whom the development of narrative cinema figures as a "carrier wave of the bourgeois ideology of representation."[8] Baumbach reminds us, in language that is more neutral even as it leads to much the same conclusion, that cinema has long been a "medium within an industry dependent on capital," which is in part why it's so important as a compelling and impure "non-art," a phrase he explores in the context of Alain Badiou but that would have considerable traction for a 1960s movie buff and dissenting modernist like Robert Smithson.[9] The high-speed photography pioneered by Marey and Muybridge is effectively slow motion's proof of concept, but it also looms in the background of Fredrick Winslow Taylor's doctrines of "scientific management," providing illustrations and empirical proof that wasted energies and inefficiencies that went by too fast for the naked eye to register—but were still manifest as losses on the bottom line—could now be rationalized out of existence with the aid of new media. Marey's "chronographic technologies," according to the artist Nicholas Salazar Sutil, anticipated an "industry of movement composition" that eventually comes to inform the "commercial kinetopoiesis" of computer animation and gaming, but long before these twenty-first-century applications, Marey marks what Sutil describes as the "wider cultural shift of practice from motion discipline to motion control, and from a modern science *of* motion, to an advanced capitalism *in* motion."[10]

None of this is meant to suggest that the ongoing project of understanding what Marx called capitalism's "laws of motion"—or even the deceptively straightforward proposition of David Harvey's that capital is "value in motion"—requires us to track the history of slow motion from Edison to Michael Bay or to connect the dots that take us from *Entr'acte* to *Chungking Express* (1994) to *Guardians of the Galaxy 3* (2012).[11] On the other hand, it seems clear that the study of time as we know it under capitalism is perversely rich in themes, motifs, and arguments that help us see that part of what slow motion does—as the technological intensification of physical action in the service of a media aesthetic—is to extract and produce a specific form of value. Slow motion does not just valorize motion by rendering it more beautiful or graceful, more visceral or graphic: It manufactures a whole world of motions that might look like dream images or virtual ballets but are also fabricated by machines that operate at the accelerated speeds and microscopic temporalities of modern capitalism. "We know that the value of each commodity," Marx famously writes in chapter 7 of *Capital* as he describes the valorization process, "is determined by the quantity of labour materialized in its use-value, by the labour-time socially necessary to produce it."[12] This is a tough passage to figure out in respect to the commodity that is slow motion, all of the ambiguities that start to loom about what counts as the "use-value" of an aesthetic form, and how we might think about the socially necessary "labour-time" that makes it. Perhaps even this short turn to Marx risks a hopelessly literal image of slow motion as the "false consciousness"—a return to the camera obscura of bad ideology—of high-speed photography's perpetually accelerating rates of "turnover time," as if producing frames per second was just like making spindles in a different form. Or as Harvey puts it, "ever since time-and-motion studies ... became fashionable around 1900, there has always been a strong link between the hardware and the software of capitalist production systems."[13] Slow motion shows us both in action. It is a paradoxical display of speed, a dreamscape of deceleration that does not simply depend on technologies that can go fast but indexes their extreme velocities with inhuman precision. And slower motion is necessarily the output of faster cameras, which, along with cheaper, faster hard drives and more efficient software for image processing and editing, has allowed for an unprecedented "degree of exploitation" in the extraction of surplus-value—as art or information or both—from microscopic intervals of time that even the most devout phenomenologist would be hard pressed to account for or reach by way of introspection.

Thus in one of *Capital*'s most beautifully deadpan citations, Marx quotes the unnamed factory inspector who observes that "'moments are the elements of profit.'"[14] Passages like these are why Marx remains so prominent in discussions of what Sarah Sharma describes as "speed theory," an expanding body of twenty-first-century work "focused on the impact of technologies built for acceleration and faster-moving capital on the democratic fate of a sped-up world."[15] But it's not like we had to wait that long to hear how Marx's insights into the temporalities of capitalism could inspire a language of resistance to various techniques of acceleration that turns on the aesthetic sensibility that was simultaneously coming into shape around slow motion. In *History and Class Consciousness* (1923), Georg Lukács returns to Marx, at least in part, we might suspect, because he wants to show his readers—when Bergson's reputation and influence were never higher—that Marx had already grasped what the concept of duration puts to work. The beginning of the section Lukács cites sounds very much like Marx in *Capital*, with its punchy metaphor suggesting that "the pendulum of the clock has become as accurate a measure of the relative activity of two workers as it is of the speed of two locomotives." This line of Marx's thinking about clocks and locomotives then arrives, as Lukács must surely know, at a complaint that sounds like Bergson on the same modernity of clocks and trains some decades later: "'Time is everything, man is nothing; he is at the most the incarnation of time. Quality no longer matters. Quantity alone decides everything: hour for hour, day for day.'" And so Lukács continues in his own words, which radiate with Bergson even as they are explicating Marx. "Thus time sheds its qualitative, variable, flowing nature," Lukács writes, "it freezes into an exactly delimited, quantifiable continuum filled with quantifiable 'things.'"[16] But of course Lukács is not explaining Bergson or slow motion, which is why I find these parallels and echoes so intriguing in the ways that they remind us how readily duration flows into the world of technologies that we might like to think oppose it but in fact determine some of its most familiar forms and values.

"If we want to grasp the complex intersections of social differences under global capital," Sharma insists, "we need to take the temporal seriously on its own terms." This means recognizing that the always high speeds at which many of us feel our lives have been resigned to go at are also signs of "the structurally excessive privilege" that distributes time unevenly as a resource for some to worry about and for others to endure in harder ways. She is arguing against the habit of Harvey, Virilio, and other critics of speed to universalize and reify the experience of acceleration as the world's default velocity when it might be more accurate to say that slowness hasn't disappeared so much as been "outsourced" to whole regions of the globe and vast numbers of people everywhere, an outsourcing obscured by the "temporal architectures" of the contemporary world.[17] Slow motion might finally be too privileged as an aesthetic form for its efforts to take time seriously—even to the point of bathos—to do justice to the inequalities that mark the distribution of temporal resources and freedoms in the present. But at the very least it gives us an artistic language that, in the ostentatious strangeness of its relationship to the technologies on which it's based, can remind us that "speed is not a phenomenon but a relationship between phenomena: in other words, relativity itself."[18] Even Virilio, whose commitment to the critique of speed did not slow down in a career that spanned five decades, here seems to understand that acceleration isn't what it used to be. "The race for the absolute intensity of time turns reality inside out like a glove," Virilio writes elsewhere, and "the yardstick of duration is no longer really 'duration' but, paradoxically, the infinite and constant deepening of 'the instant.'"[19] Slow motion does not at all resolve or reconcile this ambivalence, no matter how much grace or dreamlike style it manufactures. Better, I think, to say that it objectifies these plural and dissonant temporalities and puts them to work in film and other media, where their casually dialectical potential—to show that speed can feel like slowness and that slowness can be made from speed—is subsumed in often formulaic set pieces and now familiar genres.

This is, I concede, an impossibly unwieldy set of issues to impose upon a single media effect. At the same time, we will soon see that this is precisely what a number of literary texts that make reference to slow motion try to do. But before we turn to them—and then return to the films of the late 1960s that they anticipate or retrospectively survey—there is one last point I want to make about slow motion in its relationship to the logistics of modern "clock-time" it encodes and visualizes. Scholars interested in the sociology of time have argued for decades that we need to pay more attention to what Barbara Adam describes as the "inseparability of physical, living, and cultural existence" within and amid the incessant "focus on technologically constituted times" that too many writers, both popular and academic, take as given in their accounts of the contemporary moment.[20] Hartmut Rosa assumes the "widespread perception of a social *time of crisis*, where, paradoxically, the feeling spreads that a deep-seated structural and cultural stasis is hidden behind the permanent, dynamic transformation of social, material, and cultural structures," or as he puts it in slightly punchier language later, there is the perception of "a fundamental historical rigidity in which nothing essential changes anymore, however rapidly everything may alter on the surface."[21] As an academic of a certain age, identity, and class, I know that Rosa is very much playing my song, so to speak, which I wish would sound a little louder or more threatening despite the fact that I know that this isn't really the point of writing these sorts of books. Like Jonathan Crary's equally impassioned *24/7*—another favorite, I must admit—a lot of the best work on the contradictions of contemporary time that I've found most rich to think about are much sharper at the level of diagnosis than they are promising at the level of actual response. Crary takes this to an almost ludicrous extreme by offering up "the restorative inertness of sleep" against the violence and predations of capitalism and what it has wrought: "the deathliness of all the accumulation, financialization, and waste that have devastated anything once held in common."[22] I too would like capitalism to end after a dream sequence in delirious slow motion.

But I suspect the final scene will need to be considerably more disturbing—less harrowing and explosive, I hope, than then blood-soaked conclusion of *The Wild Bunch* but probably not as graceful as Ginger Rogers and Fred Astaire—and it is telling, I think, that what is most likely to get pictured in slow motion now are the technicalities of combat.

It's obvious to me that writing about the history of slow motion is also largely a diagnostic undertaking and marks an even deeper dive into the symptomatic forms of capitalism's culture with no more promise that we will ultimately arrive somewhere on the other side. But it does perhaps illustrate with striking clarity the paradox of what Moishe Postone has characterized as the *"treadmill effect"* of modern capitalism, which conspires to guarantee that all "increased productivity" at work and in the body appears inevitably as inertia and deceleration on the bottom line. I'm willing to concede that this is a reading of slow motion that is extravagantly loaded. It will be the labor of later chapters to show how various writers and filmmakers use slow motion to explore the shape of historical time across and beyond the twentieth century as they help us understand, borrowing again from Postone, "the movement *of time*, as opposed to the movement *in time*."[23] That this most dramatically takes place in films of the late 1960s is significant because this is also the moment when not just economists but a great many figures in the West begin to reckon with the possibility that there is no difference between capitalism and modernity at a standstill and in decline, with any sign of slowing down implying the apocalypse to come. That none of these films are set within the present they inhabit so completely is significant too, for here we see how tricky it is to know if modernity is going slower or whether it has been moving at this speed for centuries, one of the many as it takes us toward its bitter end—which we don't want to be ours too.

PART II
Modernity at Any Speed

10

Some Literary Histories of Slow Motion

In the beginning of the modern world, there was speed: This is one of the primordial mythologies of modernity as a structure of historical feeling, which need not be fully real or even very thoroughly defined to do the work that we have attributed to it in the West. Even those of us who study modernism for a living have largely stopped pretending that a single set of social, intellectual, technological, or political transformations can possibly explain the vast plurality of cultural forms and diverse practices of representation that we now correctly and routinely talk about as multiple and uneven, distributed and global, untimely and belated. We have come to agree implicitly that there never was just one way of being "modern" and nothing like a universal "we" that could speak in just one voice from all the places, periods, identities, and communities where ideas about modernity—whether true or false or both or neither—have been at issue since long before Baudelaire and Manet walked the streets of Paris or Pound, Joyce, and Eliot got to know one another.[1] We recognize these familiar constellations for the clichés and mystifications that they are and know to look for modernisms everywhere and almost all the time ("early modern," "ancient modern"), or at least when the uncertainty and contingency of human life is tangible and the fact that it's in motion is made visible. Jameson is writing from the heart of the heart of the modernism we have left behind when he declares, with his typical grandeur and mixing of categorial generalities and out-of-nowhere specifics, that "time today is a function of speed, and evidently perceptible only in terms of its rate, or velocity as such: as though the old Bergsonian opposition between measurement and life, clock time and lived time, had dropped out, along with the virtual eternity or slow permanence without which Valéry thought the very idea of a work as such was likely to die out."²

Much of this section is focused on a set of writers whose own interests in the medium of film—from such usual suspects as William Faulkner and Don DeLillo to more contemporary novelists like W. G. Sebald and Tom McCarthy—invoke slow motion as a cinematic form and adopt its refracted temporalities to help them pose a set of larger questions about the speed and shape of modern life. I am obviously not suggesting that these are the only authors who wear the influence of film on their pages or that they constitute anything like a canon or even a representative selection of novelists concerned with media and history and how these systems of meaning come to interact and serve as channels for more occult reflections on the phenomena of modernity. But as I hope to show, they share a sensibility and, perhaps more importantly, a susceptibility to certain cinematic styles that cut across and comment on the ways that I've been arguing for slow motion's minor but iconic status as a twentieth-century aesthetic.

Consider these three illustrations of "slow motion" over time: The first is a simple Google Ngram, the second was generated using the HathiTrust's Bookworm database, and the third comes from Project Arclight, which provides a way to visualize trends within the Media History Digital Library, a collection of more than 2 million pages of books and magazines focusing on film, TV, and recorded sound (figures 10.1, 10.2, 10.3).³ For both of the first two charts, we see a roughly similar increase in occurrences of "slow motion" as a phrase, with both the Ngram and the Bookworm showing a fairly steady rise from 1920 to their respective presents. The acceleration looks more dramatic for Bookworm, and there is no sign of the dip over the past few years that we find at the right edge of the Ngram. Overall, both confirm what we might guess about the ways that "slow motion" as a phrase in common usage would parallel and track the emergence of film as a popular medium of mass entertainment in the 1920s. Given that there is an even more precipitous rise in mentions of "slow motion" right around 1920 in the media history materials, it seems likely that a lot of the "slow motion" that starts appearing in the Ngram and Bookworm views refers specifically to the special effect itself.⁴ There are no doubt more sophisticated ways to map how terms and ideas linked to film begin to travel widely at the level of general culture—or at least the broad cross-sections of language captured by Google and HathiTrust. But since I'm not trying to do anything more than show that "slow motion" gets used more frequently as the twentieth century proceeds, this will have to do.

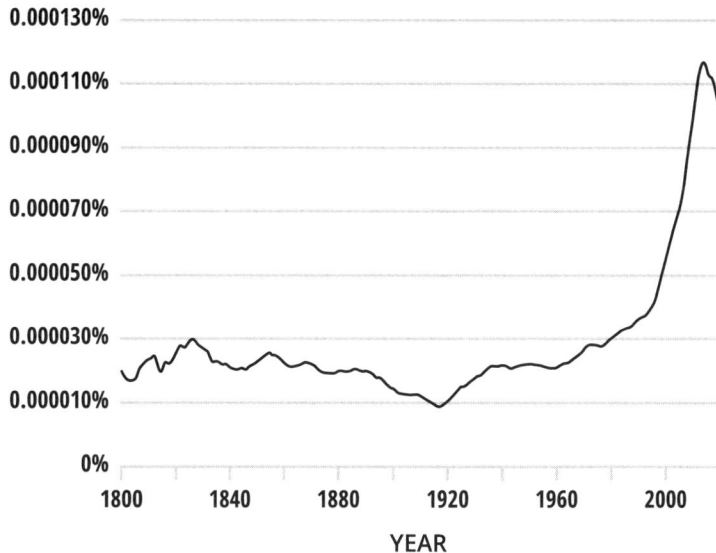

FIGURE 10.1 Google Ngram: "slow motion."

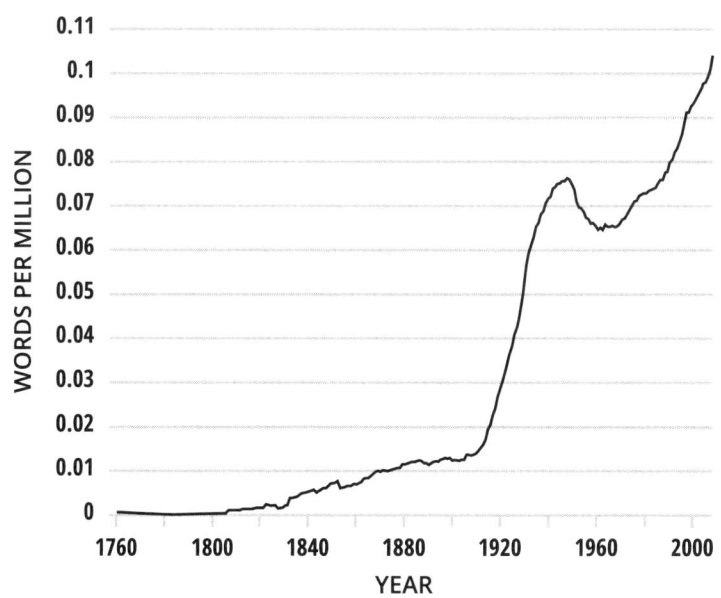

FIGURE 10.2 HathiTrust Bookworm: "slow motion."

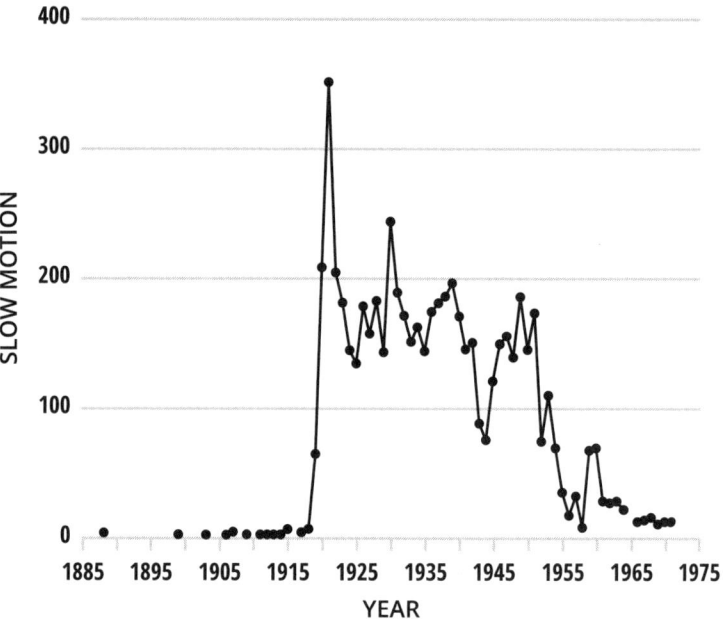

FIGURE 10.3 "Slow motion" in media studies database.

Where this short interlude in data gets more interesting is on the other side of slow motion's timeline in the twentieth century. Its trajectory on the Ngram viewer and Bookworm has its bumps and dives from 1960 forward, though it keeps on going up, particularly after 1980. But when we look at the Arclight visualization, which focuses on film and media publications, we see just the opposite: Immediately after 1920, "slow motion" starts to decline in numbers. Specific references maintain an erratic stutter across the 1930s and 1940s, drop dramatically in the 1950s, and fade by the mid-1960s. This divergence tells us several things, but not necessarily about slow motion and its popularity as a special effect, since it does not require any graphs or numbers to know that there is more slow motion now—and in the 1970s, 1980s, 1990s, and 2000s—than at any prior moment in the history of film and media. Again, just search "Action" as a Netflix genre and you'll find more movies with a fight scene, gun battle, or explosion in slow motion than you'll ever have the time to watch. The kinds of materials and publications that the Media History Digital Library collects—distributors' catalogs for nonfiction shorts and documentaries, guides to educational films for teachers and school administrators, trade magazines, etc.—were always just as devoted to the world of non-narrative, nontheatrical, and otherwise "useful" cinema, which became increasingly isolated as a commercial sector from "the movies" with the declining popularity of newsreels and shorts in the 1950s and the gradual shift to video for educational and industrial exhibition. This is not a story that need concern us in much detail, but it provides a background against which we can understand that what we are seeing in this sharp decline of "slow motion" is actually the growing obsolescence of a whole discourse aimed at advertising and describing the sorts of nonfiction films—sports highlight newsreels, documentary shorts, and more—where slow motion flourished. As broadcast TV effectively assimilated these subgenres, there is simply less reason to talk about slow motion in these specialized domains; where once it was a discrete attraction of a short or newsreel, its more frequent use in sports coverage and elsewhere becomes so utterly prosaic that its appearance goes without saying.

The fact that "slow motion" gets more difficult to find in this particular database, then, is a sign that slow motion gets easier for viewers to see—which also, of course, anticipates the media ecology in which it uncontrollably proliferates on YouTube, TikTok, Instagram, and the internet more generally. I obviously can't say how much of this slow motion looms behind these examples of "slow motion" since the 1980s that, in the case of Bookworm, seems to be growing exponentially. Most of them are merely passing. In Katherine Anne Porter's *Ship of Fools* (1962), for example, Amparo and Pepe share a dance that the narrator describes figuratively "as complicated as a ballet, in the rhythms of a slow-motion film."[5] Could I take this single cinematic reference in a novel of almost five hundred pages and make it symptomatic of the whole? Almost certainly. But it is also clear—and just as compelling to acknowledge—just how little "slow motion" can mean as a dead metaphor, where it is not trying to signal a network of histories and media archaeologies so much as letting us know, precisely by not trying to signal much of anything, how deeply media have come to pattern the languages of modern life at its most conventional and everyday. I won't risk further delay by even trying to think through the 256,000,000 hits for Googling "like moving in slow motion" or the 107,000,000 for "felt like I was in slow motion": At the top of both searches are links for "Slow Motion Feeling" as a clinical feature of anxiety, a symptom also called "The Matrix Effect" for reasons that have a lot to do with the history of media but also nothing much at all.[6]

At the most rudimentary level, every instance of slow motion offers an allegory of how we live with technology. Slow motion naturalizes those incremental aspects of reality and fleeting states of being that it lets us perceive and that take on the character of expanded moments somehow salvaged from and set against the speeds at which the present otherwise flows away from us. And yet the greater speeds required to make slow motion possible are also rendered invisible within the codes of art or genre or by our more routine but no less complicated contemporary habits of image consumption. I am interested in how slow motion becomes, drawing on Kristen Whissel's work about special effects, "emblematic" for the idea of modern life.[7] For Whissel, the historical category of the emblem provides us with an intellectual tool for reconciling the tension between narratives and attractions in film studies. Rather than viewing spectacles of visual extravagance and technological display as efforts to "arrest narrative" and put a stop to its momentum, emblems are "continuous" with the plots they mark and often represent the "conceptual obsessions" that are crucial for the story that surrounds and structures them.

How exactly does slow motion become emblematic for a modern world that only ever seems to be going faster? Stephen Kern's essential work in *The Culture of Time and Space* continues to set the terms by which we understand the artistic and intellectual consequences of the interconnected changes in technologies of communication, transportation, and industrial production that structured the everyday experiences of speed that became increasingly central to the imagery of modern life in both high art and popular expression as the nineteenth century progressed.[8] We have already seen how Marx's analysis of capitalism and its accelerationist imperatives—the double annihilations of space and time he describes in the *Grundrisse*—grounds theories of modernity and postmodernity in David Harvey and Fredric Jameson and figures prominently for social theorists like Hartmut Rosa, who speaks in less overtly political languages of a contemporary "domination of *the faster*."[9] No theorist or intellectual of the past half-century has found speed as such as worrisome as Paul Virilio, for whom it represents a kind of primal drive or "pathology of movement" that, much like Freud's model of religion in *Civilization and Its Discontents*, seems more like an innate condition of self-denial and misery that humans have always suffered than it does a historical dimension of the economy based on assembly-line production and wage labor that hasn't always been there.[10] In his fantastically persuasive *The Speed Handbook*, Enda Duffy presents us with a more properly dialectical account of what it means to see modern culture shaped by its perpetual acceleration. As Duffy argues, to identify modernity with an "increased regime of speed" and capital's need for routinized and systematic power over time is only part of the story, no matter how depressingly and pugnaciously it gets told by Virilio and others; for Duffy, it is an essential "individual pleasure" of modernity even as it drives a logic of "more intense and tighter social control."[11] Even if the speed of modernism is just the speed of capitalism with better advertising—Futurist lines of force and color dressing up the Model-T's basic black—the potential that it represents for change over time is real, no matter how conditional. This is both an echo and a helpfully concrete version of Jameson's account of modernism, too, which pursues genuine aesthetic inventions in both formal and thematic terms but also "becomes a blind," as he observes, "behind which the more embarrassing logic of the commodity form and the market can operate."¹²

Let me try to make this less terminally abstract by spelling out two lines of argument I'll be pursuing. First, I am suggesting that slow motion is a useful figure for thinking through the limits of speed as a leitmotif for modernity as such. "Toward the end of the eighteenth century," writes Reinhart Koselleck, "voices proliferated that came to see all of history from the perspective of increasing acceleration."¹³ His point is not simply that various technologies we associate with the Industrial Revolution—driven always by the imperatives of capitalism—speed up systems of production, transportation, and communication in Europe and beyond. Koselleck argues more broadly that "there is a peculiar form of acceleration which characterizes modernity" and that any reckoning with its empirical effects must also understand how the sheer rapidity of progress "abbreviated the spaces of experience, robbed them of their constancy, and continually brought into play new, unknown factions, so that even the actuality or complexity of these unknown quantities could not be ascertained."¹⁴ For many writers interested in both the formal possibilities and political imperatives that come from thinking about some of history's slower speeds, the present figures as a period where it becomes possible to wonder how much longer these dynamics—and the economic and social systems that structure them—can be maintained. Slow motion turns even the smallest increments of time into potential epochs of indeterminate size and scale; it lets the present be imagined as a period of possible deceleration that is still entirely the aftermath of speed in prior centuries. As a technique for registering not so much the velocity of an event but, returning to Herbert Zettl's helpful terminology in 1973's *Sight, Sound, Motion*, its "density," slow motion conceives of every instant as an archaeology of brief but bygone histories and almost vanished moments that look like they might linger there forever—until suddenly they don't.

But I'd also like to situate these works exploring slow motion as a literary trope and narrative effect in another context that is more visible in the short run. Some social theorists and economists have spent the years since the financial crisis of 2008 trying to determine whether modernity—or at least, the systemically linked forces of capitalist production and technological innovation—are still capable of advancing at the rates that we have come to expect across the twentieth century. Mainstream economists regularly ask "Is U.S. Economic Growth Over?" and debate the causes of a "great stagnation" that a better mix of tax policies or Keynesian investments might alleviate.[15] More radical thinkers, drawing on the work of Giovanni Arrighi and other financial historians, argue that there is, in fact, no viable set of adjustments and corrections within contemporary capitalism that will return the global economy to former levels of profits and the social expenditures that they accommodated in the West, however unevenly, in the decades after World War II. I make no strong claims for expertise in these issues, but I can appreciate how their rhetoric and historiographical assumptions place a great deal of pressure on familiar narratives of modernity and how its network of ideologies and technologies—perpetually productive and progressively accelerating—have bounded the horizons both of modernity's strongest critics and its most willing champions. The politics of speed and slowness can lead to self-contradicting logics and unlikely affiliations, with proponents of "slow growth" and sustainability defending property rights with utter militancy or "accelerationists" producing fantasies of technological transformation that imagine Marxist revolution as the ultimate deliverable of Silicon Valley venture capital. "These recent restatements of accelerationism," writes Benjamin Noys, "come explicitly against the background of ongoing financial crisis [and] the evident stasis of the world-system of capitalism." Yet Noys is just as skeptical about the "tepid, or even reactionary" character of slowness as a strategy of resistance. In a somewhat higher register of abstraction, Rosa cautions us against "forms of intentional deceleration" that are not so much directed against what he calls the "time structures" of contemporary capitalism but are instead "entirely *functional* for it."[16]

These might seem like intellectual frameworks utterly too grand to help us understand a single visual effect and the cultural work that it might do. But as I have been insisting all along, slow motion is a way of valorizing motion itself, primarily as an aesthetic attraction but also as a product of how media technologies let us see the world—and it often takes no time at all to go from these technologies to the economies that propel them. Which is why we might want to know what they look like as they slow down.

11
Modernity's Slow Start

Even if we grant, at least for now, that modernism and modernity are connected to—and often talked about like synonyms for—a culture and aesthetics of technology and speed, we should remember that it all gets off to something of a slow start. "In 1839," according to one of the more vivid details that Benjamin recovers from the archive for his *Arcades Project*, "it was considered elegant to take a tortoise out walking. This gives us an idea of the tempo of flânerie in the arcades."[1] If this is how modernity arrives—slouching toward Paris at barely three or four miles per hour—we are compelled, though not exactly rushed, to think again about the suddenness that structures so many of the stories that we are told about how it felt to be at any number of places or events that have become versions of ground zero for our accelerated present. Benjamin witnesses the emergence of modernity at a far different and dramatically reduced velocity when compared, say, to Virginia Woolf's sense of a new epoch when "in or about December, 1910, human character changed" or to Willa Cather's late realization that "the world broke in two in 1922 or thereabouts" with the simultaneous arrivals of *Ulysses* and *The Waste Land*—neither of which were, strictly speaking, written on the fly, though this isn't Cather's point.[2] Unlike the revolutions of 1848 or the massive violence of World War I, a tortoise plodding down the sidewalk can definitely sneak up on you, which is why it provides Benjamin with such a perfect image, perverse and dialectical, for a special kind of rupture between the present and the past, a moment where the temporality of modern life is hard to fathom not so much for its astonishing pace but for its inhuman capacity—both creaturely and refined—to move just barely at a gaudily lethargic tempo while everybody else goes rushing forward. Both Benjamin and his tortoise mean to teach us the same lesson about modernity: It is not simply a set of historical transformations that make everything go faster all the time but rather a new distribution of speeds across a wider range of social and economic actions, some of which become intensively compressed and valorized while others are prolonged, distended, and exaggerated to the point of virtual stasis.

"On the level of its technological operativity," writes Wolfgang Ernst, our contemporary moment "experiences an implosion of the phenomenological sense of the present into a myriad of differential timing processes." Ernst himself operates with a very broad conception of technology, but I doubt that he would place a tortoise anywhere amid the semiconductors and "delay lines" that pattern the flows of information that only ever reach their end users—the default subjectivity in Ernst's somewhat less charming vision of modernity—in "time-dilated" forms that have been slowed down for processing by humans.[3] In a world of computers, in other words, everything that has to do with us must be put into slow motion, or else we'd never have a chance to perceive it in the first place. The flâneur and his tortoise—and we'll keep the figure masculine for reasons that will come into focus later—can only go so fast if he is to process the spectacle of commodities produced on assembly lines devoted to minimizing "turnover time" and brought to the city by railroads and other systems of "fixed capital" that, as David Harvey puts it, facilitate the "fluidity and speed-up [that] are essential qualities of capital flow" but are also crucial to "the deep, crisis-prone contradiction between fixity and motion" that characterizes modern economic life.[4] The tortoise in slow motion is the measure of the larger system's speed.

Henri Lefebvre argues that it is precisely this diversity of speeds that has defined modernity from the ancient Mediterranean to late-capitalist New York and London in the 1980s. "Let us insist on the relativity of rhythms," Lefebvre writes, which he explains cannot be measured, "as the speed of a moving object on its trajectory is measured, beginning from a well-defined starting point (point zero) with a unit defined once and for all. A rhythm is only slow or fast in relation to other rhythms with which it finds itself associated in a more or less vast unity."[5] For Lefebvre, it is urban space itself that brings this assembly of velocities together, and this is worth remembering, but the fact that global capitalism not only allows for but actively requires its own distribution of speeds and temporalities across races, genders, geographies, and classes should give us pause before making a utopia from this vision of difference and flexibility. As Sarah Sharma, Jesse Matz, and others rightly caution, to conceptualize the experiences of time apart from all the vectors of identity and power that structure them can lead to empty celebrations of slowness for its own sake, which, returning to Rosa's similar warnings, serve as accelerants for the very dynamics of inequality and exploitation that they otherwise intend to moderate or repair. This has also been among the most important contributions that sociologists of time like Barbara Adams have made toward expanding and correcting the ways that some philosophical and artistic traditions have obscured the networks of power and status that render time as anything but a "unity." Adams's own early work, for example, drew on Anglo-American feminism to show how fraught attempts to reckon with a "global present . . . from a time-sensitive ecological perspective" rehearse much earlier and more immediate debates about the roles of women in the 1970s and the "differential treatment of times" and other forms of "sequencing and prioritizing" that conditioned "compromises in time allocation that [had] to be achieved on a daily basis."[6] Or, as Michael Hanchard writes in respect to the "unequal temporal dimensions" of Blackness in the United States, there is only ever "racial time," and we must continuously attend to the material practices of expropriation and white supremacy that operate through and in everyday routines of waiting and enforced delay, of "time appropriation" as a tactic of policing, or in the "ethico-political relationship between temporality and notions of human progress."[7] The figure of Benjamin's tortoise is not so confrontational as an expression of being "elegant," since consuming all this time conspicuously is one way the flâneur can put himself above, or at least an ostentatious step behind, the regimes of standard time that came to rationalize and discipline nineteenth-century Paris and beyond. "The idleness of the flâneur," as Benjamin suggests in this same section of the *Arcades Project*, "is a demonstration against the division of labor."[8]

■ ■ ■

There is nothing "elegant" about Mink Snopes, and he doesn't need a turtle to pace him, as he proceeds in the slowest motion possible through William Faulkner's second-to-last novel, *The Mansion* (1959). This is far from the greatest work of modernism that we might describe as patterned on slow motion, but it is among the most explicit. As the conclusion to the Snopes trilogy, the events that Faulkner here recounts are themselves conceived as echoes and extensions of actions that have been unfolding since *The Hamlet* (1940) and *The Town* (1957)—the first two installments of his late epic detailing the rise to power and dominance of Flem Snopes, a grotesquely empty figure for the predations of modern capital. While it's difficult to summarize all of Flem's various schemes and the plots that Faulkner constructs upon them over the course of three thick novels—not to mention earlier accounts of other Snopeses found in famous stories such as "Barn Burning"—Eck Snopes provides a good enough description in *The Town* of what his family represents when he reflects on their "long tradition of slow and invincible rapacity." When *The Mansion* opens, Mink is just being sentenced to life in prison for murdering a wealthier landowner, Houston, on whose land Mink has his own cow feed since he is too poor to pay for grain himself. Houston quietly lets Mink's cow eat with his herd but then later bills Mink for "the slow incrementation of feed converted to weight," and it is the outrage over Houston charging him for money that finally means nothing to him save the "prolongation" of Mink's embarrassment and torment in legal wranglings, that drives Mink to kill him.[9] Mink at first believes that his cousin, Flem, will help him get out of prison sooner since Flem is an increasingly important member of Jefferson's elite and central to the town's economy even if his manners and self-presentation leave him barely tolerable to the older gentry he is displacing. Flem instead abandons his cousin to the full force of the law. Knowing that this means Mink will want to kill him in revenge when he is freed, Flem contrives a plan to trick Mink into escaping so that he will suffer still more "prolongation" when extra years in Parkman Penitentiary are added to his sentence. Mink spends thirty-eight years in prison before he is released, and we have to do a little math and read too closely to untangle the convoluted timeline and realize that he goes to prison in 1908. He is incarcerated, more or less, for the whole duration of high modernism as a literary period.

The almost forty years it takes for Mink to get his revenge on Flem makes him emblematic of a quality that had always fascinated Faulkner in his fiction: endurance. In the genealogical "Appendix" added to *The Sound and the Fury* for Malcolm Cowley's 1946 compilation *The Portable Faulkner*—which helped confirm Faulkner's reputation as a major U.S. writer and arguably set him on his way to winning the Nobel Prize for literature—it is famously Dilsey, the Compson family's Black maid and maternal presence over generations of psychic trauma, whose whole life is both reduced but also monumentalized by the two-word summary that finally brings the Compsons' saga to a quick end. As many readers will no doubt remember, what Faulkner finally tells us about Dilsey and her Black family, or rather doesn't, is encrypted in the ambivalent assertion: "They endured."[10] This is more than the white Compsons manage after decades of alcoholism, parental neglect, suicide, theft, abuse, and misogyny that we follow, with considerable effort, across the fractured modernist narrative structures of Faulkner's first genuine achievement as a novelist. But the value of Faulkner's praise must of course be weighed against the suspect romanticism of the gesture and the perverted grandeur of treating Dilsey as a collective token of Black persistence in the face of suffering that white southerners like Faulkner have themselves inflicted. For all Faulkner's conflicted views on race over the decades, when he returned to the arc of his first masterpiece the least that he could do was recognize that Blacks in the United States had to be in it for the long run, or not at all.

What Mink withstands from his cousin's corruption and venality is not a racial crime so much as business as usual for Flem as he gradually transforms from petty clerk and horse trader to capitalist and banker. As Mink approaches Jefferson, he worries that he will be recognized and arrested even though, Faulkner writes, "he knew this to be a physical impossibility." The last time Mink was home, after all, the highway into town—"on which automobiles sped"—was still "a winding dirt along which slow mules and wagons, or at best a saddle horse, followed the arbitrary and random ridges." The transportation infrastructure has been so thoroughly modernized that even the topography has changed, but still Mink worries that something about "his face" or "his expression"—or "his familiar regional clothes or the way he walked"—will give him away.[11] But Mink is entirely anonymous on the slow road to Jefferson, as anonymous as another stranger on a manhunt whom Faulkner all but beatifies into an icon of duration: Lena Grove in *Light in August* (1932). She is a figure of "timeless unhaste" with the "slow palpable aura of somnolence" who is looking for the father of her expected child when she crosses the violent path that also brings Joe Christmas to Jefferson roughly thirteen years before Mink's own return.[12] It takes Lena about four weeks to cover the distance from her home in Alabama to arrive at the same place it will take Mink almost four decades to get to at a moment when his own deliberate slowness, in the context of the modernity that surrounds him, is even more pronounced.

12

Faulkner at the Speed Limit

With time enough and the vast assembly of characters in Faulkner's many fictions, we could find other parallels and analogues for Mink Snopes's exquisitely deliberate course through the novels of the Snopes trilogy and the sweeping histories they narrate. Luckily Faulkner himself cuts to the chase in a short preface to *The Mansion*. Here we see that the single figure who most closely resembles Mink Snopes in his interminable, morbid struggle with Flem Snopes over the decades is the author who creates them both:

> This book is the final chapter of, and the summation of, a work conceived and begun in 1925. Since the author likes to believe, hopes that his entire life's work is a part of a living literature, and since "living" is motion, and "motion" is change and alteration and therefore the only alternative to motion is unmotion, stasis, death, there will be found discrepancies and contradictions in the thirty-four-year progress of this particular chronicle; the purpose of this note is simply to notify the reader that the author has already found more discrepancies and contradictions than he hopes the reader will—contradictions and discrepancies due to the fact that the author has learned, he believes, more about the human heart and its dilemma than he knew thirty-four years ago; and is sure that, having lived with them that long time, he knows the characters in this chronicle better than he did then.[1]

In at least two late interviews, Faulkner approvingly compared his own ideas about time to those of Henri Bergson, and while it is hard to know when exactly Faulkner would have encountered Bergson—or if he ever really did, given

Faulkner's reading habits and propensity to talk out of his hat when performing the role of laureate and genius near the end of his career—there is no mistaking the language of vitalism, however generic, that patterns his account of what *The Mansion* represents.[2] If all Faulkner was concerned with were continuity errors in a multinovel project concluding after more than thirty years, his defense would not have had to grasp at such lofty metaphysics.

What draws me to this stately show of rhetoric at the beginning of a novel that brings a longer, slower epic to an end is that it turns on many of the same questions about the twentieth century and its speeds that I've been asking from the start. Richard Godden has convincingly written about the "dense or double temporality" that structures Faulkner's later novels, not so much because their scope gets broader or more expansive than already grand-style narratives such as *Light in August* (1934) or *Absalom, Absalom* (1936) but rather because the changes facing Faulkner and other southerners as World War II exploded made it impossible to believe there was a future for the economy of sharecropping and indentured labor that had let, in Godden's striking formulation, a "plantocracy whose regime of accumulation . . . constituted a counterrevolution running from Emancipation to Depression" live on in more grotesque and gothic forms.[3] If we read the novels of the Snopes trilogy as "studies in deferred modernization and its aftermath," then at least some aspects of their unevenness and varying quality as narrative constructions become visible as different forms of "contradiction": not bad writing by a great novelist whose better days had been two decades earlier but the concerted effort to understand the logic of capitalism when its relentless forward progress is best embodied in the grinding, unhurried normalcy of Flem Snopes, who, in over one thousand pages of fiction in the collected edition of the novels that Faulkner names in honor of his extended family, is almost never pictured doing anything that looks like the "motion" of a living human being. This is only one reason why it takes so long—thirty-four years for Faulkner, thirty-eight for Mink—to kill him faster than we can process in a show of slow motion that still takes several chapters of *The Mansion* to describe.

We can reconstruct the timeline of Mink's vengeance on his cousin without much difficulty, at least when compared to some of the other narrative mysteries that loom at the core of Faulkner's novels. Mink has been in prison for thirty-eight years, waiting to get out and murder Flem. Linda Kohl—the legal daughter of Flem and Eula, though by this point in the florid saga we know that Flem is not her biological father—pushes Gavin Stevens to petition for Mink's release, which everybody knows will set him in motion on the way to Flem. The question is how fast: Mink leaves prison on a Thursday, which is earlier than Stevens planned, which leaves him and Ratliff, Flem's equally long-suffering adversary since the first pages of *The Hamlet*, scrambling to mount a chase to stop Mink in his tracks. They don't want Flem to get away with all the decades he's spent scheming and accumulating—swindling his way from horse trader to banker and beyond, the master of both the quick sale and long-term financialization—but they don't want Mink to pay the price. Stevens and Ratliff fail to keep the worst from happening, as they have failed before, and they can't catch Mink even though he hardly takes the straightest, fastest path toward retribution. As the sheriff spells out on the following Tuesday, Mink has "had four days now, to come a hundred miles."[4] Mink travels a little farther since he takes a detour to Memphis to get a gun, but we can grant him covering closer to two hundred miles and still recognize that Faulkner sees his journey as more momentous than just a couple errands that, on the recently paved highways of northern Mississippi in the 1940s, could be completed before lunch, depending on the traffic. Mink certainly knows that time is of the essence, but he also seems incapable of hurrying. On his fateful walk toward town after some directions from a Black man who better knows the roads—a passing association that connects Mink to other marginal figures in a novel strangely crowded with representatives of the global proletariat—he recalls how he used to watch the trains from prison.[5] They were "looked at, seen, alien in freedom, fleeing, existing in liberty and hence unreal, chimeras, apparitions, without past or future, not even going anywhere since their destinations could not exist for him: just in motion a second, an instant, then nowhere."[6] The language here, as in so much late Faulkner, is not exactly streamlined and efficient. Most readers will arrive at the idea long before this line of clauses comes to a stop. We don't need to see trains fly by to know that Mink is embodied and incarnated history, a living figure of time and punishment who carries with him not just the thirty-eight years he's spent in Parchman penitentiary but the collective decades that all of Flem's antagonists—Ratliff, Stevens, Eula, Linda, and more—have spent and lost as Flem has accumulated his petty commercial empire and solidified his holdings. Mink is fast and slow at once and is driven by a mix of ancestral family grievances that Faulkner filters through his sometimes clunky gestures toward the postwar present. By the end of the chapter, Stevens will learn that Flem is already dead. And then in the next chapter, Faulkner narrates it again extravagantly and in slow motion.

The scene itself is not long. The action unfolds over two paragraphs that add up to just over six hundred words. Faulkner, as we know, could write single sentences that were twice as long and unfold paragraphs that go on for many pages.[7] There is a series of actions that in real time might take a couple seconds—Mink enters the room, then Flem turns his head and swivels toward his cousin, whose gun misfires the first time, so he spins the chamber back and shoots again—which Faulkner intersperses with short fragments of interior monologue in Mink's distinctive dialect. The narration obviously extends and dilates this moment into a passage that is hard to read, for me at least, in less than a minute, but I'm not trying to be too empirical. What makes this scene so striking as an example of slow motion is that Faulkner seems to be after some aesthetic effects that aren't really very special. The first of these two paragraphs, as the old saying goes, is where the action is:

> He didn't need to say, "Look at me, Flem." His cousin was already doing that, his head turned over his shoulder. Otherwise he hadn't moved, only the jaws ceased chewing in midmotion. Then he moved, leaned slightly forward in the chair and he had just begun to lower his propped feet from the ledge, the chair beginning to swivel around, when Mink from about five feet away stopped and raised the toad-shaped iron-rust-coloured weapon in both hands and cocked and steadied it, thinking *Hit's got to hit his face*: not *I've got to* but *It's got to* and pulled the trigger and rather felt than heard the dull foolish almost inattentive click. Now his cousin, his feet now flat on the floor and the chair almost swivelled to face him, appeared to sit immobile and even detached too, watching too Mink's grimed shaking child-sized hands like the hands of a pet coon as one of them lifted the hammer enough for the other to roll the cylinder back one notch so that the shell would come again under the hammer; again that faint something out of the past nudged, prodded: not a warning nor even really a repetition: just faint and familiar and unimportant still since, whatever it had been, even before it had not been strong enough to alter anything nor even remarkable enough to be remembered; in the same second he had dismissed it. *Hit's all right* he thought *Hit'll go this time: Old Moster don't play jokes* and cocked and steadied the pistol again in both hands, his cousin not moving at all now though he was chewing faintly again, as though he too were watching the dull point of light on the cock of the hammer when it flicked away.

So much of this is conventional, and even forced, with Flem's frozen posture ("the jaws ceased chewing in midmotion") and projected stasis ("appeared to sit immobile and detached too, watching") staging this spectacle of violence as theatrical tableau or protocinematic montage of close-ups and *plains Américains* or medium shots of figures from the knee, which is how Mink seems to loom in the glimpse we get of him from Flem's perspective as Mink fumbles at the gun when it misfires. But this seems too clever by half, and I want to resist some of the more overt analogies to cinematic form that this scene invites. The close-ups, for example, are a bit too close. Focusing on Mink's hands as they shake "like the hands of a pet coon," for example, shifts the visual scale into something more surreal and naturalistic at the same time; any Snopes would know a raccoon's hands better than I would, but he is not just reducing Mink in size and stature but also seeing him as less than human. The phantom racial epithet goes by fast but further thickens and extends the play of signifiers in a manner that is resplendently verbal. The last image is similarly excessive and goes beyond the logic of cinematic representation though appearing, at first glance, as homage to it. What Mink sees as the "dull point of light on the cock of the hammer" is an almost impossibly small detail to stress and fetishize on screen—particularly in the genres of narrative film that Faulkner knew from the inside out. We are seeing Flem as he looks to Mink as Mink looks back at Flem and assumes the power to narrate what Flem is looking at, "as though" his cousin's mind is as open to his view as his own is open to narration. Mink is never more sympathetic to his cousin—in a strictly novelistic sense, at least—than when he pulls the trigger.

But having seen Flem's death as it unfolds from Mink's perspective, we also know that even if he was murdered in slow motion, he really didn't have the time or chance to do things differently. This scene belongs to Mink as both the agent of the novel's culminating violence and as the consciousness that Faulkner's narration inhabits, giving us a version of Mink's own words as inner monologue ("*Hit's got to hit his face*") but more powerfully letting free indirect discourse decelerate the action so that we have language that Mink would never use himself qualifying and mediating his every move ("and pulled the trigger and rather felt than heard the dull foolish almost inattentive click"). We might not notice the way Mink tries to personify the gun—its "click" would not be "almost" but altogether "inattentive"—at the moment it misfires, had the narrative not paused to show us Mink catching himself in this mistake just milliseconds earlier. "*Hit's got to hit his face*," we read that Mink is "thinking," and then he backs up to think some more about what it means that, right now when it matters most, it's "not *I've got to* but *It's got to.*" Mink is too busy after the misfire and readying to kill Flem again to do more close reading of the language that the narrator is using to magnify each instant of this tawdry small-town murder—which will hardly bring an end to the Snopeses and what they represent—into a short epic of modernism at its most enduring and monumental. "Even back when they said man lived in caves," Faulkner writes once Mink is on the move again as the novel ends, "he would raise up a bank of dirt to at least keep him that far off the ground while he slept, until he invented wood floors to protect him and at last beds too, raising the floors story by story until they would be laying a hundred and even a thousand feet up in the air to be safe from the earth." Faulkner's own "stories" are also the expressions of this epoch of technology and progress, which sometimes feels like it is speeding out of control or maybe barely plodding forward. But we learn, in the same moment, that novels and other media can also go from zero to speeds beyond our own ability to perceive—and back again—and that this is what they have been doing, "story by story," for what Faulkner wants us to experience, in this brief episode, as "all the time of Man."[8]

13
Snopes at Rest

If we step back from these particular scenes and problems as Faulkner frames them in *The Mansion*, what comes into focus are three types of timelines—and the scales they register, the durations they represent—that each lay claim to capturing the experience of technological modernity. In late Faulkner, we see this network of ideas emerge with such striking clarity because he was already working in a retrospective mode that does not just look back to the past in the genre of historical fiction that he himself profoundly modernized but also broods over a series of questions—and nobody can brood like Faulkner—about the proper scale at which to picture different histories happening. This same project lets Faulkner imagine what it might mean to understand that some of the processes and transformations that seem to take place quickly in the modern world—the changes at high speed that symbolize the era—might actually feel slow or perhaps interminable when reckoned against greater, grander spans of time. And of course, all manner of inverse manipulations of the time axis are just as possible and, as we have seen, just as important to Faulkner's novels. Microscopic intervals become vast displays of violence, masculinity, introspection, physicality, and technology that expand into whole epochs of suspended narrative intensity that are nonetheless tamed by—and become more charged within—the stories that they punctuate. At his best, Faulkner often manages to achieve what, borrowing from Justus Nieland's work on modernism at scale, "fluidity of movement between microcosm and macrocosm."[1] But by the 1950s, Faulkner was not often at his best. The various slow motions that he explores—fraught and frozen seconds of concentrated fervor, the overlapping eras of industrial modernity and settler colonialism in the United States, "all the time of Man" in all its humanistic cliché—are thrown together anything but seamlessly, and the shifts of scale are rarely smooth.

At one point earlier in *The Mansion*, for example, the doomed affair of Linda and Gavin Stevens is figured against a ludicrously inflated span of centuries and millennia that, for a later modernist like Smithson, with his pretensions on geologic time, would provide the temporal leverage to evacuate all meaning from the very idea that at this late date in human history people are still going through these particular romantic motions. Faulkner, on the other hand, dives into the deep time of melodrama with abandon:

> "There,'" she said. "It's all right now. We were here. We saved it. Used it. I mean, for the earth to have come all this long way from the beginning of the earth, and the sun to have come all this long way from the beginning of time, for this one day and minute and second out of all the days and minutes and second, and nobody to use it, no two people who are finally together at last after all the difficulties and waiting, and now they are together at last and are desperate because of all the long waiting, they are even running along the beach toward where the place is, not far now, where they will finally be alone together at least and nobody in the world to know or care or interfere so that it's like the world itself wasn't except you so now the world that wasn't invented yet can begin."[2]

The sentiment is bald and bland. This is carpe diem on the order of cosmology, which doesn't so much modernize the rhetoric as demonstrate its good old-fashioned durability. It's an astonishing coincidence that Clair Cameron Patterson had just determined in 1956 the estimated age of the Earth to be roughly 4.5 billion years—which is effectively simultaneous at such vast scales with the publication of *The Mansion* in 1959. But even I am not historicist enough to suggest that this passage is somehow in communication with the highly technical findings based on the radiometric dating of meteors that Patterson used to push back the origins of the planet by more than a billion years in just a few pages.[3] The grammar of Linda's speech is challenging and abstruse enough in the dilations and inversions of time that it figures without using any big numbers. A single sentence carries us from a "beginning of time" that seems purposefully removed from any hint of human presence, with "no two people" in existence over the slowly passing, empty epochs that come down to these final seconds before Linda and Gavin can act on their desires. Or not, since what they pursue instead involves convoluted plotting and delay. She was always counting on Gavin's regret over failing to save her mother, Eula—or, as narrated at great lengths in *The Town*, to pursue his own attraction to her—in her plans for

Mink's early release and Flem's timely murder. Linda does not blame Gavin for Eula's sudden suicide, but she seems to know for years before any of the men in the Snopes trilogy that it provides the key to beating Flem once and for all. What Gavin does not quite realize—and what we as readers won't be able to puzzle out until the novel's ending—is that Linda has been playing the long game too, but proceeding so slowly that Stevens never sees it.

From the moment Linda Snopes returns to Jefferson in *The Town*, she represents a problem in the representation of motion. "She went past us still walking, striding, like the young pointer bitch," we read, "the maiden bitch of course, the virgin bitch." At one level, this language feels almost like a calculated effort at self-parody, with Stevens channeling the worst misogyny of Quentin Compson from *The Sound and the Fury* or Ike McCaslin from "The Bear." Yet Stevens still fancies himself a man of action too, and Linda will provide him with a chivalric second chance to save a woman from the machinations of Flem Snopes. "I need to reassure myself," is how Stevens puts it to himself and therefore to the reader, "that I also am Motion."[4] But this narration does not make it true, any more than Quentin can simply "say" his way to having committed incest. Gavin Steven is no Compson, and his intentions toward Eula and later Linda aren't as convoluted in their idealizing of female bodies for the purposes of subjugation. Stevens will, though, remain forever out of sync with any of the women he believes that he is serving with what are, for the most part, purely visual predations. He just can't seem to keep himself from watching. This makes him more than a little creepy, but in a fictional world full of truly monstrous men who commit travesties of racial privilege, sexual violence, and horrifying acts of both at once, the worst that we can say of Gavin Steven is that his primary scopophilia—a term I'm using to invoke Laura Mulvey as clearly as I can—means that he'll always be a step behind.

It's a few chapters before Stevens again has the chance to observe Linda in motion—as "Motion"—again as she walks by. The moment does not last long but still manages to deliver a concentrated dose of signifiers linked to high modernity and the history of cinema. And Faulkner avoids any mentions of meat or bitches, though this makes the character of Stevens's scrutiny only marginally less indecent:

> So when she passed rapidly across the plate-glass window, I didn't know her. Because she was approaching not from the direction of the school but from the opposite one, as though she were on her way to school, not from it. No: that was not the reason. She was already in the store now, rapidly, the screen clapping behind her at the same instant and in the same physical sense both running and

poised motionless, wearing not the blouse and skirt or print cotton dress above the flat-heeled shoes of school; but dressed, I mean "dressed," in a hat and high heels and silk stockings and makeup who needed none and already I could smell the scent: one poised split-second of immobilised and utter flight in bizarre and paradox panoply of allure, like a hawk caught by a speed lens.

Faulkner's syntax requires some untangling for us to know what, if anything, Linda is really wearing as Stevens gazes upon her, but there is no mistaking that she is moving "rapidly" since we're told so twice. This would be a fitting epithet, from Steven's point of view, because it seems obvious to him that Linda is already very "fast" for her young age. The repetitious references to Linda's speed might also operate as hesitations, like the "stuck" record on the Victrola in the store where Stevens is waiting to meet her that is playing "the same tune it was playing before." Her arrival lets Faulkner spin a medley of his greatest hits, mixing the heady smells of Linda's sexualized virginity with Steven's fascination with the idea of freezing her in time so as to save her from the lurid attention—chiefly his own, or so it seems—that is foreshortening her adolescence into adulthood and rendering her an object of male desire. The negations and double meanings put a stop to any reading of the scene that might go "rapidly." Linda has caught Stevens off guard; she's in the store "already" despite the fact that Stevens has been waiting for her. So Stevens strips her bare, at least rhetorically, and leaves her naked to his gaze. The intent is pornographic, though the language on the page is so circular and hazy that the impression that she makes is not so much erotic as it is effortful. But in trying to see through Linda's show of sexuality, Stevens reveals too much. He later frames himself as "what old Negroes called 'settled,' incapable now of harm," his blood "slowed" by time and his desires "untroubled . . . by turn of wrist or ankle."[5] We've seen otherwise. In the slow motion he manufactures out of flowery language and archaic sentiments, he is a real Peeping Tom.

All this is depressingly to form for Faulkner. By the late 1950s, he had been diagnosing the sexual and political pathologies of white southern men for as long as he had been chronicling the arc of Flem Snopes's career as capital made flesh. But as this excavation of *The Town* and *The Mansion* comes to an end, I don't want to look past another origin story of modernity and its media that Faulkner puts on full display. The "plate-glass window" that frames Linda's arrival in Steven's field of vision is a technology with a rich precinematic history from the arcades of Benjamin's Paris to the department stores in *Sister Carrie*; it is one of the most important objective correlatives for the "mobile virtual gaze" that Anne Friedberg famously explores as a central precursor, both materially and psychologically, to film spectatorship as such in the first years of the twentieth century.[6] Just as soon as Linda makes it into the store and we can see that she is "dressed" despite the flash of nudity that Stevens invites by cataloging what she is "wearing not," another of his senses seems like it is going to be provoked. Once she is close enough for Stevens to realize that she has put on makeup, it is a relief to know that he is talking about perfume. "I could smell the scent," Stevens confirms, and then immediately, he loses it. On the other side of the colon, we might expect a description of what, exactly, Stevens smells. Instead, we get a "poised split-second" that sets Linda in flight on the other end of a telephoto lens, too far away for Stevens to see with his lusty, naked eye—much less to catch her scent.

Faulkner is a writer who regularly indulges in the lushest olfactory details. In an interview from 1958, right between *The Town* and *The Mansion*, Faulkner offered that smell was "a sharper sense" with him than sight or hearing.[7] But probably not sharp enough, I'd venture, to catch the scent of the altogether visual and highly technological image that follows. For not only is it difficult to imagine how a "poised split-second of immobilized and utter flight" would smell, but the analogy that extends the metaphor is even more spectacularly distancing. High-speed photography in the 1950s could obviously capture the motion of an airborne hawk. In point of fact—though this is not the kind of historical specificity that Faulkner is known for—some of the first pictures that introduced the world to the motion photography of Etienne-Jules Marey, a famous precursor to cinema as we know it, were strips of images showing birds in flight. Marey used gulls and pelicans in his experiments of the late 1880s, but they wouldn't have smelled any differently since, at the risk of belaboring the "paradox" and diminishing its "panoply of allure," the image of a hawk "caught by a speed lens" is directed to a reader's sense of sight or perhaps not to any sense at all. Suddenly, at the very "split-second" when Linda is close enough to Stevens that he can get her scent, she is metaphorically released and loosed into the air. The shock of seeing Linda Snopes "already" as a woman—which is Stevens's fantasy made flesh—is too much for him in the instant, and so he tries to slow things down. Which then becomes a fast way to invoke an epoch of modernity and its media technologies from the perspective of an observer who realizes that there is maybe nothing he perceives without them.

My particular interest in the Snopes trilogy is neither a reevaluation of its merits as a novel nor an attempt to situate it alongside the much greater accomplishments of the 1930s that established Faulkner as arguably the preeminent modernist that America produced in the twentieth century. It is the sense of self-reflexivity that this stature earned him that lets him go on interminably, and occasionally with so much bombast, about the fate of "Man" in the abstract and about the experience of duration as a phenomenon of Black racial temporality that becomes more diffuse and ecumenical in the epic of Flem Snopes and his long-suffering antagonists. What does singularly mark these novels, however, is their preoccupation with slow change over time without the historical catastrophes that loom over many of his other novels. The Civil War and Reconstruction have receded into the deeper background of these fictions, which is, at one level, a sign that Faulkner was treading carefully around some of the questions of race that shaped his earlier novels. But on another level, novels like *The Town* and *The Mansion* pose a set of historical questions—in the form of the novel and, at times, in the language of visual media—that are perhaps just as significant and contemporary despite the unavoidable and indefensible fact that they turn away from race by letting its presence fade into a familiar background of minor characters and pervasive tropes. These are not his best fictions, but perhaps because they were among the last—coming at the beginning of a decade that would see other modernisms fade and falter—they are less invested in the events and transformations that make up the history and more with wondering about the long and short and slow and fast of change itself.

14
Remainder's Instant Replays

Slow motion, as we have seen repeatedly by now, has a history that is in part obscured by its contemporary prominence as a visual cliché in narrative cinema and also by the descriptive shorthand summoning this imagery across a wider cultural field. Faulkner is only one of several writers I am interested in whose references to slow motion do much more, I think, than just invoke it casually to suggest, returning to Sobchack, *"the movement of movement."* It is always worth remembering that even such fast citations of slow motion pay tribute to the appeal of its tautological lyricism—aestheticizing any and every physical action by rendering it technological. This would be a fairly cold and artificial way to describe the abiding subjects of Faulkner's fiction and feels like some particularly weak language to broach questions of white supremacy and Black freedom and the many ways the former tries, through overt and psychological violence, to deny the latter by way of violence, brutality, and sexual trauma. But in whatever terms we might use to stress different versions of his novel's themes—tenuous and gradual changes over centuries, tortured family romances of decline and suffering, racial trauma and the deformations of white identity—there is no denying that his project is entirely historical, both in its recurring constellation of significant events and shared experiences and in its brooding modes of scrutiny into how these larger contours of time come to shape the inner lives of human beings. Faulkner at his slowest still goes faster than the histories he slogs us through, which is, as Gerard Genette and others will help us see more clearly, only to confirm that most conventional written narratives—and for all the limits at which Faulkner pushes, he remains conventional enough in this respect—have a higher default velocity than we think. As "temporal close-ups," Faulkner often codes these scenes as interludes or fantasies of interrupted, blocked, or arrested progress, and, like Gavin Stevens's creepy gaze at Linda Snopes, they are often the province of white men who want to romanticize their power or indulge in their nostalgia for a past that would have granted them more status still. Yet as we should certainly have learned by now, slow motion is not the opposite of speed but rather an expression of its technologies in displaced and different iconographies. So the question really is: What else is going fast when Faulkner has us reading in slow motion?

We can start answering this question by looking at two contemporary novels that feature slow motion in utterly different contexts and emotional registers. In Tom McCarthy's celebrated 2005 novel *Remainder*, a narrator who is recovering from a traumatic event—and is now absurdly wealthy from the legal settlement it brought him—begins pursuing ever more elaborate and involving reenactments of chance meetings with strangers, mechanical mishaps, and, before the novel comes to its ecstatic end, violent crimes like bank robberies and hijackings that he himself is technically committing since only the narrator and his assistant, Naz, know that everything they're doing is still intended as a simulated version of what they're really doing. From scrupulous architectural installations to full-scale recreations of whole buildings and complex narrative scenarios, the novel's plot consists entirely of following the narrator as he spends his seemingly inexhaustible fortune on an escalating series of meticulous simulations of memories or events. Soon after it was published, Zadie Smith famously praised *Remainder* for representing one of "two paths for the novel" at the start of the twenty-first century—the preferred one, bracing and experimental instead of merely "realist"—and it has been equally admired by scholars fascinated with the theoretical problems of language, art, materiality, and media that get worked through in the black comedy of McCarthy's prose and the conceits that it pursues with astonishing relentlessness.[1] While Walter Benn Michaels sees *Remainder* as a reflection of the appeal of a materialist "literalism" that he traces back to some of the same debates between Michael Fried and Robert Smithson that we have already encountered—and will again—other critics have tended to appreciate McCarthy for all the ways he does "media archaeology," as Justus Nieland puts it, in the format of the realist novel or, as Christina Lupton argues, "an account of mediation" that tries to "make all text conceivable as the material impression left by one medium upon another."[2] The traces of film are especially visible in the novel, with the narrator's earliest memories of his compulsion for reenactment, even before the accident that erases much of what could otherwise be called a self, tied to an image of "walking down the street just like De Niro" in *Mean Streets*, and when his simulations become more baroque and comprehensive as they start to operate in locations in the city where the narrator wants them staged alongside, and finally as, versions of actuality, Naz tells him that to get permission for one reenactment to proceed, they'll need a license for a movie shoot since "the activity that it most closely resembled is filming." This is just a bureaucratic ruse—a sign of Naz's demonic aptitude for "logistics"—since the narrator has, from the very beginning of his experiments, insisted that nothing should be photographed or filmed.[3] Still, as N. Katherine Hayles suggests, a side effect of whatever injury the narrator has suffered is that now his consciousness "is free to carry out its own version of time manipulation . . . as if reality was being screened inside his head as a slow-motion film."[4] In the increasingly precise scenarios that the narrator pays more and more reenactors to perform, this is the speed at which he wants everyone to go. After several repetitions of a drive-by murder, the narrator decides that the best way to get at "what was inside, intimate" to the action is to run it "at half speed." This lets him perceive how "in this instant, this sub-instant" the victim would have "developed" a "full-blown understanding that they'd come to kill him," while at the same vanishingly short time "he would have pictured the space behind the windows" through which he wasn't able to escape. The language of photography seems almost incidental here ("developed," "pictured," "full-blown" as if the narrator is "blowing up" an image), but I doubt it is given the degree of control that McCarthy exercises in respect to every utterance of his maniacally controlling narrator. And while Benjamin and his notion of an "optical unconscious" does not seem to figure among the media theories that McCarthy has explicitly championed in interviews, the slow-motion sequences in *Remainder* soon turn into "enlargements" or "temporal close-ups" that have the narrator telling his reenactors to "slow it down," to go through the motion "as slow as it can be," "so slowly that each instant . . . each instant as though it could expand—you understand?—and be . . . if each instant was—well, that bit doesn't matter; you don't have to know that." As a local official says of the narrator near the novel's end—just after cataloging the "one hundred and twenty actors" and "five hundred and eleven props" that have been used for something that resembles, but is absolutely not, a "filming"—"this is the man who has had set up a building in which certain mundane, and, on the surface, meaningless moments are repeated and prolonged until they assume an almost sacred aspect." By this point, though, the aura of his slow-motion reenactments is already withering for the narrator. His last reenactment is a real-time bank robbery in the actual bank that he and Naz are using for the performance, which is so authentic that it leaves several actually dead and wounded. "Their fall was long and slow," the narrator observes, "I watched it buckle like a giraffe's legs do in old films when the giraffe has been shot by hunters." Watching bodies tumble, the narrator becomes the incarnation of the "speed lens" that Gavin Stevens only plays at being: "His neck seemed to move the other way—to contraflow, its flesh wrinkling back in waves towards his shoulders. It looked like the crumple zones they build into the fronts of modern cars."[5]

In a 2014 essay, McCarthy describes the end of J. G. Ballard's *Crash* as showing us the "sudden intercession of the catastrophic real."[6] The narrator's attention to the intricate physical details and microtemporalities of violence could well be a nod toward Ballard and his amazingly clinical accounts of wounded bodies, traumas, and eruptions of brutality. On the other hand, the narrator is likening what he sees to such a generic style of twentieth-century iconography that we don't need the possible allusion to get the picture. The first crash test dummy was the invention of Samuel Alderson in 1949; the popularity of the original that Alderson named "Sierra Sam," along with improved versions designed by Mercedes Benz and General Motors, eventually allowed automotive engineers to stop using human corpses in the "accidents" they staged to assess the safety of new vehicles. Versions of GM's Hybrid I and Hybrid II starred in countless public service announcements made by the U.S. Department of Transportation to raise seatbelt awareness beginning in the 1970s, and the Hybrid III—which was released in 1997 and came in more sizes, body types, and ages—remains the industry standard today, with improved sensors and a digital anatomy that can transmit impact information at the very moment that it happens.[7] This is not the sort of data that would interest the narrator of *Remainder* by the time he is watching things go horribly wrong in the actual bank robbery that he thinks he's reenacting. His investment in the events that he turns into slow motion is purely—indeed, transcendently—aesthetic. The accomplices he knows as "Two" and "Four" might be real to him, which is why he is enraptured by how "the whole scene went static" as if it "had been slowed down so much that we'd come to a standstill."[8] But he does not see them as especially human and feels less for their imminent deaths—"the only thing that moved was a deep red flow coming from Four's chest"—than we're supposed to feel for the two dummies, "Vince" and "Larry," who were finally named in dozens of award-winning safety ads in the 1980s and 1990s. They were donated to the National Museum of American History in 2010 and honored at a ceremony that had two live reenactors dressed in the familiar jumpsuits and black-and-yellow warning strip accessories that identified their respective characters.[9] The narrator of *Remainder*, though, is not out to learn a lesson or even get off on the carnage like one of Ballard's variously willing or reluctant perverts. At the sight of "Four" bleeding out onto the carpet, his reaction is simple and, within the logic of the novel, utterly sincere. "'Beautiful!' I whispered": We have to take him at his word. As Michaels argues, *Remainder* is about "taking a world where nothing is meant and turning it into a world where everything is."[10] Slow motion literally makes more meaning possible, or meaning more possible, which is not quite the same thing but almost good enough.

But meaning isn't cheap in *Remainder*, and I'm not even talking about the body count that strikes the narrator's aesthetic fancy or all the work his reenactors do along the way to play out his scenarios and fantasies. "The people we'd hired," the narrator explains, "were being paid vast amounts of money." The narrator's compulsions don't extend to bookkeeping, and so we're spared a full account of what he spends on designers, architects, builders, electricians, plumbers, actors, security guards, site managers, gardeners, props and wardrobe, hair and makeup; giant cranes, refrigerators, pianos, trucks, and vans; buildings, warehouses, and real estate across London. *Remainder* is enough of a realist novel to give us these impossibly expensive lists but not so naturalistic that it wants us to keep a running total of what the narrator has left of the gigantic settlement that lets him put his plans in motion. As a satire of the original dotcom bubble, the novel reminds us more than once that the narrator's capital is growing at a pace that outstrips his most exorbitant desires. The narrator must sell four million pounds of stocks to buy the building that he turns into his first theater of full-scale reenactments. "The amazing thing, though," he learns almost immediately, is that his "portfolio had risen back almost to the level it had been before he'd sold the shares" in just a couple weeks. His accountant tells him that "the technology and telecommunications sectors are experiencing a boom just now" and while the narrator might risk a measure of "exposure" if he doesn't also pursue "diversification," this financial jargon is supposed to sound completely empty and unreal. Thus the narrator, who is nothing if not materialist, instead conceives of his money "like yoghurt . . . or a lizard's tail, that grows back if you yank it off." The firm he hires to produce his reenactments is portentously called "Time Control," but the services they sell are just as pointedly abstract and vague. "They're a company that sort things out for people. Manage things. Facilitators, as it were." The narrator gets what he paid for, and Time Control delivers on the symbolic promise that McCarthy all but spills onto the page like the exploding "blue liquid gush" of the window-wiper malfunction that inspires a dramatic escalation in his reenactments. He is already immersed in a version of slow motion as movements "mesmerize" him, "like a bird charmed by a snake" as he watches the "gliding clamps, the gushing blue—monotonously, hypnotic, endlessly repeating."[11] The scene is happening at normal speed for the reenactors that the narrator employs and for us as readers, too, if we think about the raw sensory footage, so to speak, that he is slowing down—an organic feat of speed ramping that means the narrator is perceiving at an accelerated rate. He sees as fast as high-speed photography, which is impressive until you realize that his capital must be going up in value almost infinitely faster.

15
Austerlitz's Traumatic Pauses

In *Remainder*, the narrator's giddy aestheticism is the opposite of a historical sensibility, though McCarthy provides the novel with more than enough period details, technological motifs, and financial jargon to frame it as a story of the early twenty-first century. What the narrator pursues with amoral compulsion and economic abandon is a world experienced in short loops of endlessly repeatable scenarios that are not quite narratively coherent but legible in their respective genres (leaving the building, the mechanical mishap, the drive-by shooting, the bank robbery). If the narrator didn't have money to burn, he could have tried to get his fix with anonymous videos on YouTube or, today, TikTok. The production design and sets might not be up to his high standards, and he would sorely miss the physicality of his exquisite reenactments. But at least he could watch on repeat forever—and at any speed he wanted. *Remainder* is not exactly about digital media; as Lupton proves, the novel is devoted to exploring the "temporal extension" of objects in the phenomenal world and to the particular magic made possible by works of fiction as material relays "between paper to imagination and back again."[1] Still, it's hard for me to imagine *Remainder* apart from how it captures a specific cultural and economic moment—defined by the fantasy of the "technology and telecommunications sectors" going boom forever—that the novel studies with inhuman neutrality.

If we want to see what slow motion looks like when portrayed with a maximum of historical motivation and brooding melancholy, no recent novel takes it more seriously than W. G. Sebald's *Austerlitz* (2001), which is also set against "the dissolution, in line with the inexorable spread of processed data, of our capacity to remember." The story of a Jewish refugee raised in Wales after escaping the Nazi occupation of Czechoslovakia as part of the *kindertransport* that brought thousands of children to the United Kingdom, there is little about the history of the modern world that the novel doesn't worry over with deep shows of ethical self-consciousness: the design of European railroad stations, the architectural traces in Antwerp of Belgian atrocities in the Congo, the theaters of Prague and other cosmopolitan outposts of the fading Austro-Hungarian Empire, the stark emotional terrain of provincial Britain in the 1940s, the dysfunctional Cold War rationality of the Bibliothèque Nationale, and more, all of which evoke for Sebald's protagonist "the vortex of past time" that weighs down not only his personal history and the era that determines it but also the longer geological durations that he senses even as a child when "he used to walk beside the cliffs of Devon and Cornwall, where hollows and basins have been carved and cut out of the rock by the breakers over millions of years." This is a novel where, as Austerlitz says of Antwerp-Centraal station, "time ... represented by the hands and dial of the clock, reigns supreme among the emblems."[2] If slow motion in *Remainder* accesses the stupid pleasures of generic violence in the delirious choreography of material reality perceived in microintervals of time, in *Austerlitz* there is nothing funny about it: Slow motion is the media aesthetic of Sebald's moody reflections on human suffering and alienation. The crash-test dummy PSAs and action cinema that pattern the visual sensorium of McCarthy's narrator have no place in Sebald's older world of nostalgia and refinement. The narrator of *Remainder* might appreciate the rippling, churning flesh of a Zach Snyder movie or the overwrought car crash montage in *Death Proof* (2007); it's hard to imagine anyone in *Austerlitz* seeing such a spectacle and not worrying how much that must have hurt. For Sebald, slow motion is a historical aesthetic because it's very painful.

As every reader of the novel will remember, Austerlitz's research into the circumstances of his mother's death leads him to the surviving footage of an infamous propaganda film that Nazi officials had made at Theresienstadt in 1944. Its script and direction were supervised by Jewish prisoners at the camp, which had been staged as a benign resettlement community for a Red Cross inspection in 1943. Soon after the film was finished, its director Kurt Garron and many others who contributed to the production were sent to the gas chambers at Auschwitz. While conceived as part of an elaborate program to mask the ongoing atrocities of the Holocaust as the end of the war in Europe became inevitable, the film itself was never widely screened and then was lost in Prague in 1945, with around twenty minutes of fragments from the original feature-length version eventually discovered in different film archives and libraries. In the novel, Austerlitz watches a videocassette of the film in London's Imperial War

Museum, where he soon realizes not only that he is unable to recognize any figure in the footage who looks like his mother but that there is probably little chance of seeing her because, to his "horror," the video copy is "only a patchwork of scenes cobbled together and lasting some fourteen minutes" and consisting of "scarcely more than an opening sequence." "However hard I strained to make her out among those fleeting faces," he confesses to the narrator, he is confronted instead with the "impossibility of seeing anything more closely in those pictures, which seemed to dissolve even as they appeared."[3] Sebald's preoccupation with photography and other visual media has, not surprisingly, been of major interest to many of his critics.[4] Among Sebald's readers, Ross Posnock is by far the best at capturing the strange temporality of the photographs and film stills in *Austerlitz*. They are there, as Posnock writes, to challenge "our assumption that documentary images yield clarity and possess a privileged veracity." As in all of Sebald's fiction, he continues, "the photographs are uncaptioned, uncredited, untethered to source or fact, often blurry or enigmatic or askew; above all they slow down the reader, at once inviting and frustrating and prolonging looking."[5]

These concerns loom over *Austerlitz* with particular insistence because the novel, as Sebald himself admitted, reflected the influence of Barthes's *Camera Lucida* in many of its themes but also in the drive that shapes its spare but haunting plot as Austerlitz becomes increasingly determined to manifest a picture of his dead mother—a version of the momentous "Winter Garden" image we never see in *Camera Lucida* but that punctuates Barthes's grief. Sebald renders this complicated process of epistemological reflection, cognitive estrangement, and mediated reverie literal at the level of technology. Since there is not enough of the lost film of Theresienstadt for Austerlitz to find his mother, he effectively makes more of it by deciding to have "a slow-motion copy of this fragment made," one which "would last a whole hour" but is best captured in the single grainy still that Austerlitz produces of the woman that he believes to be his mother (figure 15.1). Much of the slow motion that Austerlitz recounts for the narrator pushes toward abstraction—though not the "deep abstraction" that he lapses into later as he tells his story. Slow motion turns the Theresienstadt footage into "patterns of bright white sprinkled with black" and transposes the music meant to inoculate the camp's brutality—light opera from Offenbach, some passages of Mendelssohn's *Midsummer Night's Dream*—into noises from "the most nightmarish depths . . . to which no human voice has ever descended."[6] At one level, the irony is obvious: The slow-motion horror show of Austerlitz's copied copy is cinematic realism, an *actualité* against all odds that reveals the tortured intentionality not only of

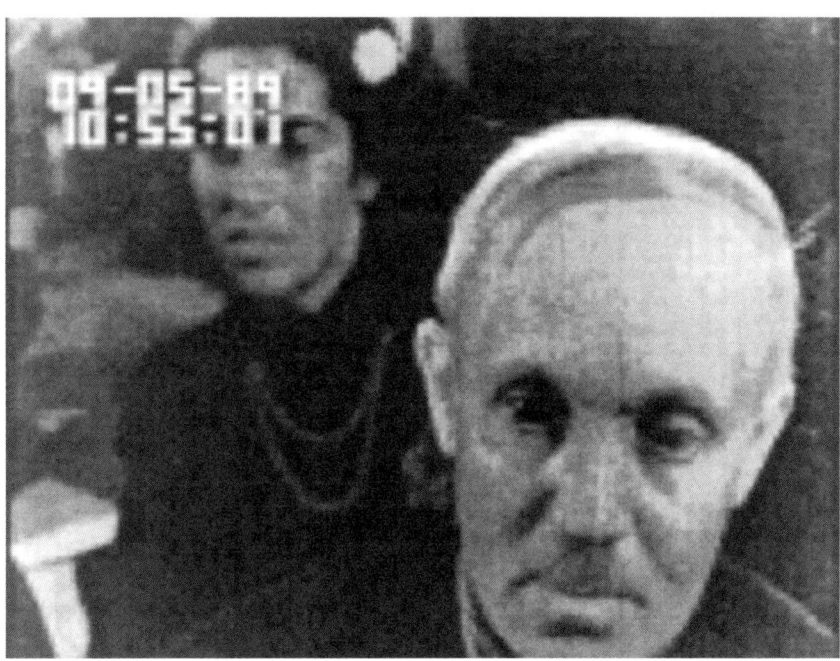

FIGURE 15.1 A time-stamped image of the Holocaust from Sebald's *Austerlitz*.

the camp but also of the Jewish filmmakers who will be murdered by their executive producers.

But we also have to ask: What does Austerlitz manage to see in this "too close" detail that he hadn't seen before?[7] He doesn't see his mother, at least not in any way that would count as proof within the fiction of his life history. The image that finally transfixes him is not exactly—or, better, not only—a photograph, despite the ease with which most critics and readers use this term for the vast majority of the illustrations in *Austerlitz* and Sebald's other novels. It's not exactly a film still either, though in keeping with Barthes's spirit as it hovers above the text, it is an image that has been isolated from a cinematic sequence and then slowed down until it stops for good, at which point, as Sebald perhaps learned from *Camera Lucida*, it turns into something else. But what Barthes would argue and what Austerlitz would seem to confirm is that these transformations can be quite emotional and also that there are certain feelings that remain distressingly medium specific. "Cinema is protensive," Barthes writes in *Camera Lucida*, by which he means it is necessarily extended toward the future, one image following another even in the slowest motion. Cinema is "in no way melancholic" because it is "sustained by the presumption that, as Husserl says, 'the experience will constantly continue to flow by in the same constitutive style.'" The problem, in short, is "flow" itself, the sense of momentum at whatever speed that makes film, for Barthes, "simply 'normal,' like life."[8] Who would ever choose to be on the 'normal' side of Barthes's devastating scare quotes? We look at photographs to find the "punctums" that evoke an overflow of affect and emotion, that figure the deepest and most otherwise unsayable meanings of a still image. Everything in film, however, devolves onto convention and mechanical routine. Every film, for Barthes, is at some level just going through the motions.

The screenshot in *Austerlitz* is technically a still, but the "excessive, monstrous mode" that Barthes finds in the way photography immobilizes time looks different when the image can't escape, much less transcend, all the traces of its prior formats and versions in other media. Slow motion at its slowest—as the very opposite of the moving image we experience as film—might be able to produce "the stasis of an *arrest*," to borrow again from Barthes, but it still isn't quite a photograph. It could not be plainer on the face that's not his mother: "09-05-89 / 10:55:01." "I run the tape back repeatedly, looking at the time indicator in the top left-hand corner of the screen," he tells the narrator, "where the figures covering part of her forehead show the minutes and seconds, from 10:53 to 10:57, while the hundredths of a second flash by so fast that you cannot read and cannot capture them."[9] As Austerlitz brings this part of his story to an end, all that slow motion shows him is more speed.

"A return to cinema's past," Mulvey writes in *Death 24x a Second*, "constitutes a gesture toward a truncated history, to those aspects of modernist thought, politics and aesthetics that seemed to end before their use or relevance could be internalized or exhausted." It might not be easy to find critics who would agree with Mulvey that modernism somehow died too young or wasn't granted enough time for us to reckon with its possibilities and consequences. Or, looked at differently, the problem Mulvey has with modernism's overly abrupt sense of an ending is that, having died, it won't now go away. "A return to the past of cinema is paradoxically facilitated by the kind of spectatorship that has developed with the use of new technologies," according to the process she details, "with the possibility of returning to and repeating a specific film fragment ... interrupting the flow of film, delaying its progress, and, in the process, discovering cinema's complex relation to time." Just in case her tone does not convey the full sweep of her argument, let me observe how Mulvey takes us from the scene of rewatching a particular sequence in a single film to an interruption in the "flow" of the medium as such and its institutions in the abstract. Yet almost as soon as Mulvey discovers in "return and repetition"—which are, of course, at the hard core of Austerlitz's way of watching movies, too—that cinematic time might register and encode an experience of modernity that has been cut short before we had a chance to see it to the end, she admits that we've already seen enough. "Needless to say, there is nothing fundamentally new here" since, as she will go on to demonstrate at length, "to see cinema through delay is to see a cinema that has always been there." "Delayed cinema" becomes for Mulvey a kind of symbol for a twentieth century that doesn't really come into its own until the 1920s (with Dziga Vertov's *Man with a Movie Camera*) and is already over by the 1970s, and while she is not, as I noted earlier, much interested in slow motion as a stylistic device or directorial technique, she is, like Sebald, intensely fascinated by "the actual act of slowing down the flow of film." As a filmmaker, Mulvey certainly did not have to wait for VCRs or DVDs to watch a movie slowly. Her landmark writings of the 1970s are predicated on the sort of scrupulous and exacting immersion in the material practice of film analysis that came with access to celluloid prints and editing stations. Yet even Mulvey insists that she was caught off guard by her belated discovery that the widespread proliferation of these viewing practices—cheap and easy enough for an amateur like Austerlitz to master in the 1990s—was in fact a version of ground zero for the medium she loved, a catastrophe that had already happened because it had been happening all along. In a bit of dry understatement both regal and devastating, Mulvey realizes that "there is a loose parallel here with Freud's concept of deferred action (*nachtraglichkeit*), the way the unconscious preserves a specific experience, while its traumatic effect might only be realized by another, later, but associated, event."[10]

Mulvey's trauma is not Austerlitz's, but like the spectacular twentieth-century destruction that Sebald catalogs—a destruction that prevents Austerlitz himself from progressing through a twentieth century that never moves past the Holocaust that he escapes—it becomes uniquely visible in slow motion. In this spirit, I would like to point out that the slow motion in *Austerlitz* is as much a video artifact from sometime in the 1990s as it is a damaged trace of the Holocaust from 1943. Mulvey also cautions us against seductively simple expressions of a "determinism inherent in the image of a void before the 'before' and the 'after' of an era that [has] suddenly ended," and while she is talking about Godard's *Histoire(s) du cinema* and their own wild experiments in archival fetishization and hybrid cinematic form, her comments are particularly useful for reminding us that *Austerlitz* was written at the end of the same "transitional period of the 1980s and '90s" when new media—like videotape, now fully obsolete—were thought to be displacing cinema, whose aura has been much slower to fade despite the waning of its connection to the materiality of photography on celluloid. If slow motion can make a few microseconds in a library basement feel like the unfolding of the entire twentieth century, we should not be shocked to see that other writers besides Sebald are drawn to it as a way of figuring the experience of modernity. Though as Faulkner might remind us, there are some aspects of modernity that must be endured for longer, as if the forces putting them in motion are all but timeless. Maybe the problem with the modern world is not that, as Faulkner famously pronounced, "the past is never dead. It's not even the past." The past might be the past and could be dying—just not fast enough for us to see or know without some help from the technologies that bury it but also keep it going in the meantime.

16
Being in Racial Time

Daughters of the Dust

There are other histories in slow motion besides those that Faulkner and Sebald track across the long arcs of their fictions. As we have seen, slow motion gave Faulkner a figurative language for organizing some of his most acute fixations: the heady aesthetics of Romantic temporality; the grinding politics of underdevelopment and peripheral modernization; the stubborn psychologies of social power as lived for generations; the almost imperceptible gradations of catastrophe that capitalism introduces along with, of course, the all-but-inescapable spectacles of change and destruction that are just as essential to its character; and how each of these elements of, and influences on, U.S. experience in the twentieth century are necessarily shaped and patterned by ideas of race that have timelines of their own that variously parallel, lag, and anticipate the different logics of modernity that Faulkner tracks. At the same time—a phrase that maybe here must take on more weight than it can bear—as Jussi Parikka insists, the only way to account for the consequences of our own modernity is to think through both "the slow duration of deep times but also the accelerated microtemporalities" that govern the economic practices and systems of the twenty-first century.[1] The present, he suggests, is equally defined by two opposite dynamics: acceleration, deceleration. But we don't need to leave the twentieth century to start seeing things in slow motion that Faulkner couldn't.

In the opening shot of Julie Dash's *Daughters of the Dust* (1991), we see an image that is utterly mysterious in the film's narrative but an explicit illustration of its title. After a brief series of short texts identifying the Gullah communities of South Carolina and Georgia as the film's subject—ending with an intertitle stressing how physical isolation helped Gullah remember "much of what their ancestors brought with them from Africa"—we fade into a severe and shallow close-up showing a pair of open hands that hold small piles of brown dirt as a breeze disperses them from the viewer's left to right. The framing is tight, and the focus is shallow. The background looks near but has been left a blurry field of earth tones that contrast with the brighter oranges and browns that distinguish the visual field of the woman, her dress, her hands, and the "dust" this "daughter" is setting free or giving up. Much later, a voiceover will establish that these hands belong to Nana, the matriarch of the extended Peazant family facing the allure of the modern world in 1902 and preparing, save for some holdouts, to leave the Georgia island and site of Ibo Landing that they've known as home for generations: "How can we plant in this dust?" she asks in a flashback of the same shot that starts the film. What we are witnessing in this poetic image—complete with wind effects on the movie's soundtrack—is a small diaspora that might involve only a "handful" of individuals but that is irrevocable. Once adrift in the north or cast onto the mainland, this small collectivity won't be easy to reassemble or hold onto. Then again, as the very ground from which the Peazants came is seen to blow away—their "peasant" traditions going everywhere as the forces of modernization appear—this might also be a picture of how they will endure. The Gullah, we read in the film's first intertitle, maintained their culture into the twentieth century "as a result of their isolation," but this culture also, as Dash's film lovingly details, is defined by African survivals of language, folklore, and both native West African and Muslim religious practices. All this has somehow managed to outlive the Middle Passage, slavery, and Jim Crow. It feels premature—and against the spirit of the film's own vibrancy and inventiveness—to say we're seeing a whole way of life just going with the wind. The Peazants will not be here forever. Traces of their culture will soon be circulating to parts unknown, at speeds they have never had to comprehend. "Movement into a new environment," Edward Said writes in his famous essay "Traveling Theory," "is never unimpeded."[2] On the other hand, we all know that dust gets everywhere.

It should probably come as no surprise that a film made in 1991 and released in 1992 would employ slow motion more or less at will; there are roughly a dozen slow-motion sequences in *Daughters of the Dust*, and most of them translate simple gestures or common physical activities into heightened instants of lyrical resplendence or poetic grace. By the early 1990s, slow motion had already achieved such saturation that it would be ridiculous to associate its prominence in Dash's film with any of the period's other highly stylized examples drawing both on the influence of the New American Cinema and on the dubious "MTV aesthetic" that was said to privilege "gloss, atmospherics, and camerawork."[3]

Daughters of the Dust makes for a strange addition to the period's slow-motion canon of films like Tony Scott's *Top Gun* (1986), where Maverick and Ice spend some free time in a game of deliriously distended volleyball on a beach that is truly a world away from Ibo Landing, and though *Daughters of the Dust* features several scenes of characters walking with a familiar aura of somber deceleration, there's no mistaking them for the petty criminals that stride through the credits of Tarantino's *Reservoir Dogs* (1992), which debuted at Sundance one year after Dash's landmark. Spike Lee's most characteristically showy trick is the double dolly shot, but he uses slow motion in *Do the Right Thing* (1989) when Mookie throws the garbage can through the window of Sal's Pizzeria and starts the riot that is retribution for Radio Raheem's murder. The elaborate lexicon of slow-motion techniques devised by Wong Kar-Wai for *Chunking Express* (1994), working with his cinematographer Christopher Doyle, remains as varied and compelling as anything done since, with countless sequences of shimmering step printing and others where the actors themselves were coached to move with excruciating slowness so that they would appear to drag and hesitate in front of background action going faster in the same frame. These parallels are deliberately scattershot and speculative, but they help us see that *Daughters of the Dust* is remarkably self-conscious about the different speeds of progress as it happens and about the various technologies that mediate its many forms. Some of which go very fast, while others that are just as modern barely move at all.

By the time Dash acquired the financing to shoot *Daughters of the Dust* in 1991, she had been interested in her father's Gullah heritage for nearly twenty years. At about this same period in her career, she studied at the American Film Institute with the Czech New Wave director Jan Kadar and with Slavko Vorkapich, whose montage of fast cuts and interpolated slow motion in *What Price Hollywood?* was, as we have seen, a signal moment in the history of Hollywood's embrace of the effect. His biography lets us track slow motion from the European avant-garde and modernism in the 1920s to the Hollywood studio system at practically the heights of its prestige and power as an industrial system for making movies and then to Dash as a figure whose career in the 1970s and 1980s reveals how some of the stylistic innovations of the New American Cinema entered the language of mainstream film almost effortlessly, while the racial politics of the film industry were so slow to change that they were effectively frozen into place. But it is not as if Dash would have needed to "learn" slow motion from Vorkapich, Kadar (whose 1971 *Adrift* features a bit of very period-specific, soft-core, slow-motion erotica), or any other single film or director. Dash's shooting script for *Daughters of the Dust* only marks two sequences for "SLOW MOTION," which suggests that at least some of the film's much more elaborate use of the effect resulted from her collaboration, on location and in production, with her cinematographer Arthur Jafa.[4] Calvin Tomkins says that it was Jafa, then also married to Dash, who rented the two 35mm cameras on which the film was shot, as well as a computer that "allowed him to weave together normal-motion and slow-motion footage."[5]

This is hardly a complete account of how *Daughters of the Dust* managed its frequent interludes and passages in slow motion, but it does at least start to explain why there are two distinctive kinds of slow motion used throughout. The first shot of the film and many others that employ slow motion—particularly those sequences that depict the ghostly future presence of the unborn child of Eula and Eli who is its narrating voice—have the stutter and blur that comes from step printing, when individual frames photographed at normal speed are then printed multiple times in editing to produce sequences of images that hesitate and jump as they proceed at their decelerated pace. But there are other moments in the film where slow motion has the characteristic ease and smoothness of action photographed at higher frame rates. We can see these two slow motions side by side in a fraught sequence early in the film. When Eli has a violent outburst that functions as the overt physical expression of his anguish over Eula's rape—the prophetic child whose presence haunts and charms the film is the product of this trauma—he attacks a bottle tree with a large board and sends shattered glass across the screen, the sheer materiality of his destructive rage made more graphic by its distention. This might be the most straightforward, even clichéd instance of slow motion in *Daughters of the Dust*: Manifesting male pain, from Penn and Dennis Hopper to Peckinpah and Leone, is perhaps the ultimate expression of slow motion's use-value in the films of the late sixties that codify its place in Hollywood. But Dash and her editors Joseph Burton and Amy Carey intercut the rising frenzy of Eli's rampage with shots of Eula writhing in the turmoil of her predicament (figure 16.1). This slow-motion diptych is strictly composed of formal and dramatic oppositions. Eli's violence is directed at the bottle tree, and the bursts of broken glass that accompany his exertions are conspicuous displays of the emotions that Nana has, just moments earlier, told him he must accept to move past Eula's trauma. Eula's distress is frantically stylized, almost as if she herself is suffering from Eli's blows as they are unleashed. He is out in the yard and lashing out; she is inside and absorbing still more punishment.

The manners in which they are respectively in slow motion are decidedly distinct. Jafa appears to have filmed Adisa Anderson, the actor playing Eli, at 48 frames per second, and the lighting on set is noticeably more intense and artificial to compensate for shorter exposure times. But when we see Eula,

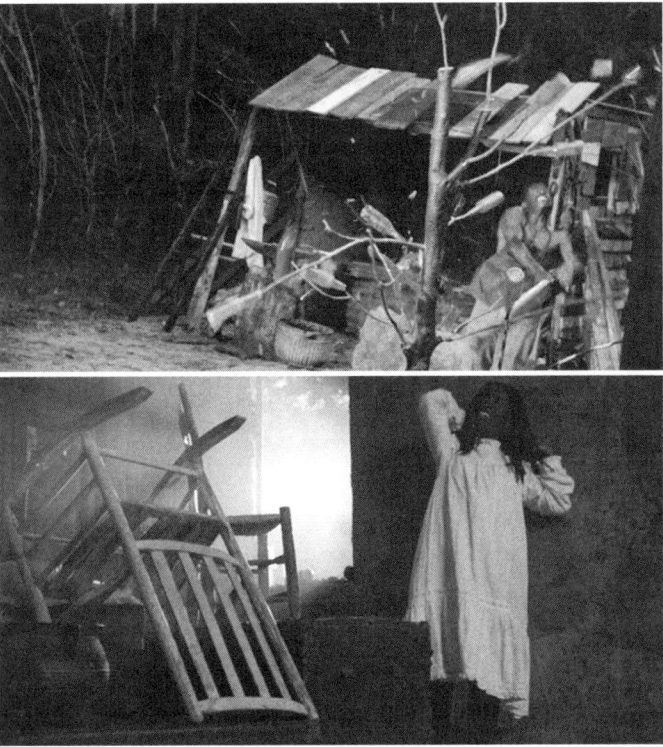

FIGURE 16.1 Slow motion and step printing in two stills from *Daughters of the Dust* (1991).

played by Alva Rogers, turn her back against the cabin wall and then roll in agony as she strains against the artificial wind that blows her dress, the action has the characteristic stuttering flow of step printing, which suggests that at least some of the scene was not filmed for slow motion but rather manufactured later in the production process. That the film shows us the difference between Eli's slow-motion tantrum and other slow-motion raptures that we witness at Ibo Landing is a measure of how seriously Dash and Jafa were willing to take it as not just a flashy signature of avant-garde style or aesthetic seriousness but as a device for registering a world of racial times that had never quite before been pictured in the history of film. *Daughters of the Dust* is also in slow motion from the beginning because it is an allegory of media technology and the modernity it both harbingers and that some people are asked to wait for longer than others—so long, Dash seems to wonder, that it begins to look like modernity is defined by its delays, distensions, and deliberate retardations.

Any version of Gullah culture that exists in 1902, the film makes clear, is already an artifact of deep modernity, a mix of West African tribal practices with Islam brought into New World contact with indigenous and Creole traditions and then recombined within a matrix of European domination and white supremacy. While the oldest forms of Gullah life are slowly vanishing—Nana Peazant's folkways, Bilal Muhammad's Islamic survivals—Dash strenuously counters the projection of anachronism or, in Johannes Fabian's more knotty terminology, the "denial of coevalness" that Western anthropologists devised with the professionalization of the discipline to frame the temporalities of non-Western or subaltern peoples as always following, at a manufactured distance, the Anglo-American horizons of modernity that are figured as the present's bleeding edge.[6] With the specter and consequences of white violence never far from Ibo Landing, this is one of the few occasions when this visceral metaphor of media culture might be truly justified.

Within the fiction of the film itself, however, an archaeology of new media does not so much reveal a traumatic break with the past as it does a gradual procession of technologies that share the present and extend its possibilities, if only formally. The fascination with the prehistory of cinema in *Daughters of the Dust* is not as dizzying as that in another film released in the same year, Francis Ford Coppola's wildly gothic adaptation of *Bram Stoker's Dracula* (1992), but it still manages to produce a version of its argument: that modern media might be inventions that depend on scientific rationality and its advances but that they also speak to and embody older systems of representation that, in their sheer persistence over time, appear increasingly uncanny in the present. We see the "Unborn Child" initially running in step-printed slow motion—an answer to Nana's prayer who gets there "just in time" after the torments that Eli and Eula have suffered in slow motion—in a long shot that frames her as the only moving thing against a minimalist landscape of faded grays and sandy browns that have been overexposed to almost white (figure 16.2). She will manifest again at several moments in the film, serving as its off-screen narrator and invisible to the other characters until she shows up in a picture (figure 16.3). A photographer from the mainland, Mr. Snead, is brought to document the Peazant family in a series of formal portraits. The Unborn Child magically appears among the men of Ibo Landing even though neither the photographer nor his subjects are able to see her. She becomes visible only through the imposition of the antique viewfinder Dash puts in the frame, linking this image to an era before cinema—it is both technically and symbolically a picture full of ancestors—and making for an exquisite invocation of modernist self-referentiality. Snead's boxy wooden camera makes him a comic stand-in for Boris Kaufman in Vertov's *Man with a*

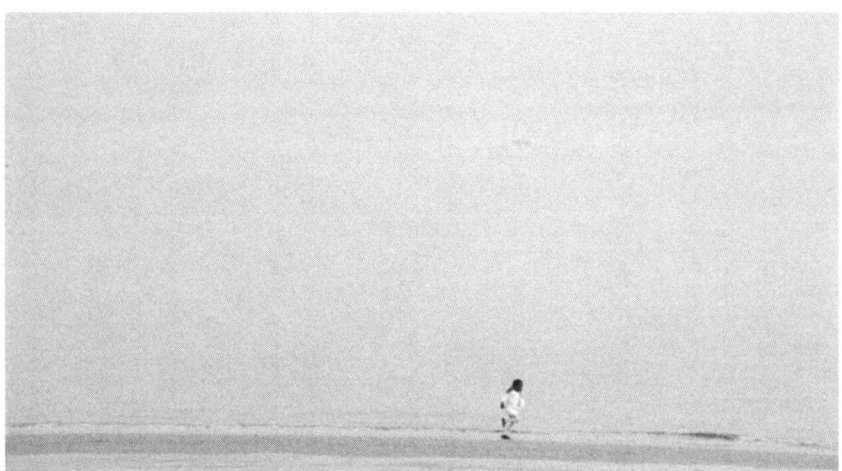

FIGURE 16.2 Still from *Daughters of the Dust* (1991).

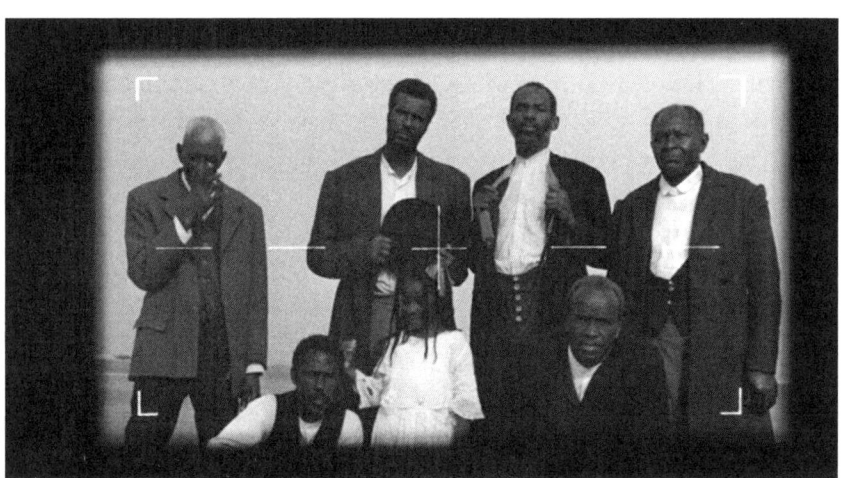

FIGURE 16.3 Still from *Daughters of the Dust* (1991).

Movie Camera, an icon of the Russian avant-garde that almost certainly Dash knew well.

Modernity has also come to Ibo Landing as entertainment and diversion (figure 16.4), with someone from the mainland having brought a stereoscope along with a few newspapers to help the children of the island pass the time while waiting for the family to assemble on the beach. With Nana's voiceover remembering

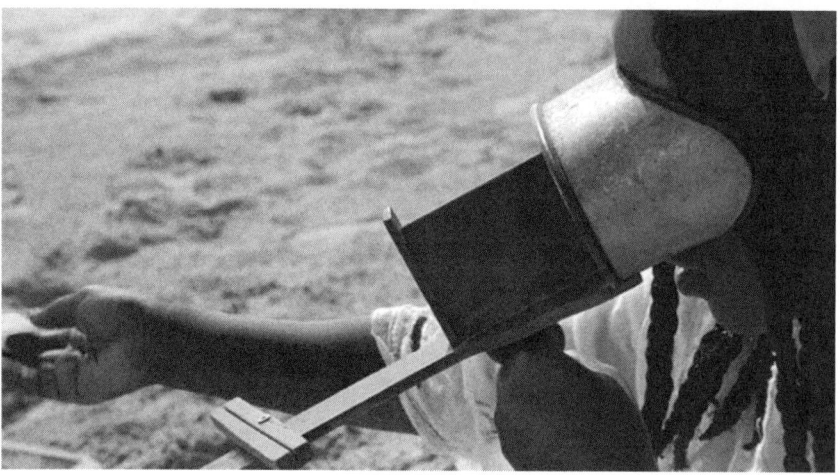

FIGURE 16.4 Still from *Daughters of the Dust* (1991).

an elder who, when she was dying, had the look of "Africa in her face," we cut to a girl looking into a stereoscope, which is less a negation of Nana's backward glance and more a fitting symbol of the multiple historical dimensions that the Peazants are trying here to reconcile. Modernity exists as double vision, an image of the past—like Ibo Landing in Dust's film of 1902—that is both preserved in media and altered by translation into a stranger version of what it was already. Over a mix of synthesizer and percussion, the Unborn Child declares in her voiceover that "it was an age of new beginnings," and what we see next is structured—by the young girl on screen as a focal character, by the logic of narrative expectation—as if it will be a version of an image from "inside" the stereoscope. Footage from an Edison short fills the screen instead. The irony of the Child's hopefulness is not lost on anyone, but her performance of these lines does suggest that they're intended as ironic. If it takes almost a century for a Black woman to direct a feature film, perhaps we shouldn't be so quick to define modernity as speed and to assume that media and technology are accelerants of progress by default.

In his *Introduction to Modernity*, Lefebvre offers an appropriately dialectical tribute to the "sleepy old village" where he is living in 1960, "vegetating and emptying, like so many other dying villages and towns" in the face of the onrushing modernity—as technology, as bureaucracy, as capitalism—that brings with it "the abstraction which rides roughshod over everyday life." But the Peazants of Ibo landing are not reluctant bourgeoisie in 1950s France, and they have already known a version of modernity—as southern chattel slavery—that, to borrow from Lefebvre, had "taken the technical division of labour to such extremes" that it is has "dismembered everything which had hitherto been organically united." There are intimations throughout *Daughters of the Dust* that Africa might once have figured as an alternative to these effects of violence and alienation, but Dash's film is far too clear-eyed to have any of the Peazants looking this far into the past or future. When Lefebvre says that in the village, "life was lived in slow motion, life was *lived* there," he means that modernity had not yet arrived to speed it up and make it something deader, colder, and more cruel.[7] But when we see that life is lived in slow motion at Ibo Landing, we must understand that the Peazants—and as always, the double meaning of this name that is their class is right there for us—have always been modern. Slavery makes it impossible for them to be anything else. "Time management," writes Michael Hanchard, "was an imposition of the slave master's construction of temporality divided along the axis of the master-slave relationship." Or as Ira Berlin and Philip D. Morgan put it, in slavery "labor was so inseparable from life that, for most slaves, the two appeared to be one and the same."[8] This is just one reason why a particular strategy of lived slow motion—the "resistance to forced labor and time [that was] seen in work slowdowns," as Hanchard notes—has such a long aftermath in the politics of performative delay that are encoded in the idea and the practices of "colored people's time." Thus Blacks from the era of slavery to the present have seized on and transformed the "racialized and racist comportments" that, in the words of Kemi Adeyemi, have been accorded to "slow subjects" and "used to justify their domination and subjugation."[9] Slow motion in *Daughters of the Dust* is neither a naturalized aesthetic of premodern freedom nor a fantasy of an already vanished way of life. Like the stereoscope, and bicycle, and, however magically, the sight of early cinema itself, slow motion is a reminder that while Ibo Landing might be separated from the mainland as a matter of geography, it has forever been a part of the same modern world, whether or not it always seems to be going at the same speeds or running on the same clocks.

But the film's own attention to the archaeology of film suggests that Dash, Jafa, and their collaborator are not simply trying to employ slow motion as the symbolization of Blackness as a temporality, though there are passages where this is powerfully the case. The ease with which slow motion would have been seen and seen *through* by the 1990s is challenged and something of its strangeness, and, I would suggest, the charge of its explicit modernity is recaptured. This becomes especially visible for me when Dash's use of slow motion is at its least imperative within the structure of the film's aesthetic argument. It might not be possible—and probably not desirable—for *Daughters of the Dust* to make running nowhere in particular into a simple spectacle of pleasure on the sands as dumb as Tom Cruise and Val Kilmer playing volleyball to Kenny Loggins in *Top Gun*. But there are moments of slow motion in *Daughters of the Dust* that seem barely motivated by more than the appeal of Gumbrecht's "athletic beauty."

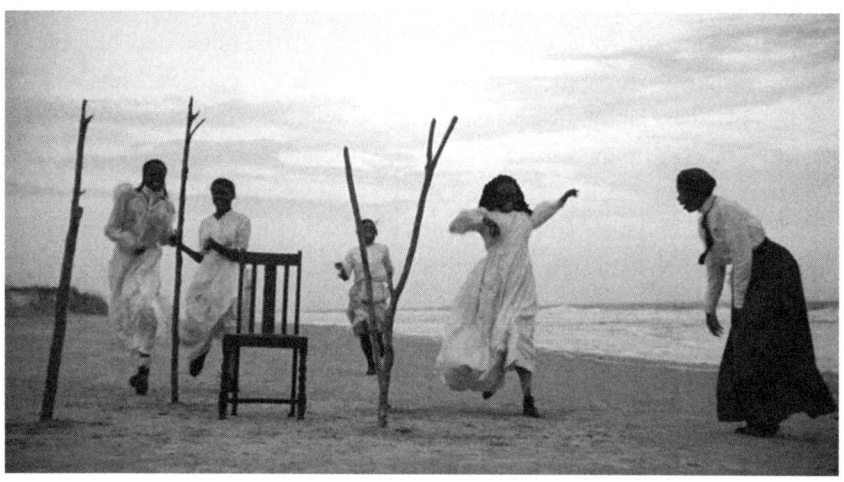

FIGURE 16.5 Still from *Daughters of the Dust* (1991).

Perhaps none of the slow motion in Dash's film can manage to be as underdetermined as so much of it can look in other movies of the period that have much shorter memories (figure 16.5). Dash and Jafa might not mean to recall the joyous lyricism of Vertov's high jumpers in *Man with a Movie Camera*, though they clearly know their avant-gardes. It is even less likely that they were citing the goofy sprinting of Harold Abrams in slow-motion footage from the 1920s or the epic long-jumping of Jesse Owens that Leni Riefenstahl captures in slow motion for *Olympia*. *Daughters of the Dust* hardly needs slow motion to establish that Dash and Jaffa were capable of mastering the idioms of cinematic modernism. Not so much belated or anachronistic, but on time in the only way the movie could imagine.

17
We Have Always Been in Slow Motion

The Discovery of Slowness

Daughters of the Dust *discovers slow motion in the shared modernity of race and early cinema, but its history might be even older. This counterfactual media archaeology is perhaps one of the least strange turns in the historical novel I turn to next, which also, anachronistically enough, makes time for the invention of film along the way to charting the fateful course that eventually takes him to his icy death while looking for the Northwest Passage. Which is, no matter how much slow motion there may have been before the 1960s, about the last place we would expect to find still more of it.

In 1983, the German writer Sten Nadolny published *The Discovery of Slowness* (*Die Entdeckung der Langsamkeit*), which was translated into English four years later and eventually appeared as a Penguin paperback in the United States in 1997. According to Robert Macfarlane, as of 2003 the book had sold more than a million copies in Germany and had been translated into fifteen languages.[1] Its success appropriately evokes the sort of "slow burn" that the novel makes central to its subject: the British naval officer and doomed polar explorer Sir John Franklin and the conceit that informs every aspect of his character in the novel, which imagines him as a figure in and of slow motion from his boyhood to his icy death. "John Franklin was ten years old," we read as the novel opens, "and he was still so slow that he couldn't catch a ball."[2] It soon becomes apparent that Franklin's slowness is not a metaphor for Nadolny, though he rarely misses the chance to indulge the symbolic meanings of Franklin's naturally decelerated temporality as it often isolates him from the modernity emerging all around him from the late eighteenth century to his disappearance in 1845—which gruesomely extended his renown, with several searches in the early

1850s hoping still to find survivors. Archaeologists did not confirm the deaths of Franklin and his crew until the 1990s. But their findings largely matched nineteenth-century reports of a stranded crew of white men witnessed by Inuit in Nunavut, Canada. Franklin's family and much of the English public rejected what Inuits said they had discovered: mass death and evidence of cannibalism. Dan Simmons's 2007 novel *The Terror* plays to the full horror of Franklin's fateful expedition and inspired a 2019 AMC series, which has a demonic monster called the Tuunbaq eat many of the crew who don't eat one another, die from disease, or succumb to exposure in the sub-Arctic cold. The version of Franklin in Nadolny's novel gets off comparatively easy. He dies from a purely fictional stroke, still believing that rescuers are on their way—making steady if not rapid progress.

Perhaps this somewhat happier ending—no demons and only the gentlest hints of cannibalistic desperation—has helped *The Discovery of Slowness*, as Macfarlane relates in a brief look at the novel from 2003 that remains one of the few signs of its English reception, inspire celebrations of its theme that feel weirdly disconnected from the morbid realities it lets us imagine, with or without *The Terror*'s CGI monster. "It has been named as one of German literature's twenty 'contemporary classics,'" Macfarlane writes, "and it has been adopted as a manual and manifesto by European pressure groups and institutions representing causes as diverse as sustainable development, the Protestant Church, management science, motoring policy and pacifism." Macfarlane says that "a center for paraplegics in Basel organizes a regular *Marsch der Langsamkeit* (a 'march of slowness' or 'of the slow')" that pays tribute to the novel and translates into disability activism the sheer literalness of Franklin's slowness, which is obviously and abundantly a metaphor, but one grounded in his biological inability to move fast for any reason, at any time.[3] When mocked by other children, an early fight leaves Franklin bleeding from a flurry of blows even as his first try to defend himself hangs "dead in midair as though paralyzed, the slap petrified like a monument." Franklin does find ways to turn his speed—or, rather, lack of it—to his advantage. At boarding school he learns that he can masturbate all but invisibly since his hands' "travel under his covers were not noticeable; he withdrew them from sight with his slow, deliberate motions." But I don't think the pleasures of what the Pointer Sisters memorably had in mind when they sang about wanting "a man with a slow hand" is enough to account for the appeal of Nadolny's imagined Franklin. Macfarlane also tells us that "a management journal in the US described *The Discovery of Slowness* as a 'major event not only for connoisseurs of fine historical fiction, but also for those of us who concern themselves with leadership, communication and systems-thinking issues.'" This somewhat appalling endorsement speaks to the values that got the novel reissued in 2005 with an introduction from Carl Honoré, the journalist and "Slow Movement" proselytizer whose *In Praise of Slow* and accompanying TED talk introduced and adapted the ideas of Carlo Petrini's Slow Food initiative into a lifestyle plan largely bled of the already attenuated politics of individual consumption that circumscribes many of this well-known project's broader ecological and environmental aims. I would like to know what lessons the business leaders Macfarlane mentions were supposed to have taken from the example of Franklin's slow life and death in Nadolny's novel. *The Discovery of Slowness* treats him as an icon of moral fixity and perseverance and even toys at times with turning him into an arch-Victorian Forrest Gump whose cognitive atypicality prompts some to call him "slow" when he alone is capable of perceiving "motions that were too gradual for human eyes." Or, as his temporal defects are described by Dr. Orme, a teacher who later comes to study Franklin as a medical curiosity, "'his apparent slowness of mind and his inertia are nothing but the result of exaggerated care taken by his brain in contemplating every kind of detail.'" Franklin is undoubtedly the hero of Nadolny's novel, which operates as a kind of bildungsroman predicated on the uneven temporality of a central character who is always and forever lagging behind the moments that are making him. Thus Nadolny must continually remind his readers that the "'enormous patience'" ascribed to Franklin by Orme is actually a virtue, despite all the action that he misses and the punishment he must endure. For long stretches of the novel—which is deeply focalized in Franklin's consciousness and distended sense of time—Franklin seems an unlikely model for MBAs and TED talks even if he doesn't, in the end, like the original on which he's based, all but get eaten alive.[4]

In recounting this aspect of the novel's reception, it would be easy to place *The Discovery of Slowness* in the company of books like Milan Kundera's *Slowness* (1995) or J. M. Coetzee's *Slow Man* (2005). I don't think this does justice, as I'll soon explain, to the deep historical peculiarity of Nadolny's novel. But there is no denying that these novels share a certain family resemblance of theme and mood, and each is centrally concerned with a figure whose attitudes toward the modern world at best reflect a knowing weariness with the imperatives of progress and at worst are muddled by nostalgia. With varying degrees of awareness, then, these novels share some of the same concerns and ideologies that, since the rise of Slow Food in the late 1980s, have informed a range of projects devoted to exploring and promoting alternatives to a contemporary culture of speed, acceleration, and the rapaciousness of capitalist productivity—though, as critics have pointed out, many "slow" movements have less to say about capitalist consumption and are eminently subject to co-optation as mere marketing strategies or worse. As I suggested earlier, the debates surrounding slow cinema in the 2000s and early 2010s had their own parallels to many of these projects, not simply because fuzzy terms like "independent film" invoke the same contradictions as "artisanal" commodities but also because slow cinema, Slow Food, and other attempts to render "slowness" as resistance share a common history as they developed out of a network of older 1960s ideas connecting the vagaries of anticorporate aesthetics to ecology and environmentalism.

It is not hard to impeach the political pretensions that distinguish some of the more haute bourgeoisie formations of the contemporary slow movement. They practically self-destruct with just a glance at the expensive asceticism of *The Kinfolk Home: Interiors for Slow Living* (2015) or with a single click on a website like "The Slow Road," which sells "luxury travel" packages to Lake Como or Provence or on slightly rougher "slow tourism" advice on "How to Be an Earth Friendly Traveler" in Kenya or Bhutan.[5] The recent "Slow Issue" of *Whalebone* magazine continues the trend, pleading that its readers take "more time to cognitively dig in" but also let their dogs "enjoy the down time" on $300 shearling pet beds.[6] These easiest of targets make it difficult to grant the premise that slowness offers a meaningful alternative to the speed that is one of capitalism's defining features, particularly when much of what is on offer is just more capitalism—only slower. The clanging ironies and obvious blind spots of the "slow" life, in all its forms, is missed by precisely no critic interested in slowness as an intellectual theme or aesthetic possibility. Koepnick, for example, points out that slow movements today can weirdly mirror the modernist cults of speed they seek to challenge and replace. They want to make their slow "adventures of ecstasy and vision" so immediately available that "they often lack the patience or ability to put things on hold for the sake of refracting the temporal exigencies of the present."[7] It doesn't take long, in other words, to shop your way to slowness if all you're really after is a nice chair or some organic jam. Sarah Sharma sees Slow Food and related programs trying, in effect, to rectify the inequalities of large-scale economic systems by decelerating the smallest fractions of their supply chains. "They assume," she writes of some Slow Food proponents, "that better time management is all that is needed. They imagine that time is something everyone has, something everyone has access to, and something that can be shaped individually, given the right choices."[8]

Many of the undertakings and institutions that Jesse Matz describes in his terrific account of "time ecology" strenuously avoid this emphasis on individual experience, and groups like Germany's Society for the Deceleration of Time (Verien zur Verzögerung der Zeit) not only have, I'd wager, more than their fair share of Nadolny fans but also "rely more heavily and explicitly," Matz writes, "upon environmental figuration" because they want to ensure that their insistence on "time autonomy" does not get reduced to a set of therapeutic slogans.[9] Wendy Parkins and Geoffrey Craig also insist that "slow living in the global everyday . . . is not an escapist pastime but is both the result of, and a response to, the radically uneven and heterogeneous production of space and time in post-traditional societies." None of these writers, though, has any interest in slow motion as, technically speaking, the first and still most popular type of "slow" movement to gain any sort of visibility in the twentieth century.

■ ■ ■

As a historical novel, *The Discovery of Slowness* is relatively generic. Franklin's life and career are duly narrated from start to finish, which means that we are treated to scenes of rural English life at the end of the eighteenth century, major naval battles of the Napoleonic Wars and the War of 1812, London's rise to an imperial metropolis, colonial life in Tasmania (where Franklin served as Lieutenant-Governor), and, of course, Victorian England's culture of exploration and discovery, which was both a product and a predicate of the imperialism that features everywhere in the background of the novel. Not surprisingly, it is the eventfulness of the period that Nadolny wants to stress in the refracted view made possible by the slowness that Franklin doesn't so much discover as just lucks into like any other accident of birth. Because Nadolny tells the story entirely from Franklin's point of view, a character who knows that "he made out things too slowly," the irony that Nadolny almost never fails for very long to signal is that whenever something happens to Franklin we are reminded that it has already happened, above and beyond the simple past tense of the narrative. Franklin moves so slowly—physically and functionally incapable of normal speed—that he continuously lags behind what is, for most of us, the imperceptible delays that structure our specious present. Nadolny often stages this formally by having episodes begin for us as readers after they have been underway for quite some time, with Franklin suddenly found somewhere different from where we left him or talking to entirely new characters whom he seems to know already. The trick is mechanical but effective, and it serves to emphasize that the novel's story—or, to borrow a narratological term from Viktor Shklovsky, the *syuzhet* we experience as readers—will be forever out of sync with the actual chronology of events—what Shklovsky calls the *fabula*—that we can infer and put together from the text as it unfolds.[10] Franklin's singular temporality brings a measure of magical realism into a novel that takes painstaking lengths to ground its story in the facts and public record of its subject, with a complete bibliography appended so that we can appreciate Nadolny's archival passion along with his technique.

Yet for all the ways that Nadolny finds to register Franklin's slowness—for all his unwavering commitment to the bit—it can still be hard to figure out what the narrative is doing with time as both its theme and medium since, on a more abstract level, "deceleration" is the default mode of art in general that, "by 'estranging' objects and complicating form . . . makes perception long and 'laborious,'" to return to Shklovsky. The idea that art depends on "defamiliarization" is, throughout Shklovsky's *Theory of Prose*, presented as a temporal phenomenon that happens not when we discover something where we don't expect to find it but rather when, "removed from the domain of automatized perception," we have to take more time and are delayed in making sense of art, where our desire and need to gain "recognition" of a scene, motif, or story is itself "impeding and retarding" us.[11] We might recall that Nietzsche has an entirely different critical tradition in mind when, in *Daybreak*, he calls himself "a teacher of slow reading," and though Marjorie Garber is not explicitly championing either Shklovsky's formalism or Nietzsche's commitment to philology, she does ask academics to embrace "slow reading" as the appropriate speed of literary study, which she insists, despite all the data now at our disposal, remains a "revelatory and potentially still deeply subversive mode of teaching."[12] As a slow reader who tends to get too close to any text I try to write about, I'm an easy sell for arguments along these lines—even if I'm not entirely convinced that they're designed to win the fights we need them to.[13] In any case, Nadolny lets Franklin take something of a victory lap for naturally possessing a temporality whose downsides can be turned to the advantage for novelists and academics alike. "'In the study of history, slowness is an advantage,'" we hear a character tell Franklin, adding that "'the scholar decelerates the fast-moving event of past days until his mind can fathom them.'"[14] After a life of never, ever feeling that he is up to speed, Franklin appreciates the sentiment. That he finally chooses a course that leads to cannibalism and hideous deaths for all involved should maybe give us pause about the virtues of the slowness he embodies.

This is not the only way that *The Discovery of Slowness* lets us think about the relationship between slow motion as a discrete effect and everyday experiences of moving slowly—or at least slower than we sometimes do. As Franklin walks the streets of the high-velocity metropolis to which he has returned after fighting in the War of 1812—"All of London," he thinks, "seemed to be in love with speed"—the contrast between his unspecified but clearly halting pace and the accelerated whirl of people moving past him is pronounced. On his last visit home before his ultimately doomed voyage to the north, his reflections take an even more explicit swerve toward the sort of language that will eventually establish Nadolny's text as an icon for various groups and projects trying to resist the pace of life in the technological West today. "London was steaming," in Franklin's steady view, and "the accretion in implements, machines, and iron constructions grew daily. This was called progress. Many worked at it, and few reaped it benefits. Most of them stared at it with glassy eyes and said admiringly, 'Madness.' Progress was madness." With his moral rectitude and emotional reserve—his feelings are usually a beat or two behind—Franklin would seem an unlikely model for any countercultural politics. His devotion to the idea of Britain and its empire, for which he does manage to die, links him just as strongly to an older order based on duty and tradition, more Edmund Burke than Timothy Leary. Franklin is deliberately at a remove from his society, but not because he has turned on it, much less tuned in or dropped out. In living his life entirely in slow motion, Nadolny's version of Franklin follows the exact same course as the historical Franklin—and gets there just as quickly. On his thirtieth birthday, Franklin wonders if he might outlive his friends since everything he tries to do is distended and decelerated. "If I'm slow like a clock," he reasons, "then it takes longer, too, until I've run down."[15] Except it doesn't, and Franklin dies on June 11, 1847, at the age of sixty-two—right on time.

Perhaps the conceit of Franklin's temporality is unnarratable, a term I don't want to freight with too much philosophical or ethical baggage but that points to a difficulty in imagining how a novel might operate in slow motion. Most of us have probably described a book as slow in an impressionistic sense, and most of us, if pressed, would admit that such judgments are at best subjective and at worst corrupted by hierarchies of literary value—many of which we blame on modernism and its real or imagined sorting of the reading public—that associate plots full of action and events with entertainment, genre fiction, or distraction. Nor is it the case that literary fiction really runs faster or slower than other genres according to the numbers, as Ted Underwood has argued in his large-scale statistical analysis of narrative fictions and the durations that are encoded in their timelines—despite the fact that we tend to think that the intense description of shorter spans of time is a mark of literature's distinctive temporality.[16] As an aesthetic judgment, slow is fungible and relative, often a synonym for dull or boring that we project onto a book we don't like anyway; one reader's interminable slog through Proust is another's palpable impatience with the inevitable set pieces in a thriller or the endlessly rehearsed history of a mythic land or magic sword. But as we already began to sense in Faulkner, there are other reasons that slow motion is so tricky to conceptualize on the page.

In his *Narrative Discourse*, Gérard Genette employs the daunting example of Proust to define what he calls the "four basic forms of narrative movement" in the dimension of time, the foundational "anisochronies" that describe the field of possible forms that duration can take in novels or short stories. By "anisochronies," Genette means simply changes in speed or, as he later tries to clarify, "effects of *rhythm*" that vary over the course of a narrative. If "*steadiness in speed*" is what characterizes the "isochronism of a narrative," all the anisochronies that are more interesting to Genette are the perceptible shifts in velocity that not only make stories complicated and compelling artifacts of human temporality but actually constitute the "reference point" or "degree zero" at which narrative as such begins: "At any level of elaboration at all," he writes, "it is hard to imagine the existence of a narrative that would admit of no variation in speed," and though he hedges a bit by admitting this is a "banal observation," the case remains that "a narrative can do without anachronies, but not with *anisochronies*." And while his language is decidedly obscure—"anisochronous" seems like it was borrowed from the chemistry of crystallization or from data processing, where it refers to processes that have transitions with unconstrained time intervals or units of duration—there are only four variations, he argues, that we need to know. Genette concedes that the empirical horizons of his project are impossible: "The very idea of 'time of the narrative'" is, in a word, fictitious since "reading time varies according to particular circumstances," and unlike what happens in movies, or even in music, there is "nothing [that] allows us to determine a 'normal' speed of execution."[17] Of course this isn't really true of movies in an age of video or streaming, but his larger point still applies in the abstract, which is why he says that we can only measure "narrative time"—the duration registered in the discourse roughly matching Shklovsky's *syuzhet*—against the "story time" that is encoded in the duration of all the events that compose the *fabula* of a narrative's background chronology. With this offhand apology, Genette anticipates a point made brilliantly by Brian Gingrich, who argues that "the greatest determinant of [narrative] pacing today is visual, cinematic, and streaming." At moments trying to narrate what Gingrich calls "[units] of kinesis, motion, action" or "the velocity of modern life," writers employ the structuring metaphors of film to register a "sense of a 'prolonged present'"—he is quoting Gertrude Stein in "Composition as Explanation"—that seems exhausted from the start, a figure of "temporal trauma" and the "unsustainable antidevelopmental pace of later modernity."[18]

Genette would rather do narratological math than thematize. "From the infinitude of possible speeds of execution" that narrative time has at its disposal, Genette maintains that there is, in fact, a remarkable economy of basic operations. And it is hard to describe them more economically than Genette does:

> We could schematize the temporal values of these four movements fairly well with the following formulas, with ST designating story time and NT the pseudo-time, or conventional time, of the narrative:
> pause: $NT = n$, $ST = 0$. Thus: $NT > ST$
> scene: $NT = ST$
> summary: $NT < ST$
> ellipsis: $NT = 0$, $ST = n$. Thus: $NT < ST$.[19]

I'm not sure if Genette explains these movements with a rigor matching his formulas. Even before *Narrative Discourse* appeared in English, Seymour Chatman had undertaken the job of refining many of Genette's terms, and, as Underwood has shown, working with these categories in the narrative wilds of the corpus is not as easy as Genette's speculative algebra might indicate.[20] Nor does this particular aspect of Genette's narratology appear to have prompted the most inspiring elaborations of, and responses to, his influential accounts of narrative time. I find it telling, for example, that Mark Currie comes back repeatedly to Genette's discussions of prolepsis (flash-forward) and analepsis (flashback) in his recent work on narrative and the philosophy of time but effectively ignores the passages in Genette that I find most striking for their definitional bravado and dubious empiricism.[21] All the more so because Genette contends, with little hesitation, that the aesthetic temporality that concerns us here is technically unworkable in narrative form. "A plain reading of this chart," he cautions, "reveals an asymmetry, which is the absence of a form with variable tempo symmetrical to the summary and whose formula would be $NT > ST$." Or, as Genette translates out of his own abbreviations, "This would obviously be a sort of scene in slow motion," which might be "feasible" as an experiment, he grudgingly admits, but not in any "form really actualized in literary tradition."[22] There is no such thing as narrative slow motion for Genette. So if no novel can deliver the "slowness" that makes slow motion slow, what else is there for Franklin to discover?

Genette's initial promise of exactitude—however shaky its foundations—does lead to one of his most revealing insights about what actually makes a novelistic scene go slow. It is not so much that "contemplation" in Proust lets the momentum bleed away from sequences of action or event; along with recollection and description, these largely inner processes become "absorbed into narration," where they can appear "intense, intellectual, and often physical" despite the way we might assume they would decelerate and retard the novel's progress.[23] What looks like narrative slow motion, in other words, are often scenes where the past experiences of other characters are brought forward as the experience of memory in the present, whether willful or involuntary, but with the effect in either case of bringing more time into the story than even the most elaborate account of a single scene allows. The fifty-page description of a four-hour dinner party in Proust, to summon one of Genette's cherished examples, might feel like a slow experience of reading (particularly when read in the daily course of work, email, and errands), but the amount of otherwise "lost" time that it recovers— whole years or decades of "story time" by way of flashbacks or elaborate, analeptic leaps into the pasts of characters—is technically much greater than whatever duration we might construct by starting our watches when the narrator punches in and then stopping them when the scene is over and the narrator goes off the clock.

There are, as Seymour Chatman explains in more detail, few examples of narratives that try to go beyond the temporal conventions of those that Genette insists preclude slow motion. Chatman cites Ambrose Bierce's famous "Occurrence at Owl Creek" as proving that the "Stretch"—his name for the kind of *scene ralentie* (in French, slow motion is usually translated *au ralenti*) that Genette dismisses out of hand—might be added to the four alternatives Genette allows. This is the same trick Nicholson Baker uses in *The Mezzanine* (1986), for example, which radically distends the timeline of a short ride up an escalator as the narrator returns to his office after a lunch break. A span of maybe thirty seconds in Genette's "diegetic time" is stretched and bloated into a novella— provocatively set in an office full of new technologies and information systems at the verge of the first dot-com decade—that is both a charming tribute to and obsessive reflection on time-axis manipulation. That said, very little of the novel happens slowly, and Baker's intermittent descriptions of the ride itself are relatively conventional. It's just that they've been radically dispersed and constellated amid long discourses on best practices for tying shoes or on bathroom manners at the office or for assembled passages of pseudomemoir or the iterative narration of the ritual and subroutines of bureaucratic labor. If even Proust— Proust!—couldn't find a way to slow down narrative time in over four thousand pages of one of the twentieth century's most elaborately conceived experiments with time, it's a lot to expect Baker or Nadolny to do much better.

So Nadolny does the next best thing and has Franklin find another form that slowness takes in a distinctly different medium. The novel shows an interest in the archaeology of cinema almost from its start. While still a boy, Franklin visits a country fair where one booth displays a "miracle turntable" that, if it turns "fast enough on its own axis," shows Harlequin and Columbine "united as a couple" despite the fact that their pictures are on opposite sides.[24] Given that this scene takes place before Franklin's first voyage with the Royal Navy in 1800, the appearance here of a thaumatrope is not outrageously anachronistic; these optical toys, as Laurent Mannoni has detailed, become something of a popular sensation in nineteenth-century Europe after various scientists and inventors began to use them in the 1820s to demonstrate the phenomenon of persistence of vision.[25] "It had to do with speed," Nadolny writes, "but John thought today he didn't have a head for it." But the novel won't keep him from encountering more evocatively precinematic spectacles for very long. Franklin serves as a test subject for Dr. Orme, who is introduced as the headmaster at his school but also moonlights as an amateur optical researcher, an overdetermined hobby that makes him very curious about Franklin and his ability to see what Orme describes as "a light of the past." When confirming that Franklin is fit for military service despite his body's slowness, Orme writes in a letter to the navy that "'John's eyes and ears ... retain every impression for a peculiarly long time,'" which Orme somewhat anxiously presents as a perceptual advantage that aids Franklin's "patience" and makes him more "dependable" than some men who might move too fast. It is 1805 when Franklin, back in London and preparing to ship off on the *Bellerophon* for what will be the Battle of Trafalgar, again sees Dr. Orme. By this point the doctor has become so devoted to the persistence of vision that he has managed to invent—almost a quarter-century too soon—a device that sounds a lot like the Phenakistiscope, "a disc that rotated around a perpendicular axle when one turned a crank," with sequential illustrations that produce the appearance of motion.[26] It became a minor Victorian sensation after its invention in the early 1830s. But in Nadolny's novel, Franklin gets there first yet is still the slowest. Franklin's slowness, perversely enough, makes him see motion faster—or at least after fewer rotations—than Dr. Orme's other subjects, who operate at normal speeds. There is literally no "slow motion" in *The Discovery of Slowness* (and no "*zeitlupe*" in the German original), though it's hard to imagine seeing Franklin in any other way.

We are supposed to think it tragic—though not as devastating, I admit, as dying on the ice alone in arctic Canada—that Franklin does not live to experience the discovery of cinema. In the novel, at least, a fictional Peter Mark Roget comes very close in 1844. Working from Orme's model of a prototype Phenakistiscope, Roget is trying to perfect a "picture rotor" every time he and Franklin cross paths in the novel. The historical Roget was also interested in Michael Faraday's optical experiments, but only as one of many curiosities that he pursued along the way to writing the first edition of his famous *Thesaurus* in 1852.

At their last meeting, Roget only has to crack the problem of capturing the actions of performers who, in a double meaning we are certainly supposed to appreciate ironically as Franklin sails off to his icy end, "have to freeze and be exposed in each phase of their movement." Roget has even figured out that he'll need "at least eighteen pictures for a single second" but is stuck because "the process is too complicated and slow" using daguerreotypes. But as Franklin has his picture taken to commemorate the launch of *Erebus* and *Terror*, he has a bolt of inspiration that he communicates to Roget before he leaves. "If one needs to use daguerreotypes for the picture rotor," Franklin writes, "one must decrease the intervals between individual picture takes so that the performers need not always relax and then reassume their positions. Perhaps one could have so many takes per second that they retain their natural movement."[27] What Franklin is conceiving, needless to say, is the course that the discovery of cinema will take from Muybridge and Marey to Edison and the Lumières, each of whom finds ways to accelerate the speed of shutters, cameras, and the various photosensitive materials they handle. His precocious talent for slow motion in Nadolny's novel comes to him naturally or automatically—as if there is a difference. This is why he understands that the future history of a medium that he won't live to see depends on technologies that must keep going faster so that the world they picture for us can look otherwise.

18
DeLillo, Slowing Down

"The art of deceleration," writes Hartmut Böhme, "is a postreligious path to healing a velocified culture."[1] I have my doubts, though I appreciate the sentiment. But the path to heaven doesn't necessarily go in slow motion. This is just one of several lessons we might take from the bad slowness we find in Don DeLillo's fiction over the past two decades. The protagonist of Don DeLillo's 2003 novel, *Cosmopolis*, for example, moves across New York from one side of the city to another at a pace that more than matches any flâneur and his turtle—which means it plods and drags along its way to an endpoint that seems just another anticlimax. The currency trader Eric Packer wakes up in his forty-eight-room apartment near the United Nations and decides he wants a haircut—"in the year 2000" and on "a day in April," two ostentatious signifiers of the times that get boldface treatment on a page of their own right after the half title since, for reasons that will become clear enough, it is crucial that this story happens in an epoch before 9/11. His bodyguard and driver, Torval, appears to know immediately what this will entail at this time and in this city. "You will hit traffic that speaks in quarter inches," he tells Packer, in dialogue that sounds more than typically absurd for all the banality of its familiar DeLillo rhythms of stop-and-go recursiveness and prosaic interruption: "I want a haircut." "The president's in town." "We don't care. We need a haircut. We need to go crosstown." Language, as is often the case for DeLillo, is jammed and moves in fits and starts. Yet there is little reason to think that Packer will change his mind, much less his mode of transportation, despite later learning that the funeral of a Sufi rapper and a series of protests have paralyzed all traffic in the city. His car might be "a tremendous mutant thing that stood astride every argument against it," yet it cannot make him any faster and even slows him down dramatically.² When *Cosmopolis* is over, after all, Packer will have died within three miles of where he started out. For a trip that Google says you can drive in less than half an hour or walk in roughly twice as long, I think it's fair to say that he makes remarkably poor time.

Packer's trip exemplifies the temporalities of DeLillo's recent writing. The first sentence of fiction that DeLillo published after his enormous and encompassing novel *Underworld* signals this new and abiding fascination. "Time seems to pass," observes the narrator of *The Body Artist*, which was released in early 2001. From the perspective of an individual—say, a currency trader stuck in traffic—this may be true enough, and a vast tradition of inquiry into the human perception of time has provided us with reflections on the complexity of everything that time "seems" to us, but maybe not to others, and almost definitely not in other scales and speeds extending beyond, beneath, and radically outside our claims at comprehension. Still, time does pass, or, as DeLillo puts it in the novel's second sentence, "the world happens, unrolling into moments."³ From Aristotle through Augustine and then William James, Husserl, Bergson, and Heidegger, we have seen how the effort to reconcile and understand the differences between these two domains of time—termed by Ricoeur "the time of the soul" and "the time of the world"—deeply structures Western philosophies of time and so links the recurrent motifs and preoccupations of DeLillo's career since 9/11 to "the search for narrative mediations between the discordant concordance of phenomenological time and the simple succession of physical time."⁴ An interest in what John Durham Peters calls the "cultural techniques of time" assumes that "large philosophical questions are usefully pursued in the workings of apparently mundane devices."⁵ Slow motion functions as this sort of technology for DeLillo. Time seems to pass both fast and slow at once in late DeLillo, and though this does not necessarily make his novels any better than they were when they were full of Cold War histories and ideologies, assassination plots and jokes about postmodernism, it does mark him as still entirely our contemporary—precisely because his fiction has lost so much of its momentum.

This is only to rephrase, in terms that I will explore more fully, something of a critical consensus on DeLillo's writing in the almost twenty years since *Underworld* appeared. Book reviewers have noted, at varying degrees of approval or dislike, that, as Sam Anderson writes, "stasis, paradoxically, has become the animating force of [DeLillo's] plots."⁶ In *Slate*, Mark O'Connell suggests that DeLillo's fascination with the "deceleration of narrative time" is "more pronounced with every new work."⁷ It is not clear how far back O'Connell intends to take us, but this language perfectly describes what Anderson calls the "metaphysical

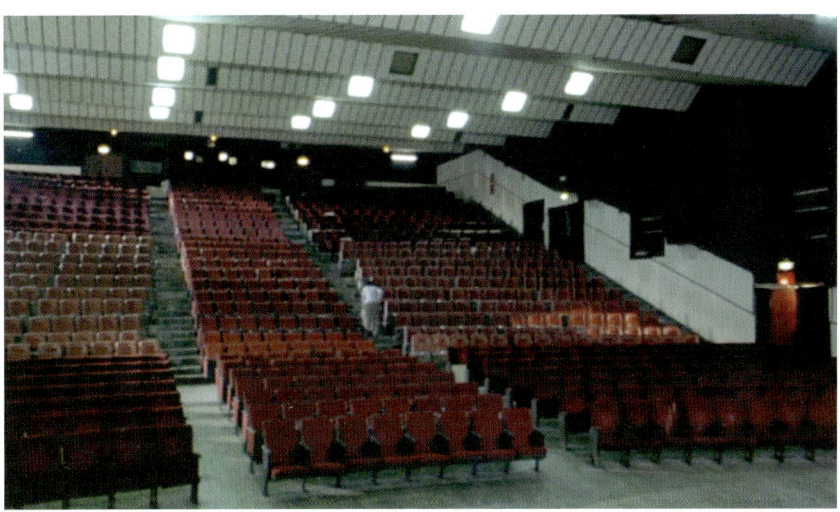

FIGURE 2.3 Still from *Goodbye, Dragon Inn* (2003).

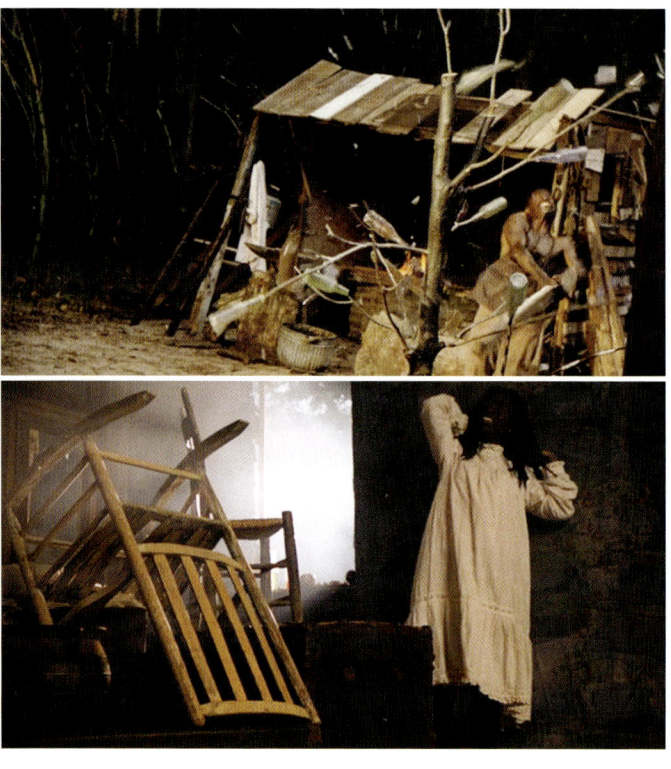

FIGURE 16.1 Slow motion and step printing in two stills from *Daughters of the Dust* (1991).

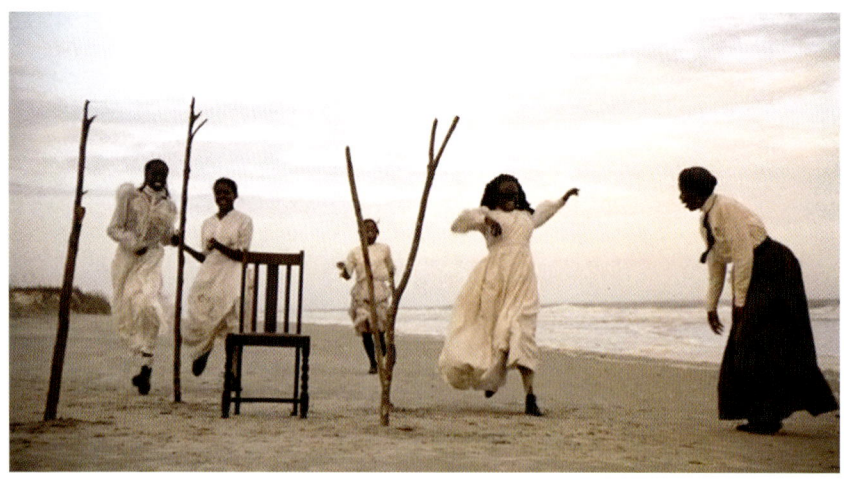

FIGURE 16.5 Still from *Daughters of the Dust* (1991).

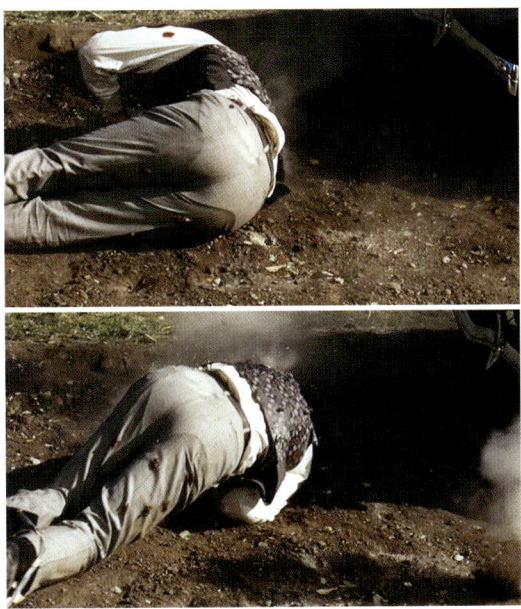

FIGURE 22.6 The agony of Clyde's postmortem ecstasy in two stills from *Bonnie and Clyde* (1967).

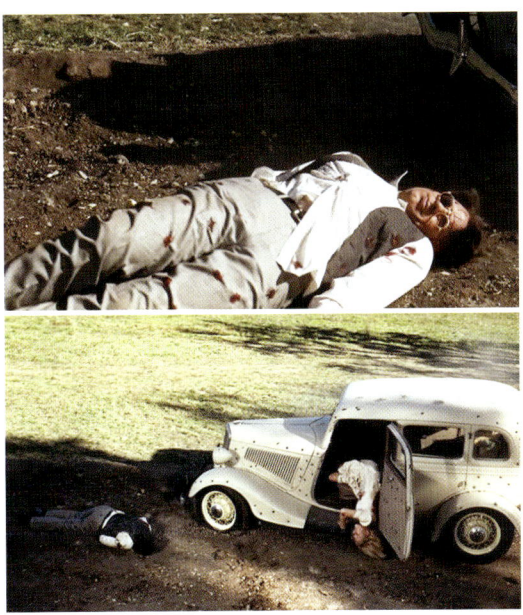

FIGURE 22.7 Stills from *Bonnie and Clyde* (1967).

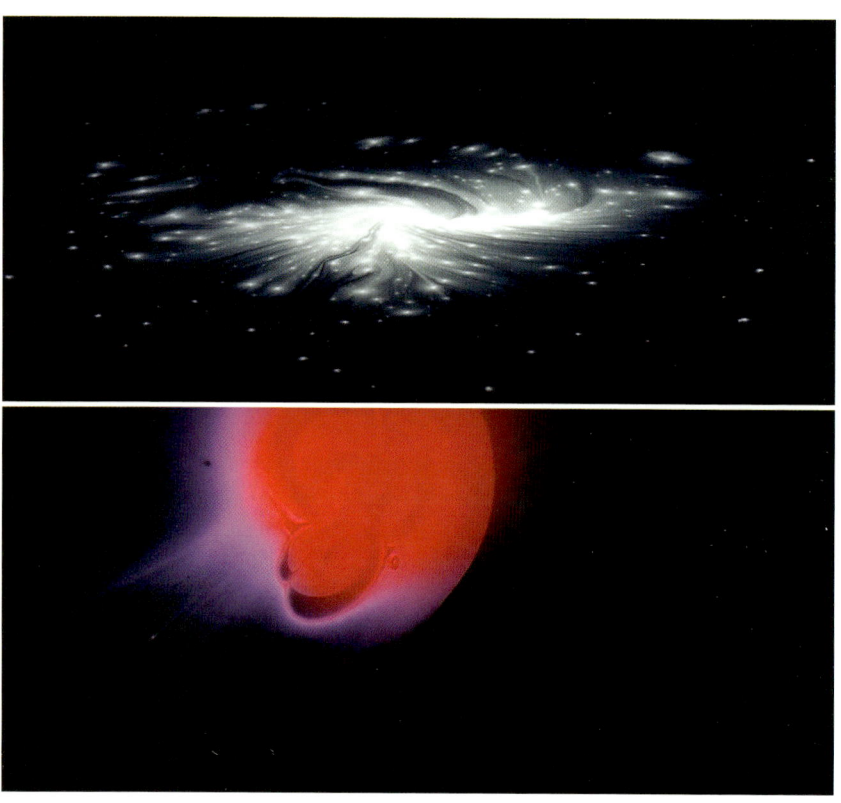

FIGURE 23.1 Stills from *2001: A Space Odyssey* (1968).

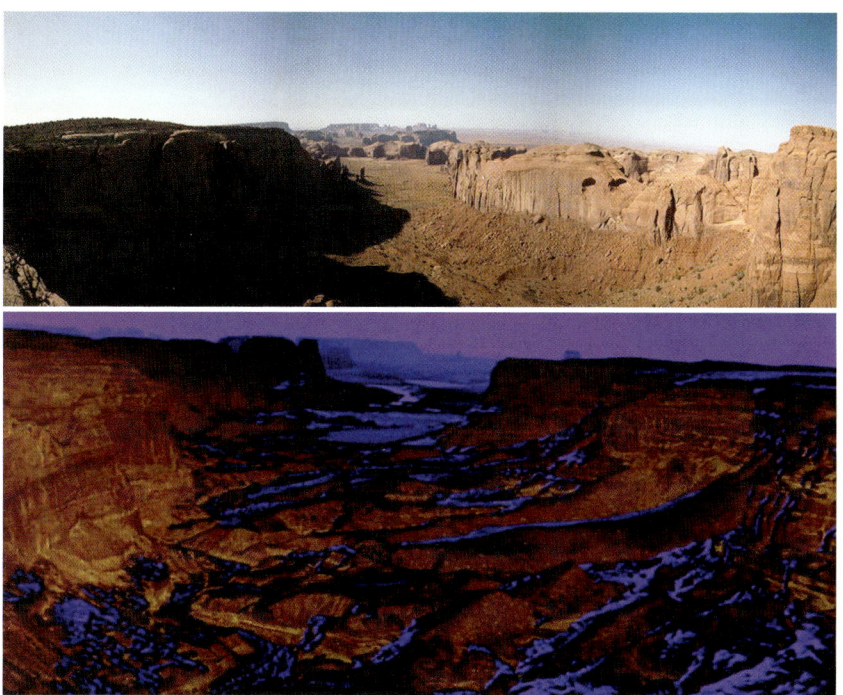

FIGURE 23.4 Monument Valley and Monument Valley on drugs in stills from *How the West Was Won* (1962) and *2001* (1968).

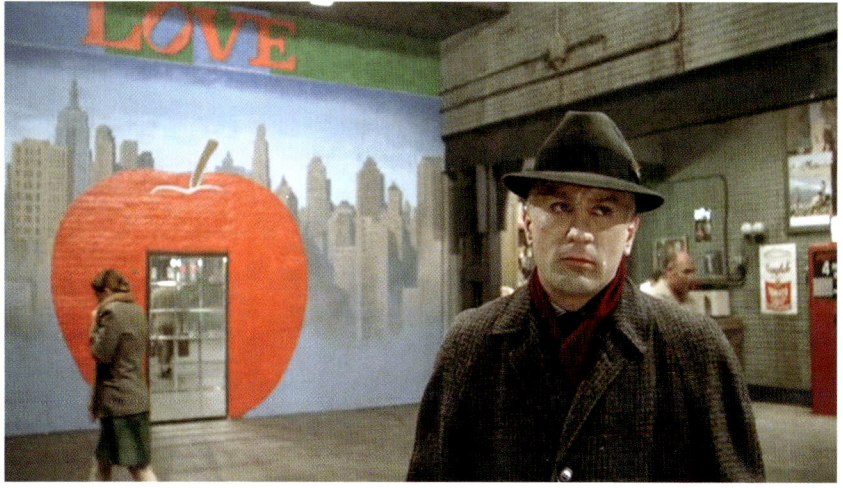

FIGURE 24.5 It's always 1968 in Leone's *Once Upon a Time in America* (1984).

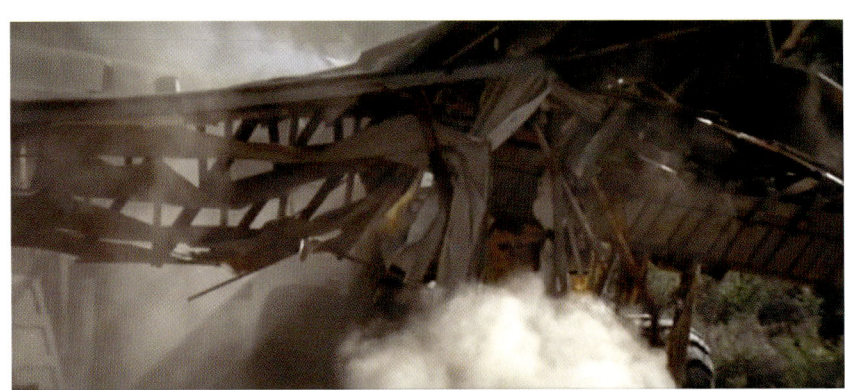
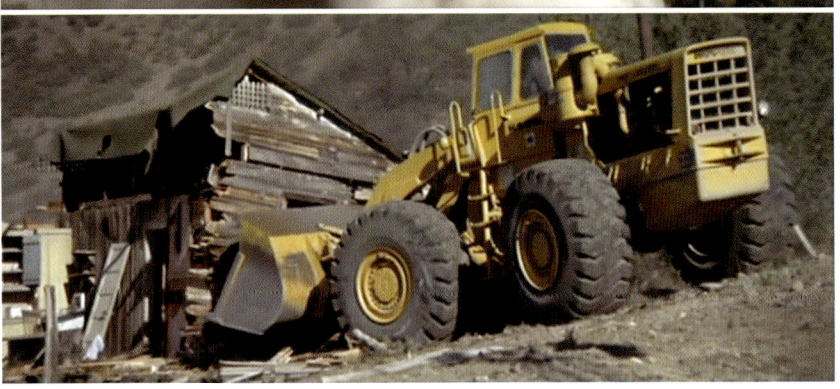

FIGURE 25.1 Stills from *Junior Bonner* (1972).

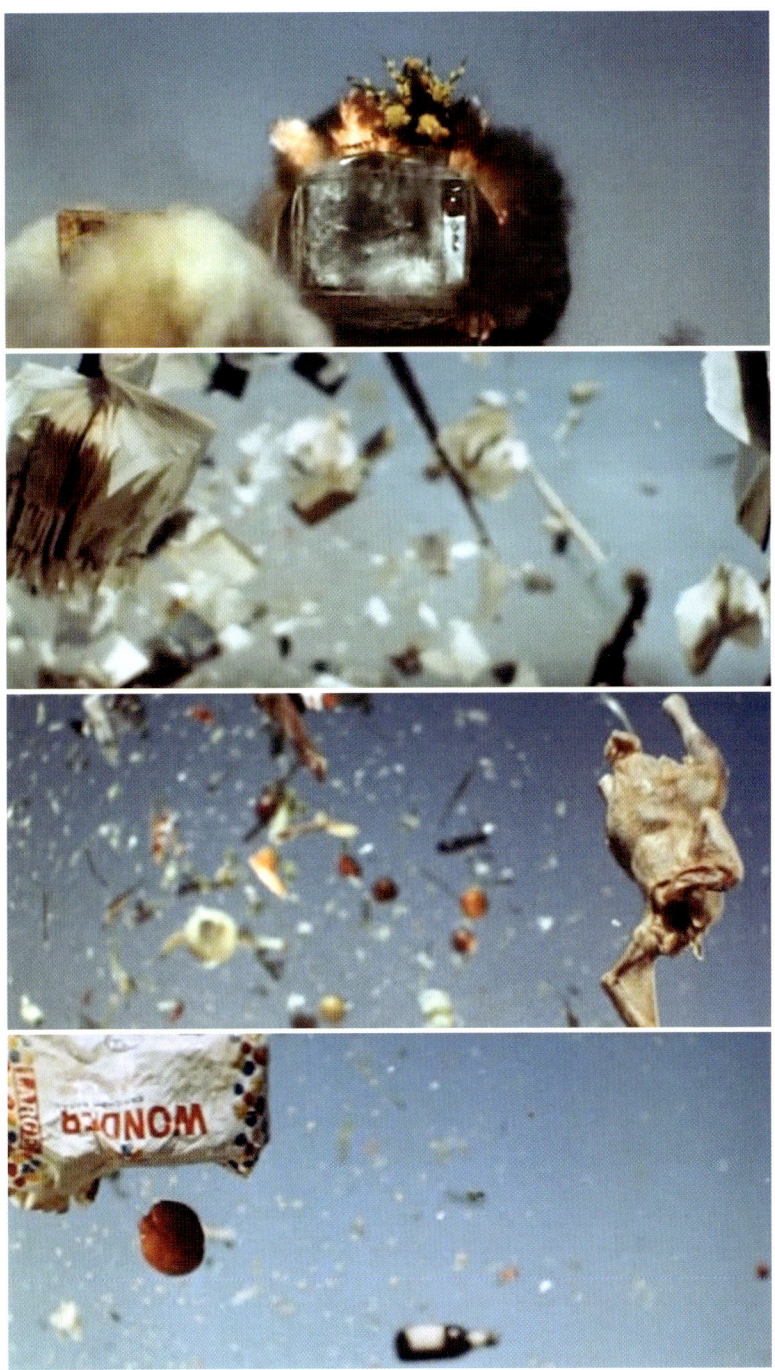

FIGURE 26.5 Stills from *Zabriskie Point* (1970).

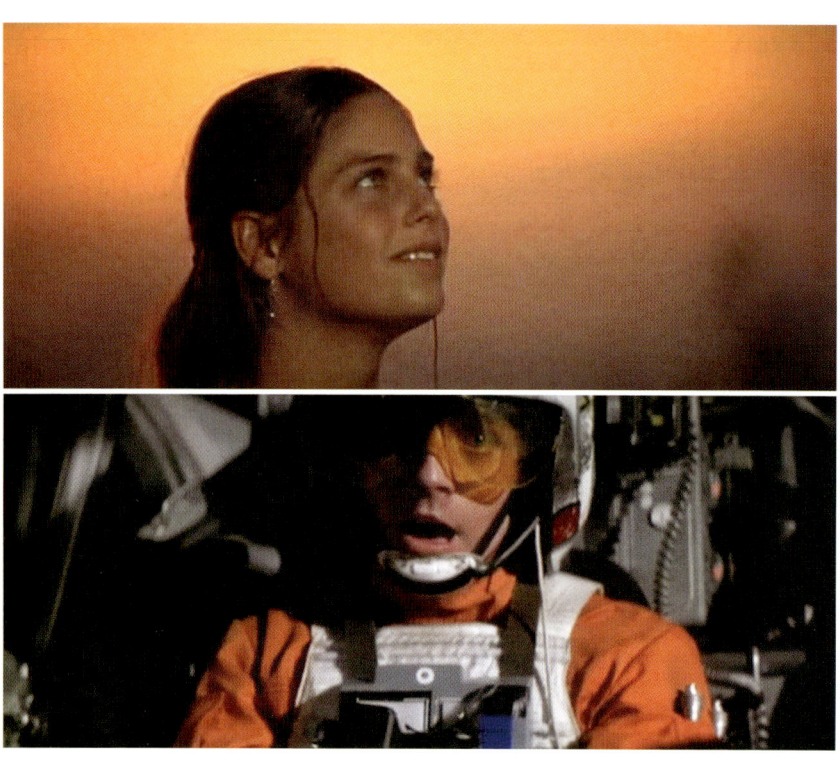

FIGURE 26.7 The thrill of victory in *Zabriskie Point* and *Star Wars* (1976).

anti-thrillers" that DeLillo has been writing and, in different forms, rewriting since *Underworld*. This is not to say that his signature concerns and stylistic gestures have radically departed from his more capacious novels of the 1980s and 1990s. His protagonists are still middle-age white men who work jobs with intentionally opaque titles and a veneer of intellectualism; they have anxieties, which they of course repress, and father-complexes that condition their relationships with older men who are yet more opaque and intellectual; there are women, but never more than one in any scene, who radiate with loss or sexual melancholy and then largely disappear; there are systems, networks, institutions, and economies, and they are doing things in DeLillo's novels that feel almost like the things their real-world analogues are doing, but with a self-conscious aestheticism and second-order theorizing that most of us do not associate with currency trading (*Cosmopolis*) or the Department of Defense (*Point Omega*). The temptation—indeed, the logic—in seeing DeLillo's twenty-first-century oeuvre as evidence of a late style, as we might see it thanks to Adorno or Said, is considerable. "They show more traces of history than of growth," Adorno says of Beethoven's last works; they are the "catastrophes" that mark "subjectivity turned to stone," which sounds like something that DeLillo would have one of his characters see in the "slow, difficult, and sometimes agonizing" performances of Lauren Hartke in *The Body Artist* or hear in Richard Elster's ruminations on deep time in *Point Omega*.[8] With its opening set piece and elaborate referencing of Douglas Gordon's *24 Hour Psycho*, *Point Omega* made plain that DeLillo, like the "Defense intellectual" whose retreat into the desert is both a displacement of and penance for the Gulf War, is mesmerized by "the depths that were possible in the slowing of motion, the things to see, the depths of things so easy to miss in the shallow habit of seeing."[9] At moments such as these, it is hard not to agree with James Lasdun's notion that late DeLillo is actually "very much about lateness: late life, late empire, hindsight, dread, disappearance."[10] Or as Lutz Koepnick notes of DeLillo's *Point Omega* in a persuasive account of its ekphrastic use of Gordon and slow motion, "slowness here [is] expected not to open a therapeutic window to redemption and the eternal, but to help deliberate the multiple and conflicting streams of time that characterize our contemporary moment."[11] Koepnick here sounds almost like one of DeLillo's gnostics, like some prior incarnation of the cryogenics scientist in 2016's *Zero K*: "Time is multiple, time is simultaneous. This moment happens, has happened, will happen."[12] DeLillo is so good at making time sound ominous and grand that simply citing him is almost argument enough.

But not quite. DeLillo's devotion to the "submicroscopic moments" of our present suggests a number of analogues between his recent fiction and, as

Koepnick also provocatively suggests, other forms of slowness that flourish now as responses and reactions to a contemporary culture of speed.[13] Many of these discourses are altogether "therapeutic," recalling Koepnick, in their gestures toward a sense that human beings have lost touch with the more basic, natural temporalities of primordial activities like eating food or having sex and can no longer withstand the speeds to which the already accelerated systems of modern life have been made to go—and then go even faster. The redemptive powers of slowness have long patterned defenses of the arts or the humanities, as we have seen, though only in the past few years has this rhetoric pitched itself in opposition to everything about the present that Google, to cite the easiest possible example, wants to ratify with its corporate mantra "fast is better than slow." Any slow at all will do: in *24/7*, Crary looks back to a "world of time-in-common" that he sees in the unmoving queues of people surveyed by the endless tracking shots of Chantal Akerman's *D'Est*, a notable precursor to work by Tsai Ming-Liang and other "slow cinema" figures, which documented life in East Germany and the Soviet Union as a life of waiting, perhaps aimlessly, but together, with no prospect of relief or satisfaction. Crary asks that we consider the potential for political resistance in "figurations of the inert or inanimate," and while there is much to recommend in his jeremiad against high-speed capitalism, I also cannot avoid a certain restlessness—and contrarian impulse to check my phone while I am reading—with some of his more strident turns against technology. "The form that innovation takes within capitalism," Crary justifiably reminds us, "is the continual simulation of the new, while existing relations of power and control remain effectively the same."[14] If this is right, what do the latest, newest calls for slowness get us? This is a question that looms over DeLillo's fiction after 9/11, though it isn't always answered, as DeLillo writes in *Point Omega*, with the "the force of geologic time."[15]

Sometimes these questions hit much harder in DeLillo. When the first plane strikes the tower in *Falling Man*—which begins in the immediate aftermath of the World Trade Center's collapse—DeLillo's protagonist, Keith Neudecker, has no idea what is happening, save that reality around him is getting unmade into something strange yet distinctly recognizable to anyone who has seen an action movie since *The Matrix* (1999) or experienced Christopher Nolan's integration of digital and practical effects in *Inception* (2010). These examples are the opposite of obscure, which is what makes this parallel scene in *Falling Man* so revealing: Hollywood slow motion is not the magic of Lauren Hartke's body art or high art like Gordon's *24 Hour Psycho* but just another technological effect—like traffic jams or financial crises or terrorist attacks—that we have come to naturalize as a basic aspect of the times in which we live. I am not suggesting that DeLillo has this in mind when he enlists slow motion at a crucial moment of dilated time in *Falling Man* but rather that its appearance is all but reflexive. It makes perfect sense to us that history happens now as acceleration and deceleration at the same time:

> He fastened his seatbelt.
> A bottle fell off the counter in the galley, on the other side of the aisle, and he watched it roll this way and that, a water bottle, empty, making an arc one way and rolling back the other, and he watched it spin more quickly and then skitter across the floor an instant before the aircraft struck the tower, heat, then fuel, then fire, and a blast wave passed through the structure then sent Keith Neudecker out of his chair into a wall. He found himself waking into a wall. He didn't drop the telephone until he hit the wall. The floor began to slide beneath him and he lost his balance and eased along the wall to the floor.
> He saw a chair bounce down the corridor in slow motion. He thought he saw the ceiling begin to ripple, lift and ripple. He put his arms over his head and sat knees up, face wedged between them. He was aware of vast movement and other things, smaller, unseen, objects drifting and skidding, and sounds that weren't one thing or another but only sound, a shift in the basic arrangement of parts and elements.
> The movement was beneath him and then all around him, massive, something undreamed.[16]

Other critics have talked eloquently about the tensions within DeLillo's treatment of 9/11, both as an event that lets him extend and complicate his longstanding fascination with political violence and also as an occasion for us to see how the languages of trauma have become central to the deeper logic of neoliberalism's model of the always isolated, radically abandoned subject.[17] I am finally interested in this passage less for its implications across the whole of DeLillo's recent novels than for its amazingly detailed description of the microseconds that it opens to narration and tries to visualize in a familiar language of special effects. Recall the floating chunks of rubble and miraculously suspended bullets in *The Matrix* or the broken glass and drops of water hanging in the air while the van falls slowly into the river in *Inception*. Or don't: Maybe DeLillo has never seen *The Matrix*, and anyway *Inception* postdates this scene in *Falling Man* by several years. My point is that the uncanny phenomenology of time and trauma—of time *as* trauma, and vice versa—happens in a kind of "slow motion" that is by definition cinematic, no matter what sequences or films it might or might not be enlisting to distend this zero point along a time axis that will become the novel's plot and then the history of the contemporary moment that traces through the wreckage after.

Like many of the writers who have contributed to the genre of 9/11 fiction, DeLillo took a few years to produce his version of the event in novel form. What makes *Cosmopolis* so fascinating is, in part, that its perverse fixation on the radically unsympathetic Eric Packer makes his death "in the year 2000" something of a preemptive strike, in retrospect, against the collective mourning that would have us grieve for this embodiment of "cyber-capital" alongside the other victims and casualties of 9/11—a category that implicitly includes, by the time of *Point Omega*, the victims and casualties of torture, drone strikes, and various war crimes that will be committed by the United States. In the immediate aftermath of 9/11, DeLillo's politics were equally ambivalent.[18] But he had, just weeks later, already discovered the language of time and temporality that has defined his fiction ever since. Invoking the riots and protests in "Genoa, Prague, Seattle and other cities" where the antiglobalization movement confronted the WTO, DeLillo is largely sympathetic to their attempts to "decelerate the global momentum that seemed to be driving unmindfully toward a landscape of consumer-robots and social instability," and he adds that "whatever acts of violence" were committed, "most of the men and women involved tend to be a moderating influence, trying to slow things down, even things out, hold off the white-hot future." Slowing down, however, is not the same as stopping, and even a drastically decelerated capitalism or war on terror can wreak damage that will endure for centuries. And though trying to arrest or reverse the flow of time would be something else entirely, DeLillo equates such an assault upon modernity to the specter of a far more violent anachronism that has come to haunt the global present: "The terrorists of September 11 want to bring back the past."[19] It may have been comforting to think so in the months after the attack, but as we saw in *Falling Man*, the terrorists of September 11 strike in spectacular slow motion too, and so we might observe that whatever "past" DeLillo thinks they might bring back has belonged to our modernity, our technologies, and our moment for longer than he could see in 2001. But maybe the intervening years have gone slowly enough for him—and us—to know it now.

19
From 9/11 to JFK in Slow Motion

Falling Man is not DeLillo's best novel by a long shot, and who knows how it will age alongside other 9/11 fictions of the period. It is, however, elegantly conceived as a temporal construct. The novel's entire *syuzhet*, revisiting Shklovksy, is the painstaking prequel to the catastrophe that gruesomely starts off its *fabula*, we might say, with a bang. The last words of the novel flow easily and inevitably into its opening sentences—a loop that's not unlike the endless repetitions of Hitchcock as distended and transformed by Douglas Gordon's *24 Hour Psycho*, the high-art emblem of the interminable "War on Terror" that *Point Omega* will brood over in DeLillo's next work of 9/11 melancholy. As one character describes the experience of watching Gordon's iconic work, "it was like watching the universe die over a period of about seven billion years." It's hard to decide if this makes *24 Hour Psycho* sound blindingly fast or just as unimaginably slow, which is maybe why the temporality of this distended and distending masterpiece—"a spectacle of excess" that filters Hitchcock through "the blur of technology"—is utterly appropriate for DeLillo's always alienated Americans to ponder while the "War on Terror" lasts forever. "How many people," we are made to ask, "will want to spend all that time looking at something so zombielike?" This is a question about *24 Hour Psycho* that is obviously a question about America after 9/11 in "the depths that were possible in the slowing of motion."[1]

Falling Man is every bit as ostentatiously high-minded as *Point Omega*, but any cinematic analogues that might be patterning its interest in slow motion are altogether more conventional than Gordon. Late in the narrative—which is also shortly before we flashback to the crucial instants that will eventually explode and reify as 9/11—we come across Keith in Las Vegas, where "there were times, in the sports book, when he glanced at one of the screens and wasn't sure whether he was seeing a fragment of live action or of slow-motion replay."[2] This could read like a particularly bleak joke about the incessant replay of the footage of the attacks, which continue to be memorially recycled for every anniversary of 9/11—a grotesque "tradition" that would only have been a few years old when *Falling Man* was published but already wearing thin. If this is DeLillo at his most deadpan, though, the effort feels a little "zombielike." Slow motion, we might say, is the traumatic cliché that we must forever suffer after living through the history of the twentieth century.

As the special effect of 9/11 in *Falling Man*, DeLillo's turn to slow motion is not even remotely original, and while there is little in this relatively humorless novel to suggest that this is, at least in part, the reason why it's there—it's been a minute, after all, since the postmodern in-jokes of *White Noise*—I think it's just as telling to see it as sheer reflex, a shorthand for a trauma that happens suddenly but also lasts much longer and reveals a trail of precedents and prior devastations as it endures. This is not a temporality of historical experience that is unique to 9/11 or DeLillo. Since my own reflexes are by training Americanist, I am especially drawn to Faulkner's fictions for the ways they explore the reach of vaster spans of white supremacy and capitalist exploitation on even the most fleeting instances of action and perception, which are then, in turn, revealed as split-second spectacles that can do little but rehearse the centuries of power and violence that have determined them. Clearly there will be no end to the Holocaust for Sebald's Austerlitz, whose obsessive search for the visual documentation of his loss is a symptom that the novel wants to cultivate in us so that we might similarly resist, with all the media at our disposal, "the dissolution, in line with the inexorable spread of processed data, of our capacity to remember." *Daughters of the Dust* salvages a more optimistic vision of the modern world in its abundance of slow motion, but it would also apply just as readily as a figure for what Saidiya Hartman describes as the "time of slavery" that continues to shape "the relation between the past and the present" as it "negates the common-sense intuition of time as continuity or progression."[3] As Jared Sexton writes, there are forms of "'colored time,'" a phrase he takes from *In the Heat of the Night* (1967), that register as "interminable, perhaps even incalculable, stalled time"; "this is the slow time of captivity," Sexton adds, "the dilated time of the event horizon, the eternal time of the unconscious, the temporality of atomization."[4]

As we have seen before, William James and other experimental psychologists of the late nineteenth century were already documenting the variability of time perception in different contexts, with occasions of great stress or risk convincing test subjects that even split seconds were dramatically longer periods to endure.

This is one of the most significant genres of the "moment" that Sue Zemka's work on the microtemporalities of Victorian literary culture discusses with great clarity, which also helps connect the era's many representations of small intervals of intense experience to the laboratory methodologies that historians of science and technology, such as Jimena Canales and Marta Braun, have traced in their accounts of figures such as Marey, Herman von Helmholtz, and Albert Michelson.[5] As Canales shows, the increasing accuracy with which short segments of time could be measured—too short for humans to track without the mediation of technologies—had the effect of internally expanding small durations that had never been explored in detail or made available for visual or narrative documentation. Contemporary neuroscientists, not surprisingly, have devised more precise ways to register just how much our perception of time slows under conditions of threat, duress, or fear. David Eagleman devised a test for students at Baylor that involved dropping them from a "Suspended Catch Air Device" (often called bungee jumping without a rope) to simulate conditions terrifying enough to alter their perceptions of time.[6] Eagleman turned to this machine—which takes people facing toward the sky and drops them, with warning, from about 150 feet in the air onto a safety net below—when none of the rides at a nearby amusement park could frighten any of his subjects into experiencing the sorts of time dilation that he hoped to measure. Having already collected as many firsthand stories as he could find from survivors of falls, car crashes, bike accidents, and more, Eagleman had confirmed a basic folk mythology where "everyone ... [seemed] to say the same thing: 'It felt like the world was moving in slow motion.'"[7] Eagleman ultimately concluded that the sense of decelerated time so frequently reported in the aftermath of life-threatening trauma is more a phenomenon of memory than of perception; his subjects were not any better able to read off the fleeting microseconds on the "perpetual chronometers" they were wearing than they were under normal circumstances. The experience of "moving in slow motion," Eagleman proposed instead, was the result of their retaining more of what they remembered feeling, thinking, and sensing as they fell. We seem to have more access to perceptions of such fateful moments—perceptions that accumulate faster at their normal speeds than consciousness can access anyway—and this might be why the "event density" of a trauma feels so much greater and protracted. We might experience almost everything in some form of slow motion if we thought that we were always dying. Which we are, of course, but not fast enough to matter to our brains.

But it takes far less expertise than researchers studying time perception to track "slow motion" as a recurrent motif in reports or reminiscences about 9/11. The easiest Googling will do: The tower "seemed to fall in slow-motion"; "time seemed to stop, or at least moved in slow motion"; "the North and South Towers both collapsed, also as if in slow motion"; "everything that I was doing—it was just playing in slow motion"; "I turned around as the first tower collapsed. It was just coming down like it was slow motion"; "It didn't make sense to me. It was quiet and eerie. People moved in slow motion."[8] All these examples come from the first stories you'll see if you search for "9/11" and "slow motion," but there are plenty more among the more than 43 million hits that Google generates. And this makes perfect sense: As we can know from Eagleman's surveys, "slow motion" has been a popular leitmotif in accounts of trauma for more than forty years and was one of the starting points for his later studies in the field and lab. The experience of time passing in slow motion—or "as if" this were the case though an individual realizes that it can't actually be happening—counts among the most prevalent time distortions that psychologists encounter in patients who report such "tachypsychic" episodes after trauma, drug use, or physical exertion.[9] Slow motion is now a perfectly recursive technology for capturing the lived experience of trauma, while also serving as a second-order allegory of how we need media—even at their most overtly stylized and artificial—to show us what we believe that we have lived through.

On YouTube, the imagery of 9/11 in slow motion is depressingly abundant, with between 170,000 and 270,000 results, depending on the precise search terms one enters.[10] Much of the footage shows sequences that are immediately familiar to anyone who watched news reports of the event on television—the number of canonical video perspectives on the World Trade Center attacks is not large—and in the intervening twenty years, advances in software have made it possible for frame rates to be easily manipulated by both amateurs and self-identified "professionals" who post versions that have been filtered for noise reduction, motion stabilization, and color correction, as well as occasionally scored with music aspiring to some flavor of cinematic emotion. It becomes apparent almost as quickly that many of these videos are posted by conspiracy enthusiasts across the fullest spectrum of extremely online ideologies and political fixations; the comments sections tend rapidly to devolve into forensic speculations about how these ten frames or that two seconds in slow motion prove that the explosions could not have been caused by the hijacked planes, which were decoys for the bombs that had already been placed inside the buildings, or that there were no planes at all but rather holograms or CGI in footage doctored for the media to distribute as part of the elaborate scheme to engineer the towers' collapse for maximum spectacle and agitate the public into supporting wars in Afghanistan and Iraq already planned and plotted in advance. This is the closest kind of reading I can possibly imagine, and slow motion does not merely allow this paranoid style to flourish so much as it becomes its objective correlative. If these four or sixty-three or 140 seconds are all but inexhaustible in the secrets that their microscopic temporalities reveal, how are we simply supposed to let them pass? There is an anxious and relentless certainty on full display in these endless loops of 9/11: The truth is out there, but you'll always miss it at full speed.

"For DeLillo the problem with representation is a matter of speed," writes Marco Abel, adding that his writing follows from a deeply felt belief that "representation is always too fast."[11] I think Abel is right, and I appreciate how sharply this throws into relief the tradeoffs that DeLillo is willing to embrace in the short and stripped-down fictions of his late style, with the six books that he published since *Underworld* nowhere matching the maximalism of its word count or its sprawling timeline and geography from the postwar Bronx to exurban Phoenix in the early 1990s. The "unremitting mood of catastrophe," as DeLillo calls it in *Mao II*, is the signature emotion of all his major novels and his lesser efforts too, with even a sketchy, vaguely science-fictional project like *Zero K* (2016) setting its thin plot about billionaires trying to extend their lives against a constant play of images that show "our climate enfolding us" in "footage of the rubbled storm path, the aftermath, houses in a shattered line ... whole streets leveled, school bus on its side, but also people coming this way, in slow motion, nearly out of the screen."[12] In the tortured alternative history of the Kennedy assassination that *Libra* (1988) imagines—with Lee Harvey Oswald as the fall guy for a plot conceived by CIA agents and Cuban exiles—there is a brief moment when, in the midst of a fight outside a bar, Jack Ruby is grabbed and pulled "down to the pavement in slow motion."[13] It's hardly more than what we see in *Falling Man*, and on its own it is just another citation of a not very special effect by the late 1980s. Just another data point for "slow motion" in a Google Ngram in a novel that luxuriates in what DeLillo calls "assassination aura" but that is also, in a later introduction, said to be about the "sense of the secret manipulation of history" that comes from living with too much of the past mediated by "modern technology." "Technology tends to represent a thrust toward the future," DeLillo writes, "an accelerated promise of microrefined systems and networks, deeper probes into the way we live and think."[14] His language is a little wonky, but since this is from 2005, he clearly wants to invoke the idea of the digital ("microrefined") and the specter of social media ("networks"). Facebook launched in 2004, and YouTube went online in February 2005—when DeLillo's new introduction to *Libra* and its "assassination aura" would already have been at the printer.

While *Libra* is a novel set almost entirely in the time of Kennedy's assassination, it is, just barely, a contemporary novel of the 1980s, too. The second chapter introduces us to Nicholas Branch, a retired analyst for the CIA whose ongoing investigation of the events of November 1963 consists exclusively of immersion in a bureaucratic archive of "legal pads and cassette tapes," along with "a massive file cabinet stuffed with documents" that represents the "data-spew of hundreds of lives" caught up in the story and the mystery of what Oswald did or didn't do. Branch has been "hired on contract to write the secret history of the assassination of President Kennedy," though we are never told by whom, and by the novel's end, we'll see Branch "almost immobilized by his sense of the dead" since "the dead are in the room" and it is full and getting fuller of dead media sent to him by some shadowy "Curator"—"the stuff keeps coming . . . a thirty-five-hour film chronology of unedited network footage shot during the weekend of November 22 . . . a computer-enhanced version of the Zapruder film . . . detailed descriptions of the *dreams* of eyewitnesses following the assassination." It seems like we're supposed to think—or at least have the nagging, paranoid suspicion that is more powerful than "thinking" anyway—that Branch has not been sent all this information because someone wants the "secret" to get out but rather because they know the best way to make sure it doesn't is to give the whole "data-spew" in its unrelenting bulk, historical suggestiveness, and piecemeal dissolution to a painstaking researcher and let his academic habits slow his progress down to null velocity. When Branch reflects on his mission, which he has chosen to accept, he understands it as the revelation of "six point nine seconds of heat and light. Let's call a meeting to analyze the blur. Let's devote our lives to understanding this moment, separating the elements of each crowded second." But these messages from the past will never fade away or self-destruct—not in five seconds, as the old spy TV show–turned–action franchise warns us, and still not for a decade and even longer. "He is in the fifteenth year of his labor," we read as *Libra* introduces us to Branch in this room where he fears he will spend the remainder of his life trying to get past seven seconds in 1963. How many days or months or years does it take Branch to determine that "the first shot came much sooner than most theories would allow, probably at Zapruder frame 186"? He has confirmed that "the shot that killed the President, crushingly, came four point three seconds after that." So he's itemized these technicalities and put a timestamp on the violence, which brings him no closer to the end. "Even though he has reached firm conclusions in this area, Branch will study the computerized version of Zapruder. He is in too deep to stop now." He has been given everything he needs to stretch out these few seconds into an epoch that he realizes he will not outlive, much less deliver as a narrative to fulfill the "contract" he has signed. "Of course they've known it all along," Branch finally comes to understand. "That's why they built this room for him." The incomparable "secret" of the twentieth century that he's been asked to write is hidden in the "microrefined" intervals of time as it at once passes too fast for us to process fully and endures too long for us to move beyond. There might well be forces conspiring against him—"they've known it all along"—but their methods aren't exactly obscure. They just have to let the files, cassettes, and movies—all the modern media that Branch needs to do his job—keep accumulating. A history that seems to go by fast until we watch it in slow motion, and then it feels interminable. Someday, it will be over, but all we can know for now is that "the stuff keeps coming."[15]

20

Underworld

How Slow Is Now?

DeLillo has had a lifelong fascination with the Kennedy assassination and its afterlife. His debut novel, *Americana* (1971), ends its shaggy road-trip narrative in Dealey Plaza, and though the Zapruder film is perhaps not the primary fetish object in his gargantuan *Underworld*, its aura and iconography are almost as important to the novel as the lost homerun ball from Bobby Thompson's 1951 "shot heard round the world" that we follow as its bounces back and forth across the late twentieth century—as close as anything the novel gives us to a plot. Even before the Zapruder film makes its appearance, footage of a murder committed by the "Texas Highway Killer"—"an act of shadow technology, of compressed time and repeated images, stark and glary and unremarkable"—anticipates how DeLillo will have us watch and rewatch Kennedy's assassination. "Taping-and-playing intensifies and compresses the event," DeLillo writes of this random videotaped act of violence, but with a portentous lack of specificity that lets us realize that there will be many other moments in the novel that are emblematic of this artificial temporality and its depressing model of better trauma through media technology. Nothing particularly significant is happening when, in a section of the novel set in 1974, Klara Sax—the artist who, along with Nick Shay, serves as this wandering sprawl's protagonist from the Bronx to the desert Southwest to Kazakhstan and back—has an accident in someone's kitchen that seems harmless enough until we sense just how it radiates with DeLillo's determination to find the symbolism of devastation everywhere he looks. How else do we account for the fact that, decades later, when Klara cuts her finger, "it was one of those microseconds that's long and slow and nuclear-packed with information"?[1] This is a moment of DeLillo's realism at its most "hysterical," as James Woods would have us disregard it for the empty application of some very special effects where they have nothing much to do; a few years before a great *Chappelle Show* skit will confirm that anything "looks better in slow motion," DeLillo had already discovered that slow motion can give any instant a sort of atomic half-life of aesthetic emphasis, with a virtual infinity of "information" being generated from the smallest possible reactions.[2] For Woods, big American novels like *Underworld* have been "embarrassed into velocity," by which he means that they try to move too fast and say too much about too many things, with the unintended consequence of leaving them fatally bogged down.

With just over eight hundred pages devoted to the forty years of U.S. history it depicts, *Underworld* cannot exactly be considered fast or slow, and we have already seen how such shorthand phrasings are unworkable gestures toward far more complicated reactions to how narrative pace is perceived and how aesthetic pleasure is or isn't subject to the time that readers might have to invest. "How deep is time?" DeLillo asks at the beginning of one chapter. "How far down into the life of matter do we have to go before we understand what time is?" These are appropriately overwhelming and serious questions for a novel that is so self-consciously trying to be both "great" and "American," and even if I wanted to go on for as many pages as DeLillo, I wouldn't really come up with any answers. They are deliberate echoes of Augustine's chapter on time in his *Confessions*, and the fact that they are voiced here as they rattle through the mind of Albert Bronzini—an old teacher and chess tutor still living in the Bronx after all the other characters have left the neighborhood—only adds to the impression that they're less in the novel to be solved and more to be admired for their old-fashioned grandeur, perhaps as monuments to the Jesuit education that Bronzini once provided to Nick Shays and his brother, Matt. (Or even to DeLillo's own: Cardinal Hayes High School, Class of 1954; Fordham, BA, 1958.) At one level, the novel's interest in "deep" time is almost stupidly literal: In its penultimate episode we follow Nick to Kazakhstan where, in his capacity as "a sort of executive emeritus" at a company called Waste Containment, he talks about "vacated military bases" in the southwest and how "they will or will not accommodate thousands of steel canisters of radioactive waste for ten thousand years. Then we eat lunch." DeLillo is at his deadpan best in these easy jokes about modernity's long tail risks—"the waste may or not explode, seventy thousand tons of spent fuel, and I fly to London and Zurich to attend conferences in the rain and sleet"—and the money that some will be trying to make right up to the second when all these old bombs from our epoch of the Bomb go off.[3]

Underworld's temporal structure is vast and labored but not especially complicated; we begin on October 3, 1951, with the "shot heard round the world," then jump immediately to a section that takes place in 1992, and from there we start moving back in time, each further set of chapters now letting us excavate an earlier moment after we have dug our way through what has happened since. Yet outside the bravura microhistories DeLillo assembles for part 5's "Selected Fragments Public and Private in the 1950s and 1960s"—a montage of pseudodocumentary anecdotes that pays homage to John Dos Passos's *U.S.A.* trilogy or the "Time Passes" interlude of *To the Lighthouse*, as well as to E. L. Doctorow's *Ragtime* (1975)—nothing in this exceedingly long novel about the Cold War actually happens in the 1960s. I almost admire DeLillo enough to believe that this is a gesture of boomer self-critique; he buries the decade most responsible for enshrining a myth of generational progress that, in the timeline that the novel does explore, has failed utterly to materialize. The novel's amazing set piece at the start is not just a thematic "cold open" onto some of DeLillo's signature preoccupations in what is coming— with baseball, the Bronx, nuclear annihilation, and race in more or less that order of importance—but also a rehearsal of its methodology throughout, its determination to discover sweeping arcs of history already "contained" within the smallest bits of time we can conceive. The play of scales is Proustian, but time in *Underworld* does not exist to be regained or magically recalled in memories summoned to our minds. DeLillo instead gives us traumatic instants that we can never know if his characters are conscious of or not. Like the nuclear waste that Nick dispassionately discusses—in a ridiculous display of repression and sublimation that still manages to work—we can't say for sure whether the past will or will not explode or just expand into a brutal present that will shade into a bleaker future, "slowly, durably, over time." This is what makes Nick's late turn toward a variety of nostalgia so despairing. "I long for the days of disorder," we read in the last words of the narrative given over to his perspective, "the days of disarray when I walked real streets and did things slap-bang and felt angry and ready all the time, a danger to others and a distant mystery to myself."[4]

Of course the split second of "slap-bang" trauma that shapes his life is not a metaphor. "Nick pulled the trigger": This is how DeLillo quickly and efficiently describes how a sad suburban husband with a cheating wife and job in waste management once shot a man. Handed a shotgun and dared to believe it isn't loaded, the manslaughter that Nick commits might technically be a convoluted act of suicide by the sad junkie, who either didn't know the gun was loaded or did know all too well. Either way, this small moment of violence was, as DeLillo writes, "a kind of history taking place," and it still seems to be exploding more than forty years later, though Nick's considerable "bunker system" of decrepit masculinity and white ethnic machismo has managed to "accommodate" the damage. Nick doesn't show much evidence that he feels guilty or remorseful, but then again, DeLillo makes it impossible for us to miss that he has risen to the status of "executive emeritus" because he is so good at burying things. The novel, on the other hand, goes to great lengths to guarantee that we see the primal scene of Nick's disordered, angry past. "In the extended interval of the trigger pull," DeLillo writes, "the long quarter second, with the action of the trigger sluggish and rough, Nick saw into the smile on the other man's face. Then the thing went off and the noise busted through the room and even with the chair and body flying he had the thumbmark of George's face furrowed in his mind."[5] After this briefest moment in slow motion—which expands a quarter-second exponentially already—DeLillo proceeds for the next sixteen paragraphs to replay and loop Nick's mental footage in deliberately short "fragments" of visual experience, a montage of what I hesitate to call "bullet points" save for the fact that this is clearly the stylistic effect that DeLillo is after. The language is brutal in its repetitions of "loaded," "trigger," "gun," and "man"—the degree zero of signifiers that the narrative requires to haunt us with the image of what went wrong, or possibly right.

While not every instance of slow motion in *Underworld* is as traumatic as this "quarter second" act of murder-suicide that DeLillo expands into a page or two of fiction and fifty years of his main character's damaged self, each one is, in its own manner, almost just as formulaic. The novel's opening requires DeLillo to transpose what is basically a sports highlight, complete with famous radio call, into the highest and most serious style of literary fiction. "The next inning seems to take a week," he writes at the beginning of the section of "The Triumph of Death" that will describe Thompson's homerun—but only in due time. Pages are spent getting runners on base, Ralph Branca out of the bullpen, and Bobby Thompson to the plate with Don Mueller and Whitey Lockman on base with one run in; "in a country that's in a hurry to make the future," as DeLillo observes with delicious grandiosity, there is nothing even slightly rushed about this scene devoted to registering "a lifetime of effort compressed into seconds." The homerun is captured as a moment of aestheticized arrest, suspended in "the scant delay, the stay in time that lasts a hairsbreadth." Russ Hodge's legendary radio call—four utterly astounded shouts of *"The Giants win the Pennant"*—is reproduced as interstitial exclamations between paragraphs that are short but still distend five seconds that are, in DeLillo's words, "excessive with a little tickle of hysteria" into a more measured refrain against the backdrop of the narrative's meticulous description of the scene and its details.[6] This deceleration and dilation of Hodge's iconic broadcast is more than just an exercise in nostalgia and extreme historicism. Which is as much to say that it is precisely this on several levels: a manufactured constellation of large and small events; cameos from Jackie Gleason, Frank Sinatra, and J. Edgar Hoover to remind us that the set piece's protagonist, Cotter Martin, is the epitome of the "average man" that Lukács says we need for scale in a properly historical novel; a homerun and a hydrogen bomb all conspiring to shape the remainder of the twentieth century around a game that DeLillo says that he remembers hearing on a dentist's radio. The formality of "The Triumph of Death," to put this differently, is more than simply DeLillo throwing around his weight as novelist and representative of a generation with an outsize claim on popular mythologies of the 1950s and beyond. "Better in slow motion" is not just a punch line for DeLillo; it's his entire theory of the American century that *Underworld* helps consecrate and lay to rest.

Since *Underworld* has so much in it, we probably shouldn't be surprised when the Zapruder film appears at last—not just as an aura or an echo but in the mediated flesh. It is 1974, and the novel is again following Klara Sax on her parallel escape from the Bronx into the world of large-scale land art where she will later "manage" the waste of Cold War armaments into a desert installation of retired painted B-52s. But before all this, we find her at a loft in New York that has been turned into "the Zapruder Museum."[7] The first time through the footage, in an gesture Øyvind Vågnes registers with wonderful precision, the images of Kennedy's assassination are described in a single paratactic sentence that "takes about as long to read . . . as it takes to project the Zapruder film."[8] DeLillo's twisty and ekphrastic sentence about the film is brilliant in its polish, another fine set piece in a novel full of them—some going faster than others. At the time this scene is set, of course, the Zapruder film had yet to be seen by the vast majority of Americans *as* film, circulating instead as stills in *Life* and in the *Warren Commission Report* for more than a decade after it—and Kennedy— were shot. The pun is grisly, I confess, but entirely in keeping with DeLillo's grand-style detachment from the horror of what Klara and the rest are seeing. On the one hand, "people in the room went ohh," and a woman "covered her face because it was completely new, suppressed all these years"; on the other, by 1997 when *Underworld* was published, there wasn't much novelty left in this footage of "the President being shot," which is both the clearest way to signify the horror of the film that Klara and the rest are watching and an especially dark figure of speech for what Zapruder's work most literally represents as an artifact of media.

It turns out that the Zapruder film has been pirated and reproduced ad nauseam, though even in the singular it should be upsetting enough. "Different phases of the sequence showed on different screens," DeLillo writes, and the "spectator's eye could jump from Zapruder 239 back to 185, and down to the headshot." For Klara, all these repetitions and manipulations of the footage—slowing it down, stopping it, assembling it into montages and grounding it in space—cannot keep the film from "being what it was, in being film." DeLillo's fiction of the "Zapruder Museum" is meant to invoke the pop-art "happenings" and conceptual gamesmanship of high culture in the 1970s, but perhaps Klara is nostalgic for the old days too. Her rapture could not possibly be more modernist in its medium specificity, which projected all sorts of metaphysics onto the materiality of what were, once upon a time, the only technologies that we had for making pictures—whether or not they moved. "It carried a kind of inner life," she thinks to herself as she watches Kennedy assassinated in slow motion, "something unconnected to the things we call phenomena."[9] Here is film "completely steeped in being what it was": Klara feels so powerfully that her own words can only circle back to where they started, "in being film." And while she doesn't necessarily need a better argument for feeling what she feels about the way she sees film "being" film at the "Zapruder Museum," it is telling—though barely circumstantial evidence—that Greenberg does not do much better than similarly reverent *koans* in his most famous and doctrinaire expression of his aesthetic ideology in his 1960 essay "Modernist Painting": "It quickly emerged that the unique and proper area of competence of each art," Greenberg intones with real grandeur in the passive voice, "coincided with all that was unique in the nature of its medium."[10] "The footage seemed to advance some argument about the nature of film itself," Klara realizes, but then her thoughts turn to how "this home movie was some crude likeness of the mind's own technology," if not "a model of the nights when we are intimate with our own dying." It gets dark for her in a hurry at the "Zapruder Museum." Thankfully somebody offers her a joint.[11]

"Here was an event," Klara imagines hearing in the voice of her companion Miles, who speaks from even deeper inside the art scene that we encounter halfway into *Underworld*, "that took place at the beginning of the sixties, seen belatedly, that now marked the conceptual end."[12] It's a remarkably tensed and twisted sentence about history. The "event" seems like it must mean JFK's assassination, since this is the act of violence captured on the Zapruder film, and so the referent for all the signs and signifiers, frames and duplications, that someone whom the novel never names has used to turn a downtown apartment into a shrine immersing us in media. "Seen belatedly" in a constellation of media technologies and aesthetics that did not exist in 1963, it is only from the perspective of 1974 that Klara can realize that the sixties have been over for a decade. Do they flash by as a traumatic blur, "twenty-some-odd seconds of a home movie" that, when sufficiently slowed down, emerge as a monumental show of action that can be almost infinitely deferred? Freud's *nachträglichkeit* in delirious slow motion as the way that history comes to us delayed and overdue? Or did the sixties get off to a slow start, with JFK's assassination as their "beginning," and then last longer than they should have on the clock and calendar? In which case it was "the sixties," according to DeLillo, from November 22, 1963, until some moment in the early 1970s when, in an apartment probably in SoHo or the East Village, the epoch was suddenly brought to a halt by a bunch of 8mm and 16mm projectors, televisions, and who knows how many bootlegged copies of the Zapruder film. How would this bring the "sixties" to an end, "conceptual" or otherwise, for anyone not there with Klara, Miles, and their artist friends? Had the "sixties" already ended for the members of the Warren Commission who were privileged to see it sooner? Stills from the Zapruder film had circulated for decades, but most Americans—unless they found their way to the right underground showings—would have, by DeLillo's logic, been living in a suspended, frozen vision of the sixties until the footage finally played on ABC as it was shot. Does this mean the sixties really didn't end until Geraldo Rivera broadcast it on an episode of *Good Night America* on March 6, 1975?

DeLillo proposes that something happens at the "beginning of the sixties"— which might also be their "conceptual end"—that makes us radically and terribly self-conscious about how time has been experienced for decades now, not just because of what we see in the Zapruder film or what we hear on the radio during the "shot heard round the world." We witness history as an unfolding sequence of catastrophes and traumas in slow motion, which happens only at high speed even if we never really come to terms with what this means in the moment, or if it finally takes a while to catch up with the technologies that go fast enough to let us see what has already happened as if we still have time to do something about it. We don't. Not in DeLillo's last word on the twentieth century or in any of the other fictions of modernity—from Faulkner years before to Sebald and McCarthy after—in which slow motion gives visual form to the experience of time passing in a world where we need technologies to see what our technologies have done to it and us already. "It ran continuously, a man in his forties in a suit and tie, and all the sets were showing slow motion now," DeLillo writes, "and the footage took on a sense of elegy, running ever slower, running down, a sense of greatness really, the car's regal gleam and the murder of some figure out of dimmest lore—a greatness, a kingliness, the terrible mist of tissue and skull." I'll admit, it is hard for me to identify with this inflated rhetoric of loss; I'm not the right generation for the fetish that DeLillo makes of JFK, though I do love his stately prose and almost certainly unconscious echo of the "standstill" that brings everything to a halt in *Mrs Dalloway* when another car that radiates with mystery and "greatness" moves at its own exquisite crawl across the page. But this is not the modernism that DeLillo has in mind here as we are made to realize "belatedly" that the sixties have maybe ended right before our very eyes or were over before we had a chance to look. Maybe I'm thinking too conspiratorially—even for DeLillo—in suggesting that Clement Greenberg and his own fetish for medium specificity can help us understand why this scene depends so much on slow motion as it tries to picture for us, in a late 1990s vision of the 1970s still carrying, as we read elsewhere in the novel, "an afterglow of sixties incandescence."[13] I might be reading too much into this moment because DeLillo is so good at playing to the nostalgias that I do have, despite my age, for baseball and formalism as they figured at midcentury. What DeLillo captures perfectly in *Underworld*—and what his later novels track into the century that comes after the one he tried to bring to a "conceptual end"—is the particular or, in perverse tribute to Greenberg, the specific impurity of slow motion as a media aesthetic. In the "compressed event" of JFK's assassination as it is captured by the Zapruder film, we find a dense network of themes that resonate across DeLillo's writing and come to function as a template for depictions of the 1960s, a way of capturing the "afterglow" and "dimmest lore" of an imagined "sixties" that was, as we'll see in films like *Bonnie and Clyde* and *Zabriskie Point*, already present in the moment and made supremely visible in slow motion. Slow motion can make the present last forever, which can turn the future into an endless half-life of a past that ruined it years or centuries in advance. "This is the whole point of technology," as DeLillo writes in *White Noise*. "It creates an appetite for immortality on the one hand. It threatens universal extinction on the other."[14] It feels a bit premature to say that it's all over when slow motion can turn "microseconds" into eons, but if the present is still irradiated by the "afterglow of sixties incandescence," then we may as well live fully in the moment since we must suffer it for the duration.

21

A "Sixties Incandescence"

Periodizing Slow Motion

That the period of historical turmoil and cultural dissent we call "the sixties" begins, in the United States at least, with JFK's assassination has become a fixture of generational mythology and popular nostalgia. "November 22, 1963," says DeLillo in an interview, "marked the real beginning of the 1960s. It was the beginning of a series of catastrophes: political assassinations, the war in Vietnam, the denial of Civil Rights and the revolts that occasioned, youth revolt in American cities, right up to Watergate."[1] This of course sounds exactly like DeLillo at his most allusive and authoritative as the rarely public figure whose relative disregard for the routines of literary celebrity only makes his pronouncements feel more grand. This also sounds like a litany of cliché and commonsense that almost any person of a certain age could utter with as much conviction. But we can also, I think, grant DeLillo a little license for the shorthand and synecdoche, given that almost everything he's written about the Kennedy assassination has almost nothing to do with Kennedy as president or even his administration's policies but rather wants to register a whole aesthetic or cultural sensibility in an instant or, to use a more specific term to capture a "structure of feeling" that exceeds whatever happened during a few seconds on November 22, 1963, but that reveals, when reckoned over longer periods of time, some of the conditions and determinants on daily life, emotions, and desires for a class or social group. As a way to talk about the "most delicate and least tangible parts of our activity" within a culture and its epoch, even Raymond Williams's original definition of his signature idea reads like something of an exercise in the nuances and ambiguities of *Libra*'s "blur analysis." A "structure of feeling," he first writes in *The Long Revolution* (1961), "is a very deep and wide possession, in all actual communities, precisely because it is on it that communication depends."² Nor am I going to make things immediately less blurry by reminding us that Williams first used "structure of feeling" in 1954's *Preface to Film* (written with the documentary filmmaker Michael Orrom) and that *The Long Revolution* is itself primarily concerned with the microscopic changes wrought by media technologies and practices of communication in Britain over centuries of uneven "progress" and "development" marked by few large-scale, high-speed cataclysms on the order of events in the United States in 1776 or France in 1789 or Russia in 1917. Modernity as a structure of feeling can come "from" almost anywhere and might be with us for all the futures that we'll live to witness. Or at least this is how we'll see it for the time it takes as an epoch "in" slow motion.

If slow motion gives writers like Faulkner or DeLillo a set of symbols, languages, and visual analogues to think through the problem of when, exactly, modernity begins and ends—and how long we must endure it—the films that I will turn to shortly do not embrace slow motion as a technological metaphor but as a technology. We probably should not be surprised to find slow motion triumph as an iconography of the U.S. 1960s, as a visual language for intensifying violence and valorizing forms of trauma that read as social transformation and vice versa. This is an imagery of the period that all but converges on some mythologies that have not aged especially well or that I would want to reproduce uncritically. DeLillo's remark about the sixties having started with JFK's assassination only amplifies a familiar boomer rhetoric of generational identity, and so too would any argument offering up slow motion as a once vibrant aesthetic form whose modernist credentials have been bled out by its proliferation. I am not interested in a story of slow motion's decline and fall from Kubrick and Antonioni to YouTube's Gav and Dan or in complaining that generic fight scenes from the nth+1 installment of the MCU are mass-market knockoffs of what *Bonnie and Clyde* or *The Wild Bunch* achieved in rendering violent action as an aesthetic tour de force. I'll do my best to guard against a certain nostalgia even as I confess that I'm often happy to indulge it. For me, though, what makes these films important is how they help us remember the sixties—whether we there or not.³ I am struck by all the ways these films turn to slow motion to extend and warp a feeling of their contemporary moment into a longer, stranger temporality of a modern world that is experienced as both accelerated and enduring.

I shouldn't need fully to rehearse the basic shape of the "'situation' of the 60s," as Jameson described it when he was significantly closer to the period, "as the sharing of a common objective situation, to which a whole range of varied responses and creative innovations [was] then possible."⁴ The movies that we will shortly be considering for their spectacular indulgence of slow motion became immediately iconic, with the exception of *Zabriskie Point*, in part because they were so easy for viewers and critics to recognize in light of their contemporary resonance with world events like the Vietnam War or for, however accidentally or unconsciously, their attention to the failings of what Theodore Roszack named "the technocracy . . . that social form in which an industrial society reaches the peak of its organizational integration."[5] Jameson and many others insist that we should understand such dynamics of what he calls "the first world 60s" in the context of the international "third-worldism," which is itself a deeply anachronistic way of talking about the period's investments in the "new revolutionary forces" of the Global South.[6] All to say, in short, that the history of the sixties still can seem, much like slow motion, outdated and ongoing at the same time. I am not suggesting that the slow motion that we see in Hollywood films of the late 1960s is anything like a direct translation of these politics into cinematic style or that a more widespread and ambient fascination with alternative temporalities in these same films is the form that "dropping out" takes, even though many of the "slow" movements of the twenty-first century can trace their genealogies to this period and sustain some of its better and worse fantasies. There are moments in these films that give us refracted glimpses of the Civil Rights Movement or mass resistance to the Vietnam War or echoes of the discourses we associate with second-wave feminism or the Gay Liberation Movement, but I don't think we need to believe that films like *Bonnie and Clyde* or *The Wild Bunch* were as radical as their most ardent champions thought in order to understand what they managed to accomplish.

We should expect to find, in other words, that the same constellation of forces, politics, and people that in the 1960s came to set themselves against the "ideal men" of "technocracy"—who always speak "of modernizing, up-dating, rationalizing, planning"—would also register their resistance to the "classical time" that Western narratives of progress have long assumed, an image of time that, in Carolyn Dinshaw's formulation, must be understood as "linear, laminar, measurably constant." Dinshaw is reflecting on a model of temporality that we have encountered before in Koselleck and others who explore the historiography of time over the centuries of our attempts to understand and represent it. Drawing on the ideas of Michel Serres and Bruno Latour, she describes this familiar cultural logic as "a modernist plot that created the image of time as moving relentlessly forward in a constant, measured flow and promoted the related, specious chronology of modernity with its abjected premodernity."[7] Though Serres comes out of a much different tradition than writers such as Heidegger or Benjamin—each of whom, for what it's worth, aren't really prominent intellectual figures in the United States until the 1960s—the "polychronic" sense of time he champions is echoed in their writings.[8] But there are also inviting parallels and rough analogies between these alternative temporalities, often discovered, as David Couzens Hoy writes, by looking at the wreckage of the West "from the point of view of [its] victims" at this particular beginning of the end of the "American century."[9]

Thus across the range of social movements and protest politics that continue to define the period in both academic histories and popular commemorations, we can find many configurations of time and temporality that try to resist the default speeds and coercive fantasies of progress that define modernity throughout the twentieth century. It is not hard to see how contemporary "slow" movements around food, fashion, and other consumer goods draw on the legacy of 1960s environmentalists or gentrify the counterculture pastoralism of "back to the land" hippies. Invocations of "Nation Time" by both intellectuals and activists working in the Black Power movement were meant to challenge and displace the chronologies of white American history, and Sun Ra's speculative cosmic flights of technoprimitivism make those same timelines seem even more imaginatively impoverished.[10] Native American and Chicano artists in the period offered images of rewilded prairies or a resurgent nation of "Aztlán" in the U.S. southwest and Mexico, among other implicit and overt attempts to turn back the clock on settler colonialism throughout the hemisphere. Postcolonial nationalisms in what was still considered the "developing" or "third world" were also assertions of new temporalities that promised "a decisive and global chapter" in a history of human freedom outside Anglo-European racial contours or that abandoned this project entirely in favor of non-Western historical teleologies shaped by non-Western discourses as Maoism (whether literal or, in Jameson's sense, "symbolic").[11] These contexts help us understand how such interventions as Johannes Fabian's critique of time as it had been traditionally employed by Western anthropologists—that is, as a tool of epistemological power meant to disenfranchise native peoples and indigenous subjects from a shared present— spoke more widely to a post-sixties politics as its radicalism moved, however tentatively, into the academy. Some of the arguments that would eventually be spelled out in Fabian's *Time and the Other* (1983) are first ventured in articles derived from fieldwork that he did in the late 1960s, and they were published in the early 1970s alongside other reflections on and statements against the neoimperialism of the field's most basic and widely held assumptions and chronologies.[12] Time was obviously not the only thing that social movements of the 1960s had to worry about, and not every postmodern turn in the humanities that introduced a note a skepticism about the shape and speed of progress was a downstream consequence of student protests in the streets of Paris or Black uprisings in Watts, Detroit, or Newark. Very little of the slow motion that we'll be tracking in the final section of the book is a direct expression of alternative temporalities, either in a global context or in respect to "those inner colonized of the first world," in Jameson's clunky but revealing phrasing, whose ongoing and imperative claim to other times—feminine time, queer time, crip time—remain unfinished business from the 1960s and suspended for durations that we're still reckoning with today.[13]

My sense of the conceptual terrain that slow motion opens up in the late 1960s is best described by Moishe Postone. As we remember, Postone identifies the epoch of late capitalism by all the ways it founders on a dynamic he calls "the treadmill effect." This is a particularly vivid figure for capturing the dialectical character of both modernity and "the temporal dimension of value," according to Postone, which simultaneously makes the continuous acceleration of accumulation necessary for capitalism to function yet also, "because each new level of productivity is redetermined as a new base level," means that greater and greater quantities of "concrete time" are required to produce the value that is only ever visible as a quantity of "abstract time." Capitalism, for Postone, is a "society marked by a temporal duality—an ongoing, accelerating flow of history, on the one hand, and an ongoing conversion of this movement of time into a constant present, on the other." We move faster—as bodies, as labor power—but feel like we are only getting slower, taking longer. "The constant hour becomes 'denser,'" Postone writes, "yet this 'density' is not manifest in the sphere of abstract temporality" that is capitalist modernity, where time is counted solely as a measure of "the socially necessary labor time required to produce a commodity." Or rather, this is how capital conspires to determine time as an "abstract constant" or "'mathematical time'" while its "historical 'content' . . . remains hidden," much like how, in classical Marxist theory, "the social 'content' of the commodity" is obscured and fetishized in everyday perception. Postone argues that the "transformation of concrete time into abstract time" is both a "temporally normative compulsion" but also changes as it gets "continually reconstituted historically."[14] To borrow a phrase that Stephen Greenblatt used memorably to characterize a different sort of treadmill that promised and contained the energies of modernity, there is no end to speed, only not for us.[15] Or, as we might say with the help of another nineties classic, as we speed up we slow down.

"It's hard to build a robust philosophy of history," write Sarah Brouillette, Joshua Clover, and Annie McLanahan, "around an economic theory for which time itself starts to slow down."[16] They are talking specifically here about the work of the American economist Alvin Hansen, who in the late 1930s suggested that signs of declining population growth and diminishing returns on technological innovation during the Great Depression might signal that there are structural limits to the amount of progress that even a thoroughly active, fully Keynesian capitalism could deliver. The unprecedented mobilization demanded by World War II, which was followed by several decades marked by high levels of Cold War investment in both domestic and international development and also by a global population boom in part made possible in the 1950s and 1960s by the Green Revolution's breakthroughs in agricultural productivity, made Hansen's economic pessimism almost immediately a period relic, an outmoded echo of J. S. Mill's vision of capitalism's dismal future as a "stationary state" where neither profits nor productivity would be likely to increase for the duration. Mill himself took comfort in the image of a "stagnant sea" replacing the frantic acceleration and destructive profiteering that counted as progress for Victorian industrialists; "I confess I am not charmed," he writes, "with the ideal of life held out by those who think the normal state of human beings is that of struggling to get on" and "trampling, crushing, elbowing, and treading on each other's heels."[17] The economic historian Robert Brenner has been arguing for years that growth in the postindustrial societies of the United States and Europe has effectively decelerated to the pace that Mill once dreamed about, though the period Brenner describes as the "Long Downturn" has obviously not seen the "better distribution of property" that Mill foresaw as stagnation's upside. Instead, as Brenner and others have pointed out, declining rates of profit—matched with perpetual austerity and the rampant financialization of the lifeworld—have returned most Western economies to high levels of income inequality and class stratification.[18] Dan Sinykin has traced the contours of these economic shifts—and the variously despairing or fateful fantasies they inspire—in late-twentieth-century and contemporary U.S. literature, suggesting that the widespread popularity of apocalypse as a narrative motif is one measure of just how interminable this period's politics otherwise can seem.[19]

In 2019, *The Economist* gloomily assessed the current world economy as defined by "slowbalisation," with international flows of services, goods, and capital continuing to increase but lagging over time as "globalization has gone from lightning speed to snail's pace in the last decade."[20] Yet there are others who hope that the "long downturn" will get slower even faster and never let the world's economies get back up to speed: In the face of climate change, some economists and environmental scientists insist that wealthy countries in particular should design policies to encourage "degrowth" as the best way to limit the damage already done by global capitalism and also manage the softest possible, though likely still brutal, landing in a world of scarcer resources to come.[21] Brenner's "long downturn" starts with the end of the postwar boom in the early 1970s, which lines up with Robert Gordon's sense that "maintaining growth at the pace of the years before 1970 proved to be beyond the realm of possibility."[22] The first public report of the Club of Rome, an international assembly of economists and politicians founded in 1968, was already forecasting—using the latest in computing technology that today would hardly be enough to run a smart refrigerator—"that under the assumptions of no major change in the present system, population and industrial growth will certainly stop within the next century, at the latest."[23] A lot of people have been quick to see things slowing down since the 1960s.

I might put this another way by suggesting that slow motion tries to visualize some of the small-scale contradictions of speed and temporality that come with the terrain of what a certain style of Marxist thinking once called "uneven and combined development."[24] From its first appearance in Trotsky's *History of the Russian Revolution* to more recent attempts to salvage and resuscitate this term for understanding the conceptual history of world literature, this idea has been contested for almost a century, with some critics trying to apply it as a model for the ways that we see global economic systems operating at their most literal and concrete and others drawing on its symbolic resonance as a figure for thinking through how different modes of cultural production can be variously belated or emergent as expressions of their contemporary moment.[25] Slow motion captures something of the combined and uneven temporality of modern life. The desire for life at different speeds—a wish that slow motion renders emblematic—is real, and the fact that we can witness it accelerating in films of the late 1960s can help us understand why, and on what historical grounds, an imagery of Western progress could seem at once to be running with abandon at the upper limits of full-speed-ahead forever and at the same time winding down and feeling almost terminal and spent, about to die at any second, no matter how long such a fateful second might take finally to happen.

As the social geographer Danny Dorling argues, across a range of demographic measures and economic statistics, "the global point of greatest change, the international pivot point" from acceleration to deceleration "came around the year 1968." I don't think slow motion begins to proliferate at roughly this same moment because artists, novelists, or filmmakers were somehow out in front of gradual trends that still might take decades to observe concretely, much less quantify or prove. But for many figures, the shocks and shifts that we can read as signs that follow on the ending of at least one especially calamitous version of the twentieth century will be so slow to materialize precisely because they will register, perhaps for decades, as just the "recoil from an earlier acceleration," to borrow again from Dorling.[26] Even for a would-be prophet of deceleration such as Dorling, the defining feature of the past fifty years or so remains the problem of all the speed we have to burn—and burn through before it does the same to us—as modern capitalism keeps slowing down. Whether or not we can stand to wait is another question from the extended moment of the sixties that maybe some answered too quickly. In this respect, at least, slow motion is not so much the end of speed but another form of the technologies that made it—which almost no one any longer thinks were built to last.

PART III
Forever '68

22

Bonnie and Clyde and Slow and Fast

Let me begin this book's last section with one thing about slow motion we can know for sure apart from any of the perhaps too free associations I have made along the way: It did not begin with *Bonnie and Clyde*, which had its debut at the Montreal Film Festival on August 4, 1967, and then, just a little less than two hours later, ended with a gruesome showpiece of decelerated gunfire that I can also say for sure must count among the most cited, imitated, and influential sequences in American film. As Jeff Menne notes, there were many films associated with the rise of New Hollywood that assimilated the influence of "location shooting, lightweight camera technology and its attendant lighting procedures," along with a political sensibility among younger filmmakers who fitfully gestured to their "labor force self-understanding" rhyming, however clunkily, with its generational appeal. But no single scene in the period offers a more spectacular assertion of these elements than the ending of *Bonnie and Clyde* and the dazzling bloodshed that marks its mix, returning to Menne, "of bravura style and modernist form."[1] Which is to suggest, I realize, that slow motion does in fact begin with the finale of *Bonnie and Clyde*.

If *Bonnie and Clyde* had not begun the process of translating slow motion from a minor technological form and modernist aesthetic into the most pervasive special effect of global narrative cinema and moving image culture, there would have been no shortage of contenders for this honor, which, strictly speaking, isn't one. Just a couple weeks after *Bonnie and Clyde* had its Montreal premiere, John Boorman's *Point Blank* appeared in theaters and featured an arresting slow-motion flashback dream sequence. *Point Blank* is a brilliant thriller—hard-boiled existentialism of the highest order—but perhaps too unforgiving to become a genuine sensation, with or without slow motion. This was obviously not the case for Kubrick's *2001: A Space Odyssey*, which had its debut in April 1968 and features a slow-motion sequence at primitive humanity's ground zero that I'm sure many can picture. Neither the May 1968 release of Frank Perry's *The Swimmer* nor the August 1968 release of Jerry Paris's *How Sweet It Is!* is remembered now for showing Debbie Reynolds and Burt Lancaster as improbable slow-motion sex symbols, though this is exactly how Ali McGraw's slow-motion nudity in Larry Peerce's adaptation of Philip Roth's *Goodbye Columbus*, which opened in April 1969, introduced her as a star. In between these three films that variously domesticate slow motion for romantic comedy or urbane realism, Sergio Leone's *Once Upon a Time in the West* opened in December 1968 and featured a sequence in slow motion that is, as we shall see, just as epic as we might expect. *Easy Rider*, which had its premiere in July 1969, has only a brief slow-motion flourish at its bitter end, but considering the film's iconic status it could, if *Bonnie and Clyde* had not done so already, have similarly rendered the effect as a default mode of countercultural ambivalence. There is precious little that is ambivalent about the slow motion that Sam Peckinpah indulges in *The Wild Bunch*, which had appeared just one month before in June 1969. In February 1970, Michelangelo Antonioni's ornately self-serious *Zabriskie Point* finally arrived in theaters after five years in production; it promptly bombed, but not for a lack of truly spectacular slow motion in its exquisitely composed finale. These ten films, released over a period of about thirty months, represent more examples of slow motion than any previous decade had witnessed. This is the last time it was possible to comprehend slow motion in some approximation of its totality as a media aesthetic.

Slow motion almost immediately becomes identified with the various restrictions on graphic content—from nudity to bloodshed—that are loosened when the Production Code is finally set aside in 1968. The unprecedented popularity of slow motion that we see at the end of the 1960s is not in any straightforward way a belated, wildly unintended consequence of the Paramount Decree and its destabilization of the studio system; nor is it simply a response to the competitive pressures film faced as an aging medium whose basic infrastructures of exhibition and distribution were not as well aligned with postwar demographics as those of TV.[2] For most of the early sixties, after all, TV was where the action was in slow motion: Sports broadcasts helped conventionalize the effect after 1963 and brought it to countless viewers unlikely to be interested in anything like cinematic modernism or in the more institutionally eccentric "useful" scientific films and other documentaries that would have shown in various classrooms, laboratories, trade shows, and factories. TV ads also began to use slow motion in the early 1960s; whether or not the plush slow-motion fall in the iconic Downy fabric softener ad from 1962 made it the first commercial to employ slow motion, the fact that even decades later Stan Brakhage was still taking credit for the shot suggests the degree to which this image figured as period shorthand for the visual culture of TV advertising and its play with avant-garde techniques.

But *Bonnie and Clyde* holds pride of place in both popular mythologies of the New America cinema and in film histories of the period that are deliberate, if no less admiring, arguments that see more continuities and compromises along the way to what J. D. Connor calls the "neoclassical" Hollywood coming into focus as early as 1970. For critics such as Connor or Jerome Christensen, the rhetoric and pageantry that many figures, both in the 1960s and long after, employed to celebrate the film as radical and epoch making remain distractions from its shrewder and more circumscribed reflections on American culture and its movie industry. From this perspective, *Bonnie and Clyde* is not so much part of a "revolution," to borrow from the journalist Mark Harris and his compelling, largely credulous account of sixties Hollywood. Rather, it is a picture of corporate reorganization that illustrates how the distressed and failing major studios would ultimately survive as media conglomerates and "brands."[3] Given that the film has acquired an outsized reputation as a symbol of generational identity and turnover—and that this reputation continues to draw writers and journalists to its rich and gossipy production history—it is no surprise that several anecdotes about the making of *Bonnie and Clyde* circulate with almost clockwork regularity.[4] Told here by its director, Arthur Penn, this one in particular has made the rounds. The two young Hollywood auteurs had to sell their movie to Jack Warner, long nicknamed the "Colonel" and the last surviving mogul of Hollywood's bygone golden era. It should come as no surprise that the three men didn't exactly speak the same language:

> We arrived with the film. The Colonel warned us, "If I have to get up and pee during this, you'll know the movie stinks."
> ... We were still in the first of the ten reels that constituted the movie when Jack arose and left the room. We looked at each other, uncertain whether or not to stop the projection. We didn't. The Film ran on. Jack returned to his seat. The film narrative began to gain velocity, and we thought we had him. No. He was up again, peed, returned, watched, peed, returned, peed, and the longest, most diuretic film in human memory, came to an end.
> Silence.
> "What the hell was that?" spake the Colonel.

Nervous small talk.

". . . the hell was that?" he said again.

Warren Beatty rose and began to speak about the great gangster films that Warner Brothers had been famous for through several decades. Finally, he concluded. "So you see, Jack, this, in a sense, an *homage* to those great films."

Silence.

". . . the fuck is an *homage*?"[5]

I want to say this anecdote is irresistible, though I know its clubby details and aura of Hollywood masculinity (new and old) are definitely acquired tastes. Penn lets Beatty make the pitch that seems to save the day, which is in keeping with the credit he is usually accorded as not just the star of *Bonnie and Clyde* but also its producer. Beatty seems to have persuaded Warner, despite how mystifying and exhausting he found the film, that it was a contemporary variation on a classic Warner Bros. genre, if not a logical extension of a form rooted in such iconic 1930s films as *The Public Enemy* (1931) and *Little Caesar* (1931). As Christensen observes, "no actor-producer since Chaplin had been as intimately involved with all aspects of a Hollywood production—including distribution and exhibition." More importantly, Christensen details just how "adroitly [Beatty] manipulated the means at his disposal to displace the corporate line of succession at Warner Bros. and to project a fundamental change in its corporate structure."[6] Beatty didn't put one over on the aging studio chief so much as grasp how a more decentralized and financially leveraged production system put more power in the hands of enterprising actors and directors who were willing to take on greater risks and break established norms, if not the law. For Penn and Beatty, time was on their side. In 1966, Warner had sold much of his share in the studio he helped found, and his reluctance to throw his full support behind *Bonnie and Clyde* at best delayed its wide acclaim by limiting the scope of its release. Though even this attempt at sabotage finally backfired to Beatty's advantage when the strong divergence of critical reactions to the film—with older, conservative writers such as Bosley Crowther for the *New York Times* attacking it repeatedly and younger reviewers, particularly Pauline Kael in the *New Yorker*, defending it with even greater ardor—became central to the publicity campaign that assured the visibility of *Bonnie and Clyde* despite some disappointing early numbers at the box office. As the winner of this battle over Warner's bladder and Warner Bros., it is easy for Penn to joke in retrospect that *Bonnie and Clyde* was "the longest, most diuretic film in human memory." For me, though, the film best comes into focus as an expression of its moment by looking at what it accomplished in slow motion—which we know today will never end.

A HISTORY OF VIOLENCE

Bonnie and Clyde memorably begins with no motion. After the appearance and disappearance of a sepia-tinted vintage Warner Brothers shield—"a relic of antiquity," in Christensen's terrifically suggestive language—the black screen suddenly gives way to a series of equally anachronistic photographs as seven black-and-white images of nameless individuals flash and fade before we read "Warren Beatty" in letters that at first match the pale brown palette of the film's cold open in the archives and then slowly turn deep red in what is literally a "bleed" that takes about three seconds, which is longer than any other picture or name will linger for the remainder of the credits.[7] Four more photographs go by at roughly the same pace before Faye Dunaway gets second billing, and about a second less on screen, as her name also bleeds to red a little faster than Beatty's. Three more pictures, and then the names of three supporting actors—Michael J. Pollard, Gene Hackman, and Estelle Parsons—who play the other members of the Barrow Gang; their names also turn to red, and then two more pictures of, first, a young girl and then a boy, each captured from the knees up and wearing hats that partially obscure their faces. Though we can't know who they are any more than all the other faces from the past in the sixteen photographs that thus far make up the film we're watching, they become "Bonnie and Clyde" when the title of the movie shows up next and fades to red and then to black to prepare us for the rest of the credits.[8]

"There's something new working for the Bonnie and Clyde legend now," according to Kael: "our nostalgia for the thirties." This was certainly among the come-ons that Penn and Beatty used to sell the film to Jack Warner when he wasn't in the bathroom, but Kael is almost as resistant to the idea of "homage" as the Colonel. Throughout her famous essay on the film for the *New Yorker*, she insists repeatedly on the degree to which *Bonnie and Clyde* is "contemporary in feeling" even though she admits, from the perspective of a very royal "we," that "our experience as we watch it has some connection with the way we reacted to movies in childhood," with "how we came to love them and to feel they were ours." I will have more to say about the structure and the temporality of the cinephilia that the film so desperately inspires, but what I find especially striking about Kael's assertive presentism—"this film expresses certain feelings of ours," there is no missing "just how contemporary in feeling *Bonnie and Clyde* is"—is that she attributes it, at least in part, to where it's coming from. "An American movie," as Kael puts it plainly, "makes a different kind of contact with an American audience from the kind that is made by European films, however contemporary."[9] There is no arguing with Kael's love for the anachronism of the film's Americana since, in keeping with the logic of her own rhetoric, you either feel it with her or you don't. She has to acknowledge that *Bonnie and Clyde* pays tribute to some of the European sources that David Newman and Robert Benton, two *Esquire* journalists trying to break into the movies, had idolized and assimilated into their earliest conceptions of the project as they shaped the screenplay, which they first tried to get made with François Truffaut and later pitched to Jean-Luc Godard, who proposed to shoot the film in Tokyo.[10] Kael does not have a lot of nice things to say about Penn as a director, and she disapproves of how he "unfortunately imitates Truffaut's artistry" in a gangster pastiche like *Shoot the Piano Player* instead of "going back to its tough American sources" in the Warner Bros. films that Beatty traded on to sell the project to Jack Warner.[11] Elsewhere Kael will wish that *Bonnie and Clyde* borrowed more heavily from Truffaut; she was opinionated, not consistent. Her main complaint is that Penn's directing keeps us "too conscious of the technical means" that give the film its character and structure. She wanted modern, not modernism.

With Truffaut and *The 400 Blows* as a strong influence on the screenplay, it is a little surprising that *Bonnie and Clyde* does not also end its story with the sort of freeze-frame that, in an example that it partially inspires, leaves the outlaws of *Butch Cassidy and the Sundance Kid* (1969) suspended, in what Garrett Stewart describes as a moment of "temporal arrest encoded with "the plot's (as well as the medium's) own nostalgia for itself."[12] Slow motion and freeze-frame are close relations; Cavell includes the latter as another of the "assertions in technique" that, along with the former, speaks to different ways that films like *Bonnie and Clyde* and *Butch Cassidy and the Sundance Kid* try to extend their subjects' hold on us by "[translating] them into immortality." He doesn't really like freeze-frames either, complaining that they have become "an uncontrollable tic" so mandatory as to seem "apparently part of the contract in television drama" when he is writing in 1971. But he does appreciate the ending of *Bonnie and Clyde*. "At the finish," he writes, "the film persists in an elegy of bullets long after the pair are dead. Society is making sure of itself. But art is not so satisfied. The camera is at once confessing its invasion of their existences and its impotence to preserve them, and our pasts in them; it is at once taking vengeance on them for their absence and accompanying them across the line of death."[13] This puts "the sting back into death" in a language and tradition of high aesthetic seriousness that could not possibly be more removed from the knowingly contemporary "put-on" that Kael admires the film for venturing with its period trappings.

No critic in the period could mistake the emphasis that Penn's style placed on violence—on very stylish violence—in whatever sort of "homage" to the gangster movie that he and Beatty were offering. In one of his almost hysterically hostile reviews of *Bonnie and Clyde* for the *New York Times*, Crowther was left at a loss to fathom why Penn filled the screen "with smears of vivid blood" since the film's "blending of farce with brutal killings is as pointless as it is lacking in taste."[14] Writing for the equally conservative *Films in Review*, it was not enough for Page Cook to call the movie "*dreck*"; she was also horrified by the "*evil in the tone*" and the mix of comedy and bloodshed to "incite in the young the delusion that armed robbery and murder are mere 'happenings.'" These are precisely the critics that Kael saw as altogether wrong about the irony that sustained the film and its triumphant play of signs and signifiers.

"This is not a case study of Bonnie and Clyde," Penn admits in answering a reporter's question about the historical accuracy of his version of the famous real-life outlaws at a press conference in Montreal after his film premiered, "we don't go into them in any kind of depth." Penn instead pulls back to frame *Bonnie and Clyde* as nothing less than an account of modernity and its evolution, sounding like an American Studies professor who has just read a lot of Paul Virilio. He improbably describes the movie as an allegory of speed, technology, and the state's monopoly on violence. For my purposes, it makes for some compelling reading. We should probably be glad, though, that Beatty did most of the talking at Jack Warner's if Penn was going to talk like this:

> When Ford made the V-8, which was sufficiently powerful to out-run the local police automobiles, gangs began to spring up. And that was literally the genesis of the Clyde and Barrow gang. What happened was that they lived in their automobile. . . . It was really where they lived. Bonnie wrote her poetry in the car, they ate ginger snaps in the car, they played checkers in the car—that was their place of abode. In American Western mythology, the automobile replaced the horse in terms of the renegade figure. This was transformation of the Western into the gangster.
>
> Meanwhile, these very rural people were suffering the terrors of a depression, which resulted in families being uprooted, farms being foreclosed, homes being taken away, by the banks, the *establishment* of their world, which in part was represented by the police.[15]

We don't have to think that Penn is right or believe that his class politics were best served by the especially glamorous vehicle he chose to "mobilize" them to start seeing the outlines of the film that even some true radicals came to admire in 1968. "Let's face it," he starts a later answer to a reporter who I hope was ready for the barrage, "Kennedy was shot. We're in Vietnam, shooting people and getting shot. We have not been out of war for any period of time in my lifetime.

Gangsters were flourishing during my youth, I was in the war at age 18, then came Korea, now comes Vietnam." Once Penn gets on a roll, there is no end to violence in his vision of what American society has been throughout the twentieth century. "We have a violent society," he says in something of an understatement of the carnage he's just cataloged: "So why not make films about it?" Penn traces the experience of violence, speed, and trauma back into the very texture of modern life even when it doesn't seem to be hurting anyone. "I don't mean 'violence' only pejoratively," he tries to clarify. "It's violent to get in an airplane and be in Montreal in an hour—it's a violent experience, an assault on the senses. It's an assault on the senses to get in an automobile and drive: it's an assault on the senses to do so many of the things that we do." Given that Penn sounds like he is impossibly ventriloquizing Walter Benjamin—the first English translation of "The Work of Art" essay would not be published in *Illuminations* until later in 1968—it perhaps should come as no surprise that he is drawn to slow motion for its uncanny way of showing us the damage that the "optical unconscious" can record without our knowing it. When Penn observes that "we live in a violent time," he is of course referring to the sixties. But even their accelerating, intensifying violence is just a matter of degrees from what we've been enduring all along. "It is the character of the modern world," as Penn has forever known it.[16]

Kael believes the movie is a triumph precisely because it trades on the short memories that viewers have on the far side of an accelerated century. For Kael, this is the best joke in all of *Bonnie and Clyde*, though it only works when Penn gets out of the way:

> We tend to find the past funny and the recent past campy-funny. The getaway cars of the early thirties are made to seem hilarious (Imagine anyone getting away from a bank holdup in a tin lizzie like that!) In *You Only Live Once*, the outlaws existed in the same present as the audience, and there was (and still is, I'm sure) nothing funny about them; in *Bonnie and Clyde* that audience is in the movie, transformed into the poor people, the Depression people, of legend—with faces and poses out of Dorothea Lange and Walker Evans and *Let Us Now Praise Famous Men*.... The writers and director of *Bonnie and Clyde* play upon our attitudes toward the American past by making the hats and guns and holdups look as dated as two-reel comedy; emphasizing the absurdity with banjo music, they make the period seem even farther away than it is. The Depression reminiscences are not used for purposes of social consciousness; hard times are not the reason for the Barrows' crimes, just the excuse. "We" didn't make Clyde a killer; the movie deliberately avoids easy sympathy by picking up Clyde when he is already a cheap crook. But Clyde is not the

urban sharpster of *The Public Enemy*; he is the hick as bank robber—a countrified gangster, a hillbilly killer who doesn't mean any harm. People so simple that they are alienated from the results of their actions—like the primitives who don't connect babies with copulation—provide a kind of archetypal comedy for us.[17]

There is too much happening too fast in this passage to address its every turn. But I am mainly interested in how Kael locates the comedy of *Bonnie and Clyde* as an effect of differential speeds. The joke or "put-on" of the film depends on audiences of the sixties recognizing that everything the characters believe is fast and modern (their cars, their crimes, their politics) looks almost inconceivably slow in 1967. Their present was already history to them—a "legend" we can still recall in photographs like those that start the film—but one too far away from Kael to count as anything but an "absurdity." It is as anachronistic now for "purposes of social consciousness" as a "tin lizzie" would be as a getaway car with a maximum velocity that couldn't reach a current speed limit. In *Bonnie and Clyde*, the best things in life and death are fast and slow at once.

NOSTALGIA FOR NOSTALGIA FOR NOSTALGIA

The first use of slow motion in *Bonnie and Clyde* might not be awful, but it isn't much to look at. After about an hour of robberies, high-speed chases, and shootouts, the full Barrow Gang—Bonnie; Clyde; their first recruit, C. W. Moss (Michael J. Pollard); and Clyde's brother, Buck (Gene Hackman), and his wife, Blanche (Estelle Parsons)—must steal a car to replace one left leaking oil from their most recent criminal adventure. The car they end up taking belongs to a minor character named Eugene Grizzard, played by Gene Wilder in his film debut, who then decides to pursue the Barrows with his girlfriend, Velma (Evans Evans), before abandoning the chase in what we know to be the exceedingly well-founded fear that they may have guns. Do they ever.

Then, for no reason whatsoever apart from Clyde's split-second impulse, the Barrow Gang starts chasing Eugene and Velma in Eugene's own stolen car, which they use to force them off the road. Eugene and Velma are made to squeeze into the back seat with Buck and Blanche, which is when they learn that they've been kidnapped by the most wanted outlaws in the nation. Eugene and Velma soon settle down from their initial shock and start cracking jokes, sharing hamburgers, and laughing at the prospect of "joining up with us," as Clyde says so effortlessly, with a sly grin and stuffed mouth, that we are supposed to think that maybe these two squares are actually going to stick around. Until, that is, Bonnie asks Eugene what he does and Wilder's character answers that he's an undertaker. Then suddenly there isn't anything funny, at least as far as Bonnie is concerned, about the two stiffs that Clyde was charming into lives of crime. Newman and Benton were more heavy-handed in the original screenplay. When Eugene states his occupation, we read: "Suddenly everyone freezes. A shudder, as if the cold hand of death had suddenly touched the occupants of the car. The atmosphere changes to cold, deadly, fearful silence in exactly one second. It is a premonition of death for the Barrows, and they react accordingly, BONNIE especially."[18] There is plenty of excess mortality in the air already, and the desolation of the field where Bonnie and Clyde reconcile after this disturbing interlude is not an inspiring backdrop for their shared future. In a genuinely stunning bit of landscape cinematography, Burnett Guffey manages to capture the deep shadows of clouds passing in an elegant and overdetermined show of what Jordan Schonig calls "contingent motion."[19] We fade into the next scene, where Clyde and the Barrow Gang meet Bonnie's mother and her extended Parker family. It might be what Bonnie wanted, but things have gotten darker still.

"*Bonnie and Clyde* is about style," declares David Newman, reflecting back on the film after more than thirty years, "and people who have style. It is about people whose style set them apart from their time and place so that they seemed odd and aberrant to the general run of society."[20] For Kael, the problem with this scene is that it has style to burn, with too much showy camerawork and other affectations. This is not to suggest that the deeply unsatisfying reunion that Bonnie has with her mother and her family is just a failure on stylistic grounds, but from the first instant of the Barrow Gang's desperate attempt to return to at least a version of "society," things aren't looking good. The shadowed skies we just saw in the cornfield have darkened further, and the visual gloom is unrelenting since Penn and Guffey shot the entire scene with filtered lenses; everything is dim and muddy, though this makes the arid, almost anaerobic landscape sound more appealing than it appears on screen. It's not that Penn and Guffey manage to make Dunaway and Beatty look bad—a feat that no filmmakers could have accomplished in 1967—but they do bleed as much life as they possibly can from the conventional markers of the future that would be waiting for Bonnie and Clyde if they weren't so "odd and aberrant" and, more importantly, so stylish. Kids and family picnics might be a fine way for the rest of the Parkers to spend an afternoon, but we aren't interested in Bonnie and Clyde as they go through the motions of domestic routine like the normies that they thrillingly are not. Nobody has ever watched *Bonnie and Clyde* and wished for more Eugene and Velma.

Kael labels this scene "the showpiece sequence" of the film, which is her way of saying that she hates it.[21] Almost every aesthetic decision she can spot is evidence of how "Penn's limitations show" when his directorial ambitions become too obvious. While she understands that the film is trying for "an effect of alienation," Kael is brutal in her assessment of what instead goes wrong as Penn creates instead "a frieze from our national past" that is both too artful in its "filtered effects" but also too simple in the sentiments and feelings it conveys, which are finally bromides, to borrow a period-appropriate idiom, about the "poetic echoes of childhood" and the "Depression of our dreams." "Our memories *have* become hazy" over time, but Kael does not approve of Penn's literalization of what is, after all, a natural historical process, in the "filtered effects" he employs as the "the technical means used to achieve this blur." She can see right through him. To understand how badly Penn has botched this Dust Bowl interlude, Kael expects her reader to recall a structurally similar scene in William Wyler's 1937 crime melodrama *Dead End* (haven't seen it), as well as the superior historicism of John Ford's 1939 biopic *Young Mr. Lincoln* (nor this one). She also pointedly compares this scene in *Bonnie and Clyde*—again, to Penn's discredit—with Truffaut's *Jules and Jim*, which not only is an exemplary model of a film that is technically about the past but would resonate with many of Kael's readers in the sixties as "contemporary in feeling" but also would have functioned as the most knowing of inside jokes between Kael and Newman and Benton: Through a series of connections in New York, Newman and Benton had pitched an early treatment of their eventual screenplay—translated into French—to Truffaut in hopes of enticing him to direct.[22]

As the reunion scene continues, we have a bit of slapstick involving Bonnie and Clyde posing for a snapshot as if they have been captured at gunpoint by a dopey member of the extended Parker clan, and Clyde gently nudges down the deadly weapon that has been aimed at them for comic effect. Then we cut to another loaded joke, so to speak: two boys playing cops and robbers at the top of a dune bring their game to its predestined conclusion (figure 22.1). At the prompting of the boy who disappears behind the hill, the other tumbles over in slow motion, rolling twice as he falls across the screen before Bonnie comes to crouch above his "dead" body with a smile that turns quickly—even in slow motion—to a more disturbed expression when she also seems to register the obvious foreshadowing we have witnessed. Guffey filmed the family reunion scene at the old-fashioned speed of 18fps, perhaps to underscore the rougher, documentary look that Penn was after, so the slow motion was achieved by shooting double-time at 36fps. These technicalities aside, Kael is dismissive of how slow motion merely functions here to convey "poetic echoes of childhood." She invokes it as a mere "echo" of a similar scene in *Jules and Jim* that shows a

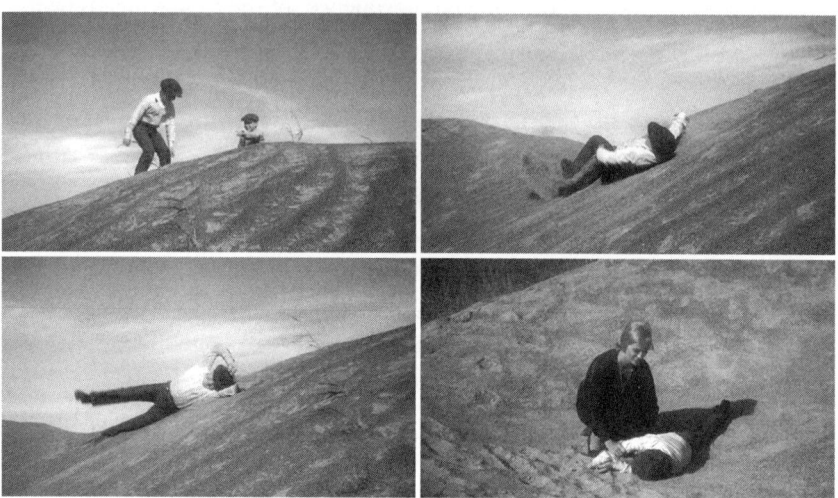

FIGURE 22.1 Stills from *Bonnie and Clyde* (1967).

"child sliding down the hill" and so undersells the originality of this moment in *Bonnie and Clyde* even as she is brutally correct to see it as cliché. The problem, at least for Kael, is that Penn's slow motion is emotionally manipulative and forced. Because the filtered lighting and soft focus visually estrange us from the past the film depicts, the additional "stylization" of slow motion isn't necessary. "The lines are good enough," Kael argues on behalf of Newman and Benton. Their screenplay—with its jokey gunplay and displays of happy children—gives us all the mournful foreshadowing we should need, and so "a simple frozen frame might have been more appropriate." And while there isn't any slow motion in *Jules and Jim*, there is a very subtle freeze-frame that pauses the action in the midst of Jules and Jim's first embrace after their time apart, a moment of photographic stillness to memorialize the brief interlude of complicated intimacy the three will share as an ideal version of a family.

So Kael dislikes the look of the reunion scene intensely, but she loves Penn's bloody and horrific ending. "The rag-doll dance of death as the gun blasts keeps the bodies of Bonnie and Clyde in motion," she simply declares, "is brilliant." We will look more closely at this second, and excruciatingly final, time that *Bonnie and Clyde* employs slow motion in a moment, but note how Kael's brief description of the scene acknowledges that, since they are corpses almost from the very second that the sheriffs and cops start shooting, whatever it is that "keeps the bodies" moving must be applied from the outside. "It is a horror that seems to go on for eternity," Kael continues, "and yet it doesn't last a second beyond what it should." She praises Dede Allen's editing for the scene's exquisite timing and duration, though in something of a parting shot she does concede that "one may assume that Penn deserves [some] credit for it."[23] Within the film, these "gun blasts" manage to produce motion out of what should be still; this isn't so much "change mummified," to recall Bazin, as movement zombified for us to witness as a brutal application of power and technology. Slow motion reveals that film has the capacity to capture life in intervals too small for human beings to perceive, but it is far more powerful as an aesthetic that reminds us that media can make dead things seem to move at any speed that we might wish to see or, even if we don't, still watch in terrifying fascination.

IMPOTENCE (BAD TIMING)

"And then there was the sex problem": While not as outrageously visible on screen as the slow-motion violence that ends the film, Newman and Benton had been determined to make this spectacle of bloodshed share top billing with another riot of broken taboos and scandalous imagery they derived from "veiled and often contradictory references to Clyde's sex life." Recounted almost as often as the story of "Colonel" Warner's bladder, the film's writers describe, as if just confirming their fidelity to archival records, how "all the sources indicated" that Clyde "wasn't quite 'normal' in either his preferences of sexual partner, or practice, or both and so much more." In a tone that is at once provoking and detached—their stylistic signature as *Esquire* trend spotters—they recount rumors of "an S-M trip," or at least some "inferred homosexuality." Though only one or two accounts suggested that Bonnie and Clyde might have been more open as a couple, it is this possibility that of course intrigued them most; as they put it in 1972, "Clyde and Bonnie and one or another of the various men in the gang at different times were involved in a functioning *ménage-à-trois*, a mini-orgy in every little motel." Shortly after Penn and Beatty joined their foursome, the prospect of having the film's hero labeled "as a sexual deviant" was abandoned. "Arthur didn't go for it, and it worried Warren, too," and so Newman and Benton not surprisingly relented "in our quest for an off-beat love affair." We instead get ample references to Clyde's impotence and a single, highly concentrated glimpse of the film's first-draft perversity in the form of the tattoo that C. W. Moss reveals as we cut from the aborted picnic of familial normalcy that includes the initial appearance of slow motion that would be even more forgotten now if Newman and Benton had had their way. Gene Hackman's Buck has to push aside the tube from the gas mask Moss is wearing to read that he has had "LOVE" inscribed beneath a female figure that he insists to Buck is not his girlfriend, though he then adds that the bluebirds that fly above his nipples were, in fact, "Bonnie's idea." The idea of a traveling three-way at the erotic center of the Barrow Gang, Newman and Benton will recall in 1972, "seemed just bizarre and somehow brave enough to fit right in with our notion of [their] avant-garde style." "We had our Bonnie in love with Clyde, to be sure," they write of the queer triangle that the film does not entirely discard, "but our Clyde, while in love with Bonnie, unable to perform sexually without the stimulation of the third (generally) unwilling sidekick."[24]

I'm willing to bet that Clyde's literal "impotence," performed by Beatty with such deliberate mannerisms in the film, is about the last thing Cavell wants to evoke in his reflections on how *Bonnie and Clyde* reveals that art can't always rise to the occasion. But this doesn't mean that we can't see it almost every time the film slows down. Clyde's impotence doesn't just pattern the narrative of *Bonnie and Clyde* by getting in the way or blocking us from seeing what potentially could have been more sex on screen to match the film's stupendous violence. There are, of course, repeated scenes that stage Bonnie's desire and its frustration as a source of conflict at the level of plot and character, and the fact that their relationship is largely chaste—against the grain of Beatty's established image as a star, as well as Dunaway's own considerable erotic dazzle—is a point the film keeps making like an argument it has to prove by citing solid evidence and counting up examples. The narrative of the movie opens in a breathless rush of erotic action and dramatic foreplay that confirms that Clyde can't go quite as fast as Bonnie wants. They flirt and banter about armed robbery, and Clyde explains his limp by telling her how he chopped off two toes to avoid forced labor while in prison. It won't be very long before his limp comes to function as the most conspicuous symbol of Clyde's condition, which Beatty signals with method-acting gusto in keeping with Penn's determination, according to John Cawelti, that both "Clyde's impotence and his shame about it" were to be "much more explicit in the film than in [the] original script."[25] Thus what follows as Bonnie and Clyde indulge in foreplay for their first crime together is a hash of phallic imagery and compensatory substitutes that let us see the couple getting turned on by Clyde's little toothpick, two bottles of Coke, and, after she mocks him for being a "faker" about his having done "hard" time, so to speak, the gun Clyde lets her fondle knowingly while she dares him to prove he has the "gumption" to use it. For this particular show of his manhood, Clyde can't go any faster: He walks into the nearest store and comes out with a bulging fistful of dollars, chased by the clerk before he fires a warning shot; somewhat belatedly he and Bonnie introduce themselves and then speed off to the appropriately frenetic bluegrass of Lester Flatt and Earl Scrugg's "Foggy Mountain Breakdown." Though no one is chasing them, the ride is not without its thrills: Bonnie—who clearly expects more in the way of action now that Clyde has proved his pistol fully operational—tries to embrace and kiss him with more passion than he seems willing to risk out on the open road.

When Clyde stops the car, she is all but in his lap and tries to pull him down on top of her, ready now to desublimate the Freudian erotics of their first encounter by pulling out the real attraction behind the substitute that Bonnie has already touched before Clyde pops off in the street. But no: She instead hears Clyde say, "Slow down, slow down, slow down, slow down" as he not only hesitates but with increasing agitation tries to fight his way from her embrace. We see Beatty step out of the car and take a theatrically measured walk, his limping leg on grand display, before he comes back to explain that he "ain't much of a lover boy." It's nothing "personal" about her, Clyde maintains, and he even tries to make the situation sound more disinterested and strictly rational by assuring her that he's "never saw no percentage" in having sex. We've already seen that armed robbery has an immediate return on minimal investment and is all but guaranteed to produce a "money" shot—Clyde brandishes a flashy stack of dollar bills as he runs out of the grocery store. Clyde says he's certain that he "don't like boys," and Beatty sells the line with a bit of physical comedy that is perfectly unsubtle in its timing. Still backing away from Bonnie—despite the fact that she is signaling that the moment, such as it is, has passed—Clyde pulls out prematurely from the car and bangs his head (figure 2.22). His hat is knocked down over his face, and the accompanying metal thump is both the rim shot for the revealing, phobic joke and the bell that tolls for the far racier set of sexual permutations that Newman and Benton's early draft of Clyde had to lose along the way.

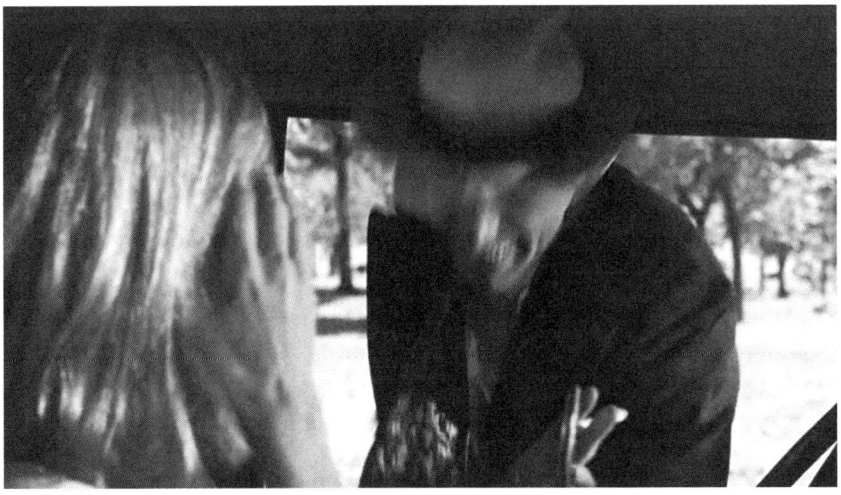

FIGURE 22.2 Queer slapstick in a still from *Bonnie and Clyde* (1967).

We shouldn't read too much into this moment of cringing slapstick as Clyde and Bonnie realize that, though they share a passion for armed robbery, they get off from its rush in different ways, at different speeds. The tone is closer to Kael's language of the "put-on" than it is to Cavell's too somber invocation of art's "impotence" in the face of time and death. Even knowing that Clyde was originally imagined as a figure of far more ambiguous sexuality, Penn and Beatty give us little reason to believe that he is lying when he says he "don't like boys"—despite the bonk he gives himself by being so quick to argue. "*Bonnie and Clyde*," Kael writes, "substitutes sexual fulfillment for a change of heart" to lend a sense of narrative development and arc to Beatty's protagonist since, unlike the products of old Hollywood and its conventions of "romanticism," there isn't a "falsified finish when the anti-hero turns hero." When Clyde finally "finishes" in the field with Bonnie after several failed attempts in variously dingy motel rooms while on the run, the fact that he can maintain an erection for the time he needs to orgasm is about the only thing that's changed about him as a character since the beginning of the movie. "Audiences sophisticated enough to enjoy a movie like this one," she proposes, "are too sophisticated for the dramatic uplift of the triumph over impotence," which is just another "fancy lyric interlude" like the slow-motion sequence in the reunion scene with Bonnie's family. "One is never for a minute convinced he's impotent," she insists, but even this "failure" is a tribute to the ways that his "slow timing works perfectly" in scenes where "there may not be another actor who would have dared to prolong" some of the lines and beats he makes us wait and wait for; "the prolongation" we suffer and enjoy because of his "non-actor's 'bad' timing" is transformed into a "kind of genius" as we are forced to watch him "*think out* his next move."[26] We don't need to read Beatty's mind to see what happens to his body when he says "slow down." Slow motion might not, as Cavell suggests, "[translate] them to immortality." But it does almost the next best thing by letting us watch while they act themselves to death.

SLOW MOTION AND THE RENOWN OF FRENZY

The second use of slow motion in *Bonnie and Clyde* is recognized as nearly perfect for the brutality of its beauty and vice versa. It is as impossible to track or quantify its actual influence on narrative cinema in America and around the world since 1967 as it is to deny its outsized presence in the history of screen violence, popular culture, and the New Hollywood. I've said the ending of *Bonnie and Clyde* was my wrong first guess for the origins of slow motion as the media effect we think we know so well—or as least see so much—today. I am too young to have seen *Bonnie and Clyde* in a theater and honestly can't remember when I first rented it on VHS after its 1990 release in this old-fashioned format that, like the film's antihero and -heroine, now is dead. *Bonnie and Clyde* was not a mark of generational identity for me or a vivid experience of something I'd never seen before—especially not slow motion, which I am old enough to have seen in impossible abundance almost entirely by accident just from watching moving images since the 1970s on many screens of different sizes. D. A. Miller acknowledges, having seen the film in 1967 and then again, just a few years ago, on DVD, that "violence in slow motion" is not just crucial to whatever "spectacle of resolution" the narrative of *Bonnie and Clyde* tries to provide but is obviously, from a retrospect of more than fifty years, "the film's most spectacular—and transmissible—stylistic innovation."[27] Everything that felt "new" in *Bonnie and Clyde*, from the texture of its actors' performances and vintage splendor of their costumes to its technically impeccable and original slow motion, now only "consummates the film's very retro-ness, as a movie made in full anticipation of the nostalgia it might one day occasion and is actually occasioning from the start." Even the slow motion that brings the film to a profoundly horrific stop manages to work because it looks like something we've already seen. Which is true, though no one ever had.

While we know that Penn, Beatty, and Towne made many changes to Newman and Benton's script, the ending of the film follows closely from the version they conceived. Maybe not quite so close that we can count as "the laws [*sic*] fire eighty-seven shots into BONNIE and CLYDE" but faithfully enough that we do, more or less, see what Newman and Benton want us to: "the bodies of CLYDE and BONNIE twisting, shaking, horribly distorted; much of the action is in slow motion."[28] They picture Clyde's body "arching and rolling from the impact of the bullets" and then Bonnie's body "jerking and swaying as the bullets thud relentlessly into her" before her corpse "slews out sideways, head first" from the car as Clyde's body "rolls over and over on the ground and then lies still." The sequence that Penn, Guffey, and Allen ultimately construct from these sketchy though certainly evocative lines is flamboyantly complex and crafted, a display of New Hollywood aesthetics that trades on the old Hollywood professionalism of Guffey and Allen in particular.

Slow motion was not a novelty to Penn, however, who would have known at least one of the two or three precedents for decelerated graphic violence in Hollywood film before *Bonnie and Clyde*. He directed it: In 1958, Penn's debut, *The Left Handed Gun*, shows Paul Newman's Billy the Kid exact his cool revenge on the brutal Sheriff Ollinger when he shoots him with a shotgun as Ollinger squints into the high sun and manages to make out the blurry figure on the nearby roof just before Billy raises his weapon and fires, a wry smile on his face and Ollinger's gun still in its holster. The relatively few instances of Hollywood slow motion from before *The Left Handed Gun*, we might recall, are either inner reveries of fantasy or psychic trauma (*Love Me Tonight*, *What Price Hollywood?*), dance sequences (in *Carefree*'s dream sequence or Astaire's solo in *Easter Parade*), or decidedly less-than-graphic action sequences (in *The Thief of Bagdad* or *The Crime of Helen Small*). A veteran of the studio system like Penn's cinematographer on *The Left Handed Gun*, J. Peverell Marley, might well have known a couple of these films since he was already an established professional by 1924, when Douglas Fairbanks wrestled with a giant underwater spider in Raoul Walsh's gloriously hand-tinted slow motion. But Arthur Penn would have been just two years old, and anyway he cites Kurosawa's *The Seven Samurai* as his model. "Certainly the slowed motion of Akira Kurosawa's great films inspired," Penn explains, but then insists that when he "did experiment very briefly" with the effect in his first film, he didn't quite realize the power of its "true use."[29]

We know a great deal about how the final scene of *Bonnie and Clyde* was shot. As Stephen Prince notes, "Penn and his crew joined four cameras side by side, each running at a different speed"; thus Penn, Guffey, and Allen had footage of the action from the same perspective that was shot at 24, 48, 72, and 96fps.[30] So it is not just slow motion but a mix of slow and slower motions—all captured without disrupting the illusion of the classical spectator as a singular observer in the space outside the screen—that helps make the violence so compelling and, perversely enough, lends it an almost unbearable momentum as the scene proceeds at breakneck speed across the final minute depicting their last split seconds. Again from Prince, who has tracked the history of cinematic violence in commanding detail, we discover—for those who haven't counted—that there are fifty-one shots in the fifty-four seconds that comprise this hail of bullets in various slow motions, a pace that not even the most aggressive action films of our contemporary era of "intensified continuity" can maintain for very long. The average shot length of *Bonnie and Clyde* is just under four seconds, which compares favorably—depending on your tastes—to the frenetic tempos of directors like Paul Greengrass in the *Bourne* trilogy (*The Bourne Identity* [2002], *The Bourne Supremacy* [2004], *The Bourne Ultimatum* [2007]) or the "Bayhem" that is particularly extreme in Michael Bay's *Transformer* films (*The Transformers* [2007], et al.), where the average shot length is closer to three seconds.[31] To almost the same degree that Jack Warner resisted seeing *Bonnie and Clyde* as an "homage" to films like *Public Enemy* or *Little Caesar*, I suspect that neither Penn nor any of his collaborators would want the credit for inspiring, however inadvertently, the perceptual challenges of *Resident Evil 2* (2004, Paul W. S. Anderson) or *Die Hard 4* (2007, Len Wiseman). "Penn was the first American filmmaker," Prince writes, "to conjoin multicamera filming, montage editing, and slow motion systematically in the visualization of screen violence."³² Apart from Kurosawa, Penn is probably the first to do this anywhere.

The ambush that kills Bonnie and Clyde is the culmination of several plotlines that unfold with deliberate and even clunky foreshadowing in the film's last act. After Buck's death, Blanche is arrested and mercilessly interrogated by Sheriff Hamer; she gives him the name of C. W. Moss, which gives Hamer the leverage that he needs to conspire with Moss's father, not that it takes much for Hamer to turn Moss's father against Bonnie and Clyde since he is already disgusted by the perversion he sees literally tattooed on his son's body. It's not clear how much of all this dawns on Clyde as he utters his final word, "hey"—the last word in the film too—and his goofy smile gives way to mild confusion and then, after an exchange of rapid glances back to Bonnie in the car, a brief realization that they've been set up. There is a lot for Clyde and us to process in the roughly twenty seconds it takes for Moss's father to draw Clyde to his truck with the ruse of a flat tire, and there are twenty-nine individual shots in the escalating action just before the gunfire starts, some tracking the approach of two Black farmers in another truck and others following a flight of birds that have been flushed by the deputies who neither Clyde nor Bonnie nor we will see until it is too late. Slow motion appears for the first time after five more quick cuts have further mapped the scene as it will tortuously unfold, with Clyde shot repeatedly in the midst of his doomed attempt to make it back to Bonnie, who is shot where she is sitting in their car, lurching back and forth as the deputies keep firing into her body, which along with Clyde's has become a corpse well before the brutally persistent forces of society, as Cavell reminds us, are satisfied. This is what Kael beautifully sums up as a "rag-doll dance of death," which combines the image of a medieval *danse macabre* with the sense that Bonnie and Clyde are just playthings for the forces of the law that kill them and hints as well that what we see on screen, for all its visceral physicality, is the product of actors who are pretending even harder in slow motion. Penn wanted to have Clyde's death "be rather like a ballet," and though the arc his body traces to the ground is not exactly graceful, it does evoke the "poetry" of the boys who tumble to the ground at Bonnie's feet in the earlier scene at the family reunion that darkly foreshadows his fall, a lyrical farce that in this case precedes the tragedy that comes second; not that Bonnie has time to register the difference since her death, which Penn directed Dunaway to mimic like a "physical shock," plays out as a writhing agony of jerks and spasms.³³

There is no shortage of slow motion on any of the many, many lists or supercuts of "worst movie death scenes" compiled by fans and critics.³⁴ Orhan Aksoy's 1973 Turkish film *Kareteci Kiz, Karate Girl* in English, became a minor meme sensation in the early 2010s for a wonderfully distended death scene that, last

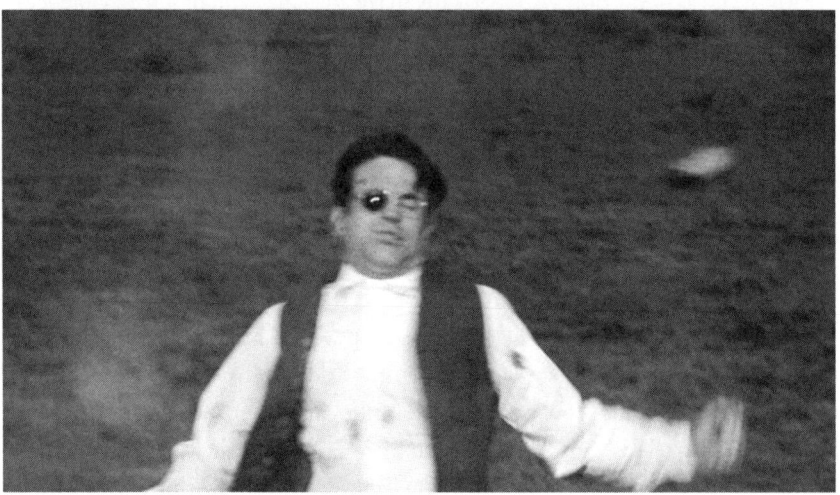

FIGURE 22.3 Zapruder film homage in a still from *Bonnie and Clyde* (1967).

time I checked, was at just under 5 million YouTube views on the two most popular threads devoted to its minute-plus of ornately stupid agony.[35] This is perhaps the worst-case scenario for the combination of elements—montage, slow motion, gunshots, bodies—that Penn and Allen handle with such conviction in *Bonnie and Clyde*. Amid all this bravura carnage, it would be easy to miss the full importance of the shot that immediately precedes the shift into slow motion—or at least it could have been if Penn hadn't explained its iconography in detail a 1968 interview (figure 22.3). At the film's debut in Montreal, Penn had begun his litany on America as a "violent society" by invoking JFK's assassination, but a few months later he revealed that there was a more direct connection between this seminal trauma of the 1960s and this image taken from the earliest split-seconds of Clyde's agony just before it becomes even more brutally extended. What we see here to Beatty's left is a bit of effects work that was made to simulate the skull fragments and brain material that are visible in the infamously graphic frame 313 of the Zapruder film.[36] Penn went to great lengths to make his version of this traumatic image. As he said, when they asked about the spectacular finale, "there's even a piece of Warren's head that comes off, like that famous photograph of Kennedy."[37] With all the other "squibs" and condoms filled with stage blood that had to be set off over the three days and six takes it took to film the ambush, this prop was just another minor technicality that crew and actors had to manage; it was attached to Beatty's head with a monofilament line and pulled away on cue.[38] Before underground copies of the Zapruder film began to circulate after Clay

Shaw's conspiracy trial in 1969, and before it was broadcast, first on local TV in Chicago and then on ABC's *Good Night America* in 1975, *Bonnie and Clyde* was as close as most viewers could get to seeing Kennedy's assassination, or at least the fatal "money" shot, in something like real time. This is certainly an allusion DeLillo would have appreciated if he was watching closely enough to catch it— though it was, in fact, too fast for almost anyone to see.

This homage to the Zapruder film is the last shot that we see before the finale so memorably decelerates its violence. Though this is not Penn's native language as a filmmaker, I think he is trying to produce what Barthes—also obsessing over Eisenstein at this very period in the late sixties—would call a "third meaning," a "specific filmic" image that "lies not in movement" nor in the frozen immobility of a "simple photograph" but emerges only "*inside* of the fragment."[39] But such "third meanings" cannot be designated in advance, and they can't move since they're only visible in the still which has "[thrown] off the constraint of filmic time." The still image of Clyde and his exploded head—at which I have no doubt Penn and Allen stared for hours in some editing room—is a signifier that, if anything, has more signifieds than it can bear. So if there is a "third meaning" to be had in the supremely choreographed display of violence from the ending of *Bonnie and Clyde*, we should find it in slow motion. Bonnie's last protracted moments are difficult to watch for the manic violence of her suffering; Clyde's, on the other hand, are equally as violent and leave him looking just a little stupid or "obtuse," to borrow a word that Barthes uses to describe the appeal of a "third meaning" in the flesh. We're awkwardly reminded that he really may have been too slow to ever be, as he had haltingly protested from the start, "much of a lover boy." Penn wanted Clyde's death to appear "balletic," but the course his body takes once all the guns begin to fire is anything but elegant.

Clyde looks pretty dead here to me (figure 22.4). The garish slash of red at his left temple matches the piece of skull that we have already seen explode away from his head; there are wounds on both his legs and another in the center of his torso. The direct quotation of the Zapruder film, though effectively subliminal, would also mark the precise moment when Clyde is assassinated by a faceless group of cops and sheriff's deputies that register as the very opposite of a "lone gunman" in their personification of state authority. There is also evidence for the other side in this highly artificial inquiry into the timing of Clyde's death—a debate I confess that I am manufacturing out of too close reading at its most attentive—in his raised right hand that still can hold the now bloodstained pear, and also his bent right knee, which might register at least a minimal sign of life. The medical term of art that we are after, which I find oddly appropriate here, is "primary flaccidity," and these two small gestures of defiance over gravity are the best that I can do to persuade myself that this is not quite yet a corpse we see before us.

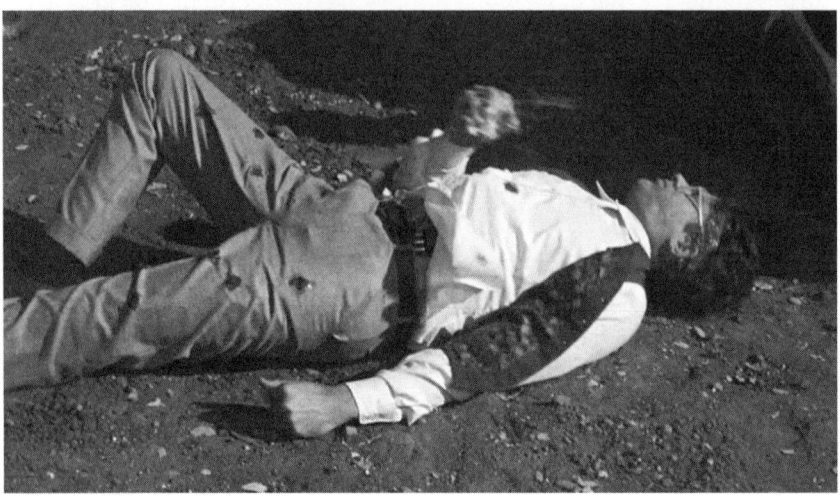

FIGURE 22.4 Still from *Bonnie and Clyde* (1967).

When the sequence shifts back into slow motion, Clyde's body is propelled again to action. In the long establishing shot at normal speed that brings him and Bonnie together in the frame for almost two full seconds, we catch a glimpse of Clyde somehow rolled over onto his right side (figure 22.5), which reveals still more bullet wounds to his back, shoulder, and legs. The dust kicked up from machine gun fire soon obscures our view of Clyde entirely, but when we cut to the next shot of him in isolation, he has been flipped onto his back again or, rather, flopped to where the momentum of his fall had left him in the first place. There are four more shots of Beatty acting out Clyde's dying agonies at differing rates of slow motion, and given that his eyes stay closed and his face has no more expression on it than it had when he originally hit the ground, I think we are supposed to understand—phenomenologically, as viewers watching with our bodies as well—that his corpse isn't moving on its own but rather being animated by the bullets pouring into it. I recall enough high school physics to know that the way his body moves here under fire is impossible, if not more literally preposterous (figure 22.6): The small mass of a bullet cannot generate enough momentum to displace, much less lift off the ground, the bulk of a human body. Its kinetic energy is concentrated at the point of impact, and the damage that it does is relatively contained at entry, which is why exit wounds are far more graphic and, in the case of *Bonnie and Clyde*, would have required larger squibs and shows of blood and tissue than Penn and Beatty ever contemplated. Need I even add at this point that "what happens when you're shot?" YouTube videos exploit slow motion to the fullest so that we can watch bullets from high-caliber

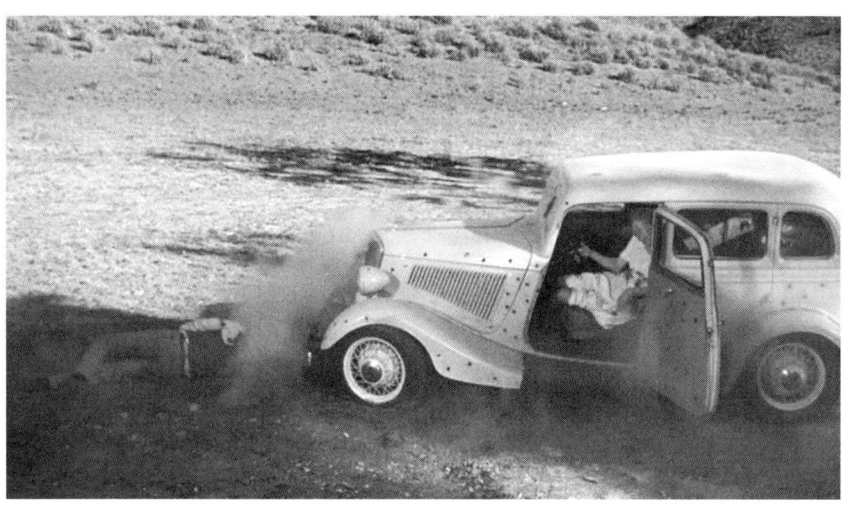

FIGURE 22.5 Still from *Bonnie and Clyde* (1967).

pistols or assault rifles go through slabs of pork or transparent torso "ballistic dummies"?[40]

We maybe can't call this method acting since Clyde has no emotions to express or inner life for Beatty to identify with and access, but we're still supposed to see this as the last indignity Clyde must endure. The ungainly and embarrassing postures that the bullets put him in—ass and backside ready for their close-ups—are meant, I think, as signs of how he is assaulted by these forces (technological, political, social) that won't just let him die even though they've already overkilled him. But if Beatty is acting up this storm that highlights Clyde's "posterity," so to speak, it is perhaps important too that this death-scene choreography draws our attention to the particular "side" of his character that might well have had to be visualized, however cryptically, as an erogenous zone in whatever ménage a trois with Bonnie and C. W. Moss that the film's writers didn't even get the chance to leave on the cutting room floor. After the shooting stops at last, Clyde's body tumbles over to give us a final look at Beatty's vacant face and the perfectly smooth and undisturbed display of pelvis, which is about the only part of the corpse where there's been no penetration (figure 22.7). If, as T. J. Clark writes of a different corpse depicted in a different medium, "what is most dreadful about the dead body is its immobility," then *Bonnie and Clyde* uses every trick at its disposal—from Guffey's technically demanding cinematography and Allen's exacting editing to Penn's auterist ambition and Beatty's "calculated" acting—to delay this particular inevitability for as long as possible. Clyde is not exactly a figure of what Clark describes as "speed stopped dead," but his ungainly and ornate demise is so moving not because it reveals a potential aspect of his queer

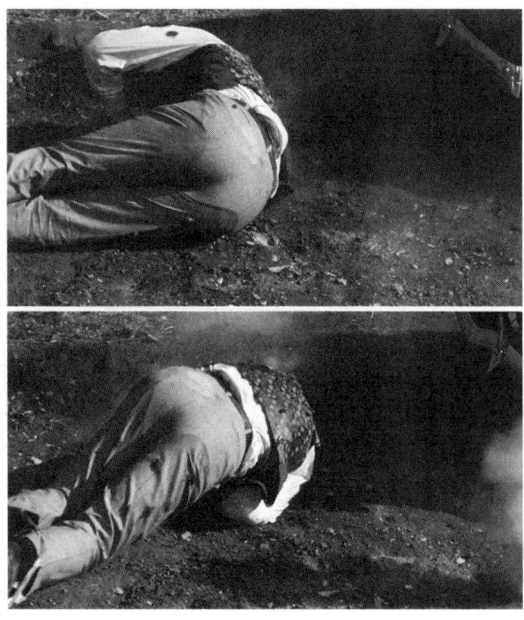

FIGURE 22.6 The agony of Clyde's postmortem ecstasy in two stills from *Bonnie and Clyde* (1967).

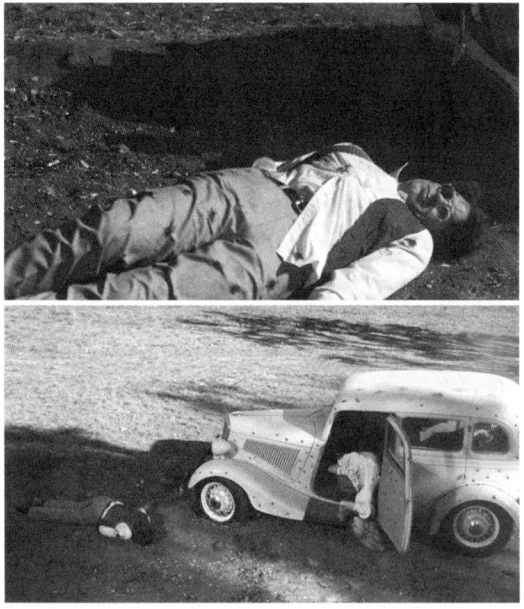

FIGURE 22.7 Stills from *Bonnie and Clyde* (1967).

identity that the film must otherwise repress but rather because it puts on display how weird and sad we all might look as human beings dying at a velocity, no matter how slow or fast, that is just another number to a machine that has all the time in the world that we don't.[41] Beatty has Clyde's profoundly dead body now do another roll to guarantee that the last image that we'll have of him is evocative of a melancholy that, in the unfolding of the scene, goes by too fast to count as a hint of anal eroticism but still leaves us with a final sight of Clyde that hardly memorializes him as a "lover boy." Unless it does, but only in a way that slow motion lets us see—or rather show us at high speed—a truth about his body that might otherwise get lost in the spectacle of violence that ultimately makes it a dead issue anyway. Two technologies of speed—cameras and guns producing "shots" at a delirious but also unfeeling and calculated pace—give us a glimpse of things that Clyde was forever too slow to tell us for himself.

ENDTIMES IN HOLLYWOOD

As I conclude this account of *Bonnie and Clyde* and the slow motion that it helps popularize in 1967 and 1968, I would like to step back a bit to consider one last way the film tries to connect its fetishistic vision of cinematic death to what I'll call, with apologies for some clunky aggrandizement, its theory of American modernity or picture of the present crisis that it dressed up in thirties iconographies and fashions. There is enough in the film—scenes of foreclosed houses, Black figures on the margins of the violence that Bonnie and Clyde giddily indulge before the forces of authority get their revenge—for us to understand why Penn and others could so confidently believe in its affiliation with the period's counterculture. On the other hand, there is everything that has happened since the sixties to make us skeptical about easy links between displays of cultural ingenuity and the structures of race and class and sexual identity that predated and, as we have learned the hard way, obviously outlived them. I could go on about how Newman and Benton pitched their original scenario to Truffaut by insisting that Bonnie and Clyde "were out of their time in the 30s" because they were "hip people" in a film "about what's going on now."[42] We know the terms of the debates from here, with eye rolls and righteous boomer condemnations matched to intimations of utopia and earnest tributes to what Christopher Leigh Connery calls "a time of eventfulness" that was itself "a stand against given time, against capitalist time, against abstract time."[43] There is a lot to be seen in Bonnie and Clyde's overwrought and anguished dying seconds.

Yet the slowest death memorialized in *Bonnie and Clyde* has already happened, and there is precious little mystery to the meaning of the corpse that it has left behind. Just minutes after meeting, we find Bonnie and Clyde walking down the ramshackle, nearly empty streets of her East Texas hometown. This early scene was shot in Venus, Texas (population 414 in 1970), and was one of several locations that Penn and his crew discovered thanks to Robert Benton, who was born and raised in the comparative metropolis of Waxahachie (population 13,451 in the same census year). Like many of the locations featured in *Bonnie and Clyde*, the iconography of peeling paint, abandoned storefronts, and fading signs and advertisements are patently intended to invoke the legendary work of photographers like Dorothea Lange and Walker Evans. Kael recognized this immediately; there are some shots throughout the film that look so much like quotations of Depression-era originals that the effect is less Pop Art "put-on" and more a perfect simulation with a difference, as if anticipating the scandalous literalism with which Sherrie Levine replicated Evans's work later in the 1980s. I don't think Penn is trying to be this conceptually adventurous. He wants his film to start in a world where, in real ways, the movies have come to a stop.

In the gloomy recesses behind Dunaway and Beatty, it is impossible to read all the posters that have been left to picturesque decay. There are three on one wall that have been torn or papered over, though their colors are improbably deep and vivid; underneath a board that reads "Closed Keep Out," we can barely make out that the last picture shown at this Texas theater was Frank Tuttle's 1930 version of the first "Philo Vance" mystery, *The Benson Murder Case*. This was a Paramount feature, not Warner Bros., and the story of a "gentleman detective" solving a stockbroker's murder, which is a far cry from the gangster movies Penn and Beatty were revisiting. This ephemeral bit of classical Hollywood at its most forgotten—it isn't streaming anywhere, and DVDs are hard to come by—seems like it is put here to index the idea of a generic "old movie" so that we can recognize another "relic of antiquity" amid these icons of the "New Cinema," as *Time* christened it in 1967. "What y'all do for a good time here," Clyde asks from the lengthening shadows of the golden hour that is turning into twilight, "listen to the grass grow?" Maybe if they could've gone to the movies, their meet-cute wouldn't have led to such a bloody crime spree, one ending only when they themselves closed out its body count.

Yet I would argue that *Bonnie and Clyde* is fascinated with the fading ruins of American film not just in its many gestures toward the studio era that had been slowly dying since the 1940s anyway. The movie theater that Bonnie and Clyde stroll past before their first date becomes armed robbery is a site of weirdly accelerated ruination, of slow historical processes of decline and decay that shouldn't be happening quite this fast. There is something prematurely ancient in the aura that this abandoned theater tries to summon, and it is easy to picture Sugimoto setting up his large-format camera inside to add it to his series of empty, haunted movie palaces. Sugimoto took his first theater photography just a couple years after *Bonnie and Clyde*, and he wouldn't have had to know Penn's masterpiece to understand that he was coming of age in an era that would witness endless variations on "last picture shows" for decades after. The mythology that Tsai Ming-liang evokes in the slow cinema of *Goodbye, Dragon Inn* is much the same in its rough outlines. Nick Pinkerton argues that Tsai's nostalgia for the theaters of his childhood—which is what we're seeing here in *Bonnie and Clyde*, at least through Benton's eyes—involves a more complex architecture of gay desire and Chinese identity. But I think that this moment on the streets of a nameless town in Texas during the depths of the Depression is supposed to register as universal. Much like the equally stock figure of a Black man in straw hat and overalls that Bonnie and Clyde proceed to walk by next, there is a sense in which this shuttered theater is just another remnant of age and history as such, an emblem of nothing in particular save the difference between the past and present in the form of changes that take place so gradually that they never seem to happen as an event that anyone might witness in real time. This small-town movie theater is, by definition, a ruin of the modern that bleeds into what Brian Dillon describes as a whole category of iconic twentieth-century sites and spaces that "now look like relics of lost futures" in the face of an abiding fear that the progress that they promised has already stopped somewhere along the way.[44] In this regard, the film's elaborate commitment to slow motion is a symbol of how it hopes to outpace oblivion by turning speed itself into an aesthetic of what it might be slightly blasphemous to call "arrested" time since no one is supposed to watch *Bonnie and Clyde* and identify with Sheriff Hamer and the faceless cops that kill our heroes in their prime. The movies can't go on and will go on. In slow motion, only more so.

This is nowhere more visible then in the film's most stagey cinematic set piece, which finds our newly murderous gang of three—having gone from clowns to killers in their first robbery with C. W. Moss—thanks in part to the slapstick delay he causes by parallel parking the stolen car in which, after a few grazed bumpers, they make their escape. The next town not only has a movie theater but is showing a release so new that in the fictional timeline of *Bonnie and Clyde* it shouldn't yet exist. The dates are hard to track: The opening credits suggest that the action starts in 1931, though in reality Bonnie and Clyde began their string of robberies and murders after his second release from prison in 1932; the historical version of the Moss character invented for the movie joined them at the end of 1932, with Buck and Blanche arriving for more crime and mayhem in March 1933. The whole saga of the Barrow Gang takes two years to unfold, a duration that feels compressed into a month or two in *Bonnie and Clyde*. Which is to say that it must be an anachronism that the next film we see within the film is no obscurity but instead one of the most iconic movies of the Great Depression, *Gold Diggers of 1933*—the Warner Bros. top box office hit for the year. It debuted in March 1933 and seems like an impossible matinee to catch after what is only Bonnie and Clyde's third robbery in the film. Unlike the poster for *The Benson Murder Case*, which comes out of nowhere, this cinematic reference was intended from the start. It is there in Newman and Benton's screenplay, where the irony of hearing and seeing Ginger Rogers sing "We're in the Money" in the traumatic aftermath of their escape is played for all its worth. "BONNIE sits, watching the movie intently. In front of her and several seats away, C. W. slouches down morosely. In the row between them is CLYDE. He is nervous and keeps watching the door. CLYDE is in a rage. He shifts in his seat. We hear the music of the song on the soundtrack."[45]

This moment in *Bonnie and Clyde* is, in its own Hollywood idiom, every bit the showpiece as Busby Berkeley's original production number. With Ginger Rogers and a chorus line decked out in strings of coins and little else—and punctuated by a verse she sings in Pig Latin as the camera zooms in to a suggestively unnerving close-up—this famous backstage musical about hustling dancers, sexual barter, and the silver standard is rightly celebrated as one of the most important artifacts of the studio system from the Great Depression, and it is easy to see why Newman and Benton, and then Penn, Guffey, and Allen, work so hard to construct a monument to New Hollywood around it. The irony is obvious and rich as Clyde and C. W. twitch and fret about the murder they have just committed while the tinny jubilance of Rogers, in all her knowing sunniness, pours out over the audience where they sit in high anxiety as Bonnie tries to give her full attention to the movie. *Bonnie and Clyde* would have its viewers think this day is past, flattering them at every turn, in fact, for seeing through such old-fashioned formal logics as the "put-on" that they always were. The film deploys slow motion as another symbol of its own modernity, an aesthetic innovation that distinguishes it from the sort of movies we watched once upon a time, like *Gold Diggers of 1933*, or didn't, like *The Benson Murder Case*. Slow motion lets us know that we are watching a film that takes place *now*, no matter what period costumes its stars are wearing or what antique cars they're driving. It is how we see the 1960s bleed into a vision of the 1930s that *Bonnie and Clyde* can't quite decide is history yet or not.

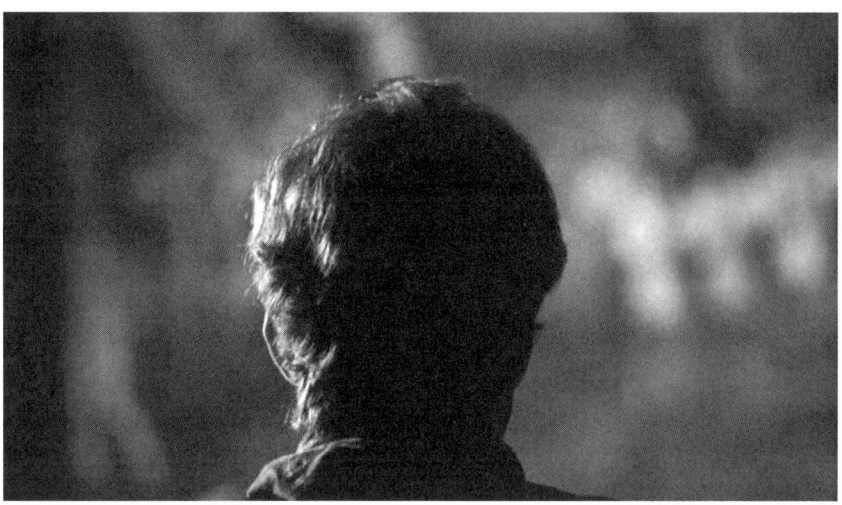

FIGURE 22.8 Still from *Bonnie and Clyde* (1967).

We see this strange temporality in the shadowy sludge that *Bonnie and Clyde* makes out of *Gold Diggers of 1933*, which turns into an enigmatic image of a haunted screen before our very eyes. For a brief moment, the back of C. W. Moss's head fills the screen (figure 22.8). The highlights in his hair and on his left ear are skillfully composed to balance the pitch-black void that looms between us and the movie he isn't really watching since, as we've already seen, he is too upset and anxious to pay attention. I won't claim to know how Guffey captured this on film, but the aperture of his camera must be wide open to get so much detail out of such faint light. The depth of field is not quite murdered out, but the Warner Bros. classic that we know that Moss is watching is reduced—or maybe just transformed, no better or worse—into a field of silver-gray abstraction. It pulses and flows at a speed that's neither slow nor fast because it isn't representing anything particular in motion but rather movement as an experience of film, the specific character of its medium even when it has nothing left to show us. This is not slow motion, but it still offers us a glimpse of what the end of cinema might look like. By the time that *Bonnie and Clyde* is over, the only question left will be what else dies with it. Or worse, what dies to keep it going.

23

Posthistoric Prehistoric Modernism

2001: A Space Odyssey

Though among the least of its superlatives, Stanley Kubrick's *2001: A Space Odyssey* was the first American film released in 1968 featuring an "iconic" sequence of slow motion—"iconic" maybe being an understatement for a scene that many of us can summon in a vivid instant, with or without having seen the film in all its monumental grandeur. Some are already picturing the bone and spaceship or remembering the throb of bass that hums along in isolation before the initial fanfare from the trumpets, surprisingly restrained at first, erupts into the full symphonic force of brass and stomping timpani in Richard Strauss's *Also sprach Zarathustra*. And then, of course, a few seconds and four million years later, we hear the even more preposterously sincere and pretty opening chords of Johann Strauss's "The Blue Danube" and see the "Pan American" logo on the spaceship taking Dr. Heywood Floyd to Clavius. After almost twenty minutes, Kubrick shows us the first human being in the film, dead asleep and blissfully unaware that his pen is floating in the empty aisle. We are still in "The Dawn of Man," according to the film's three-part narrative architecture, and in one of Kubrick's characteristically deadpan jokes, we're still having trouble as a species waking up after millennia of evolution, technology, and progress.

There isn't any dialogue in the first twenty-five minutes of *2001*, unless we count the various whoops and screams of early hominids that are barely less significant than the empty pleasantries that Floyd exchanges with the flight attendants and clerks at the Hilton on Space Station 5 after his flight lands. We don't learn much more from Floyd's brief presentation to a roomful of functionaries on the Clavius outpost that the United States has constructed on the moon; his cool prattle about "the situation" or the "the news" of "this event" is meant to be obscuring and diffuse and also slightly menacing as Floyd stands before a glowing blank white screen, with an American flag off to the side, smiling as he mentions "loyalty oaths" and laughs off a question about how much longer some mysterious "council" will require the "cover story" of a contagion to be maintained. In a film that lasted almost three hours in the version that debuted on April 2, 1968, in Washington, DC, but, shockingly for many critics, had only forty minutes or so of dialogue, it is another display of style and power for Kubrick to make us spend almost five of these listening to Floyd waste time. But nobody went to see *2001* for the language of its screenplay, which Kubrick wrote with Arthur C. Clarke from the novel Clarke composed at Kubrick's urging over the course of the years that the film spent in expensive and elaborate development.

2001: A Space Odyssey was a sensation—with box-office earnings of nearly $150 million, more than doubling the receipts for *Bonnie and Clyde*—because it was an overwhelming visual experience that employed over two hundred special effects shots at a level of technical precision and scale and that demonstrated a commitment to both realism and aesthetic abstraction unlike any film before. Words are beside the point when taking "the ultimate trip," as the film's famous marketing campaign in late 1968 described it. Scott Bukatman suggests that Kubrick helps inaugurate an extended period of films that stress "perceptual activity," "haptic engagement," and "an emphatic share of wonder" that "[moves] away from ... narrative and into the pleasures of the spectacle."[1] I don't think Bukatman sees these as a strict opposition. If anything, the slow motion in *2001: A Space Odyssey* makes for some of most densely plotted moments in the film. But this comes into focus later, long after what Annette Michelson, writing in *Artforum* in 1969, described as "the most spectacular ellipsis in cinematic history."[2] Not all late-sixties hyperbole has aged so well, but I am happy to second Michelson on this. Or maybe not exactly second, since Michel Chion, also writing on *2001* (in 2001), identifies the celebrated, wholly unexpected cut from bone to outer space as "possibly the most famous [single transition] in the history of film, certainly one of the most sublime."[3] Nor really third either, since several thousand YouTube viewers have watched this scene as "The Greatest Scene Cut in Film History" or "The Best Cut in the History of Cinema."[4] For all Kubrick's meticulously rendered innovations at the level of technique in *2001*—adoringly chronicled in production histories and biographies—the scene of his most singular achievement employed slow motion and a simple cut, two of the least special effects at his disposal in 1968. It is remarkable to witness how much mileage Kubrick got from these most primitive of tools.

I have already gotten far ahead, and also fallen somewhere very far behind, the moment in 1968 when *Bonnie and Clyde* was still playing in theaters globally and in the United States and MGM finally released the science-fiction epic on which Kubrick had been working, under various titles and growing budgets, since early in 1964, just as *Dr. Strangelove or: How I Learned to Stop Worrying and Love the Bomb* was earning him newfound, international acclaim. This expansion of the frame is almost unavoidable in the face of what *2001* becomes: a massive, charismatic giant at which critics, fans, and cinephiles still gaze with wonder and obsessive fascination for its overt metaphysics, high design, and meticulous construction as an artifact of mainstream cinema's own emerging future as a medium of blockbusters at scale and with extreme investments in technology. But speaking for the prosecution, as she always was where Kubrick was concerned, is Pauline Kael on the occasion of *2001*: "With his $750,000 centrifuge, and in love with gigantic hardware and control panels," she writes in *Harper's Magazine* the very month that Michelson takes up Kubrick's defense in *Artforum*, he is "the Belasco of science fiction."[5] In an admittedly arch and narrow context that seems almost laughably removed from, well, anything that mattered in at the time, it is hard to imagine a worse insult; though this being Kael, summoning the ghost of nineteenth-century melodrama to put a stop to Kubrick in his monumental, high-tech tracks was probably just another Tuesday. "American movie technique is generally more like technology," Kael offers, "and it usually isn't very interesting." Kubrick, she added, "had gotten carried away with the Erector Set approach to moviemaking." She was not alone in thinking that Kubrick had applied considerable, if not excessive capital to produce a vision that, for all its grandeur and ingenious engineering—indeed, because of them—"looks like the apotheosis of the fantasy of a precocious, early nineteen-fifties city boy." This nasty bit of perfect writing comes from Renata Adler's review of *2001* in the *New York Times*, and the savagery is that I'm sure she knew that Kubrick, during the period in question, would have been a "boy" of almost thirty, already married and divorced. For Adler, the problem is the pacing of a film that "is so completely absorbed in its own problems, its use of color and space, its fanatical devotion to science-fiction detail, that it is somewhere between hypnotic and immensely boring."[6] All to say that the lingering aura of Kubrick's stature as a filmmaker—an aura that emanates with special radiance around *2001: A Space Odyssey*—has everything to do with the "uncompromising slowness" he achieves, much to Adler's irritation in 1968.

Kubrick's fans thought *2001* had achieved escape velocity. "Youth in us," Michelson argues in her concluding rapture, "discarding the spectator's decorum, responds, in the movement of final descent, as to 'the slap of the instant,'" quickening in a tremor of rebirth, reveling in a knowledge which is *carnal*." This is two years before *Carnal Knowledge* (1971) is released, so the weird echo of

Mike Nichols's existential sex drama is an accidental anticipation; I also don't know why she scare quotes "the slap of the instant," a phrase that I've never been able to discover anywhere but here. But she would have no patience for my pedantic fact checking or worries that this is also a half-baked allusion to the rape fantasy of Yeats's "Leda and the Swan." She wants to save *2001* from "the clear projection of aging minds and bodies" whose "critical performance around this film" revolves "about the historical, anecdotal, sociological, concerned as it is with the texture of incident." These are terms of high disdain in the modernist tradition of Clement Greenberg, and Michelson almost certainly assumed her readers in *Artforum* would choose instead "the heightened and complex immediacy of this film." Michelson attributes most resistance to the rush of Kubrick's film to critics who cannot help but feel their age—for the record, she was turning forty-seven—but does concede that "the intensity and perfection" of *2001* is "contingent upon a conspicuous invisibility of *facture* commanded by the power of a rigorously conceptual imagination, disposing of vast amounts of money."[7] *Facture* is literally a term of art: It is used almost exclusively to refer to the manner in which a painting is made and often to invoke the medium-specific qualities of handling, layering, brushwork, and density as they are left perceptible on the surface of a canvas by the interaction of the artist's body and materials. The box-office success of *2001* did bring more prosaic attention to the designers and effects photographers whose skills and ingenuity actually disposed of the "vast amounts of money" spent by MGM to translate Kubrick's "conceptual imagination" onto the Cinerama screen. In June 1968, for example, *American Cinematographer* published a long story by Herb A. Lightman on the more than "30 technical experts" with whom Kubrick consulted "in his quest for complete authenticity," from the director of photography Geoffrey Unsworth and his assistant, John Alcott, to the designers Tony Masters, Harry Lange, and Ernie Archer and special effects supervisors Wally Veevers, Con Pederson, and Douglas Trumbull, who became the most celebrated figure of the production team that Kubrick assembled.[8] It all makes for fascinating reading of a kind I doubt that Michelson would care about. I should also add that neither Lightman nor Albert make any mention of the slow motion that expands the "redescent," as Michelson calls it, of bone and spacecraft into "nothing less than the entire trajectory of human history."[9] This effect, or so it seems, was straightforward enough for Kubrick to come up with on his own.

"Modernists put a peculiar stress," writes T. J. Clark, "on the physical, technical facts of the medium they were working in." In Kubrick's case this is a stupendous understatement of the amount of engineering, both cinematic and interpersonal, that *2001* required, not to mention a rather timid way to summon up the sheer expenditure of social and financial resources ("vast amounts of money") that Kubrick convinced MGM to endure over four years when the studio's investment looked like it might only produce some "technical facts" and not a movie. Slow motion, as I have said before, hardly registers in popular or critical discussions of how *2001* was revolutionary. It was also, as many viewers recognized immediately, the special effect on which Kubrick's image of modernity—if not his whole theory of being human—primarily depended. We saw in *Bonnie and Clyde* that Penn freighted slow motion with a history of violence in America, from the settlement of the U.S. West to the assassination of JFK. Kubrick was thinking on an even bigger, slower scale. The slow motion in *2001* could not possibly work more strenuously, for all the speed and magic of its singular match cut, to be and look iconic, even at the cost of possibly undoing, from four million years in our prehistory, the prospect of a future that Kubrick floats toward Earth in the form of the giant embryo the fills the screen at the end of *2001* (making for a very "pregnant" year). This alone would make Kubrick a modernist for Clark, who reminds us, with equal measures of regret and admiration, that "technique in modernism was not problem-solving. It made problems worse."[10] For Kubrick, slow motion shows us everything that makes us human—and terrible.

THE SHAPE OF KUBRICK'S TIME

In the beginning, Kubrick wanted slow motion in *2001* to let us picture the lights and colors of the firmament, and it was good. From Michael Benson's extensive reconstruction of the film's production history and several Kubrick biographies, we know that he had already begun to think about a work of science fiction while filming *Dr. Strangelove* (1964) in England earlier in the 1960s.[11] It was a chance conversation with a publicist at Columbia, Roger Caras, that eventually led Kubrick to track down Arthur C. Clarke, who had established himself as a leading figure in science fiction in the 1950s and who was, when a telegram arrived from Caras asking if he'd be interested in meeting Kubrick, living in Ceylon—partly to pursue his love of diving, partly to avoid the scrutiny and stigma of being gay in England. Kubrick and Clarke then devised the basic architecture of ideas that *2001* would later visualize in such spectacular form. Clarke was charged with writing his own novelistic version of the story; Kubrick relied on Clarke's draft of his own book as he was pitching the film to executives at MGM, revising the screenplay, and, quite often, asking for more time and money during the elaborate and expensive shooting and unprecedented postproduction and effects work that had to be completed before *2001* (the movie) appeared in theaters just a few months before *2001* (the novel). This timeline tracing Clarke's influence on the project is important because it reminds us how invested Kubrick was—and how much of the narrative was roughly set—when he saw two films that would figure just as decisively in the film's visual aesthetic. At the 1964–1965 New York World's Fair, *To the Moon and Beyond* (1964) debuted in the "Moon Dome," a purpose-built ninety-six-foot-high theater with a vaulting, rounded ceiling. Shot in 360 Cinerama, this documentary short not only influenced Kubrick's decision to use this format for *2001* but also inspired his hiring of Con Pederson and Douglas Trumball away from Lester Norvos's Graphic Films, the company that had made the film with funding from KLM Royal Dutch Airlines.[12]

Around this same period, Kubrick became fascinated with the Canadian documentary *Universe* (1960), which was directed by Roman Kroitor and Colin Low; narrated by the future voice of HAL, Douglas Rain; and included fantastically abstract slow-motion sequences of sunspots and solar flares, depicted in cascading flows of white, translucent haze and fields of sinuous illumination. These effects in *Universe* were accomplished by the high-speed photography of chemicals—of varying viscosities or opacity—as they were poured into glass tanks filled with ink brightly lit from above or behind. This was precisely how Kubrick, almost three years before *2001* was at last released, had shot some of the imagery that would find its way into the "Star Gate" sequence along with Trumbull's flashing corridors of "slit-scan" pulses and color-shifted landscape b-roll (figure 23.1). Kubrick tried to film the origins of the universe on 65-millimeter color stock, with assistance from a company called "Effects-U-All," at what Benson notes with a deadpan smirk, was an "abandoned brassiere factory on Seventy-Second Street and Broadway."[13] Shooting with a macro lens at 72fps, Kubrick and his effects technicians managed to achieve, according to Benson, "'galactic' slow motion." Pun entirely intended. Perhaps more revealingly, though, Kubrick named these early experiments that would constitute the first moments of *2001* "The Manhattan Project"—an appropriately pitch-black joke for a filmmaker who had already laughed at the prospect of nuclear annihilation in *Dr. Strangelove*.

I will have more to say about Kubrick's famous match cut from bone to spaceship. In the film, this is the first slow motion that we see; while the slow-motion footage that Kubrick and Effects-U-All shot in 1965 is effectively invisible or unmarked. Because we have no idea what it is that we're looking at, we're even more at sea, out here in the space of "Jupiter and Beyond," about how fast or slow

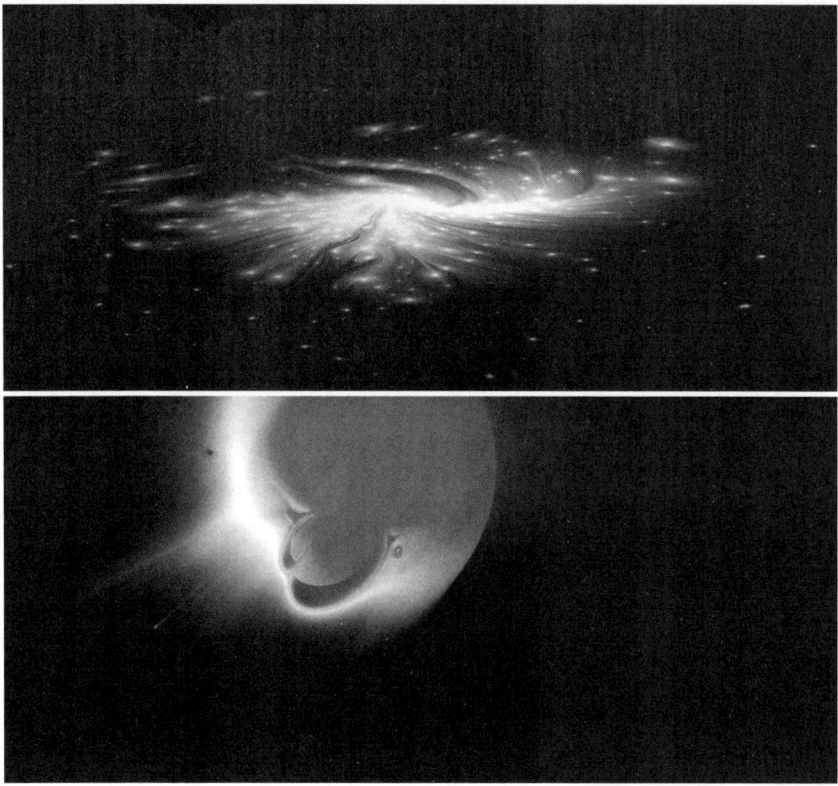

FIGURE 23.1 Stills from *2001: A Space Odyssey* (1968).

it could be moving. Trumbull's "slit-scan" cinematography was shot at normal speed and generated patterns on the screen that possessed a sense of rapid, linear momentum on both the horizontal and vertical planes, so the first time that we cut to Kubrick's macro shots of flowing chemicals, about two minutes after Bowman has entered the "Star Gate," it is clear that we are watching something else unfold. We cut to a tight close-up on Bowman's eye, fixed open for a second and then blinking, that has been processed into a garish spread of blue and orange, and then to a pulsing circle of white light that disperses into a field of tiny points that almost counts as realism for mimicking a galaxy or star cluster. There are eleven more shots of this kind—flows of hazy white and iridescent drapes of green, a weird jellyfish of fluid dynamics, an ulcerous red and orange lobe against a field of black, a vaguely sperm-shaped splatter moving through pink dots—and they comprise the middle of Bowman's journey through the "Star Gate." Which is to remember that, for all its sublime imagery and nonrepresentational, immersive spectacle, we can trace the itinerary of the "Star Gate" even if its metaphysics are indecipherable. We go from the propulsive rush of slit-scan to the flow and drift of uncannily derealized slow motion and, then, with another close-up of Bowman's eye, this time as a psychedelic pop of electric cyan and magenta, we return briefly to a set of sprawling, horizontal slit-scan images and then "land," after a final eyeball close-up, above the rocky surfaces of an unknown moon or planet. As Benson notes, much of this footage was shot by a cinematographer that Kubrick, staying in England the whole time, dispatched to Monument Valley and other sites near Page, Arizona, where different combinations of filters were used to manufacture darkly radiant landscapes that do, though only for a second, occasionally resolve into the familiar backdrops that some might recognize from John Ford westerns. I will also return to Kubrick's perhaps surprising swerve onto the terrain of this more traditional, though certainly not older, Hollywood genre.

So the first time Kubrick used slow motion was actually the second, and I want us to remember that even in its breathtaking and explicit monumentality, it's also an echo of the slightly goofier and obscure slow motion that he had reverse engineered, which is to say copied, from an educational film about the origins of the universe, a film where nobody, not a tapir or an early human or an artificial intelligence, has to die. As Robert Slifkin writes, the "daunting technological sublime" we see in *2001* has much to do with the terminal velocity that modern art had reached in 1968 and with a projected future, as conceived by many in the period, of "increased entropy, ephemerality, and technological breakdown."[14] Within the logic of *2001*, the viewer is supposed to think that we are witnessing the birth of everything we know of modern life when we experience the grandeur of slow motion as if it somehow came from out of nowhere. This was clearly not the case. If anything, slow motion was picking up considerable momentum in the fall of 1967 and spring of 1968. Kubrick had been laboring in and at slow motion for years before Penn and Beatty even started on *Bonnie and Clyde* and consecrated the effect as one of the crucial symbolic forms of the New America cinema. John Boorman's *Point Blank* appeared in August 1967 and featured a violent slow-motion dream sequence. Martin Scorsese had already completed the original version of his debut film, *Who's That Knocking at My Door* (1967–1968), which includes a precociously stylized slow-motion tracking shot of small-time gangsters and their studied gestures, guns, and physiognomies set to Ray Baretto's "El Watusi," and then months later, Scorsese adds more gloriously vulgar slow motion to guarantee its theatrical release by showing Harvey Keitel's character raining a deck of cards over the body of a naked woman as the last and thoroughly embarrassing few seconds of the Doors' "The End" concludes the montage. Even if Kubrick had gotten *2001* into theaters first, he would still not have been inaugurating Hollywood's discovery of slow motion, much less inventing the effect as a technological aesthetic. So why does *2001* go to such lengths—and so far back in time—to conceive slow motion, with the help of some divine intervention from a monolith in prehistoric Africa, as the most special effect that we could possibly imagine?

THE DEEP TIME OF THE WEST

Almost nothing about the sheer scale of Kubrick's undertaking in *2001*—as a celebrated work of popular art and complex product of an advanced culture industry—is remotely overlooked in the accounts of its accomplishment. From coffee table books to museum retrospectives, *2001* remains entirely enduring as an image of its moment, "that present moment," in Michelson's adoring prose, "which extends a century back into the past."[15] She probably didn't know how true this sense of Kubrick's historicism was in 1969 or how literally it describes at least one dimension of the film's design. We might remember *2001* as the "ultimate trip" for its abstract, kinetic visions of the future, but it started as the grandest, slowest western ever made.

Nothing about the thunderous triumphalism of *How the West Was Won*, the second and final feature ever shot in three-camera Cinerama, would seem to translate into the oblique and existential mysteries of *2001*. But when the first press releases for the film that would become *2001* announced Kubrick's collaboration with Arthur Clarke, their still untitled story was offered as a virtual sequel. Kubrick and Clarke tried out both *How the Universe Was Won* and *How the Solar System Was Won* as truly awful working titles, though it's hard to know how seriously either took the bloated grandeur of the predecessor as they designed their sleeker, cooler product. Clarke recalled in 1972 that he and Kubrick "had in mind a kind of semidocumentary about the first pioneering days of the new frontier" but that they "soon left that concept far behind" as the ridiculously grander timeline of *2001* came into focus and the remaining vestiges of the western that it never really was were swapped out for "the Odyssean parallel" that is also just as strained. *How the West Was Won* was among the signature accomplishments of an earlier and anxious urge to scale in Hollywood. Time has been kinder to Kubrick and the spectacle of human progress that he and Clarke discovered after abandoning the awkward remnants of the massive western that they momentarily considered. The traces aren't exactly buried, but they are displaced into an even starker, slower past.

The opening sequence of *2001*, again, is called "The Dawn of Man," and its events take place somewhere in sub-Saharan Africa around 4,000,000 years BCE, give or take. Since Kubrick had no intention of flying to Africa himself after discovering a landscape to his liking in pictures of rock formations and *kokerboom* trees from the Namib desert of what was then disputed territory in South West Africa, he sent location scouts, photographers, and second-unit directors to capture the various images that, in the form of large-format transparencies, would provide the photorealistic backdrops for the elaborate front-projection camera system that allowed him to stage all of this prehistoric action study in Shepperton and Borehamwood. Recalling the *Diorama* photos that Hiroshi Sugimoto started taking in the early 1970s—perfectly synchronized with his *Theaters*—it is provocative to think of Kubrick's beautifully meticulous reproductions of deep time as some of the most expensive natural history installations of the twentieth century. He sent his actors to London's Natural History Museum to look at bones and diagrams of *Australopithecus* specimens, as well as to the Regent's Park Zoo, where the American mime Dan Richter, who played the central figure in the film's first dramatic episode of accelerated, artificial evolution, apparently did some close observation, like the proper method actor that he wasn't, of the zoo's famous attraction Guy the Gorilla.[16] This isn't to suggest that Kubrick and Clarke were after scientific accuracy in their fantastic parable about the origin of our species, which seems like a niggling point since the entire fiction of this sequence is the intervention of an alien monolith that suddenly arrives one night near where "Moon-Watcher," as he is named in Clarke's novel, and his clan are sheltering in an environment of threats and brutal competition. We've already seen a leopard that would just as soon eat any of them as the zebra it has caught, and then, of course, it does exactly that. Another group of hominids, called only "the Others" and led by "One-Ear," has claimed dominion over the sole source of water in the area. It is a wild anachronism, I know, to suggest that we are supposed to see the Others as somehow conceptualizing their claim upon the water hole as ownership. But they do chase away Moon-Watcher and his group in a vivid show of dominance that makes it clear that they have no desire to share.

Elsewhere, though, a peaceable kingdom still seems possible. Moon-Watcher and the others in his group—though not, of course, the Others who are not—live easily in the desert with harmless tapirs we see in the stunning front-projection photography and layers of production design and artifice that went into recreating primordial Africa in the London suburbs. Prehistoric tapirs lived only in the Western Hemisphere, as Benson notes, and so no actual version of Moon-Watcher, who would not have had a name, could not have killed one sometime after the appearance of the monolith, which for the sake of my argument I will presume never existed. But this is precisely what we see happen in the film's first slow-motion sequence, which begins with Richter's hominid tentatively grasping with his hand the bone that will soon become a weapon and then, with increasing energy and violence, laying waste to the skeleton of the creature whose death has revealed the purpose of technology in Kubrick's universe. With the unbearable grandeur of Richard Strauss's *Also sprach Zarathustra* swelling on the soundtrack—and the even more monumental figure of Nietzsche looming in the philosophical background for at least some viewers in 1968—the slow motion that distends and magnifies this moment is not, like the last few seconds of *Bonnie and Clyde*, asking us to experience their suffering from inside a temporality that thankfully no one alive can know. At this slow-motion primal scene, we are rooting for the executioners.

According to the gospel of *2001*, "Man . . . had put his heart and soul" into "the spear, the bow, the gun, and finally the guided missile" as the narrative arrives at Clarke's version of Heywood Floyd.[17] Or to put it in terms borrowed from Adorno's *Negative Dialectics*, first published in Germany in 1966 while Clarke was back in Sri Lanka and Kubrick was making galaxies and nebulae out of basic high school chemistry, there is a "universal history that leads from savagery to humanitarianism," a history "leading from the slingshot to the megaton bomb."[18] Kubrick is not exactly illustrating Clarke's version of *2001*, no more than Clarke is novelizing the film that is more widely known for many reasons, not the least of which is that it's better. But the claggy exposition of Clarke's prose helps reveal some of the ideas and logics that remain mysterious, to Kubrick's benefit, at the level of symbols and suggestions. When Kubrick's Moon-Watcher—the name survives in early drafts of Clarke and Kubrick's screenplay, so I will keep on typing it—returns, bone club in hand, to the waterhole from which his "tribe" has previously been repelled by One-Ear, there is little mystery about what is going to happen, no matter how opaque the meaning of the monolith that we have seen already. There is no *Also sprach Zarathustra* on the soundtrack to translate the quick and brutal killing of One-Ear into a sublime event or moment of discovery; we hear the screeches and howls of monkeys and an indeterminate roar that seems to come from Moon-Watcher and then the slightly hollow Foley sound effects of thuds that land on One-Ear, seventeen in full, though he stops twitching after two or three. Some version of human society, to recall Cavell, is only seconds old and already is "making sure of itself" with excess force. After One-Ear's tribe has left, the final howl of

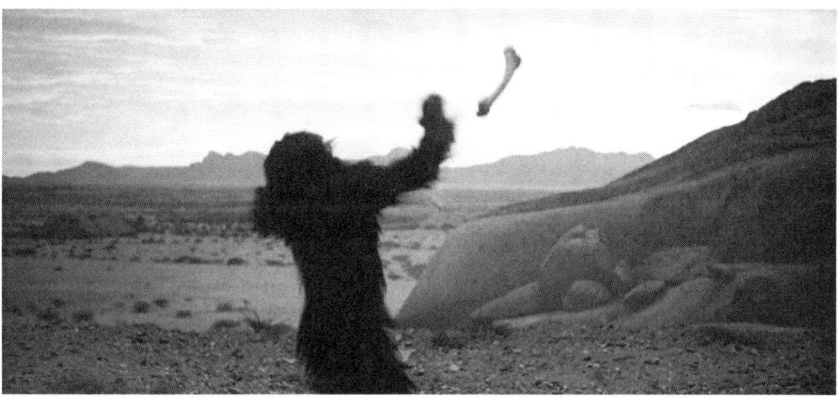

FIGURE 23.2 The fastest four million years in narrative cinema in a still from *2001: A Space Odyssey* (1968).

victory that Moon-Watcher unleashes as he launches the first piece of technology on Earth—which also is the first murder weapon—is really overkill since there are no more "Others" to frighten, which makes the several seconds that we watch it tumble up into the sky, in an echo of the original slow motion that marked Moon-Watcher's discovery, technically redundant too, a show of aesthetic aggrandizement that replays the highlight not of the winning touchdown but the victory celebration (figure 23.2). Until the cut to outer space, when we are suddenly thrown four million years ahead in story time with a single twenty-fourth-of-a-second interval in narrative time, an ellipsis that, recalling Genette's equations, goes infinitely fast.

Clarke identifies the invention of speech as humanity's "first great victory over Time," but Kubrick shows us just how easily film can do this on the fly, so to speak. What we don't see is all the history in between, and the history we can't see can't hurt us. This doesn't mean it isn't there. Though scrapped as Kubrick came to embrace the radically "elliptical" structure of the film we know, we can read in the original screenplay that the nondescript vessel whose smooth fall both mirrors and completes the slow-motion trajectory of the bone was conceived as a "thousand megaton nuclear bomb in orbit above the Earth, Russian insignia and CCCP markings," followed by an "American thousand megaton bomb in orbit above the Earth," a "French bomb," and then a "German bomb," and then a "Chinese bomb."[19] Kubrick is reported to have thought, for good reason, that such a sequence would have too closely rehearsed the grim atomic comedy of *Dr. Strangelove*. Even without hearing from the voiceover in Clarke and Kubrick's early draft that, by their imagined "2001," hundreds of giant warheads have been placed in orbit and are "capable of incinerating the Earth's entire surface," the implicit threat behind this show of ease and rhythm is still perceptible. It was for Kael anyway, who saw through the stunning leap of history that left Michelson the opposite of speechless. "*2001* celebrates the invention of tools of death," Kael writes, "as an evolutionary route to a higher order of *nonhuman* life. Kubrick literally learned to stop worrying and love the bomb; he's become his own butt [of *Dr. Strangelove*'s satiric joke]—the Herman Kahn of extraterrestrial games theory."[20] The reference she is making here is to the Cold War strategist and systems theorist widely credited with popularizing the strategy of nuclear deterrence, which rested on the likelihood of "mutually assured destruction" to prevent the United States and USSR from acting against the "Others" across the world. Evolution leads from Moon-Watcher to Dr. Strangelove or even worse. Adorno, grimly satisfied, is proved right all along.

But this trip starts and, stranger still, ends on some terrain that brings *2001* back to the iconic U.S. West that was, according to both Clarke and Kubrick, too small a canvas for the visions of technology and progress they were determined to materialize. Consider the plot of the first section of Kubrick's *2001*. This is not a sentence that would inspire even the film's most ardent fans when there are so many staggering images to pursue instead and the endless mysteries of the monolith to contemplate, stoned or not. Writing about the landscape of the Hollywood western that is and isn't what we see in Kubrick, Jane Tompkins captures the eerie sublime that *2001* tries to deliver: "In the beginning, say these shots, was the earth, and the earth was desert. It was here first, before anything.... In the instant before the human figure appears we have the sense of being present at a moment before time began."[21] Tompkins is invoking the empty expanses that establish both the historical and philosophical ground on which the genre puts its narratives in motion; she cites such iconic Ford films as *Stagecoach* (1939), *My Darling Clementine* (1946), and *The Searchers*, where we open onto the image of the world as it might have looked across the eons while our evolutionary forebears, working without the aid of any alien intelligence, had to discover the power of clubs and technologies of violence on their own. These landscapes of deep time are only figural in the westerns that she is describing, but this is the fiction that Kubrick wants us to take very seriously in the scenes of the Namib desert that he had photographed and front-projected at great expense while he stayed home at his estate in England. But we might say that *2001* begins in a desert altogether adjacent to the deserts of the western, despite being an actual continent and an imagined four million years away, because Kubrick is trying to tell a story about the limits of human progress and the dramas, both material and existential, that come with the technologies that let us think that we can beat them.

Here too, Kubrick is following the course of *How the West Was Won*, but he is going faster and straining for the longer view. The last section of the earlier film is set in 1889 and follows Debbie Reynolds's "Lilith"—just a girl in the first part of the narrative and now in heavy makeup to age her into looking like she is old enough, though four years younger, to be George Peppard's mother—as Peppard helps close the frontier by stopping a gang of train robbers in the increasingly developed territory of Arizona, where modernity and the rule of law are both arriving with a vengeance. But I don't think this is the finale that attracted Kubrick. The music grows symphonic as the camera lifts us above the land and we're pulled toward the future, facing backward—like Benjamin's "Angel of History" with Spencer Tracy narrating—as we hear that though the West is now "long gone," it will never be "buried in the compost of events" because it was "forged in freedom" and now survives in wonders of the modern world we see in glorious Cinerama. We fly over Hoover Dam and then the stratigraphic horror of the Bingham Canyon Mine in Utah, an open pit that we're supposed to celebrate for showing how the twentieth century has made it possible to extract the resources from geological times that beggar the four million years since Moon-Watcher took up a bone and used it as a club (figure 23.3). This rush of helicopter footage then leads us, with no irony whatsoever, to aerial shots that document the wonders of the LA freeway system and the bridges of San Francisco, as if the film has been an allegory of transportation infrastructure from its open scenes of dusty roads and rivers. The ideology of the voiceover is bludgeoning even if you are the kind of person who could listen to Spencer Tracy speak forever.

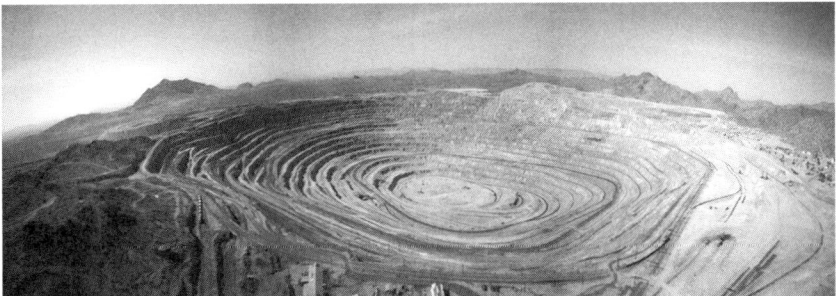

FIGURE 23.3 Bingham Canyon Mine in Cinerama in a still from *How the West Was Won* (1962).

Or put differently, this is why *2001* could be described by Gene Youngblood in 1970's *Expanded Cinema* as an example of what he called "The New Nostalgia." This was Youngblood's phrase to capture the experience of living "effectively 'outside' of time" in a world shaped by the "'dehumanizing' effects of technology."[22] The final section of the "Star Gate" consists of aerial footage, mainly shot in Scotland, that has been processed into lurid hues of deeply saturated blues and oranges, greens and browns, that are supposed to register just how alien the landscape is on the "other" side where Bowman and his pod eventually arrive, though we never see him set down anywhere in particular before we cut to find him in the suite of Regency rooms where he will live out the remainder of his life in minutes, or perhaps millennia, before the figure of the Star Child appears. But Kubrick wanted, always, more, so he sent his cinematographer Bob Gaffney to Monument Valley, a place where Kubrick had never been but, like many of us who have watched movies in the twentieth century and after, had seen repeatedly in westerns directed by John Ford (*Stagecoach, My Darling Clementine, She Wore a Yellow Ribbon, The Searchers, Cheyenne Autumn*) and also, like the more extreme and esoteric spaces he was trying to picture in *2001*, in *How the West Was Won*. Just before its concluding aerial apotheosis, this is where we find Debbie Reynolds and George Peppard reflecting on a century of progress. Kubrick inserts several shots of Monument Valley into the final version of the "Star Gate" sequence, including one that is almost an exact duplicate of a similar tableau from *How the West Was Won*, though it is difficult to recognize in the abstract, unreal tones of Kubrick's garish palette (figure 23.4). This is someplace, within the fiction of *2001*, we would need a miracle of technology and speed to get to, an evolutionary leap that is the equivalent of traveling four million years in the briefest instant of slow motion. Then again, we know exactly how to get here by covered wagon, train, or film—each of which, or so it seems, is more than capable of going as fast as any human being is ever meant to go.

KILLING TIME, KILLING HAL

That *2001* arrives at "Jupiter and Beyond" by way of Monument Valley does not make the film a western, but it does help us understand why this particular genre and its fantasies of human progress were encoded in its narrative shape from the beginning, even if the "trip" that it imagined was finally too "ultimate" for any landscape here on Earth. The cut that takes us from 4,000,000 BCE to 2001 renders billions of violent deaths invisible, and the next murder in the film

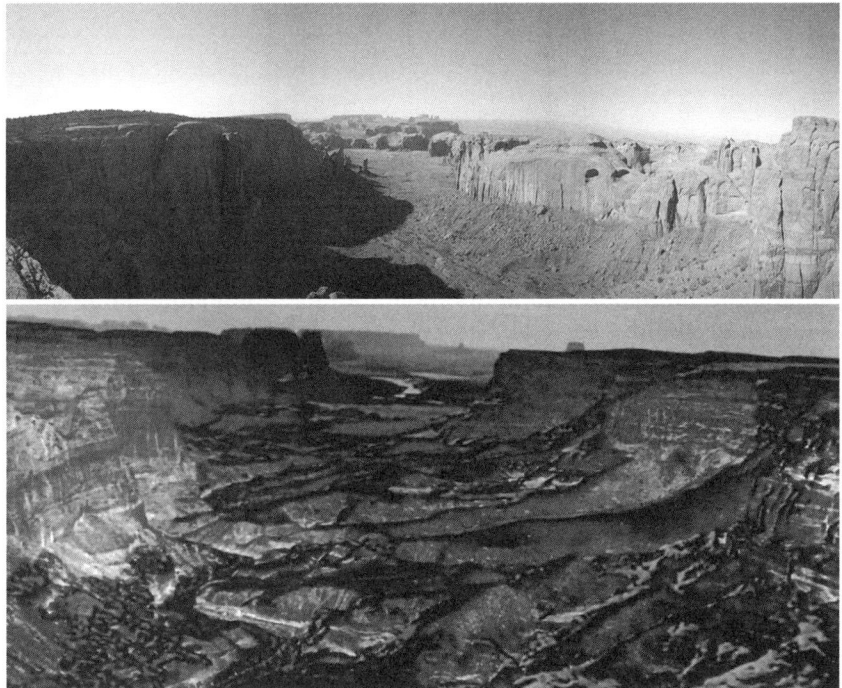

FIGURE 23.4 Monument Valley and Monument Valley on drugs in stills from *How the West Was Won* (1962) and *2001* (1968).

happens almost as quickly. Having read Poole and Bowman's lips as they plot HAL's deactivation, HAL in turn kills Poole by using the articulated arms on one of *Discovery*'s pods to cut the oxygen lines on his spacesuit in the course of a repair outside the ship—where HAL, or so it seems, has lured him. The pod approaches Poole with deliberate menace—turning slowly toward us like a silent-movie villain, unfurling its arms in a posture recalling Boris Karloff's Frankenstein—but then the scene horrifically accelerates. Five quick close-ups tighten onto the red light that figures both as HAL's Cyclopean eye and conscious being, then we see Bowman at a control panel as his attention suddenly tracks toward a window and Poole's body—in footage undercranked, like slapstick comic action—spinning, flailing, flying at high speed into the depths of space. His frantic struggles with his disconnected or severed air hose last for only a few seconds but represent about the fastest action we will see from anyone in *2001*; in the next shot his body is already spinning slower as it rushes and recedes from view. Bowman does not exactly hurry to the pod he pilots to retrieve what is now obviously a corpse, though he is under enough pressure that he forgets the helmet for his spacesuit, which will inspire the next elaborate set piece of this extended sequence, when he must regain entry to *Discovery* by propelling himself into the vacuum of an airlock. He is too late, of course, to save the remaining crew, whom HAL has murdered in their sleep.

So there has already been a quiet frenzy of bloodless violence by the time Bowman makes his way back into the ship, puts on his helmet to survive without the aid of life support (which HAL controls), and proceeds to turn HAL off for good—until he is brought back for the sequel and largely redeemed, which only confirms that he is the real star of *2001*, or at least the product of the film's most compelling performance. Much of the credit belongs to Douglas Rain, the Canadian stage actor whom Kubrick cast as HAL after hearing his preternaturally smooth voice in *Universe*, where his elegant and composed narration was definitely not the powerful attraction it would become by *2001*. The amazing tenor of Rain's voice—light and resonant, precise and measured even when it pleads ("Stop, Dave") and breaks into existential crisis ("My mind is going, I can feel it")—is, along with Bowman's relentless heavy breathing, the constant soundtrack for the nearly six minutes that it takes for HAL to die at Bowman's steady hand as one and then another of HAL's memory units are slowly disconnected. The measured pace at which each memory circuit glides out of glowing walls that house HAL on board *Discovery*—an immersive geometry of muted reds and whites that could, though again improbably, be seen as homage to Dan Flavin's fluorescent sculptures and installations from this exact period in the late 1960s—is matched perfectly to the uncanny valley that Rain's eminently composed breakdown throws us into as HAL's virtual humanity ("Will you stop, Dave?" "I'm afraid," "I can feel it") is never more resonant than when we see how artificial and massively technological it truly is. HAL is not just a voice and eye but a network of sensors, consoles, and speakers distributed throughout a giant spaceship, which also makes HAL the environment in which Poole and Bowen had to live, at least until HAL tries to kill them. And here we see that, at his core, HAL is finally just a room where memories are stored. We hear a few of them as Bowman meticulously makes sure HAL's circuits are inoperative as HAL repeats the first words he spoke when he was brought online in Urbana, Illinois, and then sang the 1892 hit "Daisy Bell (Bicycle Built for Two)." Clarke had attended an event at Bell Labs in 1962 that featured an IBM 704 computer programmed with the first synthesized human voice to sing about this antique mode of transportation that was, of course, a technological sensation in its moment.[23] This wholly artificial recording later appeared on an LP that commemorated the first Philadelphia Computer Music Festival in 1978, but Kubrick instead had Rain, his flesh-and-blood HAL, perform the song in *2001*, and it is his tremendously manipulated voice that we hear over Bowman's agitated breathing as HAL shuts down.[24]

"Daisy, Daisy give me your answer do. / I'm half-crazy all for the love of you": the question of HAL's queerness, as Ellis Hanson has argued brilliantly, is an appealing answer to the majestically opaque problem of what causes HAL to go so wrong.[25] He has spent months watching Poole and Bowman live together intimately, and Poole is a particular figure of physical fascination in the film—running around the centrifugal interior of *Discovery*'s crew quarters, working on his tan—which tempted critics and viewers to speculate about HAL's desires and jealousies. "HAL was a 'straight' computer," Kubrick insisted later to an interviewer, but the square quotes are themselves revealing of how absurd it is to say that HAL has any sort of sexuality, queer or otherwise, that can be imagined on the meager terms that glorified apes like us have managed to evolve.[26] Clarke himself was semicloseted for the majority of his career, publicly declining to say anything about his sexuality while living openly with men and personally confirming to Kubrick and many others that he was gay. An early ending of the film was conceived as having several astronauts along with Bowman land on a fantastic planet where, as Clarke remembered later, "'camp' robots...create a Victorian environment to put heroes at ease." Kubrick then returned with relish, again according to Clarke, to the "wild idea of slightly fag robots" waiting on the other side of the future put in motion, so to speak, by the arrival of the monolith on Earth some four million years before.[27] *2001* is not an especially sexy movie. This doesn't mean that it is an erotic void or quiet about the alluringly detached and plaintive character of HAL's relationship with Poole and Bowman, however unsustainable as either a ménage à trois or even a spite marriage that neither man nor machine survives.

HAL's death scene is, as I have said, protracted. From Bowman's deliberate plodding through the corridors and bulkheads of *Discovery*, now devoid of any human presence save his own, to the smooth and fluid action that marks each stage of HAL's slow death as we watch Bowman take his memory cores offline, one at a time, nothing about this scene happens with the ferocity and suddenness of Moon-Watcher's attack on One-Ear. Bowman defeats HAL without a fight, and obviously Douglas Rain did not require a stunt double for the staging of his breathtaking demise. But Kubrick—already being Kubrick to the limit—made the actor work for it. While not quite so deliciously compulsive as his now legendary insistence that Tom Cruise do ninety-five takes walking through a door for *Eyes Wide Shut*, Kubrick had Rain perform and record more than fifty versions of "Daisy Bell." According to Benson, Rain was at one point asked to sing the song five times in five different keys (E, G, B, D, and F), as well as at a range of tempos from decidedly *allegro* to something close to the tortuous *grave* that we hear in the film. For in *2001*, as many will no doubt recall, when HAL starts singing, he is already in a state of considerable decline, fatally debilitated if not technically inoperative. Kubrick and his sound editor Winston Ryder and sound mixer H. L. Bird immediately drop the register of Rain's tenor into a heavy baritone that is soon distended through the bottom of the bass clef and toward an inhuman rumble by the third or fourth line of the lyrics. Kubrick managed to achieve some of these effects by a process that is tantalizingly analogous to slow motion: Chion writes, "Rain sang several versions of the song at faster and faster speeds, after which, in the editing stage, the rerecording was done at slower and slower speeds."[28] Rain had to sing fast, in other words, so that Kubrick could then radically extend the action that he was capturing in accelerated real time so that even as the pitch and timbre slowed, the rhythm of the music that we hear stays constant. And when Kubrick wanted to go slower still, he used an Eltro information rate changer to decelerate Rain's slowest versions of the song another 15 or 20 percent.[29] The Eltro was the standard technology for audio time stretching before digital pitch shifters were introduced in 1974 (becoming popular in the 1980s and, just like the slow-motion cameras on our phones, now a default option for users of music software like Garage Band that comes standard on computers that can easily outpace HAL and remain, for the most part, squarely under our control). It is also worth pointing out that the Eltro was vintage hardware compared to many of the innovations Kubrick and his special effects designers were pursuing for *2001*. Invented in Germany in the 1920s, Eltro units were commonplace in radio and recording studios by the 1950s, where they were routinely employed to scale down (which is to say, speed up) commercials so that more ads could run in a single break in programming.

Sonic variations on slow motion would require more time to consider than I have here. This is especially true if we think about works of music that play with the absolute lower limits of tempo and melody, push the far extremes of perceptual endurance, or embrace the temporalities of sound-art installations that meditate on spans of time that are designed purposefully to defy the phenomenological experiences of continuity and flow that, in Husserl's language of retention and protention, are patterned on the qualities of music.[30] But there is at least one instance of slow motion that we hear in one very popular film before *2001* that is, if not a distant ancestor of HAL's painfully distended performance of "Daisy Bell," more resonant with his droning-unto-death than we might realize. In *Singin' in the Rain* (Stanley Donen and Gene Kelly, 1951), among the many ways we see and hear that silent film is doomed at the disastrous test screening of "The Dueling Cavalier" is the warping of Don Lockwood and Lina Lamont's voices, already terminally out of sync at this point in the film within the film, into a slow and tortured sound of comic anguish as the studio attempts to modernize two giant stars of costumed melodrama for a future of new technologies and the genres that come with them. The moment is played for laughs at their deserved expense, and like many other uses of pitch shifting as a rough approximation of slow-motion sound—often punctuating the deployment of such tropes as the "Big 'NO' " or the "Overly Long Scream"—the aesthetic often aims for bathos and an exaggerated grandeur that is meant to keep us at a distance from the suffering whose cries have nonetheless bent cinematic time around the anguish that they register.[31]

I am neither proposing *Singin' in the Rain* as an influence on the sound design of *2001* nor suggesting that HAL's distorted voice in his last sentient moments is an echo of the inhuman noises that come from the mouths of Gene Kelly and Jean Hagan as they bear witness to the destruction—or, just as catastrophically, the evolution—of a technological world they thought they'd mastered. HAL might have a lot of issues in *2001*, but being replaced by a later model—newer, younger, no doubt cheaper—is not one of them. HAL does not even get the last word in *2001*, though the distorted voice that he produces from his slowly failing circuits has more life to it than the bland recording of Heywood Floyd that starts playing, as a desperate contingency that his measured bureaucratic tone belies, to reveal to Bowman the truth about the mission that only HAL has known from the beginning. It is, however, his slurred and violently degrading voice that we remember in its painful dissolution into sounds too slow for us to understand as words. In *Singin' in the Rain*, Lina's days are numbered from the very start; she is effectively a dinosaur, and though Hagan delivers a command performance in a comic heel turn, the film definitely wants us laughing at her, not with her, when the final curtain closes, or rather opens, and Debbie Reynolds's Kathy Selden is revealed to be the body that contains the voice that the audience and Don have grown to love. Their marriage plot, or so the film suggests, is all the future Hollywood requires.

Kubrick in *2001* leaves ample space for us to imagine a hopeful ending, but not a happy one. We have spent too much time watching technology make no human being better, no matter how slow or fast it goes, for millions of years. From the "dawn of man" to HAL's sad love song from the Gilded Age, any step we take toward what we think is progress is always over somebody's dead body. In slow and slower motion, Bowman kills HAL so that he can eventually, after finishing the "ultimate trip," return to Earth in whatever form the monolith—which has been teaching us how to make weapons since before we became human—at last lets him achieve. With HAL's brutally decelerated voice still ringing in our ears or, maybe better, rumbling through our bodies, we might well wonder if we're actually just meeting the new man, same as the old. A killer to the very end.

THE DESCENT OF MAN

Though we have known for decades now that Kubrick's future did not come to pass, there are countless ways in which we are caught up in the long tail of his vision of modernity and technological existence from *2001*—a vision that depends entirely, as I have been arguing, on the slow motion that he indulges with such unselfconscious grandeur in "The Dawn of Man" and elsewhere. Or put differently, it is the utter self-consciousness of the aesthetic fanfare that surrounds this foundational moment of slow motion in *2001* that renders it so monumental. Shot primarily from below, the viewer is placed to admire with awe and wonder as Moon-Watcher smashes bones against the stark sky of the desert (on a sunny-enough day just outside London); the gigantic sounds of Richard Strauss are weaponized without a trace of the hard irony that would come with such a vengeance when the classics are deployed in *A Clockwork Orange*, where Alex and his violent "droogs" suggest an even more depressing branch of *Homo sapiens*' evolutionary family tree. We should also remember that it was no accident that Kubrick structured the soundtrack for this slow motion in *2001* around the full assault and bombast of a composer like Strauss, a late figure within a musical tradition that, as Alexander Rehding argues, aspires to two "distinct types of magnitude" in performing both a sense of "historical greatness" as a function of "collective memory and identity formation" and also "physical size" in its "marked tendency toward dramatic proportions." There are, with every year, fewer and fewer of us who have witnessed *2001* on the big screen, much less the Super Panavision or 70mm format that propelled Michelson and countless others into raptures, ecstasies, and "trips"—not always purely cinematic—that have helped consecrate Kubrick's minimally coherent spectacle into one of the period's signature examples of what Rehding would term "an aesthetics of wonderment."[32] Still, this might be a case where size doesn't matter. Even at the diminished scale of the 35mm prints most audiences saw in the late 1960s and after, and even on the smaller screens on which I've watched the film most recently—which vary from my respectably large LCD TV at home and the monitors and laptops that I write on to the iPhone that, like Moon-Watcher's bone, has become an extension of man—Kubrick's sheer determination to overwhelm us has managed to survive.

Writing about U.S. sculpture in the period, Slifkin suggests that works like Smithson's "nonsites" or the minimalist obelisks and monoliths of Barnett Newman or Donald Judd functioned as "monument[s] for a world in which the future seemed more like a distant, nearly prehistorical past than a shining new frontier."[33] There is little reason to believe that Kubrick had an interest in or much awareness of these terminal forms of twentieth-century modernism that Slifkin so powerfully describes here, which is another way of saying that slow motion is not the only way that figures in the period tried to reconcile its deeply contradictory temporalities, its anticipations of decline, deceleration, and collapse that were frequently shot through, in Kubrick's case especially, with fantasies of speed and progress at the upper limit of human possibility and beyond. Slow motion—in *2001* as Kubrick imagines it in 1968—makes perfect sense, even in a film that doesn't really try to do so, as the way modernity has looked for more than four million years and might forever without some alien or divine intervention. In cutting from our primordial past to a speculative future, Kubrick ostentatiously insists that everything that has happened in between—a whole history of people making things and killing—wouldn't show us anything we hadn't seen before, just not with the technical efficiency and exquisite beauty of slow motion. The beginning and the end of history, for Kubrick at least, has to happen in slow motion because it goes so fast that we would miss it otherwise.

But for all the ways that *2001* has settled into its monumentality in the more than fifty years since its release, there is still one dimension of the slow-motion sublime that Kubrick shows us with such bravura force that we should not let it rush past simply in the interest of time. I cannot begin to count how many repeated viewings I have made myself endure—in theaters, at my desk, in front of students, and never without a minimum of pleasure—of the perpetually tremendous scene when the first hominid to be programmed successfully by the message that the monolith-as-media brings to Earth takes bone in hand and learns to kill his way into modernity. I would guess that it took me at least one hundred or so viewings—maybe I'm not such a quick study?—before I saw what distinguished this particular moment from almost every prior instance of slow motion that we find in cinema's fossil record from the twentieth century to the 1960s, a period that can feel like it was over in a flash and also like a shadow from which there is no escape. Put simply, in most of the slow motion that I have tracked across film history before this moment, it is an aesthetic that wants to stress and amplify the consequences of an action that a body suffers, that happens *to someone*, often making weirdly sympathetic victims, if only for these decelerated seconds, of figures who we might say have it coming to them. At one level, this follows naturally or, rather, technologically from slow motion's tropism toward violence and trauma, and the dilated temporalities that it puts on display are representations or emblems of the felt intensity of the many terrible experiences that, when they are survived, are recounted as protracted intervals where time itself slows down. Slow motion is an effect of violence on a body, a form for registering an experience of sudden pain and suffering so overwhelming that it demands a different temporality in films as unlike one another as Cocteau's *Blood of a Poet*, Cukor's *What Price Hollywood?*, Pudovkin's *The Deserter*, and Kurosawa's *Sanshiro Sugata* or *The Seven Samurai*. Even *Bonnie and Clyde*, for all its revolutionary excess and manneristic detail, is also just two more slow-motion deaths where viewers have no choice but to witness the elaborate effects of violence in, but also *as*, a distended temporality that is inflicted from the outside, an application of brute force by obscure figures with whom we wouldn't want to identify even if we had the chance.

It is not simply that violence looks triumphant and bombastic in the majestic surplus of slow motion that punctuates this already profoundly aestheticized scene at the moment when Moon-Watcher raises his hand and brings it down in blows that symbolize the very "dawn of man" (figure 23.5). What we see here, quite possibly for the first time in film history, is violence in slow motion from a perspective that aligns entirely with the figure causing it to happen instead of feeling its effects. We have seen other characters pull off a version of this trick and throw their cinematic worlds into slow motion: when Maurice Chevalier in *Love Me Tonight* evokes the magic of a Shakespearean comedy as the horses he sends running into the woods, without any warning whatsoever, transform into a tableaux of fluid grace or when Fred Astaire dispenses with a string of showgirl partners and starts dancing with his cane alone in the "Steppin' Out with

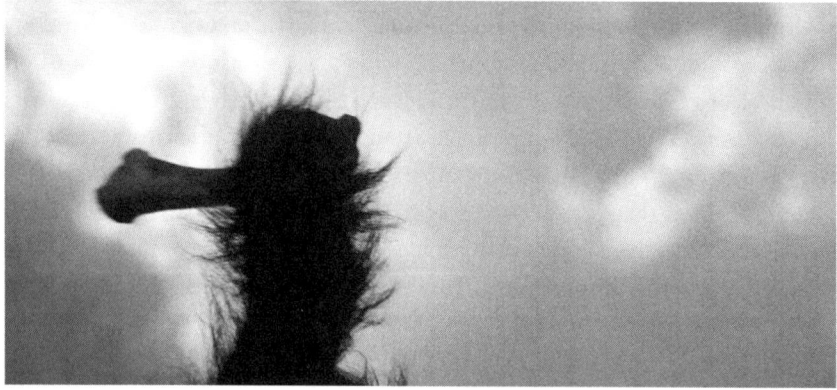

FIGURE 23.5 Still from *2001: A Space Odyssey* (1968).

My Baby" number in *Easter Parade*. The stunning shift into extreme slow motion (while the chorus line projected behind stays in normal time) is again a feat of style and form as a preternaturally powerful magic trick at the expense of physics as we know it. Moon-Watcher, to be clear, is no Astaire or Chevalier. He is another giant monkey who looks like all the rest—until he wins an evolutionary lottery and gets a software upgrade from an idealized "black box" that he cannot even use because it is technologically beyond him, just as it remains for us on the other side of the four million years that Kubrick cuts out but also reifies in slow motion. As Moon-Watcher smashes a skull and then brings down a tapir and then another, we demonstrably are not supposed to mourn the objects of his violence. There is no elegy or melancholy in this frenzied victory of technology over man and of man over everything that he can manage to destroy within his reach—which keeps getting longer as the film proceeds, but always to the same depressing end. There is something thrilling about Kubrick's utterly wild ambition and insistence that he can construct for us the slow-motion instant replay of the first moment of our history as a species. We can appreciate that we have seen nothing like it since and still reckon with the fact that almost every time—and countless times since 1968—we see slow motion turn a punch or kick or shot into a work of art, some filmmaker is, well, aping Kubrick in *2001*. In the beginning, there was slow motion. If Kubrick is right, it will probably outlive us, no matter the technology that looms behind it.

KUBRICK'S CIRCULATION CRISIS

Given what we know about the twenty-first century so far, *2001* would also seem to represent another opportunity to witness how thoroughly Kubrick failed to predict our future—though he did, perhaps, understand the times and speeds of modern life with real brilliance within the limits of his project. And we can see, by way of a final coda to *2001*, how Kubrick's film continues to reveal aspects of the modernity that is grinding slowly on as we feel like everything is only getting faster. Although there are countless science-fiction blockbusters and space epics, highbrow and otherwise, that bear witness to the influence of *2001*, I would like instead to end with a decidedly more obscure and earthbound variation on the uneven temporalities that it put into iconic form. Maruo Herce's *Dead Slow Ahead* (2015) is an almost impossibly exacting documentary about the voyage of the *Fair Lady*, a freighter traveling from Ukraine to New Orleans with a load of wheat and an Asian crew who remain entirely obscure as characters while we watch them, for just over an hour, work, sing karaoke, make calls to distant homes, and try to get a little exercise. These routines of masculine labor and sociability, much like Poole and Bowman playing chess and running laps, just barely make it possible for us to see how human beings might survive for extended periods within the utterly technological environments that contain and overwhelm them. The echoes and allusions to *2001* could hardly be more self-conscious; when *Dead Slow Ahead* was traveling around the festival circuit in 2015 and after, critics noted how the severity of its formal scale and rigorous composition, from the beeps and hums that fill its soundtrack to its stark framing and meticulous palette, seemed homages to Kubrick, with perhaps a nod to the foreboding interiors of the *Nostromo* from Ridley Scott's *Alien* (1978) as it captures the quiet horrors of trips from unnamed port to unnamed port, through straits and seas and voids of liminal geography. There are no charts or calendars to let us track the itinerary of *Fair Lady* or map its progress toward whatever destination may or may not await it. We never see where this ship is going, and its final shot—of a spinning engine rotor cast in a gothic reddish gloom—warns of an endless journey still to come, perpetually wandering while at work forever on somebody else's clock. There are ninety-seven total shots over the seventy minutes of *Dead Slow Ahead*, which is "slow cinema" to mannerist excess insofar as it renders its hour plus of running time as a virtual epoch of alienated labor and existential isolation. Then again, it is over fairly quickly for the viewer, who doesn't even have to endure a standard feature-length film to witness what feels like an eternity in and of "our present," as Deborah Cowen describes it, "as fundamentally a *time* of *logistics space.*"[34] Unlike *2001*, Herce's documentary essay is a film without a single moment of slow motion which really shows nothing else.

What *Dead Slow Ahead* helps us see in Kubrick—in part through the sheer effort of its homage—is how little sense we get from *2001* of the ways that things and people move from place to place through time. The film's narrative trajectory and course of human progress could not be rendered with greater clarity: From bone to bomb to *Discovery* to Star Gate to "hotel" to Star-Child and back to Earth, we always know exactly where we are supposed to be in *2001*, even when the film pretends that it is taking viewers where they have never gone. We might say that the essence of Kubrick's vision is that he has no patience for everything that takes place in between an evolutionary past and future and, in *2001* at least, little interest in where babies come from. Monoliths and the Star-Child suddenly appear from out of nowhere, events of pure contingency that have no precedents in any history we can experience for ourselves. Slow motion must look as beautiful and ominous as it does in *2001* because it wants to make time disappear while making sure that we admire and comprehend the power it takes to draw it out, and out of sight.

Let me add—though it sounds weird to state a fact that is so obviously true but also borders on the insignificant—that *2001* pictures a whole universe in which modernity has arrived and flourished and perhaps even been transcended without anything resembling an economy. The struggle over water in the opening section of "The Dawn of Man" may evoke the conflicts about property rights that structure so many classic westerns, but there is nothing else about *2001* that seems interested in the intervening epochs of accumulation, primitive and otherwise, that are rendered void with the flicker of a single frame. It strains even my own determined overreading to suggest that Kubrick is interested in deep allegories of resource scarcity or that his film is an object lesson in how technologies can catalyze and shape the evolution of the "animal spirits," to borrow a famous phrase from John Maynard Keynes, that define our nature as *Homo economicus*. Clarke and Kubrick wanted to produce a science fiction of the future that was plausible and textured with the protocols of realism, but they weren't exactly anticipating futures like those in Kim Stanley Robinson's *New York 2140* or *The Ministry of the Future*, where the focus is as much on the speculative horizons of our own financial systems, ideologies, and bureaucracies as it is on any feats of engineering or invention. Any progress that we see human beings make in *2001* is literally a miracle. Left to our own devices, the best our species can accomplish is a computer that kills us slower than the bones and bombs we have used for centuries and millennia already.

For the planners and economists working in the late 1960s as the Club of Rome—employing their own version of HAL so that they could use "a computer as a tool to aid our own understanding of the causes and consequences of the accelerating trends"—the only future that they could plot out for the West was static and regressive.[35] "Under the assumptions of no major change in the present system," they write in 1972's *The Limits to Growth*, "population and industrial growth with certainty stop within the next century, at the latest."[36] Though far from revolutionaries, the Club of Rome proposed an end to capitalism as the twentieth century had always known it. When they ran the numbers, the brutal logic of their rationality—displayed in charts and graphs throughout a book written in a tone of bureaucratic hauteur that Kubrick's Dr. Floyd would certainly appreciate—led them to conclude that a "self-imposed restriction on growth" was the best and only chance to avoid the inevitable "collapse" of the world system. "Economically developed countries," they argue, must "encourage a deceleration in growth of their own material output while, at the same time, assisting the developing nations in their efforts to advance their economies more rapidly." Directors like Leone and Peckinpah were more interested than Kubrick in the politics and mythologies of uneven development as the 1960s was ending for the West and for its epoch of modernity at speed. Kubrick, on the other hand, offers us the exceedingly cold comfort of the hope for what the club described as "another technological leap [that] will allow growth to continue still longer." For the Club of Rome, though, this is the riskiest and most fantastic dream of science fiction that they can possibly conceive: "We have found that technological optimism is the most dangerous reaction to our findings from the world model." Planning for another monolith to launch us toward the future is an expression of sheer wish fulfillment, and the somber grownups in the Club of Rome might well have seen Kubrick's Star-Child as the appropriately symbolic manifestation of such an epic and infantile delusion.

But if we go back in time to *2001* from the perspective not so much of the blockbusters it made possible but from a decidedly minor masterpiece like *Dead Slow Ahead*, it becomes hard to miss how little hope Kubrick finally seems to have for a future that can only grind away on the same course we have been traveling since before we became human. In the wholly artificial environments of the *Fair Lady*, the little men in their protective gear never look like anything but alienated labor. The sense of science fiction that *Dead Slow Ahead* borrows for its stylized portrayal of global shipping and commodity logistics is not ironic but entirely earnest in its insistence that the scales and temporalities of global capital require a leap of genre into expanses that lie beyond the space of documentary. As an uncanny homage to *Alien*, the film could well adapt its grisly tagline to remind its viewers that at sea no one can see you work. Yet there are no horrors on display in *Dead Slow Ahead*, just the endless everyday routines of labor on a vessel whose dreadful size and unrelentingly technological materiality are constant reminders that while flesh-and-blood workers are essential to its ongoing operation, they are functionally irrelevant to its mission. Poole and Bowman, we learn with HAL's demise, also do not know why they have been sent across the solar system at tremendous speeds that look and feel like one long, interminable working day of repetitious labor—pushing buttons on HAL's instructions, responding to HAL's sensors and alerts, keeping themselves fit enough to do the simple grunt work, trained monkeys more than heroic astronauts, until some boss back home gives them another set of orders.

Dead Slow Ahead is explicitly about the maritime spaces and variously connected "counter-sites," to use a term of art from Foucault that Allen Sekula deploys in *Fish Story* (1995), his photobook about the liminal and, for most of us, invisible "other spaces"—like brothels, colonies, or boats, to cite some of Foucault's examples—where modernity's hardest work gets done.[37] In Sekula's mordantly majestic epic of global shipping, containerization, and the complex relationships and harrowing exploitations that are necessary to create a "society of accelerated flows," Sekula observes how conceptually difficult it is to keep it all moving when it is also "in key aspects a society of deliberatively slow movement."[38] Containerized cargo movement is, as he reminds us, one of the most crucial inventions behind the decades of economic expansion after World War II, with uncelebrated pioneers such as Malcolm McLean discovering that while commodity production might demand perpetual acceleration of turnover time in search of profits, "large-scale material flows" depended on a different calculus of conservative fuel use, minimal overhead, increasing automation at ports and docks, and ships that were designed to be "deliberately slow."[39] In this respect, at least, the *Discovery* in *2001* works perfectly until it doesn't. With its skeleton crew of two—and HAL requiring no compensation that we can imagine—Kubrick's vision of space travel is profoundly lonely and not so much a romance of exploration as an exercise in surviving on the narrow margins of a technological world that we may have built, but not to do our bidding. The shipping containers that are moving, slowly, through the Port of Oakland just a few miles from where I am writing are not designed to the ideal mathematic ratios of the monolith; though at the modern standard measurements of 8′ × 8′ × 40′ per container, you could make one into a monolith that would only be a little narrower in its proportions than Kubrick's original. From the outside, their contents are equally mysterious. Their surfaces are not nearly so refined, untouchable, and flat, and while Sekula works wonders with them in *Fish Story*'s photographs, they are not built for beauty so much as they are built for speed. Which does not mean that they go fast. Unlike the humans who load and then unload them, they have all the time in the world to go as slow as necessary to make as much money as possible on whatever might be inside them. They are the opposite of singular or monolithic, and like slow motion after 1968, so familiar that we hardly see them for the strange marvels of technology they truly are. Artifacts from a twentieth century that was maybe already over by the late sixties, when the "ultimate trip" was Kubrick's grand illusion—rendered in the most spectacular slow motion—that the West still had nowhere to go but up.

24
How the West Slows Down

Sergio Leone and the Long Struggle

Between *Bonnie and Clyde* and *2001*, we might say that slow motion had already achieved escape velocity in early 1968 and that the arc of its eventual trajectory through Hollywood film and contemporary visual culture was largely set. This is not a counterfactual that I am interested in pursuing, nor am I certain—for all the iconic power of the scenes in Penn and Kubrick that we've been lingering over—that we can ignore the outsized role of Sam Peckinpah, first in *The Wild Bunch* and then throughout his subsequent career, as a popularizer of slow motion at its most flagrant and pervasive. With *Bonnie and Clyde* still playing in America and abroad for much of the year as well and *2001* commanding both critical attention and stoner devotion, this makes for a sense of 1968 as the annus mirabilis for slow motion as we know it now, the year slow motion broke into the basic syntax of studio filmmaking in the United States. But just before the year was out, Sergio Leone's *Once Upon a Time in the West* had its debut in Rome on December 20, 1968. Though it did not appear in the United States until the following May, Leone's epic of masculinity and modernization still made it to theaters about two weeks before *The Wild Bunch*. As we will see, it is finally easier to say why Peckinpah used so much slow motion than it is to understand why Leone used so little.

Even though Leone never used slow motion before the final few minutes of *Once Upon a Time in the West*, his major films of the 1960s—which we now know as the Dollars Trilogy of *Fistful of Dollars* (1964), *For a Few Dollars More* (1965), and *The Good, the Bad, and the Ugly* (1968)—had already established the distinctive temporalities that structured the schematic narratives and symbolic landscapes of his films. It is worth revisiting what contemporary critics had to say about Leone's performatively deliberate pacing and the static grandeur of set pieces that made for the barest skeletons of stories. His films, like the vast majority of spaghetti westerns, drew overt condescension from critics who, as we have seen, were willing to indulge directors such as Penn and Kubrick almost anything. Stanley Kaufmann might have admired Leone for his "touching and maniacal" commitment to the classic western but could not abide the way that every setting, "no matter how stark it is supposed to be," has to be "ornately stark"; the radiating glows captured by Leone's cinematographer, Kaufmann reports with clunky chauvinism, "has covered everything with melted parmigiana." Kaufmann insists that "the story could have been told, as it often has been, in 80 minutes or so" if not for Leone's wild determination to "[anatomize] every scene into compositions, expanding small incidents into small dramas."[1] Kael, for once, is somewhat kinder. Though she may have blamed Leone for transforming Clint Eastwood into an icon of what she saw as disturbingly regressive politics—an argument she never tired of making with each installment in the Dirty Harry franchise—Kael is relatively quiet on Leone's other films. She at least avoids the Italian stereotypes and opera jokes that Kaufmann can't resist ("this Western has the first shootout in which I expected the duellists to burst into *bel canto*"). Writing about Leone's *Once Upon a Time in America* (1984), his massive gangster saga on the order of *The Godfather*, she regrets how he "inflates" all the incidents in his more-than-three-hour film and "slows them down, and gives them a dreamy obsessiveness."[2] But I am interested in more than just the wearying slowness of Leone's stately compositions and thematically ostentatious tableaux. I think Leone goes even slower: His films explore what Jussi Parikka terms, in an admittedly much different context, "the deep times of contemporary politics" and the "long term durations that unfold as not immediate" for human perception.[3] I realize this sounds a lot like the terrain that we just covered with respect to Kubrick and the vast sweep of prehistory and history that culminates with *2001*. I should add, before we go much further, that we are also headed back to Monument Valley. We'll be taking the long way. Though slow motion gets us there faster than we might realize.

There are westerns that go even slower than Leone at his most impossibly expansive could ever have conceived. One particularly extreme example can help us save some time before we get too deep into Leone. If you plan to watch *The Searchers* with Douglas Gordon, you'll want to clear your calendar: In 1995, the Scottish artist proposed an installation version of John Ford's famous western that he hoped to realize as a site-specific screening of the film stretched out and distended so that its running time would coincide with the duration of the events it narrates. As Gordon writes in the original proposal for *5-year drive-by*, which he presented at the Biennale de Lyon in 1995, "the narrative here is pretty straightforward":

> John Wayne returns home from the Civil War, eventually, and rolls back to his brother and kin like a bad penny. It's all going swell until the Injun's turn up and do the dirty; killing the menfolks, raping the women, and stealing one of the kids to take back to their camp. Of course, all the pillage and plunder is taking place while John Wayne has conveniently disappeared from the storyline for a few moments to allow the Commanche to finish off what they started and disappear with the stolen child (Wayne's niece).
>
> So what's to be done; well, old Uncle Ethan (Wayne's character) simply embarks on an epic search for the missing child.
>
> This is the essence of the story; nothing less, and nothing more.
>
> The search lasts five long years.[4]

Gordon's cheeky play with stereotypes is supposed to get across just how preposterous he finds *The Searcher*'s plot, which works with stock characters and mythologies so broad and predetermined that it is hard to take them seriously in 1956 or after. "The story seemed too simple," notes Gordon earlier, but as with many of the "endless westerns" he remembers watching as a child of six or seven, it "made a big impression" on him—"in retrospect," he adds, invoking yet another way that *The Searchers* and its genre have managed, against the ravages of cinematic history, to nonetheless survive. For Gordon, the problem of *The Searchers* is "quite simply a question of time" and the impossibility of "anyone even [trying] to sum up 5 miserable years in only 113 minutes." Gordon says that he will "[reconstitute] the narrative, as it were," by effectively undoing the compression of information that makes for narrative itself. "This need not be so difficult, on a technical level," he adds, and then he runs the numbers as if to show that his own thinking is hardly more self-conscious than the movie's own. Thus 113 minutes of "cinema time" equals "5 years in real time," or "5 x 365 [days] + 1 [day for a leap year]"; these 1,826 days equal 43,824 hours and so on until he has 2,629,440 minutes in "real time" from which he then works backward to discover that his version of *The Searchers* will need to render just under six and a half hours of its "fabula," to revisit the term from Russian formalism, per second of the film's original duration.[5] There is no "story" at one frame per 1,015 seconds.

Though never installed in situ in the U.S. West, Gordon's *5-year drive-by* was conceived as something of a sequel to what remains his most visible and crucial work, *24 Hour Psycho*, the time-dilated screening of Hitchcock's masterpiece that helped make Gordon prominent enough to win the Turner Prize in 1996 and then go on to represent Great Britain at the Venice Biennale in 1997. For all his stature in the world of contemporary art, Gordon has yet to mount a full-scale version of *5-year drive-by*. Perhaps, as he concludes in his original proposal—in the deadpan that is de rigueur for a conceptual artist's prose—he is "still working on it."

But this unrealized Gordon project also raises, on a grander, slower scale, many of the questions that we saw DeLillo approaching by way of *24 Hour Psycho* in *Point Omega*. There, Gordon's slow art was enlisted as an exercise in learning to think deliberately about forms of violence that go too fast, which is why, when encountered by the "defense intellectual" Richard Elstir, it is supposed to help him comprehend the catastrophic failings of a War on Terror that Elstir once imagined could be as "transient" as a haiku. In the aftermath of such disastrously high-speed instances of ideology, DeLillo makes Gordon's film into an icon of the aesthetic temporality that we should now pursue instead. "It takes close attention to see what is happening in front of you," DeLillo writes of Elstir. "It takes work, pious effort, to see what you are looking at. He was mesmerized by this, the depths that were possible in the slowing of motion, the things to see, the depths of things so easy to miss in the shallow habit of seeing."[6] Given that *Point Omega*, as we have seen, has the barest architecture of the Hitchcock thriller behind its very sketchy plot, it makes sense for DeLillo to allude to Gordon's radically distended version of *Psycho*, but in the desert wastes to which Elstir has exiled himself, the mythologies of nationhood and ideology that *5-year drive-by* turns into a futile challenge of endurance would resonate as thoroughly. If you've read *Point Omega*, you can almost imagine Elstir sitting through the whole thing, the ideal audience for Gordon's punishing yet beautifully fetishistic immersion in the fiction of a heroic U.S. West.

I am particularly interested in how Gordon tries to warp and break the sense of narrative drive that, as we saw with Kubrick's detour back to *How the West Was Won* for his own supremely modern vision of the future, is patterned on the timelines of progress and development that were already losing steam in a revisionary western like *The Searchers* and that directors like Leone and Peckinpah grind to a sadomasochistic halt before our very eyes. Michael Fried has come to admire Gordon for "the revelatory power of [his] radicalization of slow motion" in relation to how projects like *24 Hour Psycho* reveal the array of gestures and bodily "automatisms"—a term of art within a discourse of modernism that he shares with Stanley Cavell—that conspire to produce the style of highly textured, naturalistic acting that we associate with studio filmmaking in the

United States after World War II. At the glacially distended speeds to which Gordon subjects these famous films, we are allowed (or forced) to see the almost frozen poses of familiar stars like Janet Leigh or John Wayne as "visually gripping in a way that has almost nothing to do with the original narrative" even if we think we know it. This provides Fried with another opportunity to confirm his priors and enlist Gordon in what has become a never-ending twilight struggle over modernist aesthetics in which Fried has outlasted any of the figures from the 1960s, like Donald Judd or Robert Smithson, who once upon a time in *Artforum* staged their own versions of the climactic showdown from *The Good, the Bad, and the Ugly* over highly technical debates about the temporality of art and objects and the medium specificity of their materials and forms. I don't think Fried would want to say that either Judd or Smithson were bad, so much as ugly—inconsistent and a little phony, like Eli Wallach's painfully inauthentic "Tuco" in perhaps Leone's greatest film—but certainly Fried sees himself still fighting the "good" fight in the "centuries-old attempt to defeat theater" that his work as both a critic and art historian has been pursuing now for several decades.[7] Though hardly a shooting war at this late date, the drama that surrounds these highly wrought and very narrow arguments from the late 1960s weirdly enough unfolds across the same intellectual terrain that Leone is exploring amid the violence, awkward dubbing, and stylized masculinity of his spaghetti westerns. It's not just that Leone's manneristic exercises in the genre work as powerful defamiliarizations of Hollywood conventions that, returning to some of Shklovsky's most important terminology, function as "estrangement[s]" revealing "the essential character of art's technique."[8] I admit that Leone's imaginary West is an exotic place to look for signs of an ongoing and interminable struggle over "certain artistic issues," as Fried puts it, "that first came to the fore around the middle of the eighteenth century in France and that a received a further, explicitly ontological inflection in the encounter between high modernism and Minimalism/Literature in the mid-1960s."[9] I doubt, in fact, that Leone would have known what Fried was talking about if somebody had shown him Fried's "Art and Objecthood" when it appeared in 1967, just as production was getting underway on Leone's last two westerns. But what Leone shows us—as his films become enamored with the many forms of slowness they discover—is that one aspect of the modernism that Smithson and Fried were fighting over, far from the deserts of Spain where we were and weren't supposed to see America, was whether its dreams of endless, accelerating progress still were possible. Or whether the narratives and technologies that kept modernity going, even when they occasionally looked good, or maybe just a little ugly, had actually turned forever bad.

THE GOOD, THE BAD, AND THE MINIMALIST

"The sites in films," writes Robert Smithson, "are not to be located or trusted."[10] Sound advice when thinking about the films of Leone and the genre of the spaghetti western he made so famous in the 1960s, first with *A Fistful of Dollars* in 1964; its two sequels, *For a Few Dollars More* in 1965 and *The Good, the Bad, and the Ugly* in 1966; and finally *Once Upon a Time in the West* in 1968. Filmed largely on locations scattered across Andalusia and other parts of Spain but with interior sequences often shot at Rome's Cinecitta studios—all the better to represent a spectacular, imaginary version of the U.S. West—the grand inauthenticity of the spaghetti western's sense of place was missed by precisely no critic or reviewer of the period and remains central to any and all contemporary discussions of the genre, popular or scholarly. It is not for nothing that Jean Baudrillard, according to Leone's biographer, once called him "the first postmodern director" and that, in the lecture "History: A Retro Scenario," Baudrillard cites Leone as registering, along with Stanley Kubrick and other filmmakers of his moment, an epistemic break whose contours and clichés feel as mythically familiar as any of Leone's set pieces or archetypes: "The great event of this period, the great trauma, is this decline of strong referentials, these death pangs of the real and of the rational that open onto an age of simulation."[11] While it can be cruel to read Baudrillard against his actual examples, this may be a case where his hyperbole is on the money. Consider Enzo Castellari's 1976 *Keoma*, a particularly baroque example of the genre whose plot is far too formulaic to interest anyone save Quentin Tarantino (figure 24.1). The "real" dies so

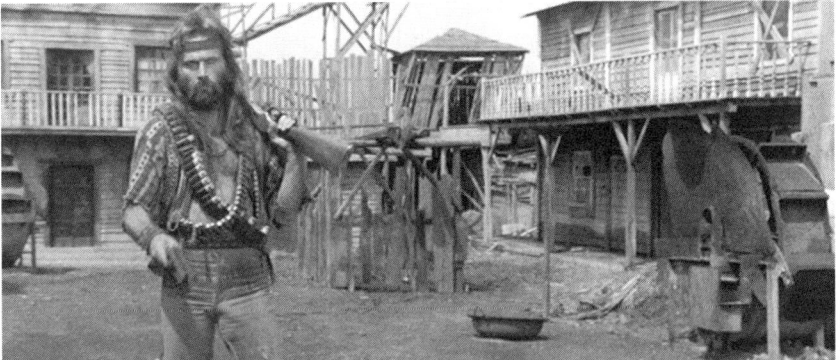

FIGURE 24.1 Franco Nero, not yet moving in slow motion, in *Keoma* (1976).

many little deaths: In Franco Nero's ethnically unlikely casting as Keoma, "half-breed Indian"; in his equally unlikely wig; in the voice behind the gunshots that *isn't* Leonard Cohen's, though this was precisely whom Castellari wanted for the soundtrack; in the claustrophobic artifice of the ruined Texas town, ripped by winds off the Deserto di Accona in Tuscany; and, most lavishly, in the spectacular slow motion that monumentalizes almost every act of violence in the film and that imparts each gunshot, fall, and rearing horse with a fatality at once auratic and absurd. As we remember from Benjamin, once upon a time in one of modernism's most cited essays, "slow motion not only presents familiar qualities of movement, but reveals in them entirely unknown ones 'which, far from looking like retarded, rapid movements, give the effect of singularly gliding, floating, supernatural motions.'"[12] Slow motion, like so much modernism according to a logic I've been challenging, appears the first time as avant-garde, then every other time as farce.

There is precious little slow motion in Leone's early spaghetti westerns, but even before his first use of the effect in *Once Upon a Time in the West*, his films had already become marked everywhere by an aesthetic of slowness, and it is this—and perhaps only this—which he shares with Smithson, whose first "earthwork," *Asphalt Rundown*, was done near Rome in October 1969, just four months after Leone's film opened in the United States. Though Smithson was capaciously receptive to odd influences, I'm not claiming that Leone figures in his career. Rather, I'm interested in a set of preoccupations that Smithson and Leone shared and rendered at a scale and sheer materiality that locates both at a certain distance from a form of modernism that, if aging noticeably by the late sixties, still flourished nonetheless. To borrow from the title of Smithson's own quasi-ethnographic writings on the Yucatan, he and Leone undertake "mirror-travels" in their respective mediums as the 1960s end, with Smithson traveling to Italy to inaugurate the major phase in his too short career and Leone at last arriving to film in the American West after the global box-office success of the Dollars Trilogy gave him the capital—in every sense—to shoot several sequences in Monument Valley, the site of countless Hollywood westerns and especially sacred ground for Leone, given its prominence in the films of John Ford. Smithson too would go west in the last years of his life, building *Asphalt Ramp* near Amarillo, Texas, in 1973 and, most iconically, *Spiral Jetty* at Great Salt Lake, Utah, in 1970. As Jennifer Roberts and others have pointed out, Smithson selected the site for *Spiral Jetty* in part for its proximity to the Golden Spike National Historic Site that commemorates the completion of the transcontinental railroad, an event whose historical shape, in patently mythic and schematic terms, looms in the background of *Once Upon a Time in the West*, whose plot concerns the coming of modernity and its predations as a widow, Jill McBain (played by Claudia Cardinale), and the robber baron, Morton, and his hired killer, Frank (played by Henry Fonda), fight for control of "Sweetwater," a piece of land located squarely in the railroad's path of progress. It is less the coincidence of this shared geography than the fact that both men use the Western landscape to explore iconographies and experiences of duration that make slowness central to the temporality of modern life, not simply as an opposing force to a twentieth-century culture of speed but as a more pervasive aesthetic speaking to a deeper condition of the technologies with which we share the world. Put differently, if we are accustomed to thinking about modernism—with its rhetorics of speed and progress, innovation and immediacy—as profoundly oriented, in Fredric Jameson's terms, toward an "already-existent technological ideology," Smithson and Leone give us a chance to see what a later, more contemporary modernism looks like when we realize that what might be most important about technology is not that it goes too fast for us to manage but that it moves too slow for us to perceive.[13]

This is perhaps too broad a canvas on which to pursue the admittedly weird connections between Smithson and spaghetti westerns that I am after. Even before Smithson undertook his earthworks, he had pursued a series of projects that confronted some of the most firmly held positions among the preferences and dogmas of late modernism in the United States. And as we saw before, these projects were preoccupied with forms of slow motion that confronted the modernism of the period with a vastly different reckoning of art and time. In particular, Smithson's writings on behalf of minimalist sculpture (his 1965 review of Donald Judd and "Entropy and the New Monuments" in 1966) articulated an aesthetic that squarely departed from the tastes and, more importantly, the modes of temporality that Clement Greenberg and, later, Michael Fried had claimed for *their* Modernism alone (and the capital *M* makes all the difference). Smithson's "nonsite" installations made his objections to Greenberg's modernism profoundly and materially plain. By installing rocks and stones from specific construction sites in plainly geometrical, shaped containers, Smithson at once invoked the kind of Duchampian gamesmanship that Greenberg never liked and violated, in decidedly concrete terms, the basic, ontological autonomy of the work of art in time and space that Greenberg and then Fried made central to the only Modernism they were willing to defend. Greenberg had long since purified his doctrines of their Marxist antecedents by the 1960s, when, in essays like "The Case for Abstract Art" and "Modernist Painting," he increasingly foreclosed on the idea that art should have either content (that it should represent something) or even permit its beholder to perceive it as an expression of or artifact in historical time; Modernism was "personal before anything else," and its proper relation to the world was to defeat our mere phenomenological immersion in it: "Pictorial art in its highest definition is static; it tries to overcome movement in time and space . . . its unity should be immediately evident . . . and this is something to be grasped only in an instant of time."[14] For the early Fried of "Art and Objecthood" (1967), the two worst things that art could do were, first, revert to being an object in a perceptual field that's shared with other bodies in specific spaces ("theatricality") and, second, produce an experience that "*persists in time*" or in any way gives "a presentment of endless or indefinite *duration*." Modern art's essential value for Fried was and very much remains—he has yet to change his mind—a function of its capacity, if only for an instant, to exist in, evoke, or constitute a "continuous and perpetual *present*" that is virtually experienced as the transcendence of everyday time but still remains within a logic patterned on a certain faith in and willing submission to the eventual fall back into temporality. "Presentness is grace," is how Fried famously ends "Art and Objecthood," and though he would never consecrate it in the terms I am using here, it should go without saying that "presentness" goes fast, and "grace" is fleeting.[15] This is a present, in other words, that comes after a past and gives way to a future, just like modernism comes after art that tried too hard to stage or manifest *its* theatricality for us, and so kept us, until the signature advances of French painting in the nineteenth century, suffering on the clock instead of freeing us, like more advanced artists later would for a moment anyway, from the hard reality that even when we think we are transported by an artwork, we're still just bodies sharing spaces with objects and one another. And some of us—and them—age much more poorly than we might want.

There is more to say about Fried's place within a larger constellation of 1960s figures who found themselves negotiating what Pamela Lee has termed the "chronophobia" of late modernism.[16] This is more or less how Smithson responded to Fried in a letter to the editor of *Artforum*, where he characterized Fried as clinging fearfully to a "state of temporal grace" precisely because he fears the "atemporal" world that minimalist sculptures and nonsites suggest, works of art that do not try to beat time but simply outlast it. For all Fried's talk of modernism's "grace" divinely saving us from lives experienced otherwise as unendurable expanses of homogenous, empty time, Smithson says that Fried's desire for instants of pure "presentness" speaks less to a strong faith in art's powers of transcendence and more to a profound anxiety about the inhumanity of time itself. Thus Smithson sees Fried as clinging, with barely sublimated dread, to the idea that art can offer fast and fleeting instants of timelessness because what a modernist like Fried can't actually abide is the image of a world where there is no change or progress that we can comprehend. Smithson sees modernists of the 1960s perpetually replaying allegories of time lost and then regained, cycling with increasing speed and desperation through played-out styles of avant-garde aesthetics, pretending—or perhaps, misbelieving—that they want to be saved from temporality when what they really want is for the story and ideology of modernism as a narrative of progress to go ever faster, for as long as it can. Modernism *needs* time to suffer through and then outpace just like the "fanatical puritan," as Smithson calls Fried, needs temptations of the flesh in order to have something to resist. So Smithson calls his bluff: Minimalism's boxes, planks, and towers, like the rocks and soils of his own "nonsites," show us all too powerfully that the world consists of things that exist in or evoke a deep time where modernism doesn't matter any more than the human beings who insist that they believe in it, a world that moves too slowly for any product of human thought or making to apprehend. "At any rate," Smithson answers back to Fried, "eternity brings about the dissolution of belief in temporal histories, empires, revolutions, and counter-revolutions—all becomes ephemeral and in a sense unreal, even the universe loses its reality. Nature gives way to the incalculable cycles of nonduration."[17]

As Lytle Shaw suggests, Smithson "points here to the theatricality not only of Fried's but of *all* critical positions" in the face of a literal eternity that Smithson's argument takes to "its truly science-fictional" conclusion.[18] This is why Smithson calls Fried, on perhaps the only occasion in his long career, a "Marxist saint" who "shall not be tempted into this awful sensibility" of timelessness or surrender to the "non-durational labyrinths of time [that] are infecting his brain with eternity."[19] Smithson doesn't care about the politics of modernism and certainly isn't trying to remind the readers of *Artforum* that Greenberg started out as a socialist and that the earliest articulations of his theories of kitsch and medium specificity were offered in the service of a left aesthetics, however half-sincere or temporized.[20] It is more that Smithson is trying, with scattershot and savage cleverness lost on almost everyone, to invoke the spirit of Hegel that resides in this discourse of Western modernism at practically the genetic level, not just evolving alongside Hegel's *Aesthetics* in the early 1800s but trying to answer some of the same questions about the purposes of art in a world where its traditional sources of authority (religion, classical philosophy) have lost a measure, if not the totality, of their power. "Hellish objecthood," Smithson writes, "is causing modernity much vexation."[21] These intimations of a stupid, brute duration without an end or human meaning render modernism as another desperate passing fancy, a period style dressed up as putative ideal. In what is effectively an appropriation of Keynes's old joke at the expense of economics, Smithson wants to remind both Fried and *Artforum*'s readers that in the long run—which is longer than they can possibly imagine—modernists and minimalists alike will all be dead. Art cannot outlive us; objects can be forever.

Smithson conceives of deep time in terms that anticipate some of the concept's more radical implications for thinking about human history, implications that both critics like Mark McGurl and philosophers like Quentin Meillassoux have addressed. Smithson here seems remarkably prescient on the problem of what Meillassoux calls "ancestrality," the profoundly disturbing notion of a potentially endless "anteriority in time" that cannot be reconciled to any form of subjectivity or consciousness we can imagine because it is "prior to givenness," by which he means it has no relationship to consciousness or correlate to any form of human thought. Similarly, McGurl points out that many recent invocations of deep time as potentially allowing for an expanded notion of politics and literary history—he departs from Wai Chi Dimock's *Through Other Continents*—significantly underrate the utter insignificance of any human project or institution across the vast temporal expanses on which evolutionary biologists and geologists, much less astrophysicists, pursue their work.[22]

I am not suggesting that Leone's westerns are about deep time exactly, but they certainly are determined to test the limits of duration—for the generic tropes and myths whose entropy they simultaneously stage and stave off, for the characters whose physical and mental suffering they explore with sadomasochistic languor, and for viewers whose attention is subjected to longer and longer spectacles of inaction between the episodes of brutal violence that punctuate their plots. Indeed, it is hard even to illustrate the temporal dimensions of Leone's later westerns because so many of the sequences—such as the roughly six minutes that the "good," the "bad," and the "ugly" will here spend staring at one another before opening fire—defy the conventions of even the most indulgent argument (figure 24.2). The entire showdown is a bravura piece of Eisensteinian montage, and the gradual acceleration of Ennio Morricone's score is so utterly compelling that it feels scandalous to point out that the whole scene is, within the logic of the narrative, a tremendous waste of time. Eastwood has already taken all of Eli Wallach's ammunition; there is no drama about whom he should shoot first as if this is some exercise in Old West game theory: He knows he has nothing to fear from the "ugly" and must kill the "bad." Leone's biographer relates an anecdote confirming that Leone was intentionally after such effects of aggressive delay and stylization and that he considered them essential to his "modernism": Leone was "upset" when American preview audiences expressed irritation at the temporal juxtapositions of slow and fast in *The Good, the Bad, and the Ugly*, finding the desert sequences especially "far too long

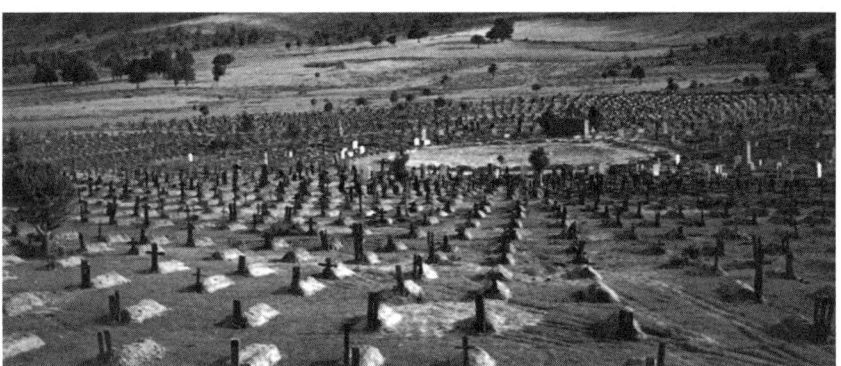

FIGURE 24.2 Still from *The Good, the Bad, and the Ugly* (1966).

and drawn-out"; so too, they were confused about why "the rhythm of the film seemed to them to have slowed down since the first two 'Dollars' films to an almost hallucinatory pace." Leone particularly resisted cuts to several sequences featuring Wallach and Eastwood, remembering later that "the worst thing was that [in America] they found the desert scenes too long. I adore them myself. Tonino Delli Colli photographed them in a way that was worthy of the great surrealist painters."[23] Delli Colli was also the cinematographer for Pasolini's *Mamma Roma*, where slow motion adds a measure of fantasy and expressionist dream-work to the neorealist syntax that the film pushes past its limits. Leone admired Max Ernst and Magritte and was more than familiar with the main currents and figures of Italian Futurism, but his favorite was Giorgio de Chirico, and Leone started collecting de Chirico in the late 1950s. Though such rough coordinates and biographical details do not exactly prove a line of influence, it is always worth remembering that one of the most crucial sites of slow motion's emergence as a special effect is in avant-garde cinema of the 1920s, including Luis Buñuel's *Un chien Andalou*, Rene Clair's *Entr'acte*, Jean Epstein's *The Fall of the House of Usher*, and Jean Vigo's *Zero for Conduct*—all works produced within the orbit, if not the sway, of surrealism at its most influential. There are several scenes in the Dollars Trilogy and *Once Upon a Time in the West* that look like they were designed as homages to paintings like de Chirico's *The Enigma of the Hour* (1910 or 1911), *The Nostalgia of the Infinite* (1911), or *The Great Tower* (1921), not simply for the austerity of space that gives so much room for variously diminished figures to be isolated from one another or for the dry intensity of the deep browns and oranges that radiate with apprehension across his largely empty canvases. Again, it is hard to know what Leone means by when he praises Delli Colli for capturing a "surrealist" experience of time, but at the very least such remarks confirm that Leone was self-conscious about the artistry behind his fantasies of time and knew that what his westerns may have lacked in authenticity—at the level of landscape, dialect, or realism—they tried to balance with their weirdly avant-garde pretensions in style and their expanded field of visual motifs that filled the many dead zones in their always skeletal narratives.

But I'm finally interested in other aspects of Leone's fascination with slowness. First, the history of the western as a cinematic genre is the history of its slowing down, and Leone all but brings it to a halt. From 1903's *The Great Train Robbery* through John Ford's 1925 epic, *The Iron Horse*, no body of silent narrative cinema is more breathtakingly kinetic than the western, and it is not simply the case that westerns depend on such set pieces as chases, shootouts, and barroom brawls that place a premium on speed and action; early Westerns often look especially fast because of the regular use of "undercranking" when filming chases or fights—action sequences were filmed at less than 24fps, so that when projected in theaters at standard speeds, movement appears accelerated, sometimes intensely, even comically so.[24] Even after the transition to sound, when stars like Tom Mix and William S. Hart give way to Gary Cooper and John Wayne—each of whom possessed an acting and speaking style that was dramatically slow—classical westerns of the 1930s, such as Ford's *Stagecoach*, proceed at more or less the same velocity, both narratively and stylistically, as their silent-era predecessors. After World War II, the western begins to change. Ford's films of the 1940s and 1950s become more static and expansive, still punctuated by sequences of visceral and accelerated action but also marked by a new emphasis on painterly composition and the sheer representation of landscape (*My Darling Clementine, She Wore a Yellow Ribbon, The Searchers*). We might also think of the ways in which Anthony Mann's classic westerns (*The Man from Laramie*), for example, explore the recesses of psychological time in the always traumatic backstories of their heroes or, perhaps most ostentatiously, in the stately formalism of George Steven's *Shane* or Fred Zinnemann's *High Noon*, whose narrative unfolds in real time—a decidedly non-avant-garde experiment in cinematic duration. Writing in 1954, it thus makes perfect sense for Robert Warshow to describe the western hero as "a figure of repose," in the last analysis defined not just by his capacity for action but by his suffering *not* to act with "nobility" until the moment has arrived.[25] The forward-looking epilogue to *How the West Was Won*—with its sweeping vistas showing the infrastructure of American modernity in Cinemascope—is a spectacle of compensation in precisely this regard. The monumentality of its scale and narrative composition may have attracted Kubrick to aspects of its style and ideology, but *How the West Was Won* is left to assert its vision of progress from a deeply retrograde perspective. Indeed, until the last shot of its final sequence, the viewer is still looking backward at a modernity that already has been accomplished, with no way to know what, if anything, is left to "win" as the camera at last turns out to the Golden Gate Bridge and the Pacific Ocean. The project of the western can still look epic enough in the 1960s, but it is also clearly over.

FAST DRAW, SLOW VIOLENCE

In this brief narrative of the genre, the 1960s mark a period in which many filmmakers produce "revisionary" westerns of one kind or another. And while I'm interested in what makes Leone's westerns specifically so slow, it's worth remembering that the emergence of slow motion as a popular special effect in Hollywood film is itself a story about the western, with Penn's *The Left Handed Gun* representing a crucial early appearance. Of course it takes the triumph of Penn's *Bonnie and Clyde* to codify slow motion as a stylistic signature of the New American cinema, but the film's self-conscious play with generic conventions is not limited to its devotion to Warner Bros. gangster movies of the 1930s, since its decidedly rural landscapes and "primitive" fragments of Americana give it the aura of a bygone western past. Yet even before Leone first employs slow motion in *Once Upon a Time in the West*, we can think about how, like Smithson, he had begun to explore temporalities that could endure beyond the limits of any genre of human narrative or action. Here, for example, is "Sad Hill Cemetery," a location Leone built for *The Good, the Bad, and the Ugly* (figure 24.3). At the center of these concentric rings of graves, one of which conceals a treasure in Confederate gold, we see a large stone circle laid out within the ruins of what may once have been walls or perhaps a low fence. This is not "earth art"—though as this 2006 image reveals, the site has endured for almost fifty years and is only slowly receding into the landscape that surrounds it (figure 24.4). Yet as a large-scale arrangement of natural materials outdoors, with a stark aura of minimalism presiding over its geometry and shape, Leone's "Sad Hill Cemetery" and Smithson's *Asphalt Ramp* are more alike than we might think. Leone's set was obviously not intended to last for the duration, but its primordial materiality—which is also crucial to the kind of landscape it wants to signify—has already let it long outlive its human maker. Like the stone mandala built by the dying scientist Powers in J. G. Ballard's 1960 short story "The Voices of Time"—read avidly by Smithson—here is a site where being-toward-death in all its Heideggerian seriousness must ground itself on terrain that has been cleared by a disreputable,

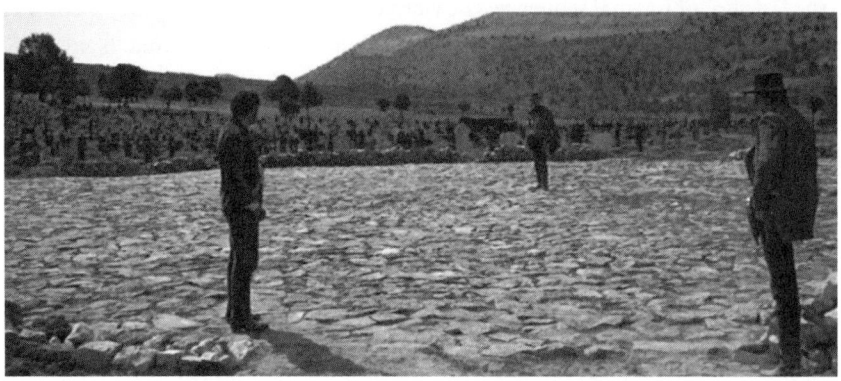

FIGURE 24.3 Still from *The Good, the Bad, and the Ugly* (1966).

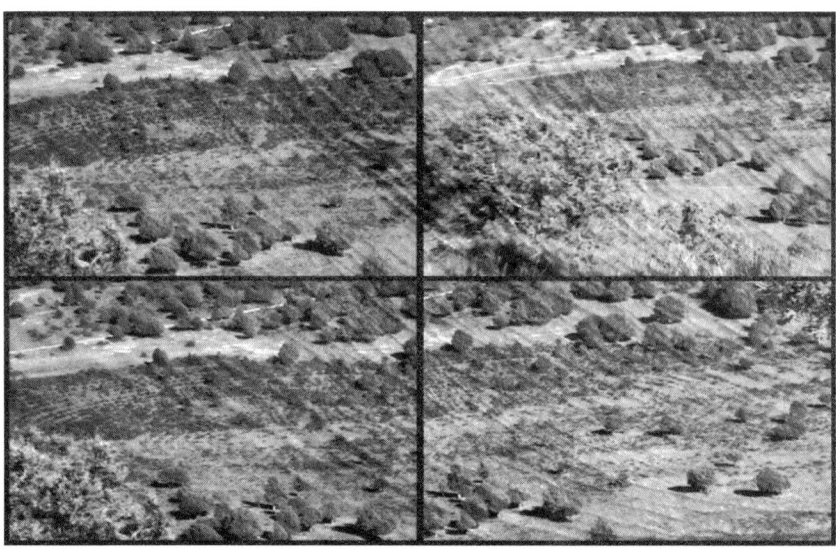

FIGURE 24.4 Google Earth photos of Sad Hill Cemetery location in Spain, circa 2006.

popular genre. "The image of the mandala," Ballard writes, "like a cosmic clock, remained fixed before his eyes, illuminating the broad surface of the stream. Watching it constantly, he felt his body gradually dissolving, its physical dimensions melting into the vast continuum of the current, which bore him out into the centre of the great channel, sweeping him onward, beyond hope but at last at rest, down the broadening reaches of eternity."[26]

Within Leone's film, the stone circle provides the ideal stage for men to reckon with their basest nature as its massive "ancestrality" suggests that is has been there for decades, if not centuries before the hastily dug and half-marked graves around it. Where better to conclude a contest between three essentially ahistorical forms of being-in-the-world (good, bad, or ugly) that are only momentarily inhabiting a Civil War terrain in which no viewer could possibly believe? In this sequence of the film, we get perhaps the purest expression of Leone's modernism not simply in the visual environment he has constructed but in the spectacle of human character it reveals. "The ontological view governing the image of man" in modernism, as Georg Lukács writes, "is by nature solitary, asocial, unable to enter into relationships with other human beings." According to Lukács, man "thus conceived is an ahistorical being," and the conditions of his existence are again captured best by Heidegger, which is of course the problem in the first place. The "hero" of a work of modernism is " 'thrown-into-the-world,' " as Lukács quotes. And then he adds, to clarify his antipathy: "meaningless, unfathomably. He does not develop through contact with the world; he neither forms nor is formed by it. The only 'development' . . . is the gradual revelation of the human condition. Man is now what he has always been and always will be. The narrator, the examining subject, is in motion; the examined reality is static."[27]

To imagine Lukács watching Leone is just short of absurd, but his account of a modernism that he loathes is almost impossibly precise in its description of the cinematic world that Leone would soon begin unfolding. Indeed, the final sequence from *The Good, the Bad, and the Ugly* has a strange affinity for the rawest materials of what makes us human in the barest sense—less as characters or individuals but as a species that uses tools, "extensions of man," to borrow from McLuhan. And though the use of guns will ultimately decide who and what wins out—we're in a western, after all—Leone seems just as fascinated by more primitive technologies, like the board that Tucco uses to start digging up the grave he thinks contains the gold or the rock on which Eastwood's Blondie writes the name of the grave where it is buried. These are the sorts of tools—or, I would say, technologies—that *Homo habilis* was using for 2.3 million years before Eli Wallach, and though writing is just an early Bronze Age baby by comparison, it is worth pointing out that Eastwood elects to use the most ancient medium at his disposal, one on which human beings have been leaving marks for over forty thousand years. Which is to say that Leone's version of the 1860s, for all its period trappings, has advanced perhaps the barest fraction of a second in deep time from Stanley Kubrick's slow-motion fantasy of the Pleistocene.

The fact that all these films about the origins of tools and men are made during a period of rapid technological advancement—one perhaps unequaled to this day—is a "historical irony" of the 1960s that, as Jameson observes, allowed intellectuals and artists of the period to conceptualize "a whole new step in the conquest of nature by human praxis" in a "kind of thought officially designated as 'antihumanist' and concerned to think what transcends or escapes human consciousness and intention."[28] Rock and bones and extraterrestrial obelisks become figures of the machines that human beings suddenly have made—from nuclear warheads to personal computers—that have left us so estranged from prior epochs of modernity that we can only understand them as objects alien to our very being and beyond our temporality as a species.

"Even the most advanced tools," writes Smithson in an essay about his earth projects, "are made of the raw materials of the earth. Today's highly refined technological tools are not much different in this respect than those of the caveman."[29] This sounds like exactly the sort of statement to which Leone would subscribe, which is to suggest that his earthworks on film, no less than Smithson's, register a larger turn at the end of the 1960s away from a particular logic of modernity—progressive, teleological, and technological—that was quickly losing momentum in the West. And with more time, it would be possible to spell out in more detail just how these sites are connected to countless others in the period where the politics of modernization are contested—and with weapons far more advanced than sticks and stones. "A first world 60s," Jameson asserts, "owed much to third-worldism in terms of politicocultural models." The terminology may sound a little dated, but it still reminds us that no critic of Leone or film historian observing the more violent turn that Hollywood takes in slow motion with the release of *Bonnie and Clyde* or *The Wild Bunch*, does not mention the war in Vietnam, for example; indeed, the Tet Offensive occurs just months after the debut of *Bonnie and Clyde* and mere weeks before the release *2001: A Space Odyssey*. The entire production histories of these films are contemporary with the long duration of America's involvement in Vietnam. Or we might look to another location where Leone's slowness seems to have resonated in a context more immediately political than I've been discussing here: *Once Upon a Time in the West* was not a global hit on the order of his previous three films, but it was a huge sensation in France, where, as Leone's biographer points out, "the students of May 1968 flocked to see [it], half a mile up the boulevard from the Sorbonne." If Jameson is right to argue that "the beginnings of what will come to be called the 60s" takes place in the "third world with the great movement of decolonization in British and French Africa," then perhaps some of these students—already set against the forces of the establishment by the firing of Henri Langlois at the Cinémathèque Français—saw in Leone's simulacrum of Civil War America another "battle of Algiers."[30] It might be hard to assess the global impact of the celebrated "Langlois Affair" outside the precincts of high culture and cinephilia where the cause of the French film archivist found its most ardent champions, but there is reason to believe, as Louis Menand writes, that it was still a "dress rehearsal" for the May '68 uprisings in France.[31] Farther afield, J. Hoberman describes a review of *Easy Rider* by the Asian-American playwright and radical Frank Chin that turns on the image of "indigenous Third World Revolutionaries like the Black Panthers and the (American) Red Guards" showing up, in Chin's own words, "'at the drive-in, whooping it up with Sergio Leone.'"[32] This might tell us less about the political unconscious of Leone's project and more about the masculinist chic that patterned certain elements of the counterculture. Still, it is appealing for those of us who love Leone's films despite their relentlessly embarrassing and occasionally archaic iconographies of sexual domination, bumbling postcolonial comedy, and shoddy racism to imagine that his vision of the modern world was resonant for some figures, or so I hope, who would have spotted the same faults.

Whether or not Leone's films earned their pride of place among the period's landmarks of the cultural left, these were associations that his work came to exploit. Though not included in prints distributed in the United States, his 1971 follow-up to *Once Upon a Time in the West*—known variously as *Duck, You Sucker!*, *A Fistful of Dynamite*, or *Once Upon a Time . . . the Revolution*—begins with a parade of text, in a patently "contemporary" sans serif font that looks like it was borrowed from the opening of Godard's *Week-End* (1967) and that eventually spells out Mao's famous slogan from his *Report on an Investigation of the Peasant Movement in Hunan*, which confirms, for those who might be wondering, that "the revolution is not a dinner party, a literary event, a drawing, or an embroidery. It cannot be done with elegance and courtesy. The revolution is an act of violence." Between Rod Steiger's formidable commitment to a bad Mexican accent and brownface and James Coburn's equally pronounced, though less noxious Irish blarney as a Republican bomb maker who gets caught up with the Zapatistas, the revolution here, whatever else it may or may not be, is overacted violently for sure. It is also in slow motion: An extended Mao quote might be a surprising start for *Duck, You Sucker!*, but slow motion is used exactly where we would expect it. The first time we flashback to memories of Coburn's character in Ireland, we drift to a green world of pastoral fantasy whose pleasures—a simple drive through the lush countryside with two friends, tweedy coats and sweaters instead of terminally stained cowboy hats and dusty tunics—are presented as a long slow-motion idyll that lasts over a minute until, in a bit of clever visual mechanics, Coburn puts his foot on the accelerator while his friend is driving and launches the car into regular speed as we watch it disappear down a manicured forest lane. Most of the slow motion in the film is used to punctuate explosions, letting us admire Coburn's prowess as a bomb maker mainly in the imagery of destruction played for laughs (when Coburn, in revenge for getting stopped by Steiger's band of guerillas, blows up the luxurious train car that they have stolen) or as solemn spectacles of revolutionary seriousness—though a couple of these action shots are undercut by janky model work that reminds us that Leone did not have Kubrick's effects budgets. The most dramatic moment of slow motion returns us to Ireland and completes the arc of trauma and betrayal that lands Coburn in Mexico. We see the same friend who was driving earlier brought into a pub by British soldiers to identify any Republican militants that might be found there; John Ford's *The Informer* (1935) casts its shadow over these proceedings, but the extended sequence in slow motion is decidedly contemporary. Leone has us spend almost two full minutes in slow motion as Coburn turns from the bar to see his friend, bruised and beaten by his interrogators, point out his former comrade to the soldiers; Coburn turns around and fires a hidden sawed-off shotgun, first at the two soldiers, who fall to the ground, blood splattered from the squibs inside their uniforms, and then, after a protracted exchange of eye contact in severe close-ups, at his fatally compromised friend, who looks like he gets shot in the stomach but whose death is marked by a garish, oozing streak of blood that trails down his forehead with almost comic gravity. The soundtrack for all this decelerated action is the bouncy Ennio Morricone theme that swings along throughout the film, perhaps in perverse tribute to the massive hit that Burt Bacharach and Hal David had with "Raindrops Keep Fallin' on My Head" in *Butch Cassidy and the Sundance Kid*, whose lighter moments seem the inspiration for much of the comic business in Leone's awkward Maoist epic. The slow motion in *Duck, You Sucker!* is only the second example from Leone's long career, and it demonstrates, if nothing else, the fast advances of the effect into the language of narrative cinema around 1968. Yet the slow motion in *Duck, You Sucker!* is not exactly revolutionary, either.

REVOLUTIONS AT A STANDSTILL

Leone went on to produce a few films later in the 1970s, but he only directed one more feature before his death in 1989. The oddly insistent Maoism of *Duck! You Sucker*—Coburn's character goes from mercenary to martyr as his sympathies for Steiger's peasant movement grow with every bomb that he sets off—would be hard to find in 1984's *Once Upon a Time in America*, his four-hour gangster epic, which is still effectively unfinished until Martin Scorsese can help Leone's children acquire the rights to the remaining footage necessary and restore the version Leone wanted to debut at Cannes. With even more pretensions to historical grandeur, here Leone tries again to pursue his trademark preoccupations—with greed and cynicism, desire and detachment, suffering and vengeance—squarely into the epoch of the twentieth century. There is only one slow-motion passage in *Once Upon a Time in America*, when the youngest member of the gang, led by David "Noodles" Aaronson (played as an adult by Robert De Niro) and Max Bercovicz (James Woods), is murdered by a rival. And while there is much that is remarkable about Leone's last film—from the sheer scope of its production and design to its difficult fixation on rape—its most elaborate temporal trick cannot be isolated to a single moment. The film unfolds across four timelines and follows its characters as immigrant children on the Lower East side of Manhattan in the early 1900s though their rise and fall as Jewish gangsters in the time of Prohibition and shortly after and then thirty-five years later, when Noodles returns to New York after decades hiding under a different name in Buffalo, having in 1933 turned his friends in to the police in hopes of saving their lives after Max convinces them to try a desperate bank robbery. In one especially "contemporary" image from the film's frame story, we see De Niro standing in front of a mural based on Robert Indiana's iconic *LOVE* design, which was first used as a MOMA Christmas card in 1964, then later cast as a sculpture in 1970 and ultimately adapted as a U.S. Postal Service stamp in 1973 (figure 24.5). We can see some signs of postmodernity in the Warhol soup can just visible over De Niro's shoulders. Maybe Max is right, and he was "chicken" Noodles all along? But despite these floating signifiers, we *know* that the "present" of *Once Upon a Time in America* is actually 1968 because Noodles and another old friend, Moe, go out of their way to confirm that it has been thirty-five years since he left the city. And so Leone, who begins his career with "sword-and-sandal" epics set in ancient Greece and Rome, then advances across centuries of history into the nineteenth before he ventures, in his last film, a story that wants to span the full sweep of the twentieth to the present. But even here, Leone remains impossibly historical—never finding the right vehicle to make something fully synchronous with the present, which means his time stays out of joint until it ends, somehow reflecting on the cataclysms of the 1960s long after they had ended or, elsewhere, centuries before they start.

History, for Leone, might as well begin in pre-Christian antiquity or ancient Rome or even the Old West. But it ends in 1968. Richard Godden has brilliantly

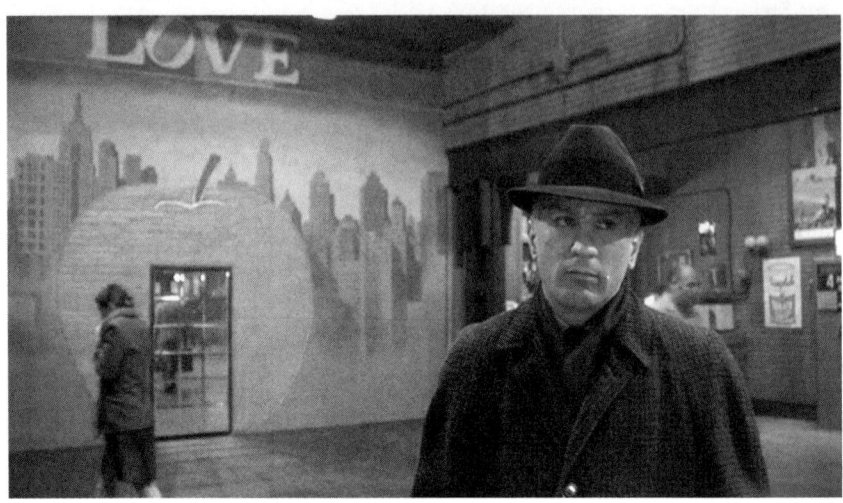

FIGURE 24.5 It's always 1968 in Leone's *Once Upon a Time in America* (1984).

argued that Leone's last gangster movie is an allegory of Fordism in crisis, which is why its dating is so peculiarly fixated on isolated segments of time even as its style speaks to capital's increasing need for "flexibility" after the global economic shocks of the early 1970s.[33] Somewhere in all the convoluted timelines of *Once Upon a Time in America* this must be true, though like the remains of Jimmy Hoffa—whose disappearance provides the model both for Noodle's haunting return after years of playing dead, as well as for Max's later evolution into a corrupt Teamsters boss—conclusive evidence is very hard to find. In the virtually prehistoric postmodernity of Leone's 1968, De Niro's old-age makeup is about as convincing as Wallach's or Steiger's accents, and though no one can say that Leone was just going through the motions in his belated gangster epic— which he was contemplating long before *The Godfather* (1972) modernized the genre—the film is still a conceptual pastiche, daringly anachronistic and disconnected from the real world. It wouldn't surprise me if the mirrored doorway behind De Niro's shoulder opened onto a Spanish desert where Italian actors meant to evoke Mexicans are having their fates decided by American actors speaking dubbed-in English. The vision is admittedly absurd, but so is much of what makes Leone's films so powerful, provided that we take them very seriously while also laughing at their excesses.

Yet this is exactly the sort of fast synchronization of work and world that is incredibly hard to sustain within the arid landscapes of Leone at his slowest. It is tempting to redeem the cynicism of even his best films—with their bleak embrace of violence and reflexive misogyny—for all the ways that they reserve their deepest scorn for any ideology of progress or development and especially for the modernity that awaits the twentieth century on the other side of the western. There is little in Leone's background or biography to suggest that he was as committed to the politics that some projected on his films in the late sixties, unlike the students rioting outside the Sorbonne or the apocryphal Black Panthers that, according to Frank Chin, embraced his films with such abandon. But I also don't want to suggest that there is nothing radical about Leone except his style. The unendurable wastes of time that his films exploit and mobilize are resonant as indexes or, in a vocabulary more appropriate to these landscapes, monuments of a moment when, like now, there was good reason to wonder how much longer the West might go on winning or if it really ever had. "The coming crisis of the US regime was signaled between 1968 and 1973," writes Giovanni Arrighi, "in three distinct and closely related spheres." The films of Sergio Leone are definitely not one of them, but it is worth pointing out that these overheated studies of capitalist accumulation, suffering, and decline are all but unimaginable in isolation from the familiar domains of crisis in the period that Arrighi describes so soberly as "serious troubles in Vietnam," the realization that it was "impossible to preserve the mode of production and regulation of world money established at Bretton Woods," and the retreat of "the US government's anti-communist crusade" as it began "losing legitimacy at home and abroad."[34] We see images and intimations of this historical terrain throughout Leone's westerns of the period, and though his ornately nihilistic skepticism is very much applied to the idea of "revolution" too in *Duck! You Sucker*—which is, despite its opening barrage of Mao not exactly certain that the future belongs to Marxism—there are still moments when Leone gives his viewers, if they can wait long enough, scenes of another world to come. But he is never in a hurry to get us there.

 We can see Leone's abiding commitment to a pace of his own in particularly majestic fashion near the end of *Once Upon a Time in the West*, where Leone employs slow motion for the first time in his career. As I have said before, there are terrifically slow sequences throughout Leone's earlier westerns—and none perhaps more famous than the strikingly unendurable opening credits of *Once Upon a Time in the West* and its more than ten full minutes of creaking windmills, buzzing flies, and dripping beads of sweat. But only in the stylized temporality of slow motion are we thrown back into recesses of time—both cinematic and geologic—from which any present seems too fleeting to matter. I doubt that many will recognize the looming shape in this still from the film's climactic showdown as Henry Fonda's ruthless killer "Frank" from *Once Upon a Time in the West* (figure 24.6). But this is what he looks like after we have waited for most of this film's three hours of plot and witnessed its staggering body count to

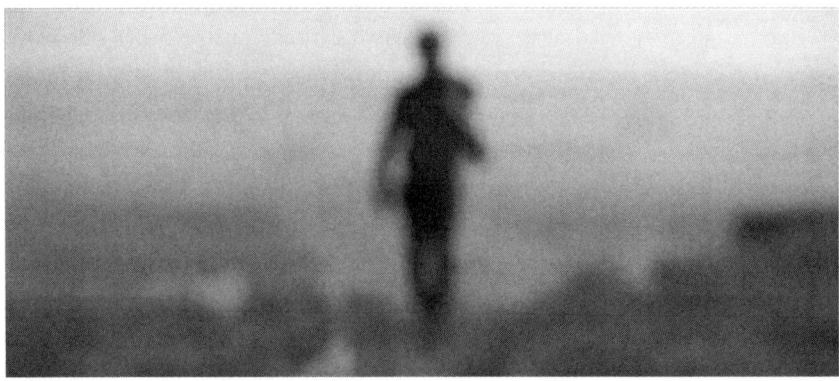

FIGURE 24.6 Henry Fonda as modernist sculpture in *Once Upon a Time in the West* (1968).

understand at last the logic behind the extravagance of style and violence we have been watching. At first, there is just this slow-motion glimpse of a strange figure, shaped like a Giacometti sculpture, striding toward us from a distance that is entirely abstracted in the blur but also utterly familiar for its western palette and horizons. About an hour later, as Fonda's Frank again comes toward us, the film completes its slow-motion flashback to at last explain the revenge plot that, along with the coming of the railroad, has driven what minimum of narrative the film has been advancing since Bronson's "Harmonica" first appeared. We learn that Frank killed Harmonica's brother, a crime whose brutality is intensified by its elaborate contrivance to technically make the young Harmonica into the tool of his brother's death—the duration of his ability to stand beneath his brother's weight is made equivalent to the duration of his brother's remaining life (figure 24.7). Frank doesn't kill Harmonica's brother by his own hand; he makes Harmonica his stand-in and turns his young underdeveloped body, up against its physical limits, into a technology for committing murder, kludgy but effective.

The use of slow motion feels entirely conventional here even though this would have been among the first times it had been featured in a narrative film in wide release throughout Europe and the English-speaking world. It is cinematic technique applied mechanically as the sign for narrative analepsis, and we would know immediately how to read it even if we were seeing it for the first time. Slow motion here is an aesthetic of ancestrality, weirdly prehistoric in the way it makes the avant-garde seem like something that has always existed in the substrata of memory and consciousness since the dawn of man. And where better for it to emerge on screen than beneath this crude, stone arch that looks to have

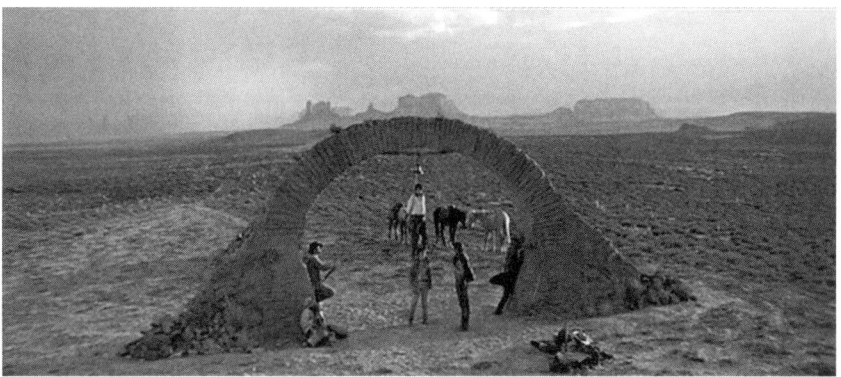

FIGURE 24.7   Still from *Once Upon a Time in the West* (1968).

been built by makers who have vanished long ago and taken with them any sign of why they may have placed it on the most hallowed, cinematic grounds of the southwestern United States. We know why, especially if we know the archaeology of the genre that Leone is bringing back to life and to an end: This is a makeshift proscenium to frame the geological formations of Monument Valley in the background and so to stage the film's inheritance from John Ford, which it is so determined to do that it uses these locations even though they look nothing like—in light, in soil, in scale—the terrain that elsewhere functions in the film as the West at its most terminally "American." All the other locations that Leone used were in Spain, but of course he did not venture to San Juan County, Utah, out of a commitment to verisimilitude or continuity. Here, and only in slow motion, can Leone recreate the signs and symbols of a genre that has almost passed—along with the stylistic codes and corporate structures that sustained the ecology of classical Hollywood cinema in the middle decades of the century.

Like Sad Hill Cemetery, though, something of this artifact too has survived, ruins that can remind us of the technologies—both cinematic and far older forms of making—that here converged in time and space (figure 24.8). After Frank is dead and Harmonica rides away, there is the briefest image of a better future in an improbable assembly of Chinese and Black laborers gathering around the figure of Claudia Cardinale, the surviving widow of the first man we saw Frank kill when this epic of exploitation started. She has faced her own share of brutalities along the way, and they are rendered as depressingly lurid as we might expect from Leone at his worst. But she also finally endures to claim the land that Frank was going to steal for himself and own in grotesque

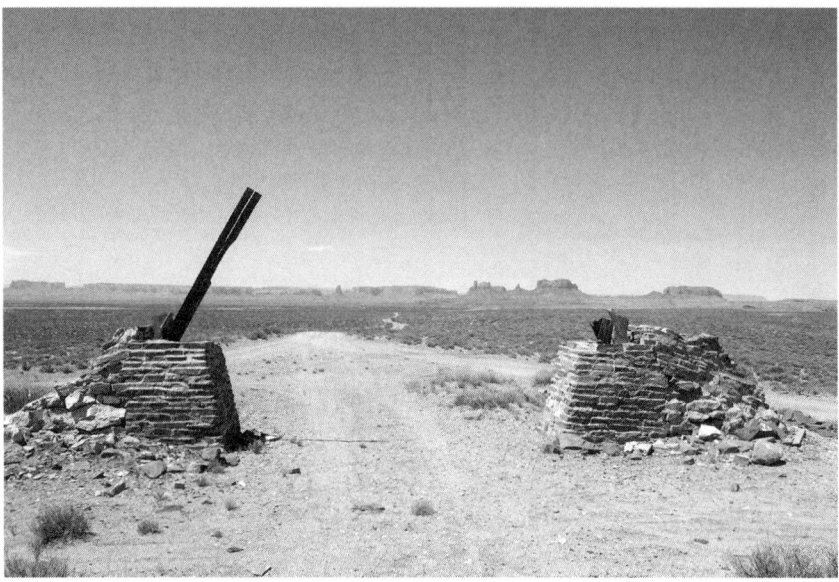

FIGURE 24.8 A Leone nonsite in Monument Valley, 2013.

perpetuity. It may have taken a whole lifetime, but Harmonica comes along and stops to gaze at what looks, from a certain distance at least, a lot like a peasant revolt that has traveled to some fantastic version of "America" in Spain or Italy from hallowed ground in Monument Valley. We're not sure where this place is or where it is supposed to be. Yet it also feels possessed, for spans of centuries we can't quite specify, with what Jussi Parikka, writing about the "damaged environments" of technological culture, calls "an odd sense of synchronized materiality [and] multiple temporalities."[35] Or, call it a Leone nonsite—where once upon a time, the West slowed down.

25
The Wild Bunch, or the Pains of Being Sam Peckinpah

Once Upon a Time in the West was not released in the United States until May 28, 1969, almost six months after its debut in Rome and just three weeks before Sam Peckinpah's *The Wild Bunch* (1969) had its New York premiere. Both films had started shooting in April 1968, and their long production histories overlapped with those of *Bonnie and Clyde* and *2001*, as well as with several other U.S. studio films from the same period that, while not nearly so iconic and controversial as Peckinpah's conflicted masterpiece, show that slow motion was rapidly emerging as a routine convention for mainstream Hollywood cinema, a standard feature of its latest style. Not everyone who saw *Bonnie and Clyde* went on to see Leone's latest or Peckinpah's half-besotted epic. There were maybe some viewers at the time—more than a few, given the popularity of at least some of the films at issue here—who perhaps remembered the brief uses of slow motion in Kurosawa's celebrated *The Seven Samurai* or recalled the Hollywood history of slow motion in earlier studio films such as *What Price Hollywood?*, *Love Me Tonight*, *Carefree*, or *Easter Parade*. *The World of Henry Orient* seems to have left an impression only on Stanley Cavell, but figures like Epstein, Cocteau, and Vigo were established presences in the modernist canon as it was discovered and asserted after World War II. It is trickier to speculate about the influence in the United States of Soviet directors such as Vertov, Pudovkin, or Dovzhenko, who had much smaller followings in the United States, but they were known among critics, film scholars and students, and many filmmakers, too. More slow motion, in short, could not have come as a surprise to audiences as the sixties ended, though I still can't imagine anybody being ready to see Debbie Reynolds run across a beach in eroticized soft-focus deceleration in *How Sweet It Is* in August 1968. Ali

McGraw made for a far more plausible sex symbol and fetish object of the camera's protracted gaze in the film version of *Goodbye, Columbus*, which was released in April 1969, just weeks before *The Wild Bunch* and *Once Upon a Time in the West*. *How Sweet It Is* and *Goodbye, Columbus* were comedies based on the broadest period clichés of sexual liberation, and these ideas also loom over *The Swimmer*, which starred Burt Lancaster in a fever dream of existential dread as he must contemplate, in an anxious middle-age of waning masculine desirability, his future as an obsolete survivor of a vanished world. Unlike William Holden's Pike in *The Wild Bunch*, Lancaster's character can't try to fight his way out either, no matter how good he looks in a luxurious slow-motion interlude of athletic prowess that he enjoys about halfway through his suburban odyssey from pool to pool in his tony Connecticut surroundings. *The Swimmer* is now recognized as a crucial work of minor genius from the late sixties, which is more than anyone would say about *How Sweet It Is* or *Goodbye, Columbus*. Though, for what it's worth, *Goodbye, Columbus* handily outearned both *The Wild Bunch* and *Once Upon a Time in the West* at the domestic box office in 1969. It did not, however, come close to the commercial success of *Easy Rider*, which had its debut just one month after *The Wild Bunch* opened. By the time Dennis Hopper's "Billy" is shot off his motorcycle and murdered by a menacingly goofy redneck in the film's last scene, there is no reason to expect to see slow motion, but there it is. *Easy Rider* didn't need a few seconds of entirely incidental slow motion to achieve its status as one of the era's absolutely defining films alongside *Bonnie and Clyde* and *2001*. Yet the stupid abundance of slow motion in *The Wild Bunch*, as we will see, does help bring Peckinpah's career back from the dead in 1969—though this is the least of what the film accomplishes for good or bad or ugly.

Before the shooting starts, though, consider the opening credit sequence of *Junior Bonner* (1972), Peckinpah's wistful romance of an aging rodeo rider, played by Steve McQueen, and the strained family relations that play out between his even older rodeo rider father, Ace Bonner, played by Robert Preston, with Ida Lupino and Joe Don Baker starring respectively as Junior's mother and brother. Like *The Ballad of Cable Hogue* (1970), *Junior Bonner* is a gentler variation on the familiar themes that drive his major films: violence and its pleasures, justified or otherwise; morality and masculinity on the ragged edges of society; technological modernity and its many failings, from the brutal efficiency of the machines it makes to kill, to the bloodless savagery that graces its economy. There is plenty of this on display in *Junior Bonner*, where the brothers come to blows over Curly's plans to turn the Bonner family homestead into a trailer park for suburbanites from the Midwest who are coming to Prescott,

Arizona, not because it is the rodeo capital of the American southwest but because of cheap land and low taxes in "clean air country." Though Curly is not exactly the heavy in *Junior Bonner*, Joe Don Baker's ample menace as an actor makes him pretty threatening as a real estate developer; nor does McQueen's Junior have much to fight for since both his parents are more or less on Curly's side, and all he earns for staying on an unrideable bull named Sunshine for a full eight seconds is enough prize money to buy his father a ticket to Australia, which he has managed to convince himself is still a version of a wild frontier in 1970. Junior beats the clock, but nothing else.

The first thing we see as *Junior Bonner* starts is Steve McQueen in a tight close-up, framed by two men in western shirts who are largely cropped out of the frame, which isn't even big enough to show the top of Bonner's cowboy hat. We hear some voices speaking, but not what they are saying; the sound of some metallic clangs and rumbling crowd noises help establish that we're at a rodeo. But the film's setting does not become entirely apparent until a quick flurry of montage gives us glimpses of the gate being opened to release the bull; then the bull's deep brown eye in a close-up so tight that it borders on abstraction; another flash of Bonner; and then another close-up of a stopwatch, half-buried in a thick palm with dirty fingers, the hand of the timer poised at zero and just beginning to sweep into action, though this is all but imperceptible since the shot lasts for less than a full second. There are six shots in the first nine seconds of the film, and the fleeting image of a stopwatch that would basically be useless if we were timing what we're watching makes for a clever inside joke, perhaps more subtle than we might expect from Peckinpah. But it goes by much too fast to land. Then we cut to a wider shot that lets us see Bonner getting launched into the ring. The crowd noises and cowbells that we've heard from the beginning are still there on the soundtrack, but as the film shifts into slow motion for almost the next seventeen seconds their naturalism feels strangely disconnected from the action as the camera tracks the giant bull as he jumps and spins from right to left trying to throw the stuntman—McQueen was known as something of a daredevil, but not to the degree that anyone would let him try to stay on Sunshine for the eight seconds that a successful ride demands. As we watch McQueen walk toward us in the next shot—now back to normal speed but proceeding at a deliberate pace that is definitely not triumphant—the credits start rolling faster, the title song starts playing, and the frame breaks into a split-screen geometry that many McQueen fans would have recognized from 1968's *The Thomas Crown Affair*, the heist film directed by Norman Jewison that introduced Christopher Chapman's "multi-dynamic image technique" to audiences in Hollywood. This might not be Peckinpah at his majestic best—a borderline fascist, as Kael accuses, but also "so passionate and sensual a film artist that you may experience his romantic perversity kinesthetically"—but it is amazingly coherent in conveying the full message of its medium, and vice versa. This is not quite the "Old West" so much as a diminished and contained performance of its exploits and their values.

So far, there is nothing in this account of *Junior Bonner* that diverges much from how we've heard critics talk about Peckinpah and—which is also to say *in*—slow motion since the 1970s and decades after. I won't try to match devout admirers like Paul Seydor or Stephen Prince in their shot-by-shot anatomies of his first and most spectacular deployments of slow motion in *The Wild Bunch*. Dukore tracks the variable frame rates that Peckinpah uses, from the normal 24 to 30, 60, 90, and 120 per second, across the 209 shots of the Bunch's first bank robbery and the "four dramatic movements" in their doomed assault on Mapache's compound. He discerns a structure that is "almost classically symmetrical" in the way the sequence starts out relatively slow, with shots that average 1.1 seconds, then picks up speed in sections where shots accelerate to .74 and .83 seconds respectively, and then return to 1.09 seconds per shot as this "orgy of bloodletting" comes to an end and stands revealed, in this frenzy of overdetermined formalism, as "sustained, carefully crafted, and masterfully modulated."[1] We know from Cameron Detig's recent and even more technically precise work on slow motion and Bordwell's notion of "intensified continuity" that 1.9 minutes, or 1.3 percent, of *The Wild Bunch* is actually in slow motion, which is more than that of *Bonnie and Clyde* (.7 minutes, or .6 percent) and *2001* (.9 minutes, or .6 percent) combined.[2] This plainly demonstrates the scale of Peckinpah's reliance on slow motion and helps us quantify our sense that it can simply happen anywhere in his major films without it seeming like any sort of singular event, in either tragedy or exaltation, that marks its monumental first appearances in Penn, Kubrick, or Leone.

But I don't think we need to run the numbers on later films like *Junior Bonner*, *The Getaway* (1972), or *Pat Garrett and Billy the Kid* to understand that Peckinpah, for all the perversity of his fixations and often excruciating limits of his ideology, should probably be remembered as the most important figure in the history of cinema for rendering slow motion utterly conventional, so inescapable that even its most graphic and disturbing contrivances of time come to look entirely routine or worse. Peckinpah's familiar style of artful damage was recognizable enough for *Monty Python's Flying Circus* to present their version of "Sam Peckinpah's *Salad Days*" in November 1972. The skit reimagined a popular West End musical of the 1950s as an accidental slapstick bloodbath of impalings and amputations, a garden party of men in striped jackets and straw boaters and women in summer gowns all soaked gloriously fake-red. Introduced by Eric Idle's presenter as one of his favorite directors for his "utterly truthful and very sexually arousing portrayal of violence," the real punch line lands after the absurdity of genteel carnage, when Idle's character is then slaughtered in a slow-motion hail of bullets, squibs firing as he writhes in desperate agony before the show's jaunty exit music and credits roll over a freeze frame of his face in full comic rictus.[3] Near the height of his fame—and particularly appealing as a target for British satire after *Straw Dogs* pictured rural Cornwall as a hellish world of atavistic male brutality—*Monty Python* makes quick work of Peckinpah, reproducing both the rhythmic shifts from fast to slow that he and his editor Louis Lombardo perfected for *The Wild Bunch* and the frequent cuts to close-up reaction shots that show the viewer the emotional responses they were almost certainly too overwhelmed to have in anything like real time. Peckinpah seems to have loved the skit, if only for the attention.

The influence of Peckinpah's abundant and gratuitous slow motion remains a visible fact of action cinema in the twenty-first century, with many of the exemplary directors in the genre—from celebrated auteurs like James Cameron and John Woo to more contested figures such as Zach Snyder, Michael Bay, or Gareth Evans—revisiting the violent choreographies of *The Wild Bunch* at more or less explicit degrees of homage. It seems likely and correct that Peckinpah will loom less large in film histories going forward than he did for critics who vividly remembered or lived through the controversies that he courted and taboos he broke; nor should we want to see the personal mythologies that surrounded his career and that his biographers often reproduce continue to perpetuate and justify the fantastic image of his self-destructive, misogynistic genius. As Sean Cubitt writes, in a superb account of *The Wild Bunch* whose implications I will be tracking to some very different ends, "Creative freedom is, in Peckinpah, the mythic freedom of the Old West, and both are dying." "The new domestic pleasures of suburbia," or so Cubitt proposes, are perceived to have "emasculated television" or at least kept a series like Peckinpah's *The Rifleman* within the limits of network censorship.[4] Cubitt poetically describes Peckinpah's films, with a nod to Adorno, as "barbaric elegies" or "songs for a vanishing world." That said, the inevitable modernity that looms over his aging cowboys and melancholy gunfighters in films like *The Wild Bunch* or *Pat Garrett and Billy the Kid* is rarely made as tangible as the signs of historical change that Cubitt, drawn into the sadly irresistible biography of Peckinpah—as I am too, of course—pictures as an accelerated montage showing how, "in a single lifetime, the open ranges will become tract housing, and the epic and epochal scales of cinema will be replaced by the corrupt and dishonorable codes of television." Again, Peckinpah and his westerns die, but his "aesthetic moment," which is above all else an aesthetic *of* the moment, will live on forever, "always temporary" and "defined by its brevity," to borrow again from Cubitt, while it endures for decades, from one century and on into the next, with no sign of going anywhere despite the fact that for it to work on us at all we must already know that it is gone. In Peckinpah, slow motion "fills the scene with itself to such an extent that its pure presence overtakes any meaning it might have." Slow motion might not come as cheap in Peckinpah as "tract housing" or be quite such a monstrosity of scale and uniformity. But what finally might matter most about slow motion in his films is that there is so much of it.

Still bruised and bandaged from his attempted ride on Sunshine that is cut up and distended across *Junior Bonner*'s opening credits, McQueen arrives back at what he thinks is still his father's home, only to discover that while the intense agonies of bull riding may be painful, at least they're over quickly, unlike the slow brutality of real estate development. It is not just that he finds his father's house has been abandoned and left to ruin, covered in torn rodeo posters, deep drifts of dust, and mementos that locate its period style in the 1930s; Junior Bonner, whose name is never more ironic than it is at this moment, which confirms an utter break between the generations, has arrived decades too late to catch his father but just in time to see his family's former house demolished. As Bonner drives past a field of heavy machinery that looks more like it is needed for a mining operation than a mobile home park, he does not encounter anyone who can direct him to his father and can only wander briefly through an artificial wasteland—"Here is no water but only rock," we might say—of outsized piles of gravel, giant furnaces and tractors, and a particularly menacing construction worker who stares Bonner down and forces his retreat while two bulldozers plow through and over his father's house, first crushing the mailbox with Ace's name on it in subtle but perceptible slow motion and then proceeding to raze the remainder of house in a montage sequence that, by 1972, would have been exceedingly familiar to audiences who knew how Peckinpah liked to show things get damaged and destroyed (figure 25.1). From start to finish, the destruction lasts for roughly ninety seconds; there are fifty-seven shots within the sequence, which begins with the crushed mailbox and returns to this same image as a flashback to the most recent past we can imagine. There are fifteen or so sections of slow motion, most of which are tightly focused on the very one-sided but no less violent action involving massively powerful modern machines and brittle structures redolent of a fading epoch—maybe not the Old West, but older than anything that will survive the onslaught. It is hard to be exact because some of the shots that Peckinpah and his editors Frank Santillo and Robert

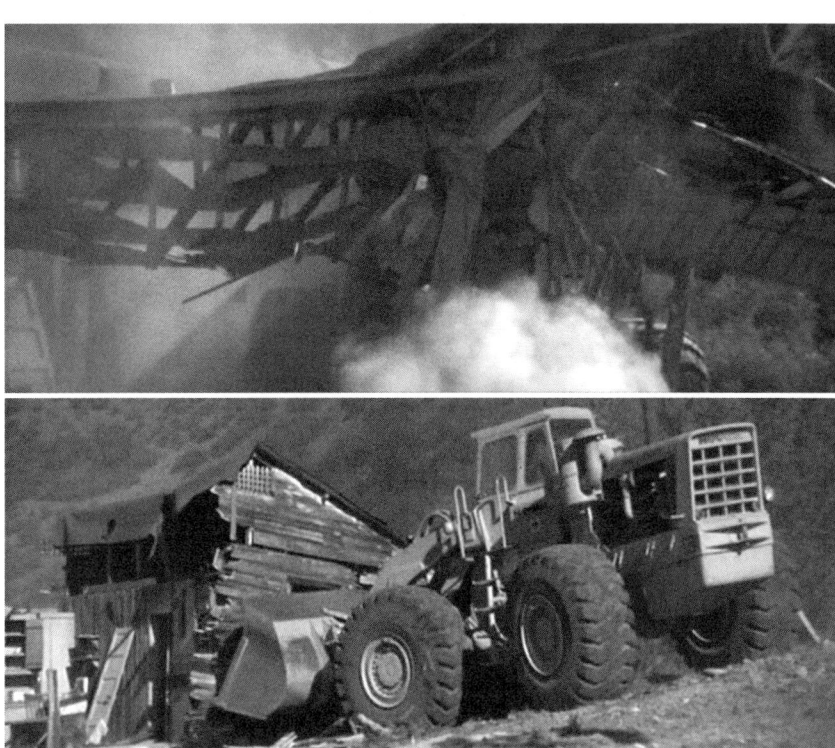

FIGURE 25.1 Stills from *Junior Bonner* (1972).

Wolfe insert last less than a second, establishing the shifts and jumps in time and temporality that Dukore, writing of *The Wild Bunch*, describes as "kaleidoscopic effects": The "intercutting of normal with slow and slower speeds gives the battle" what he calls "balletic" beauty.[5] I doubt that this sequence of artful wreckage in *Junior Bonner* informs the slow-motion spectacles of architectural destruction in, for example, *The Matrix*, when Neo and Trinity storm the office building where Morpheus is held prisoner, or in the earlier *Koyaanisqatsi* (1982), which features slow-motion footage of the televised implosions at the Pruitt Igoe housing project in St. Louis that took place in May 1972, only a month before *Junior Bonner* had its premiere. Christopher Jencks, with deliberate and ostentatious portent, pointed to this moment as signaling "the death of modernism" in twentieth-century architecture.[6]

The stakes are nowhere near as high in *Junior Bonner* and its extended scene of demolition. Peckinpah's stylistics might seem routine—though I haven't found an earlier instance of such a mechanized assault on sheer materiality, at least in Hollywood. But they let us see, I think, that even when he's not at his awful best, Peckinpah has an affinity for not just violence but also for what Pamela Lee terms "obliteration" as a motif in art of the late sixties.[7] In *Junior Bonner*, we witness a blunt-force allegory of development and modernization. Progress looks like giant machines that plow under the past with inhuman power and cruelty. A trailer park will grow out of the rubble, leaving men like the Bonners, who aren't really cowboys anyway but just athletes or entertainers, modern variations on hired guns, with nowhere else to go.

MODERNITY AS MIDLIFE CRISIS

No Hollywood director tried as hard in slow motion as Peckinpah. His concerted and ultimately aborted efforts to use slow motion for parts of the battle sequences in *Major Dundee* (1965) helped contribute to its bloated budget and extended the wearying running time of its rough cut, which led to Columbia's disastrous attempts to edit down the film without him. In the version that debuted and failed in 1965—earning barely half of its production costs at the domestic box office while also baffling or frustrating the same critics who had admired Peckinpah's far more controlled breakthrough, *Ride the High Country* (1962)—there is no slow motion left, along with precious little logic in either plot or characterization, and a mix of tones and politics that are as confusing as Richard Harris's accent as a Confederate prisoner of war in Texas who is enlisted, along with a group of racist Southern soldiers, settlers, Union misfits, and Blacks, under the command of Charlton Heston's prison warden turned Apache hunter, to find and kill a dangerous Indian named Charriba, whose forces have been ravaging farms and ranches on the U.S. border with Mexico while the Civil War is raging elsewhere to the east. It is, in short, a lot. Whatever lost slow motion Peckinpah expensively produced—several fights and, according to David Weddle's biography, an entire version of the last battle with the French—was a problem from the beginning. "On *Dundee* he just shot [slow motion] wild, there was no concept at all of how it would be used," remembers Howard Kunin, one of three editors at Columbia who was tasked with assembling a narrative feature from the four hundred thousand feet of 35mm film, or roughly seventy-four hours of material, that Peckinpah brought back from locations across Mexico.[8]

I do not want to rehearse too much of the Hollywood mythology around Sam Peckinpah's career, a story that is punctuated by the tremendous bungling of *Major Dundee*, which then, in a turn that feels like it was manufactured by a screenwriting algorithm, is redeemed by the controversial triumphs of *The Wild Bunch* four years later, where Peckinpah gets everything right—an immanent critique of the Old West, an ultraviolent moralized aesthetic, a dizzying abundance of slow motion—that he mismanaged in 1965. *Major Dundee* is the precocious mess providing proof of concept for the stylistic architecture of his later epics, however fraught in theme and tone or halfway botched by Peckinpah's decline into addiction by the early 1970s. It is perhaps better that we can't see the slow motion that he wanted here so that when we see it for the first time in *The Wild Bunch* it strikes us with the same force and show of ostentatious mastery that would have distinguished it in 1969 from the equally legendary sequences we have already seen in *Bonnie and Clyde*, *2001: A Space Odyssey*, and *Once Upon a Time in the West*. Just over ten minutes into the film, one of Pike's crew fires at Thornton's bounty hunters and causes one to tumble off a roof. The grace of his slow-motion fall is stunt work that casually demonstrates how easily and quickly death will come in the nearly two and one-half hours of existential self-reflection and triumphant gunplay that is to follow. This moment also marks the frenzied speed that drives the editing of Peckinpah's slow motion. There are sixteen shots in the nine seconds from the moment when we see this figure take a bullet to when he hits the ground; only the three shots that trace his fall are in slow motion, with the others offering a disorienting but efficient map of the action as members of the Bunch and Thornton's bounty hunters indiscriminately open fire on one another and on bystanders alike. The alternation of regular speed and extreme slow motion will become far more pronounced in the barrage of sheer technique that Peckinpah reserves for the doomed assault on Mapache's compound.

But even this first eruption of slow motion in *The Wild Bunch* tells us a lot. As Cubitt puts it, with *The Wild Bunch* "we are in the field of beauty and ugliness, not of sublimity and the vile."[9] This first fall has something of the charm—though vertical and therefore brutal—of the floating march of the funeral procession across the screen in *Entr'acte*, which is itself enlisted for the giddy revolution of the slow-motion pillow fight in *Zero for Conduct*. These are accidental associations with films that Peckinpah likely didn't know. His points of reference were instead *The Seven Samurai*, whose two scenes of death depicted in (and as) a mix of speed were the inspiration for the abandoned slow-motion sequences in *Major Dundee*. Peckinpah became a devoted fan of Kurosawa after seeing *Rashomon* in Los Angeles when it was released in the United States by RKO. He later tells an interviewer that he would "like to be able to make a Western like Kurosawa makes Westerns," a curiously double-sided formulation of respect and cultural appropriation.[10] Peckinpah had also seen *The Left Handed Gun* when it debuted and tried to bring both its darker psychology and explicit violence to his own prolific career as a writer and director of TV westerns in the late 1950s and early 1960s. Penn's influence was a more anxious matter later, and Peckinpah sometimes protested that he had not seen *Bonnie and Clyde* before he started working on *The Wild Bunch*. But we also know that Peckinpah had a print of *Bonnie and Clyde*—a Warner Bros. film like *The Wild Bunch*—delivered to the town in Mexico where he spent more than six months on location in early 1968. Though just the start of the slow-motion love affair that would eventually help define his style, he had "already answered the bell," Jeff Menne writes, by reproducing the "balletic deaths of Bonnie and Clyde on expanded scales."[11] Mixing metaphors of sex and violence feels appropriate here. Yet even when we catch Peckinpah red-handed, so to speak, in his determination to outdo the splatter and splendor of Penn's finale from *Bonnie and Clyde*, a complete provenance of the slow motion in *The Wild Bunch* is tricky. The film's editor, Lou Lombardo, came to the production for his first job on a studio feature from the TV series *Felony Squad*, where he had created a slow-motion sequence for a 1967 episode entitled "My Mommy Got Lost"—which also starred *Junior Bonner*'s Joe Don Baker as the heavy—employing step printing to give the effect of decelerated action even though the show was shot on cameras that could not achieve the rapid frame rates that action auteurs like Kurosawa had at their disposal.[12] When Baker's kidnapper, described as a "deranged wannabe country singer," is shot by the police, his death in what certainly resembles slow motion—though manufactured as an editing effect and not an artifact of high-speed photography—may well be the first show of fictional violence on TV that tried to emulate the graphic iconography of suffering that Penn bestowed upon his infinitely more glamorous outlaws. "My Mommy Got Lost" was broadcast on November 27, 1967, which means that it was written and produced in the very weeks that spanned *Bonnie and Clyde*'s initial run in U.S. theaters.

For *The Wild Bunch*, Peckinpah reunited with the veteran cinematographer Lucien Ballard, who had shot Peckinpah's *Ride the High Country*, his first and, as of 1969, only viable commercial feature film. Ballard was a true professional of the studio system at its most classical. He may have gone uncredited for his camera work on Josef von Sternberg's *Morocco* (1930), but by the early sixties, he had assembled a bewildering résumé that ranged from Kubrick's early breakthrough in *The Killing* (1956) to botched prestige pictures like von Sternberg's adaptation of *Crime and Punishment* (1935), starring Peter Lorre as Raskolnikov, as well as dozens of B movies and shorts with salacious titles like *Racketeers in Exile* (1937), *Venus Makes Trouble* (1937), *South of the Boudoir* (1940), and *The Unholy Wife*

(1957). He first met Peckinpah in 1960 when he was hired to film three episodes of Peckinpah's *The Westerner*, the series he created as a grittier and less romantic variation on the cowboy shows that still dominated network television. Ballard eventually worked on five of Peckinpah's films, including *The Ballad of Cable Hogue*, *Junior Bonner*, and *The Getaway*. Ballard was responsible for all the slow motion, except for the abandoned footage from *Major Dundee*, that is perhaps the most recognizable signature of Peckinpah's major phase, with only *Straw Dogs* shot instead on location by the Dutch-British cinematographer John Coquillon as part of the film's largely British crew.

Ballard received an Academy Award nomination for 1963's *The Caregivers* but is not widely considered a major figure and nowhere ranked among the Hollywood legends (Haskell Wexler, Conrad Hall, Gordon Willis) whose stylistic innovations helped visually define the New American cinema. There is definitely nothing remarkable about 1968's *How Sweet It Is!*, a very formulaic family comedy with James Garner and Debbie Reynolds as a settled and suburban married couple whose relationship is mildly strained—and then thoroughly resolidified—over the course of a European trip spent following their son, a hippie manqué with Monkees bangs and a peace medallion, and his high-school classmates as they mainly gawk and giggle. Fully committed to both its generational anxieties and dreary situation comedy—the script earned Garry Marshall his first screenwriting credit and is, as he probably thought the kids said, almost impossibly "square"—*How Sweet It Is!* is bad and often looks it. Though much is made of its French settings, there was no shooting on location. Aside from a couple shots of Central Park that establish Garner and Reynolds as living happily enough outside the city in Connecticut, *How Sweet It Is!* was filmed with precious little flair on the West Hollywood soundstages of the Samuel Goldwyn Studios and around Los Angeles, right down to an unconvincing version of the Louvre, where Garner, playing a magazine photographer, has all the girls on his son's trip pose before the Mona Lisa.

But there is, in this profoundly forgettable film that Ballard finishes just before he starts to film *The Wild Bunch*, which is by far his most important credit, a sequence where we see slow motion used to modernize the image of Debbie Reynolds, who was by then a fading star whose body was itself a strange anachronism in the moment. Unlike William Holden's prematurely hollowed-out physique—which Peckinpah, as we will see, treats like a ruin from some bygone age of Hollywood and the Old West—Debbie Reynolds was not yet thirty-six when Ballard shoots her running on a beach meant to be the Riviera in lascivious slow motion, coded as somewhat suspect not simply because Reynolds was not quite anybody's idea of a sex symbol by 1968 but also by the aura of infidelity that surrounds this turn within the movie's plot. Through a series of contrivances too numerous and dull to explain, she has been distracted and waylaid by a French ne'er-do-well, who is encouraging her to think the worst of Garner and the flirtatious attentions of a younger teacher also on the trip; played by Maurice Ronet, Philippe lures her to the beach, and though they never kiss, the dreamy erotic action of their suggestive jogging is already charged, and that is before they crash down onto the sand together in a clunky rehearsal of Burt Lancaster and Deborah Kerr's embrace in *From Here to Eternity* (1954). The whole scene plays like an echo of slow-motion iconography whose sexual meanings are too obvious to explicate. Though putting no more flesh on display than she did as an ingénue in *Singin' in the Rain*, Reynolds might well be the first female star in Hollywood to have slow motion symbolize her own status, within the logic of the film at least, as the decelerated object of a sexualized male gaze. It is more comforting, though, when Ballard has her reprise her slow-motion run as the film ends, with Reynolds, now fully clothed, and Garner, with his son's peace necklace dangling over his normcore polo, finally synchronized in the same aesthetic temporality that signifies their marriage will endure. This is also a happier ending in slow motion that anything that Ballard and Peckinpah will give us in *The Wild Bunch*.

The last time we see William Holden's Pike, he is dying in protracted agony but still dispensing even more destruction in slow motion from behind the Browning machine gun whose rapid firing and noise are emblematic of the camera speeds that we register as just the opposite. There is nothing pretty about what he suffers, though it is every bit as much the Hollywood ending as the lyrical and empty run across the beach that Ballard and Jerry Paris use to let us know that everything is going to be all right with Reynolds and Garner's marriage until, I guess, death do them part. A bleak and unrelenting melancholy about modernity is so utterly the abiding structure of *The Wild Bunch*—patterning both its violence and its casual misogyny—that when it erupts in full-blown allegory it feels almost too obvious to acknowledge, much less analyze. Pike takes his first visible damage in the final battle when he is shot in the back by a young Mexican woman whom he has dismissed as a threat. He kills her with a sneering cry of "bitch" but ultimately falls to an even younger foe: As Peckinpah makes clear, it is just a boy who fires the rifle that brings Pike to his knees as he dies in a hail of bullets while manning the machine gun. These moments are radically ambiguous if, as some reviewers and many critics did, we try to parse the slaughter as a blood-soaked shadow play of the U.S. war in Vietnam, a reading that Peckinpah eventually welcomed. But we don't need to worry about wondering whether the brutal General Mapache—whose shooting by Pike inaugurates both the battle and its ornate slow motion—is more like Ho

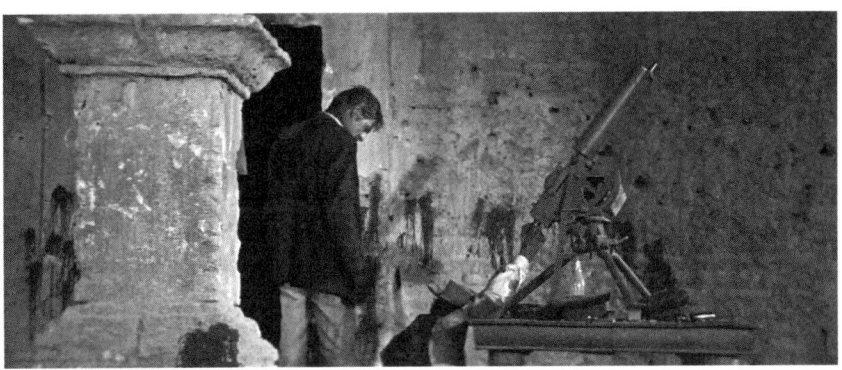

FIGURE 25.2 Pike can still get it up in a still from *The Wild Bunch* (1969).

Chi Minh or Nguyen Van Thieu to realize that two of the youngest figures that we see on screen are instrumental to Pike's downfall, however inevitable and cruel and justified and overdue. Even in death, he cannot let go of his big gun—which is ridiculously still erect long after it has stopped ejaculating bullets into any body that comes into range (figure 25.2).

Slow motion is an effect of end-stage masculinity in Peckinpah. Obviously. But then again, what isn't in *The Wild Bunch*? This is an aspect of the film that emerges with particular vividness when set against another film from 1968 that premiered about two months before *How Sweet It Is!* and that was nowhere near as trifling in its look at middle age and the wreckage it leaves behind as the years pass by—quickly or not. Nobody comes close to getting shot in Frank Perry's *The Swimmer* (1968), and there wouldn't be a place to hide a squib on Burt Lancaster's "Ned" anyway since he spends the entire film in a tight pair of bathing trunks as he makes his way from pool to pool across his neighborhood in suburban Connecticut, with each new party he encounters helping reveal his increasingly fantastic and deranged detachment from a present in which his wife and family seem no longer to exist back at the home to which he is returning. Based on a famous John Cheever short story, Perry and his cinematographer David Quaid had finished the film in the summer of 1966, but its release was significantly delayed by its producers after they fired Perry and Quaid and brought in Sydney Pollack and his cinematographer, Michael Nebbia, for elaborate and expensive reshoots. Lancaster reportedly paid $10,000 out of pocket to cover a final day on set. *The Swimmer* becomes progressively weirder and more hallucinatory as Lancaster makes his way to the abandoned house that was apparently his home, falling into a crushed heap of tears and desperation on the doorstep of the locked mansion as the film fades out. Lancaster's performance is compelling but not exactly subtle at this moment of high anguish. In this regard, his acting is much like the film's visual style, which is most effective and unsettling when it is simply documenting idle social interactions that possess an undertone of quiet dread. But *The Swimmer* also throws a kitchen sink of gimmicks from the New American cinema at its subject—crash zooms, out-of-focus long shots, overexposures, underexposures, double exposures, lens flares in bulk—and so of course there is a sequence in slow motion that feels like it goes on forever. Having picked up one of his daughter's old babysitters at the last pool—played by Janet Landgard as intrigued by Lancaster but decidedly not interested when he later tries to kiss her—Lancaster and Landgard come across a steeplechase course in an idyllic meadow somewhere in the woods. Of course they do. What follows is two full minutes of Lancaster's slightly weathered version of athletic beauty put through its paces in slow motion (figure 25.3): At almost fifty-four when *The Swimmer* was principally shot in 1967, he was well removed from his days as a circus performer, and while every scene of Lancaster in his little swimsuit is an exquisite reminder of his iconic physique, this moment turns sadly painful soon enough. When he lands his last ecstatic leap in this miniature *Olympia*, he comes down heavy on his ankle right in front of Landgard, whose close-up has figuratively charmed and haunted Lancaster's exploits as a double image on the screen. As a self-consciously lyrical, romantic interlude in a film as ultimately despairing as *The Swimmer* it makes sense that Lancaster's indulgence of artfully "slow time" can only finish with an embarrassing thud. It could be much worse for old men in the country, as Peckinpah has shown us.

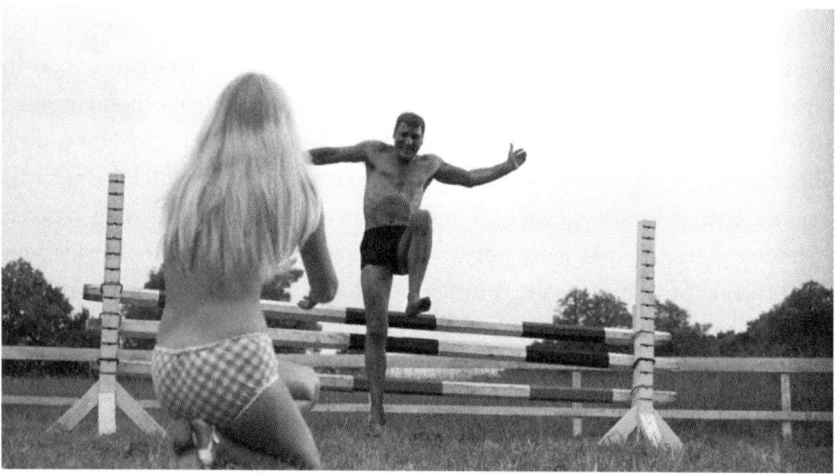

FIGURE 25.3 Burt Lancaster does not stick the landing in this still from *The Swimmer* (1968).

The Wild Bunch is also very much a film about aging, or, like *How Sweet It Is!* and *The Swimmer*, about feeling older than you think you are because a younger generation has decided you're a relic. We can't get a very good look at Holden's middle-aged physique in the rustic Mexican sauna where he enjoys a good steam with Ernest Borgnine's Dutch, and he dresses with his back to us in modesty after his later encounter with a Mexican prostitute before their doomed assault on Mapache. To be clear, Holden still looks pretty good: Perhaps he hadn't trained with quite the seriousness that marked Lancaster's preparation for *The Swimmer*, perhaps because he wasn't spending the whole movie in tiny swim trunks, either. In the steam, Dutch calls attention to a grotesque scar on Pike's left leg, a gnarled and open ridge of split flesh that causes him to limp and, at one moment of overdone embarrassment, makes him fall while trying to mount his horse, giving the crude Gorch brothers a good laugh at his expense. The strikingly young prostitute with whom Pike spends his last night alive—her inappropriate age underscored, without much subtlety, by her crying infant in the same room—doesn't seem appalled by Pike, but his sudden decision to lead his men against Mapache in the postcoital gloom seems like a moment of reckoning not so much with his mortality but with the disgust he starts to feel when, having sacrificed Angel, the youngest member and only Mexican of the Wild Bunch, to torture back at Mapache's compound, he realizes that maybe his own time should be up. Angel is effectively "fridged," turned into the sacrificial, feminized victim who inspires action and retribution from our decidedly male heroes, which is what Pike and the Wild Bunch become in the last minutes of the film when they finally unleash their wanton violence on an even worse assembly of awful men. They have endured enough in slow motion already. We can see its history on their sagging bodies and the lines cut in their faces. They were dying at the deliberate rate we all are anyway. Slow motion lets *The Wild Bunch* get it over with in a hurry and look better doing it than any of them deserve.

I don't think that Peckinpah, for all the formidable technique *The Wild Bunch* puts on display, has anything particularly original to tell us about the moral ambiguities of violent action or the raw aestheticization of masculinity, his two most favorite things to have ideas about whenever he seems to feel that his films must have ideas. As an Americanist by training, there is a wearying familiarity to the desperate calculus of honor, loyalty, and various flavors of misogyny—from casual to murderous—that there is no getting past in Peckinpah, no matter how ironically or repulsively his narratives explore its flaws and gross deformities. It is almost worse for me that Kathleen Murphy, writing in *Film Comment* shortly after Peckinpah had died, sounds entirely correct when she suggests that, while self-inflicted damage to his reputation may have left him isolated in Hollywood, "there are other, older friends in whose anachronistic company [he] should feel at home: Melville, Hawthorne, Twain, Hemingway, Faulkner."[13] To cite just one example that I've perhaps been begging since the first rodeo scenes of *Junior Bonner*, the intensely time-critical descriptions of bullfighting in *Death in the Afternoon*—many of which are based on Hemingway's huge collection of photographs depicting matadors frozen, at high speed, in motion—read like tributes to the men that Peckinpah admires for the athletic beauty of their collective death wish. "I learned the things that can be done with him," Hemingway observes of bulls that have been wounded by banderillas, "when he is properly slowed."[14] Hemingway insists he knows "no modern sculpture, except Brancusi's, that is in any way the equal of the sculpture of modern bullfighting." Hemingway makes surprisingly few references to film in *Death in the Afternoon* given that he argues throughout that neither the still image nor sculpture are sufficient for registering the spectacle of bullfighting as it happens in real time, and when he does mention slow motion, it is just a metaphor to evoke how a matador named Cagancho can "perform the usual movements of bullfighting so slowly that they become, to old-time bullfighting, as the slow motion picture is to the ordinary motion picture." Then again, almost every description of bullfighting in the book is effectively an exercise in extreme deceleration, with Hemingway devoting whole pages to a fleeting turn of hip or shoulder, a flash of cape or sword. This is how Hemingway tries to register the "growing ecstasy of ordered, formal, passionate, increasing disregard for death that leaves you, when it is over, and the death administered to the animal that has made it possible, as empty, as changed and as sad as any major emotion will leave you." There is maybe no better description of how Peckinpah wanted his viewers to feel after *The Wild Bunch*, spent and somber at the sight of animals we've finally come to see as men now put to death.

We should not be so sad to see them go. Not just because they're terrible and culpable for everything they've done until Peckinpah tries desperately to redeem them in slow motion. They are simply having too much fun—living up to the happier connotations of the name "wild bunch" in these noisy, blood-soaked minutes—while for most of the film they are so glum or ponderously dejected as they scrap for money or take on whatever work Mapache has for them. They die painfully and violently, but what we see in slow motion are demonstrably the most meaningful and vital moments of their lives. Slow motion registers and signals the "ecstasy" with which they intend to kill as many people as they can before they die, which is grotesque by any measure save that of the outmoded, ugly West that Peckinpah has shown is waiting for them as the twentieth century unfolds. This is as good as they will ever have it anyway. Or, to borrow from

Martin Hägglund on Virginia Woolf, whom absolutely nobody but me would associate with Peckinpah, "the sense of temporal irreplaceability is here what gives the sense of a singular value to the moment and precipitates the investment in a singular life."[15] Pike Bishop never has to say that he will shoot the general himself, but there is no mistaking the intensity of his "chronolibidinal investment in the fate of temporal existence." In Peckinpah's slow motion we see nothing else. Of course, "the same investment," as Hägglund argues, "may also make one susceptible to a suffering that may make it impossible to go on living." Nobody in *The Wild Bunch* must wait for very long for this to play out in a stupendous style that turns the damage that they endure into a monument to modern time, both fast and slow at once. No matter how we might ultimately remember *The Wild Bunch*, we have to admit that Peckinpah wanted his men to have their time of their lives.

MEN, WOMEN, AND SLOW MOTION

It is hard to think of another director apart from Peckinpah for whom slow motion is as much of a nearly metaphysical proposition. Slow motion, as we have seen, makes *Bonnie and Clyde* and *2001* into the icons of New Hollywood that we remember, and though Leone probably could have done without it—*The Good, the Bad, and the Ugly* (no slow motion) remains a toss-up for me with *Once Upon a Time in the West* (his first slow motion) as his most crucial film of the late sixties—the blurred image of Henry Fonda's Frank when he walks us back into Harmonica's traumatic past remains iconic and, more importantly, symptomatic of Leone's attitude toward modernity more generally. We are about to finish with Antonioni's *Zabriskie Point*, his belated and baroque attempt to make a film of 1968 that he doesn't finish until 1970. The slow motion in *Zabriskie Point* is impossibly spectacular, and the film is something of a miracle for the almost pathological sincerity of its revolutionary posture. This is not to say that slow motion is exhausted by the 1970s; there are literally countless works and figures that have proved otherwise. But even among the genuine auteurs of slow motion in the decades after Peckinpah, there are precious few—John Woo and Wong-Kar Wai come immediately to mind, the Wachowskis too, along with video artists like Bill Viola and Douglas Gordon—for whom it functions not just as a "special effect" but as the very logic of being in a world of film and all the media technologies that have materially replaced it. Michael Bay, Zach Snyder, or Justin Lin are manneristic geniuses of action cinema, but slow motion remains for them, I think, one of Cavell's "assertion[s] in technique." Their technique is wonderfully assertive, and I'm sure that others have ideas about filmmakers just as powerfully accomplished in the deployment of slow motion (Pete Travis in *Dredd*, Paul W. S. Anderson's Resident Evil series, Lexi Alexander's deeply underrated *Punisher: War Zone*), but it is still a form applied when the occasion, or the car crash or the fight scene, might demand and not, as it becomes for Peckinpah in the 1970s, a way of life and nearly categorical imperative that reveals the shape of time itself. Each of his films after *The Wild Bunch* is tremendously flawed by his own standards, and I don't intend to trace the dismal arc of his decline and his abuses. But if *The Wild Bunch* is Peckinpah at his very best in slow motion—and a film like *Junior Bonner* finds surprising charms in his critiques of progress, however self-obsessed and limited—we must also reckon with what slow motion shows us at his worst. Hopefully, this won't take very long.

There is no slow motion in roughly the first hour of *Straw Dogs*. There isn't a graphic rape scene either, until there is, and then we have a lot of both. But the connection is not as obvious as it looks. The early sections of the film have walked us through the lousy marriage of David Sumner, an American mathematician played by Dustin Hoffman, and Susan George as Amy, his English wife whose Cornish village is their home while David is on a research sabbatical. They go through the motions of rural domesticity—trips to the pub, fixing up a farmhouse, vanilla sex—while the growing tensions in their marriage start to bloom into hostilities. Amy questions whether David agreed to come to England in the first place to retreat from student politics on campus; he is treated as an oddity by most of the villagers and takes their condescension out on Amy; Amy is lewdly jeered at by the men working on their house, including an ex-boyfriend, Venner, who then contrives to distract David with a hunting invitation that becomes an elaborate ruse to let Venner sneak back to the house and assault her. Venner tries to kiss her, and she tries to make him leave. He rapes her, but there is a queasy ambiguity to their encounter that is calculated to invoke her own desire—for Venner or revenge or both—as mitigating Venner's culpability. In a draft of the screenplay by David Z. Goodman and Peckinpah, still with the working title "The Siege of Trencher's Farm" from Gordon Williams's novel, there is nothing ambiguous in their assertion that Amy is "more than willing, totally possessed" by this point.[16] The direction to have her assailant "KISSING HER . . . almost in slow motion" would have even more grotesquely rendered this rape fantasy as overtly softcore, lyricized like the vision of Ali McGraw in *Goodbye, Columbus* or the decelerated lovers' leap into a park lagoon that Peckinpah puts near the beginning of *The Getaway* to underscore the romance of McGraw's reunion with Steve McQueen when he is paroled from prison. If Amy's rape was "almost in slow motion," it might have looked even less like what it is.

What makes it to the screen is terrible enough to watch before Venner's friend, Scutt, interrupts their now ambivalently consensual sex within the rape fantasy that Peckinpah treats as axiomatic and then at gunpoint has Venner hold her down for Scutt to rape again. In the more explicit UK version, this is signaled as sodomy; the U.S. version cut this second rape to get its "R" rating and so is arguably worse for only showing Amy seeming to take pleasure in Venner's rape without requiring viewers to then endure the plain terror of her violation. The longer version is a harder watch for sure but does reveal the logic of Peckinpah's exploitative gaze: To whatever degree a viewer might come to accept the grotesque arc from rape to sex we are supposed to see with Venner, Scutt's brutal violation is unambiguously horrifying, and Venner's ultimate complicity renders his own illusions of seduction, as well as those of any viewer sharing them, horrific. Of course it never should have been that hard to see this rape for what it is from the beginning. Some critics in the early 1970s, as well as many of Peckinpah's most prominent defenders in the decades following, observed that George was directed to begin performing pleasure during the first part of the assault, and I won't try to do justice to the malice of the scene's editing, which cuts back and forth in overlapping sound between the cries of Amy as she gradually succumbs to Venner's force and David's flaccid handling of a bird he only wounds and tries to hide away in shame.[17] This all unfolds with complicated brilliance over the nearly ten minutes given over to the assault.

But for me it is more telling that the first time Venner kisses her, Amy slaps him, says "get out," and then he hits her back and she recoils onto a sofa in the very first slow motion that the film indulges. We cut to her reaction on his loud slap, and her scream of pain fades into a disturbing, abstract music cue as we watch her hair flail out as she falls. No blood is spilled, but Susan George goes down like any other body in a Peckinpah film that has received a killing blow. It is impossible to romanticize the way that Venner hits her precisely because slow motion makes its viciousness so plain, its hatred toward her obvious and palpable. Unlike the members of the Wild Bunch, Amy survives along with David, who dispenses plenty of slow-motion violence of his own—including cruelly slapping Amy in a shot that rhymes with the earlier rape scene—as he defends his home against the group of villagers, Amy's rapists included, who attack their cottage in their effort to capture and lynch another villager. The men want to punish this minor character, whom David perversely commits to protect at all costs, for another brutal crime against a woman that, in the sick calculus that governs *Straw Dogs*, we are also maybe supposed to think had it coming to her. In Peckinpah's bleak world, no deed—good or bad—goes unpunished in slow motion.

I don't have it in me to track all the slow motion in the film's ferocious final sequences. There are point-blank shotgun blasts, third-degree burns, and a nasty reprise of Amy's assault when Scutt breaks off from the attempted lynching to attempt another rape. As Hoffman hardens into a tool of vengeance amid the mayhem of Dutch tilts and horror-movie thrills, the argument that Kael makes about the fundamental fascism of *Straw Dogs* comes into focus: "This is the stupidity and moral corruption," she writes, as Peckinpah insists with every trick he knows that "it may be necessary to be violent in order to defend your home and your principles" because he thinks "that's what makes a man a man."[18] Peckinpah was apparently so upset by Kael's review and what he saw as her misreading of the film's immanent critique, an as intellectual like David might call it, that he tried to arrange a meeting to respond in person. I am not inclined to take his side long after the fact, though she does perhaps ignore how strenuously Peckinpah and John Coquillon visually frame Hoffman as just another monster in the busy final carnage, and it has never been clear to me how she turns Hoffman's nebbishy outsider into the figure of a ruthless *volk* trying to defend the territory where he knows he doesn't belong against the native mob that he has to fear would lynch him too. This is probably not a fight worth having about Peckinpah's too-violent legacy now that it is fading from the glow it still had in spades in 1971. But I will have to disagree with Kael's description of what I think is the crucial split-second of the film's endless rape scene. This is, disturbingly for Kael, "one of the few truly erotic sequences in the film, and the punches that subdue the wife have the exquisite languor of slightly slowed-down motion." With the benefit of an open copy of *Straw Dogs* on my desktop, I can confirm that there is only one "punch" and that it is a slap. More importantly, when seen as part of Peckinpah's ongoing and stylized epic of violence after 1968, this blow seems pointedly removed from the "erotic" action that Kael appreciates. I can't say I have any strong opinions about what will happen next to Amy and David; he drives back into town without her, smiling with the satisfaction of his ugly victory. It is not pleasant to think of Amy left in their cottage with the wreckage and corpses, but it might be considered nobler, or whatever tribute Peckinpah imagines he is paying her, that she is abandoned to survive apart from what we've watched David just become.

Straw Dogs is an exhausting film to watch and would be even if it never ventured into slow motion. But this was an impossibility for Peckinpah after 1968. Slow motion appears in every film he makes after *The Wild Bunch*, emerging as perhaps the most familiar signature of his style across the wayward years of his decline into addiction, illness, and increasingly mercenary projects like *The Killer Elite* (1975) and *Convoy* (1978), a disaster of half-baked populism inspired by a novelty country hit that I remember distinctly as the first of his films I ever saw—probably because it was a surprising box-office hit that played repeatedly well into the 1980s on the local UHF channel that I watched growing up. I was not especially struck by any of its slow motion, which is ample but profoundly unremarkable, which could easily serve as an epithet for the effect itself as it lives on and thrives. What Peckinpah, Lucien Ballard, and his editors discover in *The Wild Bunch* is nothing less than the complete assimilation of slow motion into the narrative syntax of action cinema, which also helps radically extend the lifespan, a term whose ironies are loaded in this context, of the various codes of masculinity and violence in the western that Peckinpah both cherished as they were and wanted powerfully to modernize. Like slow motion, this opinion is widespread and conventional. But not everything that goes slow in Peckinpah leaves behind a body, and at least a few of his tragically long-suffering characters are left with exit wounds they're able to survive.

This is what we are supposed to realize, if we haven't already, when Thornton's men descend on the remains of Bishop, Dutch, and the Gorch brothers at Mapache's blasted compound and flock to their corpses like the ominous buzzards perched everywhere around the ruins, more like gargoyles than birds, trapped there by means that, given Peckinpah's spotty record with animal welfare on his sets, I'm happy not to know.[19] While the bounty hunters cackle over their prizes—with Strother Martin's aptly named "Coffer" already reckoning the payout—Thornton walks away with measured eloquence in a terrific bit of physical acting on Ryan's part that serves as symbolic reconciliation with his old and now dead comrade. And there we see him sitting for almost the duration: Coffer and the bounty hunters leave with the bodies of the Wild Bunch strapped to their horses, in a hurry both for their money and because, as Martin's character points out, "these boys will start going ripe on us by tomorrow"; then, with the sky seeming to have darkened noticeably, a procession of villagers go past Thornton, who hasn't moved, as they cart out their own dead; over the distant echoes of gunfire, he stays right there until the only surviving member of Pike's bunch, Edmond O'Brien's supremely grizzled "Sykes," returns to the scene of his friends' slaughter to imply, with little ambiguity, that Thornton's own men have been killed, along with any of Mapache's stragglers, by the revolutionary cadre formed from Angel's village, where Sykes was left behind when he was wounded. It is about the happiest ending we could expect after the destruction we have witnessed, and though the final nod toward Third World radicalism is maybe a bit too timely for its own good—Leone manages to smuggle Maoist posturing into his spaghetti westerns with more conviction—it gives Thornton and Sykes a nicer sunset into which they can ride off then either character can possibly imagine they deserve. "Me and the boys here," Sykes grumbles with a knowing smile, "we've got some work to do." The only plan that Thornton can come up with on his own is to "drift around" in Mexico with as little purpose as his display of rueful immobility. He's ready to go back on the clock.

But before his change of heart—which is also a change of sides—how long do we think that Thornton sits there? Robert Ryan spends over three minutes of screen time barely moving, though no single shot in this last sequence is particularly long. Unlike the stunningly protracted opening of *Once Upon a Time in the West*, which this scene might well recall and answer, the slowness and duration here are naturalized into ellipsis. The changing light and color of the sky suggests that Thornton is stuck there the better part of an afternoon and evening: Bishop leads the Wild Bunch to their doomed assault on the morning after a debauched night of booze and prostitutes fails to erase the image of Angel's abandonment and torture, and Mapache's table looks set for an elaborate lunch that will be fed to machine-gun fire instead. My point, though, is not to figure out to some artificially precise second just how much diegetic time unfolds but rather simply to observe that whenever Thornton does arrive, there is plenty of daylight left for him to contemplate his empty future now that his last, worst job is over. Then Sykes rides back with a better offer. It is just the sort of bleak promotion we might expect to end one of the exemplary versions of the genre Will Wright calls "the professional Western," which later critics like Noël Carroll and Menne have explored as a crucial sixties subgenre that tries to put the tropes of U.S. frontier mythology "in service of Third World revolution."[20]

According to W. K. Stratton's helpful reconstruction of the shooting of *The Wild Bunch*—the pun is unavoidable but not intended—these scenes with Ryan sitting in the dust were filmed after several days devoted solely to the intricate logistics of the battle, which required considerable coordination and extensive labor from stunt performers, camera operators, costume designers, and prop assistants. Countless setups were required to get the coverage Peckinpah desired, with five or six cameras running simultaneously at different speeds alongside master shots in normal time. None of these scenes involved Ryan, who had to wait on set in Mexico for weeks before he had anything to do. There are apocryphal reports, which I'd very much like to believe, that Peckinpah and Ryan almost came to blows over the actor's frustration that his time was being wasted when he could have been at home campaigning for Eugene McCarthy's presidential run in 1968.[21] Ryan had left the set for several days after the assassination of Martin Luther King Jr. to meet with colleagues in SANE (National Committee for a Safe Nuclear Policy), which had become an important group for Hollywood liberals, like Ryan, Paul Newman, and Tony Randall, who had followed and embraced King's own shift toward a more radical antimilitary position and explicit critique of the Vietnam War as racist in both its impact on Black Americans and the ideology that it projected globally. But Peckinpah insisted that Ryan not fly back to California again when Robert Kennedy Jr. was killed two months later, which further weakened McCarthy's efforts to win the Democratic nomination as Kennedy's supporters at the convention largely split for either Hubert Humphrey or George McGovern. McCarthy was pilloried when he said he was open to the possibility of a treaty that would cede power to the Communists in Vietnam. Ryan was no revolutionary, but his politics were more left than many liberals in Hollywood and decidedly more radical than Peckinpah's own half-baked hash of libertarianism and nostalgia. Nor was McCarthy an ideal candidate in 1968, but even if the refined and intellectual liberalism he embodied wasn't "like it used to be," as Sykes's offer to Thornton admits, for Ryan in real life the best answer was probably Sykes's own, "but it'll do."

As much relish as I have for almost ludicrous historicism, I won't suggest that any of these flights of association were someone's reading of *The Wild Bunch* in the late sixties. But I still offer them as one way we might revisit Peckinpah's most famous film and think about how the texture of its moment can represent surprising aspects of a period that feels at once like a vanished epoch of the twentieth century yet aggressively contemporary. Peckinpah knew that the western's days were numbered and maybe understood by 1968 that its ideal version of the West was also very much on borrowed time. One way or another, though—in Bishop's agonized nobility, in Thornton's weary resignation—*The Wild Bunch* wants to remind us that, after a while, it's not just the time but ultimately the job that is the killer.

26

Antonioni's Art of Excess

Zabriskie Point

Z*abriskie Point* is exactly the European art film about the American 1960s that you would make if you wanted to lose tons of money for a major studio and have Pauline Kael make fun of you. Though its budget of $7 million now looks more like the price of a Hollywood home than a Hollywood movie, it was still a considerable investment at the time for a struggling MGM. This works out to a budget of around $53 million today—*John Wick 2* money—for what remains, by any measure, Antonioni's most divisive and politically extravagant film. Some of the critics who most ardently adore his work ignore it altogether. Peter Brunette's survey *The Films of Michelangelo Antonioni* devotes a chapter to each of the director's major films but skips from *Blow-Up* (1966) to *The Passenger* (1975) as if *Zabriskie Point* did not exist. Brunette speeds past it in a single paragraph that calls it "naïve," "tacky," and, far more cruelly—though not, alas, without good reason—the "embarrassing record of the fifty-year-old director's own presumed sexual liberation (or wish-fulfillment.)"[1] The literary critic and narrative theorist Seymour Chatman spent the second half of his distinguished career celebrating Antonioni's elusive style and enigmatic sensibility but confesses in the highly reverent *Antonioni, or, The Surface of the World* (1985) that the "cultural mistakes of *Zabriskie Point* seem so pervasive as to disable the film" and never really gets around to arguing otherwise.[2] When Chatman returns to the problem of *Zabriskie Point* about a decade later, he still regrets that "Antonioni's sudden segue in American politics was too simplistically partisan" and so is happy that, with *The Passenger*, he was able to "move back to the broader, philosophical scope that had served him so well in previous films."[3] Chatman shifts some of the blame onto the studio as "the inevitable consequence of working for the very capitalist establishment that the film was attacking." On one level, at least, Antonioni's assault on capital succeeded: *Zabriskie Point* grossed less than $900,000 and effectively brought Antonioni's run of daunting modernist successes to a stop. "For its day," writes Seymour Chatman, "it was the most expensive failure ever made."[4] What the movie failed to make in money, though, it reaped in scorn and pity. One guess which Kael's review in the *New Yorker* put on sumptuous display.

From Kael's first sentence quoting a *Variety* story on Antonioni's appearance at the San Francisco Film Festival with a new beard and "chicklette" on his arm, we know that he is in for it.[5] *Variety* had treated Antonioni's sojourn in America with cheeky condescension. "A séance to invoke the ghost of D. W. Griffith would have been conducted with less reverence," writes Rick Setlowe, who also reports with unkind irony that the thin crowds by the end of the long evening suggest that "the Antonioni mystique is apparently strong enough to endure anything but five hours of unadulterated Antonioni films."[6] It's a good line but still just barely lives up to the populist fizz of a title like "Frisco Fest Buffs Hushedly Pious Welcome for Plot-Killer Antonioni." Kael's review runs under the positively demure headline "The Beauty of Destruction" but does more damage not just to the pretensions of Antonioni's image of countercultural liberation and revolt but to his entire project as a director since his "masterwork [of] postwar alienation" *L'avventura*. "Trying to be topical," Kael argues, "Antonioni is merely obtuse and dated"; he is enamored of the "New Hollywood" mystique of *Bonnie and Clyde* and *Easy Rider*, but his vision of the sixties "is as far off America as the Italian Westerns shot in Spain." She calls Antonioni clumsy, dumb, and snobbish and takes considerable pleasure in dismissing the film's delirious closing montage of slow-motion explosions as yet another "sign of his aristocratic aesthetics" and self-indulgent formalism. Kael writes, "I doubt if he's much interested in the theme of revolutionary action; I think it's the other way around—politics provides the excuse for photogenic explosions." Just thirty months before, Kael had been left rapturously silent by the agonies that were visited on Bonnie and Clyde, but in Antonioni, "when America blows up, there are no bloody bodies, no people at all; only our material objects go up." She sees instead a grand capitulation to the logic of the market as it trades on "one of the insanities that grow out of the photographic nature of the movie medium" to use more tricks and special effects in hopes of "finding images powerful enough" to keep an audience interested when they have seen it all before. I doubt that Kael would have liked *Zabriskie Point* much better if Antonioni hadn't wasted almost five years making it, but she wouldn't have been able to call it too much, too late.

Zabriskie Point ends not with a bang but with a delirious montage of explosions. The film begins in LA, and we follow Mark Frechette's blank but beautiful protagonist—"he looks like a cross between Warren Beatty and Peter Fonda," Kael notes—as he is radicalized by police violence at a student protest. He steals a plane and flies out to Death Valley, where he meets the film's other lead, played by Daria Halprin, the secretary of a ruddy and grotesquely dashing real estate developer played by Rod Taylor, who was the only professional actor Antonioni cast for any of the film's main speaking roles. Here we see Halprin's character as she pauses on her escape from Taylor's mansion, which she flees in revulsion (figure 26.1). This isn't the actual Boulder Reign house, designed and built by Hiram Hudson outside Carefree, Arizona, where Antonioni filmed the first exterior shots and subsequent interior scenes at the deluxe property. Perhaps Antonioni would have reached the limits of MGM's largesse if he had insisted that they purchase the actual home so that he could blow it up, which is what the film's last sequence shows in Halprin's inner vision of its obliteration come to life. I am reproducing here a single still I hope is worth so many thousands of slow-motion frames (figure 26.2).

In the narrative, this sudden swerve into reverie or hallucination is the hangover of the pot she smoked back in Death Valley (good stuff, I guess, if she's still high after an eight-hour drive) or else the deferred reaction to the news of Frechette's murder on the radio. Either way, what happens next is utterly spectacular. The film's production designer, Dean Tavoularis, who had worked on *Bonnie and Clyde* and later became renowned for his work on *The Godfather*, *The Godfather II*, and *Apocalypse Now* with Francis Ford Coppola, built a full-scale exterior replica of Boulder Reign a few miles from the original; as the film's publicist Beverly Walker recalled in 1992, its load-bearing studs were sunk in

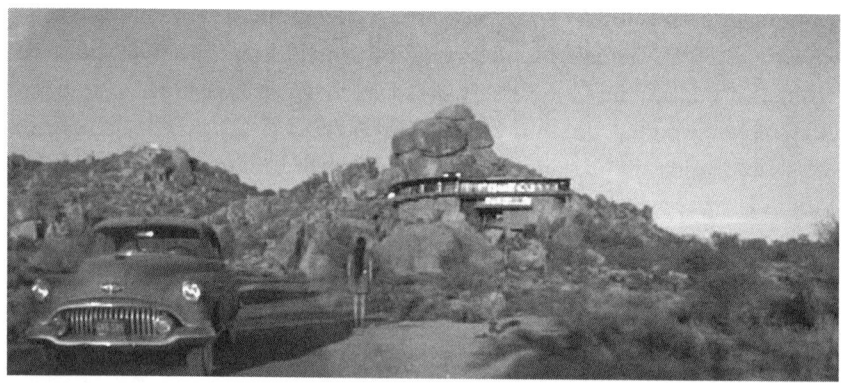

FIGURE 26.1 Still from *Zabriskie Point* (1970).

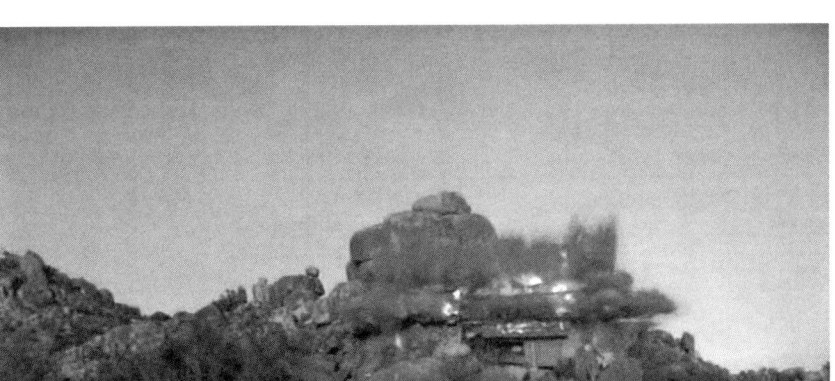

FIGURE 26.2 Still from *Zabriskie Point* (1970).

"barrels of combustible liquid" and its walls "lined with rows of dynamite sticks."[7] The resulting explosion—"said to be the single biggest explosion created for a movie," according to Walker—was captured by seventeen high-speed cameras placed in makeshift hardened bunkers around the site. Antonioni shot thousands of feet of film in a single, costly scene that nicely allegorizes what he was doing with MGM's money. Walker suggests they managed to recoup at least a fraction of their investment by using some of it as "stock footage in MGM's library," with "bits and pieces" finding their ways into many films over the years. Antonioni's slow motion may have been excessive and embarrassing, but the studio found a way to guarantee it wasn't all dead loss.

As anyone who has ever seen *Zabriskie Point* will know, Antonioni is only getting started in slow motion. The main explosion of the house is shown and heard ten times from different distances and angles, first in two long shots that reasonably reproduce what Halprin's character might be seeing—if this weren't all a fantasy—from her position on the road below the property and then in various close-ups from below or at angles that are harder to map from her perspective as a viewer. It is perhaps unnecessary to track precisely how point of view is shifted here since, when all the apocalyptic booms and bangs have stopped, the blissed-out look on Halprin's face as Roy Orbison's "Love Theme from *Zabriskie Point*" swells onto the soundtrack is the whimper that confirms that everything we have just watched has been the reverie of a fleeting moment. Kael hates this "aestheticized fantasy of blowing up America" not simply for what Halprin's being "clumpy, in a well-fed, middle class way" reveals about the "'revolutionary' youth" that Antonioni so adores; her deadly square quotes are even crueler than the "ripples of laughter" that she says greeted Halprin and Frechette's

FIGURE 26.3 Still from *Zabriskie Point* (1970).

line readings in the theater. But more than the artificial nature of Antonioni's politics, Kael hates the "aristocratic" distance of his remove from the sort of violence she lovingly admired in *Bonnie and Clyde* and at least respected in the "voluptuous, frightening" deaths in *The Wild Bunch*.[8] In *Zabriskie Point*, Kael scoffs, Antonioni "is being satiric and saying that America is nothing but garden furniture and books and the contents of our freezers—that we are a nation not of people but of objects."[9] After the tenth explosion, instead of another setup on Tavoularis's replica, we have a tighter shot of a large bookcase framed against a pool of deep black smoke and a little sky; the bookcase is absurdly out of place and in the process of exploding (figure 26.3). From the style of its paneling and general opulence, we are supposed to understand that this is another dream-image from inside the house that Halprin is destroying in her mind's eye. Next we see a metal rack of clothes subjected to the same fantastic demolition, followed by a white refrigerator, door open and perched far to the right side of the Panavision frame, that warps and crumples and flies in shiny pieces toward the screen. We are clearly in the same fantasy, but Halprin's unconscious has switched cameras and film stock. The house explosions are brighter and more sharply detailed; they look like they were probably filmed at 96fps with Panavision cameras similar to those Antonioni and his cinematographer Alfio Contini used throughout the shoot.

Because *Zabriskie Point* was, it must be said, a bomb, it has never gotten the deluxe DVD treatment, where such technical details would be unveiled on a commentary track, and so I'm sounding more speculative than I'd like. From James Williams, writing in *Film Quarterly* in 2008 with an appreciation

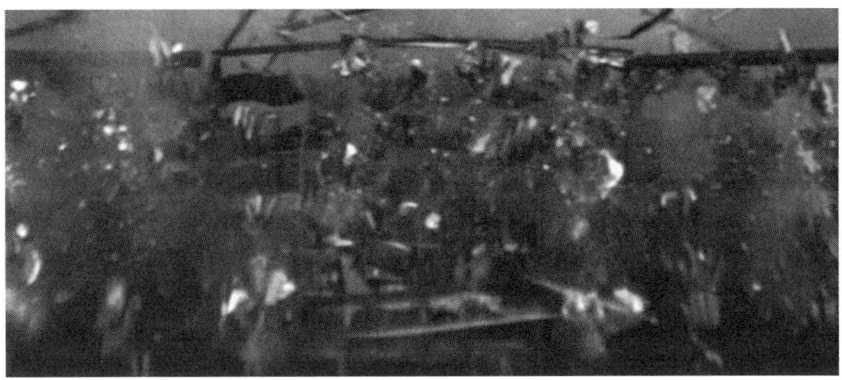

FIGURE 26.4 Still from *Zabriskie Point* (1970).

shortly after Antonioni's death, we learn that the cameras for these passages of slower motion were able to shoot at the then astounding rate of 3000fps, and we can assume that part of the diminished resolution is the result of "blowing up" 35mm footage to match the scale achieved by 70mm Panavision.[10] There is a swish pan from the burning rubble when Pink Floyd's "Come in Number 51, Your Time Is Up" becomes audible and then swirls away into a crunching blare of drums and feedback over twenty-three more shots that fill the screen for nearly three minutes with stuff exploding. We see a set of patio furniture that glancingly resembles a set in the house but then a different rack of clothes and, as the sequence ends, a different bookcase, too (figure 26.4). In between, Antonioni revisits the exploding refrigerator and detonates a television; the camera gets so close to the debris and rubble that hang magically in abstract space that there are moments that immerse us in a floating, 3D world of books that pulse like sea creatures or bewilder our attention by turning the geometry of the wide screen into a daunting, slowly vanishing work of abstract expressionism made from wires, buttons, and scraps of fabric (figure 26.5). Not that Antonioni always aims so high, as these stills prove. I can only guess how much it cost him to launch a chicken into uncanny flight with MGM's blank check and boundless technical proficiency. *Zabriskie Point* might not have been successful as a film about the sixties by the time that it debuted in 1970, but it remains, for me, a "wonder" (like the bread launched toward the viewer by one of the explosions) that tells us more about slow motion than many of its critics would have dared or deigned to guess. I've dredged up too many harsh appraisals to convince myself that it really is a work of art. But it might be even better.

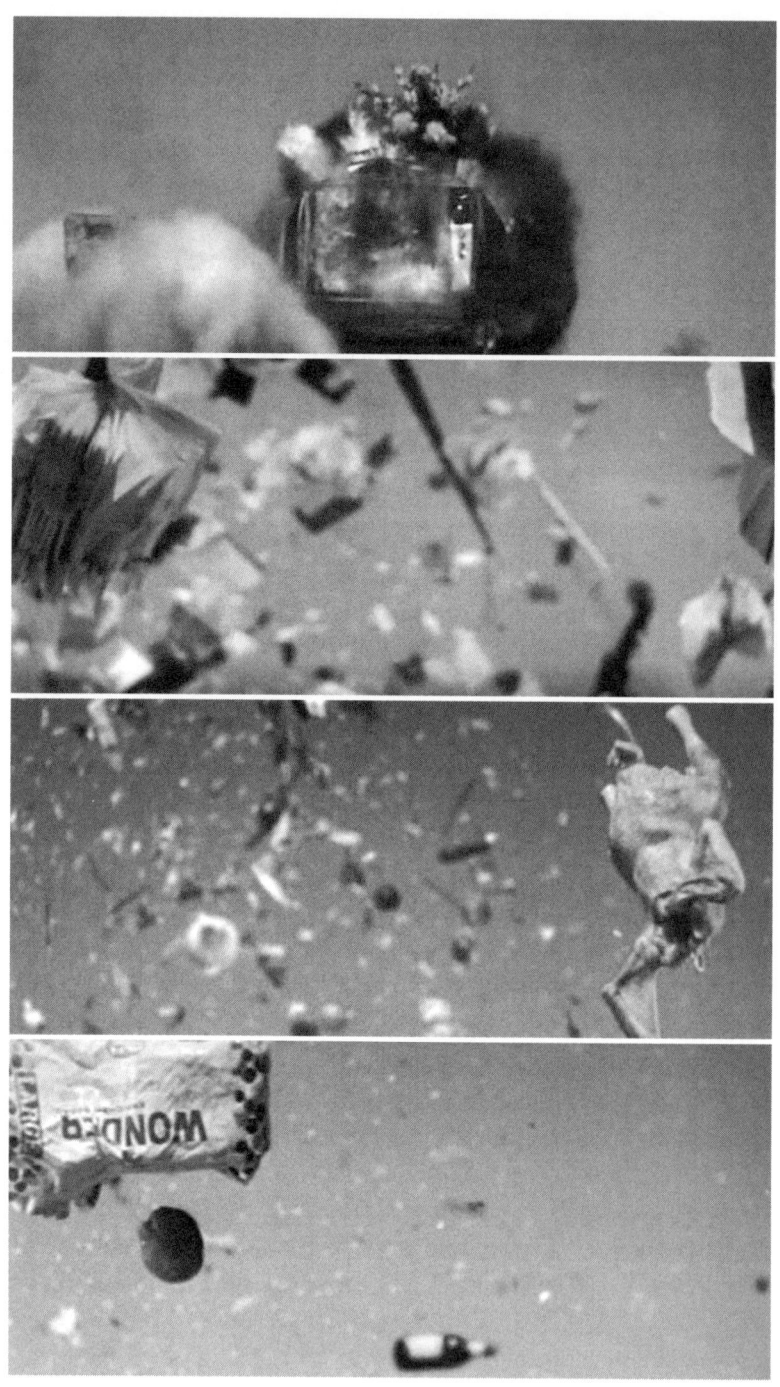

FIGURE 26.5 Stills from *Zabriskie Point* (1970).

THE IDEAL EXPLOSION

The best review that *Zabriskie Point* got in 1970 came from someone who never saw the film and wouldn't have been caught dead in any theater showing it. "Scars of damage and disruption are the modern's seal of authenticity," writes Adorno in *Aesthetic Theory*, "by their means art desperately negates the closed confines of the ever-same"—but it is the kicker to this frequently quoted passage that carries us back from Frankfurt to the golden deserts outside Scottsdale: "Explosion is one of its invariants."[11] This is from Adorno's final manuscripts for the book, on which he was still working when he died in August 1969 and which had been one of his major projects of the 1960s. When Adorno began the book, Antonioni had just become a global icon of cinematic modernism with *L'avventura* and *La notte*, and Adorno was deep in its revision over the very years Antonioni was scouting locations, meeting radicals and hippies, and meeting "chicklettes" in California, all at the expense of MGM and its blank check. This also means that Adorno was working on *Aesthetic Theory* in the months before his death when, as we know from the tense correspondence surrounding Herbert Marcuse's invitation to the Institute for Social Research in 1969, Adorno's relationship with the German student movement had turned bitter and recriminating. Since Adorno never came to terms with jazz, it is just short of absurd imagining what he would have done with David Gilmour's awesome scrawls of feedback as lingerie and loaves of Wonder Bread float with goofy majesty across the screen. If Adorno could have survived the drum fills, the flying chicken might have killed him anyway. *Zabriskie Point* bombed so thoroughly in 1970 that there is no evidence that it opened in Germany; it had brief runs in France and Greece and a single week in Italy, with its international box office estimated in the range of only $85,000, which might even be less than *Aesthetic Theory* has earned in the years since. Adorno obviously would have hated everything about *Zabriskie Point*, but the terms on which his loathing might be imagined can tell us a lot about why Antonioni chose the other side so fiercely—to the point that he'd risk destroying everything in slow motion to make sure that no one could accuse him of being one of modernism's relics.

This first explosion in *Aesthetic Theory* is metaphorical. It is a figure that he introduces to make Benjamin's "concept of the dialectical image" into something visible, a "voracious vortex" in the modern world that "lets nothing inherited go unchallenged."[12] "Even when modern art maintains traditional achievements in the form of technical resources," he continues, it does so according to a logic that has "destroyed tradition as such" and so cannot be "susceptible to correction by returning to foundations that no longer do or should exist." Adorno immediately turns this discussion toward contemporary music and the ways that it "rebels against conventional temporal order," but I think his point applies, however roughly, to Antonioni's own restless trajectory from *Red Desert* and *Blow-Up* and then *Zabriskie Point*, with each film not just introducing but deeply structured by the new "technical resources" (color in *Red Desert*, the dazzling and mystifying enlargements in *Blow-Up*, Panavision and slow motion in *Zabriskie Point*) he discovers and indulges. Or discovers *to* indulge, since it was the increasingly garish and vulgar formalism of his films that tested the patience of critics who had admired the austere, existential rigors of the black-and-white films that comprise the first installments of his tetralogy. After 1968, Antonioni announces—too loudly, and with too much slow motion—his "concept of classicism" is insufficient for the younger audience he wants to embrace. Or as Adorno puts it: "The enduring perished and drew the category of duration into its vortex." Art must change and move ahead, but at what speed? Too slow, and it risks hardening into mere tradition, but at full velocity, art becomes "paradoxically transient" in Adorno's thorny terminology, and we're left with "an eternity bare of semblance." The explosion is inevitable; the question is how fast?

L'avventura was released in West Germany in the spring of 1961, and *La notte* debuted at the Berlin Film Festival just a few weeks later. Antonioni seems to have known enough about Adorno to have the dying writer Tommaso, whose somber sickbed is the counterpoint to all the parties that we'll see later, congratulated by Marcello Mastroianni's Giovanni for his recent article on the imposing German intellectual. The contrast between the glittering novelist and the sick professor is morbid but treats Adorno as an icon, if only for the very few. By *Zabriskie Point*, though, Antonioni has no more patience for such alienated intellectuals and the quiet anguish they experience in their tailored suits at cocktail parties. The explosions that end the film look appropriately "modern," but the sublime they lust after would probably feel as artificial to Adorno as they did to Kael, who didn't need any aesthetic theory to dismiss them. "In technique," writes Adorno, "violence toward nature is not reflected through artistic portrayal" but is instead "only a reorientation of technical forces of production."[13] Translated into the rough vernacular of Kael, this is an explanation of why the film's "flash finish" is, despite its revolutionary posturing, the most embarrassingly "Hollywood" ending she can imagine.

Then again, Adorno did like fireworks. They are the occasion for an extended argument in *Aesthetic Theory* that offers some of his most forceful claims for the specific value of the experience of time that art makes possible. Adorno complains that "the phenomenon of fireworks is prototypical for artworks, though because of its fleetingness and status as empty entertainment it has scarcely been acknowledged by theoretical consideration."[14] Fireworks "are a sign from heaven yet artifactual, an ominous warning, a script that flashes up" when the ephemeral is relieved entirely of "the obligation of duration." They are not art but are still visions of the "blocked or denied sensuality" that is "poisoned by its exploitation" within the ruins that are the modern world. Adorno's fireworks reveal, in the vernacular of a minor form, an experience of the temporality that we should want from a culture's singular achievements, however impossible they might seem to us now. "Artworks are the persistence of the transient, they are concentrated in appearance as something momentary," and this is why they evoke "Benjamin's formulation of a dialectic at a standstill." But they are never not moving. "Art is profoundly akin to explosion," Adorno offers, and the "shocks inflicted by the most recent artworks are the explosion of their appearance." They are involved in the "incineration" of the world around them, which is also why they are "essentially historical" since what we see and hear exploding in and out of them is their "own inner time," now "[blasted] open" to assault us with the contents of the "history [that is] immanently sedimented in them." Adorno would prefer this history to sound like Beethoven's symphonies, where "movement at a standstill is eternalized in the instant." But sometimes, to the dismay of many who abandoned Antonioni at *Zabriskie Point*, maybe it looks like cucumbers, books, wires, picture tubes, scarves, chairs, and a box of Special K not quite but almost at the "standstill" that a work of art demands? Antonioni might not give us art according to Adorno or almost anybody else who saw the film in 1970, but we do get the pyrotechnics.

This detour through Adorno might not redeem Antonioni and *Zabriskie Point*, but it puts the gaudy excess of its ending in a slightly different light. I think it gets us closer to understanding why he used slow motion for his surpassingly committed vision of the sixties—and used so very much of it—than subsequent defenses of the film and its postmodernism. Writing on the occasion of Antonioni's centenary, for example, Angelo Restivo makes a compelling case that in the last explosions of an earnest counterculture sensibility in *Zabriskie Point* we are witness to ground zero of the "simulacrum" that would come to preoccupy Jean Baudrillard, another fancy European intellectual with a long-running love/hate relationship with America.[15] Restivo argues that "the turmoil of the film is that of the sign posting itself as its own point of referentiality, unanchored from the framing discourses which would have guaranteed both its meaning and its truth."[16] But I don't think that we have to choose between Antonioni's rather heavy "framing" of the period's politics and the unbearable lightness of his slowly exploding signifiers. Antonioni might finally give us too much of a good thing, but as his disappointed and disparaging critics realized immediately of *Zabriskie Point*, there was no mistaking the sincerity of his references to the politics of "1968." He hoped for the "persistence" of their transience in slow motion.

We can still blame Antonioni for his indulgence of slow motion and what emerges from the aftershocks of *Zabriskie Point*. At the time of its release in 1970, it was reported to have featured the largest single explosion that Hollywood had ever manufactured. I don't know how long Antonioni held this title. In 2015, Guinness gave a new "world record" to a relatively naturalistic explosion in the James Bond film *Spectre*, where the producers are said to have deployed more than 2,200 gallons of fuel and seventy-two pounds of TNT for a scene showing the destruction of Blofeld's base as Daniel Craig and Lea Seydoux look on in real time.[17] But the previous record holder has been unwilling to concede that he has been outdone, and so in 2022 Michael Bay assured his fans and critics that he believes that there is a bigger explosion in *Pearl Harbor* (2001), somewhere among the 192 explosions that Mark Hofmeyer cataloged for a full accounting of the director's boisterously inflammable career for *Rotten Tomatoes*.[18] The total number of explosions for Bay's filmography came to 1,649, and that didn't include *Ambulance* (2023)—which has plenty, I can assure you. With "decades of experience in exploding the hell out of Hollywood," Ben Travis writes, Bay makes for a perverse inheritor of whatever legacy Antonioni leaves behind with the finale of *Zabriskie Point*. When Martin Lawrence and Will Smith lead the assault on the mansion of the drug lord and rescue Gabrielle Union in *Bad Boys II*, we see what was, for a while at least, the biggest and "most expensive" explosion that Hollywood had ever put on screen (figure 26.6). I doubt that Bay was paying tribute to Antonioni or that the Slo Mo Guys are ever trying to emulate *Zabriskie Point* in their elaborate stunts and massively decelerated videos.[19] I will grant that much of the aesthetic power of explosions in *Zabriskie Point*, faster in their comparatively cheap slow motion, is perhaps already dead and gone within a few years of Antonioni's desperate museum piece of 1968. He is safely back making art cinema by 1975, and one year later, in George Lucas's far-off galaxy "long, long ago," we see another dopey kid with a blissed-out blank expression feel good about themselves because they too think that they've just blown up the evil empire (figure 26.7). In *Star Wars* (1976), it is definitely not a stoner dream when Luke Skywalker destroys the Death Star, though this big bang is less than the decisive victory for rebellion than it seems. The final explosion is also the only bit of slow motion that we see in the original *Star Wars* since Lucas, though very much a late figure of the New American cinema, filmed his space epic as a stylistic homage to old-fashioned Hollywood action serials of the 1930s, with a color palette from John Ford's westerns of the 1950s. Slow motion would have been an anachronism a long time ago, in this galaxy far, far away.

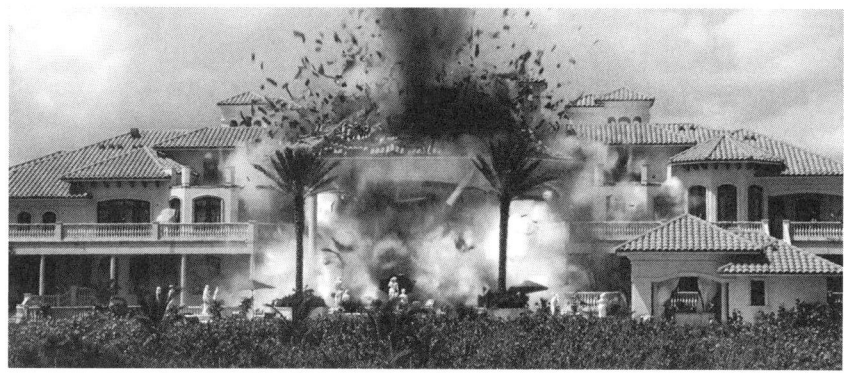

FIGURE 26.6 Real estate porn in *Bad Boys II* (2003).

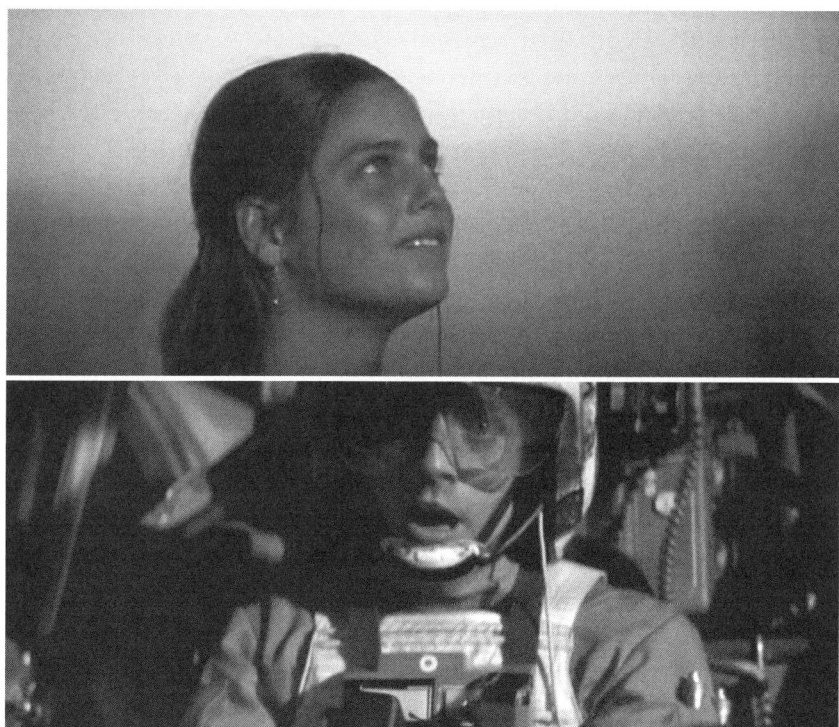

FIGURE 26.7 The thrill of victory in *Zabriskie Point* and *Star Wars* (1976).

It doesn't take much aesthetic theory or film history to figure out what's going on in *Zabriskie Point*'s other most outrageous departure from reality—aside from its plot and most of its dialogue, of course. There isn't much of either in the Death Valley interlude marking Antonioni's equally earnest tribute to the spirit of 1968, but this time in a love scene for the ages.

ON THE RUN AND GOING NOWHERE

Zabriskie Point is a road trip that takes a long time to get going. Compared to its outrageously stylized slow-motion ending, the start of the film is a special kind of drag. For more than eight minutes, Antonioni gives us a scene of student radicals across the spectrum of ideologies—Maoists and well-meaning liberals, New Left social democrats debating picket-line logistics, and Black Panthers providing the recipe for Molotov cocktails—trying to plan and work through the contingencies for an upcoming campus strike. Antonioni collaborated with the activist Fred Gardner on this section of the script, which is very much an exercise in a purist mode of neorealist aesthetics that Antonioni himself had never really practiced. Kathleen Cleaver plays a version of herself and is easily the most charismatic presence amid a wearying exchange of slogans and positions. Harrison Ford is apparently a silent extra somewhere in the background. Frechette's character emerges as a focal figure in the proceedings when he stands up and expresses his impatience with how long it all is taking; with no particular charm or magnetism, he declares his willingness to die for the cause, a statement that puts him on the side of the Black militants, whose authority is resonant in the room, and also, of course, that foreshadows his fate within the narrative. The meeting goes on without him for another couple minutes, and in what maybe counts as a joke by Antonioni's standards, the scene gives the last words to another student who complains about his early exit. "Meetings aren't his trip," another character tries to explain as Frechette leaves. But the final voice we hear is unconvinced and attacks him for the lack of patience he has demonstrated. "Even anarchists," we are reminded, "spend most of their lives talking in meetings for Christ's sake." This might be the best line in the whole movie, including any of those that can be credited to a young Sam Shephard, whom Antonioni brought in to sharpen some of the romantic dialogue between Frechette and Halprin and to give more menace to Rod Taylor's patter about the "Sunny Dunes" development his company is financing in Arizona. I'm willing to bet that I have more patience for *Zabriskie Point* than almost anyone, but I'd much rather watch Antonioni explode TVs and chickens than hear Frechette and Halprin—who were a couple throughout the shoot—attempt to flirt.

Fortunately for us, Antonioni gives us plenty to look at when they do. Frechette and Halprin have their meet-cute near the geological formation from which the movie takes its name. The scene starts as a strange homage to *North by Northwest* as the plane Frechette has stolen in LA—his getaway from the riot after the police shooting of a protester and the shooting of a police officer in turn—flies so low over Halprin's car that one take almost resulted in an on-set crash. After he lands and they are traveling west in Halprin's car, they stop at Zabriskie Point. Halprin reads the sign for us, and though there is nothing very remarkable in her flat narration about the sublime topography, if we are listening at all we know what she is describing is a landscape of deep time and its modern exploitation. This was "an area of ancient lakebeds deposited five to ten million years ago"; after dry millennia of erosion, deposits of borax and gypsum were exposed, which is why the Pacific Borax Company was first drawn to this part of Death Valley and why, when it was turned into a National Monument in 1933, it was named in honor of the company's vice president, Christian Zabriskie. Antonioni has us spend nearly twenty minutes in this commanding world of sand formations, rock, and empty canyons. The pauses and dead spaces in the dialogue give us ample time to scan the vast horizons of the scenery, which, given what Frechette and Halprin have to work with, positively chews them; Antonioni, however, dubbed much of their performances back in the studio, so we have no choice but to hear everything that they are saying even when the film has almost made them too small to see or matter. Soon Frechette and Halprin are frolicking their way down stark hillsides and saying things like "so anyway, so anyway, 'soanyway' ought to be one word." Let's not blame that one on Sam Shephard. Frechette's character provides the marijuana, and soon enough, in an inevitability that has already been self-consciously delayed, the love scene starts. The music is Jerry Garcia, the nudity and erotic action are conventional for the period, and then suddenly Death Valley is alive with hippies having sex.

It is hard to know for sure if there is any slow motion because so much of the erotic choreography that Antonioni puts on screen is stylized and highly wrought, more like the awkward exercises from an especially randy acting class than the epic orgy that he had promised. Again, as the publicist Barbara Wexler recalled in 1992, when Antonioni first toured possible locations in Death Valley with some crew from MGM, he said, "I see ten thousand people making love across the desert."[20] He fell short by well about 9,700 but did manage to assemble three hundred bodies for what starts out as a basic sex scene and then multiplies into a revelation of human being at its most primordial, which for Antonioni in 1970 is its most carnal or, put more simply, horny. San Francisco's "Summer of Love" in 1967 was Antonioni's general inspiration, and the "Human Be-in" earlier in that same year—when more than twenty thousand crowded into Golden Gate Park for one of the iconic public spectacles of the counterculture—was his direct point of reference. Getting Jerry Garcia to contribute a solo guitar piece for the soundtrack (named "Love Scene," naturally enough) was another echo of this event, which featured a legendary performance from the Grateful Dead. He arranged for several dozen members of Joe Chaikin's Open Theater to come out to California for the filming of the scene, leading to a brief FBI investigation into possible violations of the Mann Act (for transporting women across state lines for "immoral purposes") that didn't lead to any charges—or produce the "million dollars' worth of publicity" that Wexler tells us MGM hoped it might inspire.

Other extras were recruited in Los Angeles and Las Vegas, but I think we can assume that most of the performers that we see up close in this scene—which was almost universally derided in 1970 and enshrined among the film's embarrassments—are Chaikin's actors. Too much of the posing, nude or otherwise, depends on perfectly extended lines and arching backs; too many of these bodies come together like method-acted animals in an improv game or dancers following a score (figure 26.8). It's a very tasteful orgy, which is maybe why Antonioni barely intrudes upon the erotic action with a couple touches of slow motion. Near the beginning of the interlude, a couple tumbles down a hillside like the children mimicking cops and robbers in *Bonnie and Clyde*, but it is honestly almost impossible to spot without increasing the playback speed to realize that their fall looks more natural when accelerated because it must have been filmed at 36fps. A later clutching lunge of naked dusty flesh seems also like a flash of quick slow motion, but obviously this is not where the action is for Antonioni. Since the rocky sand already there was not picturesque enough to dust up in the clouds he wanted—and was too painful for the very active, largely naked actors as they rolled around—Antonioni had truckloads of industrial sand delivered from Los Angeles at MGM's expense. In a *Sight and Sound* interview with Marsha Kinder from almost a year before the film's release, he already was anticipating a degree of failure and was hoping to salvage his orgy "in a different way—just a few people and the background almost empty."[21] This is precisely what we get in the wondrous tableau of unnatural sand and naked extras that concludes the sequence as the pot that Halprin smoked is wearing off (figure 26.9). We have perhaps too vivid evidence from this amazing photograph on set that, in the moment anyway, while Antonioni might not have had the best plan to make a thousand orgasms bloom at Zabriskie Point, he definitely was willing to get his hands or white shoes dirty for the cause (figure 26.10).

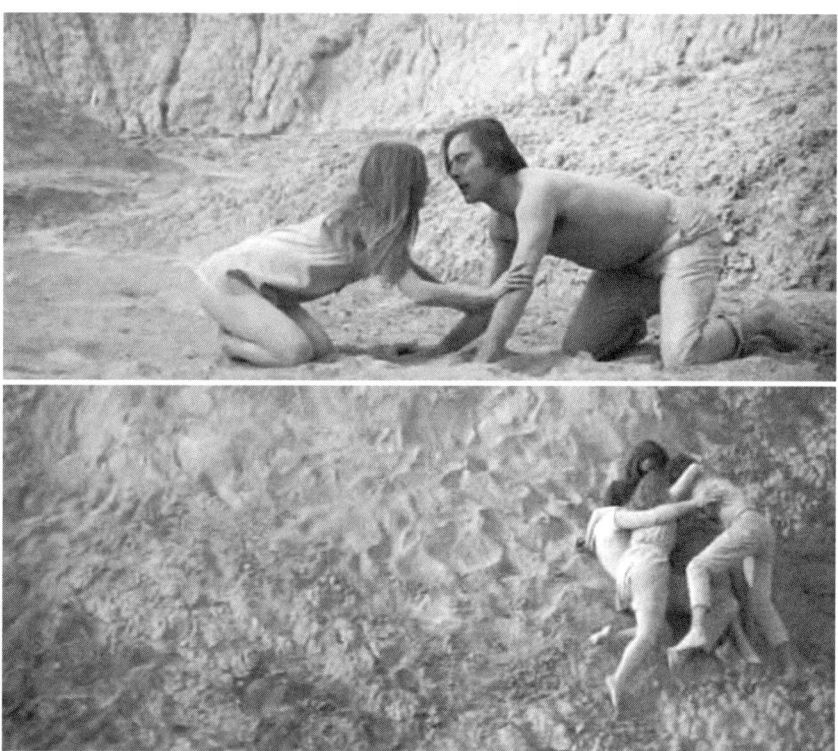

FIGURE 26.8 Stills from *Zabriskie Point* (1970).

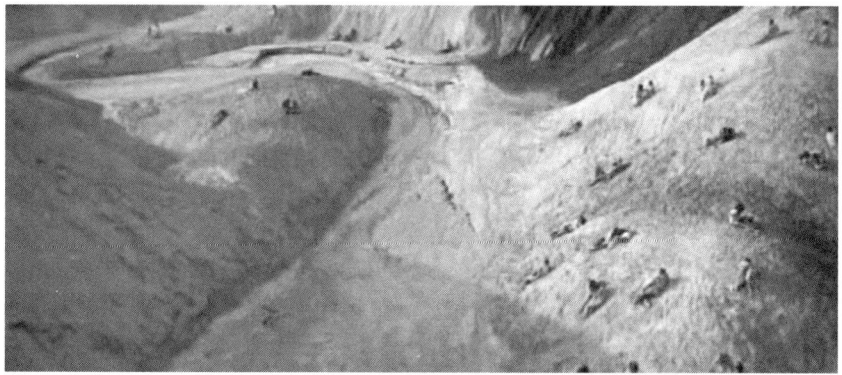

FIGURE 26.9 Still from *Zabriskie Point* (1970).

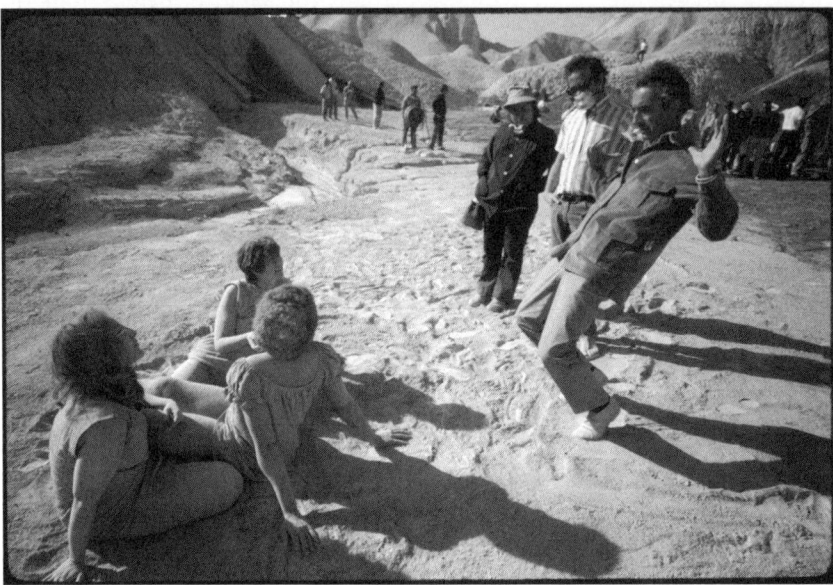

FIGURE 26.10 Antonioni showing actors what he wants on the *Zabriskie Point* set in 1969.

Source: © Bruce Davidson, "Michelangelo Antonioni on the set of *Zabriskie Point*, 1969–70." Ferrara, Achivio Michelangelo Antonioni.

This amazing Bruce Davison picture alone constitutes a critique of *Zabriskie Point* from which there is almost no recovering. Antonioni is fifty-seven here, pitched forward on his toes with his white oxfords sinking in the costly artificial sand; impassive members of the crew look idly at the spectacle of the aging auteur lording over extras probably nowhere close to half his age as he shows them how to get it on. There is no arguing that the desert orgy is anything but an embarrassment, and it helps make *Zabriskie Point* into a target broad enough to bring out Kael at her barbed best, or worst. Don't cry for Antonioni: He was still on contract to MGM and in 1972 was invited by Mao to film the documentary *Chung Kuo, China*, which was televised in a slightly abbreviated version on ABC and RAI in Italy. He never again made movies as fast as he did earlier in the 1960s, but *The Passenger* was celebrated as a return to form, and until a severe stroke in 1985, he worked for years after *Zabriskie Point* in his familiar idiom of existential dread, blank irony, and erotic tension. There isn't much of any of these on display in Antonioni's blissed-out Death Valley vision, and even with a couple flashes of slow motion it is nowhere nearly as outrageous as it would need to be to cause the scandal MGM was banking on or to break any new ground—on the real gravel or the more photogenic sand he had trucked in—for representing sexual revolution in 1970.

The valley that he imagines is uncanny, awkwardly on the way to the propaganda of Godard's Maoist spaghetti western *Wind from the East* (1970) but getting stuck in the softcore terrain of Radley Metzger's *The Lickerish Quartet* (1970) and without the slightest hope of getting near the transfixing erotic intensity of Akio Jissoji's *This Transient Life* (1970). For all its lust after scale and grandeur, the sex in *Zabriskie Point* is pretty plain apart from the glimpse of a fleeting threesome or, as we might expect from the spectacle of Antonioni on location, two women embracing. I think that there is more to see here than what Kael describes as an "inane" distraction from the film's "silly moralism," which is bad enough that she prefers Antonioni's lecturing on politics—which, to be clear, she also loathes. More than half a century later, Slavoj Žižek will still be echoing such scorn when he revisits Antonioni for a particularly tendentious sequence in his *Pervert's Guide to Ideology* where cites the "mass orgy in *Zabriskie Point*" as a "nice metaphor of what went wrong with the 1960s hippy revolution" and a symptomatic demonstration that "the authentic revolutionary energy of the sixties was already losing its strength."[22] I'm happy to stand corrected by Pauline Kael or Stanley Kaufmann, but I find Žižek's throwing more dirt on the grave of Antonioni's radicalism too much. Žižek has no patience for what, in Antonioni, amounts to little more than a fantasy of the very driest humping, now stylized into the imagery we might discover "in some publicity campaign." The problem with these complaints is that Antonioni is dreaming of a far older epoch in this admittedly ridiculous love scene.

We haven't seen much good take place in the deserts of slow motion in and around 1968. Bonnie and Clyde are not executed against a dust-bowl tableau, but the Depression-era iconography of their reunion with Bonnie's family is an arid display of a future that would almost be as barren if they lived to see it. Leone and Peckinpah set their majestic shows of violence, or the endless waiting that precedes them, in similarly stark landscapes devoid of anything that seems capable of sustaining human life. "Sad Hill Cemetery" in *The Good, the Bad, and the Ugly* is a prematurely ancient ruin in the dry Spanish mesas meant to be the U.S. southwest, and Mapache's sun-baked compound is a decadent reflection of the green oases that the Wild Bunch has encountered earlier, and we'll see nothing flow here but alcohol and blood. This is generic iconography: It is another aspect of the legacies these films are thirstily inheriting and disavowing at the same time, part of the anxieties and influences that come with the terrain of Ford and Hawks. Kubrick could well have left this world behind, but *2001* returns to the familiar landscapes of Monument Valley—shifted into the psychedelic colors of the Stargate—to render the "discovery" of intelligence beyond our own into a version of the bloated myths of progress that sprawled across the expansive Cinerama of *How the West Was Won*. And as we also saw, *2001* begins its story of human evolution with a weirdly explicit allegory of resource scarcity and escalating violence that proves how hard it was, even four million years before *Oklahoma* was on the map, for the farmer ("Moon-watcher") and the cowman ("One-ear") to be friends. I'm not suggesting that Rogers and Hammerstein figure anywhere amid the Americana that informs *Zabriskie Point*, but the desert orgy set to Garcia's gentle noodling should, I think, be taken as an answer to Kubrick's dark speculations on the primordial state of human nature in slow motion as nasty, brutish, and cruel.

Antonioni's scene of splendor in the dust, for all its gratuitous absurdity, makes for a revealing contrast despite the fact that Kubrick's hominids are both more epic and more naked. Antonioni does not frame any of his hippies as gigantic impositions on the landscape, and no one body dominates the screen; Garcia's solo playing, unlike Strauss's monumental orchestrations, isn't really going anywhere either, and while there are dozens of people getting it on with mouths and hands and hips, none of them are getting off with the highly animated passion of Moon-watcher's solo act or reveling in the violent joy he gets from, well, boning everything in sight. In *2001*, humanity is born to kill—or born by killing—and Kubrick's profound investment in slow motion is the aesthetic consecration of brutality while we must wait for superior beings with superior technology to let us take the great leap forward. In the meantime, every tool that human beings have invented—from a piece of bone to the HAL 9000—is just another weapon. Antonioni's slow motion, in this scene at least, is subtle and strangely naturalistic. Instead of Kubrick's ominous detachment and breathtaking jump cut to the stars, everything about Antonioni's fantasy of erotic humanism is deliriously earthbound. The fine sand that he imported from LA accomplishes the sense of camouflage that he was after as it physically connects the skin and hair of all his actors to the environment around them, absorbing them back into the landscape while they try their hardest—maybe too hard—to merge into each other. "The sequence closes with the whole screen going sand-colored," writes William Arrowsmith, "a single matte sheet of continuous, unindividuated being."[23]

In isolation, I might not be so enamored of this "desert vision of pure Eros," as Arrowsmith describes it, which certainly did not seduce any of the critics who sneered and snickered at it in 1970. But this is some of the only slow motion in the period, however minimal, that ends with no one getting killed. It doesn't fixate on or fetishize the single body of a star since neither Halprin nor Frechette could come close to being one on screen, but here their dullness works more democratically than in their scenes of dialogue. They are just two more pretty kids like all the others who have been manifested out of dry air, and the sexual abundance that they enjoy is less laborious and transactional than what a film like *How Sweet It Is!* tries to manufacture in slow motion around the image of Debbie Reynolds or the charmless voyeurism of *Goodbye, Columbus* and the use to which it puts Allie McGraw. Antonioni wants to give us a glimpse of heaven on and in the earth, a "realm of freedom" in the flesh, to borrow from Marx, a presiding spirit in *Zabriskie Point* no matter how aggressively juvenile we might find its translation to the screen.[24] Or, in the spirit of another set of influences and ideas that Antonioni was maybe tracking all the way out to Death Valley, this scene is trying to prove the famous Situationist cry against modernity itself in 1968. If there is truly "beach" under the paving stones—"Sous les paves, la plage"—we shouldn't be embarrassed to play around in the sand. There might be a better version of humanity in this deep-time desert of the real than the alternatives we are left with in *2001* and its history of slow and epic violence salvaged finally by a giant, floating fetus that isn't yet and might not ever be a body. At the geological low point of North America, nearly three hundred feet below sea level and in one of the planet's most arid ecologies, Antonioni finds the opposite of an Eliotic "waste land." "Here is no water but only rock," or so it seems, for as far as the eye can see, just "rock and no water and the sandy road." If this is what the twentieth century has left us, why not make the best of it and fuck around a little? It is here, like the landscape of pleasure T. J. Clark describes in a brilliant reading of Cezanne's *Bathers*, where bodies can "appear as they would in a world where . . . 'imagination,' 'mind,' 'body,' 'phantasy,' and so on would be grasped by the bodies and imaginations themselves. Then the world would be truly remade in representation."[25] This isn't quite "The Dawn of Man" or even everybody's idea of heaven on earth. It might just be a bunch of kids screwing around in the dust, but at least no one has to die—in slow motion or otherwise.

SLOW MOTION TERMINABLE AND INTERMINABLE

As seriously as I'm willing to take *Zabriskie Point*, and as much as I've come to think that we can't understand slow motion as the most special effect of 1968 without it, there are limits to its escapist violence and earthy utopianism. If revolution is one horizon for Adorno's fascination with explosions—or let's call it salvation since he is contending with the ghost of Benjamin's messianic turn throughout *Aesthetic Theory*—the other is apocalypse. The logic of *Zabriskie*

Point, with its giddy embrace of youth culture in excesses, runs counter to Adorno's pessimistic image of explosions as the "scars" of modern authenticity and even more to his darker sense that human progress has gone at too high speed "from the slingshot to the megaton bomb." Kubrick's ice-cold ironies and stately formalism are a better match in terms of tone, though it is hard to imagine the actual Adorno liking Kubrick's movies any better. When Kubrick cuts to a shot of an explosion at the end of *Dr. Strangelove*—the first of eighteen mushroom clouds that signify the end of life on Earth over the next minute or so of sublime montage—Vera Lynn's "We'll Meet Again" swells onto the soundtrack, a music-hall hit of the late 1930s that was a British standard during World War II. The song is used here with unsubtle irony because, unless there are some survivors in the fallout shelters, we won't be meeting anyone again ever. Kubrick had planned a pie fight for his conclusion but decided this was too much farce for his bleak comedy, and so he assembled the ending that we know today from footage of various nuclear bomb tests of the late 1940s and 1950s (Operation Crossroads, Operation Ivy, Operation Redwing, Operation Sandstone, and more). In the laboratory and at domestic test sites, Doc Edgerton made numerous photographs and films for the U.S. Atomic Energy Commission that captured the infinitesimally fast microseconds of atomic fusion with startling precision using his Rapatronic camera at exposure times as short as 10 nanoseconds. But in much of this iconography, the explosions have been slowed down past the point of recognition, as we can see in a representative 1952 Edgerton photograph from the Tumbler-Snapper test series (figure 26.11); the bomb platform and towers are still visible in the background, and the ground beneath the blast looks like a spotlit stage. The explosion itself, however, is weirdly embryonic. It is pocked with cavities and bulges with translucent bands and protruding spikes from the "rope-trick effect" that lend it the shape of a strange jellyfish or an amoeba with an udder. Bob Miekle, in a phrase that also speaks to Kubrick's hard-on for sublime destruction, describes these atomic ejaculations as "the expensive money shot[s] of this nuclear technoporn."[26]

Edgerton's bizarre and biomorphic images would have been useless to Kubrick, though, because he needed the end of the world in *Dr. Strangelove*, no matter what speed it was going, to look exactly like what his viewers would have expected in the sixties. I guess we can be glad that Kubrick had all this footage at his disposal so he didn't have to recreate atomic fusion in a studio at Shepperton. (For all of Christopher Nolan's fetish for practical effects, I'm glad he didn't go nuclear for *Oppenheimer*.) And while I can't say for sure that Antonioni saw *Dr. Strangelove* or *2001*, the fact that his most spectacular set pieces in *Zabriskie Point* play with variations on how Kubrick begins humanity and ends it, in two

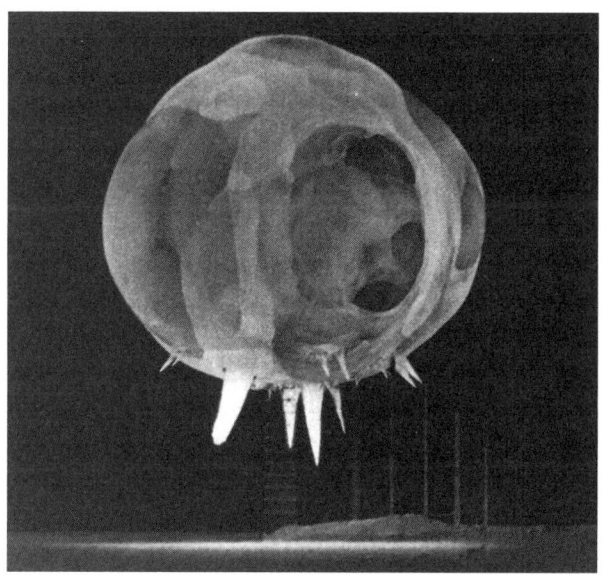

FIGURE 26.11 Harold "Doc" Edgerton, atomic explosion (1952).

of the most celebrated films from the years that Antonioni spent wandering in the desert for MGM, convince me that he was trying to find another way to use slow motion for another kind of fantasy—one not so much about apocalypse or origins but about the simpler pleasures of destroying the modern world that has happened to us in between.

I don't want to suggest that *Zabriskie Point* was altogether revolutionary or to forgive its many faults for what it gives us in slow motion. But because it took so long to finish and Antonioni tried to do so much with all the money Hollywood had given him, it remains an appropriately excessive symbol of where the energies of its moment—both before and after 1968—would go. In lusting after a "flash finish" for the sixties as an epoch, Antonioni had accidentally helped codify a cinematic language of spectacular and tamed "attractions," in Tom Gunning's still influential sense, that is now a formulaic feature of more global visual culture, from action films to YouTube channels, than anyone could ever watch.[27] Believe me, I've tried. Nor does it feel right to ignore how *Zabriskie Point* anticipates, far beyond the matter of its influence, one of the defining features of contemporary moving-image culture despite its legendary and entertaining box-office crash and burn in 1970. It will survive as long as movies do as the only film by a high modernist auteur to appear occasionally on lists of "The

15 Best Explosions in Movie History" or "The Most Impressive Real Stuff Blown Up in the Name of Blockbuster Movie-Making."[28] The Slow Mo Guys have more than fourteen million subscribers on YouTube, and there can't be many besides me who have found them thanks to Antonioni. Among their online oeuvre are thirty-one videos focusing on explosions, from such rudimentary stunts as "Melon Fragmentation at 2500 FPS" to more accomplished feats like "Blowing Up Capacitors at 187,000 FPS" and "Catching an Explosion in Water at 5 Million FPS," a fairly recent masterpiece that improbably enough has Gav and Dan getting within a couple orders of magnitude of the speeds we saw with Edgerton's Rapatronic camera. They weren't using consumer-grade electronics for this one—Google and Amazon sent them to the Colorado School of Mines, where they had access to a Shimadzu Hyper Vision HPV-X2—and like the majority of their videos, the exuberance of their technophilia is the aesthetic predicate of the plain joy they take in watching things explode. Something like this frame of "Exploding Fruit in 4K," from a video in 2018, only required the Slow Mo Guys to shoot at 100,000fps and is definitely not paying tribute to *Zabriskie Point* in any way that Gav and Dan would recognize (figure 26.12).[29] Still, we can see some fragments here of what Antonioni hoped to show us: a world exploding into a different form and a temporality that will probably come to nothing more than particularly "exciting fruit salad," as Dan promises, as we waste precious seconds online, or that could be the first sign of the fireworks to come when, if we have long enough, our time will finally be our own again.

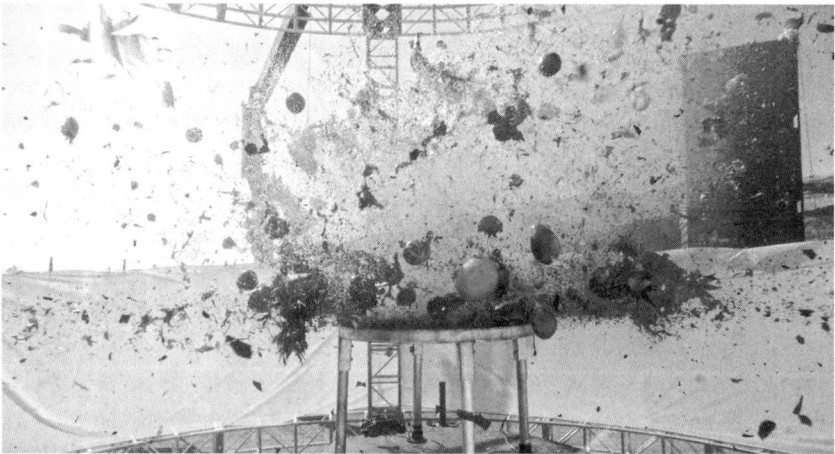

FIGURE 26.12 The Slo Mo Guys accidentally remake *Zabriskie Point* in a still from "Exploding Fruit in 4K" (2018).

I have been excavating the blast zone of *Zabriskie Point* from Kubrick to the Slow Mo Guys because it lets us trace one especially bright arc from the ruins of Antonioni in 1968 to a present in which its aftershocks are resonant even if the politics that made them matter are more obscure. Most slow motion after 1968—like most slow motion before—does not show us a better world or a worse one, just our own at speeds that are made possible by the technologies we have shaped to let us see it as it exists but goes too fast for us to otherwise appreciate. Slow motion is the most popular and, from the perspective of twenty-first-century digital media, the most primitive artifact of the modern world that still reveals, in the pointed language used by Wolfgang Ernst, "the epistemological gap between the phenomenological and the techno-mathematical conception of time." Ernst's media theory is not an easy fit with Antonioni's far more romantic Marxism, and it is not clear if there is any chance for revolution—or even a break—in the "micro-archival bubble" of a present that, as Ernst writes without much sympathy for those who might want to resist such acceleration, "no longer has time to take place." But my point is not that media archaeology can salvage *Zabriskie Point* from the ash heap of film criticism or that its entirely gratuitous slow motion is worth revisiting only because it anticipates the increasing speeds of a contemporary visual culture where "technologically-embedded algorithmic computing" has become so easy to master that almost anybody with an iPhone can be their own Antonioni or a Slo Mo Guy.[30] Antonioni is committed to the most fantastically "exploded view" of modern life he can imagine as the sixties close. Since the 1940s, which is of course the start of the Atomic Age, this is what we have come to call a genre engineering diagram: something that shows the dissembled components of a machine floating and arrested in space, as we see here in a fantastic Todd McLellan depiction of mechanical clock from 2013 (figure 26.13). Leonardo da Vinci was using this style of illustration in the Renaissance, and there were obviously complex technologies whose inner workings we needed help to visualize long before slow motion was invented. But it is precisely such an exploded view of late modernity that Antonioni wants to render for us in the last minutes of *Zabriskie Point*. What slow motion gives us is the time it takes to appreciate the complexity and sheer extent of the machines and systems and economies that have captured us. And maybe, if we watch closely enough, a sense of how to take them apart once and for all.

■ ■ ■

I am willing to concede that Antonioni makes this looks pretty easy in slow motion. But we shouldn't have to give up altogether on the pleasures that slow

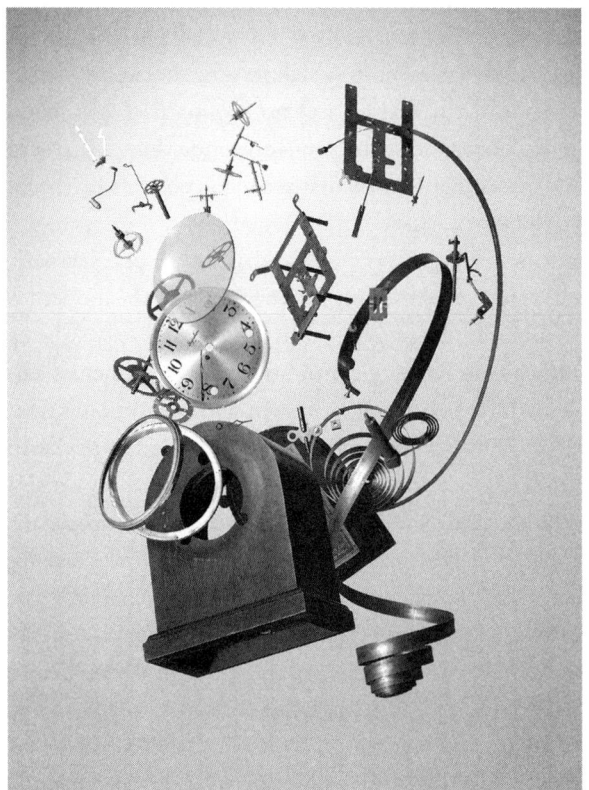

FIGURE 26.13 An especially beautiful "exploded view" of clock-time itself.

Source: © Todd McClellan, "Apart Wind-Up Clock," 2013.

motion offers, from Edison and Epstein to the Wachowskis, Michael Bay, and YouTube, just because there is so much of it that its effects might not feel as special as they did a century before, or even in and around 1968. It can still be beautiful and shocking even though, technically speaking, we have seen it all before. This is very much the case for one last film full of explosions that also takes us back to the twentieth century's most fateful ground zero in ways that neither *Zabriskie Point* nor *Dr. Strangelove* can quite imagine no matter how hard or fast or slow they try. Bruce Conner's 1975 film *Crossroads* literally begins where Kubrick's caustic nuclear fantasia ends: Assembled from footage shot in July 1946 as part of Operation Crossroads, some of the very same shots of nuclear annihilation that end the world as a dark joke in *Dr. Strangelove* are here the main attraction. This series of weapons tests at Bikini Atoll marked the first detonations of atomic warheads since the destruction of Nagasaki, and they were widely publicized by the large press contingent invited to the site. On July 1, a bomb named for Rita Hayworth's "Gilda"—her film noir of the same name was playing in theaters at the time—was dropped from a B-29 onto a target area full of empty ships, only a few of which sank, according to disappointed officials and reporters; more than 3,500 animals (goats, mice, guinea pigs, and rats) were penned or caged on the ships to measure the survivability of the blast, but only 25 percent died from the explosion or from radiation. This also was apparently a disappointment. And then, on July 25, another twenty-three-kiloton bomb, "Helen of Bikini," was detonated underwater, sinking ten ships immediately, leaving several more too irradiated for salvage, and killing who knows how much wildlife in the coral lagoon and surrounding area. A third test had to be canceled because of the intensity of radioactive contamination at the site and on surviving ships that were to be reused. A later chairman of the Atomic Energy Commission called this abandoned test "the world's first nuclear disaster," which is a decidedly Strangelovian turn of phrase that takes for granted that Hiroshima and Nagasaki were not.

The U.S. Navy required so much film stock for their exhaustive documentation of the blasts that global supplies ran short for the rest of 1946. According to Jonathan Weisgall's detailed reconstruction of the event, "nearly half" of the world's film was shipped out to Bikini Atoll, where it was loaded into more than seven hundred cameras.[31] There were eight cameras mounted on remote-controlled B17s that were set to fly too close to the blast zone for human pilots, and some planes operating at safer distances carried as many as twenty-eight still and motion picture cameras. Cameras placed on test ships were not expected to survive, but it was hoped that photographs and footage of the blasts from closer range would later be retrieved and studied. The Army Air Force planned to take 9 million photographs during Operation Crossroads and calculated that the filming of the first four seconds of the initial detonation consumed as much stock as four Hollywood features, or, put differently, four complete *Gilda*'s worth of film for four seconds of their "Gilda" in the flesh and on location. The world's largest still camera was stationed on a Navy ship at a range where its forty-eight-inch telephoto lens—which could capture the hands of a watch at a quarter-mile—would be able to get readings from instruments on board target ships at the exact ten-thousandth of a second of the blast. All these astounding data points—which I've collected from accounts of Operation Crossroads by Weisgall, Miekle, and Tung-Hui Hu—don't add up to as much, for my purposes at least, as the sixty high-speed movie cameras brought to the site, some capable of filming at 8,000fps while others, that were strictly speaking "slower," were still able to shoot at the tremendously fast frame rates of 3,500fps. By the time the cameras stopped rolling on Operation Crossroads, the United States had 1.5 million feet of film to screen and study, which translates to around 150 or 200 feature-length productions. These explosions, then, were not just "the most photographed moment" in human history to date but also represent the greatest single spectacle of slow motion that has survived the twentieth century. It is also, of course, a monument to why we almost didn't.

Crossroads takes the cheeky nihilism of *Dr. Strangelove* and returns the iconography of nuclear Armageddon to the realm of the sublime. Where Kubrick gives us a montage or, maybe better, a "supercut" of explosions that are noticeably distinct from one another, Conner asks us to confront the singular event of the "Baker" test at Bikini Atoll on July 25, 1946, in a sequence of footage assembled and reedited but, as J. Hoberman reminds us, "in no way manipulated" otherwise.[32] Hoberman points out that *Crossroads* also is a work of montage, consisting of twenty-four shots of varying lengths; the shortest are just under a minute, and the longest is a final shot of over six and a half minutes that shows, in slow motion, a lone destroyer in the test zone as it is first dwarfed against the gigantic plume of water and superheated vapor from the detonation and then, after the last cut in *Crossroads* brings us closer, gradually consumed by the advancing clouds, disappearing entirely, and then improbably emerging as a shadowy, low-contrast ghost of itself in the haze of radioactive fog as the film ends (figure 26.14). We probably wouldn't need Hoberman to tell us that *Crossroads* aspires to the sublime, but his insistence on this is clarifying. He describes *Crossroads* as an "instance of twentieth-century religious art" that is both "exemplary" and "rare," a "visual mantra" of the "nuclear sublime," a phrase he takes from Frances Ferguson's writing in the early eighties on Jonathan Schell's *The Fate of the Earth*, an especially pious work of apocalyptic worrying from the early Reagan years when all manner of Strangelovian doomsday scenarios felt depressingly plausible.[33] While I have never revisited the middle-school trauma of watching *The Day After* and never plan to, I also realize that I am probably on the very generational edge of seeing in *Crossroads* what Hoberman looks to Ferguson to help us recognize in Conner's masterful reflection on the aesthetics of explosions. This is a graceful and horribly composed apocalypse, a mutating shape of folds and billows that at some level we appreciate as monstrously technological but also experience as a formal process of expanded temporality that, at 8000fps, translates destruction at the speed of light into a show of twentieth-century human ingenuity at its most terminally inhuman. It was over in four seconds almost eighty years ago. It takes us thirty-seven minutes to watch it happen again in *Crossroads*. It is still happening at Bikini Atoll and will be long into the future. All these speeds and more are captured in slow motion.

ANTONIONI'S ART OF EXCESS   341

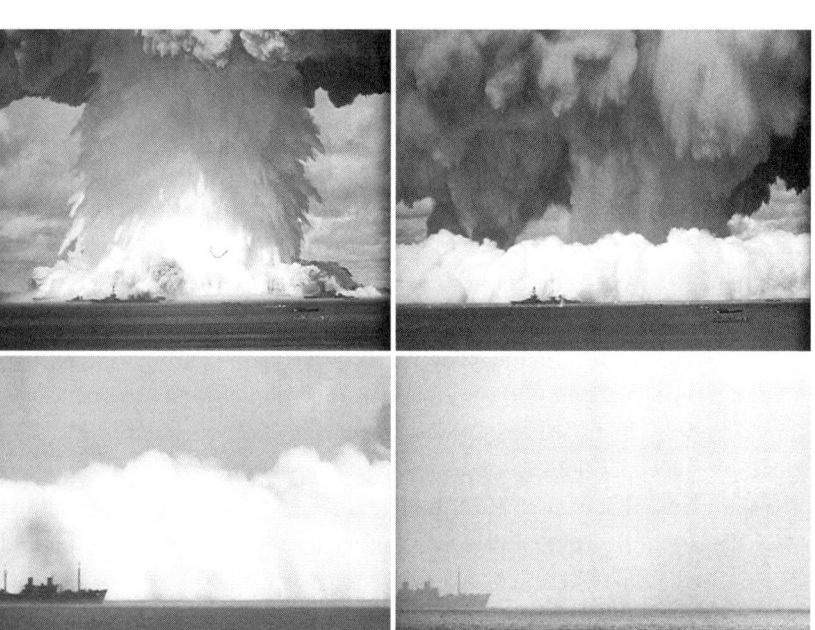

FIGURE 26.14   Stills from *Crossroads* (1975).

About a year after Operation Crossroads, the *Bulletin of Atomic Scientists* published its first "Doomsday Clock," and since 1947 we have never had more than seventeen minutes left until some awful midnight that will strike after years or centuries of recklessness and ruin. This clock is more a symbol than a timepiece. Its minute hand advances or, occasionally remains stopped or even inches backward, only when the *Bulletin* issues a yearly press release announcing that the catastrophe we always know is coming is speeding up or slowing down. Since 1991, climate change has been the main accelerant of this awful future, which has required the *Bulletin* to reconceptualize its sense of temporality—and figuratively reset its watches—for the technological devastation of the world not in the flash of nuclear holocaust but from the "slow violence" of accumulated moments of incremental damage in the name of profit that, when played back at the speed of geologic time, will have lasted only for a fleeting second. This is not a fun way to tell the time or the most helpful, since it can be paralyzing, precisely when we most need to get a move on, to understand the present as an instant that has already passed and guaranteed the suffering of future ancestors whom we will never know. In this worst possible example of slow motion, no matter how long we might wait, all there is to do is watch the course of some history set for us in the twentieth century, or even earlier, proceed exactly as we can see that it must go and precisely on the familiar arc that it has been tracing for as long as we've been watching.

It might be too late then, on every clock that matters, to remember that while *Zabriskie Point* is arguably an awful movie, it isn't a despairing one. After the fireworks, we cut back to Halprin as she drives off into a western sunset that is altogether a cliché—like slow motion was becoming thanks to Antonioni—but also more drop-dead gorgeous than any frame in *Bonnie and Clyde*, *2001*, *Once Upon a Time in the West*, or *The Wild Bunch*, each better films and masterpieces, but not so willing to embarrass themselves for wanting to show a world on the other side of 1968 and what it could still become. We see this best, I would suggest, not in the slightly goofy look on Halprin's face when the explosions stop but in the sheer deliriousness and absurd splendors of slow motion as it describes the apocalypse that comes before it. Here we might see, as Virginia Woolf wrote near the beginning of the twentieth century that Antonioni hoped was ending prematurely because it had lasted long enough already, "the terror, the exultation" of what she called "The Moment," back when the experience of modernity brought with it "the power to rush out unnoticed, alone; to be consumed, to be swept away ... to feel the glory run molten up the spine, down the limbs, making the eyes glow, burning, bright, and penetrate the buffeting waves of the wind." Or put differently, we have been at this crossroads and will be for the duration. The point is not to speed past a present that feels already doomed for all the violence it will bear into the future. It has always been the end, happening to us in slow motion in an epoch of technology that has gone in one direction, "from the slingshot to the megaton bomb" and maybe worse to come. It is the end, and will be forever, which we should hope is enough time to put things right. As fast as we can, and as slow as we must.

Acknowledgments

Books should never merely mark time, but they cannot always help the ways they keep it. This one more than most. The past few years have felt especially eventful to all of us for reasons I do not need to detail. I am definitely not the only critic or writer who has wondered if we'll ever get back to something like the "before times," or whether this phrase and fantasy is just a means of registering how quickly and how slowly things can change. I think we all have learned how hard it is to make up for lost momentum but also can now appreciate more fully that we do not always need to rush so much in the first place. I may never know if this book came out at the right time. What I do know, however, is that some thanks are overdue. I am grateful to colleagues in the English department and beyond at the University of California, Berkeley, for their intellectual generosity and encouragement through the years. Elizabeth Abel, Josh Gang, Dorothy Hale, Donna Jones, Jeffrey Knapp, Colleen Lye, Tom McEnaney, and Samuel Otter have done so much to keep me going. The support of chairs Genaro Padilla, Steven Justice, and Eric Falci was both spirited and timely. Kent Puckett, Scott Saul, and Bryan Wagner have been terrific readers, and in making this book better they have shown Berkeley at its best. I am singularly indebted to Kevis Goodman, not only for her friendship but for serving as a guide into New Hollywood and the underworld Sam Peckinpah embraced. *Straw Dogs* will always be the hardest watch, but at least now I know where to look. Tim Hampton and Damon Young asked the right questions at the right time while I was a Fellow at Berkeley's Townsend Center for the Humanities.

Philip Leventhal has been part of this project from the beginning. His advice, enthusiasm, and belief have been sustaining. He is a patient and discerning editor, and I very much appreciate his faith in what academics do. Emily Simon, Michael Haskell, Elliott Cairns, and Julia Kushnirsky continue to make everything about working with Columbia University Press a pleasure. Without the copy editing of Robert Fellman and the indexing of Sarah Osment this book would be far less readable and useful. I am grateful for their careful labors.

Readers for the Press offered sharp and substantive responses to the manuscript and did so much to help it find its final shape. J. D. Connor and Justus Nieland have been teaching me about media and the modern world with their own books for years, and I can only hope that their advice at a critical stage in this project's development has brought it closer to their examples.

Audiences at Columbia University, the University of Illinois–Chicago, Yale University, Princeton University, Vanderbilt University, the University of Michigan, Pomona College, the University of Louisville, the University of Notre Dame, the University of North Carolina, Michigan State University, the University of California–Santa Barbara, the University of California–Los Angeles, the Freie Universität Berlin, the University of Oslo, and the National Humanities Center heard earlier versions of this project. It would not have become this book without the attention, care, and good advice I received along the way. I am particularly grateful to friends and colleagues who have extended so much generosity to me over the years and given me a chance to share work, meet deadlines, and figure out the book I was really writing: Sara Blair, Leslie Bow, Stuart Burrows, Russ Castronovo, Jerry Christensen, Florence Dore, Jen Fay, Jonathan Freedman, Andy Hoberek, Aaron Jaffe, Joseph Jeon, Martin Lüthe, Kate Marshall, Mark McGurl, Walter Benn Michaels, Eivind Røssak, Christian Refsum, Mark Seltzer, Scott Selisker, Alexander Starre, and R. John Williams. Laura McGrath and Dan Sinykin pointed me in the right direction when I went looking for some slow motion that I wouldn't have found otherwise. I am thankful for conversations I had with Arden Reed and Mark Wollaeger, both of whom are missed. Carl Smith has been the best teacher, mentor, and model for everything that we should try to be as scholars. Peter Coviello, Chris Spilker, and Samuel Zipp are in it for the long run. Their friendship means more to me than I have ever told them and has kept time flying for years that we can count in decades now. But let's not.

I learned to think better, bigger, and more variously thanks to my time on the "Motherboard" of ASAP: The Association for the Study of the Arts of the Present. Invitations from the English Institute and Post45 gave me the opportunity to present material from this book to the most demanding and inspiring audiences. Leslie Bow, Russ Castronovo, Christina Lupton, Joshua Miller, R. John Williams, and Cindy Weinstein were terrific editors of pieces that let me work through earlier versions of material on Faulkner, DeLillo, and Leone that appear in parts 2 and 3 ("Faulkner at the Speed of History," in *The Oxford Handbook of Twentieth-Century American Literature*, ed. Leslie Bow and Russ Castronovo [Oxford University Press, 2022]; "How the West Slows Down," *ELH* 85, no. 2 [Summer 2018]; "DeLillo, Slowing Down," in *A Question of Time: American Literature from Colonial Encounter to Contemporary Fiction*, ed. Cindy Weinstein [Cambridge University Press, 2018]). Material from another essay ("Weird Times," in *The Cambridge Companion to Twenty-First-Century American Fiction*, ed. Joshua Miller [Cambridge University Press, 2021]) had to be left on the cutting room floor that is my hard drive, but I know that some of ideas have found a second home here. My thanks to *ELH*, Oxford University Press, and Cambridge University Press for their permission to include these materials.

I am grateful to the Andrew W. Mellon Foundation, the Division of Arts and Humanities at the University of California, Berkeley; the Office of the Vice Chancellor for Research at the University of California, Berkeley; the Townsend Center for the Humanities at the University of California, Berkeley; and the Global Urban Humanities Initiative at the University of California, Berkeley. This book would not exist without the time to write and the subventions for the reproduction of images that these programs and institutions have provided.

I lost both my parents over the years when I was finishing this book. Ben and Cary Goble lived long lives, hard and well. Their memories are a blessing. Every second matters because of Elisa Tamarkin and Edith Tamarkin Goble. It is all for them.

Notes

INTRODUCTION: SLOW MOTION, VERY QUICKLY

1. Cynthia Ozick, *The Messiah of Stockholm* (Knopf Doubleday, 1988), 68.
2. Ozick, *The Messiah of Stockholm*, 6.
3. Ozick, *The Messiah of Stockholm*, 8.
4. Kim Stanley Robinson, *The Ministry for the Future* (Little, Brown, 2020), 471, 417–18.
5. Karl Marx, *Grundrisse: Foundations of the Critique of Political Economy* (Penguin UK, 2005); David Harvey, *The Condition of Postmodernity: An Enquiry Into the Origins of Cultural Change* (Wiley, 1992).
6. Robinson, *The Ministry for the Future*, 419.
7. Susan Sontag, *Against Interpretation and Other Essays* (Eyre & Spottiswoode, 1967), 12, 14.
8. William Faulkner, *Light in August* (Vintage, 1990), 210. I have discussed slow motion in *Light in August* in Mark Goble, "Faulkner at the Speed of History," in *The Oxford Handbook of Twentieth-Century American Literature*, ed. Leslie Bow and Russ Castronovo (Oxford University Press, 2022).
9. "Opening a Condom in a Wind Tunnel," January 30, 2019, by the Slo Mo Guys, YouTube, 12:09, https://www.youtube.com/watch?v=LovoT3eXI2k; "Diving Into 1000 Mousetraps in 4K Slow Motion" May 10, 2017, by the Slo Mo Guys, YouTube, 6:20, https://www.youtube.com/watch?v=ewGAmiLuYCw. The Slow Mo Guys' mousetrap video was shot on a Phantom Flex 4, which sell used for $75,000–120,000 in 2024, which would buy a lot of iPhones with relatively primitive slow motion capabilities but also represents about .00045 percent of the budget for 2023's *The Marvels*.
10. Shane Denson, *Discorrelated Images* (Duke University Press, 2020), 22, 2.
11. Friedrich Kittler, "Real Time Analysis, Time Axis Manipulation," trans. Geoffrey Winthrop-Young, *Cultural Politics* 13, no. 1 (March 2017): 1–18; Friedrich A. Kittler, *Gramophone, Film, Typewriter*, trans. Geoffrey Winthrop-Young and Michael Wutz (Stanford University Press, 1999), 11. I'm indebted to Denson's sharp articulation of Kittler and Ernst in the context of postcinema for aiding the direction of my arguments throughout.
12. Peter Sellars, in *Bill Viola: The Passions*, by Bill Viola et al. (J. Paul Getty Museum, 2003), 165.
13. Roland Barthes, "Textual Analysis of a Tale by Edgar Poe," trans. Donald G. Marshall, *Poe Studies (1971–1985)* 10, no. 1 (1977): 3. My special thanks to Kent Puckett for bringing this essay to my attention.

14. Malcolm Jones, "Slow Reading: An Antidote for Fast World?," *Newsweek*, June 22, 2010, https://www.newsweek.com/slow-reading-antidote-fast-world-73395; Patrick Kingsley, "The Art of Slow Reading," *The Guardian*, July 15, 2010, https://www.theguardian.com/books/2010/jul/15/slow-reading; D. Mikics, *Slow Reading in a Hurried Age* (Harvard University Press, 2013).
15. Lutz Koepnick, *The Long Take: Art Cinema and the Wondrous* (University of Minnesota Press, 2017), 4.
16. Barthes, "Textual Analysis of a Tale by Edgar Poe," 3, 10.
17. Denise Riley, *Time Lived, Without Its Flow* (Pan Macmillan UK, 2019), 9, 24, 67, 75.
18. Koepnick, *The Long Take*, 189.
19. Kristen Ross, *Fast Cars, Clean Bodies: Decolonization and the Reordering of French Culture* (MIT Press, 1996), 4.
20. For some of the broadest articulations of these arguments, see Kohei Saito, *Marx in the Anthropocene: Towards the Idea of Degrowth Communism* (Cambridge University Press, 2023); Kohei Saito, *Slow Down: The Degrowth Manifesto*, trans. Brian Bergstrom (Astra, 2024).
21. Enda Duffy, *The Speed Handbook: Velocity, Pleasure, Modernism* (Duke University Press, 2009); David Harvey, *A Companion to Marx's* Capital: *The Complete Edition* (Verso, 2018).
22. Hartmut Rosa, *Social Acceleration: A New Theory of Modernity*, trans. Jonathan Trejo-Mathys, New Directions in Critical Theory (Columbia University Press, 2013), 15, 45, 10.
23. Andreas Malm, *Fossil Capital: The Rise of Steam Power and the Roots of Global Warming* (Verso, 2016), 8.
24. Rob Nixon, *Slow Violence and the Environmentalism of the Poor* (Harvard University Press, 2011).
25. Jonathan Sachs, "Eighteenth-Century Slow Time: Seven Propositions," *Eighteenth Century* 60, no. 2 (Summer 2019): 185–205.
26. Jean Louis Schefer, *The Ordinary Man of Cinema*, trans. Max Cavitch, Noura Wedell, and Paul Grant (MIT Press, 2016), 178.
27. Laura Mulvey, *Death 24x a Second: Stillness and the Moving Image* (Reaktion, 2006), 150.
28. Mulvey, *Death 24x a Second*, 67.
29. Alix Beeston, *In and Out of Sight: Modernist Writing and the Photographic Unseen* (Oxford University Press, 2018); Stuart Burrows, *A Familiar Strangeness: American Fiction and the Language of Photography, 1839–1945* (University of Georgia Press, 2010); Louise Hornby, *Still Modernism: Photography, Literature, Film* (Oxford University Press, 2017).
30. Jordan Schonig, *The Shape of Motion: Cinema and the Aesthetics of Movement* (Oxford University Press, 2022), 11.
31. Mulvey, *Death 24x a Second*, 70, 79.

1. AT THE MOVIES TO THE END OF TIME

1. Robert Smithson, "A Cinematic Atopia," in *The Collected Writings*, ed. Jack Flam (University of California Press, 1996), 138. Subsequent citations internal, abbreviated as necessary.
2. I take this from Smithson, "Entropy and the New Monuments," in *The Collected Writings*, ed. Flam, 11, 139.
3. All citations from Smithson, "A Cinematic Atopia," in *The Collected Writings*, ed. Flam, 138.
4. Michael Ned Holte, "Shooting the Archaeozoic (on Robert Smithson)," *Michael Ned Holte* (blog), http://michaelnedholte.com/2005/01/shooting-the-archaeozoic-on-robert-smithson/.
5. Annette Michelson, "Forward in Three Letters," in Peter Gidal, "FOREWORD IN THREE LETTERS," *Artforum* 10, no. 1 (September 1971): 8–8.
6. John Roberts, *Revolutionary Time and the Avant-Garde* (Verso, 2015), 123.

7. Miriam Bratu Hansen, "The Mass Production of the Senses: Classical Cinema as Vernacular Modernism," in *Disciplining Modernism*, ed. Pamela L. Caughie (London: Palgrave Macmillan UK, 2009), 242.
8. Smithson, "Entropy and the New Monuments," in *The Collected Writings*, ed. Flam, 11.
9. Smithson, "Illustrations of catastrophe and remote times," 1966, Robert Smithson and Nancy Holt Papers, Archives of American Art, Smithsonian Institution, Box 4, folder 28.
10. Stephen Kern, *The Culture of Time and Space, 1880–1918* (Harvard University Press, 1983), 29.
11. Leo Charney and Vanessa R. Schwartz, eds., *Cinema and the Invention of Modern Life* (University of California Press, 1995).
12. Susan McCabe, *Cinematic Modernism: Modernist Poetry and Film* (Cambridge University Press, 2005), 5. See also Sara Danius, *The Senses of Modernism: Technology, Perception, and Aesthetics* (Cornell University Press, 2002).
13. Hansen, "The Mass Production of the Senses."
14. Hansen, "America, Paris, the Alps: Kracauer (and Benjamin) on Cinema and Modernity," in *Cinema and the Invention of Modern Life*, ed. Charney and Schwartz.
15. Mary Ann Doane, *The Emergence of Cinematic Time: Modernity, Contingency, the Archive* (Harvard University Press, 2002), 11.
16. André Bazin et al., *What Is Cinema?*, vol. 1 (University of California Press, 2005).
17. Wolfgang Ernst, *Chronopoetics: The Temporal Being and Operativity of Technological Media*, trans. Anthony Enns (Rowman & Littlefield International, 2016), 9–11.
18. Jonathan Sterne, *MP3: The Meaning of a Format* (Duke University Press, 2012).
19. Martin Heidegger, *The Question Concerning Technology, and Other Essays* (HarperCollins, 1982).
20. Gary Shapiro, *Earthwards: Robert Smithson and Art After Babel* (University of California Press, 1997); Pam M. Lee, *Chronophobia: On Time in the Art of the 1960s* (MIT Press, 2004).
21. Blaise Cendrars, *Modernities and Other Writings*, trans. Monique Chefdor (University of Nebraska Press, 1992), 50, 53.
22. George Kubler, *The Shape of Time: Remarks on the History of Things* (Yale University Press, 1962), 87–88, 69.
24. Donald Davidson, *Inquiries Into Truth and Interpretation* (Oxford University Press, 2001); Susan S. Friedman, *Planetary Modernisms: Provocations on Modernity Across Time* (Columbia University Press, 2015); Johannes Fabian, *Time and the Other* (Columbia University Press, 2014).
25. Lutz Koepnick, *On Slowness: Toward an Aesthetic of the Contemporary* (Columbia University Press, 2014).
26. Walter Benjamin, *The Writer of Modern Life: Essays on Charles Baudelaire*, ed. Michael William Jennings (Harvard University Press, 2006), 146.
27. Erin Hogan, *Spiral Jetta: A Road Trip Through the Land Art of the American West* (University of Chicago Press, 2008); Elaine Jarvik, "At 50, the Spiral Jetty, Utah's Most Iconic Land Art Sculpture, Keeps Drawing a Crowd," https://www.visitutah.com/articles/utahs-spiral-jetty.
28. Siegfried Zielinski, *Deep Time of the Media: Toward an Archaeology of Hearing and Seeing by Technical Means* (MIT Press, 2006), 5 and *passim*.
29. Smithson, "The Monument: Outline for a Film," in *The Collected Writings*, ed. Flam, 357.

2. ALMOST FREEZE FRAME

1. Quoted in Michael Fried, *Why Photography Matters as Art as Never Before* (Yale University Press, 2008), 5; and Hiroshi Sugimoto, "My Inner Theater," in *Hiroshi Sugimoto: Theaters* (Éditions Xavier Barral, 2016).

2. André Bazin et al., *What Is Cinema?* (University of California Press, 2005), 1:9–16.
3. Jennifer Fay, *Inhospitable World: Cinema in the Time of the Anthropocene* (Oxford University Press, 2018), 91.
4. Mary Ann Doane, "Has Time Become Space?," in *Thinking Media Aesthetics: Media Studies, Film Studies, and the Arts* (Peter Lang, 2013), 97.
5. Fried, *Why Photography Matters as Art as Never Before*, 13.
6. Wolfgang Ernst, *Digital Memory and the Archive*, ed. Jussi Parikka (University of Minnesota Press, 2013), 156–57.
7. Susan Stewart, *The Ruins Lesson: Meaning and Material in Western Culture* (University of Chicago Press, 2020), 259.
8. Joann Greco, "The Psychology of Ruin Porn," *The Atlantic: Cities* (blog), January 6, 2012, http://www.joanngreco.com/wp-content/uploads/2011/01/The-Psychology-of-Ruin-Porn-Design-The-Atlantic-Cities-20120106.pdf; John Patrick Leary, "Detroitism: What Does 'Ruin Porn' Tell Us About the Motor City?," *Guernica* (blog), January 15, 2011, https://www.guernicamag.com/leary_1_15_11/.
9. Nick James, "Passive Aggressive," *Sight and Sound* 20, no. 4 (April 2010): 4–5.
10. Erika Balsom, *Ten Skies* (Fireflies, 2021), 67.
11. Harry Tuttle, "Slow Films, Easy Life," *Unspoken Cinema* (blog), May 12, 2010, https://unspokencinema.blogspot.com/2010/05/slow-films-easy-life-sight.html; Steven Shaviro, "Slow Cinema, Fast Films," *The Pinocchio Theory* (blog), May 12, 2010, http://www.shaviro.com/Blog/?p=891.
12. Manhola Dargis and A. O. Scott, "In Defense of the Slow and the Boring," *New York Times*, March 6, 2011, https://www.nytimes.com/2011/06/05/movies/films-in-defense-of-slow-and-boring.html.
13. Katherine Fusco and Nicole Seymour, *Kelly Reichardt* (University of Illinois Press, 2017), 53. See also Song Hwee Lim, *Tsai Ming-Liang and a Cinema of Slowness* (University of Hawai'i Press, 2014); T. de Luca, *Slow Cinema* (Edinburgh University Press, 2015).
14. Ira Jaffe, *Slow Movies: Countering the Cinema of Action* (Columbia University Press, 2014), 7. For more of the cinematic avant-garde's relationship to "slow cinema," see Justin Remes, *Motion(Less) Pictures: The Cinema of Stasis* (Columbia University Press, 2015).
15. Arden Reed, *Slow Art: The Experience of Looking, Sacred Images to James Turrell* (University of California Press, 2017), 9.
16. D. A. Miller, *Second Time Around: From Art House to DVD* (Columbia University Press, 2021), 5.
17. Michel Chion, *Film, a Sound Art*, trans. Claudia Gorbman (Columbia University Press, 2009), 107, 112.
18. Hiroshi Sugimoto, *Snow White* (Damiani, 2017).

3. FROM ZERO TO SLOW

1. In Terry Ramsaye, *A Million and One Nights: A History of the Motion Picture* (Taylor & Francis, 2012), 173; Georges Sadoul, *Histoire générale du cinéma* (Denoël, 1946), 89. No mention in these texts: Charles Musser, *The Emergence of Cinema: The American Screen to 1907* (University of California Press, 1994); Noël Burch, *Life to Those Shadows*, trans. B. Brewster (University of California Press, 1990); Laurent Mannoni, *The Great Art of Light and Shadow: Archaeology of the Cinema*, ed. and trans. Richard Crangle (University of Exeter Press, 2000).
2. Barry Salt, *Film Style and Technology : History and Analysis* (Starword, 1983), 48.
3. *The Indian Chief and the Seidlitz Powder* (British Film Institute, 1901), https://player.bfi.org.uk/free/film/watch-the-indian-chief-and-the-seidlitz-powder-1901-online.

4. Rudolf Arnheim, *Film as Art* (University of California Press, 1957), 117.
5. Siegfried Kracauer, *Theory of Film: The Redemption of Physical Reality* (Oxford University Press, 1960), 183.
6. Walter Benjamin, *The Work of Art in the Age of Its Technological Reproducibility, and Other Writings on Media*, ed. Michael W. Jennings, Brigid Doherty, and Thomas Y. Levin (Belknap Press of Harvard University Press, 2008), 67.
7. Arnheim, *Film as Art*, 116.
8. "Picture Plays and People," *New York Times*, December 16, 1923.
9. Hans Ulrich Gumbrecht, *In Praise of Athletic Beauty* (Belknap Press of Harvard University Press, 2006), 8.
10. Jimena Canales, *A Tenth of a Second: A History* (University of Chicago Press, 2010), 10.
11. Friedrich Kittler, *Optical Media*, trans. Anthony Enns (Wiley, 2010), 163.
12. Wolfgang Ernst, *Chronopoetics: The Temporal Being and Operativity of Technological Media*, trans. Anthony Enns (Rowman & Littlefield, 2016), 38–39.
13. Paul Rotha, *The Film Till Now: A Survey of World Cinema* (Twayne, 1960), 174. I am indebted to Rotha's neglected book for bringing *The Thief of Bagdad* and Dovzhenko's *Zwenigora* to my attention. Along with Kracauer, Rotha is the only film historian of the period who identifies slow motion as an effect in feature films before the 1930s, though of course he points to different films than Kracauer.
14. Tom Gunning, "The Cinema of Attraction[s]: Early Film, Its Spectator, and the Avant-Garde," in *The Cinema of Attractions Reloaded*, ed. Wanda Strauven (Amsterdam University Press, 2006), 387.
15. Kracauer, *Theory of Film*, 91.
16. Jean Epstein, *The Intelligence of a Machine*, trans. Christophe Wall-Ramona (University of Minnesota Press, 2015), 29.
17. Béla Balázs, *Béla Balázs: Early Film Theory: Visible Man and The Spirit of Film* (Berghahn, 2010), 165.
18. Trond Lundemo, "A Temporal Perspective," in *Jean Epstein*, ed. Sarah Keller and Jason N. Paul (Amsterdam University Press, 2012), 212–13. See also Malcolm Turvey, "Jean Epstein's Cinema of Immanence: The Rehabilitation of the Corporeal Eye," *October* 83 (1998): 25–50.
19. Rotha, *The Film Till Now*, 238–39.
20. Charles Acland and Haidee Wasson, *Useful Cinema* (Duke University Press, 2011); Justus Nieland, *Happiness by Design: Modernism and Media in the Eames Era* (University of Minnesota Press, 2020).
21. Rampo Edogawa, *The Edogawa Rampo Reader*, ed. Takayuki Tatsumi, trans. Seth Jacobowitz (Kurodahan, 2008), 139, 12.
22. [Sidonie-Gabrielle] Colette, *Colette at the Movies: Criticism and Screenplays* (Ungar, 1980), 61.
23. Dorothy Richardson, "Continuous Performance XI: Slow Motion," in *Close Up: Cinema and Modernism*, ed. James Donald, Anne Friedberg, and Laura Marcus (A&C Black, 1998), 182, 183.
24. Richard Abel, *French Film Theory and Criticism: 1907–1929* (Princeton University Press, 1993).
25. Stanley Cavell, *The World Viewed: Reflections on the Ontology of Film*, enlarged ed. (Harvard University Press, 1979), 145.
26. John Velasco, "I Just Tested Samsung's AI-Powered Instant Slow-Mo Video on the Galaxy S24 and It Actually Looks Legit," *Tom's Guide*, January 22, 2024, https://www.tomsguide.com/features/i-just-tested-samsungs-ai-powered-instant-slow-mo-video-on-the-galaxy-s24-and-it-actually-looks-legit.
27. Cavell, *The World Viewed*, 133–34.
28. Cavell, *The World Viewed*, 136, 133.
29. Cavell, *The World Viewed*, 135.
30. Cavell, *The World Viewed*, 133.

4. EXPERIMENTS IN TIME

1. Lutz Koepnick, "Riefensthal and the Beauty of Soccer," in *Riefenstahl Screened: An Anthology of New Criticism*, ed. Neil Christian Pages, Ingeborg Majer O'Sickey, and Mary Rhiel (Bloomsbury, 2008), 56–62.
2. Marianne Moore, *The Complete Prose of Marianne Moore* (Viking, 1986), 310–11.
3. Maya Deren, *Essential Deren: Collected Writings on Film*, ed. Bruce Rice McPherson (McPherson, 2005), 47. Deren's "An Anagram" appears as an "Appendix" in this volume and does not continue with the regular pagination of the main text.
4. Bob Rehak, "The Migration of Forms: Bullet Time as Microgenre," *Film Criticism* 32, no. 1 (2007): 26–48.
5. "Slow-Motion Drop," TV Tropes, https://tvtropes.org/pmwiki/pmwiki.php/Main/SlowMotionDrop.

5. SLOW-MOTION MODERNISM

1. Mark Goble, *Beautiful Circuits: Modernism and the Mediated Life* (Columbia University Press, 2010).
2. I am indebted to Stuart Burrows for bringing this film to my attention.
3. András Bálint Kovács, *Screening Modernism: European Art Cinema, 1950–1980* (University of Chicago Press, 2007).
4. David Bordwell, *The Way Hollywood Tells It: Story and Style in Modern Movies* (University of California Press, 2006); David Bordwell, "Intensified Continuity Revisited," *Observations on Film Art* (blog), May 27, 2007, http://www.davidbordwell.net/blog/2007/05/27/intensified-continuity-revisited/.
5. Noël Burch, *Life to Those Shadows*, trans. B. Brewster (University of California Press, 1990); David Bordwell, Janet Staiger, and Kristin Thompson, *The Classical Hollywood Cinema: Film Style and Mode of Production to 1960* (Routledge, 2003).
6. Kovács, *Screening Modernism*, 41.
7. Gilles Deleuze, *Cinema II* (Bloomsbury Academic, 2005), 12.
8. Kovács, *Screening Modernism*, 42, 22.
9. Deleuze, *Cinema II*, 59.
10. Siegfried Kracauer, *Theory of Film: The Redemption of Physical Reality*, 1997 ed. (Princeton University Press, 1997), 53. I am very grateful to Andrew Hoberek for bringing Masumura's film to my attention. It might also feature a glancing moment of slow motion in its opening car-crash sequence, but it is so subtle to be almost impossible to say for sure.
11. Raymond Williams, *Marxism and Literature* (Oxford University Press, 1977), 121–27.
12. Fredric Jameson, *A Singular Modernity: Essay on the Ontology of the Present* (Verso, 2002), 145, 7.
13. There has been some work in cinemetrics from which I've learned a lot that begins to approach slow motion from the "quantitative" perspective, such as Cameron Detig's fascinating study of slow motion as a feature of Bordwell's "intensified continuity" model for contemporary film style. Detig notes the percentage of scenes in slow motion across a selection of films from the late 1960s to the present and shows that there is distinctly more slow motion or speed ramping in twenty-first-century cinema. But it would be a project on another scale entirely to assemble the sort of film database that would correspond to something like Google's NGRAM text archive and then use shot-detection software to find how much slow motion there is in, say, the top hundred films of 1978 as opposed to 2011, etc. At earlier stages of this project, I considered limited experiments

in a more empirical approach to slow motion: looking at the top films at the U.S. domestic box office over a period of years, looking at the ten most expensive films over a period of years, or other ways to delimit the otherwise impossible archive of moving images from the 1970s to the present. Time and technology conspired against me, which is perhaps not a very serious intellectual excuse but does, in its way, capture the problem of slow motion's sheer abundance over the past fifty years—which is, of course, a function of the even greater abundance of film, TV, video, and digital moving-image culture. For now, I'll have to be satisfied with the argument here, which is also something of a wager: that slow motion in 1970s film increases geometrically with respect to prior decades and then exponentially in the 1990s and into the twenty-first century as digital filmmaking and speed-ramping technologies become widely available. See Cameron Detig, "Slow Motion in the Age of Intensified Continuity," *Film Matters* 12, no. 1 (2021): 7–16.

6. ESCAPE VELOCITIES

1. Ray Gamache, *A History of Sports Highlights: Replayed Plays from Edison to ESPN* (McFarland, 2010), 105–19. Tony Verna, *Instant Replay: The Day That Changed Sports Forever* (Creative Book Publishers International, 2008).
2. Verna, *Instant Replay*, 11.
3. Henri Lefebvre, *Introduction to Modernity: Twelve Preludes, September 1959–May 1961* (Verso, 1995), 124.
4. Fredric Jameson, *Valences of the Dialectic* (Verso, 2009), 540.
5. Sarah Brouillette, Joshua Clover, and Annie McClanahan, "Introduction: Late, Autumnal, Immiserating, Terminal," *Theory & Event* 22, no. 2 (April 2019): 330.

7. TECHNOLOGICAL AESTHETICS

1. Laura Mulvey, *Death 24x a Second: Stillness and the Moving Image* (Reaktion, 2006), 7, 102.
2. For an especially compelling and comprehensive account of the motion aesthetics of film, see Jordan Schonig, *The Shape of Motion: Cinema and the Aesthetics of Movement* (Oxford University Press, 2022). Schonig's stress on the phenomenology of perception allows him to avoid rehearsing many of the more familiar problems and issues that get discussed in film criticism based on the ideas explored by Bazin and others who root film as a medium in the ontology of the photographic image. See also Rudolf Arnheim, *Art and Visual Perception: A Psychology of the Creative Eye*, exp. and rev. ed. (University of California Press, 1974), 372.
3. E. H. Gombrich, "Moment and Movement in Art," *Journal of the Warburg and Courtauld Institutes* 27 (1964): 20.
4. Jay Lampert, *Simultaneity and Delay: A Dialectical Theory of Staggered Time* (A&C Black, 2012), 1.
5. Stanley Cavell, *The World Viewed: Reflections on the Ontology of Film*, enlarged ed. (Harvard University Press, 1979), 16.
6. Mary Ann Doane, "The Indexical and the Concept of Medium Specificity," *Differences* 18, no. 1 (May 1, 2007): 146.
7. Mary Ann Doane, "Indexicality: Trace and Sign: Introduction," *Differences* 18, no. 1 (May 1, 2007): 136, 134.
8. Lev Manovich, *The Language of New Media* (MIT Press, 2001); Sean Cubitt, *The Cinema Effect* (MIT Press, 2005). Manovich works against the ontological arguments for analog media and their

distinctiveness from digital media by tracing the deep continuity in stylistic and formal practices across a long series of art-historical, cinematic, and computing "traditions," so to speak. Cubitt takes on these classic arguments for the distinctiveness of analog media at an even more material level by observing structural similarities between the way chemical molecules work on film emulsions and pixels work on digital sensors. I'm not able to comment on the science Cubitt enlists, but he does make a fascinating case for there being an equally discrete quality of pixelation—familiar to film photographers as grain, for example—that suggests less of a break from analog to digital image making than certain strains of photography criticism and new media theory have traditionally been willing to admit.

9. Cavell, *The World Viewed*, 20.
10. Friedrich Kittler and Geoffrey Winthrop-Young, "Real Time Analysis, Time Axis Manipulation," *Cultural Politics* 13, no. 1 (March 1, 2017): 5.
11. Marco Abel, *Violent Affect: Literature, Cinema, and Critique After Representation* (University of Nebraska Press, 2007); Linda Williams, *Hard Core: Power, Pleasure, and the "Frenzy of the Visible,"* exp. ed. (University of California Press, 1999).
12. Leo Bersani and Ulysse Dutoit, *The Forms of Violence: Narrative in Assyrian Art and Modern Culture* (Schocken, 1985), 38–39, 34.
13. N. K. Hayles, *Unthought: The Power of the Cognitive Nonconscious* (University of Chicago Press, 2017), 88, 10, 93, 41.
14. Wolfgang Ernst, *Digital Memory and the Archive*, ed. Jussi Parikka (University of Minnesota Press, 2013), 205.
15. Jimena Canales, *A Tenth of a Second: A History* (University of Chicago Press, 2010); Marta Braun, *Picturing Time: The Work of Etienne-Jules Marey (1830–1904)* (University of Chicago Press, 1994).
16. Sue Zemka, *Time and the Moment in Victorian Literature and Society* (Cambridge University Press, 2011), 9, 67.
17. Edmund Husserl, *The Phenomenology of Internal Time-Consciousness* (Indiana University Press, 2019), 50–52.
18. Henri Bergson, *Time and Free Will: An Essay on the Immediate Data of Consciousness* (Courier Corporation, 2012); Henri Bergson, *Matter and Memory* (Dover, 2012).
19. William James, *The Principles of Psychology* (Dover, 1950), 1:618.
20. David Bordwell, "Cognition and Comprehension: Viewing and Forgetting in Mildred Pierce," *Journal of Dramatic Theory and Criticism*, March 1, 1992, 136–7.
21. Quentin Meillassoux, *After Finitude: An Essay on the Necessity of Contingency* (Bloomsbury, 2009), 16.
22. Vivian Sobchack, "'Cutting to the Quick': Techne, Physis, and Poiesis and the Attractions of Slow Motion," in *The Cinema of Attractions Reloaded*, ed. Wanda Strauven (Amsterdam University Press, 2006), 342, 341, 349, 345.
23. Ryan Bishop and John Phillips, *Modernist Avant-Garde Aesthetics and Contemporary Military Technology: Technicities of Perception* (Edinburgh University Press, 2010).
24. Sobchack, "'Cutting to the Quick,'" 341, 348, citing Heidegger, *The Question Concerning Technology, and Other Essays* (HarperCollins, 1982), 316–17.
25. Malcolm Turvey, *Doubting Vision: Film and the Revelationist Tradition* (Oxford University Press, 2008), 3, 5.
26. Dziga Vertov, *Kino-Eye: The Writings of Dziga Vertov*, ed. Annette Michelson, trans. Kevin O'Brien (University of California Press, 1984), 131.
27. Turvey, *Doubting Vision*, 113.
28. Noël Burch, *Life to Those Shadows*, trans. B. Brewster (University of California Press, 1990), 183, 248.

29. Vertov, *Kino-Eye*, 19.
30. Ernst, *Digital Memory and the Archive*, 144.

8. NEW MEDIA, SLOW MEDIA

1. Andrew V. Uroskie, *Between the Black Box and the White Cube: Expanded Cinema and Postwar Art* (University of Chicago Press, 2014), 130.
2. Michael Fried, *Four Honest Outlaws: Sala, Ray, Marioni, Gordon* (Yale University Press, 2011), 191.
3. Philip Monk et al., *Double-Cross: The Hollywood Films of Douglas Gordon* (Art Gallery of York University, 2003), 76.
4. Fried, *Four Honest Outlaws*, 245; Monk, *Double-Cross*, 76.

9. WHAT WE SEE IN SLOW MOTION

1. William James, *The Principles of Psychology* (Dover, 1950), 1:624. David Eagleman, *Incognito: The Secret Lives of the Brain* (Knopf Doubleday, 2011); David Eagleman, "Time Perception," August 24, 2020, https://eagleman.com/science/time-perception/.
2. Lutz P. Koepnick, "Riefenstahl and the Beauty of Soccer," in *Riefenstahl Screened: An Anthology of New Criticism*, ed. Neil Christian Pages, Ingeborg Majer O'Sickey, and Mary Rhiel (Bloomsbury, 2008), 67.
3. Jane V. Curran and Christophe Fricker, eds., *Schiller's "On Grace and Dignity" in Its Cultural Context: Essays and a New Translation* (Boydell & Brewer, 2005), 140; cited in Michael Fried, *Four Honest Outlaws: Sala, Ray, Marioni, Gordon* (Yale University Press, 2011), 231.
4. Johannes Fabian, *Time and the Other* (Columbia University Press, 2014), 22–25.
5. Wolfgang Ernst, *Digital Memory and the Archive*, ed. Jussi Parikka (University of Minnesota Press, 2013), 144.
6. Nico Baumbach, *Cinema/Politics/Philosophy* (Columbia University Press, 2018), 97.
7. Herbert Zettl, *Sight, Sound, Motion: Applied Media Aesthetics*, 2nd ed. (Wadsworth, 1990), 280.
8. Noël Burch, *Life to Those Shadows*, trans. B. Brewster (University of California Press, 1990), 6.
9. Baumbach, *Cinema/Politics/Philosophy*, 114.
10. Nicolás Salazar Sutil, *Motion and Representation: The Language of Human Movement* (MIT Press, 2015), 46–47.
11. David Harvey, *A Companion to Marx's* Capital: *The Complete Edition* (Verso, 2018), 90.
12. Karl Marx, *Capital: Volume I* (Penguin, 2004), 293.
13. Harvey, *A Companion to Marx's* Capital, 173.
14. Marx, *Capital*, 352.
15. Sarah Sharma, *In the Meantime: Temporality and Cultural Politics* (Duke University Press, 2014), 5.
16. György Lukács, *History and Class Consciousness: Studies in Marxist Dialectics* (MIT Press, 1971), 89, 90.
17. Sharma, *In the Meantime*, 19.
18. Paul Virilio, *Open Sky* (Verso, 1997), 12.
19. Paul Virilio, *Polar Inertia* (Sage, 2000), 42.
20. Barbara Adam, *Timewatch: The Social Analysis of Time* (Wiley, 2013), 146.

21. Hartmut Rosa, *Social Acceleration: A New Theory of Modernity*, trans. Jonathan Trejo-Mathys (Columbia University Press, 2013), xxxix.
22. Jonathan Crary, *24/7: Late Capitalism and the Ends of Sleep* (Verso, 2013), 128.
23. Moishe Postone, *Time, Labor, and Social Domination: A Reinterpretation of Marx's Critical Theory* (Cambridge University Press, 1995), 289, 294.

10. SOME LITERARY HISTORIES OF SLOW MOTION

1. I am alluding here to Bruno Latour's argument that "we have never been modern" but am taking its insistence on the arbitrary nature of the distinctions between the modern and its counterparts (nature, history, the classical) in a slightly different direction to stress the way speed has been an essential constant to the various formulations he criticizes. Bruno Latour, *We Have Never Been Modern* (Harvard University Press, 2012).
2. Fredric Jameson, *The Seeds of Time* (Columbia University Press, 1994), 8.
3. "Arclight," accessed June 3, 2021, http://search.projectarclight.org/; "HathiTrust+Bookworm—Documentation—HTRC Docs," https://wiki.htrc.illinois.edu/pages/viewpage.action?pageId=26705922.
4. "The Movie Theater Boom of the 1920s," *Classic Film Haven* (blog), May 25, 2015, https://classicfilmhaven.wordpress.com/2015/05/25/the-movie-theater-boom-of-the-1920s/.
5. Katherine Anne Porter, *Ship of Fools* (Little, Brown, 1962), 224.
6. "What Is the Matrix Effect? It Feels Like You're Moving in Slow Motion," *Bustle*, https://www.bustle.com/p/what-is-the-matrix-effect-it-feels-like-youre-moving-in-slow-motion-69207; "The Matrix Effect: When Time Slows Down," *Psychology Today*, July 2017, https://www.psychologytoday.com/us/blog/sense-time/201707/the-matrix-effect-when-time-slows-down.
7. Kristen Whissel, *Spectacular Digital Effects: CGI and Contemporary Cinema* (Duke University Press, 2014), 6.
8. Stephen Kern, "Speed," in *The Culture of Time and Space, 1880–1918* (Harvard University Press, 1983), 109–30.
9. Hartmut Rosa, *Social Acceleration: A New Theory of Modernity*, trans. Jonathan Trejo-Mathys (Columbia University Press, 2013), 12.
10. Paul Virilio, *The Art of the Motor* (University of Minnesota Press, 1995), 57, 85.
11. Enda Duffy, *The Speed Handbook: Velocity, Pleasure, Modernism* (Duke University Press, 2009), 4–5.
12. Fredric Jameson, *A Singular Modernity: Essay on the Ontology of the Present* (Verso, 2002), 154.
13. Reinhart Koselleck, *Sediments of Time: On Possible Histories*, trans. Sean Franzel and Stefan-Ludwig Hoffmann (Stanford University Press, 2018), 96.
14. Reinhart Koselleck, *Futures Past: On the Semantics of Historical Time*, trans. Keith Tribe (Columbia University Press, 2004), 22.
15. Robert Gordon, "Is U.S. Economic Growth Over? Faltering Innovation Confronts the Six Headwinds," National Bureau of Economic Research Working Paper 18315 (National Bureau of Economic Research, 2012); see also Tyler Cowen, *The Great Stagnation: How American Ate All the Low-Hanging Fruit of Modern History, Got Sick, and Will (Eventually) Feel Better* (Dutton, 2011); and Larry Summers, "The Age of Secular Stagnation: What It Is and What to Do About It," *Foreign Affairs*, February 15, 2016, https://www.foreignaffairs.com/articles/united-states/2016-02-15/age-secular-stagnation.
16. Benjamin Noys, *Malign Velocities: Accelerationism and Capitalism* (Zero, 2014), 95, 87.

11. MODERNITY'S SLOW START

1. Benjamin Noys, *Malign Velocities: Accelerationism and Capitalism* (John Hunt, 2014).
2. Virginia Woolf, *Mr. Bennett and Mrs. Brown*, 2nd impression, the Hogarth Essays (L. and Virginia Woolf, 1924), 4; Willa Cather, "Prefatory Note," in *Not Under Forty* (University of Nebraska Press, 1988), v.
3. Wolfgang Ernst, *The Contemporary Condition: Introductory Thoughts on Contemporaneity and Contemporary Art* (Sternberg, 2016), 9, 24.
4. David Harvey, *A Companion to Marx's* Capital: *The Complete Edition* (Verso, 2018), 461.
5. Henri Lefebvre, *Rhythmanalysis: Space, Time, and Everyday Life* (Bloomsbury, 2013), 89.
6. Barbara Adam, *Timewatch: The Social Analysis of Time* (Wiley, 2013), 95.
7. Michael Hanchard, "Afro-Modernity: Temporality, Politics, and the African Diaspora," in *Colored People Time*, ed. Meg Onli and Amber Rose Johnson (Institute of Contemporary Art, 2020), 54–55.
8. Walter Benjamin, *The Arcades Project*, trans. Howard Eiland and Kevin McLaughlin (Belknap Press of Harvard University Press, 1999), 427.
9. William Faulkner, *Snopes: The Hamlet, The Town, The Mansion* (Modern Library, 1994), 378, 689.
10. William Faulkner, *The Sound and the Fury*, ed. David Minter, 2nd Norton Critical ed. (Norton, 1994), 215.
11. Faulkner, *Snopes*, 1030–31.
12. William Faulkner, *Light in August* (Vintage, 1990), 10.

12. FAULKNER AT THE SPEED LIMIT

1. William Faulkner, *Snopes: The Hamlet, The Town, The Mansion* (Modern Library, 1994), 677.
2. Cleanth Brooks, *William Faulkner: Toward Yoknapatawpha and Beyond* (Louisiana State University Press, 1989), 251–53.
3. Richard Godden, *William Faulkner: An Economy of Complex Words* (Princeton University Press, 2007), 75, 5.
4. Faulkner, *Snopes*, 1027–28.
5. Linda Kohl, neé Snopes, is, as readers of *The Mansion* will recall, a character whom Faulkner uses to represent a leftist trajectory through modern culture that was definitely not his own. She takes part in the Spanish Civil War against Franco's fascist forces and is married to a Jewish communist in New York. As a quasi-Marxist femme fatale she adds a political dimension to Mink's revenge plot against Flem that would take more space than I have here to explore fully. But it does anticipate in interesting ways some of the links and associations between slow motion and radical politics that become prominent in later works of or about the 1960s.
6. Faulkner, *Snopes*, 1038.
7. "This 1,288-Word Run-On Sentence by William Faulkner Broke Records," https://mymodernmet.com/longest-run-on-sentence-william-faulkner/.
8. Faulkner, *Snopes*, 1047, 1065, 1064.

13. SNOPES AT REST

1. Justus Nieland, *Happiness by Design: Modernism and Media in the Eames Era* (University of Minnesota Press, 2020), 81.

2. William Faulkner, *Snopes: The Hamlet, The Town, The Mansion* (Modern Library, 1994), 900.
3. Claire Patterson, "Age of Meteorites and the Earth," *Geochimica et Cosmochimica Acta* 10, no. 4 (October 1, 1956): 230–37.
4. Faulkner, *Snopes*, 464, 467.
5. Faulkner, *Snopes*, 536–37.
6. Anne Friedberg, *Window Shopping: Cinema and the Postmodern* (University of California Press, 1994).
7. Cited in Jane Haynes, "Faulkner's Verbena," *Mississippi Quarterly* 33, no. 3 (1980): 355–62.

14. *REMAINDER*'S INSTANT REPLAYS

1. Zadie Smith, "Two Paths for the Novel," *New York Review of Books*, November 20, 2011, https://www.nybooks.com/articles/2008/11/20/two-paths-for-the-novel/.
2. Walter Benn Michaels, *The Beauty of a Social Problem: Photography, Autonomy, Economy* (University of Chicago Press, 2015), 78; Justus Nieland, "Dirty Media: Tom McCarthy and the Afterlife of Modernism," *MFS: Modern Fiction Studies* 58, no. 3 (Fall 2012): 569–99; Christina Lupton, "The Novel as the Future Anterior of the Book: Tom McCarthy's *Remainder* and Ali Smith's *The Accidental*," *Novel* 49, no. 3 (November 1, 2016): 506.
3. Tom McCarthy, *Remainder* (Vintage, 2007), 24, 195, 196.
4. N. K. Hayles, *Unthought: The Power of the Cognitive Nonconscious* (University of Chicago Press, 2017), 93–94.
5. McCarthy, *Remainder*, 212, 214, 223, 236, 290.
6. Tom McCarthy, "Writing Machines," *London Review of Books*, December 18, 2014, https://www.lrb.co.uk/the-paper/v36/n24/tom-mccarthy/writing-machines.
7. "Crash Test Dummy," *I Didn't Know That*, YouTube video, https://www.youtube.com/watch?v=3vDQmoqIYio; Tabea Tietz, "Samuel Alderson and the Crash Test Dummies," *SciHi Blog* (blog), October 21, 2020, http://scihi.org/samuel-alderson-crash-test-dummies/; "September 1959: First Crash Test at Mercedes-Benz," marsMediaSite, https://media.daimler.com/marsMediaSite/en/instance/ko/September-1959-First-crash-test-at-Mercedes-Benz.xhtml?oid=9908016; "The History of Crash Test Dummies and Air Bag Safety," http://www.theinventors.org/library/inventors/blcrashtestdummies.htm.
8. McCarthy, *Remainder*, 291.
9. "Vince and Larry Crash the National Museum of American History," YouTube video, https://www.youtube.com/watch?v=oD6p1uGrOic.
10. Michaels, *The Beauty of a Social Problem*, 75.
11. McCarthy, *Remainder*, 111–13, 121, 81, 180.

15. *AUSTERLITZ*'S TRAUMATIC PAUSES

1. Christina Lupton, "The Novel as the Future Anterior of the Book: Tom McCarthy's *Remainder* and Ali Smith's *The Accidental*," *Novel* 49, no. 3 (November 1, 2016): 508.
2. W. G. Sebald, *Austerlitz* (Random House, 2011), 286, 129, 88, 12.
3. Sebald, *Austerlitz*, 246.
4. Lise Patt and Christel Dillbohner, *Searching for Sebald: Photography After W. G. Sebald* (Institute of Cultural Inquiry, 2007); Samuel Pane, "Trauma Obscura: Photographic Media in W. G.

Sebald's *Austerlitz*," *Mosaic: An Interdisciplinary Critical Journal* 38, no. 1 (March 3, 2005): 37–54.
5. Ross Posnock, "'Don't Think, but Look!': W. G. Sebald, Wittgenstein, and Cosmopolitan Poverty," *Representations* 112, no. 1 (November 1, 2010): 121.
6. Sebald, *Austerlitz*, 246, 252, 250.
7. D. A. Miller, *Hidden Hitchcock* (University of Chicago Press, 2017). Miller's beautifully suggestive discussions of Hitchcock turn on "too close" readings that discover fragments of visual detail in the smallest sections of Hitchcock's films that suggest larger readings of the works themselves. That it requires slow motion (or stills) to "see" these details is not necessarily central to Miller's arguments but parallels the work of Laura Mulvey, Garrett Stewart, and other scholars who have reflected on how video and digital technologies have effectively democratized the practices of textual analysis at the level of the frame that once were reserved for critics with the access to, and skills to employ, celluloid prints and editing stations.
8. Roland Barthes, *Camera Lucida: Reflections on Photography* (Macmillan, 1981), 90.
9. Sebald, *Austerlitz*, 251–52.
10. Laura Mulvey, *Death 24x a Second: Stillness and the Moving Image* (Reaktion, 2006), 8.

16. BEING IN RACIAL TIME: *DAUGHTERS OF THE DUST*

1. Jussi Parikka, *A Geology of Media* (University of Minnesota Press, 2015), 135.
2. Edward W. Said, *The World, the Text, and the Critic* (Harvard University Press, 1983), 226.
3. Marco Calavita, "'MTV Aesthetics' at the Movies: Interrogating a Film Criticism Fallacy," *Journal of Film and Video* 59, no. 3 (2007): 15–31.
4. Julie Dash, *Daughters of the Dust: The Making of an African American Woman's Film* (New Press, 1992), 118, 184.
5. Calvin Tomkins, "Arthur Jafa's Radical Alienation," *New Yorker*, December 10, 2020, https://www.newyorker.com/magazine/2020/12/21/arthur-jafas-radical-alienation.
6. This is a central term in Fabian's *Time and the Other*, where he uses it to describe how modern anthropologists construct a sense of differential temporality that removes their racialized objects from the "present" that defines modernity, which is implicitly and explicitly racialized as white. Assumptions about progress and the everyday speed of life are crucial to these formations. Johannes Fabian, *Time and the Other* (Columbia University Press, 2014), 25–35.
7. Henri Lefebvre, *Introduction to Modernity: Twelve Preludes, September 1959–May 1961* (Verso, 1995), 120, 118.
8. Michael Hanchard, "Afro-Modernity: Temporality, Politics, and the African Diaspora," in *Colored People Time*, ed. Meg Onli and Amber Rose Johnson (Institute of Contemporary Art and the University of Pennsylvania, 2020), 52.
9. Kemi Adeyemi, "The Practice of Slowness: Black Queer Women and the Right to the City," *GLQ: A Journal of Lesbian and Gay Studies* 25, no. 4 (October 1, 2019): 550.

17. WE HAVE ALWAYS BEEN IN SLOW MOTION: *THE DISCOVERY OF SLOWNESS*

1. Robert Macfarlane, "Read It on the Autobahn," *London Review of Books*, December 18, 2003, https://www.lrb.co.uk/the-paper/v25/n24/robert-macfarlane/read-it-on-the-autobahn.

2. Sten Nadolny, *The Discovery of Slowness* (Penguin, 1997), 3.
3. Macfarlane, "Read It on the Autobahn."
4. Nadolny, *The Discovery of Slowness*, 9, 28, 47.
5. *Slow Road Luxury Travel Blog*, https://www.butterfield.com/blog/; Nathan Williams, *The Kinfolk Home: Interiors for Slow Living* (Artisan Books, 2015); "Slow Travel: Let's Get Connected!," *Ecotourism-World* (blog), December 7, 2020, https://ecotourism-world.com/slow-travel-lets-get-connected/.
6. "The Slow Issue," *Whalebone*, 2023.
7. Lutz Koepnick, *On Slowness: Toward an Aesthetic of the Contemporary* (Columbia University Press, 2014), 254.
8. Sarah Sharma, *In the Meantime: Temporality and Cultural Politics* (Duke University Press, 2014), 125.
9. Jesse Matz, *Modernist Time Ecology* (Johns Hopkins University Press, 2018), 178–79.
10. Viktor Shklovskiĭ, *Theory of Prose.*, trans. Benjamin Sher, 1st pbk. ed. (Dalkey Archive, 1991).
11. Shklovskiĭ, *Theory of Prose*, 6, 12, 39.
12. Friedrich Nietzsche, *Daybreak: Thoughts on the Prejudices of Morality* (Cambridge University Press, 1997), 5. Marjorie Garber, "Shakespeare in Slow Motion," *Profession*, 2010, 162.
13. See my "DeLillo, Slowing Down" in *A Question of Time: American Literature from Colonial Encounter to Contemporary Fiction*, ed. Cindy Weinstein (Cambridge University Press, 2018).
14. Nadolny, *The Discovery of Slowness*, 158.
15. Nadolny, *The Discovery of Slowness*, 146, 257, 175.
16. Ted Underwood, "Why Literary Time Is Measured in Minutes," *ELH* 85, no. 2 (2018): 341–65.
17. Gérard Genette, *Narrative Discourse: An Essay in Method*, trans. Jane E. Lewin (Cornell University Press, 1980), 94, 86–88.
18. Brian Gingrich, *The Pace of Fiction: Narrative Movement and the Novel* (Oxford University Press, 2021), 179, 176, 173, 165.
19. Genette, *Narrative Discourse*, 95.
20. Underwood, "Why Literary Time Is Measured in Minutes"; Seymour Chatman, "Genette's Analysis of Narrative Time Relations," *L'Esprit Créateur* 14, no. 4 (1974): 353–68.
21. Mark Currie, *About Time: Narrative, Fiction, and the Philosophy of Time* (Edinburgh University Press, 2007).
22. Genette, *Narrative Discourse*, 95.
23. Genette, *Narrative Discourse*, 105.
24. Nadolny, *The Discovery of Slowness*, 31.
25. Laurent Mannoni, *The Great Art of Light and Shadow: Archaeology of the Cinema*, ed. and trans. Richard Crangle (University of Exeter Press, 2000), 205.
26. Nadolny, *The Discovery of Slowness*, 31, 40, 47, 113.
27. Nadolny, *The Discovery of Slowness*, 304, 309.

18. DELILLO, SLOWING DOWN

1. Markus Brüderlin and Hartmut Böhme, *The Art of Deceleration: Motion and Rest in Modern Art from Caspar David Friedrich to Ai Weiwei* (Hatje Cantz, 2012), 2.
2. Don DeLillo, *Cosmopolis* (Scribner, 2003), half title page, 11, 10.
3. Don DeLillo, *The Body Artist* (Scribner, 2001), 9.
4. Paul Ricoeur, *Time and Narrative*, trans. Kathleen Blamey and David Pellauer (University of Chicago Press, 1988), 3:22.

5. John Durham Peters, *The Marvelous Clouds: Toward a Philosophy of Elemental Media* (University of Chicago Press, 2015), 176.
6. Sam Anderson, "White Noise: Don DeLillo's Latest Brings Us as Close to Pure Fictional Stasis as We're Ever Likely to Get," *New York,* January 24, 2010, http://nymag.com/arts/books/reviews/63210/.
7. Mark O'Connell, "The Disembodied: For Don DeLillo's Characters, All Technologies Are Technologies of Death," *Slate,* May 2, 2016, https://slate.com/culture/2016/05/don-delillos-novel-zero-k-reviewed.html.
8. Theodor Adorno, "Late Style in Beethoven," in *Essays on Music,* ed. Richard Leppert, trans. Susan H. Gillespie (University of California Press, 2002), 564, 567; DeLillo, *The Body Artist,* 111.
9. Don DeLillo, *Point Omega* (Scribner, 2010), 13.
10. James Lasdun, "*Point Omega* by Don DeLillo," *The Guardian,* February 26, 2010, https://www.theguardian.com/books/2010/feb/27/don-delillo-point-omega.
11. Lutz P. Koepnick, *On Slowness: Toward an Aesthetic of the Contemporary* (Columbia University Press, 2014), 276.
12. Don DeLillo, *Zero K* (Scribner, 2016), 244–45.
13. For more on contemporary slowness, see Koepnick, *On Slowness,* 2–8; and also Hartmut Rosa, *Social Acceleration: A New Theory of Modernity,* trans. Jonathan Trejo-Mathys (Columbia University Press, 2013), 80–90.
14. Jonathan Crary, *24/7: Late Capitalism and the Ends of Sleep* (Verso, 2013), 122, 100, 40.
15. DeLillo, *Point Omega,* 19.
16. Don DeLillo, *Falling Man* (Scribner, 2007), 239–40.
17. See Sally Bachner, *The Prestige of Violence: American Fiction, 1962–2007* (University of Georgia Press, 2011); and Rachel Greenwald Smith, *Affect and American Literature in the Age of Neoliberalism* (Cambridge University Press, 2015).
18. For more on DeLillo's response, see Marco Abel, "Don DeLillo's 'In the Ruins of the Future': Literature, Images, and the Rhetoric of Seeing 9/11," *PMLA* 118, no. 5 (October 2003): 1236–50.
19. Don DeLillo, "In the Ruins of the Future," *Harper's,* December 2001, 34.

19. FROM 9/11 TO JFK IN SLOW MOTION

1. Don DeLillo, *Point Omega* (Scribner, 2010), 46–47, 13.
2. Don DeLillo, *Falling Man* (Scribner, 2007), 211.
3. Saidiya Hartman, "The Time of Slavery," *South Atlantic Quarterly* 101, no. 4 (October 1, 2002): 759.
4. Jared Sexton, "The Social Life of Social Death: On Afro-Pessimism and Black Optimism," *InTensions Journal* 5 (Fall/Winter 2011): 4–5.
5. Sue Zemka, *Time and the Moment in Victorian Literature and Society* (Cambridge University Press, 2011); Jimena Canales, *A Tenth of a Second: A History* (University of Chicago Press, 2010); Marta Braun, *Picturing Time: The Work of Etienne-Jules Marey (1830–1904)* (University of Chicago Press, 1994).
6. Jad Abumrad and Robert Krulwich, "Why a Brush with Death Triggers the Slow-Mo Effect," *NPR,* August 17, 2010, https://www.npr.org/templates/story/story.php?storyId=129112147.
7. Abumrad and Krulwich, "Why a Brush with Death Triggers the Slow-Mo Effect"; David Eagleman, *Incognito: The Secret Lives of the Brain* (Knopf Doubleday, 2011); David Eagleman, "Time Perception," August 24, 2020, https://eagleman.com/science/time-perception/.

8. "Opinion | 9/11 Coverage from the Journal Editorial Page," *Wall Street Journal*, September 10, 2021, https://www.wsj.com/articles/9-11-coverage-from-the-journal-editorial-page-11631225595; "The Indelible Impacts of 9/11," Office of the President, University of Nevada, Las Vegas, https://www.unlv.edu/news-story/indelible-impacts-911; Woody Woodburn, "Woodburn: 9/11 Seems Like Yesterday and a Lifetime Ago," *Ventura County Star*, September 11, 2021, https://www.vcstar.com/story/opinion/columnists/2021/09/11/woodburn-9-11-seems-like-yesterday-and-lifetime-ago/8261047002/; "Echoes from the Pentagon, 20 Years After Sept. 11," *DCist* (blog), September 10, 2021, https://dcist.com/story/21/09/10/echoes-from-pentagon-20-years-after-sept-11/; "A Tuesday Like No Other: State Dept. Remembers Its 9/11 First Responders and a New Generation of Diplomats," *Federal News Network*, September 10, 2021, https://federalnewsnetwork.com/workforce/2021/09/a-tuesday-like-no-other-state-dept-remembers-its-9-11-first-responders-and-a-new-generation-of-diplomats/; Jack Kelly, "20 Lessons Learned 20 Years After September 11," *Forbes*, September 11, 2021, https://www.forbes.com/sites/jackkelly/2021/09/11/twenty-lessons-learned-from-twenty-years-after-911/.
9. Jan Dirk Blom, Nutsa Nanuashvili, and Flavie Waters, "Time Distortions: A Systematic Review of Cases Characteristic of Alice in Wonderland Syndrome," *Frontiers in Psychiatry* 12 (May 7, 2021): 668633.
10. The hits generated by a YouTube search for the search terms related to 9/11 came back as follows: 270,000 hits for a Boolean search of "9/11" and "slow motion"; 170,000 hits for "9/11 video slow motion." Weirdly enough, I did this particular experiment on September 11, 2021.
11. Marco Abel, "Don DeLillo's 'In the Ruins of the Future': Literature, Images, and the Rhetoric of Seeing 9/11," *PMLA* 118, no. 5 (2003): 1239.
12. Don DeLillo, *Mao II* (Penguin, 1992), 72; Don DeLillo, *Zero K* (Scribner, 2016), 36.
13. Don DeLillo, *Libra: With a New Introduction by the Author* (Penguin, 1991), 264.
14. DeLillo, introduction to *Libra*, viii.
15. DeLillo, *Libra*, 15, 441, 445.

20. *UNDERWORLD*: HOW SLOW IS NOW?

1. Don DeLillo, *Underworld* (Scribner, 1997), 159, 387.
2. James Wood, "Human, All Too Inhuman," *New Republic*, July 24, 2000, https://newrepublic.com/article/61361/human-inhuman; "Better in Slow Motion—Uncensored," *Chappelle's Show*, Comedy Central, https://www.cc.com/video/81g5h3/chappelle-s-show-better-in-slow-motion-uncensored.
3. DeLillo, *Underworld*, 222, 804.
4. DeLillo, *Underworld*, 810.
5. DeLillo, *Underworld*, 780.
6. DeLillo, *Underworld*, 32, 47, 42, 43.
7. DeLillo, *Underworld*, 495.
8. Øyvind Vagnes, "Inside the Zapruder Museum," in *Zaprudered* (University of Texas Press, 2011), 73.
9. DeLillo, *Underworld*, 495.
10. Clement Greenberg, *The Collected Essays and Criticism*, vol. 4: *Modernism with a Vengeance, 1957–1969*, ed. J. O'Brian (University of Chicago Press, 1995), 86.
11. DeLillo, *Underworld*, 496.
12. DeLillo, *Underworld*, 496.
13. DeLillo, *Underworld*, 496, 404.
14. Don DeLillo, *White Noise* (Penguin, 1985), 285.

21. A "SIXTIES INCANDESCENCE": PERIODIZING SLOW MOTION

1. Stéphane Bou and Jean-Baptiste Thoret, "A Conversation with Don DeLillo: Has Terrorism Become the World's Main Plot?," *Panic* 1 (November 2005): 90–95, http://perival.com/delillo/interview_panic_2005.html. Translated from the French by Noel King.
2. Raymond Williams, *The Long Revolution* (Broadview, 2001), 64.
3. Sean McCann and Michael Szalay, "Introduction: Paul Potter and the Cultural Turn," *Yale Journal of Criticism* 18, no. 2 (2005): 209–20.
4. Fredric Jameson, "Periodizing the 60s," *Social Text*, no. 9/10 (1984): 178.
5. Theodore Roszak, *The Making of a Counter Culture: Reflections on the Technocratic Society and Its Youthful Opposition* (Doubleday, 1969), 5.
6. Jameson, "Periodizing the 60s," 181.
7. Carolyn Dinshaw, *How Soon Is Now? Medieval Texts, Amateur Readers, and the Queerness of Time* (Duke University Press, 2012), 9, 18.
8. Michela Beatrice Ferri, *The Reception of Husserlian Phenomenology in North America* (Springer, 2019). Cf. Thomas Sheehan's "Reception of Heidegger's Phenomenology in the United States," where Sheehan argues that the 1962 translation of *Being and Time* into English gives a new readership access to Heidegger's work at a moment where it becomes part of a "postmodern" turn in Western culture even though it was, of course, conceived at a moment of modernism's cultural dominance.
9. David Couzens Hoy, *The Time of Our Lives: A Critical History of Temporality* (MIT Press, 2012), 195.
10. Jonathan Eburne, *Outsider Theory: Intellectual Histories of Unorthodox Ideas* (University of Minnesota Press, 2018).
11. Jameson, "Periodizing the 60s," 180–81.
12. Johannes Fabian, *Time and the Other* (Columbia University Press, 2014), xix–xx.
13. Jameson, "Periodizing the 60s," 181.
14. Moishe Postone, *Time, Labor, and Social Domination: A Reinterpretation of Marx's Critical Theory* (Cambridge University Press, 1995), 293–94, 300, 292, 295, 301.
15. Stephen Greenblatt, "Invisible Bullets: Renaissance Authority and Its Subversion," in *New Historicism and Renaissance Drama*, ed. Richard Dutton and Richard Wilson (Longman, 1992). I am evoking this essay's concluding declaration: "There is no end of subversion, only not for us." Greenblatt is trying to capture the way that potentially disruptive social energies are channeled back into the forms and ritual of culture. This is not the same sort of economic dynamic that Postone analyzes, but they are similarly powerful assertions of the homeostatic logics that seem to govern so many seminal accounts of modern life.
16. Sarah Brouillette, Joshua Clover, and Annie McClanahan, "Introduction: Late, Autumnal, Immiserating, Terminal," *Theory & Event* 22, no. 2 (April 2019).
17. John Stuart Mill, "John Stuart Mill on the Stationary State," *Population and Development Review* 12, no. 2 (1986): 319.
18. Robert Brenner, "The Long Downturn," *New America*, http://newamerica.org/economic-growth/policy-papers/the-long-downturn/.
19. Dan Sinykin, *American Literature and the Long Downturn: Neoliberal Apocalypse* (Oxford University Press, 2020).
20. "The Steam Has Gone Out of Globalisation," *The Economist*, January 24, 2019, https://www.economist.com/leaders/2019/01/24/the-steam-has-gone-out-of-globalisation.
21. Jason Hickel, *Less Is More: How Degrowth Will Save the World* (Random House, 2020); Kelsey Piper, "Can We Save the Planet by Shrinking the Economy?," *Vox*, August 3, 2021, https://www.vox.com/future-perfect/22408556/save-planet-shrink-economy-degrowth.

22. R. J. Gordon, *The Rise and Fall of American Growth: The U.S. Standard of Living Since the Civil War* (Princeton University Press, 2017), 22.
23. Donella H. Meadows, Dennis L. Meadows, Jørgen Randers, and William W. Behrens III, *The Limits to Growth: A Report for the Club of Rome's Project on the Predicament of Mankind* (Potomac Assoc. Books, 1972), 126.
24. Michael Löwy, *The Politics of Combined and Uneven Development: The Theory of Permanent Revolution* (Haymarket, 2010); Jeff Diamanti, Andrew Pendakis, and Imre Szeman, *The Bloomsbury Companion to Marx* (Bloomsbury, 2019); Leon Trotsky, *History of the Russian Revolution* (Haymarket, 2008).
25. Warwick Research Collective et al., *Combined and Uneven Development: Towards a New Theory of World-Literature* (Oxford University Press, 2015); James Christie and Nesrin Degirmencioglu, eds., *Cultures of Uneven and Combined Development: From International Relations to World Literature* (Brill, 2019).
26. Daniel Dorling and Kirsten McClure, *Slowdown: The End of the Great Acceleration and Why It's Good for the Planet, the Economy, and Our Lives* (Yale University Press, 2020), 141, 324.

22. BONNIE AND CLYDE AND SLOW AND FAST

1. Jeff Menne, *Post-Fordist Cinema: Hollywood Auteurs and the Corporate Counterculture* (Columbia University Press, 2019), 17, 30.
2. Jerome Christensen, *America's Corporate Art: The Studio Authorship of Hollywood Motion Pictures* (Stanford University Press, 2012); J. D. Connor, *Hollywood Math and Aftermath: The Economic Image and the Digital Recession* (Bloomsbury, 2018); T. Balio, *The American Film Industry* (University of Wisconsin Press, 1985).
3. Christensen, *America's Corporate Art*, 257, 275.
4. The story of the film's initial screening for Jack Warner was first published in a 1997 essay by Arthur Penn for a Cambridge Film Handbook, then retold by Peter Biskind in his *Easy Riders, Raging Bulls: How the Sex-Drugs-and-Rock 'n' Roll Generation Saved Hollywood* (Simon & Schuster, 2011), as related from interviews with Penn and Warren Beatty he does in 1993. I first encountered it in Biskind's book, which is also where Christensen takes it for his own ingenious reading of its backlot, corporate implications.
5. Arthur Penn, "Making Waves: The Directing of *Bonnie and Clyde*," in Lester D. Friedman, *Arthur Penn's Bonnie and Clyde* (Cambridge University Press, 2000), 29.
6. Christensen, *America's Corporate Art*, 274–75.
7. Christensen, *America's Corporate Art*, 278.
8. Friedman, *Arthur Penn's Bonnie and Clyde*, 42.
9. Pauline Kael, *Kiss Kiss Bang Bang* (Bantam, 1969), 53, 47–49.
10. "François Truffaut's 'Bonnie and Clyde': How the French New Wave Legend Nearly Directed the Iconic Film," *IndieWire* (blog), March 3, 2020, https://www.indiewire.com/2020/03/francois-truffaut-bonnie-and-clyde-serge-toubiana-1202215097/.
11. Kael, *Kiss Kiss Bang Bang*, 54.
12. G. Stewart, *Between Film and Screen: Modernism's Photo Synthesis* (University of Chicago Press, 1999), 49.
13. Stanley Cavell, *The World Viewed: Reflections on the Ontology of Film*, enlarged ed. (Harvard University Press, 1979), 134.
14. Quoted in John G. Cawelti, *Focus on Bonnie and Clyde*, Film Focus (Prentice-Hall, 1973), 22–23, 25.

15. Arthur Penn, quoted in S. Wake and N. Hayden, *The Bonnie & Clyde Book* (Simon & Schuster, 1972), 7.
16. Penn, quoted in Wake and Hayden, *The Bonnie & Clyde Book*, 9–10.
17. Kael, *Kiss Kiss Bang Bang*, 52.
18. Wake and Hayden, *The Bonnie & Clyde Book*, 114–15.
19. Jordan Schonig, *The Shape of Motion: Cinema and the Aesthetics of Movement* (Oxford University Press, 2022), 22.
20. Friedman, *Arthur Penn's Bonnie and Clyde*, 38.
21. All Kael quotations in this paragraph are from Kael, *Kiss Kiss Bang Bang*, 61.
22. "François Truffaut's 'Bonnie and Clyde.'"
23. Kael, *Kiss Kiss Bang Bang*, 62, 62, 61.
24. Wake and Hayden, *The Bonnie & Clyde Book*, 27–28.
25. Cawelti, *Focus on Bonnie and Clyde*, 138.
26. Kael, *Kiss Kiss Bang Bang*, 53–54, 48, 53, 58.
27. D. A. Miller, *Second Time Around: From Art House to DVD* (Columbia University Press, 2021), 83, 84.
28. Sandra Wake and Nicola Hayden, *Bonnie and Clyde: Directed by Arthur Penn: Produced by Warren Beatty: Screenplay by David Newman and Robert Benton*, Faber Classic Screenplay Series (Faber and Faber, 1998), 162, 164.
29. Friedman, *Arthur Penn's Bonnie and Clyde*, 21.
30. Friedman, *Arthur Penn's Bonnie and Clyde*, 135.
31. Stephen Follows, "How Many Shots Are in the Average Movie?," July 3, 2017, https://stephenfollows.com/many-shots-average-movie/; Eric Snider, "What's the Big Deal?: *Bonnie and Clyde* (1967)," *MTV News*, https://www.mtv.com/news/2763794/whats-the-big-deal-bonnie-and-clyde-1967/.
32. Friedman, *Arthur Penn's Bonnie and Clyde*, 135.
33. Cawelti, *Focus on Bonnie and Clyde*, 16.
34. "Worst Death Scene in Movie History—So Bad, It's Good!," YouTube video, 2017, https://www.youtube.com/watch?v=te3v4y_dGuw; Ally Forward, "What Are the Worst Movie Death Scenes of All Time?," *The Guardian*, October 8, 2012, https://www.theguardian.com/film/filmblog/2012/oct/08/worst-movie-death-scenes; "The 10 Worst Death Scenes in Movie History," *ScreenCrush*, https://screencrush.com/worst-death-scenes/.
35. "Worst Dead Scene Ever ! Original Video," YouTube video, https://www.youtube.com/watch?v=nAdniWncWu4.
36. At Zapruder's request, this frame was not printed in the original *Life* magazine story that appeared soon after the assassination on November 29, 1963; it was, however, published in volume 18 of the Warren Commission Report in 1964 and appeared again in Josiah Thompson's controversial *Six Seconds in Dallas*, a fetishizing microanalysis of Kennedy's murder that featured realistic charcoal drawings of Zapruder frames that Thompson produced specifically to avoid the family's claims of copyright.
37. Cawelti, *Focus on Bonnie and Clyde*, 16.
38. "Dance of Death—Bonnie and Clyde," https://www.dga.org/Craft/DGAQ/All-Articles/0804-Winter-2008-09/Shot-To-Remember-Bonnie-and-Clyde.aspx. The allusion has since become a standard point of reference in critical and popular discussions of both these iconic movies, with Ted Gioia, for example, citing Penn's citation of Zapruder frame 313 as further evidence that this Kennedy assassination footage is "The Most Important Film of All Time." Ted Gioia, "The Most Important Film of All Time: 26.6 Seconds by Abraham Zapruder," *Daily Beast*, November 22, 2015, https://www.thedailybeast.com/articles/2015/11/22/the-most-important-film-of-all-time-26-6-seconds-by-abraham-zapruder.

39. Roland Barthes, *Image-Music-Text* (Macmillan, 1977), 67.
40. "What Happens When You Are Shot? | Secrets of Everything | Earth Lab," YouTube video, 2016, https://www.youtube.com/watch?v=v7XX8W2X2d8; "Taran's Unofficial Test with Some of the Most Popular Calibers w/ Ballistic Dummy Lab," YouTube video, 2019, https://www.youtube.com/watch?v=UfWXfnOPivg.
41. T. J. Clark, *The Sight of Death: An Experiment in Art Writing* (Yale University Press, 2006), 208.
42. Wake and Hayden, *The Bonnie & Clyde Book*, 19.
43. Rob Wilson and Christopher Leigh Connery, *The Worlding Project: Doing Cultural Studies in the Era of Globalization* (North Atlantic, 2007), 87–88. See also Michael Szalay, *Hip Figures: A Literary History of the Democratic Party* (Stanford University Press, 2012).
44. Brian Dillon, "Fragments from a History of Ruin," https://cabinetmagazine.org/issues/20/dillon.php.
45. Wake and Hayden, *The Bonnie & Clyde Book*, 71.

23. POSTHISTORIC PREHISTORIC MODERNISM: *2001: A SPACE ODYSSEY*

1. Scott Bukatman, *Matters of Gravity: Special Effects and Supermen in the Twentieth Century* (Duke University Press, 2003), 116–17.
2. Annette Michelson, "BODIES IN SPACE," *Artforum*, February 1, 1969, 2579358801, Artforum Archive.
3. Michel Chion, *Kubrick's Cinema Odyssey* (Bloomsbury, 2019), 118.
4. "The Greatest Scene Cut in Film History (*2001: A Space Odyssey*)," YouTube video, 2018, https://www.youtube.com/watch?v=xkNV_wALoYc; "*2001—A Space Odyssey* (1968)—Best Cut in the History of Cinema," YouTube video, 2008, https://www.youtube.com/watch?v=Xe3utnBqUsM.
5. Pauline Kael, *The Age of Movies: Selected Writings of Pauline Kael*, ed. Sanford Schwartz (Library of America, 2016).
6. Renata Adler, "The Screen: '2001' Is Up, Up and Away: Kubrick's Odyssey in Space Begins Run," *New York Times*, April 4, 1968, https://www.nytimes.com/1968/04/04/archives/the-screen-2001-is-up-up-and-awaykubricks-odyssey-in-space-begins.html.
7. Michelson, "BODIES IN SPACE."
8. "Filming *2001: A Space Odyssey*," American Society of Cinematographers, https://ascmag.com/articles/filming-2001-a-space-odyssey.
9. Michelson, "BODIES IN SPACE."
10. T. J. Clark, "Modernism, Postmodernism, and Steam," *October* 100 (2002): 162, 173.
11. Michael Benson, *Space Odyssey: Stanley Kubrick, Arthur C. Clarke, and the Making of a Masterpiece* (Simon & Schuster, 2019).
12. "Sloan Science & Film," http://scienceandfilm.org/articles/2656/graphic-films-and-the-inception-of-2001-a-space-odyssey.
13. Benson, *Space Odyssey*, 81.
14. Robert Slifkin, *The New Monuments and the End of Man: U.S. Sculpture Between War and Peace, 1945–1975* (Princeton University Press, 2019), 183, 139.
15. Michelson, "BODIES IN SPACE."
16. Benson, *Space Odyssey*.
17. Benson, *Space Odyssey*, 31.
18. Theodor W. Adorno, *Negative Dialectics* (Bloomsbury Academic, 1973), 320.

19. "2001 A Space Odyssey Script by Stanley Kubrick and Arthur C. Clark," http://www.dailyscript.com/scripts/2001.html.
20. Kael, *The Age of Movies*.
21. Jane P. Tompkins, *West of Everything: The Inner Life of Westerns* (Oxford University Press, 1993), 70.
22. Gene Youngblood and R. Buckminster Fuller, *Expanded Cinema*, fiftieth anniversary ed. (Fordham University Press, 2020), 139, 142.
23. "Why Does HAL Sing 'Daisy, Daisy' in 2001: A Space Odyssey?," kottke.org, https://kottke.org/06/04/hal-daisy-2001.
24. "First Philadelphia Computer Music Festival," https://www.vintagecomputermusic.com/.
25. Ellis Hanson, "Technology, Paranoia and the Queer Voice," *Screen* 34, no. 2 (July 1, 1993): 137–61.
26. Claire Mulkerin, "HAL in *2001: A Space Odyssey* Explained," *Looper*, August 21, 2019, https://www.looper.com/163074/hal-in-2001-a-space-odyssey-explained/; Gerry Flahive, "I'm Sure You'll Agree There's Some Truth in What I Say," *POV*, May 10, 2018, https://povmagazine.com/im-sure-youll-agree-theres-some-truth-in-what-i-say/.
27. Benson, *Space Odyssey*, 76.
28. Chion, *Kubrick's Cinema Odyssey*, 103.
29. Benson, *Space Odyssey*, 377.
30. I have explored questions of slow sound more fully in "The Slowest Music in the World," forthcoming in *Diacritics*.
31. "Big 'NO!,'" TV Tropes, https://tvtropes.org/pmwiki/pmwiki.php/Main/BigNo; "Slow 'NO!,'" TV Tropes, https://tvtropes.org/pmwiki/pmwiki.php/Main/SlowNo.
32. Alexander Rehding, *Music and Monumentality: Commemoration and Wonderment in Nineteenth Century Germany* (Oxford University Press, 2009), 27.
33. Deborah Cowen, *The Deadly Life of Logistics: Mapping Violence in Global Trade* (University of Minnesota Press, 2014), 5.
34. Slifkin, *The New Monuments and the End of Man*, 33.
35. Donella H. Meadows, Dennis L. Meadows, Jørgen Randers, and William W. Behrens III, *The Limits to Growth: A Report for the Club of Rome's Project on the Predicament of Mankind* (Potomac Association Books, 1972), 23.
36. Meadows et al., *The Limits to Growth*, 126, 142, 195, 152–53, 154.
37. Michel Foucault and Jay Miskowiec, "Of Other Spaces," *Diacritics* 16, no. 1 (1986): 22–27.
38. Allen Sekula and centrum voor hedendaagse kunst Witte de With, *Fish Story* (Art Pub, 2002), 116, 50.
39. Sekula, *Fish Story*, 74.

24. HOW THE WEST SLOWS DOWN: SERGIO LEONE AND THE LONG STRUGGLE

1. Stanley Kauffmann, "TNR Film Classics: 'Once Upon a Time in the West' (June 21, 1969)," *New Republic*, April 14, 2012, https://newrepublic.com/article/102692/tnr-film-classics-once-upon-time-in-the-west-june-21-1969.
2. Pauline Kael, *5001 Nights at the Movies* (Henry Holt, 2011), 548.
3. Jussi Parikka, *A Slow, Contemporary Violence: Damaged Environments of Technological Culture* (Sternberg, 2016), 11.

4. Douglas Gordon, "5 year drive-by; proposal for a public artwork," 1995, http://e-flux.com/aup/project/douglas-gordon/.
5. Viktor Shklovsky, *Theory of Prose*, trans. Benjamin Sher (Dalkey Archive, 1990). See also Gérard Genette, *Narrative Discourse: An Essay in Method*, trans. Jane E. Lewin (Cornell University Press, 1980), 86–112.
6. Don DeLillo, *Point Omega* (Scribner, 2010), 29, 13.
7. Michael Fried, *Four Honest Outlaws: Sala, Ray, Marioni, Gordon* (Yale University Press, 2011), 187, 188, 192.
8. Ross Posnock, "'Don't Think, but Look!': W. G. Sebald, Wittgenstein, and Cosmopolitan Poverty," *Representations* 112, no. 1 (Fall 2010), 112–39. "Estrangement" and "defamiliarization" are the two most frequent translations of Shklovsky's original *ostranenie*.
9. Fried, *Four Honest Outlaws*, 191.
10. Robert Smithson, "A Cinematic Atopia," in *Collected Writings of Robert Smithson* (1971; University of California Press, 1996), 141.
11. Christopher Frayling, *Sergio Leone: Something to Do with Death* (University of Minnesota Press, 2012), 492; Jean Baudrillard, *Simulacra and Simulation* (University of Michigan Press, 1994), 46.
12. Walter Benjamin, "The Work of Art in the Age of Its Technological Reproducibility [second version]," in *The Work of Art in the Age of Its Technological Reproducibility, and Other Writings on Media* (Belknap Press of Harvard University Press, 2008), 37.
13. Fredric Jameson, *A Singular Modernity: Essay on the Ontology of the Present* (Verso, 2013), 154.
14. Clement Greenberg, "Modernist Painting," in *The Collected Essays and Criticism*, vol. 4: *Modernism with a Vengeance, 1957–1969* (1961; University of Chicago Press, 1995), 80.
15. Michael Fried, "Art and Objecthood," in *Art and Objecthood: Essays and Reviews* (1967; University of Chicago Press, 1998), 166, 168.
16. Pamela Lee, *Chronophobia: On Time in Art of the 1960s* (MIT Press, 2006).
17. Smithson, *Collected Writings of Robert Smithson*, 66–67.
18. Lytle Shaw, *Fieldworks: From Place to Site in Postwar Poetics* (University of Alabama Press, 2013), 204.
19. Smithson, *Collected Writings of Robert Smithson*, 67.
20. T. J. Clark, "Clement Greenberg's Theory of Art," *Critical Inquiry* 9, no. 1 (1982): 139–56; Michael Fried, "How Modernism Works: A Response to T. J. Clark," *Critical Inquiry* 9, no. 1 (1982): 217–34.
21. Smithson, in *Collected Writings of Robert Smithson*, 67.
22. Quentin Meillassoux, *After Finitude: An Essay on the Necessity of Contingency* (Continuum, 2010); Mark McGurl, "The Posthuman Comedy," *Critical Inquiry* 38, no. 3 (Spring 2012).
23. Frayling, *Sergio Leone*, 230–31.
24. For more on the use of undercranking in slapstick comedy, particularly in the silent era, see M. Hennefeld, *Specters of Slapstick and Silent Film Comediennes* (Columbia University Press, 2018); and J. R. King, *The Fun Factory: The Keystone Film Company and the Emergence of Mass Culture* (University of California Press, 2008).
25. Robert Warshow, "The Westerner," in *The Immediate Experience: Movies, Comics, Theatre, and Other Aspects of Popular Culture* (1954; Harvard University Press, 2001), 105–24.
26. J. G. Ballard, "The Voices of Time," in *The Complete Stories of J. G. Ballard* (Norton, 2009), 193. Tacita Dean's recent film *JG* powerfully explores the connection between Ballard and Smithson and uses passages from this story to renarrate both her own footage at the site of "Spiral Jetty" and Smithson's own film of the project.
27. Georg Lukács, "The Ideology of Modernism," in *Realism in Our Time: Literature and the Class Struggle*, trans. John Mander and Necke Mander (Harper & Row, 1962), 20–21.
28. Fredric Jameson, "Periodizing the 60s," *Social Text* 9/10 (Summer 1984): 191.
29. Smithson, *Collected Writings of Robert Smithson*, 101.

30. Jameson, "Periodizing the 60s," 180.
31. Louis Menand, "After the Revolution," *New Yorker*, October 12, 2003, https://www.newyorker.com/magazine/2003/10/20/after-the-revolution-4.
32. J. Hoberman, *The Dream Life: Movies, Media, and the Mythology of the Sixties* (New Press, 2005), 321.
33. Richard Gooden, "Maximizing the Noodles: Class, Memory, and Capital in Sergio Leone's *Once Upon a Time in America*," *Journal of American Studies* 31, no. 3, pt. 1 (December 1997): 376.
34. Giovanni Arrighi, *The Long Twentieth Century: Money, Power, and the Origins of Our Times* (Verso, 2010), 309.
35. Parikka, *A Slow, Contemporary Violence*, 27.

25. *THE WILD BUNCH*, OR THE PAINS OF BEING SAM PECKINPAH

1. Bernard F. Dukore, *Sam Peckinpah's Feature Films* (University of Illinois Press, 1999), 77, 94.
2. Cameron Detig, "Slow Motion in the Age of Intensified Continuity," *Film Matters* 12, no. 1 (2021): 8.
3. *Monty Python's Flying Circus*, season 3, episode 7, "Salad Days," *Dailymotion*, https://www.dailymotion.com/video/x85rkdo.
4. Sean Cubitt, *The Cinema Effect* (MIT Press, 2005), 191, 190, 190, 211, 211.
5. Dukore, *Sam Peckinpah's Feature Films*, 77.
6. Mariana Mogilevich, Ben Campkin, and Rebecca Ross, "Pruitt Igoe: Blowing Up This St. Louis Housing Project Was Easier Than Demolishing the Myth It Created," *The Guardian*, December 10, 2014, https://www.theguardian.com/cities/2014/dec/10/pruitt-igoe-st-louis-myth-harder-demolish-social-housing-modernism; Stefan Novakovic, "Charles Jencks, 1939–2019: Postmodernism with a Capital P," *Azure Magazine* (blog), October 16, 2019, https://www.azuremagazine.com/article/charles-jencks-obituary-postmodernism/.
7. Pamela M. Lee, *Chronophobia: On Time in the Art of the 1960s* (MIT Press, 2004), 199.
8. David Weddle, *If They Move—Kill 'Em!: The Life and Times of Sam Peckinpah* (Grove, 2000), 249–50.
9. Cubitt, *The Cinema Effect*, 197.
10. Weddle, *If They Move—Kill 'Em!*, 107.
11. Jeff Menne, *Post-Fordist Cinema: Hollywood Auteurs and the Corporate Counterculture* (Columbia University Press, 2019), 54.
12. *Felony Squad*, "My Mommy Got Lost," 1967, https://www.youtube.com/watch?v=iI9nZ5tddOE.
13. Weddle, *If They Move—Kill 'Em!*, 10.
14. Ernest Hemingway, *Death in the Afternoon* (Scribner, 1960), 98, 14, 207.
15. Martin Hägglund, *Dying for Time* (Harvard University Press, 2012), 78, 75, 75.
16. David Z. Goodman and Sam Peckinpah, "The Siege of Trencher's Farm [Screenplay]," 1970, 74. I am grateful to Kevis Goodman for bringing this early version of the screenplay to my attention; it provides a fascinating look into the production history of the film, as well as showing where Peckinpah's familiar stylistic mannerisms by this point in his career were and weren't put on the page.
17. Editing by Tony Lawson, Paul Davies, and Roger Spottiswoode; Dukore and Prince both offer impassioned defenses for the treatment of rape in *Straw Dogs*, and they are persuasive in their claims. But the estrangement of the viewer's point of view from that of Amy's attackers does not necessarily excuse the excesses of the scene or its lurid fixation on the moments of pleasure that Amy is shown to experience in the midst of Venner's rape.

18. Pauline Kael, "Straw Dogs: Peckinpah's Obsession," *Scraps from the Loft* (blog), January 18, 2018, https://scrapsfromtheloft.com/movies/straw-dogs-peckinpahs-obsession-pauline-kael/.
19. W. K. Stratton, *The Wild Bunch: Sam Peckinpah, a Revolution in Hollywood, and the Making of a Legendary Film* (Bloomsbury, 2019), 266.
20. Noël Carroll, "The Professional Western: South of the Border" in *Back in the Saddle Again: New Essays on the Western*, ed. E. Buscombe and R. Pearson (Bloomsbury, 1998), 46–62; Menne, *Post-Fordist Cinema*, 54.
21. J. R. Jones, "Actor Robert Ryan Was the Wild Bunch's Party Man," *Chicago Reader*, May 27, 2015, http://chicagoreader.com/film/actor-robert-ryan-was-the-wild-bunchs-party-man/.

26. ANTONIONI'S ART OF EXCESS: *ZABRISKIE POINT*

1. Peter Brunette, *The Films of Michelangelo Antonioni* (Cambridge University Press, 1998), 23.
2. Seymour Chatman, *Antonioni, or, The Surface of the World* (University of California Press, 1985), 161.
3. Seymour Chatman and Paul Duncan, *Michelangelo Antonioni: The Investigation* (Taschen, 2004), 126.
4. Chatman, *Antonioni*, 160.
5. Pauline Kael, "The Current Cinema: The Beauty of Destruction," *New Yorker*, February 2, 1970, https://archives.newyorker.com/newyorker/1970-02-21/flipbook/094/.
6. Rick Setlowe, "Pictures: Frisco Fest Buffs Hushedly Pious Welcome for Plot-Killer Antonioni," *Variety (Archive: 1905–2000)* (Penske Business Corporation, November 6, 1968), 1505776773, Entertainment Industry Magazine Archive; Periodicals Index Online.
7. "Michelangelo and the Leviathan: The Making of *Zabriskie Point* (1992)," *Michelangelo Antonioni* (blog), June 25, 2021, https://antonioni9.wordpress.com/2021/06/25/michelangelo-and-the-leviathan-the-making-of-zabriskie-point-1992/.
8. "*The Wild Bunch*," *New Yorker*, https://www.newyorker.com/goings-on-about-town/movies/the-wild-bunch.
9. Kael, "The Current Cinema."
10. James S. Williams, "The Rhythms of Life: An Appreciation of Michelangelo Antonioni, Extreme Aesthete of the Real," *Film Quarterly* 62, no. 1 (2008): 55.
11. Theodor W. Adorno, *Aesthetic Theory*, ed. Robert Hullot-Kentor (University of Minnesota Press, 1997), 23.
12. Adorno, *Aesthetic Theory*, 23, 27.
13. Adorno, *Aesthetic Theory*, 46.
14. Adorno, *Aesthetic Theory*, 81, 84, 85.
15. Laura Rascaroli and John David Rhodes, *Antonioni: Centenary Essays* (Bloomsbury, 2011).
16. Adorno, *Aesthetic Theory*, 95.
17. James Barber, "Michael Bay Insists 'Pearl Harbor' Had the Biggest Movie Explosion Ever," Military.com, February 22, 2022, https://www.military.com/off-duty/movies/2022/02/22/michael-bay-insists-pearl-harbor-had-biggest-movie-explosion-ever.html.
18. "Breaking Down Bayhem: The Sweet Science of Explosions in Michael Bay Movies," *Rotten Tomatoes*, https://editorial.rottentomatoes.com/article/breaking-down-bayhem/; "Michael Bay Has a 'Special Sauce' for Movie Explosions: 'It's Like Making a Caesar Salad'—Exclusive Image," *Empire*, 2022, https://www.empireonline.com/movies/news/michael-bay-special-sauce-explosions-making-caesar-salad-exclusive/.

19. Sam Haysom, "A Capacitor Exploding in Extreme Slow Motion Looks Like Something from Outer Space," *Mashable*, March 2, 2022, https://mashable.com/video/slow-mo-guys-exploding-capacitor.
20. "Michelangelo and the Leviathan."
21. Marsha Kinder, "Zabriskie Point," *Monthly Film Bulletin* (British Film Institute, Winter 1969), 28, 740631824, Performing Arts Periodicals Database.
22. Slavoj Žižek, *The Pervert's Guide to Ideology*, 2013, http://archive.org/details/the-perverts-guide-to-ideology-2012-hd.
23. William Arrowsmith and Ted Perry, *Antonioni: The Poet of Images* (Oxford University Press, 1995), 141.
24. Karl Marx, *Capital: A Critique of Political Economy*, vol. 3 (Penguin, 1993).
25. T. J. Clark, "Freud's Cézanne," *Representations* 52 (October 1, 1995): 94–122.
26. Bob Mielke, "Rhetoric and Ideology in the Nuclear Test Documentary," *Film Quarterly* 58, no. 3 (2005): 28–37.
27. Tom Gunning, "The Cinema of Attraction: Early Film, Its Spectator, and the Avant-Garde," *Wide Angle* 8, no. 3–4 (1986): 63–70.
28. "The Most Impressive Real Stuff Blown Up in the Name of Blockbuster Movie-Making," *MEL Magazine* (blog), June 13, 2020, https://melmagazine.com/en-us/story/biggest-best-movie-explosions; "The 15 Best Explosions in Movie History," *Paste*, https://www.pastemagazine.com/movies/top-15-explosions-in-movie-history/2.
29. "Exploding Fruit in 4K," YouTube video, 2018, https://www.youtube.com/watch?v=oyxvYfJ5gjY.
30. Wolfgang Ernst, *The Contemporary Condition: Introductory Thoughts on Contemporaneity and Contemporary Art* (Sternberg, 2016), 36, 30.
31. Jonathan M. Weisgall, *Operation Crossroads: The Atomic Tests at Bikini Atoll* (Naval Institute Press, 1994), http://archive.org/details/operationcrossrooooweis.
32. J. Hoberman, "The Creepy World of Bruce Conner," *New York Review of Books*, July 15, 2016, https://www.nybooks.com/online/2016/07/15/creepy-world-of-bruce-conner/.
33. Frances Ferguson, "The Nuclear Sublime," *Diacritics* 14, no. 2 (1984): 4–10.

Bibliography

Abel, Marco. "Don DeLillo's 'In the Ruins of the Future': Literature, Images, and the Rhetoric of Seeing 9/11." *PMLA* 118, no. 5 (2003): 1236–50.
———. *Violent Affect: Literature, Cinema, and Critique After Representation*. University of Nebraska Press, 2007.
Abel, Richard. *French Film Theory and Criticism: 1907–1929*. Princeton University Press, 1993.
Abumrad, Jad, and Robert Krulwich. "Why a Brush with Death Triggers the Slow-Mo Effect." NPR, August 17, 2010, https://www.npr.org/templates/story/story.php?storyId=129112147.
Acland, Charles, and Haidee Wasson. *Useful Cinema*. Duke University Press, 2011.
Adam, Barbara. *Timewatch: The Social Analysis of Time*. Wiley, 2013.
Adeyemi, Kemi. "The Practice of Slowness: Black Queer Women and the Right to the City." *GLQ: A Journal of Lesbian and Gay Studies* 25, no. 4 (October 1, 2019): 545–67.
Adler, Renata. "The Screen: '2001' Is Up, Up and Away: Kubrick's Odyssey in Space Begins Run." *New York Times*, April 4, 1968, https://www.nytimes.com/1968/04/04/archives/the-screen-2001-is-up-up-and-awaykubricks-odyssey-in-space-begins.html.
Adorno, Theodor W. *Aesthetic Theory*. Ed. Robert Hullot-Kentor. University of Minnesota Press, 1997.
———. *Negative Dialectics*. Bloomsbury Academic, 1973.
Anderson, Sam. "Review: *Point Omega*, by Don DeLillo." *New York*, January 21, 2010, https://nymag.com/arts/books/reviews/63210/.
Antonioni, Michelangelo. "Michelangelo and the Leviathan: The Making of *Zabriskie Point* (1992)." June 25, 2021. https://antonioni9.wordpress.com/2021/06/25/michelangelo-and-the-leviathan-the-making-of-zabriskie-point-1992/.
Arnheim, Rudolf. *Art and Visual Perception: A Psychology of the Creative Eye*. Exp. and rev. ed. University of California Press, 1974.
———. *Film as Art*. University of California Press, 1957.
Arrighi, Giovanni. *The Long Twentieth Century: Money, Power, and the Origins of Our Times*. Verso, 2010.
Arrowsmith, William, and Ted Perry. *Antonioni: The Poet of Images*. Oxford University Press, 1995.
Bachner, S. *The Prestige of Violence: American Fiction, 1962–2007*. University of Georgia Press, 2011.
Balázs, Béla. *Early Film Theory: Visible Man and the Spirit of Film*. Berghahn, 2010.
Balio, T. *The American Film Industry*. University of Wisconsin Press, 1985.
Ballard, J. G. "The Voices of Time." In *The Complete Stories of J. G. Ballard*. Norton, 2009.

Balsom, Erika. *Ten Skies*. Fireflies, 2021.
Barber, James. "Michael Bay Insists 'Pearl Harbor' Had the Biggest Movie Explosion Ever." *Military.com*, February 22, 2022, https://www.military.com/off-duty/movies/2022/02/22/michael-bay-insists-pearl-harbor-had-biggest-movie-explosion-ever.html.
Barthes, Roland. *Camera Lucida: Reflections on Photography*. Macmillan, 1981.
———. *Image-Music-Text*. Macmillan, 1977.
———. "Textual Analysis of a Tale by Edgar Poe." Trans. Donald G. Marshall. *Poe Studies (1971–1985)* 10, no. 1 (1977): 1–12.
Baumbach, Nico. *Cinema/Politics/Philosophy*. Columbia University Press, 2018.
Bazin, Andre. *What Is Cinema?* Vol. 1. Ed. and trans. Hugh Gray. University of California Press, 2005.
Beeston, Alix. *In and Out of Sight: Modernist Writing and the Photographic Unseen*. Oxford University Press, 2018.
Benjamin, Walter. *The Arcades Project*. Trans. Howard Eiland and Kevin McLaughlin. Belknap Press of Harvard University Press, 1999.
———. *The Work of Art in the Age of Its Technological Reproducibility, and Other Writings on Media*. Ed. Michael W. Jennings, Brigid Doherty, and Thomas Y. Levin. Belknap Press of Harvard University Press, 2008.
———. *The Writer of Modern Life: Essays on Charles Baudelaire*. Ed. Michael W. Jennings. Harvard University Press, 2006.
Benson, Michael. *Space Odyssey: Stanley Kubrick, Arthur C. Clarke, and the Making of a Masterpiece*. Simon & Schuster, 2019.
Bergson, Henri. *Matter and Memory*. Dover, 2012.
———. *Time and Free Will: An Essay on the Immediate Data of Consciousness*. Courier, 2012.
Bersani, Leo, and Ulysse Dutoit. *The Forms of Violence: Narrative in Assyrian Art and Modern Culture*. Schocken, 1985.
Bishop, Ryan, and John Phillips. *Modernist Avant-Garde Aesthetics and Contemporary Military Technology: Technicities of Perception*. Edinburgh University Press, 2010.
Biskind, Peter. *Easy Riders, Raging Bulls: How the Sex-Drugs-and–Rock 'n' Roll Generation Saved Hollywood*. Simon & Schuster, 2011.
Blom, Jan Dirk, Nutsa Nanuashvili, and Flavie Waters. "Time Distortions: A Systematic Review of Cases Characteristic of Alice in Wonderland Syndrome." *Frontiers in Psychiatry* 12 (May 2021): 668633.
Bordwell, David. "Cognition and Comprehension: Viewing and Forgetting in *Mildred Pierce*." *Journal of Dramatic Theory and Criticism* (March 1992): 183–98.
———. *The Way Hollywood Tells It: Story and Style in Modern Movies*. University of California Press, 2006.
Bordwell, David, Janet Staiger, and Kristin Thompson. *The Classical Hollywood Cinema: Film Style and Mode of Production to 1960*. Routledge, 2003.
Bou, Stéphane, and Jean-Baptiste Thoret. "A Conversation with Don DeLillo: Has Terrorism Become the World's Main Plot?" Trans. Noel King. *Panic* 1 (November 2005): 90–95. http://perival.com/delillo/interview_panic_2005.html.
Brenner, Robert. "The Long Downturn." *New America*, April 21, 2010. http://newamerica.org/economic-growth/policy-papers/the-long-downturn/.
Brooks, Cleanth. *William Faulkner: Toward Yoknapatawpha and Beyond*. Louisiana State University Press, 1989.
Brouillette, Sarah, Joshua Clover, and Annie McClanahan. "Introduction: Late, Autumnal, Immiserating, Terminal." *Theory & Event* 22, no. 2 (April 2019): 325–36.
Brüderlin, Markus, and Hartmut Böhme. *The Art of Deceleration: Motion and Rest in Modern Art from Caspar David Friedrich to Ai Weiwei*. Hatje Cantz, 2012.
Brunette, Peter. *The Films of Michelangelo Antonioni*. Cambridge University Press, 1998.

Bukatman, Scott. *Matters of Gravity: Special Effects and Supermen in the Twentieth Century.* Duke University Press, 2003.

Burch, Noël. *Life to Those Shadows.* Trans. B. Brewster. University of California Press, 1990.

Burrows, Stuart. *A Familiar Strangeness: American Fiction and the Language of Photography, 1839–1945.* University of Georgia Press, 2010.

Buscombe, Edward, and Robert E. Pearson, eds. *Back in the Saddle Again: New Essays on the Western.* Bloomsbury Academic, 1998.

Calavita, Marco. "'MTV Aesthetics' at the Movies: Interrogating a Film Criticism Fallacy." *Journal of Film and Video* 59, no. 3 (2007): 15–31.

Canales, Jimena. *A Tenth of a Second: A History.* University of Chicago Press, 2010.

Cather, Willa. *Not Under Forty.* University of Nebraska Press, 1988.

Cavell, Stanley. *The World Viewed: Reflections on the Ontology of Film.* Enlarged ed. Harvard University Press, 1979.

Cendrars, Blaise. *Modernities and Other Writings.* Trans. Monique Chefdor. University of Nebraska Press, 1992.

Charney, Leo, and Vanessa R. Schwartz, eds. *Cinema and the Invention of Modern Life.* University of California Press, 1995.

Chatman, Seymour. *Antonioni, or, The Surface of the World.* University of California Press, 1985.

———. "Genette's Analysis of Narrative Time Relations." *L'Esprit Créateur* 14, no. 4 (1974): 353–68.

Chatman, Seymour, and Paul Duncan. *Michelangelo Antonioni: The Investigation.* Taschen, 2004.

Chion, Michel. *Film, a Sound Art.* Trans. Claudia Gorbman. Columbia University Press, 2009.

———. *Kubrick's Cinema Odyssey.* Bloomsbury, 2019.

Christensen, Jerome. *America's Corporate Art: The Studio Authorship of Hollywood Motion Pictures.* Stanford University Press, 2012.

Christie, James, and Nesrin Degirmencioglu, eds. *Cultures of Uneven and Combined Development: From International Relations to World Literature.* Brill, 2019.

Clark, T. J. "Clement Greenberg's Theory of Art." *Critical Inquiry* 9, no. 1 (1982): 139–56.

———. "Freud's Cézanne." *Representations* 52 (October 1, 1995): 94–122.

———. "Modernism, Postmodernism, and Steam." *October* 100 (2002): 155–74.

———. *The Sight of Death: An Experiment in Art Writing.* Yale University Press, 2006.

Colette, [Sidonie-Gabrielle]. *Colette at the Movies: Criticism and Screenplays.* Ungar, 1980.

Connor, J. D. *Hollywood Math and Aftermath: The Economic Image and the Digital Recession.* Bloomsbury, 2018.

———. *The Studios After the Studios: Neoclassical Hollywood (1970–2010).* Stanford University Press, 2015.

Cowen, Deborah. *The Deadly Life of Logistics: Mapping Violence in Global Trade.* University of Minnesota Press, 2014.

Cowen, Tyler. *The Great Stagnation: How America Ate All the Low-Hanging Fruit of Modern History, Got Sick, and Will (Eventually) Feel Better.* Dutton, 2011.

Crary, Jonathan. *24/7: Late Capitalism and the Ends of Sleep.* Verso, 2013.

Cubitt, Sean. *The Cinema Effect.* MIT Press, 2005.

Curran, Jane V., and Christophe Fricker, eds. *Schiller's "On Grace and Dignity" in Its Cultural Context: Essays and a New Translation.* Boydell & Brewer, 2005.

Danius, Sara. *The Senses of Modernism: Technology, Perception, and Aesthetics.* Cornell University Press, 2002.

Dargis, Manhola, and Scott, A. O. "In Defense of the Slow and the Boring." *New York Times*, March 6, 2011, https://www.nytimes.com/2011/06/05/movies/films-in-defense-of-slow-and-boring.html.

Dash, Julie. *Daughters of the Dust: The Making of an African American Woman's Film.* New York: New Press, 1992.

Davidson, Donald. *Inquiries Into Truth and Interpretation.* Oxford: Oxford University Press, 2001.

Deleuze, Gilles. *Cinema 1: The Movement-Image.* Continuum, 2005.
———. *Cinema II.* Bloomsbury Academic, 2005.
DeLillo, Don. "American Blood." *Rolling Stone*, December 8, 1983.
———. *The Body Artist.* Scribner, 2002.
———. *Cosmopolis.* Scribner, 2004.
———. *Falling Man.* Scribner, 2008.
———. "In the Ruins of the Future: Reflections on Terror and Loss in the Shadow of September." *Harper's,* December 2001.
———. *Libra: With a New Introduction by the Author.* Penguin, 1991.
———. *Mao II.* Penguin, 1992.
———. *Point Omega.* Scribner, 2010.
———. *Underworld.* Scribner, 1997.
———. *White Noise.* Penguin, 1985.
———. *Zero K.* Scribner, 2016.
Denson, Shane. *Discorrelated Images.* Duke University Press, 2020.
Deren, Maya. *Essential Deren: Collected Writings on Film.* Ed. Bruce Rice McPherson. McPherson, 2005.
Detig, Cameron. "Slow Motion in the Age of Intensified Continuity." *Film Matters* 12, no. 1 (2021): 7–16.
Dinshaw, Carolyn. *How Soon Is Now? Medieval Texts, Amateur Readers, and the Queerness of Time.* Duke University Press, 2012.
Doane, Mary Ann. *The Emergence of Cinematic Time: Modernity, Contingency, the Archive.* Harvard University Press, 2002.
———. "Has Time Become Space?" In *Thinking Media Aesthetics: Media Studies, Film Studies, and the Arts.* Peter Lang, 2013.
———. "The Indexical and the Concept of Medium Specificity." *Differences* 18, no. 1 (May 1, 2007): 128–52.
———. "Indexicality: Trace and Sign: Introduction." *Differences* 18, no. 1 (May 1, 2007): 1–6.
Donald, James, Anne Friedberg, and Laura Marcus. *Close Up: Cinema And Modernism.* A&C Black, 1998.
Dorling, Daniel, and Kirsten McClure. *Slowdown: The End of the Great Acceleration and Why It's Good for the Planet, the Economy, and Our Lives.* Yale University Press, 2020.
Duffy, Enda. *The Speed Handbook: Velocity, Pleasure, Modernism.* Duke University Press, 2009.
Dukore, Bernard F. *Sam Peckinpah's Feature Films.* Urbana: University of Illinois Press, 1999.
Dutton, Richard, Richard Wilson, and Leslie Wilson. *New Historicism and Renaissance Drama.* Longman, 1992.
Eburne, Jonathan. *Outsider Theory: Intellectual Histories of Unorthodox Ideas.* University of Minnesota Press, 2018.
Edogawa, Rampo. *The Edogawa Rampo Reader.* Ed. Takayuki Tatsumi. Trans. Seth Jacobowitz. Kurodahan, 2008.
Epstein, Jean. *The Intelligence of a Machine.* Trans. Christophe Wall-Ramona. University of Minnesota Press, 2015.
Ernst, Wolfgang. *Chronopoetics: The Temporal Being and Operativity of Technological Media.* Trans. Anthony Enns. Rowman & Littlefield, 2016.
———. *The Contemporary Condition: Introductory Thoughts on Contemporaneity and Contemporary Art.* Sternberg, 2016.
———. *Digital Memory and the Archive.* Ed. Jussi Parikka. University of Minnesota Press, 2013.
Fabian, Johannes. *Time and the Other.* Columbia University Press, 2014.
Faulkner, William. *Light in August.* Vintage, 1990.
———. *Snopes: The Hamlet, The Town, The Mansion.* Modern Library, 1994.
———. *The Sound and the Fury.* Ed. David Minter. 2nd Norton Critical ed. Norton, 1994.

Fay, Jennifer. *Inhospitable World: Cinema in the Time of the Anthropocene.* Oxford University Press, 2018.
Ferguson, Frances. "The Nuclear Sublime." *Diacritics* 14, no. 2 (1984): 4–10.
Ferri, Michela Beatrice. *The Reception of Husserlian Phenomenology in North America.* Springer, 2019.
Forward, Ally. "What Are the Worst Movie Death Scenes of All Time?" *The Guardian,* October 8, 2012, https://www.theguardian.com/film/filmblog/2012/oct/08/worst-movie-death-scenes.
Foucault, Michel. "Of Other Spaces." Trans. Jay Miskowiec. *Diacritics* 16, no. 1 (1986): 22–27.
Frayling, Christopher. *Spaghetti Westerns: Cowboys and Europeans from Karl May to Sergio Leone.* I. B. Tauris, 1998.
Fried, Michael. *Art and Objecthood: Essays and Reviews.* University of Chicago Press, 1998.
———. *Four Honest Outlaws: Sala, Ray, Marioni, Gordon.* Yale University Press, 2011.
———. "How Modernism Works: A Response to T. J. Clark." *Critical Inquiry* 9, no. 1 (1982): 217–34.
———. *Why Photography Matters as Art as Never Before.* Yale University Press, 2008.
Friedberg, Anne. *Window Shopping: Cinema and the Postmodern.* University of California Press, 1994.
Friedman, Lester D. *Arthur Penn's Bonnie and Clyde.* Cambridge University Press, 2000.
Friedman, Susan S. *Planetary Modernisms: Provocations on Modernity Across Time.* Columbia University Press, 2015.
Fusco, Katherine, and Nicole Seymour. *Kelly Reichardt.* University of Illinois Press, 2017.
Gamache, Ray. *A History of Sports Highlights: Replayed Plays from Edison to ESPN.* McFarland, 2010.
Garber, Marjorie. "Shakespeare in Slow Motion." *Profession,* 2010, 151–64.
García-Moreno, Laura. "Strange Edifices, Counter-Monuments: Rethinking Time and Space in W. G. Sebald's Austerlitz." *Critique: Studies in Contemporary Fiction* 54, no. 4 (October 2, 2013): 360–79.
Genette, Gérard. *Narrative Discourse: An Essay in Method.* Trans. Jane E. Lewin. Cornell University Press, 1980.
Gidal, Peter. "FOREWORD IN THREE LETTERS." *Artforum* 10, no. 1 (September 1971): 8–8.
Gingrich, Brian. *The Pace of Fiction: Narrative Movement and the Novel.* Oxford University Press, 2021.
Gioia, Ted. "The Most Important Film of All Time: 26.6 Seconds by Abraham Zapruder." *The Daily Beast,* November 22, 2015, https://www.thedailybeast.com/articles/2015/11/22/the-most-important-film-of-all-time-26-6-seconds-by-abraham-zapruder.
Goble, Mark. *Beautiful Circuits: Modernism and the Mediated Life.* Columbia University Press, 2010.
Godden, Richard. *William Faulkner: An Economy of Complex Words.* Princeton University Press, 2007.
Gombrich, E. H. "Moment and Movement in Art." *Journal of the Warburg and Courtauld Institutes* 27 (1964): 293–306.
Gooden, Richard. "Maximizing the Noodles: Class, Memory, and Capital in Sergio Leone's 'Once Upon a Time in America.'" *Journal of American Studies* 31, no. 3, pt. 1 (December 1997).
Gordon, R. J. *The Rise and Fall of American Growth: The U.S. Standard of Living Since the Civil War.* Princeton University Press, 2017.
Greco, Joann. "The Psychology of Ruin Porn." *The Atlantic: Cities* (blog), January 6, 2012, http://www.joanngreco.com/wp-content/uploads/2011/01/The-Psychology-of-Ruin-Porn-Design-The-Atlantic-Cities-20120106.pdf.
Greenberg, C. *The Collected Essays and Criticism.* Vol. 4: *Modernism with a Vengeance, 1957–1969.* Ed. J. O'Brian. University of Chicago Press, 1995.
Greenblatt, Stephen. "Invisible Bullets: Renaissance Authority and Its Subversion." In *New Historicism and Renaissance Drama,* ed. Richard Dutton and Richard Wilson. Longman, 1992.
Gumbrecht, Hans Ulrich. *In Praise of Athletic Beauty.* Belknap Press of Harvard University Press, 2006.
Gunning, Tom. "The Cinema of Attraction[s]: Early Film, Its Spectator, and the Avant-Garde." In *The Cinema of Attractions Reloaded,* ed. Wanda Strauven, 381–88. Amsterdam University Press, 2006.
Hägglund, Martin. *Dying for Time.* Harvard University Press, 2012.

Hanchard, Michael. "Afro-Modernity: Temporality, Politics, and the African Disapora." In *Colored People Time*, ed. Meg Onli and Amber Rose Johnson. Institute of Contemporary Art and the University of Pennsylvania, 2020.
Hansen, Miriam Bratu. "The Mass Production of the Senses: Classical Cinema as Vernacular Modernism." In *Disciplining Modernism*, ed. Pamela L. Caughie, 242–58. London: Palgrave Macmillan UK, 2009.
Hartman, Saidiya. "The Time of Slavery." *South Atlantic Quarterly* 101, no. 4 (October 1, 2002): 757–77.
Harvey, David. *A Companion to Marx's Capital*. Complete ed. Verso, 2018.
———. *The Condition of Postmodernity: An Enquiry Into the Origins of Cultural Change*. Wiley, 1992.
Hayles, N. Katherine. *Unthought: The Power of the Cognitive Nonconscious*. University of Chicago Press, 2017.
Haynes, Jane. "Faulkner's Verbena." *Mississippi Quarterly* 33, no. 3 (1980): 355–62.
Haysom, Sam. "A Capacitor Exploding in Extreme Slow Motion Looks Like Something from Outer Space." Mashable, March 2, 2022, https://mashable.com/video/slow-mo-guys-exploding-capacitor.
Heidegger, M. *The Question Concerning Technology, and Other Essays*. HarperCollins, 1982.
Hemingway, E. *Death in the Afternoon*. Scribner, 1960.
Hennefeld, M. *Specters of Slapstick and Silent Film Comediennes*. Columbia University Press, 2018.
Hickel, Jason. *Less Is More: How Degrowth Will Save the World*. Random House, 2020.
Hoberman, J. "The Creepy World of Bruce Conner." *New York Review of Books*, July 15, 2016, https://www.nybooks.com/online/2016/07/15/creepy-world-of-bruce-conner/.
———. *The Dream Life: Movies, Media, and the Mythology of the Sixties*. New Press, 2005.
Hogan, Erin. *Spiral Jetta: A Road Trip Through the Land Art of the American West*. University of Chicago Press, 2008.
Holte, Michael Ned. "Shooting the Archaeozoic (on Robert Smithson)." January 2005. http://michaelnedholte.com/2005/01/shooting-the-archaeozoic-on-robert-smithson/.
Hornby, Louise. *Still Modernism: Photography, Literature, Film*. Oxford University Press, 2017.
Hoy, David Couzens. *The Time of Our Lives: A Critical History of Temporality*. MIT Press, 2012.
Husserl, Edmund. *The Phenomenology of Internal Time-Consciousness*. Indiana University Press, 2019.
Jaffe, Ira. *Slow Movies: Countering the Cinema of Action*. Columbia University Press, 2014.
James, Nick. "Passive Aggressive." *Sight and Sound* 20, no. 4 (April 2010): 5–5.
James, William. *The Principles of Psychology*. Vol. 1. Dover, 1950.
Jameson, Fredric. "Periodizing the 60s." *Social Text*, no. 9/10 (1984): 178–209.
———. *A Singular Modernity: Essay on the Ontology of the Present*. Verso, 2002.
———. *The Seeds of Time*. Columbia University Press, 1994.
———. *Valences of the Dialectic*. Verso, 2009.
Jones, J. R. "Actor Robert Ryan Was the Wild Bunch's Party Man." *Chicago Reader*, May 27, 2015, http://chicagoreader.com/film/actor-robert-ryan-was-the-wild-bunchs-party-man/.
Jones, Malcolm. "Slow Reading: An Antidote for Fast World?" *Newsweek*, June 22, 2010, https://www.newsweek.com/slow-reading-antidote-fast-world-73395.
Kael, Pauline. *The Age of Movies: Selected Writings of Pauline Kael*. Ed. Sanford Schwartz. Library of America, 2016.
———. *5001 Nights at the Movies*. Henry Holt, 2011.
———. *Kiss Kiss Bang Bang*. Bantam, 1969.
———. "Straw Dogs: Peckinpah's Obsession." *Scraps from the Loft* (blog), January 18, 2018, https://scrapsfromtheloft.com/movies/straw-dogs-peckinpahs-obsession-pauline-kael/.
———. "The Wild Bunch." *New Yorker*, March 24, 2016, https://www.newyorker.com/goings-on-about-town/movies/the-wild-bunch.
Kauffmann, Stanley. *Figures of Light: Film Criticism and Comment*. Harper & Row, 1971.

———. "TNR Film Classics: 'Once Upon a Time in the West' (June 21, 1969)." *New Republic*, April 14, 2012, https://newrepublic.com/article/102692/tnr-film-classics-once-upon-time-in-the-west-june-21-1969.

Kellog, Carolyn. "Don DeLillo's Prescience Is a Mystery Even to His Acolytes." *Los Angeles Times*, October 9, 2020, https://www.latimes.com/entertainment-arts/books/story/2020-10-09/don-delillos-new-novel-the-silence-and-his-enduring-influence.

Kelly, Jack. "20 Lessons Learned 20 Years After September 11." *Forbes*. https://www.forbes.com/sites/jackkelly/2021/09/11/twenty-lessons-learned-from-twenty-years-after-911/.

Kern, Stephen. *The Culture of Time and Space, 1880–1918*. Harvard University Press, 1983.

Kinder, Marsha. "Zabriskie Point." *Monthly Film Bulletin*, Winter 1969.

King, Rob. *The Fun Factory: The Keystone Film Company and the Emergence of Mass Culture*. University of California Press, 2008.

Kingsley, Patrick. "The Art of Slow Reading." *The Guardian*, July 15, 2010, https://www.theguardian.com/books/2010/jul/15/slow-reading.

Kittler, Friedrich A. *Gramophone, Film, Typewriter*. Trans. Geoffrey Winthrop-Young and Michael Wutz. Stanford University Press, 1999.

———. *Optical Media*. Trans. Anthony Enns. Wiley, 2010.

Kittler, Friedrich A. "Real Time Analysis, Time Axis Manipulation." Trans. Geoffrey Winthrop-Young. *Cultural Politics* 13, no. 1 (March 2017): 1–18.

Koepnick, Lutz P. *The Long Take: Art Cinema and the Wondrous*. University of Minnesota Press, 2017.

———. *On Slowness: Toward an Aesthetic of the Contemporary*. Columbia University Press, 2014.

———. "Riefensthal and the Beauty of Soccer." In *Riefenstahl Screened: An Anthology of New Criticism*, ed. Neil Christian Pages, Ingeborg Majer O'Sickey, and Mary Rhiel. Bloomsbury, 2008.

Koselleck, Reinhart. *Futures Past: On the Semantics of Historical Time*. Trans. Keith Tribe. Columbia University Press, 2004.

———. *Sediments of Time: On Possible Histories*. Trans. Sean Franzel and Stefan-Ludwig Hommann. Stanford University Press, 2018.

Kovács, András Bálint. *Screening Modernism: European Art Cinema, 1950–1980*. University of Chicago Press, 2007.

Kracauer, Siegfried. *Theory of Film: The Redemption of Physical Reality*. Oxford University Press, 1960.

Kubler, George. *The Shape of Time: Remarks on the History of Things*. Yale University Press, 1962.

Lasdun, James. "Point Omega by Don DeLillo." *The Guardian*, February 27, 2010.

Latour, B. *We Have Never Been Modern*. Harvard University Press, 2012.

Leary, John Patrick. "Detroitism: What Does 'Ruin Porn' Tell Us About the Motor City?" *Geurnica* (blog), January 15, 2011, https://www.guernicamag.com/leary_1_15_11/.

Lee, Pamela M. *Chronophobia: On Time in the Art of the 1960s*. MIT Press, 2004.

Lefebvre, Henri. *Introduction to Modernity: Twelve Preludes, September 1959–May 1961*. Verso, 1995.

———. *Rhythmanalysis: Space, Time, and Everyday Life*. Bloomsbury, 2013.

Lim, Song Hwee. *Tsai Ming-Liang and a Cinema of Slowness*. University of Hawai'i Press, 2014.

Löwy, Michael. *The Politics of Combined and Uneven Development: The Theory of Permanent Revolution*. Haymarket, 2010.

Luca, Tiago de, and Nuno Barradas Jorge. *Slow Cinema*. Edinburgh University Press, 2015.

Lukács, György. *History and Class Consciousness: Studies in Marxist Dialectics*. MIT Press, 1971.

———. "The Ideology of Modernism." In *Realism in Our Time: Literature and the Class Struggle*, trans. John Mander and Necke Mander. Harper & Row, 1962.

———. *The Theory of the Novel: A Historico-Philosophical Essay on the Forms of Great Epic Literature*. MIT Press, 1971.

Lundemo, Trond. "A Temporal Perspective:" In *Jean Epstein*, ed. Sarah Keller and Jason N. Paul. Amsterdam University Press, 2012.

Lupton, Christina. "The Novel as the Future Anterior of the Book: Tom McCarthy's *Remainder* and Ali Smith's *The Accidental.*" *Novel* 49, no. 3 (November 1, 2016): 504–18.
Malm, Andreas. *Fossil Capital: The Rise of Steam Power and the Roots of Global Warming.* Verso, 2016.
Mannoni, Laurent. *The Great Art of Light and Shadow: Archaeology of the Cinema.* Trans. Richard Crangle. University of Exeter Press, 2000.
Manovich, Lev. *The Language of New Media.* MIT Press, 2001.
Marx, Karl. *Capital.* Vol. 1. Penguin UK, 2004.
———. *Capital: A Critique of Political Economy.* Vol. 3. Penguin, 1993.
———. *Grundrisse: Foundations of the Critique of Political Economy.* Penguin UK, 2005.
Matz, Jesse. *Modernist Time Ecology.* Johns Hopkins University Press, 2018.
McCabe, Susan. *Cinematic Modernism: Modernist Poetry and Film.* Cambridge University Press, 2005.
McCann, Sean, and Michael Szalay. "Introduction: Paul Potter and the Cultural Turn." *Yale Journal of Criticism* 18, no. 2 (2005): 209–20.
McGurl, Mark. "The Posthuman Comedy." *Critical Inquiry* 38, no. 3 (Spring 2012).
Meadows, Donella H., Dennis L. Meadows, Jørgen Randers, and William W. Behrens III. *The Limits to Growth: A Report for the Club of Rome's Project on the Predicament of Mankind.* Potomac Association Books, 1972.
Meillassoux, Quentin. *After Finitude: An Essay on the Necessity of Contingency.* Bloomsbury, 2009.
Menand, Louis. "After the Revolution." *New Yorker*, October 12, 2003. https://www.newyorker.com/magazine/2003/10/20/after-the-revolution-4.
———. *The Free World: Art and Thought in the Cold War.* Picador, 2022.
Menne, Jeff. *Post-Fordist Cinema: Hollywood Auteurs and the Corporate Counterculture.* Columbia University Press, 2019.
Michaels, Walter Benn. *The Beauty of a Social Problem: Photography, Autonomy, Economy.* University of Chicago Press, 2015.
Michelson, Annette. "BODIES IN SPACE." *Artforum*, February 1, 1969.
Mikics, David. *Slow Reading in a Hurried Age.* Harvard University Press, 2013.
Mill, John Stuart. "John Stuart Mill on the Stationary State." *Population and Development Review* 12, no. 2 (1986): 317–22.
Miller, D. A. *Hidden Hitchcock.* University of Chicago Press, 2017.
———. *Second Time Around: From Art House to DVD.* Columbia University Press, 2021.
Mogilevich, Mariana, Ben Campkin, and Rebecca Ross. "Pruitt Igoe: Blowing Up This St. Louis Housing Project Was Easier Than Demolishing the Myth It Created." *Guardian*, December 10, 2014, https://www.theguardian.com/cities/2014/dec/10/pruitt-igoe-st-louis-myth-harder-demolish-social-housing-modernism.
Monk, Philip, and Douglas Gordon. *Double-Cross: The Hollywood Films of Douglas Gordon.* Art Gallery of York University, 2003.
Moore, Marianne. *The Complete Prose of Marianne Moore.* Viking, 1986.
Mulvey, Laura. *Death 24x a Second: Stillness and the Moving Image.* Reaktion, 2006.
Musser, C. *The Emergence of Cinema: The American Screen to 1907.* University of California Press, 1994.
Nadolny, Sten. *The Discovery of Slowness.* Penguin, 1997.
Nieland, Justus. "Dirty Media: Tom McCarthy and the Afterlife of Modernism." *MFS: Modern Fiction Studies* 58, no. 3 (Fall 2012): 569–99.
———. *Happiness by Design: Modernism and Media in the Eames Era.* University of Minnesota Press, 2020.
Nietzsche, Friedrich. *Nietzsche: Daybreak: Thoughts on the Prejudices of Morality.* Cambridge University Press, 1997.
Nixon, Rob. *Slow Violence and the Environmentalism of the Poor.* Harvard University Press, 2011.
Noys, Benjamin. *Malign Velocities: Accelerationism and Capitalism.* John Hunt, 2014.

O'Connell, Mark. "The Disembodied." *Slate*, May 2, 2016, https://slate.com/culture/2016/05/don-delillos-novel-zero-k-reviewed.html.

Onli, Meg, and Amber Rose Johnson, eds. *Colored People Time*. Philadelphia: Institute of Contemporary Art, 2020.

Ozick, Cynthia. *The Messiah of Stockholm*. Knopf Doubleday, 1988.

Pages, Neil Christian, Ingeborg Majer O'Sickey, and Mary Rhiel. *Riefenstahl Screened: An Anthology of New Criticism*. Bloomsbury, 2008.

Pane, Samuel. "Trauma Obscura: Photographic Media in W. G. Sebald's Austerlitz." *Mosaic: An Interdisciplinary Critical Journal* 38, no. 1 (March 3, 2005): 37–54.

Parikka, Jussi. *A Geology of Media*. University of Minnesota Press, 2015.

———. *A Slow, Contemporary Violence: Damaged Environments of Technological Culture*. Sternberg Press, 2016.

Patt, Lise, and Christel Dillbohner. *Searching for Sebald: Photography After W. G. Sebald*. Institute of Cultural Inquiry, 2007.

Patterson, Claire. "Age of Meteorites and the Earth." *Geochimica et Cosmochimica Acta* 10, no. 4 (October 1, 1956): 230–37.

Peters, John Durham. *The Marvelous Clouds: Toward a Philosophy of Elemental Media*. University of Chicago Press, 2015.

Piper, Kelsey. "Can We Save the Planet by Shrinking the Economy?" *Vox*, August 3, 2021, https://www.vox.com/future-perfect/22408556/save-planet-shrink-economy-degrowth.

Porter, Katherine Anne. *Ship of Fools*. Little, Brown, 1962.

Posnock, Ross. "'Don't Think, but Look!': W. G. Sebald, Wittgenstein, and Cosmopolitan Poverty." *Representations* 112, no. 1 (November 1, 2010): 112–39.

Postone, Moishe. *Time, Labor, and Social Domination: A Reinterpretation of Marx's Critical Theory*. Cambridge University Press, 1995.

Ramsaye, Terry. *A Million and One Nights: A History of the Motion Picture*. Taylor & Francis, 2012.

Rascaroli, Laura, and John David Rhodes, eds. *Antonioni: Centenary Essays*. Bloomsbury, 2011.

Reed, Arden. *Slow Art: The Experience of Looking, Sacred Images to James Turrell*. University of California Press, 2017.

Rehak, Bob. "The Migration of Forms: Bullet Time as Microgenre." *Film Criticism* 32, no. 1 (2007): 26–48.

Rehding, Alexander. *Music and Monumentality: Commemoration and Wonderment in Nineteenth-Century Germany*. Oxford University Press, 2009.

Remes, Justin. *Motion(Less) Pictures: The Cinema of Stasis*. Columbia University Press, 2015.

Ricoeur, Paul. *Time and Narrative*. 3 vols. Trans. K. McLaughlin, D. Pellauer, and K. Blamey. University of Chicago Press, 1984, 1990, 2014.

Riley, D. *Time Lived, Without Its Flow*. Pan Macmillan, 2019.

Roberts, J. *Revolutionary Time and the Avant-Garde*. Verso, 2015.

Robinson, Kim Stanley. *The Ministry for the Future*. Little, Brown, 2020.

Rosa, Hartmut. *Social Acceleration: A New Theory of Modernity*. Trans. Jonathan Trejo-Mathys. Columbia University Press, 2013.

Ross, Kristen. *Fast Cars, Clean Bodies: Decolonization and the Reordering of French Culture*. MIT Press, 1996.

Røssaak, Eivind. *Between Stillness and Motion: Film, Photography, Algorithms*. Amsterdam University Press, 2011.

Roszak, Theodore. *The Making of a Counter Culture: Reflections on the Technocratic Society and Its Youthful Opposition*. Doubleday, 1969.

Rotha, Paul. *The Film Till Now: A Survey of World Cinema*. Twayne, 1960.

Sachs, Jonathan. "Eighteenth-Century Slow Time: Seven Propositions." *Eighteenth Century* 60, no. 2 (Summer 2019): 185–205.
Sadoul, Georges. *Histoire générale du cinéma*. Denoël, 1946.
Said, Edward W. *The World, the Text, and the Critic*. Harvard University Press, 1983.
Saito, K. *Marx in the Anthropocene: Towards the Idea of Degrowth Communism*. Cambridge University Press, 2023.
———. *Slow Down: The Degrowth Manifesto*. Trans. Brian Bergstrom. Astra, 2024.
Salt, Barry. *Film Style and Technology : History and Analysis*. Starword, 1983.
Schefer, Jean Louis. *The Ordinary Man of Cinema*. Trans. Max Cavitch, Noura Wedell, and Paul Grant. MIT Press, 2016.
Schonig, Jordan. *The Shape of Motion: Cinema and the Aesthetics of Movement*. Oxford University Press, 2022.
Sebald, W. G. *Austerlitz*. Random House, 2011.
Sekula, Allen, and Centrum voor hedendaagse kunst Witte de With. *Fish Story*. Art Pub, 2002.
Sexton, Jared. "The Social Life of Social Death: On Afro-Pessimism and Black Optimism." *InTensions Journal*, no. 5 (Fall/Winter 2011).
Shapiro, G. *Earthwards: Robert Smithson and Art After Babel*. University of California Press, 1997.
Sharma, Sarah. *In the Meantime: Temporality and Cultural Politics*. Duke University Press, 2014.
Shaviro, Steven. "Slow Cinema, Fast Films." *The Pinocchio Theory* (blog), May 12, 2010. http://www.shaviro.com/Blog/?p=891.
Shaw, L. *Fieldworks: From Place to Site in Postwar Poetics*. University of Alabama Press, 2013.
Shklovskiĭ, Viktor. *Theory of Prose*. Trans. Benjamin Sher. Dalkey Archive, 1991.
Sinykin, Dan. *American Literature and the Long Downturn: Neoliberal Apocalypse*. Oxford University Press, 2020.
Slifkin, Robert. *The New Monuments and the End of Man: U.S. Sculpture Between War and Peace, 1945–1975*. Princeton University Press, 2019.
Smith, R. G. *Affect and American Literature in the Age of Neoliberalism*. Cambridge University Press, 2015.
Smith, Zadie. "Two Paths for the Novel." *New York Review of Books*, November 20, 2008, https://www.nybooks.com/articles/2008/11/20/two-paths-for-the-novel/.
Smithson, Robert. *The Collected Writings*. Ed. Jack Flam. University of California Press, 1996.
———. *Spiral Jetty*. Videorecording. Electronic Arts Intermix, 2000.
Snider, Eric. "What's the Big Deal? *Bonnie and Clyde* (1967)." *MTV News*. https://www.mtv.com/news/2763794/whats-the-big-deal-bonnie-and-clyde-1967/.
Sobchack, Vivian. " 'Cutting to the Quick': Techne, Physis, and Poiesis and the Attractions of Slow Motion." In *The Cinema of Attractions Reloaded*, ed. Wanda Strauven, 337–52. Amsterdam University Press, 2006.
———. *The Persistence of History: Cinema, Television, and the Modern Event*. Routledge, 1996.
Sontag, Susan. *Against Interpretation and Other Essays*. Eyre & Spottiswoode, 1967.
Sterne, Jonathan. *MP3: The Meaning of a Format*. Duke University Press, 2012.
Stewart, Garrett. *Between Film and Screen: Modernism's Photo Synthesis*. University of Chicago Press, 1999.
Stewart, Susan. *The Ruins Lesson: Meaning and Material in Western Culture*. University of Chicago Press, 2020.
Stratton, W. K. *The Wild Bunch: Sam Peckinpah, a Revolution in Hollywood, and the Making of a Legendary Film*. Bloomsbury, 2019.
Sugimoto, H. *Snow White*. Damiani, 2017.
Sugimoto, Hiroshi, and Corinne Atlan. *Hiroshi Sugimoto: Theaters*. Éditions Xavier Barral, 2016.
Summers, Larry. "The Age of Secular Stagnation." *Larry Summers* (blog), February 17, 2016. https://larrysummers.com/2016/02/17/the-age-of-secular-stagnation/.

Sutil, Nicolás Salazar. *Motion and Representation: The Language of Human Movement*. MIT Press, 2015.
Szalay, Michael. *Hip Figures: A Literary History of the Democratic Party*. Stanford University Press, 2012.
Tomkins, Calvin. "Arthur Jafa's Radical Alienation." *New Yorker*, December 10, 2020, https://www.newyorker.com/magazine/2020/12/21/arthur-jafas-radical-alienation.
Tompkins, Jane P. *West of Everything: The Inner Life of Westerns*. Oxford University Press, 1993.
Trotsky, Leon. *History of the Russian Revolution*. Haymarket, 2008.
Turvey, Malcolm. *Doubting Vision: Film and the Revelationist Tradition*. Oxford University Press, 2008.
———. "Jean Epstein's Cinema of Immanence: The Rehabilitation of the Corporeal Eye." *October* 83 (1998): 25–50.
Tuttle, Harry. "Slow Films, Easy Life." *Unspoken Cinema* (blog), May 12, 2010, https://unspokencinema.blogspot.com/2010/05/slow-films-easy-life-sight.html.
Underwood, Ted. "Why Literary Time Is Measured in Minutes." *ELH* 85, no. 2 (2018): 341–65.
Uroskie, Andrew V. *Between the Black Box and the White Cube: Expanded Cinema and Postwar Art*. University of Chicago Press, 2014.
Vågnes, Øyvind. "Inside the Zapruder Museum." In *Zaprudered*, 69–78. University of Texas Press, 2011.
Velasco, John. "I Just Tested Samsung's AI-Powered Instant Slow-Mo Video on the Galaxy S24 and It Actually Looks Legit." *Tom's Guide*, January 22, 2024, https://www.tomsguide.com/features/i-just-tested-samsungs-ai-powered-instant-slow-mo-video-on-the-galaxy-s24-and-it-actually-looks-legit.
Verna, Tony. *Instant Replay: The Day That Changed Sports Forever*. Creative Book Publishing International, 2008.
Vertov, Dziga. *Kino-Eye: The Writings of Dziga Vertov*. Ed. Annette Michelson. Trans. Kevin O'Brien. University of California Press, 1984.
Viola, Bill, Peter Sellars, John Walsh, Kira Perov, and Hans Belting. *Bill Viola: The Passions*. J. Paul Getty Museum, 2003.
Virilio, Paul. *The Art of the Motor*. University of Minnesota Press, 1995.
———. *Open Sky*. Trans. Julie Rose. Verso, 1997.
———. *Polar Inertia*. Sage, 2000.
———. *Speed and Politics: An Essay on Dromology*. Columbia University Press, 1986.
Wake, Sandra, and Nicola Hayden. *The Bonnie & Clyde Book*. Simon & Schuster, 1972.
———. *Bonnie and Clyde: Directed by Arthur Penn: Produced by Warren Beatty: Screenplay by David Newman and Robert Benton*. Faber Classic Screenplay Series. Faber and Faber, 1998.
Warshow, Robert. *The Immediate Experience: Movies, Comics, Theatre, and Other Aspects of Popular Culture*. Enlarged ed. Harvard University Press, 2001.
Warwick Research Collective (WReC), Sharae Deckard, Nicholas Lawrence, Neil Lazarus, Upamanyu Pablo Mukherjee, and Graeme Macdonald. *Combined and Uneven Development: Towards a New Theory of World-Literature*. Oxford University Press, 2015.
Weddle, David. *If They Move—Kill 'Em!: The Life and Times of Sam Peckinpah*. Grove, 2000.
Weisgall, Jonathan M. *Operation Crossroads: The Atomic Tests at Bikini Atoll*. Naval Institute Press, 1994.
Whalebone. "The Slow Issue." 2023.
Whissel, K. *Spectacular Digital Effects: CGI and Contemporary Cinema*. Duke University Press, 2014.
Williams, James S. "The Rhythms of Life: An Appreciation of Michelangelo Antonioni, Extreme Aesthete of the Real." *Film Quarterly* 62, no. 1 (2008): 46–57.
Williams, Linda. *Hard Core: Power, Pleasure, and the "Frenzy of the Visible."* Expanded ed. University of California Press, 1999.
Williams, Nathan. *The Kinfolk Home: Interiors for Slow Living*. Artisan, 2015.
Williams, Raymond. *The Long Revolution*. Broadview, 2001.
———. *Marxism and Literature*. Oxford University Press, 1977.
Wilson, Rob, and Christopher Leigh Connery. *The Worlding Project: Doing Cultural Studies in the Era of Globalization*. North Atlantic, 2007.

Wood, James. "Human, All Too Inhuman." *New Republic*, July 24, 2000, https://newrepublic.com/article/61361/human-inhuman.

Woodburn, Woody. "Woodburn: 9/11 Seems Like Yesterday and a Lifetime Ago." *Ventura County Star*, September 11, 2021, https://www.vcstar.com/story/opinion/columnists/2021/09/11/woodburn-9-11-seems-like-yesterday-and-lifetime-ago/8261047002/.

Woolf, Virginia. *Mr. Bennett and Mrs. Brown.* 2nd impression. The Hogarth Essays. L. and Virginia Woolf, 1924.

Youngblood, Gene, and R. Buckminster Fuller. *Expanded Cinema.* 50th anniversary ed. Fordham University Press, 2020.

Zemka, Sue. *Time and the Moment in Victorian Literature and Society.* Cambridge University Press, 2011.

Zettl, Herbert. *Sight, Sound, Motion: Applied Media Aesthetics.* 2nd ed. Wadsworth, 1990.

Zielinski, Siegfried. *Deep Time of the Media: Toward an Archaeology of Hearing and Seeing by Technical Means.* MIT Press, 2006.

Žižek, Slavoj. *The Pervert's Guide to Ideology.* 2013. http://archive.org/details/the-perverts-guide-to-ideology-2012-hd.

Index

Pages in italics refer to images

Abel, Marco, 187
Abel, Richard, 51
Acland, Charles: on "useful cinema," 61
action film, 2, 71, 335
Adams, Barbara: on gendered time, 127
Adeyemi, Kemi, 163
Adler, Renata: on *2001: A Space Odyssey* (Kubrick), 240
Adorno, Theodor, 295; *Aesthetic Theory*, 321–23; on explosions, 321–22, 333; on late style, 179; on universal history, 248, 250
aesthetics; anticorporate, 168; aristocratic, 315; avant-garde, 275; of cinema, 16; and early cinema, 47; of explosions, 340; modernist, 25, 125, 152, 270; neorealist, 326; New Hollywood, 225; of slow motion, 11, 76, 81, 83, 85, *103*; in Schiller, 102; of Smithson, Robert, 22; of wonderment, 258
Akerman, Chantal: *D'Est*, 180
Alexander, Lexi: *Punisher: War Zone*, 89, 308
Alien (Scott), 262, 264
allegory, 78, 186; in *Bonnie and Clyde* (Penn), 215; in *Daughters of the Dust* (Dash) 159; in *How the West Was Won* (Ford), 251; in *Junior Bonner* (Peckinpah), 298; in *Once Upon a Time in America* (Leone), 286; in *The Seven Samurai* (Kurosawa), 104; in *The Thief of Bagdad* (Walsh), 47; in *24 Hour Psycho* (Gordon), 96; in *2001: A Space Odyssey* (332); in *The Wild Bunch* (Peckinpah), 302

Anderson, Paul W.S.: *Resident Evil* franchise, 89, 226, 308
Anderson, Wes, 73
Anger, Kenneth, 21; *Eaux d'Artifice*, 61
Antichrist (Von Trier), 4
Antonioni, Michelangelo, 21, 38, 66, 77, 199, 210, 307, 314–37, 342; *L'avventura*, 315, 321–22; *Blow-Up*, 314; *La notte*, 321; *The Passenger*, 314, 330; *Red Desert*, 322; *Zabriskie Point*, 6, 15, 197, 200, 210, 307, 314–38, 342
apocalypse, 15, 113, 204, 316, 333, 335, 340, 342
apparatus theory, 83–84
Army of Darkness (Raimi), 39
Arnheim, Rudolf, 56, 80, 86, 104–105; on *Ent'racte* (Clair), 434; on motion, 81; on slow motion, 44–46, 104
Arrighi, Giovanni, 124; on US crisis, 287
Arrowsmith, William, 332
Astaire, Fred, 59–60, 105, 113, 226, 260, 261
avant-garde film, 20
Augustine: *Confessions*, 178, 191
Austerlitz (Sebald), 148–53, 184; photographs in, 150, 152; screenshot in, 152; slow motion as historical aesthetic in, 149

Bad Boys II (Bay), *325*
Baker, Nicholson: *The Mezzanine*, 174
Balázs, Béla, 56; on slow motion and the psyche, 47
Balsom, Erika, on slow cinema, 37

INDEX

Ballard, J. G., 25; *Crash*, 145; *JG*, 27; "The Voices of Time," 279–80
Ballard, Lucien, 300–302, 311
Barthes, Roland: *Camera Lucida*, 150–52; "Textual Analysis of a Tale by Edgar Poe," 10, 11; on "third meaning," 229
Baumbach, Nico, 107, 109
Bay, Michael, 11, 70, 71, 97, 109, 226, 295, 307, 338; *Bad Boys II*, 335; *Pearl Harbor*, 324; *The Transformers*, 81, 226
Bazin, André, 80; "change mummified," 221; on ontology of photographic image, 32; on realism, 24, 81–82, 86
Baudrillard, Jean, 323; on Sergio Leone, 271
Beatty, Warren, 212–15, 218, 221–25, 228, 230–31, 233–34, 245, 316
Beckman, Karen, 81
Beeston, Alix, 16
Benjamin, Walter, 57, 80, 84, 86, 139, 200; angel of history, 251; on the dialectic image, 321, 323; on "messianic time," 105, 333; the "optical unconscious," 83, 144, 216; on "petrified unrest" of modernity, 28; on slow motion, 44, 104, 272; on the speed of flânerie, 125, 127
Benning, James: *Casting a Glance*, 27–28
Benson Murder Case, The (Tuttle), 234, 236
Benton, Robert, 218–23, 225, 233–36
Bergson, Henri, 33, 106, 108, 111, 117, 130, 178; on "durée," 85
Berlin, Ira, 163
Bersani, Leo: on erotic stimulation, 83
Bishop, Ryan, 88
Boccioni, Umberto, 92
Böhme, Hartmut, 177
Bolter, Jay: "remediation," 95
Bonnie and Clyde (Penn), 15, 35, 38, 57, 75–76, 97, 101, 197, 199–200, 209–37, 239, 242, 245, 248, 266, 279, 279, 282, 291–92, 294, 299, 300, 307, 315, 316, 318, 328, 331, 342; ending of, 214, 226–37; iconography of, 331; impotence in, 221–24; and nostalgia, 213–14, 217, 225, 235; ruination in, 234–35; slapstick in; slow motion in, 208–209, 210–12, 214, 216–17, 219–21, 2124–28, 230, 233, 235, 236; violence in, 213–16, 221–22, 224–27, 229, 233, 242; and the Zapruder film, 228–29
Bordwell, David; on "intensified continuity" editing, 101, 294; on slow motion, 86–87

Brakhage, Stan, 211; *Dog Star Man*, 74
Bram Stoker's Dracula (Coppola), 160
Braun, Marta, 85, 185
Brenner, Robert, 203–204
Brouillette, Sarah: on history and stagnation, 79, 202
Brunette, Peter, 314
Bukatman, Scott, 239
Buñuel, Luis, 65, 68, 70; *Un chien andalou*, 48, 277; *Los olvidados*, 65
Burch, Nöel, 42; on narrative, 96, 109; on photography, 92; on slow motion, 90
Burrows, Stuart, 16
Butch Cassidy and the Sundance Kid (Hill), 214, 284
By the Bluest of Seas (Barnet), 63–64

Canales, Jimena, 46, 84–85, 185
capitalism, 12–13, 23, 35, 70, 109–10, 112–13, 122–24, 124, 131, 162, 168, 180, 182, 202–203, 205; and catastrophe, 155; ideological crisis of, 13; the "long downturn," 203–204; speed of, 13, 122, 180; and stagnation, 79
Carefree (Sandrich), 59, 105, 226, 291, 316
Cather, Willa: on emergence of modernity, 125
Cavell, Stanley, 269, 291; on freeze-frame, 214; on photography, 82; on slow motion, 53–59, 73, 80–83, 85, 90, 107, 222, 224, 227, 248, 308
Cendrars, Blaise, 51; "High Speed and Slow Motion," 26
Charney, Leo, 23
Chatman, Seymour, 174; on *Zabriskie Point* (Antonioni), 314–15
Chimes at Midnight (Welles), 76
Chin, Frank, 283, 287
Chion, Michel: on "ritualized film," 38; on *2001: A Space Odyssey* (Kubrick), 239, 256
Christensen, Jerome, 211–13
Chunking Express (Wong), 157
Clark, T. J., on Cezanne's *Bathers*, 333; on corpses in painting, 231; on modernism, 241–42
Clarke, Arthur C., 239, 242–43, 246–50, 254, 255, 263
climate crisis, 5, 203, 341
Clover, Joshua: on history and stagnation, 79, 202
Club of Rome: *The Limits to Growth*, 263
Cocteau, Jean, 51, 65, 68, 291; *La belle et la bête*, 65; *The Blood of a Poet*, 48, 260; *Orphée*, 65
Colette, Sidonie-Gabrielle, 51

Connery, Christopher Leigh: "time of eventfulness," 233
Connor, J. D.: on "neoclassical" Hollywood, 211
Contini, Alfio, 318
Corbett-Fitzsimmons Fight, The (Veriscope), 41
Cowen, Deborah, 262
Craig, Geoffrey, 169
Cranes Are Flying, The (Kalatozov), 68
Crary, Jonathan: *24/7*, 112, 180
Crime of Helen Stanley, The (Lederman), 53, 226
Crossroads (Conner), 338, *341*
Cubitt, Sean, 82; on *The Wild Bunch*, 295–96, 299
Currie, Mark, 173

dance sequences, 49, 61, 121, 220, 226–27
Danius, Sara, 23
Dargis, Manohla, 37
Darwin, Charles, 14
Daughters of the Dust (Dash), 14, 155–65, 184; as allegory, 159; media archaeology in, 165; modernity in, 159–63, 165; trauma in, 158, 160
Davidson, Donald, 26
Dead Slow Ahead (Herce), 261–62, 264
Dean, Tacita: *JG*, 27
death: in *Austerlitz* (Sebald), 149; being-towards-, 106, 279; in *Bonnie and Clyde* (Penn), 214, 217–18, 220, 224, 227, 229, 231, 233, 234, 300; in DeLillo, 182, 193, 194; in *The Discovery of Slowness* (Nadolny), 165–67, 170; in *Dredd* (Travis) 2; in Faulkner, 134; in Hemingway, 306; in Leone, 284, 288, 299; in *Mamma Roma* (Pasolini), 68; of modernism, 297; in Peckinpah, 303, 318; in *The Seven Samurai* (Kurosawa), 98, 100–103; and slow motion, 12, 16, 47, 63, 84; as trope, 16; in *2001: A Space Odyssey* (Kubrick), 255–56
de Chirico, Giorgio, 277: *The Enigma of the Hour*, 277; *The Great Tower*, 277; *The Nostalgia of the Infinite*, 277
Deleuze, Gilles, 67, 107
DeLillo, Don, 9, 14, 118, 177–84, 187, 190–99, 269; *Americana*, 190; *The Body Artist*, 178, 179; *Cosmopolis*, 177–78, 179, 182; deceleration in, 177–78, 181; *Falling Man*, 180–81, 182, 183–84, 187; late style of, 179, 187; *Libra*, 187–89; *Mao II*, 187; *Point Omega*, 179–80, 182–83; *Underworld*, 178–79, 187, 190–97; *White Noise*, 184; *Zero K*, 179, 187

Delli Colli, Tonino, 68, 277
demolition: in *Junior Bonner* (Peckinpah), 297. *See also* destruction
Denson, Shane, 9
Deren, Maya, 61–62, 65; "An Anagram of Ideas on Art, Form and Film," 61; *Divine Horseman*, 61; *At Land*, 61; *Meditation on Violence*, 61; *Meshes of the Afternoon*, 61; *Ritual in Transfigured Time*, 61; *A Study in Choreography for Camera*, 61
Deserter, The (Pudovkin), 51
Detig, Cameron, 294
Dickson, William, 41, 42
digital filmmaking, 7, 74
Dimock, Wai Chee, 276
Dinshaw, Carolyn, 200
Do the Right Thing (Lee), 157
Doane, Mary Ann, 38, 81, 109; on indexicality, 82; on modernity's temporality, 23–24; on Sugimoto, Hiroshi, 33
Doherty, Willie, 95
"Doomsday Clock," 341
Dorling, Danny, 204–205
Dredd (Travis), 1–4, 8, 308
DuBois, R. Luke: *Fashionably Late for the Relationship*, 94
Duffy, Edna: on modernity and acceleration, 12, 122
Dukore, Bernard F., 294, 297
Dutoit, Ulysse, on erotic stimulation, 83–84

Eagleman, David, 185–86
early cinema, 6, 7–8, 47, 87, 92, 109, 163, 165
Easter Parade (Walters), 59, *60*, 105, 226, 261
Easy Rider (Hopper), 77, 210, 283, 292, 315
economic stagnation, 79, 124, 202–204
Edgerton, Harold "Doc," 62, 92, 334–36
Edison, Thomas, 40–42, 83, 109, 162, 176, 338; *Serpentine Dance*, 40–42
educational films, 49, 61, 70, 121, 245
Entr'acte (Clair), 43–44, 65, 78, 83, 85, 107, 109, 277, 299
Epstein, Jean, 47, 50, 65, 67, 277, 291, 338; *The Fall of the House of Usher*, 47, 67; *The Intelligence of the Machine*, 47
Ernst, Wolfgang, 9, 24, 34, 46, 84, 91, 107, 126, 277, 337; on intermediality, 34; on technology and time, 24, 126, 337

eroticism: in *Adrift* (Kabar), 157; in *Bonnie and Clyde* (Penn), 222, 223; in *Carefree* (Sandrich), 41; in early film, 41, 83; in *How Sweet It Is!* (291); in *Straw Dogs* (310); in *Zabriskie Point* (Antonioni), 327–32

Evans, Walker, 216, 234

Evans, Gareth, 89, 295

explosions, 15, 58, 105, 120, 333; and 9/11, 186; atomic, 39, 92, *335*; in *Crossroads* (Conner), 338–40, 342; in *Dr. Strangelove* (Kubrick), 39, 334; in *Duck, You Sucker!* (Leone), 284; in early cinema, 42, 45; in *Star Wars* (Lucas); in *Transformers: Revenge of the Fallen*, 81; in *Zabriskie Point* (Antonioni), 315, 317–24

Fabian, Johannes: "denial of coevalness," 103–104, 106; *Time and the Other*, 201

Fall of the House of Usher, The (Watson and Webber), 47, 67, 277

fantasy: capitalist, 13, 148; in *Cranes Are Flying, The* (Kalatozov), 68; in dance sequences, 59, 105–106; in *Entr'acte* (Clair), 44; masochistic, 84; in *Mamma Roma* (Pasolini), 277; rape, 241, 308–309; and slow motion, 226; in *2001: A Space Odyssey* (Kubrick), 281; 335 in *Zabriskie Point* (Antonioni), 318, 331, 332

Faulkner, William, 6–7, 9, 14, 118, 127–43, 154–55, 171, 184, 196, 199, 306; *Absalom, Absalom*, 131; "The Bear," 138; endurance in work of, 128; *The Hamlet*, 127, 132; *Light in August*, 6–7, 129, 131; *The Mansion*, 127–38, 139, 140, 141; *The Sound and the Fury*, 128, 138; *The Town*, 127, 128, 137–38, 140, 141

Fay, Jennifer, 33

Felony Squad: "My Mommy Got Lost," 300

Ferguson, Frances, 340

Fiore, Robert, 28

Flash, The (Kreisberg and Helbing), 92, *93*

Fluxus, 74

Ford, John, 219, 245, 250, 252, 267, 272, 278, 284, 289, 325, 331; *Cheyenne Autumn*, 252; *The Informer*, 284; *The Iron Horse*, 278; *My Darling Clementine*, 250, 252; *The Searchers*, 250, 252, 267, 268, 269, 278; *She Wore a Yellow Ribbon*, 252, 278; *Stagecoach*, 250, 252, 278

forensics, 11, 45, 62, 186

Foucault, Michel, 264

Frampton, Hollis: *Maxwell's Demon*, 21

Free, Gavin David, 8

freeze frame, 53, 66–67, 214, 295

Fried, Michael, 102, 143, 273–76; "Art and Objecthood," 274; on Gordon, 269;–70 on modernism, 2; on theatricality, 33–34, 95–96

Friedberg, Anne, 139

Fusco, Katherine: on slow cinema, 37

Gance, Abel: *Au secours!*, 43; *Napoléon*, 44

Garber, Marjorie, 170

Garcia, Jerry, 327, 328, 332

Gaspard-Félix, Tournachon, ("Nadar"), 33

Genette, Gerard: on narrative time, 172–74, 249

Gingrich, Brian, 172

Gitelman, Lisa, 25

Godard, Jean-Luc, 3, 4, 21, 67, 68, 153, 214, 283, 331; *Histoire(s) du cinema*, 153; *Pierrot le fou*, 68; *Suave qui peut*, 4, 67; *Week-End* 67, 283; *Wind from the East*, 331

Godden, Richard; on late Faulkner, 131; on *Once Upon a Time in America* (Leone), 285

Gold Diggers of 1933 (Berkeley), 236, 37

Gombrich, E. H., 81

Good, The Bad, and the Ugly, The (Leone), 266, 270–71, 276–77, 279–81, 307, 331; iconography in, 331

Goodbye, Columbus (Peerce), 77, 210, 292, 308, 333

Goodbye Dragon Inn (Tsai), 35–38, 96, 235

Gordon, Douglas, 307; *5-year drive-by*, 267–70; *24 Hour Psycho*, 81, 95–97, 179, 180, 183

Greenberg, Clement, 241; "The Case for Abstract Art," 273; on medium specificity, 195, 197, 275; "Modernist Painting," 195, 197, 273

grace, 1, 29, 45, 47, 49, 50, 63, 67, 75, 83, 102, 110, 112–13, 156, 227, 260, 274, 292, 299

Greenblatt, Stephen, 202

Gruchy, Daniel Charles, 8

Grusin, Richard: "remediation," 95

Gumbrecht, Hans Ulrich: on "athletic beauty," 45, 163

Gunning, Tom: on "tamed attractions" of early cinema, 47, 60, 87, 335

Hägglund, Martin: on Woolf, 307

Hanchard, Michael: on "racial time," 127, 163

Hansen, Alvin, 203

Hansen, Miriam, 109; "hegemonic modernism," 21, 23;

Hanson, Ellis: on HAL's queerness, 255

Hard Day's Night, A (Lester), 76

Hartman, Saidiya: "time of slavery," 184
Harvey, David, 12, 122; on capital as "value in motion," 109–11, 126
Hayles, N. Katherine, on new technologies, 84–85; on *Remainder* (McCarthy), 144
Headey, Lena, 1, 2
Hegel, G. W. F.: *Aesthetics*, 11, 275
Heidegger, Martin, 106, 108, 178, 281; "being-towards-death," 106, 279; "The Question Concerning Technology," 25–26; on frenzied technology, 88
Hemingway, Ernest: *Death in the Afternoon*, 306
Henri Matisse (Campaux), 66
High Noon (Zinnemann), 278
history: 10, 78–79; and acceleration, 123, 181, 189; ideologies of, 70; philosophy of, 202
Hitchcock, Alfred, 20, 21, 38, 62–63; *The Birds*, 62, 63; *Jamaica Inn*, 63; *North by Northwest*, 20; *Psycho*, 81, 95–96, 183, 269; *Rear Window*, 63; *Young and Innocent*, 62
Hoberman, J., 283, 340
Hollywood, 6, 19, 21, 25, 37, 55, 59, 63, 66, 76, 77, 80–83, 95, 97, 180, 200, 209, 246, 266, 270, 291, 313–15, 324, 339; classical, 234, 289; ending, 302, 322; neoclassical, 71, 211, 224; silent-era, 46, 47; violence in, 282. *See also* New Hollywood
Holt, Nancy, 28–29
Holte, Michael Ned, 20
Hornby, Louise, 81
How Sweet It Is! (Paris), 77, 291–92, 301, 303, 305, 333
How the West Was Won (Ford), 246, 251–52, 278, 332
Hoy, David Couzens, 201
Hu, Tung-Hui, 25
Husserl, Edmund\, 106, 108, 151, 178, 256; on phenomenology of music, 85

Ichikawa, Kon: *Tokyo Olympiad*, 74–75
Inception (Nolan), 180, 181
Indian Chief and the Seidlitz Powder, The (Heyworth), 42
Industrial Revolution, 14, 123

Jafa, Arthur, 158, 159, 163, 164
Jaffe, Ira: on slow cinema, 37
James, Nick, 36
James, William, 108, 178, 184; on duration, 85

Jameson, Fredric, 122, 198; on history, 78, 79; on modernism, 117, 123, 273; on technological progress, 70–71, 273; on the sixties, 199, 200, 202, 282; on time and speed, 117
Jencks, Christopher: on *Koyaanisqatsi* (Reggio), 297
Judd, Donald, 22, 34, 96, 259, 270, 273
Junior Bonner (Peckinpah), 77, 292–97, 300, 301, 306, 308; as development allegory, 298

Kadar, Jan, 157
Kael, Pauline: on *Bonnie and Clyde* (Penn), 212–19, 224, 227, 234; on *Once Upon a Time in America* (Leone), 267; on *Straw Dogs* (Peckinpah), 294, 310; on *2001: A Space Odyssey* (Kubrick), 240, 250; on *Zabriskie Point* (Antonioni), 314–18, 322, 330–31
Karate Girl (Aksoy), 227
Kaufman, Boris, 54–56, 65, 76, 107, 160
Kaufman, Mikhail, 54
Kaufmann, Stanley, 267, 331
Kennedy, John F., 75; assassination of, 75, 187–88, 190, 194–95, 198, 215, 228–29
Keoma (Castellari), 271–72
Kern, Stephen: *The Culture and Time and Space*, 23, 122, 349
Keynes, John Maynard, 124, 203, 263, 275
Kierkegaard, Søren, 85
Kittler, Friedrich, 46; on "time-axis manipulation," 9,
Koepnick, Lutz, 11; on contemporary slowness, 26, 95, 168; on DeLillo, Don, 179–80; on modernity, 12; on slow motion, 58, 102
Koselleck, Reinhart, 123, 200
Kovács, András Bálint, 66–67
Kracauer, Siegfried, 57, 80, 83; on *Entr'acte* (Clair), 44, 46–47; on "temporal close-ups," 69
Kubler, George: *The Shape of Time*, 26, 27
Kubrick, Stanley, 8, 15, 39, 77–78, 105, 199, 210, 238–69, 271, 278, 281, 284, 294, 300; *A Clockwork Orange*, 78, 258; *Dr. Strangelove or: How I Learned to Stop Worrying and Love the Bomb*, 39, 240, 242–43, 249–50, 334, 338, 340; *Eyes Wide Shut*, 255; *2001: A Space Odyssey*, 6, 8, 15, 38, 77, 105, 210, 238–65, 266, 267, 282, 291, 292, 294, 299, 307, 331–34, 342
Kunin, Howard, 298

Kurosawa, Akira, 20–21, 38, 57, 63, 65, 71, 98n100–101, 103–104, 226–27, 260, 291, 299, 300; *Drunken Angel*, 63, 65; *Rashomon*, 299; *Sanshiro Sugata*, 63, 100, 260; *The Seven Samurai*, 75, 98–100, 102, 104, 106, 226, 260, 299

Lampert, Jay: on delay, 81
Lancaster, Burt, 292, 302–305
Lange, Dorothea, 216, 234
Lasdun, James, 179
Last Year at Marienbad (Resnais), 68
Latour, Bruno: *We Have Never Been Modern*, 200, 356n1
Lead Shoes, The (Peterson), 61
Lee, Pamela: on "chronophobia," 274; on "obliteration" as motif, 298
Lefebvre, Henri: *Introduction to Modernity*, 78, 126, 162–63
Left-Handed Gun, The (Penn), 74
Leone, Sergio, 55, 68, 77, 84, 158, 210, 263, 266–67, 269–73, 276–79, 281–91, 294, 307, 312, 331; *Duck, You Sucker!*, 283, 284, 287; duration in, 276; *A Fistful of Dollars*, 266, 271, 283; *For a Few Dollars More*, 266, 271; *The Good, the Bad, and the Ugly*, 266, 270–71, 276–77, 279–81, 307, 331; *Once Upon a Time in America*, 267, 285–86; *Once Upon a Time in the West*, 6, 15, 38, 77, 210, 266, 271–72, 277, 279, 283, 287–92, 299, 307; revolution in, 283–84, 287
Lévi-Strauss, Claude, 14
Lickerish Quartet, The (Metzger), 331
Lin, Justin, 307
Little Caesar (LeRoy), 212, 226
Lombardo, Louis, 295, 300
Lot in Sodom (Sibley and Weber), 60
Love Me Tonight (Mamoulian), 53, 226, 260, 291
Lukács, Georg: on duration, 111; on the historical novel, 194; on man in modernism, 281
Lundemo, Trond, 47
Lupton, Christina: on *Remainder* (McCarthy), 143, 148
Lyell, Charles, 14

Maciunas, George: "Disappearing Music for Face (Fluxfilm no. 4)," 74; "Eyeblink (Fluxfilm no. 9)," 74
Malevich, Kazimir: *White on White*, 33

Malm, Andreas: on non-contemporaneous time, 13
Man from Laramie, The (Mann), 278
Manovich, Lev, 82
Mantle, Anthony, 2, 4
Martin, Agnes: *White Stone*, 33
Marx, Karl, 333; on capitalist accelerationism, 122; on space-time compression, 5, 12; on valorization, 109–11
masculinity; in DeLillo, 192; in Faulkner, 136; Hollywood, 212; in Leone, 266, 270; in Peckinpah, 292, 303, 305
Masumura, Yasuzo: *Black Test Car*, 68
Matrix, The (Wachowskis), 14, 64, 97, 121, 160, 180–81, 297
Matz, Jesse, 126; on "time ecology," 168–69
McCabe, Susan, 23
McCarthy, Tom, 9, 14, 118; *Remainder*, 143–46, 148–49
McClanahan, Annie: on history and stagnation, 79, 202
McGurl, Mark, 276
McLuhan, Marshall, 89, 281
McPhee, John: *Basin and Range*, 29
media archaeology, 24, 33, 143, 165, 337
Meillassoux, Quentin, 86–87; "ancestrality," 276
Méliès, Georges, 42–44; *A Trip to the Moon*, 43; *Under the Seas*, 43
Menand, Louis: on the Langlois Affair, 283
Menne, Jeff: on *Bonnie and Clyde* (Penn), 300; on New Hollywood, 209; on Peckinpah, Sam, 300; on the professional western, 312
Merry Widow, The (Stroheim), 49
Michaels, Walter Benn: on literalism, 143, 146
Michelson, Annette, 21–22; on *2001: A Space Odyssey* (Kubrick), 239–41, 246, 250, 258
Miekle, Bob, 334, 339
Miller, D. A.: on *Bonnie and Clyde* (Penn), 38, 225
Million Dollar Legs (Clune), 52
Ministry for the Future, The (Robinson), 5, 263
modernism, 14, 15, 26, 33, 86, 90–91, 96, 102, 107, 117, 122–23, 125, 127–28, 132, 136, 141, 152, 157, 171, 197, 214, 242, 259, 269–70, 272–76, 281; cinematic, 44, 164, 210, 321; global, 62; hegemonic, 21; high, 128, 270; ideology of, 275; late, 96; and slow-motion, 65–67, 70, 76–77; speed of, 122, 125, 273

modernity, 5–6, 9–10, 12, 21–26, 30, 78, 103, 105, 107–109, 111, 113, 115, 118, 122–26, 138–40, 153–55, 159–65, 182, 191, 200–202, 215, 233, 236, 251, 258–59, 261, 263–64, 270, 273, 275, 282, 285–87, 292, 295, 302, 307, 333, 342; aesthetic of, 15; capitalist, 13, 15, 202; crisis of, 13, 113, 298; late, 172, 337; mythologies of, 117, 196; resistance to, 3; and slow motion, 5, 79, 87–88; speed of, 9, 14, 26, 38,117; as structure of feeling, 199; and technology, 70; vanishing of, 34
Monk, Philip, 96
Monty Python's Flying Circus, 294, 295
Moore, Marianne, 60, 86, 94
Morgan, Philip D., 163
Morricone, Ennio, 276
Mr. Frenhofer (Peterson), 61
Mulvey, Laura, 16, 80–81, 138, 152–53; *Death 24x a Second*, 15, 152; "delayed cinema," 153
Murphy, Kathleen, 305–306
musicals, 3, 53, 62, 236, 294
Muybridge, Eadweard, 7, 45–46, 49, 62, 82, 92, 104, 109, 176

Nadolny, Sten: *The Discovery of Slowness*, 14, 165–67, 169–71, 174–176
neorealism, 66, 277, 326
Nero, Franco, 271, 272
New American Cinema. *See* New Hollywood
New Hollywood, 3, 66, 156–57, 209, 224–25, 236, 301, 307, 315, 325, 343
New Wave film, 21, 66–68, 157
Newman, Barrett, 259
Newman, David, 214, 218–22, 225, 233, 236
newsreels, 7, 8, 13, 45, 49, 73–75, 92, 121
Nieland, Justus, 136, 143
Nietzsche, Friedrich: *Daybreak*, 170, 248
9/11: in DeLillo, 181–87
"1968," 13, 15, 25, 78, 97, 204, 239–40, 266, 286, 324, 326
Nixon, Rob: "slow violence," 14
Nolan, Christopher, 180, 334
nonnarrative film, 11
nonsites, 22, 259, 273–75, 290
Nope (Peele), 7
nostalgia, 82, 143, 149, 167, 192, 197–99, 213–14, 217, 225, 235, 277, 313
Novagraph Film Corporation, 45–46
Noys, Benjamin: on accelerationism, 124

O'Hara, Frank: "To the Film Industry in Crisis," 19
Once Upon a Time in the West (Leone), 6, 15, 38, 77, 210, 266, 271–72, 277, 279, 283, 287–92, 299, 307
Operation Crossroads, 334, 338–41
optical unconscious, 44, 62, 83, 104, 144, 216
Ordinary Man of Cinema, The (Schefer), 15
Øyvind, Vågnes, 195
Ozick, Cynthia: *The Messiah of Stockholm*, 2, 3

Painlevé, Jean, 61–62 *The Fourth Dimension*, 62; *The Sea Horse*, 62
Parikka, Jussi: on deep time, 155, 267, 290
Parkins, Wendy, 169
Pasolini, Pier Paolo, *Mamma Roma*, 68, 277
Patterson, Clair Cameron, 137
Pawnbroker, The (Lumet), 55, 76
Peckinpah, Sam, 55, 63, 77, 83–84, 158, 210, 263, 266, 269, 291–313; career of, 298–99; and conventionalizing of slow motion, 294; *Convoy*, 311; *The Getaway*, 78, 194, 301, 308; *Junior Bonner*, 77, 292–97, 300, 301, 306, 308; *Killer Elite*, 311; masculinity in, 292, 303, 305; *Major Dundee*, 298, 2099, 301; *Pat Garrett and Billy the Kid*, 294, 295; *Ride the High Country*, 298, 300; *The Rifleman*, 295; *Straw Dogs*, 295, 308, 310; *The Westerner*, 301; *The Wild Bunch*, 6, 15, 77, 83, 101, 113, 199–200, 210, 266, 282, 291–92, 294–95, 297, 299–303, 305–13, 318, 331
Peirce, Charles Sanders, 82
Penn, Arthur, 63, 74, 76, 84, 98, 158, 193, 211–31, 233–36, 242, 245, 266–68, 279, 294, 300; *Bonnie and Clyde*, 15, 35, 38, 57, 75–76, 97, 101, 197, 199–200, 209–37, 239, 242, 245, 248, 266, 279, 279, 282, 291–92, 294, 299, 300, 307, 315, 316, 318, 328, 331, 342; *The Left Handed Gun*, 74
Peters, John Durham, 25, 178
phenomenology, 85, 106, 107, 18, 353n2
Phillips, John, 88
photography, 16, 24, 81, 82, 108, 144, 150, 152, 154, 235, 247; high-speed, 25, 45, 62, 70, 89, 92, 109, 110, 140, 243, 300; long-exposure; motion, 7, 104; slow-motion, 28; time-lapse, 33; trick, 52
Plato: *Timaeus*, 104
Point Blank (Boorman), 76–77, 209, 245
Porter, Katherine Anne: *Ship of Fools*, 121

Posnock, Ross: on *Austerlitz* (Sebald), 150
Postone, Moishe: "treadmill effect," 113, 202
Pound, Ezra, 70, 117
Prince, Stephen, 294; on *Bonnie and Clyde* (Penn), 226
Proust, Marcel, 171–74, 192
Public Enemy, The (Wellman), 212

Rampo, Edogawa: "The Horrors of Film," 50–51
Reed, Arden: on slow art, 93–95
Rehak, Bob, 63
Rehding, Alexander, 258
Remainder (McCarthy), 143–46, 148–49; slow-motion reenactment in, 144–47; traces of film in, 143–44
Reservoir Dogs (Tarantino), 157
Revolution, 49, 90, 124, 125, 131, 200, 203, 204, 242, 260, 263, 275, 283–84, 287, 299, 307, 311–13, 315, 317, 330–31, 335, 337
Richardson, Dorothy, 51, 57, 86
Riefenstahl, Leni: *Olympia*, 58, 74, 92, 164
Riley, Denise: *Time Lived, Without Its Flow*, 11
Roberts, Jennifer, 272
Roberts, John, 21
Rosa, Hartmut, 12; on "social time of crisis," 112, 122, 177
Ross, Kristin: on modernization, 12
Rosetti, Dante, 85
Rossellini, Roberto: *Paisan*, 66, 68
Roszack, Theodore, 200
Rotha, Paul, 47, 49, 86
Ryman, Robert: *Bridge*, 33

Sachs, Jonathan, 14
Said, Edward: "Traveling Theory," 156
Saratoga (Conway), 59
Schiller, Friedrich: on "grace," 102
Schonig, Jordan: "contingent motion," 16, 218
Schwartz, Vanessa R., 23
scientific and industrial film, 11, 13, 104
Sebald, W. G., 9, 14, 118, 196; *Austerlitz*, 148–53, 184
Sekula, Allan: "counter-sites," 264–65
Sellars, Peter, 10, 11
Serres, Michel, 200
Seven Samurai, The (Kurosawa), 75, 98–100, 102, 104, 106, 226, 260, 299; slow motion as aesthetic form in, 102–103

Sexton, Jared: "colored time," 184
Seymour, Nicole: on slow cinema, 37
Shane (Steven), 278
Shapiro, Gary, 26
Sharma, Sarah, 110, 111, 126, 168
Shaviro, Steven: on slow cinema, 37
Shaw, Lytle: on Smithson, Robert, 275
Shklovksy, Viktor; defamiliarization, 170, 270; *syuzhet*, 169, 172, 183
Shooting, The (Hellmann), 77
Sidney, George, 62
Singin' in the Rain (Donen and Kell), 105, 257, 302
Sinykin, Dan, on apocalypse in literature: 203
Situationists, 333
Slapstick, 39, 53, 88, 219, *223*, 224, 235, 294
Slifkin, Robert: on minimalist sculpture, 259; on *2001: A Space Odyssey* (Kubrick), 245
slow cinema, 3, 36, 37, 168, 180, 235, 262
slow food, 3, 38, 167–68
Slow Mo Guys, the, 69, 73, 88
slow motion: in the 1960s, 4, 5, 158, 199, 210, 291, 323; aesthetics of, 81, *103*; as allegory, 121; and death, 2, 12, 16, 32, 47, 63, 84, 100–103, 106, 112, 130, 145, 167, 170, 217–18, 220, 224, 227, 229, 231, 233–34, 255–56, 260, 284, 299, 300; digital, 95; dismissal of, 9, 25; as dream-work, 14, 49, 59, 63, 65, 68, 70, 76, 83, 86, 87, 90, 104–106, 110, 112, 188, 209, 226, 245, 277, 318; in early cinema, 40–54; and embodied motion, 87–88; eroticism of, 83–84; grace of, 1, 29, 45, 47, 49, 50, 63, 67, 75, 83, 102, 110, 112–13, 156, 227, 260, 274, 292, 299; and graphic content, 110, 158, 210, 220, 228, 230, 294; growth of, 74; histories of, 13, 29, 40, 61, 71, 90–91, 95, 109, 113, 291; in literature, 71, 78, 171; as machine perception, 84; –85; as metaphor, 121; and modernism, 25, 65–67, 70, 76–77, 90, 108; and modernity, 5, 79, 87–88, 123, 162; and perspective, 260; as special effect, 2, 4–6, 13, 22, 30, 39–40, 46, 49, 78, 89, 102, 118, 187, 191, 209, 242, 246, 277, 279, 307, 315, 333; and speed, 9, 12, 15, 38, 78, 82–89, 110, 123, 143, 340; and value, 110; valorization of motion in, 108–10, 124; and violence, 7, 12, 14, 15, 48, 63, 67, 84, 86, 133–34, 136, 145, 188, 190, 199, 214–16, 221, 225, 227, 229, 233, 242, 260, 272, 309, 341

slow movements, 3, 38, 168
slowness: as contemporary aesthetic, 26–27, 95, 272; geopolitics of, 111; as human condition, 81; as resistance, 124, 168, 180; and perception, 84; and speed, 38, 112, 180, 202, 341
slow reading, 3, 10, 170
Smith, Jack: *Flaming Creatures*, 74
Smith, Zadie: on "two paths for the novel," 143
Smithson, Robert, 14, 19–22, 25–30, 34, 36, 39, 64, 87, 90, 96, 109, 137, 143, 259, 270–76, 279, 282; *Asphalt Rundown*, 272, 279; "A Cinematic Atopia," 20–21; "Entropy and the New Monuments," 15, 20–22, 30, 245, 273, 276; on film sites, 271; "The Monument: Outline for a Film," 30; nonsites, 22, 259, 273–75, 290; *Spiral Jetty* (earthwork), 14, 19, 20, 27–29, 64, 87, 272; *Spiral Jetty* (film), 14, *29*
Snyder, Zach, 11, 58, 71, 73, 89, 101, 149, 295, 307; *The Justice League*, 58
Sobchack, Vivian: on slow motion as "movement of movement," 87–88, 105, 108, 142
Sontag, Susan: "Against Interpretation," 5–6
spaghetti westerns, 55, 267, 271–73, 312
special effects, 2, 4–6, 13, 22, 30, 39–40, 46, 49, 78, 89, 102, 118, 187, 191, 209, 242, 246, 277, 279, 307, 315, 333
speed: aesthetics of, 235; contradictions of, 204; culture of, 273; and modernity, 26, 30, 94, 117–18, 122–26, 162, 168, 264; and narrative, 96, 172; ramping, 7, 53, 58, 70, 71, 101, 105, 147; and slowness, 38, 112, 180, 202, 341
Sporting Life, The (Anderson), 75
sports highlights, 11, 40, 57, 70, 75, 193
Stanford Jr., Leland, 7, 49
Star Wars (Lucas), 324, *325*
Stein, Gertrude: "Composition as Explanation," 172
step printing, 4, 63, 158–59, 300
Sterne, Jonathan, 25
Stewart, Garrett, 81
Stewart, Susan: on ruins, 34–35
stillness, 16, 34, 80–81, 84, 220
Stratton, W.K., 312
Strauss, Richard: "Also Sprach Zarathustra," 238, 248, 258, 332, 334
sublime, the, 26, 87, 245, 248, 250, 259, 322

Sugimoto, Hiroshi, 31–35, 38–39, 90, 96, 235, 247; *Proctor's Theater, Troy*, 34–35, 38–39; *Tri-City Drive-In, San Bernadino*, 31; *Snow White*, 32, 38
Sun Ra, 201
surrealism, 47–48, 107, 277
Sutil, Nicholas Salazar, 109
Swimmer, The (Perry), 210, 292, 303–305

Tavoularis, Dean, 316, 318
Taylor, Fredrick Winslow, 109
Taylor-Johnson, Sam, 95
Thief of Bagdad, The (Walsh), 47, 59, 226
time: cinematic, 24, 47, 81, 153, 257; contradictions of contemporary, 112; deep, 29, 137, 179, 246–47, 250, 275–76; geological, 27, 149, 180, 251, 287, 341; imperceptible, 45, 166; intersubjective, 103; machine, 62, 106; physical, 103, 178; racial, 127, 155, 159; and temporality, 14, 24, 26–27, 35, 47, 81–85, 87, 95–96, 103, 106–107, 127, 137, 141, 155, 163, 172–73, 184, 200, 202, 204, 213, 237, 248, 260, 269–70, 273–75, 282, 287, 297, 302, 323, 336, 340, 341; and trauma, 181, 184. *See also* Bergson, Henri; Genette, Gerard; Heidegger, Martin; Husserl, Edmund
Tompkins, Jane: on *2001: A Space Odyssey* (Kubrick), 250
Top Gun (Scott), 157, 163
Transient Life, This (Jissoji), 331
trauma, 28, 75, 106, 185–86, 216, 226, 260, 271, 340; and 9/11, 181; in *Austerlitz* (Sebald), 153; in *Bonnie and Clyde* (Penn), 228, 236; in *Daughters of the Dust* (Dash), 158, 160; in *Falling Man* (DeLillo), 181, 184; in Faulkner, 128, 142, 199; in *The Pawnbroker* (Lumet), 55; in *Remainder* (McCarthy), 143, 148; and slow motion, 48; and time, 101, 172, 181, 184; in *Underworld* (DeLillo), 192–93, 195, 199; in westerns, 278, 284, 307; in *Young and Innocent* (Hitchcock), 62
trick shots, 43
Trotsky, Leon: *History of the Russian Revolution*, 204
Truffaut, Francois, 3, 67–68, 214, 233; *Jules and Jim*, 68, 219–20; *Les mistons*, 67
Trumbull, Douglas, 244
Turvey, Malcolm, 89
24 Hour Psycho (Gordon), 81, 95, 96, 179, 180, 183, 269

2001: A Space Odyssey (Kubrick), 6, 8, 15, 38, 77, 105, 210, 238–65, 266, 267, 282, 291, 292, 294, 299, 307, 331–34, 342; conception of, 242–43; match cuts in, 242–43; "slit-scan" cinematography of, 243; slowness in, 240, 247, *249*, 257–60, 263; sound design in, 238, 248, 251, 254, 256; as western, 250–54, 331

unconscious, the, 3, 44, 95, 106, 109, 153, 184, 318; political, 283. *See also* optical unconscious, the; slow motion: as dream-work,
Underwood, Ted, 171
uneven development, 263
Universe (Kroitor and Low), 243, 254
Uroskie, Alex V., 95
utopianism, 5, 12, 333

Vertov, Dziga, 4, 49–50, 54, 58, 65, 83, 89–92, 153, 160, 164, 291; *Man with a Movie Camera*, 49–50, 153, 164; *Three Songs about Lenin*, 58
Vigo, Jean, 53–54, 65–67, 76, 78, 85, 107, 277, 291; *Àpropos de Nice*, 54; *L'Atalant*e, 53, *54*; *Taris*, 53, 67; *Zéro de Conduite*, *55*, 107
Viola, Bill, 10, 93, 307; *The Passions*, 10; *The Quintet of the Astonished*, 94; *The Quintet Series*, 93
violence, 7, 12, 15, 25, 35, 48, 59, 84, 322; in *Bonnie and Clyde* (Penn), 214–16, 216, 221–229, 233, 242, 248, 318; of capitalism, 112; in *Daughters of the Dust* (Dash), 158, 160, 163; in DeLillo, 182, 188, 190, 192; in Faulkner, 133, 134, 136, 138, 142; in Leone, 272, 276, 286, 288, 331; in Peckinpah, 298, 300, 302, 305, 310, 311, 331; in *Remainder* (McCarthy), 149; in *The Seven Samurai* (Kurosawa), 63, 99, 100; slow, 14, 341–42; and slow motion, 7, 12, 14, 15, 48, 63, 67, 84, 86, 133–34, 136, 145, 188, 190, 199, 214–16, 221, 225, 227, 229, 233, 242, 260, 272, 309, 341; in *This Sporting Life*, 76; in *2001: A Space Odyssey*, 25, 42, 60, 261, 332, 333; and the Zapruder film, 195
Virilio, Paul, 111–12, 122, 215
Vorkapich, Slavko, 65, 157
voyeurism, 83, 87, 333

Warhol, Andy, 22, 74, 78, 93, 285; *Empire*, 74
Warner, Jack, 213, 214, 226
Warshow, Robert; on the western hero, 278
Wasson, Haidee: on "useful cinema," 61
Weisgall, Jonathan, 339
westerns, 19, 55, 245, 246– 250, 252, 263–79, 287–88, 293, 296, 299, 312, 315, 325, 331, 342; slowness in, 246, 278; spaghetti, 55, 267, 271–73, 312
What Price Hollywood? (Cukor), 51, *52*, 106, 226, 260, 291
Whissel, Kristen, 122
Who's That Knocking at My Door (Scorsese), 76
Wild Bunch, The (Peckinpah), 6, 15, 77, 83, 101, 113, 199–200, 210, 266, 282, 291–95, 297, 299–313, 318, 331
Williams, James, 318
Williams, Raymond, 70; "structure of feeling," 198–99
Wong, Kar-Wai, 73, 157
Woo, John, 73, 89, 295, 307
Woods, James: "hysterical" realism
Woolf, Virginia, 307; on emergence of modernity, 125, 342; *Mrs Dalloway*, 197
World of Henry Orient, The (Hill), 56, 76, 291
Wright, Will, 312

Youngblood, Gene: *Expanded Cinema*, 20, 252; "The New Nostalgia," 252
YouTube, 4, 8, 40, 58, 69, 88, 97, 103, 121, 148, 186, 187, 199, 228, 230, 239, 335–38. *See also* Slow Mo Guys, the

Zabriskie Point (Antonioni), 6, 15, 197, 200, 210, 307, 314–38, 342; explosions in, 315, 317–24, 336; mass orgy in, 327–30, 332;
Zapruder film, 188, 190, 194–97, *228*, 229
Zemka, Sue, 85, 185
Zettl, Herbert, 108, 123
Zielinski, Siegfried: on the deep time of media, 29
Žižek, Slavoj: on *Zabriskie Point* (Antonioni), 331
Zwenigora (Dovzhenko), 48–49